"A reporter from *The Boston Globe* humanizes two of the worst tragedies of the 1990s."
—*The Atlanta Journal-Constitution*

"Elizabeth Neuffer is a brave and gifted reporter who personally hunted down those she believed responsible for massacres. . . . It is hard not to be possessed of a cold fury while reading this."
—*The Times* (London)

"Gives a human face to the horrors of Bosnia and Rwanda."
—*The Economist*

"Neuffer juxtaposes scenes of almost unbearable suffering with daring accounts of the inaction of world leaders."
—Salon.com

"A revealing portrait of the two international tribunals where survivors eventually sought justice."
—*The Nation*

"*The Key to My Neighbor's House* captures the human drama at the core of the [war crimes] trials. . . . Neuffer manages to convey in intimate and sometimes painful detail the trauma of [the victims'] personal ordeals and the importance of their search for justice. . . . Prodigious research and excellent reporting."
—*The New York Times Book Review*

"A moving, heartbreaking, and distressing look into the functions and dysfunctions of the machinery of international justice, from the perspective of the victims in whose name that machinery has been erected . . . harrowing and intense."
—*The Boston Globe*

"It's a terrible thing to want justice. Very few besides the victims think it is necessary or cost effective. But tell that to the victims of the Balkan wars or the horrors of Rwanda; tell that to the subjects of Elizabeth Neuffer's compelling documentary in words on the quest for justice by those who think it is an essential ingredient for humanity. Her book will convince you that we're doomed if we don't seek justice."
—Leslie H. Gelb, President, Council on Foreign Relations, former editorial page editor, *The New York Times*

"A gripping human journey through the landscape of atrocity of the early 1990s whose moral compass is the newly revived laws of armed conflict, and the impassioned drive by jurists, prosecutors, and forensic pathologists to apply them. As the story moves from the mass grave to the courtroom, the reader is left not with drama, but, almost incredibly, a certain feeling of triumph. Superbly researched and written."
—Roy Gutman, Pulitzer Prize–winning author

"A tremendously valuable comparative study, with all its shameful conclusions in place."
—*Kirkus Reviews* (starred review)

"A compelling journey . . . Award-winning journalist Elizabeth Neuffer weaves an intricate tale of hostile criminals, trial systems, and those left in their wake. The victims' determination to rectify the wrongs done them, no matter the cost, is a triumphant testimony to the power of human will."
—*Gotham*

"Goes beyond the standard news reports of genocide in Rwanda and Bosnia to present the victims and villains in this astonishing look at human cruelty . . . Very personal and painful interviews . . . This is a very graphic, disturbing look at the failure of foreign policy and the difficulty of administering justice."
—*Booklist*

Elizabeth Neuffer

THE KEY TO MY NEIGHBOR'S HOUSE

Seeking Justice in Bosnia and Rwanda

PICADOR NEW YORK

For information, address Picador, 175 Fifth Avenue, New York, N.Y. 10010.

www.picadorusa.com

Picador ® is a U.S. registered trademark and is used by St. Martin's Press under license from Pan Books Limited.

For information on Picador Reading Group Guides, as well as ordering, please contact the Trade Marketing department at St. Martin's Press.
Phone: 1-800-221-7945 extension 763
Fax: 212-677-7456
E-mail: trademarketing@stmartins.com

Library of Congress Cataloging-in-Publication Data

Neuffer, Elizabeth.

The key to my neighbor's house : seeking justice in Bosnia and Rwanda / Elizabeth Neuffer.

p. cm.

Includes bibliographical references and index.

ISBN 978-0-312-30282-5

ISBN 0-312-30282-7 (pbk)

1. Yugoslav War, 1991–1995—Atrocities. 2. Yugoslav War, 1991–1995—Bosnia and Herzegovina. 3. Rwanda—History—Civil War, 1990–1993—Atrocities. 4. Rwanda—History—Civil War, 1994—Atrocities. 5. Neuffer, Elizabeth. I. Title: Seeking justice in Bosnia and Rwanda. II. Title.

DR1313.7.A85 N48 2001
949.703—dc21 2001036342

First Picador Paperback Edition: November 2002

P1

In memory of my mother, Meredith, my father, Robert,

and my brother Dan, for all they taught me.

And to my brother Mark,

my teacher, guide, and inspiration still.

CONTENTS

"I do not know that you could give me a complete answer, but perhaps you can help me to understand since I am not from that area. How could you explain some of the atrocities that we have heard that have been committed?... Given your background, your experiences, knowing that Serbs and Muslims lived together, went to school together, how did that happen?" asked Judge Gabrielle Kirk McDonald of the witness before her in the first international war crimes trial since World War II.

Hamdo paused. "It is difficult to answer, this question," he replied. "I am also at a loss. I had the key to my next-door neighbor's [house] who was a Serb, and he had my key. That is how we looked after each other...."

—Testimony of Hamdo Kahrimanović before
International Criminal Tribunal for the former Yugoslavia

PROLOGUE

Let me begin as it began for me: glimpsing evil in a man's soul.

The man I've been expecting has just swaggered up to my table in this smoke-filled café, followed by one of his henchmen and the aroma of cheap cologne. Like any city tough, his hands are jammed into his pants pockets and his muscular shoulders strain at the seams of his cheap black leather jacket. But when he looks at me, his eyes are as empty of expression as pure glass.

He pulls up a chair, summons the waitress, and sends her scurrying to get brandy, beer, more coffee, with the arrogance of a Mafia don. He sits down on my right, blond and mustachioed, and cocks his eyebrow. The war-hardened soldiers slouching at nearby tables, their cigarettes drooping from their lips, nod with approval. They believe this man, a fellow soldier, to be a hero. But I've been searching for him for six weeks because I believe him to be something else: executioner.

I am in the Bosnian-Serb half of Bosnia and Herzegovina and it is 1996. Peace is so newly minted here in the city of Bijeljina that civilians still don't venture onto the streets. Only a mere seven months have passed since this man and others in the Bosnian Serb 10th Sabotage Unit rounded up 1,200 unarmed Bosnian Muslim men and led them to an abandoned, grassy meadow at a collective farm just down the highway from here. They ordered the men to turn their backs and kneel on the ground. Then, as their captives wept and pleaded for their lives, they shot them.

At the time, I'd been reporting from Bosnia for more than two years, and I still couldn't understand what turned neighbors of long standing into killers, rapists, torturers: whether it was ideology or hate or madness or history or blood lust that made civilization's constraints vanish.

I had wanted to talk to this man's commander, General Radislav Krstić. But Krstić has quit Bosnia for neighboring Serbia, where I was rarely granted a visa. So I had set out tracking down this young soldier instead, whose name I had gotten from Bosnian Muslim war crimes investigators. I've spent nights searching for him in drafty bars filled with grimacing thugs and pounding rock music, and days hunting him down, the car jogging along like a child's pogo stick on roads pitted by shelling and years of communist neglect. I've come too far now to turn back. Never mind that I am the only woman in the room, save for my translator, Alex, and the waitress; never mind that suddenly the interview karma doesn't seem quite right. Much later I would offer the typical journalistic defense: The interview had been my editor's idea. Because Marko "Macak" Boškić was not in a cooperative mood.

"Do you have a tape recorder? Let's see," Boškić said with a growl, as he rifled through our coat pockets, scattering pieces of old gum, gas receipts, and shredded Kleenex across the table. Discovering my small Sony portable, he debated stealing it, but simply removed one of the batteries and the tape. The waitress, giggling at the cloak-and-dagger preparations, was shooed away with a scowl, and Boškić got down to business.

"Where did you get my name?" he demanded, leaning over the wooden table.

"From Erdemović," I lied, naming a soldier from his unit, Dražen Erdemović, who had recently confessed to the executions to international war crimes prosecutors in The Hague, Netherlands. In truth, Erdemović would later identify Boškić as part of the massacre squad.

"That traitor." Boškić sneered. I took this as an opening.

"Look, I'd like to talk to you about Srebrenica—I want to talk to you about *your* side of the story," I gushed nervously, referring to the massacres, which I had been told he participated in, that followed the fall of the UN safe area of Srebrenica and left thousands of Muslim men and boys dead. "Were you ordered to kill those men? Why did you do it?"

Silence.

The coffee in my cup suddenly tasted like silt. The dreary café began to look as welcoming as one of those graffitti-scarred, inner-city gas stations, where the cashier is encased behind thick, bulletproof glass. There comes a moment in every interview when you realize things are not going as planned; in this case, I'd just realized Boškić was not going to tell me why he had executed those men, after all.

Instead, a flush appeared on Boškić's cheeks and grew steadily darker. His hands, when he raised them, were trembling, even as he held them out toward my translator and me as if he would strangle us like chickens whose necks he'd break with a wrench of their heads.

"Would you like to get whacked?" he hissed. "I want you to forget this street and this restaurant. It doesn't exist any more for you. Don't come looking for me any more. I cannot guarantee the safety of your lives."

And with that he stood up and strode from the restaurant, stopping only to point us out to several Bosnian Serb military soldiers sitting at a nearby table, still carrying guns and clad in camouflage, despite the war's end. One winked at us. Another glared. The waitress arrived with more coffee. We drank it, wiser—and yet no wiser—than we had been before.

PERHAPS I WAS naïve in trying to interview Boškić, although I had known killers to brag about their exploits. Though I found out nothing new about the Srebrenica massacres, I did learn something else, something that had eluded me in the many months I'd spent reporting on one atrocity in Bosnia after another: why victims, particularly those who knew their tormentors, struggled so to put the demons of those memories to rest. Before I met Boškić, he was a name; afterward, he became a nightmare. Once you put a human face to evil, it will not let you go.

The evil I glimpsed in him had nothing to do with ideology; in some ways, if I could have chalked up his actions to a kind of nationalist brainwashing, I would not have felt so disturbed. Nor did it have anything to do with his being a member of the Bosnian Serb forces. While Serb paramilitaries and troops had committed the majority of the war crimes, there were atrocities on all three sides of the Bosnian war, and Boškić was actually a Bosnian Croat. The evil I glimpsed in him was the potential for evil we all share, for being human is no guarantee of our humanity. What's most chilling when you meet a murderer is that you meet yourself.

This young man had allegedly killed unarmed men who had surrendered—a heinous crime, by any measure—and yet he walked away from my table, *free*. The more I thought about the fact that Boškić had flouted society's rules with impunity, the more I felt a growing sense of injustice.

For nights afterward, I would relive my interview, providing different, more satisfactory endings that unreeled in my mind like Hollywood movies. I'd fantasize about reaching across the table, slapping on handcuffs and arresting Boškić. I'd imagine NATO troops storming the restaurant and doing the job for me. I'd envision one of the Bosnian Serb soldiers drunkenly lounging in the café suddenly becoming so outraged by Boškić's participation in an execution that he would stand up, draw his gun, and shoot him.

What I realized was that there is an innate human need for some kind of reckoning, an accounting. Like everyone I met in Bosnia, I wanted something that would assuage my guilt, answer my fears, and punish those who were responsible. I wanted order imposed on a world that would right the wrong that Boškić and his men had committed that day. I wasn't sure what outcome was best: Boškić on trial, Boškić forced to apologize for his crimes, Boškić forced to pay reparations.

But I did know this: I wanted some kind of justice for Boškić—whatever "justice" meant.

This is not a book about evil, although you will read plenty about it. It is a book about the pursuit of justice, about the people whom I met who were also trying to understand what it meant in the wake of full-scale atrocities. Many of the people I will introduce you to are from Bosnia and Rwanda, where I traveled as a reporter for the *Boston Globe*. Politicians and policy makers had prescribed "justice" as the means through which both countries could shake off the nightmare of their recent past, move beyond cycles of hatred and the sense of grievance to achieve reconciliation. But while everyone wanted justice, not everyone was sure just what that meant—or how best to deliver it—particularly in such devastated societies.

Vengeance was not an option: One need only look at the mass graves littering the hillsides in both Rwanda and Bosnia to understand that. Facing the past, looking "the beast in the eye" lest it "haunt you horrendously," as Archbishop Desmond Tutu once put it, certainly seemed to be part of the answer. Yet as I traveled from Sarajevo to Kigali, from Srebrenica to Kibuye, as I met weary prosecutors and unrepentant war criminals in shabby courtrooms and flea-infested prisons, families searching for their missing loved ones and forensic experts exhuming mass graves, questions multiplied. How much should a society remember and how much should it forget? Where does the boundary fall between enough justice to destroy impunity and so much "justice" that it becomes revenge? How can any punishment, in the wake of mass atrocities such as those Bosnia and Rwanda have seen, ever address the needs of the thousands of people raped, maimed, tortured, or homeless?

Questions like these, which I heard posed by a Tutsi woman living in a simple mud-brick home as well as by a Bosnian Muslim woman knitting a sweater in a refugee camp, suggested that, for all the culture and geography that separated Bosnia and Rwanda, the two countries had much in common. Both were rugged, beautiful lands laid waste by war and by hate. In both, conflicts had erupted in the shifting era of post–Cold War politics, when power-hungry politicians used history's unsolved grievances to fan the embers of ethnic discontent. In both, wrongs had been unpunished and vengeance often triumphed over the rule of law. In both, staggering atrocities set neighbor against neighbor, friend against friend.

Yet Bosnia and Rwanda shared something else, and that was the legacy of Western shame. American and European leaders largely stood by, wringing their hands even as the killing in both countries rocketed around the world in televised images: Rwandans macheted to death, emaciated Bosnian Muslims behind the barbed wire of concentration camps. Pleas for help buzzed along the Internet. UN peacekeepers, under orders to shoot only in their own defense, stood by helplessly as killings took place around them.

Stung by world outrage, desperate to lay the foundations for a lasting peace, the United Nations Security Council had clutched for a face-saving solution and found one in the creation of international war crimes tribunals. Trials, applying international humanitarian law, would bring Rwanda's and Bosnia's tyrants to heel. And so, as Rwanda and Bosnia unearthed mass graves and counted the dead, as rubble was swept up and rebuilding began, the hope was that with war crimes trials both countries would take a different path than in the past. This time they would walk on the far side of revenge—toward justice and even reconciliation.

DELIVERING JUSTICE, HOWEVER, has proved easier in theory than in reality. The two war crimes tribunals, once created, were undermined by a lack of political will and funding in their early years. UN bureaucracy snarled their workings into knots. The result was a limited number of accomplishments achieved against incredible odds. The Yugoslav Tribunal's decisions revolutionized the field of international humanitarian law, but for the first few years of its existence, it had no high-ranking defendants behind bars, thanks to Western leaders' reluctance to have their troops in Bosnia arrest them. The Rwanda Tribunal would deliver the first genocide verdict by an international war crimes court. Yet prosecutors working on the case remember throwing doors on top of orange crates to serve as a desk, arguing over whose motion was the most important to be printed out from the scarce paper supply, and being stymied by a court administration riddled with mismanagement.

Yet as verdicts were handed down, as war crimes law was expanded and refined, as more alleged war criminals were arrested, convicted, and put behind bars, it became clear that judgments had little immediate deterrent value: The 1998 fighting in the Serbian province of Kosovo raged long after the Yugoslav Tribunal was established. In addition, thousands upon thousands of victims knew little about the war crimes trials, ongoing outside their homeland. Increasingly, the courts' decisions seemed remote to each country's survivors, forcing many to turn elsewhere for their sense of justice. And there were so many victims and so many cases and just so much either war crimes tribunal could do.

Could a war crimes tribunal—much less any court—caught in that delicate interplay between judge, prosecutor, and defense attorney ever cope with all the cases at hand? "Perhaps what you end up with in a post-genocide society is not justice at all," Gerald Gahima, Rwanda's then deputy minister of justice, told me in 1996, as he contemplated his country's jails, crowded with 125,000 people accused of taking part in the genocide. "Maybe we should think of another word for it."

Justice, I learned, was not so simple as the lessons the Nuremberg trials would have us believe. During the years I traveled in Bosnia and Rwanda, my home base was Berlin, Germany, where fifty years after the end of World War II questions of justice and injustice, guilt, and forgiveness were still being actively debated. Almost every dinner party, every social outing, at some point came back to the same, haunting questions: Who knew what and when—and can Germany ever afford to stop remembering the Holocaust? "Facing the past, reconciliation," said former German president Richard von Weizsäcker, "is too much of a burden for a court. That has to come outside. . . . this has to be done not only by institutions, but by individuals." Von Weizsäcker should know: One of the most outspoken Germans to urge his country to face its Nazi past, the stately, white-haired diplomat had once defended his own father at the Nuremberg trials. (His father, the state secretary at the German Foreign Ministry, was convicted of crimes against the peace, although the judgment was later reversed.)

Justice is not just a court verdict, it is also a personal journey. When people say they want justice after a war, what they really mean is that they want to be able to put the ghosts of their past to rest, to lay down the burden of their guilt, to unearth the truths they seek. "Justice is not only in the end result," noted Justice Albie Sachs, the South African Supreme Court justice. "It is also in the process." As I learned from the people in this book, achieving "justice" is as much a process of questioning what justice is for them and their country as it is a court verdict. The longer I knew them, the clearer it became over time that each had traveled his own path to find justice.

I admit, chasing after war criminals and conducting interviews next to mass graves was not what I'd had in mind when I moved to Berlin in 1994. My mother, perhaps my closest friend, the magnetic north on my emotional compass, had just died; I wanted to immerse myself in Europe to forget my pain. I had visions of cozy chats with French filmmakers in chic Paris bistros, trips to Rome to investigate the intricacies of Italian politics, an investigation into Nazi gold allegedly hidden away in Switzerland.

No sooner had I arrived, though, than the Bosnian war reignited. So I had to learn quickly about things alien to me: massive shelling, indeterminate sniper fire, ethnic cleansing, and war crimes. Rather than visiting Europe's museums, I toured its battlefield in Bosnia, and then went on to Africa's version, in Rwanda. Instead of tasting the fruits of Western civilization, I felt as if I were witnessing its collapse. After watching an elderly woman gunned down in front of me in Sarajevo, in full view of two UN peacekeepers with orders not to return fire, my grief vanished, replaced by outrage.

That anger fueled my interest in Bosnia's and Rwanda's search for justice. I wanted to see wrong made right. I had begun my career as a reporter covering the Boston Mafia in trials before U.S. federal court, and I loved the soothing logic of the law, how it took moral chaos and rendered some kind of order. Over time, however, as I listened to Bosnians and Rwandans tell their stories, I always heard the echo of my own.

Who hasn't wanted revenge, when betrayed by a close friend? Who hasn't struggled to face the dark truth, about their family, themselves? Who hasn't grieved over the untimely death of a family member or lover? I myself knew the most meaningful "justice" often comes about in the very personal act of searching for it. My family, riven by a long-running emotional war, had been struggling to find its own balance. By the time I was sent to Bosnia, my feud with my father had shifted into an uncertain cease-fire. Our reconciliation played out on trips back home between Bosnia and Rwanda, and there was good reason that it did. My father had been a U.S. Marine at the battle of Bloody Ridge at Guadalcanal, a man who still bore the burden of what he had witnessed. In Bosnia's war, we found a common language and, in its horrors, shared experiences. That war crimes should not go unpunished was important to him: Among his firm beliefs, which he ran up the flagpole along with Old Glory on every public holiday, was that justice and peace went hand in hand. He was as appalled as I by the reluctance of NATO troops to arrest war criminals after Bosnia's war ended. He followed the stories I was writing about the people in this book as if they were close friends. He wanted them to get their day in court—and to reconcile with their former friends as we had learned to do.

It took turning on the television one day in 1995, however, for me to understand the connection between Bosnia and Rwanda's search for justice and the United States. As I listened to Americans bitterly dispute the verdict in the O. J. Simpson murder trial, I heard the same voices, the same arguments, the same hatred, the same strained political correctness I had heard just a few days before in Bosnia. We too have our racial prejudices, tensions, and misunderstandings and yet live side-by-side. We also have those who accept intermarriage and those adamantly opposed to the mixing of America's ethnic groups. While we have seen no recent genocide or war, we have had our share of killings spawned by divisive propaganda: lynchings, deadly riots, hate crimes.

Whenever I returned to the United States to visit, people used to say that Rwanda's and Bosnia's slaughters seemed so unimaginable to them.

I answered them this way: Imagine, say, that New York's Little Italy or Chinatown, in the midst of an economic crisis and brainwashed by ethnically divisive propaganda, decided to secede from the United States, arm itself, declare war, and then ethnically cleanse Harlem of its inhabitants. Put that way, the tragedy of mass ethnic killings seemed less incomprehensible, although still unlikely: Our democracy, our rule of law, our economy, and our overarching belief in the ideal of America help prevent it.

The stories of the people searching for justice in this book matter because they are powerful human tales. But they should also speak to us because their narratives parallel our own. They tell us something about what justice could mean, as Americans struggle to reconcile as individuals to misfortunes and as a society to our hatreds. And they show us the path so many other countries around the world are traveling, as strife, often driven by perception of ethnic differences, erupts into war.

That is why, long after my job was over in Europe, I packed my bag and traveled again to Bosnia and Rwanda. I wanted to find out how far beyond hatred these countries had traveled. That tyrants are punished, that societies heal, that individuals find justice are the responsibilities of us all—in order that they not become our fate.

Book One

BEARING WITNESS

1

BLOOD TIES TO BLOOD FEUDS

Which of us has known his brother? Which of us has looked into his father's heart?

—Thomas Wolfe, *Look Homeward, Angel*

Into the courtroom limped the defendant, tall and thin, favoring his right leg. "All rise," intoned the court clerk, and in swept the judges in their long flowing black robes. They settled into their chairs, shuffled their papers, adjusted their glasses; the prosecutors did the same. The defense attorney cleared his throat. For all the apparent ordinariness of their behavior, this might have been just an everyday trial about an everyday dispute, but it was not. This was a case about genocide, and these were the judges of the International Criminal Tribunal for the former Yugoslavia, the first international war crimes court since Nuremberg and Tokyo.

The man before them, General Radislav Krstić, was accused of the massacres of more than 7,000 Bosnian Muslim men and boys, killed by his troops as they captured a Bosnian town named Srebrenica guarded by Dutch United Nations peacekeepers. This—finally—was Marko Boškić's commanding officer. Already, much had been heard in this courtroom: the testimony of men who escaped execution squads, of mothers searching for their sons, of UN peacekeepers who saw civilians slain in cold blood. On November 1, 2000, the evidence was a telephone call, allegedly recorded between Krstić and one of his deputies, which appeared to link him beyond a shadow of a doubt to the horrors to which survivors had already testified.

"Kill all in turn," said the voice identified as General Krstić's. "Fuck their mothers!" The general, hearing the words, paled. "Don't leave a single one alive!"

In another courtroom a continent away on a different day, another witness would also testify to man's barbarity against man. The topic, again, was genocide: of how nearly 1 million Tutsi and moderate Hutu were slain in 100 days in a massacres of astonishing speed. This witness, General Romeo Dallaire, the Canadian head of UN forces in Rwanda, wept as he spoke of his frustration that the additional troops he requested were not provided in time. "All the member states of the UN have Rwandan blood on their hands," he said slowly as tears coursed down his cheeks. "It seems inconceivable that one can watch thousands of people being massacred every day . . . and remain passive. . . ."

Europe and America had no military response when these crimes occurred in Bosnia and Rwanda. But they did have a judicial one. Under the auspices of the United Nations Security Council, they had taken the unprecedented step of creating a war crimes tribunal for the former Yugoslavia, largely as a way of appearing to react to violence there without dispatching troops. World leaders then created a similar court for Rwanda, but this time out of shame: both for the slaughter they had failed to stop as well as for one they feared might still arrive.

The two courts, representing a dream nourished by human rights advocates since long before Nuremberg, had high-reaching aims. They would bring tyrants to justice, destroy cultures of impunity, uphold the rule of law, help reconcile the war-torn countries. They would shed light on the murky shadows of the past, on that troubling question of how people who once broke bread together killed each other. They would explain how madness came to grip two nations. Certainly no Rwandan could have predicted his country's tensions would be transformed into genocide. No Bosnian foresaw that their country would erupt into war. In fact, when anyone ever told me a story about life in Bosnia in the years before the war, it seemed always to be summer.

FAMILY AND FRIENDS would be sitting out in their gardens eating fruit plucked from their trees, or sipping thickly brewed Turkish coffee in a neighborhood café and chatting about trips to the beach or the mountains. The air was full of laughter, the sun was shining, the mood one of good fortune.

You could all but hear camera shutters clicking, preserving Bosnia and the country to which it belonged—Yugoslavia—if not in photographs then in someone's mind's eye. *Click.* See, we all got along, Muslim, Croat, and Serb. *Click.* Our town had a mosque, but it also had an Orthodox cathedral; we weren't religious, but we'd feast to celebrate the Muslim holiday of Bayram or the Serb holiday of Petrovdan; everyone went to Christmas Eve mass at the cathedral. *Click. Click.* See, we spent the summers at Croatia's beaches along the turquoise-hued Adriatic, the winters skiing the rugged mountains of Slovenia, visited Sarajevo to idle away the hours in cafés in the old Turkish quarter, went to the opera or the museums in Belgrade. *Click.* We were communists, but we experimented with capitalism; here we are in front of our holiday home, our *vikendica*, which we built from the money we earned working in Munich. We were open to the West; we crossed to Trieste, Italy, to buy our clothes, and look: Here are the photos of us all hosting international tourists at the 1984 Winter Olympics in Sarajevo.

Click.

This was the world in which the Bosnian families I came to know had once lived. In fact, it was the *only* world they knew. Yugoslavia's leader, wartime resistance hero Josip Broz Tito, had governed the country from 1945 until his death in 1980. Under his rule, being Yugoslav mattered more than one's ethnic origin, than being Muslim, Croat, or Serb. Suddenly, within a few years of Tito's death, everything that happened to people depended on their ethnicity. Consider the story of Hasan Nuhanović, who came from Vlasenica, a small town deep in the lush, thick forests of north-central Bosnia. In 1988, the year nationalism began to sweep across Yugoslavia in earnest, he arrived in Sarajevo to study mechanical engineering.

It was to Sarajevo that Bosnians always flocked, to this city that embodied the historic waves of culture, religions, and traditions that had swept across their country over the centuries. Its Baščaršija market quarter, with its small wooden-fronted shops and cobblestone streets filled with the smell of spicy roast kebab, recalled the days of the Ottoman Empire. The Europa Hotel and other buildings, with their rich architectural swags and cornices, bore the stamp of Austro-Hungarian rule. The tall, graceless apartment buildings on the city's outskirts, on streets named after slogans, like "Brotherhood and Unity," bespoke its communist days. With mosques, Orthodox churches, and Catholic cathedrals, Sarajevo was a blend of Europe and the Orient, a city whose population was as intermarried as they were multiethnic, and who loved nothing better than to while away the hours sitting around smoking, drinking, and talking about anything at all.

Bosnians tend not to be overly tall, and at six-foot-three Hasan towers above almost everyone. Dark-haired, lean, and peering downward through his glasses with piercing hazel eyes, I imagine him standing in a crowd of students, hands on his hips, the crook of his head twisting the shape of his body into a question mark.

His days at the University of Sarajevo, Hasan would recall years later, were spent skipping classes and hanging out with his friends, discussions that began in the morning and ended late at night over brandy, in the student bar. As pop music blared loudly and cigarette smoke floated through the air, he and his friends talked about girls, the latest movie from the West, music—Hasan himself played the electric guitar. They clinked their glasses and toasted: After all, they were students at one of the best universities in the country, headed for the best days of their lives, in what they considered the best country of the world, Yugoslavia, with its six differing yet united republics: Croatia, Serbia, Montenegro, Macedonia, Bosnia and Herzegovina, and Slovenia.

All the young men looked the same in their student chic, dressed in T-shirts and blue-jean jackets, cigarettes dangling from their fingers, an occasional growth of late-night stubble. Sure, they came from different parts of the country, with different histories and religions, but no one who looked at Hasan and his friends could distinguish them along ethnic lines, and frankly, none of them cared to do so. They'd all grown up in the same way: drunk the popular Montenegrin beer "Nikšićko" or the Slovenian drink Cockta while eating Bosnian ćevapčići and listening to the Sarajevo hit group Bjelo Dugme (White Button). The same influences had touched them all. It was no different from being an American and having grown up eating Southern fried chicken and Boston cream pie.

Which was why Hasan was so surprised one day in 1989 when hundreds of students from the university cut classes to attend a rally given by a rising nationalist politician named Slobodan Milošević from Serbia. He watched as the buses wheeled up in front of the university dorms. Hundreds of well-dressed students, some carrying posters emblazoned with Milošević's stolid face topped by his bristly porcupine haircut, clambered on, laughing and singing songs. They were headed for the Serbian province of Kosovo, where Milošević intended to commemorate the six hundredth anniversary of the battle of Kosovo Polje, where Serb forces tried to defend Christendom against the Ottoman Turks and lost.

Looking back on it later, Hasan realized that was when he first sensed that his life, as he knew it, was over. The event seemed so very innocent—the battle, after all, had been in 1389—but what struck Hasan was this: Everyone he knew getting on the bus was of Serb origin.

Merely by getting on those buses, those students had separated themselves from Hasan, had defined themselves not as Yugoslav but as Serbs. Hasan was a Muslim. All that meant to him was that his mother, Nasiha, made baclava for her parents when they broke the traditional Muslim feast of Bayram. Now, suddenly, his being a Bosnian Muslim had become who he was, whether he liked it or not.

Nearly 1 million Serbs went to Kosovo Polje that day and cheered wildly for Slobodan Milošević, and things were never the same again. Differences, not similarities, began to matter. At Hasan's university, students began singing long-banned Serbian or Croatian songs and enthusiastically marking long-forgotten holidays. Serbs in the dorms, drunk, would dance their native circle dance, the kolo, in the hallways. For the first time students began to divide up dormitory rooms along ethnic lines. All Hasan had to do was walk down the hall of the university dorms and look at the names on the door—ethnic background was not reflected in anyone's appearance but by their names—to realize that a major transformation was occurring.

What was happening was this: Communism was collapsing across Eastern Europe, and an atavistic nationalism was taking its place, spawning new leaders hungry for power. In Yugoslavia, the stirrings of political change came in the wake of Tito's death and the burgeoning economic crisis he had left behind. Once hailed as the richest and most open of the communist economies, Yugoslavia was on the verge of financial collapse, with some $20 billion in foreign debt.

For years, Yugoslavia's economy had prospered, in part artificially. In 1965 Tito replaced state socialism—and its unprofitable, subsidized industries—with a Western-style market socialism. Factories, left in the hands of their workers, downsized to compete and unemployment soared. The economy was rescued because neighboring European countries had labor shortages. Travel was visa-free and nearly 1 million Yugoslavs ended up in Germany or Austria working for several years, returning with dollars and Deutschemarks. The money in everyone's pockets not only boosted the economy but also contributed to a false sense of prosperity.

In the 1980s, economic hard times arrived. Europe, in recession, cut back on jobs for the Yugoslavs, and unemployment soared again. Inflation surged—hitting 2,500 percent in 1989. Industries, still indebted and not yet profitable, foundered. Workers went out on strike. Political chaos reigned. The collective presidency Tito created to succeed him swiftly proved unworkable. It failed to keep hold of Yugoslavia, allowing power to devolve back to republics—many of which were dominated by one ethnicity—whose relations dissolved into political backbiting and feuding.

The situation played right into the hands of a ruthless, power-hungry, forty-eight-year-old Serb politician by the name of Slobodan Milošević. Nothing in his background augured that Milošević would become a political mastermind or lead Yugoslavia into war. Born into poverty in the dusty, unremarkable town of Požarevac, 55 miles southeast of Belgrade, Milošević grew up in a household marked by loss: His father, a Serbian Orthodox cleric, abandoned the family and killed himself. Years later Milošević's mother committed suicide, as did his uncle. Milošević went on to study law at Belgrade University and then became a banker, eventually spending time in New York.

Returning to Yugoslavia, Milošević skillfully sidelined his rivals and, aided by his equally ruthless wife, Mirjana Marković, climbed his way up through the ranks to become head of the Serbian Communist Party. Shrewdly, he built a power base: transforming the Yugoslav People's Army (JNA) through purges, outfoxing his liberal opponents by appearing to be on their side. His political genius, however, lay in recognizing the rallying power of nationalism. In 1987 Milošević had become an overnight sensation after a speech in the Serbian autonomous province of Kosovo in which he trumpeted the cause of the Kosovo Serbs over that of the ethnic Albanian majority.

Kosovo had long been a source of anxiety for ethnic Serbs, who had left the province due to harassment by Albanian extremists, a problem that Tito simply ignored. But Milošević promised the Serbs that Kosovo was still theirs. (In 1989 he stripped the province of the autonomy granted to it by Tito in the 1960s.) Propelled into the limelight, Milošević and his followers gained power, purging the media of critics and winning over sympathetic journalists as allies in state television and the principal newspapers. Soon all that was being published was Milošević's pro-Serb nationalist propaganda. His message was simple: Drawing on the myths, legends, and poetry long suppressed under communism, Milošević created a sense of Serb victimization. The Serbs, he preached, are a heroic and glorious people who have suffered centuries of injustice because of their frustrated efforts to have their own state. Now is the time of reckoning: when the Serbs will have their reward—a "greater Serbia," a state for all the Serbs.

His drive for a greater Serbia would destroy Yugoslavia. Aided by another nationalist who acted as his foil, Croatian leader Franjo Tudjman, Milošević stirred up existing ethnic rivalries and, through propaganda, introduced new ones. Soon Croatia and Serbia were at war, riven by nationalist and ethnic discontent. Milošević then imported the war to Bosnia, multiethnic since the early Middle Ages. He fanned the flames of nationalist hatred until Bosnia burst into ethnic conflagration. Neighbor would turn on neighbor, Serb against Muslim, Serb against Croat. The result was a kind of collective madness that spawned the worst atrocities and war crimes Europe had seen since World War II: mass executions, torture, the expulsion of millions of civilians from their homes, concentration camps.

Serbs, Croats, Muslims; nationalism began to define everything as Yugoslavia splintered apart. Once legends surrounding the region's history were let loose—with their accompanying message of long-standing historical injustice—the past suddenly became more important than the future.

"We were brave and dignified and one of the few who went into battle undefeated," said Milošević at that same rally in 1989 that Hasan's fellow students attended, describing the battle of 1389 to the adoring Serbs who'd assembled to hear him. Then, in a portent of what his policies would bring to the region, he added: "Six centuries later we are again in battles and quarrels. They are not armed battles, though such things should not be excluded yet."

HOW DID BOSNIA, where people had long intermarried and intermingled along ethnic lines, erupt into savage hostilities that would shatter the country? During the war, President Bill Clinton at one point dismissed Bosnia's slaughter as the product of intractable ethnic hatreds. But history is never so simple. If there were a generalization to be made, it was quite the opposite one. Until World War II, Bosnia's history, unlike that of some of its neighbors, was more one of ethnic coexistence than ethnic enmity, despite the steady ebb and flow of kingdoms, empires, and religions across it.

Broadly speaking, it was the Serbs and the Croats, more than the Bosnians, whose animosities had historic roots. While all the Serbs, Croats, and Muslims of the former Yugoslavia came from the same stock—the southern Slavs who settled across the region in the seventh and eighth centuries—over the generations the arrival of Christianity, domination by the feuding Ottoman and the Habsburg empires and nationalism divided them. The first fault line came with Christianity's schism into the Western Roman Empire and the Eastern Empire of Byzantium. The boundary between the two religious empires, set along the river Drina, separated one group of Slavs into two different cultures and religions and ultimately into rivals. By the Middle Ages the Croats, with their kingdom to the west, looked to Europe and to Rome: They were Catholic and used the Latin alphabet. To the east, the Serbs looked to Constantinople and the Orient: They were Orthodox and used the Cyrillic alphabet. Over the centuries both were occupied by competing empires and then hungered for their own, independent ethnic states.

Bosnia's experience, however, was somewhat different. While it lies sandwiched between Serbia and Croatia, its geography makes it distinct. Bosnia is a land of rugged mountains, plunging valleys, thick forests, and fast-moving rivers, which carve it into distinct regions and separate it from neighboring Croatia to the north, south, and west, and from Serbia to the east. Those natural barriers, while giving Bosnia its own character, did not make it impregnable. As the Croat, Serb, and Bosnian medieval kingdoms waxed and waned, amid disputes for territory and rivalry between the Catholic and Orthodox church, parts of Bosnia would be gained and lost and regained. Both the Serbian and Croatian kingdoms at times laid claim to parts of Bosnia, something nationalists centuries later would exploit to justify their desire for the country.

Bosnia's geographical separateness gave it a sense of independence, particularly in affairs of religion. Emerging from a period of Hungarian rule, Bosnia in the thirteenth century severed its ties with Rome—although not with Christianity—and established its own independent church, whose followers were known as the Bogomils. In this patchwork of a country, carved by its geography and the ebb and flow of conquests into regions with varying traditions and religions, lived Bogomil Christians, Orthodox, and Croat Catholics. At a time when their neighbors thought of themselves as "Serbs" or "Croats," they called themselves "Bosnians." While there were struggles for power and territory, Bosnians in the Middle Ages did not fight on ethnic grounds.

But by the fourteenth century, the territorially ambitious Ottoman Empire had designs on the strategically important Balkan peninsula and beyond. Its armies clashed with those of the Serbian empire to Bosnia's east on several occasions, but the best known was the battle of Kosovo Polje, on June 28, 1389. There was a reason Milošević picked that battle to launch his nationalist career, and it was not for the battlefield's beauty: It was then ringed by industrial chimneys belching smoke in the distance and strewn with trash. Milošević chose it for its symbolism. Kosovo Polje, enshrined in legend, glorified in ballad, was as important a battle to Serbs as Gettysburg is to Americans.

Petko Grubač, a psychiatrist from the Bosnian city of Konjic whom I came to know, explained to me how he had grown up on the legends surrounding Kosovo Polje. Petko, who originally hailed from the rugged Yugoslav Republic of Montenegro, was a Serb. Like many Serbs, he grew up believing that the battle was pivotal to the region's history, a place where Serbian forces struggled to defend Christian Europe from the Turks and failed, ushering in 500 years of repressive Ottoman rule and the end of the Serbian state, but the start of a proud and successful fight to preserve Orthodoxy under Islamic domination. Passed down in poem and ballad by traveling Serb minstrels playing a one-stringed fiddle, or *gusle*, the story of Kosovo Polje defined what it meant to be a Serb—whether one came from Bosnia, Croatia, Serbia, or Montenegro.

Legend had it that, before the battle, the Serb prince Lazar was offered a choice by God: an empire on earth, which meant he would live, or an empire in heaven, which would require his death as a Christian warrior on the battlefield. Lazar, vowing it is "better to die in battle than to live in shame," went on to die nobly—sacrificially—at Kosovo Polje. Generations of Serbs would be raised to see themselves as a distinct Balkan race: martyrs to Christianity and Western civilization and heroic fighters whose duty was to resist any occupying power. "There's an old saying—either be a colonel, or be dead," Petko explained to me once. "There is nothing in between. We Serbs focus on our heroes, like Prince Lazar. We are into fairy tales. People like to say Einstein did not come up with his own ideas. It was his wife, a Serb from Novi Sad, who put all the ideas in his head."

Of course, the reality of Kosovo Polje bears little resemblance to any of the accounts Petko learned as a child. The battle was somewhat inconclusive; the Balkan troops, not exclusively Serb; and the Ottoman Empire would not actually annex Serbia and Bosnia until 1463. Ottoman rule, however, forever altered the history of the region and Bosnia, ushering in new forms of government as well as a new religion, Islam. Founded in the thirteenth century, the Ottoman Empire stretched across parts of Asia, Europe, and Africa.

Those governing the province brought with them many things Turkish, from the style of brewing coffee to Islamic mosques. But they respected the region's tradition of religious tolerance and diversity and did not force large-scale conversions. Those who did convert, which turned out to be many Bosnians and fewer Serbians, found that Islam, as practiced in that far-off corner of the empire, was lax; women didn't even necessarily wear the veil.

The mix of Bosnia's religious groups continued; Muslim, Catholic, and Orthodox coexisted, sometimes side by side, other times divided in regions by the jagged peaks of the country's mountains. Sephardic Jews, forced out of Spain, arrived at the end of the fifteenth century. Bosnians celebrated different religious holidays, wore different attire, had different songs and traditions. The division that provoked the most tension was economic. Muslim landowners occupied positions of importance in cities like Sarajevo, while Christians—often Serbs—worked for them as peasants out in the rugged hills or lush valleys of the countryside. The peasants had hereditary rights to their land but had to pay taxes to Muslim landowners. Resentment, spurred along by the Ottomans' harshness, stirred among the Christian peasants.

As the Ottoman Empire reached the height of its power in the sixteenth century, its viziers would rule Bosnia from three of its cities, leaving their stamp on different parts of the country. But it would be Sarajevo that would become one of the empire's leading cities, bustling with wealthy merchants—a town of "beautiful streets, fine and well-made bridges of stone and wood and 169 beautiful fountains," noted a contemporary French traveler. (The city's name comes from a Turkish word, *sara*, or seraglio, the sultan's residence.) Sarajevo boasted 170 mosques.

While Serbia and Bosnia were under the Ottoman thumb, Croatia had come under the rule of the Hungarian crown, eventually allied with Austria's Habsburg monarchs. The armies of the two rival empires clashed repeatedly on Balkan battlefields. To protect itself against the Ottomans' territorial designs, the Austro-Hungarian Empire enlisted Serbs to live on its border, or *krajina*, with promises of freedom of religion and property in exchange for their wholehearted military support. Thus, significant numbers of Serbs came to live in Croatia—a fact that would further complicate the region's ethnic mix and play out disastrously not only in World War II but also fifty years later.

In a sense, the next empire that swept across the Balkans came in the form of an idea: nationalism. The French Revolution in 1789 ushered in ideas of independence and statehood in the Balkans and arrived even as the Ottoman Empire, riddled with corruption and infighting, slid into decline. The Turks suffered defeats at the hands of Russia and lost control over Greece and Egypt. Desperate for funds to support their military needs, Ottoman rulers demanded more and more taxes from the populace under their thumb. In Bosnia, Christian peasants began to look to the Serbs and Croats for an identity and a political solution. Outside of Bosnia, dreams flourished: of a Serbian state, free of the Ottomans, of a Croatian state, free of Austria-Hungary.

By the mid-nineteenth century, nationalism had sparked uprisings across Europe, and the Balkans were no exception. The rebellious Serbs had won autonomy from the Ottomans, inspiring the Serbs of Bosnia, reeling under increasingly heavy taxes and oppressive means of collecting them, to revolt. In 1875 peasant rebellions across Bosnia were violently repressed, forcing hundreds of thousands of mostly Christian refugees to flee, many toward Serbia. Within a year Serbia had declared war against the Ottoman Empire and was soon joined by Russia and Montenegro.

In 1878, Europe's leaders gathered in Berlin to make the boundaries of southeastern Europe. Serbia and neighboring Montenegro were defined as their own states. But—to Serbia's great distress—Bosnia was given to the Austro-Hungarian Empire, which still included Croatia, to administer, although the Ottoman Empire still retained a shadowy suzerainty. The Ottomans had neglected Bosnia and their retreat left the country in economic disarray. Roads had crumbled and bridges had collapsed. Sarajevo was a shadow of its former glory. The majority of Bosnians were illiterate. Thousands of Bosnian Muslims quit their country for Anatolia. It would take the Ottomans' great rival, the Austro-Hungarians, to modernize the country and prepare it for the turn of the century. The Austrians built thousands of miles of railroads, roads, and hundreds of new bridges. They erected iron, steel, and coal-mining industries and introduced compulsory education. In addition to schnitzel on restaurant menus and ornate, pompous friezes on many public buildings, their legacy included a Catholic political hierarchy that eventually served as a rallying point for Bosnia's Catholic Croats.

By the beginning of the twentieth century, Bosnia had no long-simmering ancient ethnic feuds. But it did have three separate ethnic and religious groups—Muslim, Croat, and Serb—with different political identities, different histories, and different resentments.

I OFTEN HEARD from middle-age Bosnians that their parents and grandparents could not remember the region at peace. Indeed, the countries surrounding Bosnia were almost consistently in conflict from 1912 to 1945, largely due to resurgent nationalism. Serbia was drawn into wars against Turkey in 1912 and Bulgaria in 1913. (Croatia and Bosnia, still part of the Austro-Hungarian Empire, did not take part.) Both wars involved brutal attacks on civilians and the destruction of property, events that would become a hallmark of the war in Bosnia in 1992. "The burning of villages and the exodus of the defeated population is a normal and traditional incident of all Balkan wars and insurrections," concluded the Carnegie Endowment inquiry into the two wars conducted in 1913. "It is the habit of these peoples. What they have suffered themselves, they inflict in turn upon others."

The shot that ignited World War I, however, was fired in Bosnia, when a young Bosnian Serb nationalist, Gavrilo Princip, a member of a nationalist group that wanted Austria-Hungary to relinquish Bosnia, killed Habsburg archduke Franz Ferdinand in Sarajevo on June 28, 1914, the anniversary of the battle of Kosovo Polje. (The legend's sway was as strong as ever.) Within six weeks Austria-Hungary had declared war on Serbia and Germany had invaded France. While many Bosnians were drafted to fight for the Austro-Hungarian Empire, many Bosnian Serbs volunteered to fight for Serbia. At the war's end little fighting had occurred in Bosnia. Serbia, where most of the battles had played out, emerged victorious, but it had lost nearly 40 percent of those mobilized.

With the end of the war in 1918, the dream of South Slav nation-builders across the Balkans became a reality: the kingdom of the Bosnians, Serbs, Croats, and Slovenes came into being, ruled by the Serbian royal family. Finally the era of oppressive empires was gone, and self-governance was at hand. However, Yugoslavia, as it was renamed in 1929 ("the land of southern Slavs"), knew little domestic tranquillity. The nationalities it joined together had never been united, had their own distinct cultures, and were former rivals on the battlefield. The Croats and Serbs, divided for centuries by religion and culture, quarreled bitterly in their new union. (So strong were the tensions that even Muslims chose sides, calling themselves "Muslim Croats" or "Muslim Serbs.") Disillusionment and infighting were rife. After the assassination of the Yugoslav king Aleksandar in 1934 by terrorists in the pay of fascist Croats known as Ustasha, Croatia gained some autonomy within the kingdom. Lumped with it was Bosnia, which, from that point onward, many Croats would come to see as their own.

HAMDIJA (HAMDO) KHARIMANOVIĆ was a history teacher I came to know from Kozarac, a village nestled in the Kozara Mountains in northwest Bosnia. He had a full shock of white hair, velvety brown eyes, a middle-age paunch, and a bustling air of importance. No doubt you have met men like him: jolly but at the same time officious, a man who liked being the big fish of the small pond of Kozarac.

Had you sat in one of his World War II history classes, you would have learned all about Kozarac. Some of the most famous battles—and some of the more horrible massacres—of the war were carried out in the shadows of the rugged Kozara Mountains, and residents were proud of their reputation as fierce fighters. As a local saying goes: "People of Kozara love their guns like a girl, they love song, and their glass of brandy, but most of all they love their freedom." Since Hamdo was teaching the official Yugoslav version of history, rarely would he mention Serb, Croat, or Muslim. World War II so bitterly divided the region's different groups, turning fighting into fratricide, that Tito decided the only way to settle scores was to recast them. Little or no mention of who sided with whom was allowed. The war's heroes were Tito's Partisans; its losers, the Ustasha, the Nazis, and the Chetniks.

The reality was far more ethnically complicated. On April 6, 1941, the German Luftwaffe bombed Belgrade, and shortly thereafter German and Italian troops invaded Yugoslavia. In Croatia, the narrowly based fascist Ustasha threw its support behind the Italians and Germans and was given control over both Croatia and Bosnia. The Ustasha, welcomed at first because they had won Croatia its long-desired "independent state," quickly lost favor as it gained a reputation for brutality. Gangs of Croatian Ustasha slaughtered Serbs and Jews by the thousands. Entire villages of Croatian Serbs were rounded up and slain, women and children alike. Crossing the border into Bosnia, the Ustasha murdered thousands more Bosnian Serbs, rounding up those they didn't kill and dispatching them to concentration camps. At Jasenovac, one of the most infamous concentration camps in Croatia, the Ustasha killed tens of thousands of Serbs, Jews, Gypsies, and other Croats.

Jasenovac, like the battle of Kosovo Polje hundreds of years before, would become a symbol for Bosnian Serb nationalists in the early 1990s. Quarrels raged over how many died there—Serb nationalists say 600,000; Croat nationalists, 68,000. (Historians are still trying to settle the dispute.) Many times, interviewing Bosnian Serbs in Kozarac about local atrocities against the Bosnian Muslims, I would be told defensively: "But remember Jasenovac!"

But World War II's bitter fratricide was not waged solely on a Croat-Serb axis. The Ustasha sought to lure Bosnia's Muslims to their side. (Croat nationalists, after all, believed that most Muslims were really

Croats who had converted to Islam.) Many Bosnians Muslims, anxious to protect their property, did cast their lot with the Ustasha and the Nazis. One group of volunteers, the Handschar (Scimitar) Division, was deployed as a Waffen SS unit that cut its own bloody path across Bosnia. Yet many other Bosnian Muslims joined a partisan resistance movement led by Tito and his communist fighters.

Headquartered in central Bosnia's jagged mountains, the Partisans fought guerrilla-style battles from their rocky strongholds. They gained the loyalty of the Bosnians of the Kozara region, many of whom joined their ranks. (Some sided with the Nazis.) When Germans and the Ustasha surrounded the region in 1942 and captured it, tens of thousands of residents, mostly Serbs, were rounded up and killed or marched off to Jasenovac—they included 4,000 children, a handful of whom would become Bosnia's war criminals of the 1990s. Communist-era textbooks, describing the battle as "among the most dramatic and bloodiest in the people's fight for freedom," estimated that 25,000 area residents were killed or starved.

The Partisans soon found themselves fighting not only the Germans and Italians but another guerrilla group, Serbian Chetniks. Led by Draža Mihailović, a Serbian officer, the Chetniks were royalists who initially resisted Hitler. Eventually they threw their support behind him, joining with the Nazis in military campaigns, slaughtering Muslims and Croats alike. So heinous were the associations surrounding the word "Chetnik," in fact, that Bosnia's Muslims used it to characterize their Bosnian Serb foes during the war of 1992 to 1995.

World War II dissolved into many subwars in Bosnia, pitting neighbor against neighbor, brother against brother. No matter which way you turned, there was fratricide: The Chetniks battled the Partisans, and Serbs battled the Croat Ustasha; the Muslims joined both the Ustasha, whose atrocities were particularly brutal, and the Partisans. The fighting was bitter, bloody, brutal. No one could overlook the destruction, the savagery, the concentration camps, the tens of thousands who were uprooted, the tens of thousands who died. The country that Tito presided over at the war's end was divided by a central enmity between the Serbs and Croats, hundreds of regional disputes, and thousands of individual hatreds.

Tito was faced not only with restoring his war-torn land but also with knitting together a concept—Yugoslavia—that had failed under the 1918 monarchy. The son of a Croat father and a Slovene mother, Tito represented Yugoslavia's potential for diversity. He decided the best way to preserve that diversity was to do away with ethnic identity in favor of a nationalist one. Declaring a policy of *Bratstvo i Jedinstvo*, or "Brotherhood and Unity," Tito mandated that Croats, Serbs, Macedonians, and all the rest no longer existed: All were Yugoslavs. Their ethnic past was to be forgotten. (Even humming a Croatian folk tune could land someone in prison.) Only one religion existed, and that was Titoism.

The war became known as the People's Liberation Struggle. Past disputes between Serbs, Croats, and various Serb resistance movements were largely swept under the carpet. Hundreds of monuments to the Partisans were erected around the country—nearly every town had one—with no reference to the fact that any one ethnic group had suffered at the hands of another.

Although Tito officially ignored ethnic identities, at least at first, behind the scenes there was an awareness of the latent perils of Yugoslavia's heterogeneous mix. Tito kept the peace by a principle dubbed "the ethnic key," which ensured parity among the various groups. In Bosnia, which in 1948 had a multiethnic population consisting of 1.1 million Serbs, 890,094 Muslims, and 614,123 Croats, top positions in each municipality were represented by a Croat, a Muslim, and a Serb. Textbooks were written by two or more authors of varying ethnic backgrounds. The principle was even adhered to in the country's court system, whether the case be one of murder or a simple fender-bender. If the defendant was Serb, then the judge must be Serb as well.

It is one thing to rename a war; it is another to dispel its memories. "Brotherhood and Unity" demanded there be no postwar reckoning. Questions of which ethnic group was responsible for which atrocity—or which ethnic group suffered the most—were largely ignored in the hopes that people would forget them. A handful of high-profile show trials of alleged war criminals took place, but typically, impunity reigned, and many of the most notorious war criminals, including the head of the Ustasha, fled the country.

Tito's efforts to lionize the Partisans and World War II as the victory of the noble partisans over the evil fascists, however, romanticized war even as it focused attention on its brutality. Dozens of movies aired on

Yugoslav television glorifying the fighting, including *Neretva*, which starred the Welsh actor Richard Burton as Tito. An entire generation grew up on a diet of films depicting bloodthirsty Chetniks (Serb royalists), savage Ustasha (Croats), and noble Partisans. (These terms, Chetnik and Ustasha, became synonymous with "killer," so much so that the terms were revived in the propaganda of Milošević and Tudjman).

Yugoslav schoolchildren, in fact, were required as part of their education to read about wartime atrocities—torture, beheading, physical mutilation, and execution—described in bloodthirsty terms that would make most American teachers shiver. For example, the poem "The Pit" by Ivan Goran Kovačić, which described torture committed by Croatian Ustasha, was part of the elementary school curriculum. "I'm lying on the corpse: pile of cold meat" reads verse 35 of 50, "Sluggish, mucous, souring in blood / But salvation is bringing me from the ice and chills: /Flashes in my consciousness, when a woman screams. / I turned around, in a fever, towards the scream / I reached out: felt a slippery wound."

Such glorification was typically Balkan and communist and Tito made no effort to halt it. The region was famous for its epic poems and folk tales, a way of keeping history alive in a country where illiteracy had long reigned. Yet it meant that a generation of Yugoslavs grew up with particular notions about history as well as war. Everyone accepted that there was an official history, as proclaimed by movies, textbooks, and war memorials; then there were the unofficial histories, the wartime injustices that lived on in the collective memory of each ethnic group as crimes that demanded recognition, if not punishment and vengeance. Hatreds were whispered privately, passed down from parents to children. Every once in a while, someone's grandmother would let slip that a local Serb was a "Chetnik" or a Croat, "an Ustasha."

At the same time, young Yugoslav men grew up believing that war was noble, glorious, and just. A just war by necessity entailed death, no matter how it arrived. So when Tito's "Brotherhood and Unity" collapsed in the 1980s and Yugoslavia erupted into war, the fighters had not been raised to think about their conduct on the battlefield toward civilians or prisoners. They had been raised to think that war—perhaps by virtue of its sheer glory—encompassed actions that noncombatants would classify as war crimes.

THESE WERE THE students that Hamdo Kahrimanović had in his school in Kozarac, first as a teacher, then as a principal. Hamdo was proud of his school, and rightly so. His school, the Rade Kondić school, was the largest elementary school in Bosnia.

The school's size reflected the fact that Kozarac, while having a population of just 4,000, was no ordinary town. It was renowned as one of the centers of Partisan resistance, and one of the more famous World War II monuments stood on the mountain above it. It was a wealthy town, profiting from the many tourists who passed through. Numerous village fathers and sons also made good money working at factories in Germany and Austria and had returned to live in Kozarac in style. (Others were employed in the region's iron ore and lumber industries.) Nearly every family in Kozarac had a washing machine. Even though the main street was only a few blocks long, it boasted a movie theater, a health clinic, and an old Turkish fort.

Hamdo, whose family had lived in Kozarac for generations—the town dated itself back to the fourteenth century—couldn't imagine living anywhere else. The kind of man who likes to know things, Hamdo was paying attention to what was happening in Bosnia. He had noticed the ascendancy of Serb nationalist Slobodan Milošević. But given Kozarac's close proximity to the Croatian border—a mere twenty miles away—Hamdo also had his eye on an equally virulent nationalist politician, closer to home: Croatian Franjo Tudjman.

When Milošević first preached of a greater Serbia for the Serbs, Tudjman was silent. But, slowly, the war of words and symbols between the two men intensified. As the Serbs revived their Serbian folk songs, so the Croats brought back their red-and-white checkerboard flag, a historic symbol used by World War II Ustasha forces and banned by Tito. Then, in 1990, Tudjman began to speak of a greater Croatia as well.

To many Croats in Yugoslavia—and some 5 million living abroad—these were welcome words. Many began to think of Tudjman, a former Partisan fighter, military general, and self-taught historian, as the man to lead an independent Croatia. He looked the part with his jowls, and his regal, stolid manner. And he had the perfect pedigree: Sixty-eight years old, after leaving the Yugoslav Peoples Army (JNA) he had been imprisoned for his nationalist views and made no secret of his yearning to lead a free Croatia.

Between Milošević and Tudjman, little seemed to be holding Yugoslavia's republics together, save the memory of Tito. In January 1990 the fragile political equilibrium shattered when Slovenia, outraged at Serbian efforts to gain more power in running the country, walked out of the Congress of the League of Communists of Yugoslavia. Croatia later followed suit. There was no federal institution left to bind the country together, only its army. With the collapse of the communist congress, ideas of democracy looked attractive. Croatia announced it would hold its first elections, and Tudjman swept to a resounding victory as the leader of the 4.5 million-strong republic, all the time spewing nationalist Croatian rhetoric. Unlike Milošević, who saw nationalism as a means to gain power, Tudjman was a hard-core nationalist, and an intemperate one at that. Campaigning, he once remarked, "Thank God my wife is not a Jew or a Serb."

His arrival on the political scene terrified the 600,000 Serbs who lived in Croatia—12 percent of the country's population—descendants of Serb fighters settled by the Austro-Hungarian Empire along the border in the eighteenth century as defense against the Ottomans. Tudjman's political campaign revived memories of Serb suffering at the hands of the Ustasha in World War II. His victory raised questions about their future in a Croatian country. Their fears were not assuaged when Tudjman removed Cyrillic street signs, dismissed Serbs from jobs, and declared them an ethnic minority. Angered, they formed their own political party, the Serbian Democratic Party.

Suddenly nationalist parties sprouted like weeds across Yugoslavia, and Bosnia proved to be fertile ground. Hamdo, a staunch communist, found it a bewildering time. In the place of Tito-style socialism were three political parties, organized, as they were in Croatia and Serbia, along ethnic lines. First came the Muslim nationalist Party of Democratic Action (SDA), founded by the rumpled and professorial Alija Izetbegović, an Islamic scholar jailed by Tito. Then the Serbian Democratic Party (SDS), headed by Radovan Karadžić, a psychiatrist with a distinctive, unruly mop of hair, who worked for the the Sarajevo football team and then the Croatian Democratic Union, the Bosnian branch of Tudjman's party.

But which political party to join? Other emerging parties were trying to dampen the nationalism dividing Bosnia, which threatened to split it off from Yugoslavia. The Yugoslav Federal prime minister, Ante Marković, a Croat, launched his own civic party, hoping to rally nonnationalists behind him; in July 1990, tens of thousands attended a rally he held in the Kozarac Mountains announcing "an alliance of reformist forces."

As Bosnia held its first democratic election in November 1990, Hamdo refused to take part. He was surprised at the enthusiasm with which his colleagues at the Rade Kondić school and his neighbors embraced Bosnia's new nationalism. Simo Drljača, a lawyer who worked in Prijedor but also served as the legal advisor to the Rade Kondić school, was one.

Quiet and brooding, Drljača's only social activity was trout fishing, and even then it took some convincing to get him to join in when other fishermen, pulling a trout out from the river Sana, grilled it on the spot for all to share. Yet Drjlača not only joined the local Serb nationalist party, the SDS, he also became a leader in it.

Even one of Hamdo's former students and neighbor, Dušan Tadić, had picked up the Serbian nationalist cause. Hamdo was stunned. Tadić's father had been a famous Partisan and a loyal advocate of "Brotherhood and Unity"; his mother, an equally devoted Partisan, had been an inmate at the Jasenovac camp during World War II. Dušan, whom most people called by his nickname, "Dule," had grown up just a few hundred yards from Hamdo's house, and the families knew each other well. Dule, short and darkly handsome, was the married father of two, a local café owner and a karate instructor. He was known for a sometimes volatile temper, not for his political passions. But he too joined the Bosnian Serb political party, the SDS.

People, Hamdo observed, had started thinking differently. Both he and his wife, Firdesa, noticed how ordinary feuds were transformed into ethnic grievances. Tadić, one of Kozarac's few Serbs—the town was predominantly Muslim—attracted much of the controversy. Someone smashed the windows in the Tadić family café; Dule then received a threatening letter he attributed to local Muslim nationalists. Soon Muslim investors called in business loans they had granted to him. In response, Tadić banned all the local Muslims from the café. The situation had become an ugly, ethnic tit-for-tat.

As these events unfolded in Kozarac, the village suddenly found itself with a ringside seat at a far greater battle: War broke out between Croatia and Serbia in the summer of 1991. As had long been the case in the Balkans, the great Serb-Croat divide—that ancient rivalry of Rome versus Constantinople, the Austrians versus the Ottomans—would hover over Bosnia, shaping the events to come.

Hostilities had been escalating for months. The Serbs of Croatia's Krajina region—armed by Slobodan Milošević for their own "self-protection" and goaded by his propaganda—rebelled against Croatian president Tudjman and declared themselves an autonomous region in January of 1991. As Milošević began to gear up for war, thousands of students and members of the political opposition took to the streets in Belgrade in protest. Milošević sent in tanks and soldiers to halt them but demonstrations continued, with students singing "Give Peace a Chance." It was in vain.

Yugoslavia's nine-member presidency, quarreling among themselves, effectively disbanded. Milošević, having recruited the Yugoslav People's Army to his side, declared that the republic of Serbia would no longer recognize any decisions issued on a federal level. "Yugoslavia," he said, "has entered into its final phase of agony." In June 1991 two of Yugoslavia's republics, Croatia and Slovenia, took the process a step further. Each declared its sovereignty and independence.

It didn't take long for Serbia and Croatia, building on centuries of frustrated nationalism and mutual antagonism, to go to war. Milošević swiftly dispatched JNA troops from Belgrade toward the newly independent Croatia. Dnevnik 2, the evening news from Belgrade broadcast across Yugoslavia, echoed Milošević's line by reporting on the Serb "fight for freedom." Federal authorities sent troops to Slovenia to protect the border with Austria and Italy that had been lost with Slovenia's declaration of independence. The Slovenes, seeing this as a hostile act, successfully cast themselves as the David fighting the Goliath of Belgrade. Largely by virtue of their organization and the rawness of the JNA soldiers they were fighting, the Slovenes swiftly emerged the victors. Milošević had no fight to pick with the Slovenes; they were not central to his plans for "greater Serbia."

But Serbia's war with Croatia lasted into 1992. In the torpor of a Bosnian summer, the unfolding war took on the quality of a mirage.

Children ran from their yards in Kozarac down to the highway, waving to the tanks as if they were part of a holiday parade. Farmers looked up from their crops of tomatoes and cabbage, annoyed at the column of dust kicked up by the trucks manned by JNA soldiers bearing guns and munitions en route to Croatia. No one in Kozarac could quite believe it. One day the country was united; the next, the people were at war. How, Hamdo kept asking his friends, could the JNA—composed of all Yugoslavs—suddenly turn on its own people? Unbeknownst to him, Milošević had transformed the army through purges, retirement, and recruitment drives into a force that was predominantly Serb.

As the stream of soldiers and trucks and tanks continued to rumble along the highway, the war became very real. Kozarac was abuzz with news of the brutality of Serb paramilitary gangs, particularly the "Tigers," led by former Belgrade gangster Željko Ražnatović, better known as Arkan.

On top of that, there were ominous political developments: In Banja Luka, the Serb-dominated city just to the east, Serbs declared themselves an autonomous region, saying they wanted to unite with Croatia's Serbs. Then came more worrying military developments: A heavy armored JNA brigade, ostensibly bound for Croatia, had taken up residence by the Prijedor airfield, not far from Kozarac. Thuggish groups of men not visibly identified with the army hunkered down in the nine-story Hotel Prijedor. Soldiers returning from fighting in Croatia were allowed to keep their weapons.

War, in fact, had already been planned for Bosnia. Just as Serbia and Croatia, at various points over the centuries, had seen parts of Bosnia as its own, so did Tudjman and Milošević. The men were foes, yet allies in their nationalist ambitions, and so they had met in spring of 1991 with the intention of carving up Bosnia. But before the plan could be put in effect, they began fighting each other.

Milošević was hungry for power and anxious to avoid the economic disaster facing Yugoslavia. He could take care of both concerns by playing the nationalist card, by attempting to create a "greater Serbia," that long-dreamed-of-state for the Serbs. He planned to do so by linking the Serb-dominated areas of Croatia with Serbia, gerrymandering together a country along ethnic lines. But Bosnia lay between the two Serb populations.

To realize his plan, Milošević needed a Serb-controlled corridor stretching across northern Bosnia. Secretly, Milošević began laying his plans, sowing discontent among the Bosnian Serbs in the north: giving them guns and unleashing a steady stream of pro-Serb speeches and anti-Muslim, anti-Croat propaganda. Inspired, in September 1991 several Bosnian Serb areas in the north announced they were "Serb autonomous regions."

The corridor Milošević envisioned included two of the largest Serb-dominated cities, Prijedor and Banja Luka. But there was a problem with his scheme. An array of Muslim-dominated villages—including tiny Kozarac—stood directly in the way.

AS NATIONALIST PROPAGANDA swept across northern Bosnia, so it also floated down the long, sinuous Neretva River as it ran southward from Sarajevo through the city of Konjic to the Croatian seacoast. Turning on his television set one morning in 1990, Petko Grubač, the swarthy Montenegrin Serb psychiatrist who had made Bosnia his home, was amazed to see one of his former colleagues on the screen, delivering a nationalist speech—forty-five-year-old psychiatrist Radovan Karadžić.

Radovan Karadžić? Petko could not believe his eyes. Karadžić wasn't even a Bosnian; like Petko, he was from neighboring Montenegro. All that Karadžić had ever aspired to, other than psychiatry, was writing poetry. He had been a decent enough doctor when Petko had worked alongside him in Sarajevo's psychiatry clinic, but he had a reputation for being lazy, a compulsive gambler, and something of a goof. He had ended up as the sports psychiatrist for the Sarajevo football team. And now Karadžić was the head of the Serbian Democratic Party, the SDS, which had just won seats in the Bosnian assembly? He was preaching about how Serbs in Bosnia needed equal cultural, religious, and economic rights?

Things were certainly changing in Bosnia. Even though Petko didn't want to face it, they were changing in Konjic as well.

He had made the city that straddled the Neretva River his home for nearly thirty years. Still, there was no mistaking him as a Montenegrin: Short and swarthy, Petko was a passionate, talkative man, who waved his hands in the air as he talked with an Italianate flair, telling stories and jokes. "Verbal expression," he would confide with a broad, slightly self-deprecating smile, "is *very* Montenegrin." And that was after he had talked for a half hour, nonstop. Petko loved Konjic, and the surrounding area for its rugged beauty and its multi-ethnicity: half the populace were Muslim, the rest Croat and Serb. In the countryside, the mighty Neretva—the river that had once brought Venetian traders up the coast into Bosnia—did divide ethnic groups somewhat; Croats tended to live to the west, Serbs up in the mountains to the east. But the city of Konjic was heterogeneous.

That Petko was a Serb made no difference. Nobody knew who was who when they met and mingled at the restaurants that offered fresh-caught trout or succulent, spit-roasted lamb. Petko and his wife, Gordana, a Serb from a neighboring village, so believed that ethnic origin was unimportant that they deliberately chose their children's names, Minja and Oleg, to sound Slavic, not Serbian, Croat, or Bosnian. Over the years Petko had garnered a reputation for himself as both a general doctor and a psychiatrist, and his clients, as well as his best friends, were Croat and Muslim and Serb. The couple's "kum"—the best men at their wedding—were Croat and Muslim.

Yet as 1990 slipped into 1991, nationalist parties—and the divisions that went with them—took root in Konjic. Some of those who embraced the SDA, the Muslim party of Alija Izetbegović, greeted Petko with "Salaam Aleikum," the traditional Arab greeting. In fact, people who had never had any interest in politics started claiming allegiances to one party or the other.

Sophisticated as they were in many ways, Bosnians, like other Yugoslavs, were creatures of the Tito-era propaganda machine. They believed what was said on television and reported in the newspapers. As the media fell sway to nationalist leaders of all stripes, three slightly different versions of the same events would emerge, each with a different nationalist spin. Karadžić was a particularly skillful demagogue, adept at playing to primitive emotions. He preached a kind of Serb chauvinism, arguing that the Serbs are glorious, heroic warriors who over the generations had nobly sacrificed themselves, from Kosovo Polje through to World War II. Karadžić replaced individual experience—and the sense of being a Yugoslav—with a kind of collective identity of being "Serb."

He also portrayed other nationalist parties in the starkest, most fear-mongering manner. Bosnia was the most heterogenous of Yugoslavia's republics: Of Bosnia's 4.3 million people, 43.5 percent were Muslim, 31.2 percent Serbian, and 17.4 percent Croat. When Bosnian Muslim SDA leader Izetbegović foolishly asked if Bosnia could join the Organization of Islamic States, Karadžić swiftly denounced the move as a sign that Izetbegović wanted "Bosnia-Herzegovina to become an Islamic republic."

Questions of Bosnia's future were paramount in the spring and summer of 1991. It was clear that Croatia and Slovenia were going to go their own way, splintering Yugoslavia. That left Bosnia in a bind. There was no choice that appealed to all its ethnic groups, because none wanted to be a minority in whatever new country emerged.

When Croatia and Slovenia declared their independence in the summer of 1991, nationalist parties hardened their positions. Karadžić, and his Serbian Democratic Party, wanted Bosnia to stay in Yugoslavia, which then consisted of Serb-dominated Montenegro, Serbia, and Macedonia. Croatian nationalists in Bosnia, also not wanting to be a minority in the new country, pushed for a kind of federation between the various republics. Bosnian Muslims—the sole group without a parent country to ally with—saw an independent Bosnia as their only option.

That frightened Bosnia's Serbs; even Petko, who still refused to believe his country was moving toward division, felt nervous at the idea of being a Serb in an independent Bosnia. He knew in his heart that Serbs had a tendency toward paranoia, but there were already signs that Serbs might be discriminated against if Bosnia was a separate republic like the newly autonomous Croatia. In 1991, a health care company Petko worked for relieved him from a management position simply because he was a Serb.

Across Bosnia there were frantic attempts to avoid violence and find a political solution. Deals were struck and then abandoned to keep Bosnia in Yugoslavia. Proposals were floated and swiftly dismissed to try to divide Bosnia along ethnic lines, which was simply impossible. By September 1991 the United Nations Security Council was alarmed enough to slap an arms embargo on all of Yugoslavia. In October, however, it would be Karadžić and his deputies who took the first move toward the country's disintegration.

They stalked out of the Bosnian Parliament to declare their own assembly, dividing the country politically over the issue of Bosnia's independence. "You will take Bosnia-Herzegovina down the same highway of hell and suffering" that Croatia and Slovenia were experiencing, Karadžić warned the Bosnian Muslims. He added ominously: "Do not think you will not perhaps lead the Muslim people into annihilation, because the Muslims cannot defend themselves if there is war."

In Konjic, as elsewhere around the country, local Serbs followed suit. Petko was shocked when he heard that the Serbs had walked out of the municipal assembly and announced they were forming their own government out of the Serb-dominated villages that ringed the mountains around the city. That left local Muslims and Croats to quarrel over what to do. Local Croats wanted Konjic to join Croatian-dominated areas to the south in Herzegovina, a region that had announced its autonomy and was calling itself "the Croatian community of Herceg-Bosna." (The area's Croats, having watched war rage in Croatia, had formed their own military force, the Croatian Defense Council, or HVO.) For the time being, however, they were persuaded to support Izetbegović and his call for a united, independent Bosnia.

The new year, 1992, dawned with the promise of peace: Former U.S. secretary of state Cyrus Vance, acting on the UN's behalf, got Serbia and Croatia to agree to a cease-fire to be overseen by UN peacekeepers. In Bosnia, people heaved a sigh of relief. Perhaps with the end of the Serb-Croat war, questions of Bosnia's and Yugoslavia's future could be resolved peacefully. But in January, Bosnian Serb politicians declared their own Serbian Republic, announcing it was part of the Yugoslav Federation. Then, many of the Yugoslav National Army troops loyal to Milošević—retreating from Croatia with their tanks, armored personnel carriers, planes, and helicopters—took up position in Bosnia instead of returning to Belgrade.

In early 1992, there were some 100,000 JNA troops in Bosnia answering to Belgrade. Milošević—who the year before had quietly changed recruitment procedures in Bosnia so that mostly ethnic Serbs joined the armed forces—had secretly ordered all Bosnian Serb officers from Bosnia back home, in essence creating a force loyal to his plan for a greater Serbia. When Milošević ordered JNA troops home in May 1992, these soldiers simply became the Bosnian Serb Army instead.

Bosnia's referendum on independence, held on February 29 and March 1, was boycotted by many of the country's Serbs. The rest of the

Bosnians—67 percent of the population—voted for independence. At first, it looked like Serb nationalists would not respect the election; Serb gangs threw up roadblocks around Sarajevo and Konjic. Yet when thousands of people—Serb, Muslim, and Croat alike—took to the streets in Sarajevo in favor of the country's independence, not a shot was fired. It seemed that Bosnia's march toward independence might proceed peacefully.

By April 1, however, Bosnians knew better.

PARAMILITARY SQUADS, SENT in from neighboring Serbia, fired the first shots. Milošević was not going to let Bosnia slip from his grasp. Gun-toting thugs poured into Bijeljina, a quiet city hard by the Yugoslav border. Among them were the feared Arkan's Tigers, who killed local Muslim leaders and took up sniper positions around the town. Street battles left several dozen dead.

That was all Hasan, deep in his studies at the University of Sarajevo, needed to hear. Ever since the engineering student had heard tanks grinding along the streets past his dorm window en route to Croatia, he had been frightened that war would spread to Bosnia. Hearing news of the attack on Bijeljina on the morning of April 2, Hasan sprinted back to his dorm room. It was his twenty-fourth birthday.

Inside lay his girlfriend, Mirza, still sleeping. Mirza, a chemistry major, was a striking dark-haired woman with bewitching brown eyes, whom Hasan had sought out as the smartest and prettiest girl at the university. That morning, still curled up in her pajamas, she looked particularly adorable. He shook her awake.

"We have to get out of here," Hasan snapped. "There's going to be war."

Mirza laughed sleepily. "Hasan, you're just a coward," she said teasingly. Hasan stared at her, frustrated. He wished to make his point quite clear. So he picked up the edge of the bed and flattened it—and Mirza—against the wall. As she peeped her head over the edge of the mattress and from the tangled bedclothes, she realized he was serious.

Within hours she had packed a bag and was on a bus to her family's home in the Sandžak, a part of Serbia heavily populated by Muslims. Hasan was on his way home to Vlasenica. His plan was to gather up his mother, Nasiha, his father, Ibro, and his brother, Muhamed, and get them all to Sarajevo, where they could take a bus or plane to somewhere in Europe.

The Nuhanović family was well educated and upper middle class. Hasan's father, Ibro, was the head of one of Bosnia's largest forestry concerns, a respected businessman. His mother, Nasiha, was a refined blond woman with a sweet manner. Hasan was particularly close to his younger brother Muhamed. The two shared a love of music: Hasan played the guitar, Muhamed, or "Braco," little brother, the drums.

Ibro listened and agreed to Hasan's plan. Nasiha, Muhamed, and Hasan would go on ahead to Sarajevo and buy tickets for the first flight leaving for any European country. Ibro would settle up a few business details and then join them shortly. Hasan, along with his mother and brother, hurriedly packed bags and left for Sarajevo as planned. But Ibro, after going into the office and talking to his Serb employees—as one of the region's largest employers, he had quite a few—changed his mind about leaving the country. War, he was told, was the furthest thing from their minds. An attack by Serbia on Bosnia? Preposterous.

On April 4, 1992, trying to calm the tensions rippling across Bosnia, Izetbegović announced: "Citizens of Sarajevo, sleep peacefully, there will be no war," although he ordered local defense forces mobilized. So Ibro summoned his family back. Far better, he said, that they go to the family's country house in the tiny hamlet of Stoborani, deep in the woods and about 20 miles from the biggest city, Srebrenica. There they could hunker down amid the thick groves of pine, oak, and beech trees until everything blew over.

But things did not blow over. On April 6 the European Community recognized Bosnia's independence, followed by the United States. Then Serbian forces and paramilitary groups answering to Milošević again crossed into Bosnia to launch another attack. This time it was on the city of Zvornik, also near the Serbian border and home to Hasan's maternal grandfather. The city, with both rail and bridge links to Serbia, was strategic to the Serbs' aims.

Within two days Zvornik, 60 percent Muslim, was cleansed of all its non-Serb inhabitants and occupied by Arkan, his paramilitary irregulars, and Yugoslav Army soldiers. Men, women, and children were rounded up, thrown on trucks, and expelled from the city. Dozens of bodies lay on the streets. Anyone watching the official Yugoslav news heard Milošević's distorted version of events: Muslim extremists had attacked the city, and Zvornik had been "liberated."

Ibro watched news of the attack on the television in the family's country hideaway and cursed. Madness was sweeping over Bosnia: Thousands of people killed and swept from Zvornik simply because they were Muslim. He had miscalculated the nationalism that had grabbed Bosnia by the heart. He had been wrong not to flee Bosnia. There *would* be war.

Now how was he going to get Hasan, Nasiha, and Muhamed out of Bosnia?

2

THE TRIUMPH OF THE UNDERWORLD

Once the concept of "otherness" takes root, the unimaginable becomes possible.

—Slavenka Drakulić, *The Balkan Express*

It was war, and it was war aimed at civilians. Launched by Serbian nationalist Slobodan Milošević, the war's initial goal was "ethnic cleansing," moving vast numbers of Bosnia's Muslim and Croats out of key parts of Bosnia so that they could be populated by Serbs, as part of Milošević's dream of a "greater Serbia." Within months the Bosnian conflict would summon forth a vocabulary that Europe had hoped had long been forgotten, words so dreadful they were uttered with a shudder: war crimes, crimes against humanity, genocide. Since World War II, with the lessons of the Holocaust still starkly clear, nations had adopted a series of conventions and treaties aimed at protecting civilians. Yet in Bosnia, it was as if all the evils Europe and America thought had been put to rest were unleashed, loathsome genies escaping their bottle.

Western powers helped pull out the cork. As Bosnia headed toward conflagration, Western nations condemned but took no strong military or diplomatic action to halt the ravages wreaked by Serbian troops in Croatia—the bombing around the graceful coastal port of Dubrovnik, the obliteration of the city of Vukovar—all but giving Serbian leader Slobodan Milošević a green light to continue in Bosnia. Once he did so, the West turned a deaf ear to pleas from Bosnian leader Alija Izetbegović to lift the arms embargo. The Bosnian war, from the beginning, was an unequal contest: pitting the might of the Yugoslav Peoples Army—many of whose munitions, officers, and soldiers would end up in the new Bosnian Serb Army—against a ragtag opposition scraped together from territorial defense forces, something like our National Guard. At first, one side fought with artillery; the other, with old hunting rifles.

When Bosnian Serb leader Radovan Karadžić began pounding Sarajevo with artillery, setting buildings aflame, and filling the city's morgues, Western leaders sought a diplomatic solution. There were talks and talks and more talks. In the interim, it fell to the United Nations—whose peacekeepers were on the ground, charged with supervising the cease-fire between Serbia and Croatia—to oversee the delivery of humanitarian aid to Bosnia. As the airport at Sarajevo opened to what would become the airlift that surpassed even the American airlift to Berlin, Bosnia's war became defined in the eyes of Western leaders not as a pressing strategic crisis but as a humanitarian one. It was a shift in perception that shaped the Western response to the escalating crisis, further encouraging Milošević and Karadžić to press on avidly with their campaign. The only show of Western might, as far as the Serbs were concerned, were blue-helmeted peacekeepers of the United Nations Protection Force, or UNPROFOR, whose mandate was to be neutral and not to intervene militarily.

By the end of 1992, nearly 2 million Bosnians, mostly Muslim, had lost their homes. Thousands of civilians were dead. War crime after war crime had been committed. The Bosnian Serb Army occupied nearly two-thirds of Bosnia's territory and had nearly everything it wanted. As the war continued over the next three years, front lines hardly budged. But the lives of Hasan, Hamdo and his wife, Firdesa, and Petko and his wife, Gordana, would be irrevocably altered. They would learn what it would mean to be victims of crimes against humanity.

IN THE SPRING of 1992 everyone in Kozarac, where Hamdo the history teacher lived, had seen the gun-toting paramilitaries from Serbia—often clad in ski masks, bandanas, or sunglasses, the sartorial preference of modern-day war criminals—strutting the streets of the nearby city of Prijedor. Some said they were Arkan's men, the *Arkanovci*, the paramilitaries from Serbia loyal to archcriminal Željko Ražnatović, who had attacked the city of Zvornik. Others thought they were just local hoodlums trying to look the part. As the Serb campaign to oust Bosnia's Muslims gathered steam, it had picked up local converts, appealing to thugs, petty criminals, and gangs of disaffected, unemployed youths. In this war the underworld triumphed: Ethnic cleansing brought with it the chance to loot empty houses and rob prisoners, a chance to get rich as well as to gain power.

For months, northwest Bosnia had been barraged with nationalist rhetoric. Milošević dispatched Serb nationalist Vojislav Šešelj to Prijedor, one of Bosnia's largest Serb-dominated cities, where he told local Serbs how foolish they were to live with non-Serbs. Ever since paramilitary forces had seized the local television transmitter in March, the only news available was inflammatory, anti-Muslim, anti-Croat diatribes out of Belgrade. Television programs would be interrupted with news breaks giving accounts of fresh threats to the Serbs from Muslim "extremists" and Croatian "Ustasha." Terms like "jihad," "Muslim warriors," and "Ustasha massacres" were tossed around as if they were fact.

The not-so-subtle message was that Serbs were to join together and arm themselves, because the Muslims were going to attack. No one should trust their Croat or Muslim neighbors. The propaganda was clever, stirring up unresolved grievances that Serbs had carefully collected since World War II, like misers hoarding their coins. Remember the concentration camp of Jasenovac: now the "Ustasha" and "the Turks" were planning another campaign of "genocide." In many of the smaller, Serb-dominated hamlets tucked in the crags of the Kozara Mountains, rumors whipped like wildfire in a culture that thrived on storytelling. The Muslims, it was whispered, had death lists with Serb names on it. The man who ran the café down the street had seen it! The Muslims were arming themselves; they had guns stockpiled in their mosques! Encouraged by Serb nationalist speeches, television and newspaper propaganda, a sense of collective fear took hold, often replacing individual friendships unmindful of ethnic distinctions.

Cooler heads in the region tried to prevail, forming committees and holding talks. In Kozarac, Hamdo was an active member of the Citizens Peace Committee, which aimed to find some kind of multiethnic solution. But on April 30, the first blow was struck to divide the region along ethnic lines: The city of Prijedor was seized in a bloodless coup. The man leading the charge was Hamdo's former colleague Simo Drljača. The antisocial fisherman and lawyer-turned-Serb-nationalist had become a militant. Drljača, crooned the local newspaper, had done his job so well that "the take-over of power [by the Serbs] was successfully achieved in only 30 minutes, without any shots fired." Serbian flags, bearing the four Cyrillic S's that symbolized the Serbian unity motto fluttered from the office buildings in the formerly Muslim-dominated regional seat of power. Yugoslav Peoples Army soldiers occupied the bank and the radio station.

Drljača, ruling the city, enforced ethnic divisions. His armed gangs threw up barricades and military checkpoints, making it impossible for Muslims to leave. They were forced to resign their job, or to wear white armbands designating their ethnic status. In nearby Kozarac, one of a handful of villages that was mostly Muslim, the phone lines were cut, then the electricity. Along with his fellow Serb nationalists, intent on transforming the region into a Bosnian Serb state, Drljača demanded the loyalty of the inhabitants. The town's Citizens Peace Committee, still dreaming of a peaceful, multiethnic solution, balked at the idea.

Drljača responded with an artillery barrage that left hundreds dead and destroyed Kozarac's homes, mosques, and school. Among those who identified targets to the gunners was Hamdo's former student, Dušan "Dule" Tadić.

IT WAS MAY 24, 1992. Hamdo had awoken thinking it was just another tense day in the standoff that had gripped Kozarac. For several days he and others on the local peace committee had been trying to negotiate with Drljača and the other Serb nationalists who held Prijedor. Things were tense, but war? Then came the whine of the shells, as unexpected as everything else over the past few months. Hamdo sprang out of bed, threw on his work shirt, pants, and boots, and stumbled outside: *Bože moj*, he thought. My god; Kozarac was under attack. At least he had had the foresight a few days before to insist his wife and their daughter leave to visit their son Enes, working in Austria.

Hamdo loped down the street, trying to alert his neighbors. The Fazlić and Sarić families, pulling on their clothes as they ran, followed in a panic. Together, they all headed for the Kusurans' home: They had the biggest cellar on the block. As Hamdo reached the cellar door, he turned around, only to see a shell explode, sending dirt and grass spinning upward, in his own front yard. *Bože moj!*

For two days Hamdo and his neighbors stayed trapped underground, waiting for the firing to halt. The shelling was constant enough that everyone stopped flinching after a while. There was nothing to do but wait and pray in the stifling darkness, filled with the wail of children and the acrid smell of fear.

Finally, on May 26, the noise abated. For the first time, there was relative quiet. The group could hear loud voices outside; shouting, screams, and even curses in the street. "Hamdo, will you go up and see what is happening?" one of the neighbors begged. Hamdo, having been made principal of the Rade Kondić school a few months before, was considered an unofficial leader.

Emerging from the cellar, Hamdo saw a long, nearly endless column of people snaking down the main street of Kozarac. Everyone was leaving! He scurried back to the basement and yelled the news. It was time to go! He ran home, packed a bag, and joined the crowd. The town was probably being evacuated to safety for a few days, he thought, until all this craziness was over. Yet it wasn't an evacuation: it was something else. As the line Hamdo was standing in snaked around a corner, he spotted a military checkpoint. Soldiers in uniform, carrying AK-47s, along with thugs wearing black ski masks, were roughly separating the men and the women. As Hamdo watched, aghast, many of Kozarac's civic leaders were pulled aside and executed by the gunmen, who appeared to be a mix of JNA troops, paramilitary gangs, and local Serbs, aflame with a newly gained power.

Serb nationalist leader Milošević had ordered all JNA troops who were not Bosnians to leave the country. But nearly 80 percent of them, primarily Serb, simply joined up with the newly formed Bosnian Serb Army instead. Trapped in the crowd, Hamdo was shoved and pushed and prodded onto a waiting bus along with those men not targeted for execution. Kozarac was under Serb control, the gunmen snapped at them. They were all prisoners and would be taken somewhere for questioning. All the armed Muslim extremists had to be identified before they could be released.

Armed extremists? No one in Kozarac had any guns, thought Hamdo.

"What is going on?" Hamdo asked the man sitting next to him on the bus. "Where are we going?"

"They say Trnopolje, maybe Omarska," whispered his neighbor, his voice shaking, identifying villages just down the road. "They've set up some kind of camps for the Muslims there—" He did not finish his sentence.

SOME 150 MILES to the south, in the city of Konjic, Petko Grubač decided that while he was an astute observer of the individual human psyche, he was not a good judge of mass psychology. He had not believed there would be war, and after the attacks in northeastern Bosnia at the end of March, he had contented himself with the fact there would be no violence in Konjic. By mid-April, it was clear he was wrong. He hadn't considered that the Neretva River valley was strategic as well as beautiful; it was Bosnia's only link to the coast. The river, the highway, and the railroad all paralleled one other, racing from Sarajevo down to the Adriatic. The region was a key military asset. By April 1992 Bosnian Muslims, Croats, and Serbs were all jockeying to control it.

Local Serb leaders, who had broken away and declared their own Serb municipality, began distributing weapons. Local Croat leaders put their territorial defense units on the ready. Inside the city, a war presidency had been formed, headed by the mainly Muslim SDA party. Troops of the Yugoslav Peoples Army—which had halted in Bosnia on their way back from Croatia toward Serbia—were also in the vicinity. They threw their sympathies behind the local Serb minority.

By the middle of April, roadblocks surrounded the city, manned by armed Serbs. Within weeks road and trail traffic was halted, telephone lines severed. Konjic, once a bustling throughfare of north-south traffic, was almost completely cut off from the rest of Bosnia. Bosnian Muslim leaders ordered the country's territorial defense units to be mobilized, and inside the city, gangs of men were toting guns and trying to form an army. The streets teemed with Muslim and Croat refugees who had fled, terrified, from nearby villages. Every spare room in the city was taken. Shop shelves had been stripped empty, as people stockpiled provisions in wave after wave of panic buying. Konjic, filled with suspicions and rumors, braced for the storm.

Petko and Gordana found themselves isolated. They were Serbs living in a city that was now packed with Muslim and Croat refugees, who regarded them with suspicion. At the same time, they were surrounded by heavily armed Serbs, with whom they had ethnic affinity but no allegiance. Not having taken any side in the conflict, they were regarded warily by everyone.

In their neighborhood, dozens of apartments and homes had been locked and shuttered by Serb families who long ago had quit Konjic, fearing the worst. When close friends of Petko's—a doctor and her surgeon husband—packed their bags and left, Petko simply pretended it hadn't happened. He couldn't believe that Bosnia—part of Europe—could be spiraling into war. Then, a few weeks later, a Serb was killed right near the Orthodox church. For the first time, Petko did not feel safe in the city he called his own.

He and Gordana sent the children out to stay with their grandparents in the Serb-dominated hamlet of Bradina, about a half hour's drive away. One weekend they went to visit and upon their return to Konjic found the words "in the army BH" scrawled in ink on their apartment door; it appeared to have been seized by the Bosnian Army. They had no choice but to retreat to Bradina. Unfortunately, that was no quiet country village. It, too, was in a strategic position: hard by a tunnel on the road between Konjic and Sarajevo. Whoever controlled the tunnel would, of course, control the road.

So on May 4, when Serb artillery began pounding Konjic—setting buildings aflame, killing hundreds of civilians and reducing graceful architecture to rubble—the city's mostly Muslim troops punched northward toward Sarajevo. They attacked the tunnel near Bradina first, on May 10, and the village two weeks later. Petko, the man who had not believed war was possible, found himself fleeing a burning village, his wife and children with him.

They spent several nights hunkered down by a creek, huddled along with about thirty other families. But the woods proved no escape; the attacks drew nearer. They could hear the staccato sound of gunfire, see the flames leaping from the burning homes, filling the forest with a dense, dark smoke.

The group decided it was better for everyone to return to Bradina and find the advancing army commander at the checkpoint, and for Petko, whom everyone knew in Konjic, to explain they were unarmed civilians and wished to surrender. Surely reason would prevail. Yet no sooner had Petko, two other men, and several dozen women and children given themselves up than the camouflage-clad soldiers brusquely pushed the men to one side.

Had the psychiatrist known what lay ahead of him, he might well have chosen not to surrender. As far as anyone wielding a gun was concerned, he was no longer Petko Grubač, the psychiatrist; he was Petko Grubač, the Serb.

IT WAS EARLY June 1992 when the war caught up with Hasan and his family. Hasan was just awakening from a nap—he'd been out on a village patrol the night before—when he heard his father bellow. "The Serbs are coming," yelled Ibro. "Get out of the house immediately!" Hasan was unsure at first whether he was still dreaming.

Next door things were similarly surreal. People were scrambling around, yelling and crying. His aunt and uncle were arguing over how best to get a sofa out through the window and then to the makeshift hut the Nuhanović clan had built deep in the woods. Finally—after more confusion, more shouting—all twenty-five members of the extended family clan met at a prearranged spot in the woods.

Eleven days they spent there, sheltered under the thick firs' branches, huddled in makeshift huts, quivering as heavy shelling and shooting and explosions surrounded them, seemingly coming from all sides at once. Hasan and his relatives, even deep in the forest, could hear the distinctive *pop-pop-pop* as roof tiles on the houses in nearby villages exploded into fire. Day and night; night and then day; rain and then sun; and then rain again.

The worst was the day when jets flew overhead. Hasan, Ibro, Nasiha, and Muhamed could do nothing more than hug the thick, sap-covered trunks of the fir trees, hoping they would protect them. Everywhere, bombs whizzed and wheezed and—*boom*!—exploded, far louder than anything Hasan had ever heard before. He closed his eyes and tried to convince himself that this was just a scene from a film.

After days, heavy rain fell. And silence, except for the whir of helicopters. Finally Hasan raised his head, looking dumbly at his father, mother, and brother: All were alive.

As the family stumbled out of the forest into a grassy clearing, a warm sun broke through the clouds. Mist wreathed the trees. Vapor rose from their wet clothing as they stood, drinking in the sun. Everything seemed bathed in a glorious gold: the moss underfoot, the grass in the breeze, the tree trunks, their faces. They had survived, and it was a miracle.

"If I get the chance to take you out of this forest," Ibro vowed to his family, "we'll go to Australia. I'm making the decision now; we will move to Australia and never see Bosnia again, for the rest of our lives." As the sun danced in the pine needles and the birds sang, Hasan dreamed of the beaches of Australia, white, ringed with surf, beckoning. The summer was young, they were alive, anything seemed possible. Even escape.

THERE WAS NO dreaming of escape, however, for Hamdo, by now in the concentration camp of Omarska—a name that would come to symbolize all the bestial passions of Bosnia's war. Whatever the original purpose of the camps in the Omarska mine, the Keraterm ceramics factory, and the Trnopolje school (many of Bosnia's Serbs still insist they were merely transit centers to disarm the Muslims), they disintegrated into a sadistic underworld, places where days and nights were measured by a prisoner's ability to avoid starvation, torture, rape, or death. Six years had passed by the time Hamdo told me about his incarceration there, yet he still flinched at the name: *Omarska.*

Although Omarska was just ten miles down the road from Kozarac, Hamdo was unfamiliar with it. He had few friends there and no business at the town's main industry, its iron ore mine. He was surprised to see that the entrance to the mine complex was just past a row of houses with laundry flapping in the backyard. Anyone hanging up washing had a bird's-eye view.

Ordered to get off the bus, the men filed into a filthy room, small and slippery with mud. The guards, cradling AK-47s, screamed at them—*Put your hands over your heads!*—and pushed them up against the wall, legs apart. They grabbed one man and beat him savagely. When he finally slumped over like a floppy doll, he was dragged outside. A scream; a shot was fired. Hamdo recoiled.

Daily, it would prove, Omarska echoed with such screams: the screams of those being "interrogated" by Serb camp guards determining who took part in the "Muslim rebellion." Those targeted for the worst treatment were the rich, the political leaders, and the intelligentsia. The guards would call out their victim's name, drag him out of the room, and then beat him: with wooden batons, metal rods, rifle butts, knives, hammers, pipes filled with lead, and long lengths of thick industrial cable with metal affixed on both ends. Hamdo kept waiting for his name to be called, for the blows to fall on his neck and shoulders, to hear the sound of the rifle shot aimed at his back. But after the first day, when he was questioned about whether he had weapons, the names called out were those of other Muslims from Kozarac and Prijedor. Some returned, broken, forced into signing false confessions; others never returned.

Packed in a filthy, lice-infested room in a two-story white garage with about 150 men, mostly from Kozarac, Hamdo spent his days and nights hungry and thirsty. Men passed out. They cried for water. With no toilets available, their feces fouled the room. When food did arrive—the once-per-day plate of watery potato soup and a slice of bread—jeering guards made Hamdo and the others run a gauntlet to the canteen to get it, pouring water on the tiles to make them slippery. Whoever fell got beaten or, sometimes, shot. For sport, the guards forced the prisoners to crawl on their knees, like animals, to pick up food while the guards peppered the ground with bullets. When one of the men, gasping with thirst on those hot summer days, would beg for a drink, guards often forced them to sing Serbian songs: "You say Serbia's small / Liars one and all / She's not small at all / Not small at all . . ."

For the three dozen women at the camp, Omarska meant rape. Separated from the men, they spent their days crammed in the mining complex's glass-walled restaurant, their nights in the guards' offices, where some of the interrogations took place. After forcing the women to clean the blood from the walls, the guards assaulted them. If they didn't cooperate, they'd join the corpses they saw on a daily basis being thrown over the hedges or stacked like cordwood on the grass.

Some 2,000 Bosnians are believed to have died at Omarska. But who had assembled the gangs of petty crooks, small-time gangsters, and corrupt policeman who murdered them? One day, allowed to take some fresh air out in the concrete courtyard, Hamdo spotted a familiar face striding across the grounds, a tall, dark-haired man with a nose like a knife, to whom the guards bowed and scraped in deference. *Simo—was that Simo Drljača?* Hamdo was taken aback. Hamdo knew Drljača had transformed himself almost overnight from school legal advisor to Serb nationalist, seizing control of Prijedor. He knew Drljača had taken over that city's government, becoming head of its wartime "crisis committee," the emergency group convened to rule during the violence. But this?

Indeed, Omarska and the other camps were largely Drljača's idea. He had become head of the secret police. Aided by his deputy in the "crisis committee," the mustachioed, bejowled Milan Kovačević—born in the World War II camp of Jasenovac and with a past to avenge—Drljača oversaw the camps. He ordered secret and civil police to interrogate inmates in what he called "informal chats" and then torture and kill them.

What a transformation, Hamdo marveled, as he watched his former colleague stalk across the Omarska grounds. Drljača's stoop-shoulder walk had been replaced by a swagger; his aura of loneliness, by deadly arrogance. Plucking up his courage, Hamdo approached him, albeit penitently, reflecting his new status as a prisoner. *"Dobar dan,"* said Hamdo. *"Kako ste?"* "Hi, how are you?" Drljača simply walked on without a flicker of recognition in his empty eyes, as if no one had spoken to him at all.

Drljača's was not the only familiar face at Omarska. Within days Hamdo saw former student Dule Tadić. He was as changed as was Drljača, now dressed like a soldier, his manner brusque and harsh. Hamdo did not approach Tadić. After his encounter with Drljača, he had decided to keep his head down. It proved a wise strategy. When it came to beatings and torture, the men from Kozarac were often singled out. As a result of their experiences, inmates knew which of the camp staff had a reputation for sadism, such as camp commander Željko Mejakić.

Tadić, however, wasn't a guard at Omarska. He was one of the gangs of local riffraff who seemed to have permission to come to the camp at will to deal out punishment. Such power allowed violent payback for old rivalries, whether over a girl or a karate match. Mehmedalija Huskić, who had known Tadić for twenty years, was brutally pistol-whipped by him. Mehmed Alić of Prijedor, who knew the Tadić family well, heard his son Enver being dragged off shouting "Dule, brother, how have I wronged you; why do you beat me?" Fikret Harambašić was beaten until he was naked and bleeding; Tadić then ordered another prisoner to bite his testicles off.

Beatings were commensurate with a prisoner's importance. Some men were beaten to a pulp and then killed; others, barely touched. Some bribed their way out, pledging their homes. Judging from the screams, those in the red house, near the garage and the gas station, got the worst of it; prisoners who went there never returned alive. Perhaps Hamdo was considered too insignificant among the thousands of men crammed in Omarska to warrant special torture. He was not a high-ranking politician, a wealthy merchant, or a clever doctor. He was just a school principal, a solid communist yes-man and Kozarac loyalist. Although he was spared the worst of Omarska's beatings, he was robbed of his money and his watch, forced to lie down on the hot pavement outside for hours at a stretch, and whacked as he sprinted to the toilet or to the canteen for soup. In less than a month, Hamdo lost sixty-six pounds.

Hamdo was released with several other men in July 1992, albeit to a kind of house arrest in Prijedor, where he worked as a kindergarten teacher. Simo Drljača and Dule Tadić, however, contrived to bully him. The duo prowled Prijedor, with their thumbs tucked in their pants pockets. Hamdo tried to disguise himself—growing a beard, sporting dark glasses—but from time to time Drljača hauled him in to police headquarters for questioning. It was when Hamdo, after being released, faced Drljača across a desk for the first time—former colleagues turned into police chief and his prisoner—that he understood what had changed Drljača: *unbridled power*. The war was his opportunity to extort money at will from the families of prisoners at Omarska and become rich, to command respect and authority in a way he never could as a little-known lawyer in Prijedor and Kozarac. Power: It elated Drljača, Serbian colleagues who knew him later told me. It even allowed him to rewrite history.

"See what your people have done!" Drljača hissed to Hamdo that day. Drljača leaned back behind his desk. He waved a hand and ordered Hamdo a cognac, the European drink of choice for Bosnians. "You see what your people have done," he continued. "They have killed such a good man. . . . They have killed so and so, and so and so." Drljača droned on. The war was the Muslims' fault. They had armed themselves first and shot first. Hamdo shrugged. He said nothing. He had learned at Omarska that prisoners never talk back.

When he returned to visit Kozarac, Hamdo found the village was burned to the ground, save for those buildings that were Serb property, carefully marked in advance to avoid destruction. In despair, he signed over his property to the local Serbs. Local convoys were leaving regularly, ushering Muslims out of Prijedor, and Hamdo got on one going to the Muslim-dominated city of Travnik, to the northwest and not far from the Croatian border. His Kozarac was no more. All the things he had believed in, trusted in, put his faith in had vanished; there was no future for him in Bosnia. Dule Tadić and Simo Drljača—he thought he had known them well.

But he hadn't known them at all.

Hamdo left vowing he would never see Bosnia—much less Tadić and Drljača—again. But life—and a desire for justice—would make him change his mind.

THE VAST MAJORITY of the concentration camps that sprang up in 1992 were for Bosnian Muslims, but not all. Some were for Bosnian Croats; others for Bosnian Serbs. And that is how Petko Grubač ended up interned at the Čelebići camp.

He was confined, along with other prisoners, to a hangar with two small high windows. After being informed that he would be treated according to the Geneva Conventions, a guard cursed at him, then ripped his glasses out of his shirt pocket and stomped them into pieces on the floor. Petko was assigned to treat the prisoners, but found he had only old sheets to use as bandages, no surgical instruments, and nothing with which to sterilize wounds. The number of injuries far outpaced the amount of supplies. The patients who streamed in, some barely able to walk, had been badly beaten with guns, rods, or other hard objects; one of the particularly ruthless guards always strutted around with a baseball bat. Some men had been burned on their palms, legs, and faces, after one of the guards had poured gasoline on them and set them on fire.

Sometimes Petko was taken to treat wounded prisoners kept in tunnel number 9. The ceiling wasn't tall enough for people to stand, and the tunnel declined downward into the earth, so men were half lying, half sitting. There was no fresh air and no bathroom, and the stench was terrible. Petko could just glimpse the entrance to the tunnel from one of the small windows in his hangar, and he knew prisoners there were beaten frequently.

Meanwhile, Gordana Grubač was frantic. All she knew was that Petko, along with her father and her two younger brothers, was being held in the village of Čelebići, about a half hour south of Konjic, on the grounds of a JNA army compound. Nothing in her life had quite prepared her for what she had to do: figuring out how to get them out of the Čelebići camp. She had spent her life working with facts and figures in a bank in Konjic, not plumbing the depths of human psychology, as Petko had. Her logical mind, however, stood her in good stead. She knew she first had to find out which city official had responsibility for the camp. Then she knew she would have to convince him to let her family go. Her inquiries, as well as her entreaty, would have to be discreet: She was one of the very few Serbs left in Konjic, swollen now with refugees from Muslim and Croat villages. The city was under daily artillery barrage from Karadžić and what had become the Bosnian Serb Army. She knew any question she asked could be regarded as a form of spying, subjecting her to arrest.

As the days passed, the city of Konjic quivered under the ongoing barrage. Artillery pounded the bank, the post office, the apartment buildings; food supplies ran short. Gordana learned the realities of ethnic divisions during war: She didn't qualify for aid. When her friends and neighbors passed her in the street, they acted as if they didn't know her, as if they had never gone out drinking together, never sat down around a dinner table together Ahmed Jusufbegović, one of the couple's "best men" from their wedding, had acquired some power in the wartime presidency. But he also made no move to help her, even though he must have known that Petko had been taken away. Gordana was pierced to the heart; in Bosnia, there is no greater sign of friendship and personal commitment than acting as someone's *kum*, or best man. This was a betrayal both of friendship and ideals: Gordana had been a loyal advocate of Tito's "brotherhood and unity" all her life. Was she now only just another "Serb," automatically considered an enemy?

By midsummer, Gordana determined there was one key person to approach: Zejnil Delalić, a wealthy businessman who people said was responsible for military logistics in the region. The Grubačs had mingled with Delalić socially before the war, and several members of his family were patients of Petko's. Before she could reach him, however, a note arrived one day from Petko, smuggled out by a friendly guard. "Don't come," read the hand-scribbled note on a piece of paper. "Don't come to Čelebići. Horrible things are happening to women here."

What was happening, she later learned, was that the few women in the Čelebići camp were being raped every night.

Gordana ignored the note.

Several days after hearing from a friend that Čelebići prisoners "haven't been given food for three days," Gordana screwed up her courage. She took the train down to Čelebići with her sister-in-law, who hoped to see her husband, Gordana's brother. Together, they walked to the camp. Turning in the gate, she saw a long line of women, each carrying food parcels. She felt as if she had stepped back into a World War II documentary. After being kept waiting, Gordana and her sister-in-law were finally called into the camp's main office by the camp commander, Pavo Mucić. She all but burst into tears when she saw Petko and her brother. Petko was a wraith: thin, white as sheet, and crying, with tears streaming down his cheeks. Her brother, equally thin, had had many of his teeth knocked out, his nose was broken, and he could barely stand. In hushed voices, Gordana and Petko talked for about fifteen minutes about strategies for getting him out before he was taken away. "It is better that you leave on your own than me having to force you out," joked Mucić before Petko. It didn't seem a very funny thing to say.

On her return to Konjic, Gordana noticed cars and soldiers outside the house of Zejnil Delalić. She resolved to telephone him and beg for his help in getting her husband released. When she did, it was as if no war had broken out at all.

"How are you, Gordana?" said Zejnil. "And how are the children?"

She broke into tears. "Zejnil, why has my Petko been in prison for two months? I've been to see him, and he is in very bad condition. He will die there."

"Gordana," he answered, "I do not understand anything anymore." He described how it had been Ahmed Jusufbegović who had insisted Petko had wanted to stay at the camp and treat the "Chetniks."

"How could anybody normal agree to be there to treat those people?" Gordana sobbed, learning of this new betrayal by their close friend. "If he needs to treat them, he can do that going there from his own home." She pleaded for Petko to be released.

Delalić, she knew, was powerful. But she had no idea just how powerful. The very next day, Petko was indeed released. The couple immediately began trying to find a way out of Konjic, someplace where it would be safe. Yet they didn't get very far. Less than two months later, the police arrived at their doorstep and dragged both of them off to the local prison. Gordana was dressed only in her housecoat and slippers. From October until December, the couple was imprisoned, and their children were left alone to fend for themselves. Once again their crime boiled down to this: They were Serbs.

NEWS OF CONCENTRATION camps swirled through the Bosnian refugee community, particularly among the Muslims, who made up the vast majority of immigrants. Refugees were leaving Bosnia in droves, usually landing in Croatia before begging asylum from Germany and other European countries that had opened their doors. In the summer of 1992 reporters first broke stories about "rape camps," where Bosnian Muslim women had been taken and repeatedly sexually violated en route to being expelled from their homeland. By August, reports about the horrors of the Omarska camp appeared. Bosnian Serb leader Radovan Karadžić, confronted by accounts, denied anything inhumane was happening there and invited the Western press to visit. A British print and television reporter offhandedly managed to enter both the Omarska and Trnopolje camps. Their dispatches were horrifying. Around the world, people turned on their television sets and recoiled at seeing images they thought relegated to the past—skeletal men, ribs protruding, eyes blank and empty with terror.

International outrage was swift, and domestic outcry nearly as loud. The United States was in the midst of a presidential campaign, and U.S. policy in Bosnia was a bone of contention for President George Bush and his Democratic challenger, Bill Clinton. It also became a source of embarrassment to the Bush administration, as news emerged that U.S. intelligence agencies were aware of the camps and had kept the White House informed of them. The U.S. Senate Foreign Relations Committee, producing a detailed report on the camps, chastised the administration and the United Nations, whose peacekeepers were overseeing the humanitarian airlift into Sarajevo, for their failure to act.

There was much rhetoric and little action in the face of the discovery of the first concentration camps in Europe since World War II. Not until August of 1992 was there a concrete response, and it from a country familiar with the poisonous legacy of war crimes. It was German foreign minister Klaus Kinkel who demanded that an international criminal court be created to try those responsible for war crimes in Bosnia. "What is happening here is genocide, and this we condemn before the world community," Kinkel told the more than thirty countries and international organizations that had convened in London in August 1992, to try to halt Bosnia's mounting horrors. "An international court of justice has to be created."

The idea of a modern-day war crimes tribunal had first surfaced in 1991, as war raged between Serbia and Croatia. A respected Belgrade journalist, Mirko Klarin, writing for the Belgrade daily *Nasa Borba*, had called for a "Nuremberg" for the former Yugoslavia. He wrote: "Things being the way they are, would it not be better if our big and small leaders were made to sit in the dock instead of the negotiating table? And if, with the help of world-famous experts in international laws of war, we had a Nuremberg Trial of our own, no matter how small and modest? Not when 'this is all over,' but instead of whatever might soon befall us."

Klarin's call had fallen on deaf ears, embraced only by a few in the human rights community. So did Kinkel's. Attending that London conference in 1992 as honored guests were at least two of the men considered most responsible for war crimes in Bosnia, Slobodan Milošević and Radovan Karadžić. European countries and the United States did not want to label them as war criminals; they were eager only for the short-lived Bosnian conflict to end.

The West was desperate for peace and unlikely to halt future atrocities. Gleeful from their victories in Bosnia, the two nationalists promised diplomats they would dismantle the camps, halt the siege of cities in Bosnia, and turn their heavy weapons over to international supervision. In turn, American and European diplomats hailed their cooperation and agreed talks should continue, under the guidance of former U.S. secretary of state Cyrus Vance and former British foreign secretary Lord David Owen. Within weeks, of course, it was clear that Milošević and Karadžić had no intention of keeping their promises.

In September 1992, reacting to accounts of horrors on the ground in Bosnia, fearful of what would happen to civilians in the cold winter's onslaught, UN Secretary-General Boutros Boutros-Ghali announced that thousands of peacekeepers would be sent to Bosnia to guard the delivery of humanitarian aid. Approximately 8,000 troops, many from Britain and France, arrived, becoming the United Nations Protection Force. A week later the UN declared Bosnian air space a "no-fly" zone.

Earlier that year the United Nations had slapped a trade and air embargo against Serbia and Montenegro, banning financial transactions and the delivery of oil.

It was a period of newfound optimism for UN peacekeeping. With the end of the Cold War, decades of deadlock in the United Nation's fifteen-member Security Council had finally given way to cooperation. President Bush hailed "a new world order" in which UN peacekeeping would play a greater role. The belief that the UN—with troops contributed by its members—could oversee complex tasks abroad led to an explosion in peacekeeping missions, of which Bosnia's would prove one of the most demanding.

Although war was raging in Bosnia, the lightly armed UN peacekeepers were sent there under strict peacekeeping rules of engagement. They were to remain impartial, and were not allowed to use military force except in self-defense or defense of their mandate, which initially was to supervise the delivery of humanitarian aid. As the war intensified, and civilians were increasingly placed at risk, the peacekeepers' neutrality and limited use of force made them appear both callous and ineffective, undermining the UN mission in Bosnia.

Facing the prospect of their troops on the ground as UN peacekeepers, European nations proved increasingly reluctant to support the concept of a war crimes tribunal, even in the face of Kinkel's appeal. The United States, in the middle of an election campaign, was otherwise preoccupied. On the ground in Bosnia, however, the killing and ethnic cleansing only intensified, as the Balkan henchmen drove to finish their handiwork before UN troops arrived and the American elections took place. Finally, when Milošević and Karadžić openly flouted the agreements made in London, the UN Security Council took a half-measure in response. On October 6, 1992, it unanimously voted to establish a commission of experts to investigate allegations of war crimes.

Of course, it is one thing to approve a commission; it is another to ensure that it accomplishes anything—as its members would soon discover.

NEWS OF THE UN Commission of Experts did not reach Hasan Nuhanović in Australia—where, had his fantasies been realized, he and his family would be. The news never reached him at all, because by October 1992 the Nuhanović family, having progressed only some 25 miles from where they began, were trapped in another city under siege: Srebrenica.

It was not their first choice of refuge, but there had been no alternative. Eastern Bosnia was awash with Serb troops, and every escape route out to territory held by the Bosnian government was blocked. Hunkered down in a small, remote village hamlet called Luka, the family feared running short of food as the winter approached. Rumors reached them that refugees were gathering in Srebrenica, and the Nuhanovićs decided to join them. For days they hiked up and down mountains, picked their way through craggy canyons, braved a hair-raising trip on a rickety boat along the Drina River under sniper and shell fire, and plodded, exhausted, through burned-out villages. Finally, on August 28, they reached the crest of the wooded hill above the city and gazed down into the valley at it. After months of living hand to mouth in tiny villages in the forest, to the family the view of Srebrenica—with its minarets, churches, famous communist-era health spa, and rows of tidy homes—looked downright welcoming. They congratulated themselves: They had made it to Srebrenica! Surely everything would be better now.

Hasan, knowing that several of his best friends from the university had family living in villages nearby, almost sprinted down the hill in anticipation. The war had ruined his plans for his university life. Now he at least hoped to find some of his buddies and get back to doing what Bosnians in their twenties do: chat about music and the opposite sex. He was mainly concerned about the fate of his best friend, Ćamil, from the nearby city of Bratunac. Rumors had reached the family, passed along from hamlet to hamlet, of a terrible massacre there. But if Ćamil was alive, he was bound to be in Srebrenica.

As soon as they hiked down the hill into the former silver-mining town, the Nuhanović family discovered it was swollen with hundreds of refugees, driven from towns and villages nearby by paramilitary gangs and the troops of the Bosnian Serb Army. Srebrenica's proximity to Serbia—the border was just ten miles away—had also made it a logical, early target. The area's inhabitants had stubbornly resisted. In fact, it was one of the very few places in eastern Bosnia where local Muslims—led by twenty-five-year-old former bodyguard to Milošević named Naser Orić—had actually beaten back the Serbs. Srebrenica had become something of a symbol of the hopes that an independent Bosnia could prevail.

Hasan went hunting, house to house, asking for Ćamil. He fantasized that if only he and his friends could be together, they could turn the clock back. They could forget the war. Finally someone recognized Ćamil's name and pointed out his house.

Hasan, thrilled, pounded on the door.

Ćamil's parents opened it. They were surprised to see Hasan. Ćamil, they said, was at the border with the other young men. "They're in position," they explained. "They're defending us against the Serbs. Everybody has to. We are all trapped here."

Reality dawned, piercing Hasan's dreams that he might reclaim something of a normal life in Srebrenica. He looked up at the mountains ringing the city, steep and dark, their crest clearly visible from where he stood. Suddenly Hasan saw Srebrenica for what it was—a prison.

Supplies had all but disappeared. There was no medicine for the wounded in the already overburdened hospitals. Native Srebrenicans had food stockpiled, but the thousands of new arrivals were desperate and hungry and the shops were empty. Historically, the city of Srebrenica had been renowned for its mineral resources. "Srebro" means silver, and over the centuries kings and nobles in Bosnia and Serbia had battled over the city's rich silver mines. In just one fifty-year period—1410 to 1460—Srebrenica was five times Serbian, four times Bosnian, and three times Turkish. But that meant little in a city then without electricity, water, telephone lines, cultivatable land, and no natural salt deposits.

The Bosnian Serbs were desperate to gain Srebrenica—home to one of the largest concentrations of Bosnian Muslims remaining in eastern Bosnia and threatening to ruin Serb hopes of annexing that part of Bosnia to their "greater Serbia." And grievances ran deep in the region. In World War II, waves of slaughter had devastated the city. The fighting had been almost exclusively between Bosnians—the Chetniks and the Partisans. Grudges were still nursed against those Muslims who had joined up with the Croatian Ustasha, and those who enlisted with Nazi SS troops, active in the region.

Surrounding Serbs also had new grievances to hold against Srebrenica: the marauding raids its fighters carried out on neighboring villages. Naser Orić, a Bosnian Muslim who was the unofficial head of the town, oversaw several gangs of local fighters and controlled what few resources Srebrenica did have, treating it like his private fiefdom. He had acquired a hero's status among the city's residents for defying the Serbs. Some of the attacks he and others led on nearby Serb villages were brutal. After firing on a community until its defenses crumbled, Orić and his men would swoop through, killing the Serbs and burning their homes, using the same techniques of "ethnic cleansing" as were practiced on them. As cemetery plots began to fill up with the Serb dead, tales of Orić and Srebrenica became infamous among the Bosnian Serbs. Orić, reveling in his role, videotaped his raids and openly bragged about them. "This is a dirty war with no rules," he told a Reuters reporter. "At the start we had a problem with weapons. Now we have enough with what we have captured from the Serbs we have killed."

Each time Orić and his men foraged outward, killing and pillaging, the Bosnian Serbs stepped up their shelling of the town. Artillery was their greatest asset: Guns, located on nearby mountains, pounded Srebrenica, sometimes dropping over 2,000 shells a day. The Bosnian Serb Army's bellicose, bullish commander, General Ratko Mladić, was angered at Srebrenica's resistance, outraged at Orić's raids. He pledged he would starve the city into submission. But the lack of food only prompted more raids by Orić. Often, gangs of hungry residents snuck out at night, bags over their shoulders, past the minefields surrounding the city, to raid the fields of nearby Serb farmers. Others followed in the wake of the military attacks, fighting and even killing local civilians in their desperation to eat.

The Nuhanović family was hungry. They had arrived with just 44 pounds of corn flour, and their supply was swiftly dwindling. By autumn Hasan measured his life by two rhythms: shelling and thinking about food. Either the family whiled away hours in the basement of the apartment building, waiting for the artillery onslaught to stop, or he dreamed about eating. The family subsisted largely on corn, pork fat, and a little flour. To distract himself from the constant grumbling in his stomach, Hasan—who had been assigned to coordinate refugees as part of his duties in the town—pored over dog-eared, musty English textbooks he had discovered, teaching himself English.

Winter arrives swiftly in the Balkans. One day it is a crisp and sunny fall day; the next, snow has fallen in drifts. Bosnians recall the winter of 1992 as one of the bitterest in memory, with temperatures dropping to thirteen below. Snow poured down on Srebrenica, adding a thick white canopy to the blackened, bombed hulks of buildings where people made their homes. A thick haze of smoke from acrid wood fires hung in the air, swirling around the desperate people that trudged along Srebrenica's streets. Fuel as well as food now became Hasan's chief preoccupation. Daily, he would hike into the hills—praying he wouldn't get shot—chop down a tree, and spend the afternoon wrestling it back home. At first, he chopped down green trees, too young to be used for fuel, much to the delight of the peasant folk who laughed at him. "Hey, you city boy, you chopped down the wrong tree!"

The vast majority of refugees in Srebrenica came from local mountain villages, where inhabitants clung to the old ways. The women still wore the colorful head scarves and the baggy trousers, or *dimije*, once native to the region but long ago abandoned by women in the cities. The men had rugged, callous hands as used to wielding an ax as a gun. The sweep of Yugoslavia's modernization had reached their villages but not penetrated it. Many lived according to the precommunist ways, embracing religion if not superstition and, most certainly, the land. The Nuhanović family—with their education, their white-collar jobs—were at a distinct disadvantage.

By early 1993, as fighting intensified around Srebrenica, thousands more hungry, desperate refugees poured into the area held by Orić and his men. The Serbs were retaliating in full force for one of Orić's more vicious maneuvers: On Serb Orthodox Christmas Day, January 7, he had attacked the Serb village of Kravica, killing dozens of Serb civilians. Now, as the Serbs claimed back Orić's land gains, hundreds of new refugees—some 60,000—were cramming into an ever-smaller Srebrenica. Twenty-five families packed into the home Hasan and his family had been living in. Hundreds of others, with nowhere to go, camped out on the snowbound streets. What few supplies that had been available vanished. While United Nations peacekeeping forces were to ensure humanitarian aid reached places like Srebrenica, the soldiers, restricted in their mandate, could do little when the rebel Serbs blocked them from entering the city. Only one humanitarian aid convoy was able to get in.

By February of 1993 the Nuhanović family had run out of money, and, after Nasiha bartered her earrings and the family ate the scraps she had purchased in exchange, they ran out of food. Hasan was desperate and hungry enough that when news came across the radio of a UN convoy due to arrive at the city of Žepa, some 30 miles away—he convinced his reluctant father to hike there with him.

Nearly 100 people set out in column across the Sušica Mountains early one February morning, in snow so deep and thick walking in it was like wading through quicksand. The sun, rebounding off the snow, was dazzling; the wind so strong it sucked the energy right out of one's bones. One hour, two hours, three hours of walking: of planting a foot, then another, then pulling each out of the snow and heaving yourself forward. Hasan's feet felt like anchors. Four hours, five hours, six hours; Hasan was cold to his very essence. Seven hours, eight hours, nine, ten: The group had finally struggled to the outskirts of Žepa when Hasan, weak and exhausted, fainted. He could not go on.

"How can you do this to me now?" he heard his father yelling to him as he passed out. "It was your idea to come here!"

They had to let the group go ahead. Hasan cried, as if he were a small boy, so ashamed was he of not being able to carry on. Local villagers took them in, gave him a cup of tea, and let them sleep on the floor. The next morning he felt stronger, and he and Ibro began trudging through the snow toward Žepa again. As they neared the town, the two men met the line of men and women—carrying 65 pounds of food on their backs—singing happily as they trudged through the snow. Hasan salivated. *I am going to eat*, he thought.

"Where do we go to find this stuff?" asked Hasan.

"Do you have papers to show you are from Žepa?" answered one of the women, wearing thick heavy socks but no shoes.

"No," Hasan said, puzzled. No one had said anything about needing papers.

"They won't give you food unless you can prove you're from Žepa. But you know, there probably isn't much left now for you to get anything anyway." The woman waved good-bye and started off.

Ibro glared at Hasan. The column of people walked by, headed back to Srebrenica.

"It was your idea to come!" Ibro yelled. "Now we will get nothing!"

"It's not my fault!" Hasan screamed. "It's all your fault we got stuck in Srebrenica!" He still blamed his father for not having followed his advice to quit the country for Europe, back in 1992.

Their angry voices echoed off the jagged mountains. They were alone on the mountain, alone in the wind and the snow and their fury. Hasan shoved his father. Ibro shoved back. The pair wrestled in the deep snow, slipping and sliding. Ibro, his feet trapped in the white drifts, fell to his knees.

He put his head in his hands, defeated.

Hasan, looking at his father—humiliated—began to cry, the tears freezing down his cheeks. *What had they come to?* Oddly, living together under siege in Srebrenica, Hasan had felt closer to his family than ever before. Yet now he and his father were acting like animals. Never in his life had Hasan felt so ashamed, so hungry, so cold, so disheartened.

Hasan helped his father up, and father and son staggered toward Žepa; they were too exhausted to return to Srebrenica. On a whim, they stopped at a house on the city's outskirts that belonged to a friend of Hasan's grandfather, who had once served as Žepa's mayor. Ibro pounded on the door. It swung open: inside was warmth, a blazing fire, the smell of food. Luck, for the first time in that horrific journey, was on their side.

The family gave them tea, with sugar: Hasan could feel the shock of it to his stomach, so long had it been since he had tasted its sweetness. It turned out the family owed Hasan's grandfather a debt for saving their father's life in World War II. That night their generosity was boundless. After the two slept in front of a warm fire, their backpacks were filled with untold riches: one pound of smoked meat, five pounds of wheat flour, two pounds of powdered milk, Danish cheese, two tins of corned beef.

Hasan and Ibro picked up their backpacks and began the ten-hour hike back across the mountains to Srebrenica.

REPORTS COMING OUT of Srebrenica that February 1993 from relief workers with the United Nations High Commissioner for Refugees depicted hell. Refugees were camped out on snowbound streets. Starving families were gnawing on tree roots and eating leaves. Scabies and lice were rampant. A World Health Organization doctor who hiked past Serb lines into Srebrenica estimated people were dying at a rate of twenty to thirty a day, and recommended that at least 18,000 women and children be evacuated.

A group of Srebrenica residents, including its wartime mayor, somehow made it to Sarajevo, demanded meetings with Bosnian government officials, and called for help. Alerted to the city's plight, the head of the UN Protection Force, French general Philippe Morillon, an independent, strong-minded commander, decided to go to Srebrenica himself and take a look.

His plan was to meet with the rest of Srebrenica's officials, reassure them, and then leave. But Srebrenica's mayor in exile sent a coded message telling the city's commander, Naser Orić, to prevent Morillon from leaving until he guaranteed the city's safety. Fatima Huseinović, the short, feisty owner of a Srebrenica perfume store who had emerged as one of the leaders among the city's women, was enlisted. To underscore how difficult the situation was when Morillon arrived, she organized the women to give him pictures of flowers that they had drawn, as putting a normal bouquet together was clearly impossible. Later, going house to house, she gathered hundreds of women in the hopes that they could persuade the UN general not to desert them. The women made makeshift posters out of what remained of Srebrenica's dwindling supply of paper. "We want bread not snow!" proclaimed one. "In the name of women and children don't leave, Mr. Morillon, or we will be killed," read another.

When Morillon clambered into his armored personnel carrier, the women surrounded it. Some lay down in front of it. He was, in effect, hostage. Retreating to the city's post office to meet with local officials, Morillon responded with a promise that would haunt him, and the United Nations. "You are now under the protection of the UN forces," he said, bellowing through a megaphone to the crowds outside. "I will never abandon you."

Anxious to get aid to Srebrenica's residents, Morillon led a humanitarian aid convoy into the city on March 19. Amid ever more desperate efforts to negotiate Srebrenica's future with the rebel Serbs who pressed onward with their attacks, the UN evacuated some 9,000 frantic residents, over the objections of the Muslim-led Bosnian government. Some of the city's refugees died, trampled underfoot in the desperate push to be one of those evacuated to safety.

By the beginning of April, Srebrenica's demise seemed all but certain. The United Nations was in a quandary: It could arrange a large-scale evacuation of all civilians from Srebrenica—and be accused of the same kind of "ethnic cleansing" the Serbs were known for—or it could try to protect the area and get in more relief supplies. The Bosnian Muslim-led government was opposed to a large evacuation, which in their minds amounted to surrendering the territory, about all it still held in eastern Bosnia. Many UN officials, particularly those on the ground in Sarajevo, had by now become as skeptical of the Bosnian government's objectives as they were of those of the rebel Serbs. When the Bosnian army did launch an offensive, it often did so in a manner that delayed aid convoys from getting to Bosnians themselves—a tactic many in the UN saw as a way of trying to force the West to intervene militarily. Some UN peacekeepers believed the Bosnian Muslim government exploited its own people's suffering as a way of garnering Western attention. It had gotten to the point that UN commanders, hearing descriptions of atrocities, wondered if they were exaggerated.

That spring, however, there was no denying that the Serbs had intensified their attacks on Srebrenica. The city was being pounded by artillery, multiple rocket launchers, and attack helicopters daily. The Nuhanović family never left their basement. In Belgrade, in New York, in Washington, diplomats frantically tried to stop the Serb onslaught; even Serb nationalist leader Milošević agreed to try to intervene. By April 13 the Bosnian Serbs announced they were poised to take the city; three days later Morillon informed the United Nations that the town was prepared to surrender.

In desperation, late on the night of April 16, the UN Security Council passed a resolution declaring Srebrenica to be a "safe area," a concept previously applied to protect Kurdish civilians in northern Iraq in 1991. The idea had been discussed for months as a way of protecting civilians from the fighting. Among UN diplomats the idea was unpopular, as it required UN peacekeepers to protect the "safe area." But it was the only way to honor Morrillon's promise and do something for Srebrenica at the same time. Passage of the resolution demanded that the Bosnian Serbs halt their attacks and withdraw and that Orić and his fighters hand over their weapons. Thus, Srebrenica would be demilitarized. In turn, UNPROFOR troops, still under a restrictive mandate, would be dispatched to the city to monitor its humanitarian situation.

It took some time for the news to catch up to the action on the ground. On the morning of the seventeenth, the shooting was getting closer and closer; shells were exploding every minute. Suddenly Hasan heard what he thought was the sound of outgoing artillery directed at the Serbs. He ran upstairs and looked out the window to see Naser Orić and some 100 men running up the hill. His heart leapt: Had Orić pushed back the Serbs? Listening to the radio, the Nuhanović family finally grasped what had happened. The UN had acted! The city was a "UN safe area"! Laughing and crying, Hasan, Nasiha, Ibro, and Muhamed jumped up and down and embraced each other.

The next morning 170 UN Canadian troops rolled into Srebrenica, ready to oversee a cease-fire. In need of a translator, they hired that self-taught English speaker, Hasan Nuhanović. Hasan could not believe his luck. Srebrenica would be safe. He had a job. It had all unfolded just like one of his favorite movies about the Partisans, with the good guys coming in to save the day at the last minute. Surely, with the United Nations and its troops committed to being in Srebrenica, there would be an end to the war. In fact, the UN Security Council—with the United States in the lead—would move to expand the "safe area" to five other cities: Bihać, Žepa, Tuzla, Goražde, and Sarajevo.

But life is not a movie script. As Hasan and his family would find in just a few years' time, living in a safe area did not necessarily entail being safe.

3

SINCE UNHAPPILY WE CANNOT ALWAYS AVOID WARS

Last of all—in an age when we hear so much of progress and civilization, is it not a matter of urgency, since unhappily we cannot always avoid wars, to press forward in a human and truly civilized spirit the attempt to prevent, or at least to alleviate, the horrors of war?

—Henri Dunant, *A Memory of Solferino*

The mass deportation of civilians is a war crime. The unlawful confinement of civilians is a war crime. The indiscriminate bombing of civilians, the destruction of cultural property and monuments, the torture and execution of surrendered prisoners or civilians are all war crimes. I knew none of this until I went to Bosnia and witnessed war crimes firsthand. I was just three days into my first visit to Sarajevo when a shell—arching over the city on an unnaturally warm day—slammed into a crowded outdoor market, transforming it into a morgue, killing 68 and wounding more than 200. It was a rude awakening to the Bosnian war.

War. I'd reported from Kuwait, Saudi Arabia, and Iraq during the Gulf War, so I thought I knew what to expect when my editors decided I should go to Bosnia. I was all bravado and bustling know-how, a master of checklists who presided over an ever-growing stack of supplies. Pack the boots, buy the flak jacket (what do I do about the attached groin protector?), don't forget the Mag-lite flashlight, the spare batteries, the freeze-dried energy food, the water purification tablets, the long underwear. I believed I could survive the siege of Sarajevo with enough brightly colored Polartech and L.L. Bean camping gear. When you grow up in the rarefied suburbs of middle-class Connecticut as I did, you figure preparation is everything: SAT prep course for college, dancing school for social functions, the Girl Scouts for survival training. How little I knew then. I'd never been directly under heavy bombardment; never been targeted by a sniper; never seen a freshly killed corpse awash with blood; never watched anyone shot dead in front of my eyes; never had a woman collapse in my arms, crying for her dead son, his head blown off.

All of those things happened in the course of my first weeks in Sarajevo. Of course, such things had been happening to the people of Sarajevo for months by the time I got there, because I did not arrive until February 1994, nearly two years into the war. As I quickly realized, it would have been wiser to bring a copy of the Geneva Conventions and other relevant laws of war than my outdated travel guide to Yugoslavia. Bosnia's war was not a war between two armies. At that point it was a war in which one heavily armed army belonging to the rebel Bosnian Serbs clearly and deliberately targeted civilians, while the underequipped Bosnian army tried to hold its own. In the case of Sarajevo, this translated into what is known as siege warfare, a practice as ancient as war itself. Unable to conquer Sarajevo, its houses tightly clustered in the valley along the Miljacka River, the rebel Serbs tried to beat it into submission.

Their guns, perched atop the tall mountains that ringed the city as tightly as a fortress, rained death and destruction on civilians below. On bad days up to 3,500 shells pummeled the city, their whistles and bangs broken only by the baying of packs of hungry dogs. Nearly every house bore shrapnel scars, a missing roof, or the plastic sheeting given out by the UN to replace windows.

What artillery couldn't hit, snipers did. Perched high up in communist-era apartment buildings, the snipers—some of them former Olympic sharpshooters—easily picked off those unlucky enough not to have dodged behind the rows of bullet-riddled buses thrown up as sniper barricades. *Ping-poof!* A bullet zipped from nowhere; a man cowers; a woman carrying jugs of water falls over, hit in the leg. I was taken aback when this happened right in front of me, but the people around me shrugged. It was an ordinary event in Sarajevo, just another scene from a very surreal war. And it was surreal, a war in which UN peacekeepers, clad in baby-blue flak jackets and helmets, witnessed this scene and did nothing, restrained by their mandate from firing at the snipers unless directly targeted themselves. A war in which European Union monitors, looking like ice cream vendors in uniforms as white as snow, wandered through the darkened chaos. A war in which Bosnian Serbs who remained in Sarajevo in support of an independent Bosnia were shelled by their fellow Bosnian Serbs. A war in which Bosnian Serb leader Radovan Karadžić regularly denied that his troops, led by General Ratko Mladić, were shelling Sarajevo, claiming the Muslims were doing it to themselves. Even the marketplace bombing, he argued, had been staged: "It is quite clear from TV material that corpses several hours old were being manipulated on the marketplace and these 'corpses' even included plastic and textile human-size dummies," Karadžić wrote in a letter sent to President Clinton and Russian president Boris Yeltsin. The bombing was a "gross deception."

It was a war in which those who lived in Pale, the bucolic alpine village that served as Karadžić's capital, believed him. "They took existing dead bodies," shopkeeper Bozidar Bogdanović told me when I got to Pale several days after the bombing. "And then they dragged them out onto the marketplace and threw blood over them. And you were fooled! And then they pinned the blame on the Serbs!" Bogdanović, his eyes twinkling under his eyebrows, smiled at me indulgently, like a father to a doltish daughter who had just flunked her driving test. "You'd know this if only you'd watch Serb TV," he added.

Along with the shelling and the sniping that surrounded Sarajevo there was also the coldness and the darkness, for the Serbs had long ago cut off electricity to Sarajevo. Candles, or a string of Christmas lights hooked up to a car battery, took the place of lamps. Wood-burning stoves, fueled by books, furniture, or the children's toys, served as the family hearth, while electric stoves languished nearby. Running water was a thing of the past, replaced by daily sprints to the river, dragging plastic jerry cans, or a few outdoor water taps. Dreaming of food had taken the place of eating it. Nedim, the nine-year-old son of Nela and Mirsad Hosić, friends in Sarajevo who served as my barometer of the war, used to draw pictures of the watermelon and bananas he could no longer taste. The lightly armed UN troops were foiled by the fact that they were peacekeepers in the midst of a war in which food and fuel were the weapons of choice. Their delivery of humanitarian aid depended on the rebel Serbs' consent, and while generals and leaders might agree to let them proceed in principle, those manning checkpoints regularly did not. UN humanitarian aid convoys arrived infrequently, and food prices, as a result, were sky-high in 1994. Coffee hit $60 a pound; a banana could cost nearly $6; an egg, $3. *"Nema ništa,"* Sarajevans would say, when you would ask them how they were. "There is nothing."

So on February 5, 1994, on a day seductively warm—the temperature nearly 50 degrees, the sun balmy—Sarajevans were lured into leaving the smoke-filled, dank, cold tombs of their homes for the outdoors. There had been almost no shelling that morning, and the day promised to be quiet. The weather drew an even larger crowd than usual out to the market, an outdoor square pinched between buildings lining Marshal Tito Street, the main road bisecting the city. There was little to buy—some withered vegetables—but people often came to the market to barter possessions for what little food there was. And a trip to the market was a chance to pretend, for one achingly short moment, that life was normal.

It was 12:37 P.M. when the 120-millimeter mortar shell, lobbed skyward, turned down and hit the marketplace with deadly accuracy and a resounding *thump*. It was the single largest attack on civilians since the war began. I arrived shortly after it hit, and what I remember was Belma, a flower seller, screaming: one hand up to her mouth, the other at her chest, her cries those of primeval pain. The paper flower wreaths she had been selling to adorn graves lay scattered at her feet.

Around her, the rickety market stalls had shattered like matchsticks. Tables on their side, buckets overturned, vegetables mashed with the imprint from running people's feet. A leg, its foot in a boot still attached, lay on the ground. A vast pool of blood, dark and red, washed over the back of the market, coursing around the cabbages and potatoes and shopping bags strewn about the ground. A piece of head—or possibly brains—was impaled on a metal post. Bloodstained rags were draped over unidentified body parts, and men, wailing and crying, hefted bodies into cars doubling as ambulances.

It looked like a war crime to me. And, according to the 1949 Geneva Conventions and the 1977 Additional Protocols, the targeting of civilians—which this appeared to be—was a war crime. Indeed, almost everything the rebel Serbs had done to Sarajevo contravened international humanitarian law, the laws and conventions of war that regulate the conduct of war. Besieging forces are not to target civilians, deprive them of food, or target their water supply as part of daily combat. In Sarajevo, shells had already killed people standing in line for bread and the brewery, where many fetched water. Even though UN experts, determined to stay neutral, could not "conclusively" rule that the rebel Serbs had lobbed the shell, the marketplace bombing fit an already established pattern of deliberate attacks on civilians.

There had been no military response to atrocities like this. But there could be a judicial one. In 1993 the United Nations Security Council, eager to pacify critics of its policies in Bosnia, had taken the unprecedented step of creating an international war crimes court to investigate and try those charged with war crimes in the former Yugoslavia.

Pessimists saw the court as a fig leaf, aimed at hiding Western leaders' failure to intervene militarily. Others believed it was a bold step, sending the message that no one is above the law. "The lesson that we are all accountable to international law," declared the U.S. ambassador to the UN, Madeleine K. Albright, on February 22, 1993, as she announced the court's creation, "may have finally taken hold in our collective memory." A month later the UN Security Council unanimously approved a resolution that dictated the scope of the new court. Criminal justice—and the prospect of peace and reconciliation—were linked in Bosnia. For the first time since the Bosnian war had begun, there was at least the promise that those who committed war crimes would be held accountable. The question remained how substantial that promise might prove.

DISCUSSION OF A war crimes tribunal for the former Yugoslavia had percolated since German foreign minister Klaus Kinkel raised it in the fall of 1992. But in December 1992, Acting U.S. Secretary of State Lawrence Eagleburger went a step further. Arriving for peace talks in Geneva, Eagleburger stunned European leaders by announcing that the United States had identified ten suspected war criminals who should answer for their atrocities "in a court of law, I hope." He named them: Slobodan Milošević, Radovan Karadžić, General Mladić, "Arkan" (Željko Ražnatović, Serbian paramilitary leader), and Zejnil Delalić (of the Čelebići camp), among others. There was silence in the room as European diplomats pondered their dilemma. Several of the men with whom they were still desperately trying to negotiate a peace in Bosnia had just been classified as alleged war criminals. For Eagleburger and the Bush administration, on its way out of office, it was an attempt to clear the record. Eagleburger, who had once served as ambassador to Yugoslavia, had been soundly criticized for being too accommodating of Milošević, and several of his foreign service officers had resigned over the State Department's failure to investigate war crimes in Bosnia vigorously.

Once President Clinton took office in January 1993, a war crimes tribunal became a policy option simply because it was the least risky step to take. Bosnia was emerging as a troubling blip on the administration's radar screen. No matter how much the presidential campaign had been about "It's the economy, stupid," once Clinton was in the White House, it was thought that foreign policy—rather than the passage of domestic legislation—would shape his presidential legacy. And Bosnia was the first test. "Clinton's handling of Bosnia could define his presidency," noted the *Christian Science Monitor*, one of many newspapers, as well as congressional leaders, to call immediately on the White House to act in the Balkans. Policy options were limited, and all involved taking steps that a risk-adverse new administration was hesitant to take. On the campaign trail, Clinton had pushed for lifting the arms embargo and using air strikes to cripple Serb artillery, what became known as "lift and strike." Once Clinton was in the White House, European leaders made it clear this was not an option they favored. Their lightly armed soldiers in UN peacekeeping forces faced retaliation if there were air strikes. They wanted American troops on the ground as well—something the Pentagon, still under the shadow of Vietnam, was reluctant to consider.

Negotiations also seemed to be going nowhere. The two negotiators, Cyrus Vance and Lord David Owen, had crafted a plan in 1993 that called for Bosnia to remain as one country but be decentralized into ten semi-autonomous provinces, of which six would have no ethnic majority. The plan, however, required having troops on the ground to enforce it, something the United States was not willing to provide. The Clinton administration procrastinated over what to do with the Vance-Owen plan which it ultimately rejected. (The only glimmer of hope was not until the spring of 1994, when warring Muslims and Croats agreed to form a federation.)

Meanwhile, the UN Commission of Experts, created in 1992 to examine allegations of war crimes in the former Yugoslavia, had filed an interim report concluding that there were serious violations of international humanitarian law in Bosnia and that some kind of action was necessary. A war crimes tribunal emerged as a nearly risk-free way to do something forceful that involved no troops on the ground. A tribunal resonated with the romantic legacy of Nuremberg and provided convenient political cover. For European leaders, sunk in the quagmire of endless peace talks, and the United Nations, its blue-helmeted peacekeepers in Bosnia looking more ineffective by the minute, a war crimes tribunal seemed like a solution, indeed. "It was a way [for the administration] to avoid doing other things," recalled one human-rights advocate who lobbied for the tribunal. Noted Michael Scharf, then in the State Department's legal advisor's office: "It was sort of a Band-Aid to hemorrhaging credibility."

And it was an idea that appealed not only to an increasingly vocal American human rights community—Human Rights Watch had been actively calling for a tribunal for months—but also to the U.S. ambassador to the United Nations. Albright, an international affairs specialist who was the daughter of a former Czechoslovak ambassador to Tito's Yugoslavia, was a zealous advocate of U.S. activism abroad. ("What's the point of having this superb military you're always talking about, if we can't *use* it?" Albright once asked the chairman of the Joint Chief of Staff, Colin Powell.) She so actively lobbied the UN Security Council for a tribunal that European diplomats opposed to the idea—including the French Ambassador—called it "Madeleine's folly" behind her back. Albright later recalled having another name for her effort, one that reflected the outrage many women felt over news of mass rapes in the former Yugoslavia. "We called ourselves the G-8," she told an American Bar Association dinner in 1999, describing a caucus she formed of women permanent representatives to the UN. "We were determined that there be a war crimes tribunal for the former Yugoslavia, and we wanted there to be women judges."

The war crimes tribunal was not created by treaty but by a Chapter VII resolution, a measure the Security Council takes when it considers that a "threat to international peace and security" exists. In passing this resolution, the Security Council created a court with a dual mandate, its role not just to punish but also to deter and to reconcile. Its life span would be linked to "the restoration and maintenance of international peace and security of the territory of the former Yugoslavia." Officially called the International Tribunal for the Prosecution of Persons Responsible for Serious Violations of International Humanitarian Law Committed in the Territory of the Former Yugoslavia since 1991, it soon became known as the International Criminal Tribunal for the former Yugoslavia—or the Yugoslav Tribunal, or ICTY. Initially the new tribunal would consist of two trial chambers and an appeals chamber and a prosecutor's office and registry, which would serve as the court's administrative arm. It could try crimes of genocide, crimes against humanity, grave breaches of the Geneva Convention, and violations of the customs and laws of war but only those violations of international humanitarian law committed in the territory of the former Yugoslavia after January 1, 1991. There would be eleven judges, at least to start.

It was unlike any court many American lawyers had ever seen. But war crimes courts are their own unique breed. And international humanitarian law—the conventions, codes, and norms that govern modern warfare—are themselves unlike any other laws.

THE LAWS OF war are as ancient as they are modern. Reading the Geneva Conventions is a little like stepping into one of those musty bric-a-brac stores on the back roads of New England where junk gathers dust along with collector's items. International humanitarian law is a similar hodgepodge of ideals that date back centuries: language that reflects a vigorous nineteenth-century humanism and sexism, international agreements that were signed in the twentieth-century but rarely enforced. Prosecutors, as they tried cases of alleged crimes in Bosnia, would be building on the ideals of thinkers as diverse as St. Augustine of Hippo, Hugo Grotius, Jean-Jacques Rousseau, and Henri Dunant.

As long as there has been war, there have been discussions about how to regulate it, as contradictory as that seems. The Old Testament warned against killing those who surrender. Sun Tzu, in the fourth century B.C., counseled that attacks should be made against enemy armies, not cities. St. Augustine reflected on when war is just (when it turns dissension into peace) or unjust (when committed with a malicious intent to destroy). The Hindu *Book of Manu* in India, which regulated land warfare, had provisions protecting noncombatants. From antiquity into the Middle Ages, agreements were struck as to when war should be waged and who should be shielded from it.

Chivalrous codes emerged and war become more specialized, a matter for armies and their soldiers, not just a clash between countries in which civilians were necessarily part of the battle. As Shakespeare tells us in *Henry V*: "Kill the boys and the luggage! 'Tis expressly against the law of arms. . . ." In 1474 Peter von Hagenbach was tried by the first reported international war crimes court on charges of having trampled under foot the laws of God and man in Breisach, a town on the Upper Rhine. Hagenbach was accused of rape, illegal taxation, and wanton confiscation of private property. While he argued that he was just following orders—a defense that would be used centuries after his time—the ad hoc tribunal of twenty-eight judges concluded that the brutality with which he and his soldiers acted was his own contribution. He was condemned and sentenced to death.

As nation-states emerged and religious rule waned in the seventeenth-century, a Dutch scholar, Hugo Grotius, collected and wrote down the various values and beliefs concerning warfare. Grotius, who traveled widely and was something of an internationalist, is now remembered as "the father of international law." A century later, French philosopher Jean-Jacques Rousseau took his ideas a step further, arguing that war was the work of nations. "War is in no way a relationship of man with man but a relationship between States, in which individuals are enemies only by accident," the philosopher wrote.

But it was during the nineteenth century—with its flourishing idealism, philanthropy, breakthroughs in science and communications, and rash of wars in Europe and in America—when norms governing warfare became codified. War by then had qualitatively changed, as had the resulting public outrage about it. New weapons meant fighting had become somewhat more brutal. While weapons were more precise, the injuries they inflicted were often more damaging. For example, weapons such as the percussion cap, the revolver, the smooth-bore cannon, and the exploding dum-dum bullet mangled men as well as killed them. Thanks to the invention of the telegraph and developments in photography, the public was better informed about such injuries than ever before. By the mid-nineteenth century, what occurred on a battlefield could be quickly and graphically reported. Week-old dispatches that glossed over the horrors of war were replaced by up-to-date reports that emphasized war's brutality. War correspondents would file stories from battles that would prompt public reactions as never before.

In 1854, for example, the news that thousands of British soldiers in the Crimean War were dying as a result of atrocious hospital conditions prompted Florence Nightingale and her nurses to travel to the Crimea to tend the wounded, forever changing the nature of wartime nursing. Unsparing photograph and newspaper accounts of the American Civil War describing massive casualties, scenes of the wounded left to die on battlefields from gangrene, and the lack of medical care, water, or food prompted President Abraham Lincoln in 1863 to commission his War Department to promulgate a code governing the Union Army's conduct. Known as the Lieber code, after the German-Austrian political philosopher who authored it, it marked the first effort to codify all the existing laws and customs of war.

Yet it was a battle in a tiny Italian town called Solferino that most revolutionized how armed combat would be seen in the future. There, on the fertile, wine-bearing plains south of Lake Garda, the armies of Austria clashed with those of Sardinia and Napoleon III of France in 1859. The dreadful battle took place on June 24, a battle of blood and saber and bayonet thrusts, of dust and rain and heat, of men yelping with pain and horses screaming under fire, of the crack of artillery, the galloping of cavalry. Six thousand perished and more than 30,000 were wounded, left to die in agony, stranded in the winding vineyards, the thickets of mulberry trees, and the ditches that surrounded Solferino. Henri Dunant, a young Geneva businessman down on his luck, had come to the battlefield in the hopes of talking to Napoleon about his failing enterprises. Horrified by the sight of the wounded lying untended, he organized people to help treat and transport the injured soldiers. His short memoir, *A Memory of Solferino*, stirred public anguish over the battle and overwhelming support for the idea it suggested: a corps of volunteers to care for the wounded.

"No quarter is given . . . it is a sheer butchery; a struggle between savage beasts, maddened with blood and fury . . ." wrote Dunant. When the fighting had ended, he noted, "the stillness of the night was broken by groans, by stifled sighs of anguish and suffering. Heart-rending voices kept calling for help . . . [I]s it not a matter of urgency, since unhappily we cannot always avoid wars, to press forward in human and civilized spirit to attempt, or at least to alleviate, the horrors of war?"

Today a small yellow and white church atop a hill in Solferino memorializes the horrors of the battle Dunant witnessed. Pass through the entrance under the brilliant gold and blue mosaic of St. Peter into the still interior. Once your eyes adjust to the darkness, the church's decor becomes clear. Lining the rotunda behind the alter are rows of bones; the church is not just a sanctuary but an ossuary. More than 1,400 skulls and the bones of 7,000 soldiers of several nationalities are there, the remains of the battle's unidentified dead.

Outside, a plaque honors Dunant, who went on to make his vision a reality by establishing the International Committee of the Red Cross in 1863, the first international organization to care for wounded soldiers in battle and to advocate for international laws governing war time behavior. A year later, the group had achieved its first resounding victory. Gathering in Geneva's Hôtel de Ville, representatives of sixteen countries, somber in their dark suits and mutton-chop whiskers, adopted the first Geneva Convention, which laid out rules governing the care and protection of the wounded in war. For the first time in history, there were international laws limiting the impact of man's deadliest activity.

While not every country immediately ratified the convention—it took the United States until 1882—its ideals struck a sympathetic chord. In 1868 Czar Alexander II held an international conference at which it was agreed to ban the use of certain weapons and noted that civilians as well as combatants should be protected. By the turn of the century several decades of heady discussions had resulted in two schools of law: the laws of the Hague, or laws regulating the means and methods of war and warfare, and the laws of Geneva, or the laws governing the treatment of potential victims, whether soldiers or civilians.

The forces of history and the continuing evils of war—from the devastation of World War I to the horrors of World War II—have shaped international humanitarian law as we know it today. But it took the atrocities committed in Nazi concentration camps; the flight of tens of thousands of refugees; the extermination of 6 million European Jews; and the rape and ill-treatment of thousands in Asia to focus attention on a new victim of war—the civilian—and the need to specify certain violations of international humanitarian law as "war crimes offenses worthy of prosecution." When the UN in 1993 created its new war crimes tribunal, it was the 1945 Nuremberg war crimes trials and the Tokyo military tribunal—and the subsequent 1949 Geneva Conventions—that were its guide.

THE ALLIED WAR crimes trials, the first of their kind, came about largely at American prodding. British prime minister Winston Churchill, for example, had advocated summary executions for top Nazi leaders. Instead the two international military tribunals would hold high-ranking government and military officials individually responsible for violations of the laws of war. The Nuremberg and Tokyo trials were not the first international effort to prosecute war crimes. The Treaty of Versailles had recommended that Kaiser Wilhelm II of Germany be tried by an Allied court, although he sought refuge in Holland, which then refused to extradite him. Allied efforts to bring Turkish and German war criminals to justice after World War I also ended in fiasco.

Of the two World War II tribunals, it was Nuremberg that had the greatest impact. "Ask the passerby what the words 'war crimes' bring to his mind, and the chances are that the reply will be 'Nuremberg,' noted Telford Taylor, a Nuremberg prosecutor. The international military tribunal actually held only one joint trial, in 1946; the U.S. military and other allies separately conducted twelve additional trials in Nuremberg from 1947 to 1949. (Cold War politics intervened in gathering the Soviet, French, British, and American judges together as they had been in 1945.) Certainly the military tribunal's first and only trial was the stuff of history. Twenty-two high-ranking German officials were tried, including Hermann Göring, Hitler's number-two man. With the resources of the Allied armies at its disposal, no detail was spared. Teams of Allied engineers and German prisoners of war worked to rebuild parts of Nuremberg, bombed into rubble during the war, to accommodate the hordes of staff and journalists who arrived. Hundreds of staff bustled through the halls of the Justizgebäude, the city's brooding Palace of Justice, preparing for the trial. Teams of assistant prosecutors, researchers, document specialists, and translators worked seventy-hour weeks. Nearly 200,000 affidavits were evaluated as evidence.

When the trial opened in courtroom 600 on November 19, 1945—just six months after Germany's surrender—the soaring oratory of U.S. Supreme Court Justice Robert Jackson and Great Britain's Sir Hartley

Shawcross was featured in newspaper articles. The trial was to be the triumph of reason over revenge, as Jackson, the chief prosecutor at the trial, eloquently put it. "That four great nations," he said in his opening statement, "flushed with history and stung with injury, stay the hand of vengeance and voluntarily submit their captive enemies to the judgment of the law is one of the most significant tributes that power has ever paid to reason." After 113 witnesses on the stand (and 143 questioned in interrogatories), 1,800 photographs, more than 4,000 documents, and 216 days of trial, the four judges delivered their verdict: three acquittals, twelve death sentences (by hanging), seven prison terms. The trial transcripts, which extensively documented Nazi war crimes in twenty-two volumes of court hearings, became part of the postwar record. "It is safe to say that no litigation approaching this in magnitude has ever been attempted," Justice Jackson reported in his resignation letter to President Truman.

This and subsequent trails in Nuremberg, in fact, became postwar legends. Immortalized in Hollywood's 1962 movie *Judgment at Nuremberg*, starring Spencer Tracy, war crimes trials came to represent the triumph of law over impunity as well as the success of international efforts, like the creation of the United Nations in 1945. Two years after Nuremberg, the UN Law Commission, flushed with a sense of hope, called for the establishment of a permanent international court, a dream nurtured to the present day. As the years passed, the Nuremberg trials received much of the credit for the German nation's self-awakening about its role in the Holocaust. But many Germans argue it was the country's own efforts, through its war crimes trials, documentaries, and histories written in the 1950s and 1960s, that made them confront the past. "The German public was not interested in Nuremberg," argues German author Jörg Friedrich. "There was no great echo in the population at the time."

There was, actually, much to criticize about the Nuremberg trial—and as much for the new war crimes court to avoid as to adopt. Romanticized as a trial spurred by discovery of the horrors of the concentration camps, Nuremburg's prosecutors actually focused on prosecuting the Nazi leaders for waging a war of aggression. That, critics charged, was retroactive justice; aggressive wars had been waged over the centuries but never prosecuted before. Nuremberg's critics also accused the court of delivering "victor's justice"; indeed, none of the Allies whose judges sat in judgment was ever prosecuted by the tribunal for war crimes, such as the Allied firebombing of Dresden. Writer Rebecca West, reporting on the trial, described it as biased against Germany, the place "where the world's enemy was being tried for its sins." Finally, the Nuremburg trial was critiqued for failing to adequately ensure defendants' rights.

In both its statute and its rules, the Yugoslav Tribunal was determined to be different, incorporating the best of Nuremberg while avoiding the worst. "This will be no victor's tribunal," U.S. Ambassador Albright told UN diplomats on the day the tribunal was approved. "The only victor that will prevail in this endeavor is the truth." With the war still raging on the ground in Bosnia, there was no "victor's" side to take. Instead, the hope was that the tribunal would act as a deterrent, curbing crimes against civilians if not pushing the parties down the road to peace. To counter the criticism that law was being applied retroactively, the UN Security Council notified warring parties in the former Yugoslavia that they had been—and continued to be—in violation of international law. Nor was the new war crimes court to prosecute crimes against peace (waging war) as had the Nuremberg tribunal. It was empowered to prosecute crimes against humanity, genocide, grave breaches of the Geneva Conventions, and violations of the laws or customs of war. The court would provide defense attorneys, if needed, and pay their wages. Decisions could be appealed before an appeals chamber. While the new war crimes court was created in response to atrocities against Bosnia's Muslims, it was understood that it would try violations of international humanitarian law on all sides.

"Crimes against humanity," or inhumane acts committed against any civilian population committed in a widespread or systematic manner, were first introduced in the 1945 London Charter creating the Nuremberg tribunal. The term, "crimes against humanity" reflected moral indignation over the fact that crimes against noncombatants (Germans as well as citizens of enemy states) were part of a larger, planned attack. Increasing the law's reach, the Yugoslavia Tribunal added the crimes of rape, torture, and imprisonment. In deciding to prosecute genocide charges, the tribunal also was looking to the 1948 Genocide Convention, which defined genocide as acts committed to destroy in whole or in part an ethnic group.

In prosecuting "grave breaches" and "violations of the laws and customs of war," the Yugoslav Tribunal was also drawing from the 1949 Geneva Conventions. The diplomats, military experts, legal scholars from the sixty-three countries (then nearly every country in the world) that gathered in 1949 to update the laws of war differed greatly from the small huddle of reformers from sixteen countries who had convened nearly a century before. Replacing the heady idealism of 1864 was a sober realism born of two world wars and the prospect of total war raised with the development of the atom bomb. "If war denies worth and dignity, it will proceed to unlimited destruction," warned Max Huber, the honorary president of the International Committee of the Red Cross (ICRC), which initiated the conference and invited delegates to attend.

Diplomats agreed on the need to update the conventions, but there was vast disagreement over how to do so. The wounds of World War II were still fresh and resulted in sharply conflicting points of view. The formerly occupied countries of Europe, with an eye to the Soviet Union, argued vigorously for sweeping and detailed protections for civilians. But the Soviet Union, mindful of the United States' and Britain's successful bombing campaigns, pushed for restrictions on bombing.

Tensions between the United States and the Soviet Union culminated in a diplomatic showdown when, without warning, the Soviets introduced a draft resolution banning atomic weapons. They pushed for the Geneva Conventions to serve as an enforceable international penal code, while other countries argued the conventions should serve simply as a source of guiding principles for behavior during war. The Soviet resolution was voted down. Finally, on August 12, 1949, after fourteen weeks of negotiations, bartering, heated discussion, and diplomatic compromise, four conventions totaling some 400 articles were ready for signature and ratification. (By contrast, the first Geneva Convention was only ten articles long.)

The four Geneva Conventions represented a revolution in thought: guaranteeing, for the first time, protections for civilians; defining criminal violations of the conventions and obligating states to prosecute them, even if not party to the conflict; applying limited parts of international law to internal, as well as international, armed conflicts. Three of the conventions updated those agreements already in existence. The fourth, however, was groundbreaking. It guaranteed safeguards for "protected persons," including civilians on the opposite side in occupied territory.

Also new was the delineation of universal "grave breaches," or what would constitute criminal violations of the conventions. It was the first time the Geneva Conventions had attempted to specify which transgressions of international humanitarian law required punishment and obligated countries to prosecute them. Diplomats quarreled long and hard over defining "grave breaches" and whether to call them "war crimes." The resulting list was restrictive, applying only to conflicts between different countries and to people defined as "protected." It was also somewhat vague. While some grave breaches—unlawful deportation, transfer, or confinement of a civilian—were clear, others, such as "wilfully causing great suffering," were not. The precise penal sanctions for violations were not specified. Each country, instead, was obligated to provide such sanctions.

Last, the 1949 conventions included a new provision known as Common Article 3, which addressed itself to internal wars and sets minimum protections for civilians or wounded combatants in conflicts "not of an international character." For the first time, any internal conflict, or civil war, would be governed by certain provisions of international law. The provision had proven controversial, challenging the nature of international law as pertaining to matters between states. What emerged was very much a compromise: For example, Common Article 3 was imprecise about just what constituted conflicts "not of an international character." Even those in attendance weren't quite sure, commentators would later remark. But the conventions were meant to be adapted to future conflicts and wars. "A choice had to be made between drawing up very full and detailed rules covering all possible eventualities, and formulating general principles sufficiently flexible to be adapted to existing circumstances in each country," noted Jean Pictet, the legal scholar whose commentary is used to interpret the conventions.

Yet it was one thing to draft the statutes for the new Yugoslav Tribunal. It was another to staff and equip such a tribunal and investigate war crimes, particularly when hostilities were ongoing. People like Bill Haglund, an American forensic expert, would get their first taste of the difficulties war crimes investigators would face. In Haglund's case, that challenge lay in the hope that forensic evidence, for the first time in history, would be introduced as evidence in an international war crimes court.

THERE WAS VERY little that forty-nine-year-old William Haglund—Bill to everybody—hadn't seen when it came to dead bodies. As a medical and legal death investigator for the King's County Medical Examiners office in Seattle, Washington, Haglund's job took him to every murder site, no matter where it was—in a bar, in a field, or in a bed. In the fall of 1993, however, Haglund found himself at a very different kind of crime scene: one guarded by UN peacekeepers, strewn with bullet casings and bearing all the hallmarks of an execution-style slaying.

He was in Croatia, temporarily assigned to the UN Commission of Experts, whose work detailing atrocities in the former Yugoslavia was to become the mainstay of the Yugoslav Tribunal's first cases. The commission, underfunded and short-staffed, had a difficult time getting off the ground, opposed from the outset by Britain and France, which feared that official proclamations of "war crimes" in Bosnia would endanger ongoing peace talks.

Haglund was part of the mission because of his unusual combination of skills. He was accustomed to criminal investigations and dealing with multiple bodies. It was during his work on the Green River serial murders—in which nearly fifty women's bodies had been scattered across rural areas—that he had met the eminent American forensic anthropologist Clyde Snow. That meeting prompted Haglund to return to school to become a forensic anthropologist, someone who specializes in the science of identifying a body through its bones. He had concentrated on "taphonomy"—the study of how earth, water, and insects affect human remains after death. When Snow, along with Eric Stover, the director of Physicians for Human Rights, discovered a mass grave in Croatia in 1992, which they believed contained civilian bodies, Haglund was just the man they wanted to help exhume it.

And mass graves were vital to the UN Commission of Experts. With a war fiercely raging in ex-Yugoslavia, investigators knew they couldn't count on finding a paper trail detailing various war crimes, as victorious Allied troops had done when they defeated the Nazis. In the place of documents, mass graves were important evidence of civilian killings. "Bones," Snow once said, "are often our last and best witnesses; they never lie and they never forget."

Haglund, short and bespectacled, with a scraggly, graying beard, glasses, and a puckish air, looked more like a comp lit professor than a man whose pet passions were snakes and country music and whose profession centered around dead bodies. But Haglund had had an unusual childhood. Born to a waitress mother and a party-hopping mechanic father, Haglund's earliest memories were of bars: the smell of pretzels, which sometimes were his only meal, the fistfights between drunken patrons, the wild music. The family moved frequently, forcing him to miss school; Haglund couldn't read until the fourth grade.

By the age of eleven, he had gone to live with his grandparents in Oregon. When he hit seventeen, they quarreled, and Haglund, desperate for a place to live, moved into the local mortuary, where he helped the owner in exchange for a room upstairs. To get to the floor where he slept, he'd have to wind past the embalming room and then up the stairs past the casket room. It was a creepy experience, but he got used to working with the dead. ("I've been around dead people more than living people," Haglund joked to me after I got to know him, adding in one of his typically self-deprecating comments, "That's why I have no social skills.") After studying biology—and periods teaching folk mythology and playing country music on his guitar—Haglund became a medical examiner and eventually chief investigator.

Still, none of this had prepared him for Croatia: the concertina wire, the soldiers, the checkpoints, the sandbags, the destruction. Driving along, he'd notice the tank muzzles sticking out of barns, gullies, wheat fields. Everyone had guns, and half of them seemed to be pointed at the investigators. "For three days we measured the area [of the gravesite], used the metal detector to locate spent cartridges and were harassed by the Ukrainian soldiers who became increasingly belligerent as each day wore on and as their vodka took effect," wrote Haglund, a prodigious diary writer. "This was my first experience with high security amidst a country occupied by armies . . . walking to mess we carefully avoided the posted areas where it had been mined."

The land mines scattered across many of the mass graves made the prospect of exhumations daunting. The plan had been for Haglund to assist a team of some seventeen other forensic scientists to exhume the grave believed to contain the bodies of patients and staff from the Vukovar hospital, who had been shot by Serb soldiers, a clear violation of international humanitarian law. Serb commanders, however, ignoring the permission papers granted from Serbian authorities in Belgrade, refused to let the mission proceed. No one cared that they were UN representatives on an official mission.

If it was like this to exhume in Croatia, a UN "protected area" where there was a cease-fire, Haglund hated to think what it would be like to exhume in Bosnia. Within just a few years' time he had the opportunity to find out.

IF THE REALITIES of war were a shock to Haglund, then the realities of war crimes law were an equal surprise to Gabrielle Kirk McDonald, a fifty-one-year-old former federal district judge. When first asked about "international humanitarian law"—as the laws of war are formally known—McDonald recalled saying: "Could you repeat that again?"

Nothing—and yet everything—in Gabrielle Kirk McDonald's life would lead her toward what happened in 1993, when she was appointed as a judge to the newly created international criminal tribunal for the former Yugoslavia. The tall, elegant, lawyer, en route to becoming a professor at Texas Southern University's Thurgood Marshall School of Law in Houston, was no expert on the Balkans or international law. Like many Americans, she'd barely heard of Bosnia before the war began. What she knew about the former Yugoslavia came from information she had gleaned from the newspapers, and by 1993 untangling the conflicts there was not easy. There wasn't just one war, but two: Serbia's shaky cease-fire with Croatia and the war within Bosnia itself. There weren't just two sides, but seemingly five: the Serbs, the Bosnian Serbs, the Bosnian Muslims, the Croats, and the Bosnian Croats. There wasn't just one peace plan, but several, and a long parade of Balkan politicians whose names had far more consonants than vowels.

Nor was McDonald, with her nine years on the federal bench, a war crimes expert. She knew little about the Geneva Conventions and only just slightly more about the Nuremberg war crimes trials. (Pentagon lawyers paid attention to the laws of war, as did some academics and diplomats, but few others did.) But one thing McDonald did know about was injustice. As a civil rights lawyer, she'd spent her life using the law to combat it; as an African American, she'd lived it. Born to a biracial mother who looked white (McDonald's grandmother was Swedish) and a black American father, who began his working life as a waiter in a railroad dining car, McDonald was well aware of the prejudices that played out because of the color of one's skin. When her mother, an editor, and her stepfather, a jazz musician who had played with Count Basie, showed up in Riverdale, New York, the managers of the apartment they had rented took one look and wanted to evict them. In high school in Teaneck, New Jersey, McDonald was one of two African Americans in her class of 380. Before her law school graduation, McDonald made an appointment at the hair salon where her mother had just gotten a new hairdo only to be turned away when she arrived. "We don't do your kind of hair here," they said dismissively.

She also knew about using the law creatively to combat such prejudice. She began her career at the NAACP legal defense fund, working on employment discrimination cases under Title VII of the 1964 Civil Rights Act. She successfully sued Philip Morris for discrimination in its seniority system. She carried on this work in a joint practice with her then husband, Mark T. McDonald, winning Title VII claims against major American companies. That brought her to the attention of Texas senator Lloyd Bentsen, who nominated her for a position on the federal court. She would be only the third African American woman to sit on the bench. Her experience as a judge taught her that the law could triumph over discrimination: When the local Grand Dragon of the Ku Klux Klan in Houston tried to get her removed from his case because she was "a Negress," he failed.

So when Conrad Harper, an old friend from the NAACP and partner in Cyrus Vance's law firm who was the State Department's legal advisor, called her in 1993 to see if she'd be interested in a judgeship at the newly created war crimes tribunal, McDonald was intrigued. Here was a job that would combine all her legal experience, her years on the federal bench, her background in civil rights. She was fascinated by the thought of using laws untested and untried for the last fifty years. It was important for a court to make sense of why a small, multiethnic country had suddenly dissolved into ethnic hatreds. McDonald believed that the rule of law could bring about peace and reconciliation in Bosnia and create a society open to all. Most of all, she had dedicated her life to harnessing justice to the cause of civil rights. The tribunal would allow her to continue that work.

And so, on November 13, 1993, Gabrielle Kirk McDonald found herself in The Hague, the Netherlands, the Dutch capital that was home to the new tribunal. She was taking an oath to become a judge in a war crimes court so new it had no staff, no courtroom, no rules of evidence.

McDonald—a determined, hardworking lawyer with an irreverent sense of humor—laughed at herself that November day, as the winds roared across the North Sea to her beachfront hotel, plunging the city into what she would learn was its normal gray cast. Here she was, a divorced mother of two preparing to sit judgment on hardened Balkan war criminals; an activist who had retired from the federal court now teaching herself the precepts of international humanitarian law.

"My goodness," thought McDonald, "what *am* I doing here?"

MCDONALD–GABY TO her friends—would ask herself that question repeatedly in the months to come. Just like its predecessor, the UN Commission of Experts, the International Criminal Tribunal for the former Yugoslavia immediately suffered from a lack of support and funds. In what one UN insider later described as "obvious stalling," it took the United Nations months just to decide who should be the chief prosecutor. Political infighting among Britain, France, Bosnia, and the United States jeopardized every candidate. (Bosnia had become a member of the UN after it declared independence.) That fall, the UN finally settled on the court's prosecutor, Ramón Escobar Salom, the former attorney general of Venezuela.

Once the prosecutor had been chosen, the court existed in name only. It had no budget; the judges were being paid on an ad hoc basis. The court's president, Judge Antonio Cassese, had to search for office space, eventually renting a dingy wing of a building owned by a Dutch insurance company.

The judges' first task was to hammer out the tribunal's rules of procedures and evidence, which would govern the court's day-to-day workings. This would prove no easy job. First of all, the issues themselves were complex: determining what kinds of evidence would be admissable, what kinds of pleas would be allowed, what measures should be taken to protect witnesses, whether trials in absentia would be allowed. In addition, the judges had to merge two differing legal traditions—that of continental Europe, or civil law, and that of Britain and the United States, or common law. Civil law is more inquisitorial and allows judges more power to investigate and question; common law is more adversarial, granting a greater role to a defense attorney, who has a prosecutorial role.

The judges also wrestled with the language of the Geneva Conventions, trying to determine just what diplomats and legal experts half a century before them had intended. What was meant by "wilful killing" or "wilfully causing great suffering"? Or by an "armed conflict not of an international character"? Justice, in terms of the law, is made up of such definitions, such interpretations, such phraseology. McDonald and her colleagues labored late into the evening in what was the insurance company's Winston Churchill conference room—an irony given the late British leader's initial coolness toward a postwar war crimes tribunal. Finally, on February 11, 1994, the judges took the first concrete step toward preparing the tribunal for trials: They adopted 75 pages of rules, a total of 125 rules in all. McDonald and Cassese, who had sparred over the issue of trials in absentia, were photographed shaking hands on the compromise. The new court would have "Rule 61" hearings, in which evidence could be presented in court without a defendant present if that evidence supported an indictment.

The judges' mood should have been as buoyant as that snapshot of the grinning McDonald and Cassese, but it was not. Chief Prosecutor Salaom had announced his resignation in order to pursue his political career back home. The new tribunal had no prosecutor.

At the same time, UN Secretary-General Boutros Boutros-Ghali, the somewhat moody Egyptian who held that post for much of Bosnia's war, announced that the UN Commission of Experts had to finish its investigations within months. The move so imperiled ongoing war crimes investigations that Sadruddin Aga Khan, then the UN High Commissioner for Refugees, warned that international leaders appeared to be engaged in a "monumental whitewash" of atrocities for "reasons of political expediency." (Some investigations were never completed.) Judge McDonald, "smelling a rat," as she later put it, decided to confront Boutros Boutros-Ghali when he next visited The Hague. "Do you believe the General Assembly has sufficient will to support the tribunal?" she asked. He strongly reassured her the UN was committed to the tribunal.

In Bosnia, too, there was another dramatic resignation in January. The Belgian commander of the United Nations peacekeepers, Lieutenant General Francis Briquemont, had asked to be relieved of his command after six months, saying he was "very disappointed" with the UN mission in Bosnia. Only 2,000 of 7,600 peacekeepers had arrived by the end of 1993. In fact, UN peacekeeping operations around the world were stretched beyond their capacity: In July 1993 the UN had 78,000 civilians, police and troops abroad in fourteen different missions, and it was difficult recruiting new peacekeepers, much less good ones.

And it had become increasingly clear that the UN peacekeepers were in a country where peace was far from at hand. The rebel Serbs held 70 percent of Bosnia—almost all the territory they wanted, save for Sarajevo—and they fought largely just to preserve what they had. Peace plans came and went, from one that would divide Bosnia into ten provinces (Vance-Owen) to one that would divide it into three, with Serbs receiving 52 percent (Owen-Stoltenberg). There seemed no end to it all. Even President Clinton, speaking early in 1994, inaccurately attributed the war to ancient ethnic tensions. "Bosnia-Herzegovina, which always had these three different factions, basically degenerated back to the conflict which had been there for hundreds of years," the president said, adding: "the truth is, people there keep killing each other."

But the marketplace shelling was so outrageous an attack on civilians that it galvanized Western leaders into action. The United Nations, its peacekeepers lightly armed, was powerless to militarily threaten the Serbs. The heavily armed sixteen-member NATO Alliance could. NATO, prodded into action by the United States and France, decided to intervene in Bosnia for the first time. NATO's governing body, the North Atlantic Council, issued an ultimatum to the rebel Serbs to stop shelling Sarajevo or face air strikes. Under the threat of NATO airpower, both sides agreed to a cease-fire—provided the rebel Bosnian Serbs withdrew their heavy artillery from the hills around the city (a thirteen-mile heavy weapons exclusion zone) and put them under the control of the UN peacekeepers; the Bosnian government was also to put its weapons under UN control. UN troops would then act as a buffer between the two sides.

In Sarajevo, I watched to see if NATO would make good on its threats.

Even after a few short weeks in Bosnia I had learned that Western policy consisted of far more threats than action. The Serb artillery poised on the hills ringing the city did fall silent for the first time in more than 600 days. But as NATO's February 21 deadline dawned, few Serb weapons had been withdrawn. UN commanders on the ground, who had made no secret of their loathing for the Bosnian Muslim government, did not call on NATO to deliver air strikes. Instead, they allowed the rebel Serbs to extend deadlines and make up their own rules. In the end, the unfolding drama was a near farce that played out in front of the Western press corps. The Serbs finally did remove several hundred weapons from the thirteen-mile heavy-weapons-exclusion zone, but putting weapons "under UN control" translated into letting Serb guns stay in Serb-held territory on the perimeter of Sarajevo, where UN troops would have to guard them. In order to placate the Bosnian Serbs—even though they were besieging Sarajevo—some 800 Russian (and, as fellow orthodox Christians, pro-Serb) peacekeeping troops were sent as part of the deal.

And there were no NATO air strikes. NATO's first use of airpower came a week later, when six Serb jets violated the UN no-fly zone. The lessons Sarajevo presented to the Serbs were that the undermanned UN was going to let them bend the rules and that NATO was not going to punish them harshly even when they failed to comply. It was a bad omen for how things would evolve in Bosnia in the following months.

Before Bosnia's war erupted again, however, Western policy makers were distracted from their push for peace. Reports of atrocities and war crimes were streaming in from another part of the world, a tiny country in Africa almost no one knew anything about: Rwanda. So horrible were the war crimes there that those in Bosnia paled by comparison. It was a vast, bloody campaign of genocide that would leave no one in Rwanda untouched.

4

THE LAND OF 1,000 GRAVES

The past is the textbook of tyrants....

—Herman Melville

One day in April 1994 I turned on my shortwave radio to hear the news, certain that the violence in the former Yugoslavia would be the lead story. Through the static, I heard the familiar, clipped tones of the BBC announcer. He was not talking about Bosnia but an African country called Rwanda, and in sober tones he revealed the latest bulletin: massive killings of the Tutsi minority by Hutu extremists; corpses piled in heaps on the streets.

I was still in the Balkans. My first reaction to the news was shaped by my utter ignorance. Hutu, Tutsi, Rwanda, Africa—the ongoing killings sounded like tribal violence to me. The corpses floating in lakes, jamming the rivers, and scattered across the streets I automatically attributed to the unleashing of ancient hatreds. I made the same assumptions about Rwanda that I would criticize people for making about Bosnia and gave Rwanda little further thought.

It was only later, when I went to Rwanda, that I would learn that the country—and its genocide—was not at all what I, in my ignorance, had first thought.

Rwanda looked nothing like the landscapes that a childhood of leafing through *National Geographics* filled with pictures of Africa had led me to believe. It was not a tangled, steamy jungle or a dry, arid desert. Instead, it was a land of swirling mists and sudden rain showers; of clouds of pink, orange, and purple bougainvillea; of groves of avocado trees, fields of coffee, stands of fragrant eucalyptus; of cattle grazing by the roadside and rows upon rows of crops planted neatly in the raw red earth. It was a land of dazzling vistas; of mountain gorillas in forests atop conical volcanoes; of deep, crystal-clear lakes.

Tourist literature brags that Rwanda is the land of one thousand hills, and indeed the hills define everything. Ridges, hills, and mountains ripple across Rwanda, pleating its terrain as neatly as the folds of a man's tuxedo shirt. The mountains of the Rift Valley pierce the country to the west, the Virunga volcanoes parade along its north, and smaller hills and innumerable valleys punctuate its east and south. Farmers' fields must defy gravity by marching up hills; homes do not huddle together in a village but are spread out along a ridge. In fact, when people talk about where they come from in Rwanda, they do not say my village but "*ma colline*"—my hill.

Despite its rugged and fertile geography, Rwanda is overpopulated and poor. About the size of Maryland, it lies in Central Africa, bordered by Uganda to the north, Tanzania to the east, Burundi to the south, and the Democratic Republican Congo (formerly Zaire) to the west. Before the genocide, it was the world's most populous country per square mile after Bangladesh, with a population of 7 million.

Everywhere there are signs of habitation. Paths crisscross the hills and valleys, wander through the lower pastures grazed by long-horned cattle, past the houses that dot the coffee and tea fields, up and down the many hills. Nearly every available piece of visible land is planted in neat rows: crops of banana, beans, maize, sorghum, cassava, and sweet potato. (Despite this, Rwanda has not fed its own population since the mid-1980s.) No matter where you go, you are never alone. Rwanda, most of all, is its people.

Life is lived in the open and in a crowd. On bustling city streets, women in high heels and print dresses hurry to the outdoor market; men, sporting jackets and Western-style jeans, stop to dictate a letter to someone perched on the sidewalk with a typewriter. In the countryside, women wrapped in bright, multicolored skirts known as *pagnes* wash their laundry in streams, while men squat by the roadside, selling vegetables. Tall and short, stocky and slender, the country's three different groups, Tutsi, Hutu, and Twa, are on the streets everywhere, talking in a mixture of French and their native tongue, Kinyarwandan. And everywhere there are children, hard to miss as they play by the side of the road in their distinctive, bright blue school uniforms.

Of course, this is what I saw of Rwanda at first glance. But I came to know a different Rwanda through the people with whom I became friends. From them I learned of a country where thousands upon thousands of people picked up their machetes and slashed their friends, their neighbors, and sometimes their own family to death. I came to know a land where between half a million and 1 million people, mostly Tutsi, were slain within a mere 100 days. I came to see a country where even a church altar was no guarantee of sanctuary from machete-waving killers.

Many who survived told me their stories. But this is what happened to just two of them, Anonciata Kavaruganda and a woman whom I will call JJ. It is through them I came to understand how Rwanda, this country of 1,000 hills, became the land of many more than 1,000 graves.

ANONCIATA IS A short fireplug of a woman whose energy far outstrips her petite height. At fifty-three, she is a forceful matriarch whom, had she been an American, one could envision as a feisty, outspoken member of the PTA. The mother of five, she is an organizer, a woman who never stops talking, acting, doing.

Before the genocide in Rwanda, Anonciata was part of the country's small, well-to-do elite in Kigali, the country's capital, a moderate-size but cosmopolitan city of broad avenues shaded by eucalyptus and jacaranda trees. Her husband, Joseph Kavaruganda, serious and distinguished, was the Belgian-educated head of Rwanda's Constitutional Court and its Court of Appeals. Along with their children, they lived a life of modern luxury in a graceful one-story home surrounded by gardens filled with palms and bougainvillea, hibiscus and roses. They had a television, a refrigerator, a stereo, and traveled frequently overseas.

But in Rwanda before 1994, all you needed to know about Anonciata and her family was this: Their ethnic identity cards identified them as Hutu.

JJ is as tall and willowy as Anonciata is short and stout, as ethereal as Anonciata is energetic. She has the awkward grace of a newborn deer: her eyes soft and luminous, her movements alternately lithe and clumsy. While Anonciata had the life of privilege, JJ's was that of a rural subsistence farmer like most Rwandans. Hers was a life dictated by nature: by when the land is fertile and when it is fallow; by when the sun rises and when it sets; by the big rains, from February to June, and the small rains, from the middle of September to December. And her life was dictated by one other detail: Her identity card labeled her as a Tutsi.

And it is from these differing classifications—Hutu and Tutsi—that the tragedy of Rwanda springs.

Both women will tell you that they considered themselves Rwandans, first and foremost, and scoff at the idea of any real racial differences between them. Indeed, contrary to what I believed, Hutu and Tutsi, by most anthropologists' definitions, are not different ethnic groups at all: They speak the same language, share the same customs, have the same religion, have intermarried, with as many as 25 percent of all Rwandans believed to have mixed ancestry. "I cannot say there are no Tutsi in my family, nor can any Hutu household," Anonciata told me once. "No Tutsi can say they do not have Hutu in them." Rwanda did not have a history of centuries of ethnic violence, although there had been violent clashes and massacres in the twentieth century. "We knew who was classified as who," JJ explained. "But we had always lived together peacefully as Rwandans." Indeed, the first major outbreak of violence between the two was in 1959.

Rwanda's history did not produce the genocide. It took opportunistic leaders—with their hands on the levers of power and propaganda—to manipulate that history into a tale of grievances and racism and treachery. It took weaponry, streaming in from surrounding countries with the help of Western dollars. It took the international community, and its utter miscalculations, to spur on the killing once it was under way.

And it took demagogues calling forth the ghosts of race and superiority. To understand where those ghosts hail from—and how they would determine the fate of Anonciata and JJ—you must step back several hundred years, to the days of the arrival of Europeans in Africa.

FOR GENERATIONS THERE were two kinds of Rwandans: those who raised cattle and those who farmed the land. Over the centuries cattle came to be seen as a sign of wealth, and many who came to rule Rwanda were well-to-do cattleholders. By the late eighteenth century, those rich in cattle had come to be known as Tutsi. Just about everyone else was called Hutu, or followers. A small minority, who were forest dwellers, were known as the Twa. They were not different ethnic groups, but more like castes, differentiated by their professions or habits; it was even possible for someone who acquired cattle, for example, to move from the Hutu to the Tutsi.

So it was when the Europeans began to arrive in Africa in the nineteenth century. Idealistic adventurers, greedy businessmen, power-hungry politicians, and devout missionaries: All left their mark on Africa and on Rwanda. Racial divisions and distinctions fascinated Europe and its explorers, and as avidly as they mapped out the continent's geography they also classified Africa's people. Nile explorer John Hanning Speke was among them.

In 1863 the explorer put forward the theory that the taller, more European-looking Africans were really descendants of King David, possibly one of the lost tribes of Israel. Distinguishing them from the average African "negro," he believed them to be superior in intelligence and ability. Speke never visited Rwanda. But those Europeans who did were versed in his "Hamitic theory" and found what they thought was evidence to back it up: The Tutsi chiefs, who tended to be taller, finer featured, and more European looking than the Hutu, were in their opinion consequently superior to the Hutu. (They overlooked the fact that in Rwanda, there were Hutu chiefs as well as Tutsi chiefs.) It was a myth that firmly took hold as colonists arrived at the end of the century. Missionaries, spinning the myth further, suggested the Tutsi originated in the Garden of Eden.

European nations, discovering Africa's vast mineral and labor potential, vied for pieces of it, carving it up along largely arbitrary lines that did not respect local tribes or cultures. Rwanda fell to Germany, becoming a small part of German East Africa in 1885. By the time the Germans arrived, Rwanda had become a strictly hierarchical society, as feuding chieftains had come to be consolidated under the rule of a king, or Mwami. And it was a society in which the Tutsi had the upper hand: Mwami Kigeri Rwabugiri, a Tutsi, put his fellow Tutsi into positions of power as he pushed to expand his kingdom. The Germans followed suit, backing the Tutsi when a mostly Hutu rebellion broke out in the northwest in 1912.

The Great War touched Africa even as it devastated Europe. Belgian forces occupied Rwanda in World War I; in 1919 the League of Nations assigned Rwanda and Burundi to Belgium as a trusteeship territory.

(Rwanda and neighboring Burundi, which also has a mixture of Tutsi and Hutu, were then one country.) Even more so than the Germans, the Belgians ruled by overtly favoring the Tutsi over the Hutu, deposing Hutu chiefs and replacing them with Tutsi. And they governed with a firmer and less sympathetic hand, indicative perhaps of their own history of colonial exploitation in the neighboring Congo.

By the 1920s all Europe was abuzz with theories of racial science, and Belgium was no exception. In the eyes of the Belgian administrators in Rwanda, the Tutsi and Hutu were not just differentiated by occupation but also by race. Deciding to institutionalize them as two different races, the Belgians cast one as superior to the other. Declaring that only Tutsi could serve in official posts, they stripped Hutu from any positions they held and banned them from higher education.

Rwanda proved the perfect testing ground for Belgian ethnologists, as eager to classify differences between ethnic groups as explorers were to map the continent. They arrived, wielding measuring tapes and calipers, in an effort to categorize Rwandans as Tutsi or Hutu, typically measuring noses and foreheads. A Tutsi nose, Belgian scientists claimed, was 55.8 millimeters long and 38.7 millimeters wide; a Hutu's, 52.4 millimeters long and 43.2 millimeters wide. Belgian administrators, seizing on this, required all Rwandans to register and carry ethnic identity cards that identified them as Hutu, Tutsi, or Twa. Eighty-four percent would be registered as Hutu; 15 percent as Tutsi; and 1 percent, Twa.

With identification cards, the ethnic differences imposed on Rwandans became the means to determine who got what in a country of scarce resources. Those classified as Tutsi had the right to go to school and then into the country's civil service. The Belgians soon ruled Rwanda side by side with a small Tutsi aristocracy, enforcing the belief among Europeans that Rwanda was a country with a master race, the Tutsi, and a lesser race, the Hutu. The Tutsi aristocrats wore flowing long robes as befitted their rank; their Hutu servants carried their wives and daughters around on litters. Those classified as Hutu, the majority of the country's population, had far fewer options. They could become farmers. Or, in a country that had become staunchly Catholic, Hutu men eager for an education could become priests.

Ethnic identity cards, and the distinctions they provided, became a lasting part of Rwandan society. Rwandans carried ethnic cards up to and through the genocide. While many Tutsi and Hutu intermarried and struck up long-lasting friendships, many resented the ethnic distinctions imposed on them. Differences were not always based on ethnicity; less advantaged Tutsi, excluded from the small, aristocratic class, disliked Tutsi chiefs who demanded as much labor from them as from the Hutu. Still, they flaunted their alleged ethnic superiority over the Hutu.

After World War II, Rwanda had become a United Nations trust territory under Belgium, with an eye to its eventual independence. The 1950s brought sweeping changes to Rwanda. Nationalism, and the independence it would bring, was stirring across Africa. This was the era in which Anonciata and Joseph Kavaruganda came of age.

As a Hutu, Joseph Kavaruganda had accepted that his only choice for education lay in pursuing the priesthood. An intense, intelligent man, his looks stamped him as a Hutu: a broad nose, thick lips, a stocky build. Born and raised in Kigali, he would go to seminary, where he took to religion with great devotion. He embraced Christianity's strictures and its scriptures, its emphasis on honesty, its call for poverty and love. It suited his solitary, contemplative, and disciplined nature.

But as Belgian power waned in the 1950s, so did Tutsi hegemony. By 1957 a revolution of thought was under way: Hutu intellectuals published a manifesto underscoring their political, social, and economic oppression and suggesting that the Hutu, because of their greater numbers, should share power with the Tutsi. The Tutsi elite retaliated, but did so by supporting their own monarchy, annoying their Belgian allies. As Rwanda moved from colony toward independence, Belgium—under mounting criticism for letting an elite minority rule—replaced Tutsi local officials with Hutu. Political parties, emerging in anticipation of the country's independence, defined themselves along ethnic lines. And a new belief was created, as divisive, although not so unfounded, as that created by Speke: that the Hutu had been grievously mistreated by the Tutsi, that they were the country's "suppressed masses."

While dubbed the Hutu Revolution, the Hutu's rise to power was less a revolution and more a transfer of power from the Tutsi elite to the Hutu elite, with Belgium's blessing. But it did mark the first real violence between the Hutu and the Tutsi. In 1959, following the death of the Tutsi king in what his followers thought were suspicious circumstances, fighting broke out. Skirmishes between Hutu and Tutsi escalated into full-scale anti-Tutsi violence. Hundreds were slain, their houses burned, while the Belgians, now supporting the Hutu, looked on. Thousands of Tutsi fled the country in panic. As they sought to reclaim power, crossing from neighboring countries in nighttime border raids, they called themselves "inyenzi," or cockroaches.

Ten times over the next six years, Tutsi in exile in neighboring countries would attack Rwanda, seeking to reclaim power. The Hutu would drive them back and, in reprisal, vented their frustration on the Tutsi within Rwanda, claiming they had aided those outside. Some 20,000 Tutsi were killed and hundreds of thousands fled to the Congo, Burundi, Uganda, and elsewhere. Soon another belief became popular among the Hutu in Rwanda: that oppression of the Tutsi was allowed in the name of self-defense.

In 1960 the Belgians established a provisional Rwandan government headed by Gregoire Kayibanda, whose Hutu party had swept the country's local elections that year. When Belgium granted self-government to Rwanda in 1962, Kayibanda became its first ruler. Everything had changed—Rwanda appeared to be a democracy—but in some ways nothing had changed. Kayibanda was simply an autocratic king disguised as a democrat. Turning the tables, he discriminated against Tutsi as ferociously as Hutu had been discriminated against before, banning them from jobs. As a UN report then noted, Rwanda was in the grip of the "racial dictatorship of one party . . . an oppressive system has been replaced by another one."

Yet the change in power opened new avenues for Hutu like Joseph Kavaruganda. For the first time in his life, Joseph had the choice to become something other than a priest. While he would remain a devout Catholic all his life, he transferred his passion for a religious vocation to the law. In 1962, empowered by the reigning Hutu government, he went to Brussels to study, becoming not only one of the very few Rwandans to study law, but also one of the very few to study it in Europe. Anonciata, after marrying Joseph in Rwanda in 1966, went to Belgium with him. Their years in Brussels shaped their outlook and their hopes for Rwanda. Both were impressed by how, in the wake of World War II, Europe's once-warring countries lived side by side without violence. They were struck by Europe's respect for human rights and how its laws preserved them.

So impressed was Joseph with the country of Belgium, he would insist all five of his children bear Belgian names and study abroad. Adopting European ways, he claimed one family name—Kavaruganda—rather than giving each child a specific last name that reflected his or her character, as was Rwandan custom. And he dreamed of exporting Belgium's ideals back to Rwanda, transforming it into a country based on a rule of law for Tutsi and Hutu alike.

Under Kayibanda, however, Rwanda had become a totalitarian nation. He was secretive, authoritarian, and controlling, deciding democracy had little to do with choice and everything to do with demographics: As there were more Hutu, they would rule. In the 1970s, Kayibanda imposed quotas on the Tutsi, based on the size of their population; they could make up only 10 percent of places in schools, universities, or the civil service.

As Rwanda failed to prosper economically, however, so Kayibanda's popularity faltered. His authoritarian approach also seemed out of step in an Africa swept by discussion of socialism and revolution. The country's Hutu divided, with northerners coming to see themselves as superior and challenging Kayibanda's power. Desperate to consolidate his power, Kayibanda rallied his people around their ethnic enemy, the Tutsi, whom he blamed for Rwanda's problems. In the resulting violence, thousands more Tutsi were killed or fled abroad. Indeed, between 1959 and 1973, some 300,000 Rwandans, mostly Tutsi, left their country.

Like many Tutsi farming the land up and down the spines of Rwanda's hills and ridges, JJ's family watched as friends fled, often to Uganda. But the call of the land was greater than their fear. Politicians, and their politics, they reasoned, came and went. But family, land, love: That was forever.

JJ and her family came from Taba. It was a small group of houses strung out on a ridge surrounded by banana and sorghum fields to the west of Kigali. By Taba standards, JJ's parents were reasonably well-to-do; they had eight children, making them rich in available labor. They had two one-story mud-brick homes—more than eight rooms combined—and a large outdoor kitchen and a barn. They owned goats, cows, lambs, and chickens.

The six girls and the two boys kept the farm going, with plenty of chores that occupied them from dawn until dusk. But Sundays were always the day of rest. Then the entire family would walk the hour-and-a-half round trip down Taba's red-dust roads to church together, laughing and swapping stories. JJ was her father's favorite. Her soft, vulnerable eyes, her winsome, slow-spreading smile, and her optimistic nature singled her out from all the other children.

Even JJ's privileged role in the family could not help her escape the domestic burdens that fell on the shoulders of Rwandan peasant women. In the villages scattered along Rwanda's hills, it was the women who worked in the fields to raise the food that the family ate. In addition, they walked miles to fetch water for the family, collected brush and banana leaves to burn, and then cooked meals over a woodfire. Submissive and hardworking: These are the qualities JJ was raised to believe a woman should possess, along with fertility. A woman's value was judged by her ability to bear children, which were the principal source of a family's wealth. Men handled the finances and inherited the property. Women had no such rights, not even the right to complain. As the Rwandan proverb went: "In a home where the woman speaks, there is discord."

Still, that was her life and, as JJ would recall, she was happy—except at school. There teachers stood at the front of the classroom and asked who was Tutsi and who was Hutu. As soon as JJ raised her hand to proclaim herself a Tutsi, she was forever teased and bullied by Hutu children. They would corral her in the schoolyard and repeat what their parents had told them about how "evil" the Tutsi were. When the teacher was frustrated with the students, as they stumbled over their sums or their grammar, he would simply blame the Tutsi in the class. "Oh, you Tutsi, wake up!" the teacher claimed with exasperation.

History classes were also awkward. There the teacher would talk about Rwanda's history: the history of the Tutsi "oppressors" and their injustices to the Hutu. JJ used to stare down at her feet, wishing she could vanish. But then whispers about the Tutsi were something she had grown up with. "Those Tutsi," she would hear people say, "you know how arrogant they are." "*E-é*," JJ would say to herself, using the Rwandan singsong expression, which, like "okay," punctuates just about every Rwandan sentence, just ignore them.

School quotas for the Tutsi were mandated when she was fourteen. So-called Committees of Public Salvation were organized to ensure all schools and universities and the country's civil service followed the government directive. JJ, to her regret, was forced to stop her education. She returned to working on the family farm, and her life took on a different cadence: family prayers in the early morning, the day spent in the fields, the evening at home with her family. Her days were predictable, although her growth spurts were not: Overnight, it seemed, she went from being a small girl to a willowy, attractive woman. She had what was considered a distinctively Tutsi face: a high forehead, prominent cheekbones, a long, slim nose.

Men began to notice her. She noticed them too. Her favorite was a handsome, beguiling man who ran a beer and banana wine stand in Taba's outdoor market, perched alongside the red-dirt road that was the backbone of the village. She passed the market every morning en route to church. He told her she was beautiful. She beamed at him. He wooed her in turn.

So in 1973, when Rwanda's senior army commander, General Juvenal Habyarimana, seized power from Kayibanda in a bloodless coup, JJ barely noticed. She had a good excuse: She was madly in love.

RWANDANS, WHETHER TUTSI or Hutu, tend to remember the first years of Habyarimana's rule with some nostalgia. He opened Rwanda to the West. For a decade and a half, the country was tranquil and more prosperous. Foreign aid dollars flowed in—reaching 22 percent of gross national product by 1991—and the country's economy improved, particularly for the rich.

Of course, Habyarimana proved as autocratic as his predecessor. He had seized power promising to restore national unity, and backed by the troops of the Rwandan Armed Forces (FAR) and his own elite forces, the Presidential Guard, he set about consolidating control. He demanded Rwanda be a one-party state, controlled by his party, which he established in 1975. Exploiting the country's hierarchical administration for his own and his party's ends, he created a country in which everyone had his or her exact place, in which people couldn't even move to cities or villages without permission.

It was as if a biologist had come along and identified each person's genus, species, and subspecies. At the top were prefectures, something like American states; then communes, something like counties; then sectors, smaller still; and finally cells, each consisting of about 1,000 people. Communes were run by burgomasters, something like mayors, all of whom were political appointees. Even today, if you ask any Rwandan where they come from, they rattle off which prefecture, commune, and sector as reflexively as an American giving his social security number.

Under Habyarimana, Rwanda became one of the strictest, most tightly controlled noncommunist countries in the world. But its lack of violence, at a time when chaos wracked the rest of Africa, also garnered it the nickname the "Switzerland of Africa." It was an African state with no problems: no crime, prostitution, or unrest. It was orderly, clean, and Catholic, and its population was reasonably satisfied. While still barred from government posts, the country's Tutsi had more opportunities; they were allowed to take part in business, and many became successful entrepreneurs.

Anonciata and Joseph Kavaruganda also looked to their future with optimism. Joseph, who had held several low-ranking jobs in the Kayibanda administration, rocketed to prominence under Habyarimana. The two were acquaintances from seminary, although Habyarimana, unlike Joseph, had not finished his studies. Nonetheless, in recognition of Joseph's background in the law, Habyarimana made him Rwanda's attorney general, one of country's most powerful positions.

Yet the two men soon clashed. Joseph was the stickler for the fine points of the law. He believed in the law's power, its infallibility. Habyarimana, in the way of most autocrats, preferred either to ignore the law or to dictate it. Annoyed, in time he moved Joseph to a less powerful although equally prestigious job: president of the Constitutional Court and Court of Appeals. Joseph's ability to check Habyarimana's dictates had been slightly diffused. Meanwhile, the Kavarugandas were able to stay in their house in the same quarter of Kigali with other government ministers, and they prospered in other ways. Between 1967 and 1981, Anonciata and Joseph had three boys and two girls.

For Rwanda, however, the good times were coming to an end. In 1986 the Rwandan economy stumbled. The price of coffee, one of the country's primary exports, dropped sharply. A drought produced food shortages. Prosperous families like the Kavarugandas weathered the hardships, but in the village of Taba, JJ and her family suffered. Their greatest resource—their land—was scorched to nothingness. Withered stalks hung limply in their fields. They prayed for rain. By 1988 Rwanda depended on foreign aid to feed itself, and the conditions of foreign loans became increasingly strict, pushing up prices. The country's gross domestic product per capita fell by 40 percent in just four years. By the early 1990s, 50 percent of Rwandans were hungry and unable to feed themselves. As the population increased, land became more and more scarce, a situation that particularly affected the rural areas.

From hill to hill across the country, there was discontent with Habyarimana. Lacking popular support, the Rwandan president became increasingly isolated, relying only on a small circle of insiders, his "akazu," for advice. Many of those he turned to were either his relatives or a small group of advisors from his own region in the north, a greedy clique whose wealth stemmed from their nearness to power. Meanwhile, those Rwandans excluded from influence and power called for sweeping changes: Rwanda, they said, should become a multiparty democracy. It was a call echoed by foreign aid donors supporting the country. Habyarimana, reluctantly, accepted.

Yet just as these political changes were about to occur, in October 1990 Rwanda came under military attack from Tutsi in exile in neighboring Uganda. Since fleeing in 1959, Rwandan Tutsi living in Burundi, Uganda, and Tanzania had not been warmly welcomed by their host countries, often not allowed to become citizens or even to own land. Many still lived lives of squalor, camped out in refugee camps. They dreamed of returning home, but Habyarimana refused to contemplate this possibility. Finally, under pressure from Uganda, anxious to rid itself of thousands of Rwandans, Habyarimana agreed to establish a joint commission to study the situation. Few believed he was serious; among the most skeptical was the Rwandan Patriotic Front (RPF), a party of Rwandans that had emerged in Uganda.

The RPF, made up largely of exiled Tutsi, hoped to appeal to their fellow Rwandans, Hutu and Tutsi alike, across the border, with their call for democracy and an end to Habyarimana's corrupt regime. But aided and encouraged by Uganda, they decided to bring their aims home in the form of a military attack. In October, thousands of Tutsi soldiers in the Rwanda Patriotic Army (RPA) crossed the border into Rwanda. The country was at war.

But soon the conflict was transformed from a matter of returns, land

and politics to one of ethnicity, to a Hutu-Tutsi struggle. (The Twa, small in number, did not figure prominently in the dispute.) As far as Rwanda's government and certain political groups were concerned, the enemy was not just the Tutsi-led RPF, it was all Tutsi. The Tutsi—every Tutsi—were RPF accomplices; they were snakes and cockroaches; they were sneaky, manipulative, and seductive. The Tutsi had to be eliminated.

And so Rwanda, its leaders turning to ancient myths about the Tutsi to consolidate their power, spiraled downward—into ethnic hatred, chaos, and bloodshed.

IN TABA, THE open-air marketplace along the main dirt road buzzed with news of the RPF attack in 1990. It was all anyone talked about, even as they haggled over vegetables, inspected chickens, bought glasses of banana beer. Rumors of all kinds were heard along the red-clay paths that wound past houses and through the banana groves: The Tutsi wanted to rule Rwanda again. They wanted to oppress the Hutu. That Tutsi man, he's with the RPF. That Tutsi woman, she's a sympathizer.

JJ, shopping in the marketplace, was jostled by Hutu she had known all her life and accused of taking part in the war. "Your relatives are attacking!" they said, glaring at her as if she herself carried a gun, stuck in the waist of her gaily patterned *pagne*. "How do I know you aren't friends with those cockroaches?" JJ protested that she knew no one in the RPF, but few villagers paid any heed. Instead they sat tuned to their portable radios, listening to government-controlled Radio Rwanda, talking hour after hour about "Tutsi" attacks. It was from the radio that JJ first heard that the Tutsi-led RPF had attacked Kigali—a mere five days after its troops had crossed the border. As villagers moaned and cried with the news, it seemed like a fateful moment, a dramatic shift in Rwanda's history.

Unbeknownst to her and thousands of other Rwandans, the RPF actually had not attacked Kigali. In fact, their troops were forty-five miles away from it. Habyarimana had staged the attack, using his own troops in a desperate propaganda ploy to gain sympathy. It worked, galvanizing international attention to Rwanda's plight. France and Belgium, Rwanda's long-standing allies, swiftly dispatched troops to safeguard their own citizens and aid the Rwandan Army. They drove the RPF back to the Ugandan border. (The French, in fact, continued to support and defend Habyarimana's regime, their generals advising him up to the time of the genocide.)

Fighting continued for nearly three years, as the RPF advanced only to be beaten back again. Ironically, the military struggle came even as Habyarimana allowed Rwanda to continue on the road toward democracy. New parties sprang up like jungle underbrush. Newspapers were formed as Habyarimana relaxed controls on the state media. The new media, however, was shrill, unfettered by the most rudimentary professional standards. Swiftly they became a tool for propagandists with their message of ethnic differences.

Right-wing parties emerged, calling for "Hutu Power," gaining thousands of converts among the young, impoverished Hutu who found themselves homeless with each new RPF incursion. Their propagandists, gathering thousands of surly, disaffected youths at alcohol-filled rallies, preached of the need to rid Rwanda of the Tutsi. Under pressure from the right, the Habyarimana government launched a series of anti-Tutsi crackdowns. Some 13,000 Tutsi and moderate Hutu were arrested after the "attack" on Kigali; each major clash with the RPF resulted in the retaliatory killing of local Tutsi by Hutu extremists. Rwanda's justice system had always answered to the whims of politics, and in the 1959 massacres of the Tutsi, few had been punished. There was impunity for killers, and so they killed: From October 1990 to February 1994, thousands of Tutsi were killed in as many as eight different well-orchestrated attacks.

For whatever reason, the massacres passed Taba by. But JJ noticed how the anti-Tutsi messages intensified. Now the mother of three, and living on her own after her marriage to the banana-beer seller had ended, JJ increasingly realized how radio and newspapers were singling out Tutsi women for suspicion. Myths had always surrounded them, like the mists that wrap themselves around the country's hills. They were said to be more beautiful, more charming, more seductive, and, indeed, many Hutu leaders took them as wives. But no sooner had the RPF crossed the border than Tutsi women, once idolized, were demonized. They were accused of using their beauty to help the invader.

Only three months after the RPF invasion, a new newspaper called *Kangura* published the "Ten Commandments of the Hutu," insisting on the need for Hutu purity. To JJ's horror, they accused Tutsi women of treachery, arguing they aroused Hutu men in order to undermine them. "Wherever she is [she] works for the interest of her Tutsi group," one of the commandments read. "We consider as a traitor any Hutu who marries a Tutsi woman."

Increasingly, it was longer safe to be a Tutsi, JJ realized, much less a Tutsi woman.

IT WAS ALSO proving unsafe to be a Hutu moderate. Joseph Kavaruganda was finding himself an unpopular man, as his beliefs and actions put him on a collision course both with President Habyarimana and with the emerging right-wing Hutu power movement in Rwanda.

He would quarrel repeatedly with Habyarimana over issues of the law. In 1991, when the Rwandan leader denied the new opposition parties the same privileges afforded his own, including air time on government-controlled Radio Rwanda, Kavaruganda ruled that the president's efforts were unconstitutional. It was simply the opening salvo in a long battle between the two men over transforming Rwanda into a democracy.

His fellow Hutu also began to see Kavaruganda as suspect. Both government and extremist parties dedicated to Hutu power had gained converts among the Hutu elite, its businessmen, and its political leaders. But Kavaruganda was not among them. Ever the lawyer, he believed the Tutsi exiles had the legal right to come back to Rwanda. Ever the conciliator, he believed the government should be negotiating with the RPF.

Hutu acquaintances began to shun the family. Unpopularity, however, didn't trouble Joseph Kavaruganda. Although the family always had Tutsi as well as Hutu friends, Joseph never let friendships interfere or influence his work. The family tended to keep to themselves. They preferred simple pleasures, anyway; listening to classical music; swimming on Sundays in the glistening pool behind the multistory Hotel Mille Collines; spending the weekend in their country home, about an hour from Kigali. Even there, Joseph's idea of pleasure were about as complicated as walking his beloved dog, Filou, or planting yet another tree in his ever-growing groves of eucalyptus.

Then came the death threats. The first was an attack on their country home, located just down the street from Habyarimana's. Someone blew up Joseph and Anonciata's bedroom late one Saturday night, a night they would typically have been in the house. But that weekend the children had begged to go back to Kigali, and so the family had left early and narrowly escaped. After the bomb attack came the threatening letters, one after another, making it clear that Kavaruganda's moderate views had made him a target of extremists.

"You have lots of enemies," read one 1991 letter he received. "Everyone wants you to be dead."

RWANDA ARMED ITSELF in 1992, even as there was talk of a peace agreement with the RPF. The government spent nearly 70 percent of its budget on the military. Under the tutelage of the French, the Rwandan Army grew nearly five times in size. Recruits—most of them extremist Hutu—had access to an array of weapons, from grenades to Kalashnikov rifles. At the same time, Rwanda's political parties formed their own youth militias and then armed them, passing out machetes, small arms, hand grenades. Among the most violent militias were Habyarimana's right-wing Mouvement Révolutionaire pour le Développement party (MRND), known as the Interahamwe, and the followers of another extremist party, the Coalition pour la Défense de la République (CDR). The two groups openly clashed with each other on Rwanda's streets, disrupting political rallies.

Habyarimana flirted with the idea of peace. He signed a cease-fire with the RPF and agreed to share power with the political opposition. In the first of what would be known as the Arusha accords, Habyarimana consented to a transitional government and assembly in which the Tutsi RPF could take part.

The Hutu right wing protested; the Rwandan Army mutinied. In an about-face, Habyarimana quickly denounced the accords as no more than a "scrap of paper" and refused to abide by them. Tutsi in Rwanda were then hunted down and killed in an outpouring of rage at Habyarimana's action. It was a pattern that would repeat itself endlessly over the next few years: Habyarimana would agreed to a more democratic Rwanda, only to waffle, deny, or retreat. He made agreements and then swiftly broke them.

Kavaruganda, as head of the Supreme Court and the country's Court of Appeals, became tired of his president's obstructionism. It was clear that Rwanda's leader had no respect for the law. By 1993 Joseph was annoyed enough to send an angry letter to Habyarimana, detailing all the various times he had violated the country's laws and broken the agreements he had signed.

"When you violate the law, do you do it in the interest of the Rwandan people?" Kavaruganda asked in the typewritten missive. "In the spirit of the Constitution? No."

As Habyarimana waffled, anti-Tutsi propaganda grew in virulence. A new, popular radio station, Radio Mille Collines, spewed forth increasingly racist ideology, and the pictorial newspaper *Kangura* heightened its attacks. "A cockroach cannot give birth to a butterfly," the newspaper wrote in 1993. "The history of Rwanda shows us clearly that a Tutsi stays always exactly the same, that he has never changed. The malice, the evil, are just as we knew them in the history of our country."

Rwanda appeared to be teetering on the edge of catastrophe, and Rwandan and European human rights groups sounded the alarm. European diplomats dashed off worrying cables (with the exception of the French, who provided $15 million in military aid to the Rwandan government). Waly Bacre Ndiaye, the UN Special Rapporteur of the Commission on Human Rights, was dispatched to Rwanda to investigate after human rights groups there clamored for his presence.

He spent only ten days in Rwanda. But it was long enough for him to discover that some 2,000 Tutsi civilians had been victims of summary executions since 1990. It was behavior that appeared to be genocidal, he concluded in a report to the UN, as Tutsi were being killed "solely because of their membership of a certain ethnic group." He called on the UN to act immediately, recommending that international human rights observers and civilian police be placed in high-risk areas to sound the alarm if killings recommenced.

Inside the UN headquarters on New York City's East River, in one of the many miscalculations made by UN diplomats, Ndiaye's recommendations were overlooked—or ignored.

INSTEAD, THE UNITED Nations focused on getting Habyarimana—his country bankrupt from fighting, foreign aid donors threatening to withdraw—to agree to the Arusha accords and let the Tutsi return. The accords provided for a transitional government—composed of representatives of the RPF as well as moderate and extremist Hutu parties—to be followed by democratic elections. The Tutsi-led army, the RPA, would be integrated into the Rwandan Army. When Habyarimana signed the accords in August 1993, the UN Security Council agreed to dispatch a neutral peacekeeping force to Rwanda to help implement them.

Joseph Kavaruganda was relieved at the news that his country was finally taking a step forward. As president of the Supreme Court, he had been intimately involved with putting together the Arusha accords, so much so that he had again become the target of virulent attacks. Opening *Kangura* one day, he found a caricature of himself in his judicial robes, hanging by a rope from a tree. At his feet were copies of the Arusha accords. "You work with the Tutsis," it read. "If the Hutu and Tutsis take [i.e., share] power, we will hang you. That's what you deserve."

Having UN peacekeepers in Rwanda, Joseph believed, would change everything. Peace, democracy, and, most important, the rule of law would finally prevail. And just in time: In October 1993 Tutsi rebels in neighboring Burundi killed their Hutu president in an unsuccessful coup attempt, a move that sent thousands of Hutu refugees into Rwanda and rattled even the country's Hutu moderates.

After the Arusha accords had been signed, however, UN diplomats no longer saw Rwanda as a priority. There was little enthusiasm among member states for a peacekeeping mission there. Costs were rising sharply, the UN was spread thin with its many peacekeeping missions overseas, and the United States was balking at paying 30 percent of peacekeeping costs. Most of all, however, the United Nations—and particularly the United States—were reeling from their disastrous foray into Somalia that October.

Intended as a test case for international peacekeeping, the Somalia mission ended in disgrace. When Somalia dissolved into anarchy in 1991, the UN sent a small security force to ensure that aid reached those who needed it. Outgunned and outmanned, the UN troops appealed to the United States for help in disarming the country's increasingly violent gangs, and in December 1992, American troops stormed Somalia's beaches in a raid photographed by waiting television crews. But Somalia's violence proved not so easy to quell. On October 3, 1993, eighteen American soldiers under U.S. command were killed in an attempt to capture Somali warlord Mohammed Aidid. The UN was blamed even though it had not been consulted on the military operation. In the United States, the backlash was immediate. No longer was the UN peacekeeping seen as the wave of the future. Instead, on Capitol Hill and inside the White House, the agreement was that peacekeeping missions were costly, poorly planned expeditions in which no U.S. soldier should serve. Unfortunately, the shadow of Somalia would hover for years over peacekeeping efforts, dooming not only the UN mission in Rwanda but that in Bosnia as well.

"Somalia was perceived as the worst debacle since Vietnam; it poisoned the well for the whole idea of U.S. intervention in humanitarian situations," recalled one senior Pentagon official. "I can't tell you how that changed everything."

As a result, caution and a clear lack of support dominated plans for the UN mission to Rwanda. An early reconnaissance operation suggested 5,000 troops; the United States pushed for 500. Just days after the Somalia debacle, the UN Security Council approved a small mission. In the end, 2,548 military personel and 60 civilian police were approved to go as part of the UN Assistance Mission to Rwanda (UNAMIR), consisting of partial battalions from Belgium and Bangladesh and one from Ghana. Theirs was an even more restricted mission than that undertaken by UN peacekeepers in Bosnia. The troops would be based only in Kigali, and they would clear mines, assist with delivery of humanitarian aid, and monitor the repatriation of Tutsi refugees moving back from neighboring countries and contribute overall to the cease-fire. The mission was slow to get off the ground: By the end of December, there were only 1,300 peacekeepers in Rwanda, 400 of them Belgian soldiers. Arriving, they found they lacked trucks, armored personnel carriers, spare parts, ammunition, and fuel.

What the UN troops did have was a dedicated, highly disciplined commander, Canadian Brigadier General Romeo Dallaire. Born in Holland but raised in Canada, the forty-seven-year-old Dallaire, distinctive with his penetrating, deep-set eyes and jaunty mustache, was considered to be a hardworking, dedicated officer. He knew the military well: His father had been in the Canadian army, and Dallaire had held command, staff, and training appointments in Canada and Germany. Dallaire was appalled at the state of his mission. His troops carried Motorola radios, unsuitable for transmitting privileged communications. The Bangladeshi contingent had less than a third of the equipment they needed. Only five out of eight armored personnel carriers worked. He lacked an intelligence staff. "It is a wonder that we were able to conduct any operational activities on the ground even six months after the mandate approval," Dallaire said later, explaining his shock at how poorly the UN had equipped the mission. "In my opinion, no state would have permitted its troops and its operations to be put into such a predicament."

The intelligence pouring into Dallaire's office—as well as into the hands of American and European diplomats—made it clear that the mission had to be strengthened to be effective.

Alarmed, the Canadian general repeatedly appealed to the UN for more troops and supplies, and the chance to intervene aggressively if violence did break out. Indeed, as Rwanda sank further into ethnic violence—and as the Arusha accords became an agreement on paper only—he asked the UN to better define his mandate, specifically asking for permission to let his troops use force in response to "ethnically or politically motivated criminal acts." UN headquarters in New York never formally responded.

Cables flew back and forth with the UN in New York, as the Canadian general tried to sound the alarm about Rwanda's swift descent into violence. He informed his UN superiors on January 6, 1994, that recent killings were carried out by those "well-organized, well-informed, well-motivated, and prepared to conduct premeditated murder." Five days later Dallaire cabled the senior military advisor to the UN Secretary-General, General Maurice Baril, that the Interahamwe militia of Habyarimana's MDR party were being trained to "kill up to 1,000 Tutsis in 20 minutes." An informant had volunteered to lead the UN to a weapons cache in exchange for protection. Dallaire asked for permission to seize the cache.

The UN's Department of Peacekeeping Operations, then headed by Undersecretary General Kofi Annan, insisted that Dallaire take no action beyond the UN mandate and urged him to share the news with President Habyarimana. Habyarimana promised that immediate action would be taken, but a few weeks later weapons were distributed to some 4,000 extremist "Hutu Power" supporters gathered for a rally in the Kigali stadium.

By mid-January, Rwanda had become the scene of violent political assassinations, nightly grenade attacks, and eruptions of ethnic violence. The Interahamawe met openly, drawing up lists of Tutsi to be killed.

Time and time again Dallaire appealed for more troops and a stronger mandate, begging that UN troops be given permission to seize the weapons increasingly were being distributed around Rwanda. Hutu extremists, realizing UN peacekeepers would not stop them, gathered more arms and recruits.

On February 17 the UN Security Council expressed "deep concern" about the deteriorating security situation and urged all sides to press ahead with implementing the Arusha accords. That same day Dallaire learned of a serious assassination plot: a group calling itself the "Death Escadron" had plans to kill Landoal Ndasingwa—a leading Tutsi opposition-party member who was minister for labor and social affairs in the transitional government—and Joseph Kavaruganda.

The UN sent guards to both men's houses: The Kavaruganda family was told the UN peacekeepers were there because of overall security concerns. Whether Joseph Kavaruganda was told of the threat against him, however, remains unclear.

ASSASSINATING JOSEPH KAVARUGANDA was entirely logical. Not only was he responsible for implementing the Arusha accords, but also, if anything happened to any of Rwanda's political leaders—which, given the daily assassinations, seemed likely—he was in charge of swearing in a new government.

In light of the daily mayhem, the rumors, the threats, Kavaruganda found the presence of the UN guards reassuring. Indeed, all Kigali looked to the UN peacekeepers, sporting their blue helmets, with a sense of relief. Unaware of how low Rwanda ranked on the UN Security Council's priority list, they interpreted the men's presence to mean that the international community had a stake in Rwanda. Rwandans also saw the troops as military protection. While the troops were peacekeepers, they were nonetheless armed, capable of intervening if things took a turn for the worse. Indeed, Joseph, Anonciata, and the two children still at home—Julithe and Julien—slept all the more soundly with UN troops outside their door.

Little did they know of the increasing mood of desperation in Dallaire's headquarters. On February 23 the general wrote to his UN superiors with renewed alarm. "Time does seem to be running out for political discussions," he noted, "as any spark on the security side could have catastrophic consequences."

ON APRIL 6, 1994, the plane carrying Habyarimana back from a meeting in Tanzania was shot down outside of Kigali, killing all aboard. It sparked the beginning of the genocide.

The Kavaruganda family was at home, laughing while watching a *Columbo* videotape on their VCR. Recent events had left Joseph reassured that the situation would soon improve. Foreign donors had threatened to withdraw their aid money and the UN Secretary-General had threatened to "reexamine" the UN's presence in Rwanda unless the Arusha accords were implemented. Even Rwanda's neighbors were fed up with the Habyarimana's stalling; on that day in April, he had received a tongue-lashing from neighboring heads of state at the Tanzania meeting. As Kavaruganda earlier in the week had reassured his son Guillaume, "I think the bad times are behind us."

So the Kavaruganda family planned a relaxed evening: dinner and a movie. It was a pleasant night. Tree frogs chirped. The scent of flowers from the gardens in front and back of the house drifted in through the windows. Joseph, Anonciata, Julien, and Julithe gathered for dinner around 6:00 P.M.

When they had finished watching Peter Falk as the trench-coated inspector Columbo, the foursome switched to the soccer match in which Ghana was playing. Anonciata threw open the shutters so the Ghanian UN guards outside could see the game. The soldiers looked on with delight, yelping with joy each time their team won a goal. When Ghana won the match, Anonciata cooked the guards a celebratory snack of tilapia, a Rwandan white fish. After all, as far as she was concerned, the UN guards were practically family.

It was late—nearly 11:30—when the phone rang. It was their eldest son Jean-Marcel, calling from Brussels. He was in a panic. Belgian television was reporting that Habyarimana's plane had been shot down. Hadn't they heard?

Anonciata turned on the radio, but there was no news, only funereal music. Joseph strode out the door to warn the UN soldiers. "We've heard the president may have been assassinated," he said. "Be on guard."

Little did he know then how useless his warning would be.

Like the detonation of an atomic bomb, Habyarimana's death would unleash a maelstrom of horrors that would hold Rwanda in its grip for nearly three months. For the Kavaruganda family, however, the horrors arrived at their doorstep in just a few hours.

5

OUR ENEMY IS ONE

No reasonable definition of reality could be expected to permit this.

—Albert Einstein (from the article "Can Quantum Mechanical Descriptions of Physical Reality Be Considered Complete?")

The telephone rang incessantly that night in the Kavaruganda home, punctuating the tense silence that descended over the family as completely as one of the Rwanda's sudden, thick mists. There was still no official news on the radio. But clearly something terrible had happened. It was long past bedtime, yet the ministerial neighborhood where the Kavarugandas lived was ablaze with light, every home in a state of activity. Car doors slammed. Trucks ground their gears. There was the murmur of people talking out on the street.

Shortly after midnight one of the family's next-door neighbors, Frederic Nzahorambaho, the minister of agriculture and a moderate Hutu like Joseph Kavaruganda, telephoned. Everyone in the neighborhood who belonged to the president's party was being evacuated, he reported. Joseph, hanging up the phone, pondered this latest detail.

Then Jean-Marcel, anxious, called again from Brussels. Joseph tried to allay his fears. The country was still waiting for the official announcement of the president's death, he said. After that, a replacement would surely be proposed. Kavaruganda, as president of Rwanda's Constitutional Court, would then swear in the new president; everything would be fine.

When the phone next rang, it was Nzahorambaho once more. The neighborhood had been surrounded and sealed off by armed members of Habyarimana's personal troops, the Presidential Guard. But the only people left in the neighborhood were opposition party members, such as he and Kavaruganda! Joseph tried to reassure him, even as his own sense of discomfort grew. *Why seal off the neighborhood?*

Dawn brought with it the first ripple of gunfire, just as the birds began twittering in the lush gardens surrounding the Kavaruganda home. The noise startled Julien and Julithe from their sleep; Anonciata and Joseph had not been able to rest. Joseph ordered his two children to take cover in one of the home's small bathrooms while he and Anonciata went into another.

Amid the distant *rat-a-tat-tat*, a knock startled them, soft and tentative at first, then louder and more insistent, at the window of Anonciata and Joseph's bedroom. It was one of their Ghanian UN guards. "There are military men here. They've come to take you away for safekeeping," he said.

Anonciata and Joseph looked at each other with amazement. The UN was supposed to be protecting the family, not turning them over to the first soldiers who came along. And just whose military was this? Joseph went to the front door.

On the threshold stood a man in a Rwandan military uniform. The soldier gave Joseph a snappy salute. "Captain Kabera, of the Presidential Guard. My orders are to take you to join the other opposition leaders."

Joseph peered past him, into the garden. It was filled with at least forty Rwandan soldiers, all armed. On the terrace stood the UN Ghanian guards, their guns in a pile on a table.

Joseph stalled for time. "Give me time to get dressed," he said curtly. He was the severe figure of authority, the president of the Constitutional Court, even in his pajamas. He closed the door and locked it, leaving the key dangling in the door. Immediately he called the Belgian contingent of the UN troops in Rwanda. Backups were needed at his house, he pleaded. The family was under attack. He then called the Ghanian and Bangladeshi UN outposts, his fingers stumbling over the telephone buttons. "Please send reinforcements!" He was assured that additional UN peacekeepers would be on their way.

Joseph hung up. There was nothing to do but wait.

The Rwandan soldiers, patrolling the gardens, showed no sign of leaving. The UN guards stood by. Inside the house, Joseph paced. There was no sign of any UN reinforcements.

Again the telephone rang. But it was Jean-Marcel, not the local UN.

Belgian radio was broadcasting reports of violence breaking out across Kigali, and opposition party members being killed. "You have to leave the house immediately; you're going to get killed," said Jean-Marcel.

"It's too late," Joseph replied. "They're already here. The neighborhood is closed off, and all the government ministers are evacuated."

"And the UN—are they protecting you?"

As the two spoke, the troops of the Presidential Guard began to break into the house. Using their rifle butts, they smashed windows and pounded on the front door.

"What's that noise!" Jean-Marcel could hear the commotion, even in Brussels, on the other end of the crackling telephone line.

"It's the Presidential Guard. They're trying to break down the door. . . . For us, it's the end," Joseph told his son. "For you, outside, have courage. . . . They're arriving—good-bye!" Joseph and Anonciata hurried back into the bathroom and locked the door.

It was five minutes past seven in the morning of April 7, 1994. In Brussels, Jean-Marcel stared at the phone receiver. Instead of his father's voice, there was only a dial tone.

THE SOLDIERS, LED by Captain Kabera, burst in through the Kavarugandas' front door. They raced from room to room, half crouched, like commandos on a raid. They found Julithe, cowering in a shift, in one bathroom. Dragging her out into the hallway, they put a gun to her head as Julien looked on. "Where is your father?" they screamed.

She flinched. "Please, Father. Open the door. They are going to kill me."

Joseph came out of the other bathroom. Looking over at Captain Kabera, Joseph surrendered, but on his own terms. "I want to get dressed before I go," he said.

"There's no need," replied the Captain. "Come right away."

"I'm *always* dressed correctly before leaving the house," insisted Joseph, grabbing trousers and a shirt and changing while the soldiers watched. Anonciata, quickly packing a bag, handed it to Joseph as the soldiers marched him to the door.

Captain Kabera caught her eye. "Where he's going, he won't need that," he said haughtily. Joseph started to hand his wallet to his wife, when one of the soldiers snatched it from him and threw it at Anonciata.

They grabbed Joseph by the arm and marched him through the open front door. "You've forgotten your ethnic identity card!" Anonciata yelled after him.

"He won't need it," the captain said.

Outside, the garden—its flowers fragrant as the early morning sun burned off the dew—was filled with armed Rwandan soldiers.

The Ghanian UN troops stood in a group to one side, watching as the soldiers dragged Joseph down the driveway. Captain Kabera ordered Joseph and all but ten of the soldiers into a waiting truck.

Wheeling around, Kabera snapped when he saw the family assembled in the driveway. "Where are you taking them?" he yelled to his soldiers. "Quickly, take them back to the house." As the family, confused, backtracked across the garden, the truck started up with a roar and pulled out of the driveway.

There was no chance to protest. There was no chance to think. There was no chance to say good-bye. That was the last time Anonciata, Julithe, and Julien saw Joseph Kavaruganda.

THE GENOCIDE'S PLANNERS moved swiftly in the early hours of April 7. The Interahamwe militia erected roadblocks on the streets of Kigali, and the Presidential Guard blocked Belgian UN troops at the airport. Colonel Théoneste Bagasora, a retired officer with extremist Hutu leanings, seized control of elite units of the army. It wasn't difficult: The minister of defense was out of Rwanda on business, and the army's chief of staff had been killed along with the president when his plane crashed.

The extremists' first goal was to kill off all opposition politicians who stood in their way. They went after Kavaruganda as well as his good friend Landoald Ndasingwa, who, as a candidate for the presidency of the transitional assembly, could have replaced Habyarimana under the Arusha accords. The gunmen killed Landoald's wife, a Canadian, and their two children. They then sought out the prime minister, Hutu moderate Agathe Uwilingiyimana, also in line to succeed Habyarimana. At first, she escaped her armed pursuers and hid at the home of neighbors, but by midday she had been discovered and murdered. Her half-naked corpse was left sprawled on a terrace, a beer bottle shoved up her vagina. The ten Belgian peacekeepers guarding her were rounded up, taken to a nearby military camp, and then set upon by a mob, who killed them.

Across Kigali, other UN peacekeepers were surrounded, disarmed, and blocked from moving.

Anonciata harbored few illusions about what lay ahead for the Kavaruganda family. Her suspicions were confirmed when one of the Presidential Guard soldiers, whom she vaguely recognized, sidled up to her in the garden.

"Try to flee before the UN troops leave," he advised.

"Why?"

"Once they go," he said, "you will be killed." He nodded at her; he had seen what had happened elsewhere that morning.

Yet how to escape? If the UN guards would fight, there might be a chance, Anonciata thought; they were outnumbered, but only by two to one. But the Ghanians, who as UN peacekeepers had orders to use force only in self-defense, showed no inclination to defend the family. Instead they stood in the garden chatting with the Rwandan soldiers in broken Kinyarwandan. They even made no protest when soldiers began looting the house. Soon, riches many Rwandans could only dream of—the radio, the television, foreign currency, telephones—were heaped in the garden. They took everything they could lay their hands on, even raiding the refrigerator for food.

Huddled together in the garden, the Kavarugandas could hear sounds of soldiers shouting and shooting next door in the home of their friends the Nzahorambahos. Anonciata shuddered. As if reading her thoughts, one of the Rwandan soldiers whipped his gun up to her head and made as if to fire. He then laughed and pulled away, giggling. Now, here was a new sport to engage in: taunting the Kavaruganda family. The soldiers grabbed and fondled Julithe, a weapon pressed to her head. They pointed their guns at Julien's face, only to raise their hands and slap him instead. One of the soldiers, waving his gun, then ordered the two children to act as his servants. "Pack the cars with all the stuff!" he ordered.

And so Julien and Julithe began dragging the valuables across the garden to put them in the family's two Peugots. As they stood with the car door open, a hoarse whisper reached them. It was young Ferdinand Nzahorambaho, hiding by the fence that divided their properties. His voice was shaking.

"Everybody here is dead," he said. "When you leave, can you take me with you?" The two whispered back: "We will try."

Perhaps it was greed that made the Presidential Guard soldiers decide not to kill the Kavaruganda family on the spot. Perhaps it was a lack of orders, or even a lack of bloodthirst. But as soon as the children had crammed the cars with the soldiers' booty, the soldiers roared off, leaving the Kavarugandas behind. Ferdinand, hearing them depart, snuck over and hid in the family's garage.

A UN truck pulled up next, with orders to take the Ghanian troops away. "Take us with you!" Anonciata pleaded. "They will return and kill us if you leave."

The driver shook his head. The UN was being stopped at every checkpoint by armed soldiers, he said. They would discover Anonciata. "I don't want you to die in our hands," he replied, and drove away.

In the garden of her own home, Anonciata wept: tears of frustration, tears of rage, tears of sorrow, tears of fear, tears because the family had been abandoned, if not betrayed. All that remained was for them to be killed.

RESCUE CAME FROM the most unlikely source: a neighbor, Casimir Bizimungu, a Habyarimana loyalist. He had been evacuated the night before and had returned to retrieve documents and clothing. Running over to his house, Anonciata pleaded with him.

"I know Joseph is dead, and they are coming back to kill us," Anonciata cried. "Can you help us?"

Bizimungu, startled to see her, became annoyed. "I can't take you with us. Where we are going, they hate your husband."

"Just drive us to the home of the Canadian ambassador," she said. The Kavaruganda family was renting a house to embassy staff and had gotten to know the ambassador.

One of the soldiers accompanying Bizimungu spluttered with anger at the audacity of the request. "Mr. Minister," he said, "leave this woman and her children. They are accomplices of the RPF."

But Bizimungu reluctantly agreed to help. He drove Anonciata, Julien, Julithe, and Ferdinand to the Canadian ambassador's home. There Anonciata rang the bell. "Don't come here" was the answer through the intercom at the gate. "Go to the embassy. It's open." The embassy was three kilometers away. Anonciata turned and again pleaded with Bizimungu. Tight-lipped with anger, he drove them and left them outside the embassy gates.

The watchman, Thomas, appeared. "What are you doing here? The embassy is closed."

"They sent us here from the ambassador's house," said Anonciata. "I can't leave now that I'm here. They are looking for us. We have nowhere else to go."

The night watchman looked at Anonciata and the children. They certainly looked like people on the run. Anonciata had had time only to throw on a T-shirt and wrap a *pagne* around her. In her hand she clutched her handbag; she had had the presence of mind to grab the family's passports. Julien was dressed in a T-shirt that fell to his knees, shorts, and flip-flops. Julithe was wearing just a simple shift. Disheveled, exhausted, and scared, they waited.

The watchman unlocked the gate and swung it open. "Come in," he said, waving them through.

TO: ANNAN/GOULDING/HANSON/UNATIONS, NEW YORK

typed the UN officer in Rwanda, as he prepared to send the communiqué to UN headquarters on Manhattan's East River.

INFO: KITTANI

FROM: BOOH-BOOH, UNAMIR, KIGALI

DATE: 8 APRIL 1994

SUBJECT: SUPPLEMENTARY REPORT ON UNAMIR HUMANITARIAN ACTIVITIES.

.... ON 7 APRIL, 1994, THE FIRST DAY OF THE CONFLICT UNAMIR RECEIVED HUNDREDS OF CALLS FOR ASSISTANCE. AS MANY WERE RESPONDED TO AS POSSIBLE. UNFORTUNATELY, NOT ALL COULD BE ANSWERED DUE TO THE ROADBLOCKS, FIRING AND DIRECTED FIRE AT UNAMIR VEHICLES. SOME OF THESE UNFORTUNATELY RESULTED IN DEATH OR HOSTAGE TAKING....

ALL UNAMIR CAMPS HAVE SHELTERED CIVILIANS TERRIFIED BY THE RUTHLESS CAMPAIGN OF ETHNIC CLEANSING....

CIVILIAN CASUALTIES ARE IMPOSSIBLE TO EVEN ESTIMATE AT THIS TIME BUT INITIAL INDICATIONS ARE THAT THEY ARE QUITE HEAVY AND PRI-

MARILY ETHNIC IN NATURE. IN ADDITION BANDITRY IS BEING CONDUCTED AND POLITICAL CLEANSING OF THE OPPOSITION HAS OCCURRED. . . ."

It had taken a mere twenty-four hours for the genocide to begin.

Colonel Théoneste Bagasora had assembled an interim government composed of Hutu extremists, including interim Prime Minister Jean Kambanda, an economist and banker. With key moderate Hutu now dead, extremists began focusing on Tutsi, particularly the educated elite, as their chief target. Their aim was to exterminate them. Gangs of Interahamwe prowled the streets of Kigali, working their way from door to door, demanding to see ethnic identity cards. Corpses of teachers, lawyers, school inspectors, priests, nuns, and doctors began to pile up on the city's streets.

In addition to genocidal killings, there was also renewed war. As part of the Arusha accords, some Tutsi-led RPA troops were in Rwanda so that they could merge with the Rwandan Army. With peace dissolving, they joined the fighting. As the Interahamwe militia killed Tutsi, the RPA battled the Rwandan Army. The conflict played directly into the hands of the genocide's architects. The formidable propaganda machine they had assembled—including the popular radio station of Radio Mille Collines and Radio Rwanda—drummed home their message: Rwanda was at war, and the Tutsi RPF was the enemy. That meant all Tutsi were enemies. All our enemies are one. All good Hutu must join in.

Rwanda's hierarchical society was well suited to organizing a genocide. Its structure, from prefects down to cells, made people easy to mobilize. All it took to join the mass murder, killers would admit later, was a lack of courage to say no. (Many who resisted were slain, from the heads of prefectures on down.) To be sure, many young unemployed Hutu men with few prospects didn't need much persuading that the genocide offered them a chance of power in a society of elites. With a few swipes of a machete, a man could be transformed from a nobody into a member of a club of killers, with the hope of some booty as well. So they used whatever weapons were handy—machetes, guns, clubs, even hoes—as they killed and looted from Cyangugu in the south to Gisenyi in the north.

No one was safe, not women, not children, not the elderly, not priests, not nuns. The first massacre of the genocide, early on the morning of April 7 in Kigali, took place at the Centre Christus, a Jesuit retreat house. The Presidential Guard, separating the Europeans from the Rwandans gathered in the chapel, killed all of the latter, including seven priests.

Tutsi sought sanctuary anywhere they could, but there were few safe havens. Two thousand took shelter with Belgian UN troops at the Ecole Technique Officielle in the Kicikuro section of Kigali. Hundreds of civilians gathered in the church of Ntarama, on the outskirts of Kigali, were slain by machete-wielding killers, their bodies carpeting the floor of the sanctuary, like leaves from a drought-stricken tree. In the small parish of Nyange, west of Kigali, it was the priests who became the killers; one allegedly ordered his church to be bulldozed, crushing to death the several thousand Tutsi cowering inside. Within the first five days of the genocide, some 20,000 Tutsi and moderate Hutu were slain by the Rwandan Army, Interahamwe, and party militias.

In Europe, the three Kavaruganda children feared the worst as they listened to the radio and scanned for news about their country's spiraling descent into anarchy. On April 8 the Belgian daily *Le Soir* reported their father's murder in an article that appeared under the headline "A Political Change Dissolves into a Bloodbath." Their only comfort was that the story did not mention a similar fate for the rest of the family.

And, indeed, they were safe. Anonciata, Julien, and Julithe, along with Ferdinand Nzahorambaho, were camped out in a small generator shed in the tranquil gardens of the Canadian Embassy. Nestled among bougainvillea, hibiscus, and avocado trees, the family could hear the shooting and shouting outside the embassy gate, still manned by Thomas the watchman. They could not get inside the embassy itself, as its Canadian staff had been evacuated and the building locked shut.

From time to time the family followed the news on Thomas's transistor radio, trying to decipher reality from propaganda. One day the radio broadcaster gleefully announced Joseph Kavaruganda's death. Anonciata, weeping, told her children, "Your papa has been assassinated." She thought to herself: *And we will be next. I have to find a way out.*

She already had a good idea of what the family's fate would be. From her perch in the embassy garden, she had watched the road below as panicked families, bedrolls on their heads, tried to get past the checkpoint thrown up by gun-toting Interahamwe soldiers. But the guards searched everybody. Anyone with a Tutsi ID card, or even anyone who looked Tutsi, was swiftly killed.

Once she watched with disbelief as an Interhamawe soldier ripped a baby off its mother's back, and—holding it by its feet—swung it up in the air and slammed it to the pavement, shattering its skull. As incomprehension slipped across the mother's face, he killed her too.

Anonciata fell to her knees and began praying for her country.

NOT ALL RWANDANS joined in the slaying. Some Hutu sheltered Tutsi, even battled alongside them. Hundreds of Hutu fled their homes in Kigali to shelter with relatives in the countryside, hoping to avoid being gang-pressed into taking part. Some officials staunchly resisted joining.

Such was the case in Taba, where JJ lived: The village burgomaster, or mayor, Jean-Paul Akayesu, refused to become part of the killing. His reasons were as political as they were moral: A member of a moderate opposition Hutu party, Akayesu was not sympathetic to either the government's party or its Interahamwe militia.

Akayesu, a handsome, well-spoken former school inspector, was a popular and well-respected leader. Villagers looked up to him with admiration and love; his word was law in his community. So when he assembled the villagers and told them to resist the genocide, they did so. The largely Hutu village chased away the Interahamwe when they attacked and looted some of Taba's homes. And they applauded when Akayesu ordered his police to fire on the marauding gang, killing the militia members and then confiscating their weapons.

JJ and her family believed Taba was one of the few places that might survive Rwanda's violent chaos. They reassured themselves that they had nothing to fear. Akayesu knew what to do. Akayesu would protect them.

ON THE THIRD day of the genocide, as bodies lay heaped at checkpoints in Kigali and machete-wielding militiamen mowed people down like weeds, the international community finally reacted.

It did not respond to the cries for assistance from General Dallaire. "Give me the means and I can do more," the general had cabled to New York within hours of the plane crash. But no supplies, no troops, and not even an updated, more rigorous mandate was granted. The order for him and his lightly armed troops were as restrictive as ever: They could fire only when UN troops were fired upon. "I could have stopped them," General Dallaire would say later. "We could have stopped the militia at that time with force. All I needed were the troops I had on the ground plus another 2,500 men."

No weapons, no additional troops, not even drinking water and rations were forthcoming for the general. Instead, the C-120 cargo planes that swooped in Kigali from April 9 onward carrying 1,500 Belgian, Italian, and French troops were there for what was perceived to be a more pressing reason: to evacuate embassy staff, dependents, and other foreign nationals. So urgent did the UN deem the evacuation that it was the only time during the genocide that Dallaire was authorized "to act beyond [his] mandate" and provide assistance.

For the Kavarugandas, the evacuation proved a possible avenue of escape. One day Anonciata snuck out of the Canadian Embassy and made her way to the nearby Red Cross office. She managed to call a close family friend and begged him to call Jean-Marcel in Brussels. Time was of the essence, she told him; every day the genocide crept closer. Already at least ten corpses were piled outside of the embassy gates, and she knew the family's presence had not gone unnoticed by the Presidential Guard patrolling the neighborhood.

Years later Anonciata admitted that even she didn't know if her children in Belgium could help. She was as amazed as anyone a few days later when two small armored personnel carriers pulled up in front of the embassy. She, Julien, Julithe, and Ferdinand clambered aboard, along with Belgian paratroopers and three UN Senegalese soldiers, and were taken to the airport, where they were put on a plane for Nairobi.

As the plane zoomed into the clouds above Kigali, the hills of Rwanda falling away beneath her, Anonciata's heart was heavy. Hers was a double grief. Her husband was dead. *But he was dead because UN peacekeepers had handed him over to his killers.* Some day, she vowed, she would return to Rwanda. She would find Joseph's body. She would find out the truth: about why the United Nations soldiers—those peacekeepers who, with their blue helmets, represented the ideal of international cooperation—had allowed armed militiamen to take her husband away without a word of protest.

THE UN MISSION, already weakened by a lack of support, was dealt a death blow: Belgium, after rescuing its own citizens on the ground in Rwanda, withdrew all its soldiers from the UN force, nearly a third of the contingent. As Belgian soldiers boarded the cargo planes—joined by some frightened Ghanians and Bangladeshis—General Dallaire was abandoned, with a force of less than 500 military men.

The West could not have provided a clearer signal of its indifference to the genocide's planners. Not only was there domestic impunity for slaughter, there appeared to be international impunity as well. No one was going to stop them. Not the UN, not the world. The massacres escalated almost immediately.

For example, at the Ecole Technique Officielle in Kigali, where Interahamwe were literally camped outside the gates, Tutsi begged the Belgian UN contingent not to abandon them. They cried, they pleaded. "We kept saying, 'It's not possible—don't leave us,' " recalled Jean-Paul Biramvu, a human-rights activist and lawyer who was among those who sought refuge at the school. "Don't abandon us." Some asked the peacekeepers to shoot them rather than abandon them. No sooner had the Belgian UN soldiers roared off in their jeeps than the Interahamwe swooped in, slaughtering the Tutsi on the spot. Some Tutsi, fleeing, tried to reach another UN outpost. En route, Rwandan soldiers captured them and marched them up the road to a lonely ridge. There, 2,000 people were killed by grenades and machetes in a single afternoon.

> THE STOPPING OF THE MASSACRES MAY BECOME MORE AND MORE DIFFICULT AS THE LOCAL GROUPS/MILITIAS ARE BECOMING SEEMINGLY BOLDER.

Dallaire wrote in an April 17 cable, demanding that the UN act.

> BODIES LITTER THE STREETS AND POSE A SIGNIFICANT HEALTH HAZARD. RTLM RADIO BROADCASTS INFLAMMATORY SPEECHES AND SONGS EXHORTING THE POPULATION TO DESTROY ALL TUTSIS. . . .
>
> IF THIS MISSION IS TO BE CHANGED INTO A PEACE ENFORCEMENT SCENARIO TO STOP THE MASSACRES AND RESCUE THREATENED CIVILIANS THEN

A CHANGE IN MANDATE WILL BE REQUIRED AND THE MISSION MUST BE REINFORCED WITH MEN, WEAPONS AND EQUIPMENT. . . .
THE FORCE SIMPLY CANNOT CONTINUE TO SIT ON THE FENCE IN THE FACE OF ALL THESE MORALLY LEGITIMATE DEMANDS FOR ASSISTANCE/PROTECTION. . . .

Ever since Habyarimana's plane crash, the U.N. Security Council had been slow to react. There was no sense of immediacy concerning Rwanda; reports relayed to diplomats were sketchy and UN Secretary General Boutros Boutros-Ghali was absent. (Later, it would turn out that key information—like Dallaire's early telegram about the weapon's caches—was never passed on to the diplomats.) So the Security Council focused at first on finding a diplomatic solution to the violence and withdrawing UN troops. A suggestion to strengthen the UN peacekeepers' mandate so they could intervene militarily was quickly dismissed, and there was no thought of reinforcements. "The reaction was, how do we get back on to the peace track? Where is the diplomatic fix? As opposed to talking about the military fix," David Scheffer, then an aide to U.S. Ambassador to the UN Madeleine Albright, later recalled.

But Rwanda's killers moved swiftly while international diplomats debated. Tutsis were being killed at a rate of 4,000 a day. It was a well-organized, government-sponsored campaign of extermination. Lists of names were distributed to execution squads. Radio stations, denouncing people as Tutsi spies, publicized their addresses and urged people to track them down and destroy them.

The incessant propaganda, mixing truth with rumor, myth, or outright falsehood, cleverly stirred up all the age-old resentments and fear of the RPA, the Tutsi-led army. To rally the Hutu, whose various political factions had not all united behind the genocidal leaders, radio broadcasts and newspapers called on citizens to act together and fight the enemy. A popular song went: "Our enemy is one / We know him / It is the Tutsi." Radio Mille Collines, the private extremist Hutu radio station, was more inflammatory. "Finish them off, exterminate them, sweep them out of the country!" screamed one broadcast. "Just look at one person, their physique and their physical appearance, look at their cute little nose, and then break it."

Thousands of Rwandans—Rwandan Army members, the Presidential Guard, militia members, businessmen, local politicians, unemployed youth—did so. The country's churches remained silent; some priests and nuns joined in the slaughter. Even Jean-Paul Akayesu, the mayor of Taba, changed his mind.

As more RPA troops arrived in Kigali, the extremist government that Théoneste Bagasora had assembled fled to the prefecture of Gitarama, where Taba is located. On April 18 Akayesu and other local officials were summoned and received a tongue-lashing. They were exhorted to join in the united battle against the common enemy, the Tutsi. Those who opposed the genocide were the same as enemy accomplices—and would have to face the consequences of their treason.

Jean-Paul Akayesu returned to Taba later that afternoon a changed man. He knew that his political survival depended on one thing: joining the genocide.

He called together a group of bloodthirsty armed Hutu youths. When fighting had broken out in Kigali, some Tutsi had fled to Taba for refuge. Akayesu handed over eight of them to the gang of young men. "Messieurs," he told them, "right now I can no longer have pity for the Tutsi, especially the intellectuals. Even those who are with us, those we have kept here, I want to deliver them to you so that you can render a judgment unto them." The Tutsi were killed on the spot.

Then he gathered Taba's residents to deliver his new orders. They were to cooperate with the Interahamwe in killing the Tutsi. It was the Tutsi who wanted to exterminate the Hutu. It was the Tutsi who were the enemy.

The killers began their work the very next day.

THEY REACHED JJ's house by nightfall. That night they destroyed the family's homes and killed the livestock while JJ and her relatives hid in the fields nearby. The next day they returned. After slaying a teacher next door, following Akayesu's orders to execute the intellectuals first, the group attacked the ruins of the house where JJ and her family, some ten in all, had returned to sleep. They blew whistles, yelled, and tore off the tin roof. The killers ran after JJ's father, killed him, and threw his body into the latrine. Rampaging, wielding their machetes, they went after the younger men in the family first, killing JJ's brothers. Pools of blood spread out across the dirt. JJ, her youngest child on her back, ran with her three other children into a nearby forest. Her youngest sister, streaming with blood from a machete wound, followed. Everyone was running and dodging and hiding. In the panic, JJ and her children got separated.

JJ ran, hunted down like an animal by the Interahamwe, her baby on her back. She kept trying to find her older children while avoiding gangs of killers out prowling for Tutsi. JJ's tall, thin frame, elongated forehead, thin nose, and chiseled cheekbones stamped her as a Tutsi immediately. Finally, JJ's sister was too weak from blood loss to run anymore. She begged and pleaded to rest. JJ left her lying, hidden from view, in a sorghum field while she went to search for food. When she returned, however, her sister was gone. JJ assumed the Interahamwe had found her.

Crossing into another village, JJ came upon the home of a farmer, a man who ran a small coffee plantation. The man was a Hutu, but, as she knew, not all Hutu had savage hearts. He cared nothing for extremist politics. Exhausted, bereft, she begged him to let her rest. He was too frightened to allow her to stay in his house, but he agreed to let her spend the night in the coffee fields. JJ, taking off her *pagne*, placed it in a secluded corner of a field not far from the house and lay down with her baby for the first time in days. The farmer left scraps of food for them on his doorstep that night. Creeping out, before the moon rose too high, JJ pounced on the offerings.

The next morning the farmer woke her. "You need to go to the mayor's office in Taba," he said. "There are other Tutsi refugees there. The word has gone that those of us hiding Tutsi must give them up. It is too dangerous for you to stay here." *E-é,* JJ thought, *I have no other choice.* She picked herself up and left the coffee farm. Hiding behind banana trees, creeping on her hands and knees through fields, she made her way back to Taba. It was risky to return, she knew, but she trusted Akayesu. She had known him ever since she was a girl. She still could not believe that he had been behind the Interahamwe attacks.

In Rwandan villages such as Taba, the Bureau Communale, similar to a mayor's office, is one of the key gathering places, after the marketplace and the church. There people assemble to bring their problems to the burgomaster. In Taba, the Bureau Communale was an imposing, one-story, red-brick building with wrought-iron grilles on the windows.

Akayesu's office was in the front, not far from the main door and the steps where people sat, waiting to talk to him. Two more humble buildings, whitewashed ochre with tin roofs, flanked the main building. All three surrounded a courtyard of dusty red earth.

JJ turned into that courtyard. Her worst fears were swiftly confirmed: She was greeted by a group of Interahamwe, their guns and machetes drawn, standing over a group of cowering villagers. As Akayesu stood quietly in the background, one policeman lifted his gun and clubbed a villager crouched before him. The others joined in, beating any Tutsi they could lay their hands on. One grabbed JJ, beating her on the head, kicking her in the ribs, hitting her sharply in the left leg. Akayesu said nothing.

Protected, or imprisoned? The Tutsi of Taba were both. At night JJ slept with her baby at the Bureau Communale; during the day she foraged for food, trying to hide from the gangs of Interahamwe in the fields. The rainy season had begun, and she was grateful for shelter in the evening.

But Akayesu soon put an end to that. One night he ordered JJ and the other refugees out. "Wicked people," he said coldly, "no longer have a right to shelter." A policeman standing next to him grabbed JJ and soundly beat her around the head, grabbing her as she tried to pick up her baby. As soon as he let her go, she limped, cold, hungry, and wet from the rain, off into the banana field.

She slept out in the rain that night. JJ was dirty. She was hungry. Her baby was wailing constantly. She could no longer bear life on the run. A staunch Christian, JJ at this point believed death would bring her far more peace than life. She didn't mind dying; she just didn't want to die under the blows of a machete. She remembered the Interahamwe, and how their machete blows had split her brothers' bodies as easily as if they were pieces of fruit. In her mind's eye she had seen the killers so many times over the past days: their arms raised, then a downward slash that severed flesh and bone—and then slashing, again and again and again—until the dusty roads turned into abattoirs.

She and a group of ten other Tutsi refugees decided to ask to die. They returned to the Bureau Communale, where they confronted Akayesu. They told him that they were too tired to run anymore, that they could no longer bear the uncertainty of knowing if they were refugees, protected by him, or targets, hunted by the Interahamwe.

"Kill us," JJ told the mayor, drawing up her thin body to stare him in the eye. "Kill us like the others, shoot us if you will."

"There are no more bullets," replied Akayesu. "Even if there were, we would not waste them on you."

Then the Interhamwe standing nearby turned on the group and started beating them.

BY APRIL, THE dead piled in stinking heaps on Rwanda's streets or scattered in masses along the fields, numbered nearly 100,000. And still, the United Nations had not acted.

The United Nations Security Council met constantly that month. But there was little or no agreement among its diplomats as to what to do in the face of the mounting violence in Rwanda. UN diplomats—U.S. ambassador Madeleine Albright chief among them—labored under the widespread perception that Rwanda was gripped by civil war, not genocide. (Human Rights Watch, the prominent New York–based human rights organization, had written to the Security Council asserting otherwise.) Even UN Secretary-General Boutros-Ghali's report on Rwanda's violence, delivered to diplomats on April 21, failed to mention the organized nature of the massacres.

Security Council diplomats knew the UN peacekeepers' mandate, to oversee a peaceful transition in Rwanda, was no longer appropriate. But should they be reinforced, as General Dallaire had requested, or be withdrawn? The United States, ever the dominant and often determining member of the Security Council, made it clear it was determined not to intervene. The failed U.S. mission in Somalia had so shaken the Joint Chiefs of Staff that they pushed for limits on U.S. involvement in any UN mission. The result was a new presidential directive that set strict conditions on U.S. support for any peacekeeping force.

In addition, Albright told Security Council diplomats that Washington was opposed to the mission's being reinforced under any circumstances. The U.S. position was that all UN peacekeepers should be withdrawn. When Ibrahim Gambari, Nigeria's ambassador to the UN—one of the few diplomats calling for intervention—pushed for reinforcements for

General Dallaire, arguing the troops could protect civilians—the United States made it clear it would vote against the idea.

America's reluctance proved infectious. After halfheartedly calling for a cease-fire, the UN Security Council on April 21 voted to *reduce* the number of UN troops on the ground to a mere 270 soldiers who would try to establish a cease-fire.

Six days later the Interahamwe massacred 4,000 Tutsi in Muyaga. But the Security Council responded only with a statement condemning the "violence" in Rwanda. The Council chose its words carefully; had it been termed a "genocide," it would have been obligated to act under the terms of the 1948 Genocide Convention.

It took the sight of 250,000 refugees fleeing into Tanzania on April 29–30—five miles of people—for Boutros Boutros-Ghali to urge the Security Council to reconsider its decision. The refugees were actually Hutu fleeing the advance of the RPF, but the prospect of chaos in the region impelled the Secretary-General to act. The "scale of human suffering," he wrote, called for "forceful action." An estimated 200,000 Rwandans, he said, had already died.

Yet the United States was still reluctant to get involved. President Clinton called on the Rwandan government and the military to end the slaughter, while Albright repeatedly stalled votes on a new response to the violence, reflecting the administration's caution. "We have serious reservations about proposals to establish a large peace enforcement mission," she said.

In Rwanda, the interim government escalated its campaign of killing, ordering the Interahamwe to track down and kill any Tutsi who remained. There were to be no survivors.

IT WAS NEAR dawn, one day in early May. JJ had simply collapsed in a field near Taba, like a punctured balloon. She had lost so much weight her cheeks were sunken, her face nearly skeletal, her teeth protruding. That morning, when she looked up to see men wielding machetes, guns, and hoes towering over her, she didn't even protest. She had given up. *E-é; so death would come now.* Days before, reeling with hunger, she had handed off her baby son to a Hutu family who said they would take care of him. She hated herself for that. She had lost her other three children in the first wave of chaos, and now the fourth was gone too. She just wanted to die.

The men looked down at JJ. "This one's already dead," said one.

"Where are your children, you Tutsi?" taunted another.

She let them strip her naked. They dragged her over to a small pit and threw her in it. She didn't care; let the red dirt of Taba be her shroud. She listened, indifferent, as they debated how best to kill her. One proposed burying her alive, and a second gripped his machete. But a third had a crisis of conscience.

"Don't kill a woman," he said. "It will not be good for you." The group pondered this. Taboos, suspicions, moral qualms raced through their heads. They had their orders, but they had their doubts too.

"Poison," declared one. "It will kill her, we won't. I have insecticide. We will make her drink it." The men clapped their friend on the back with approval; it was a good solution. The Tutsi would die, but their hands would remain clean.

JJ was only too grateful it would not be death by machete. "Thank God," she prayed, "this will be my last day on earth to suffer." She knelt, naked, before the men, her spindly ribs and shriveled breasts exposed.

The man returned from his house with the jug of insecticide. He raised it aloft and uncorked it. JJ tipped back her head and opened her mouth, like a penitent receiving a sacred wafer from a priest. The liquid splattered across her lips, burning them. It seared a trail down her throat and curdled, burning in her stomach. But JJ opened her mouth even wider, wanting death, wanting not to have to run anymore, wanting it all to end. On and on they poured, until the jug was empty, until JJ crumpled to the ground.

Years later she described to me what happened this way: "God did not put my name on the list of genocide victims that day." JJ threw up instead of dying. Once, twice, three times. Her throat was raw and blistered, her mouth sore, her stomach felt like it was being stabbed with a thousand pins. But she did not die.

Somehow—even she can't explain how—she summoned the shreds of will that remained to her. She climbed out of the ditch. She wrapped her dirt-encrusted *pagne* around her. She stumbled on. Luckily for her, the Tutsi-led Rwandan Patriot Army had been pressing ahead with its campaign, pushing back the Rwandan Army and the Interahamwe and seizing territory from Kigali toward Taba. One day JJ stumbled into the hands of the RPA.

AFTER SIX WEEKS of frenzied killing that left 300,000 Rwandans dead, the United States and the UN finally agreed on a proposal for a new peacekeeping force. On May 17, 1994, the UN Security Council voted to expand the number of UN troops on the ground to 5,500. But the troops' mandate was still restricted. They could use force, but only to protect civilians in danger and help get aid to them. To satisfy the Americans, only 850 troops and 150 observers would arrive in the first wave, and report back. The remainder would be dispatched later, if needed.

Tired of being asked to send their soldiers abroad to missions that were often ill-conceived and poorly planned, no country wanted to donate troops, not even by the end of May, when nearly half a million Rwandans lay dead and international observers returned from the country with tales of carnage and bloodlust. The UN Secretary-General was disgusted. Finally declaring the slaughter a "genocide," he condemned the United Nations member countries for their failure to act. "It is a scandal," he said.

Ultimately, the force that turned the tide of the genocide in Rwanda would not be the United Nations or any other Western presence. The Tutsi-led RPF and its army successfully pushed back Rwandan forces. In the middle of July, Bagasora and other members of the interim government fled the country. On July 18 the RPF declared victory—months before the UN force approved in May had been assembled, much less left for Rwanda.

In the absence of a UN force, in June the French dispatched troops with the UN's blessing to Rwanda for "humanitarian reasons." Given France's support for the Habyarimana regime, the move seemed like a last-minute ploy to prop up their former ally, particularly as the French had not volunteered troops for the UN mission. Dubbed "Operation Turquoise," the French carved out a "safe area" in the southwest of Rwanda, ostensibly to distribute aid to thousands of displaced refugees. But the safe area proved a haven for the architects of the genocide, including the leading members of the extremist interim government. As the RPF pushed ahead with its military gains, Hutu leaders fled to the

French-controlled sector. France, honoring its ties to Habyarimana and eager to retain its influence in Africa, looked the other way. It allowed, even aided, in some cases, key leaders of the genocide to slip over the border into neighboring Zaire.

The killers were now free, harbored by one of the most corrupt regimes in Africa, that of Zairean leader Mobutu Sese Seko. It was only natural they would begin plotting their return to Rwanda.

AND SO THE time came to count the dead, to calculate the losses, to ponder the question of accountability.

Rwanda was not just a country full of skeletons, it was a skeleton of itself. Entire villages were destroyed, government offices looted and trashed. Nearly 80 percent of the country's cattle were stolen or slain, fields left untended or burned. There was no working water, electrical power, or telephone system. Everywhere—in churches, schools, hospitals, gardens, latrines—there lay bodies amid millions of accompanying flies.

JJ barely recognized Taba when she finally returned to her hometown. Her family's homes had been burned and gutted. The fields were fallow, choked with tangled weeds; the livestock long since gone. Where to begin mourning? Of her immediate family, only a handful remained: Her mother had survived, along with one of her sisters, who had been kept as a sexual slave during the genocide and repeatedly raped. She looked at JJ with shamed, hurt eyes, unable to articulate her pain. Against all odds, two of JJ's children—a son and a daughter—separated from her at the beginning of the genocide had survived. The baby she had left with the Hutu family had been killed.

Bereft, impoverished, JJ focused on survival. Simmering inside of her was a sense of betrayal by the man she thought would serve as her protector, but who had become a predator instead: Taba's mayor, Jean-Paul Akayesu. He, however, had disappeared from the village, leaving few traces.

A continent away, in Brussels, Anonciata was also counting up the missing and the dead. More than forty members of her extended family had been killed, despite the fact they were Hutu. Some were killed during the genocide itself. Others, more distressingly, were killed afterward, suspected of having taken part in it. The conquering RPA troops had committed their own share of atrocities. They executed groups of unarmed Hutu, many rounded up in refugee camps, and would continue to do so, killing between 2,000 to 4,000 at the Kibeho camp in April 1995. Also slain by the RPA were the Roman Catholic archbishop of Kigali and three bishops and ten priests.

Struggling to hold vengeance in check, the Tutsi-led rebels focused on forming a government. Proclaiming a new "Government of National Unity," they assured their countrymen they stood for a Rwanda for all. They swiftly appointed a government composed of both Tutsi and Hutu. They called on the country's Hutu to join with them in building a new nation. Indeed, many who had fled to the countryside returned to their homes and jobs.

But over a million Rwandan paid them no heed. Terrified of vengeance, provoked by the Interahamwe in their midst, assaulted by anti-RPF propaganda, 1.2 million Rwandans picked up their bedrolls, their few pots and pans, and left, streaming out of the country toward Zaire, Burundi, and Tanzania. From militia leaders and machete-wielding henchmen to thousands of simple followers, their ranks included everyone, from the guilty to the guileless.

Ironically, it was the wretched situation of the Hutu refugees that finally focused the world's attention on Rwanda. Camped out in squalid refugee camps in Zaire, nearly 50,000 had died when cholera and dysentery raced through the area. That devastation prompted the world to respond—although attention was largely paid to those who had perpetrated the genocide, not those who had suffered from it.

President Clinton ordered an emergency humanitarian airlift to aid the sick and dying. Television crews and reporters arrived in droves. As the crisis passed, the refugees became entrenched in their camps, swiftly transformed by Hutu extremist leaders into small fiefdoms. Aid was distributed to those who toed the party line; Interahamwe and other militia leaders got the best treatment. Rumors circulated as to what would happen to those Hutu who returned home, everything from having their eyes gouged out to worse. Indeed, many of those who went back were killed.

What to do with Rwanda's obvious thirst for vengeance? How to assuage the West's guilt? The answer was the same as for the former Yugoslavia: create a war crimes tribunal.

THE INTERNATIONAL CRIMINAL Tribunal for Rwanda—known as ICTR or the Rwanda Tribunal—was conceived partly out of shame, developed in an atmosphere of dissent, and finally born in a version that the Rwandan government voted against it.

It didn't begin that way. The RPF government first asked the UN to set up a war crimes tribunal for Rwanda, like that for the former Yugoslavia, in May 1994, as machete-wielding Hutu militiamen were killing Tutsi with ease. The RPF's prime minister delegate was outraged at the international community's apparent resistance to consider a tribunal. "Is what is happening different from what happened in Nazi Germany?" he asked reporters at a press conference. "Is it because we're Africans that a court has not been set up?" But the UN Security Council, still reluctant to characterize the killings in Rwanda as "genocide," balked. So did the United States.

By the end of June, as international observers and reporters finally arrived in Rwanda, reporting on the carnage and its aftermath, the full dimensions of the country's tragedy began to clear. While the UN and its member countries stood by, well over a half million people had been killed, nearly three-quarters of the country's Tutsi population. Stung by shame, criticized for failing to react swiftly, both the UN and the United States searched for a solution.

Inside the State Department, many were already pushing for a war crimes tribunal. "There had to be something comparable to the Yugoslav Tribunal," recalled John Shattuck, then assistant secretary for democracy, human rights, and labor. "Particularly as there had been no military response to stop the genocide." In June, U.S. Secretary of State Warren Christopher labeled what had happened in Rwanda a "genocide" and later called for an international tribunal. Shortly afterward, the UN established a Commission of Experts to investigate the killings and determine if there had been a genocide.

The newly installed Rwandan government, however, was no longer so sure about an international war crimes court, which they feared would take too long to establish. Plus "they [the government] were genuinely skeptical about the whole UN operation," recalled Shattuck, who negotiated with Rwanda over the emerging tribunal. Instead, the RPF announced its own plans to prosecute and possibly execute some of the key leaders among the over 30,000 Hutu already in prison. State Department diplomats were horrified, fearful that a campaign of vengeance would ensue. Through letters, cables, and personal visits, Shattuck and others tried to woo the Rwandans back to the idea of a war crimes court. The RPF government reluctantly agreed to delay its own trials until a UN tribunal could be established.

The UN reacted, but with foot-dragging and indecisiveness. Instead of recommending a separate court in Africa for Rwanda, most of the initial proposals simply recommended expanding the existing war crimes court for the former Yugoslavia, in The Hague. Bickering over the shape of the new tribunal stretched through October. Every detail was debated: where the court should be located, whether it would encompass allegations of RPF crimes as well as those by the extremists who carried out the genocide, how far back in time its jurisdiction would stretch, and whether it would include the death penalty.

The death penalty was one of the most bitterly disputed points. The RPF government wanted it delivered. But the issue was not negotiable for the United Nations, committed since 1968 to eradicating capital punishment. Chief prosecutor Richard Goldstone, one of those trying to hammer out the new tribunal, finally alleviated some Rwandan concerns by proposing that those sentenced to life imprisonment serve their terms in jails in Africa, rather than in Europe, as originally proposed.

Almost as divisive was the question of who would be prosecuted: General Paul Kagame, the strapping head of the RPA and now the new Rwandan minister of defense, did not want to rule out prosecuting the French for their role in propping up Habyarimana. Finally, on November 8, 1994, the UN Security Council voted on the proposal for the new tribunal, hashed out after numerous discussions with the Rwandan government. The court's future home was left temporarily undetermined, although it was agreed that it would be in Africa, and the door was left open for some trials to be held in Rwanda. The chief prosecutor in The Hague, Richard Goldstone, would oversee both tribunals and travel back and forth.

Unlike its sister court in The Hague, the Rwanda Tribunal would focus mostly on crimes committed during an internal armed conflict, rather than an international one, and many of its prosecutions would be for genocide. Moreover, its focus was only a discrete period of time, between January 1, 1994, and December 31, 1994.

Like the Yugoslav Tribunal, however, the Rwanda Tribunal was tasked with contributing to national reconciliation and the maintenance of peace and security in the region. The Security Council voted overwhelmingly in favor of the proposal. But there was one crucial exception: Rwanda, then one of the temporary members of the UN Security Council, symbolically voted no.

Six months after the genocide had begun, the United Nations had finally taken concrete action. It delivered a chance for international justice. Rwanda reluctantly agreed to cooperate with the tribunal, even though it fell far short of its expectations. But in the years to come, the divide between Rwanda and the UN war crimes tribunal would only fissure and deepen. And both JJ and Anonciata would find themselves teetering on the edge of that divide as they sought to find a workable—and acceptable—justice.

6

NO SAFE HAVENS

The soldier, be he friend or foe, is charged with the protection of the weak and unarmed. It is the very essence and reason of his being. When he violates this sacred trust, he not only profanes his entire code, but threatens the fabric of international society.

—General Douglas MacArthur, confirming the death sentence for General Yamashita at the Tokyo Military Tribunal

The spring and summer of 1994 proved to be fateful for Bosnia as well as Rwanda. April had marked the beginning of the Rwandan genocide and the humiliation of UN peacekeeping efforts there. That month also saw the first successful attack by the rebel Bosnian Serbs on a UN "safe area" in Bosnia—revealing the UN and NATO's reluctance to defend the protected zone and forever altering the course of Hasan Nuhanović's life.

At the time, Hasan and his family had no sense of foreboding. Since the arrival of Canadian UN peacekeepers in 1993, life in Srebrenica had improved slightly. The relentless shelling had eased; Hasan and his family no longer risked death every day. Hunger still gnawed at people's stomachs, and they hunted for scraps in the garbage the UN trucks poured into the dump. But food was at least available at a price, thanks to regular smuggling runs over the mountains and the arrival of some humanitarian aid. There was occasional electricity: Someone had had the ingenuity to build small water wheels in the Križevica River, and dozens now turned with the water's flow, powering batteries and generators. Even the movie cinema worked sporadically, with films available for the cost of a few cigarettes. Given that Hasan was getting paid to translate for the UN, the Nuhanović family counted themselves lucky to be in Srebrenica, one of Bosnia's six UN "safe areas."

But UN military commanders in Bosnia and neighboring Croatia were hardly so sanguine about the safe areas, which also included Sarajevo, Tuzla, Bihać, Goražde, and Žepa. From the start, it was thought foolhardy to assume that the presence of lightly armed UN peacekeepers, coupled with the moral indignation of the UN Security Council, would deter attacks by rebel Serbs. Enforcing a safe area was a mission better designed for heavily armed troops than lightly armed peacekeepers, and there weren't even enough peacekeepers to do the job properly. Calls for UN member states to cough up more personnel to guard the safe areas had gone unheeded. UN Secretary-General Boutros Boutros-Ghali—who had originally thought the safe areas would need 32,000 peacekeepers—settled for a mere 7,000 when Security Council members objected.

Yet fewer than 3,000 had arrived, many of them with inadequate equipment. And so the nearly 15,000 UN troops in Bosnia found themselves with multiple tasks: shepherding humanitarian aid, attempting to monitor borders, overseeing political negotiations, and guarding safe areas. "We really have gotten a second mission here, haven't we," bemoaned the commander of UN forces, Lieutenant General Sir Michael Rose. The only good news was that the feuding Muslim and Croats had agreed to stop fighting and form a Federation. The war again had narrowed to two sides: the rebel Serbs and everybody else.

Guarding the safe areas was a frustrating task for the UN. They were defined only vaguely. Although the safe areas were theoretically demilitarized, Bosnian Muslim soldiers among the civilians living in them never surrendered their weapons and continued to launch attacks. There was also a huge gap between the UN's assigned role and what the Bosnians thought the peacekeepers were there to do.

The UN Security Council had given UN troops a limited mandate: the troops were to deter attacks, monitor the cease-fire and the area's demilitarization, and ensure the delivery of humanitarian aid. Yet like the Rwandans in Kigali, the starving, desperate Bosnians living in the besieged safe areas saw the peacekeepers, patrolling in flak jackets and blue helmets and armored personnel carriers, as their protectors.

All UN commanders could do was hope the Bosnian Serbs would not put them to the test. But in April 1994, the Bosnian Serbs besieged Goražde, a UN safe area along the Drina River. Swiftly, the fact that the UN and NATO did not have the political will to defend the safe areas became clear. "There was no doubt from the beginning that the safe area concept was unworkable, and that the UN Security Council knew it," later recalled John MacInnis, a Canadian who was then the UN deputy force commander in Zagreb, Croatia. "But Goražde was the nail in the coffin."

Since March 31, ham radio reports out of Goražde depicted a region under desperate bombardment. "Nineteen villages have been burned and destroyed," cried Fahrudin Beslić, a local official from Goražde, his voice crackling over the radio as I listened. "The people have no accommodation and are taking shelter in the ruins . . . the humanitarian situation is very critical here." But General Rose was convinced such reports were "a campaign of lies designed to involve the West in a war with Bosnia." Determined that the UN would not be drawn into the conflict, he insisted on pursuing negotiations with the Bosnian Serbs for ten days before calling on NATO jets to deliver close air support on targets threatening the UN peacekeepers. The result was a debacle: 150 UN peacekeepers held hostage, a NATO Sea Harrier aircraft shot down, Serb tanks proudly patrolling the streets of Goražde. In the end, NATO would threaten broader, punitive "air strikes"—instead of "close air support" to protect UN personnel—although none was carried out. The Bosnian Serbs finally retreated from Goražde, but only because they lacked the troops to hold the city.

Their commanders came away with something more valuable than territory: the knowledge that despite the UN's presence there was little political will to defend the safe areas. They were, thus, easy targets. Moreover, the Serbs learned that NATO commanders were loath to use their air power, especially when its peacekeepers were held hostage.

These were lessons that would serve the Bosnian Serbs well, in just a year's time.

THE UN SECURITY Council had also done little on behalf of the Yugoslav Tribunal. The war crimes court it had created in The Hague by the spring of 1994 was still in a state of limbo. Its budget was laughably small and doled out on an ad hoc basis. What staff it had was busy trying to find desks and office equipment. And there was still no chief prosecutor.

Not until July 1994—18 months after the tribunal had been created—did the UN Security Council name a new chief prosecutor, South African judge Richard Goldstone, well-known for having chaired a governmental commission of inquiry into his country's violence. Goldstone, fifty-six years old, had a bespectacled, professorial appearance and a savvy understanding of the media. What he did not have was courtroom experience: "I have not ever been a prosecutor," Goldstone told his visibly shocked staff, participants later recalled.

But Goldstone understood that the tribunal's success depended on its public image. He made sure it had one. Indeed, his first appointment on his first day of work in August was an interview with Mike Wallace of *60 Minutes*. In his first few months, he logged thousands of miles flying between The Hague, Geneva, New York, and other capitals, courting politicians and reporters and forging contacts with refugee groups and even within the UN itself. He convinced UN bureaucrats to authorize one-year contracts for his new hires and to double his staff to eighty by the year's end. In return, the UN Security Council told him that to justify a budget for 1995 at least one indictment had to be issued by November of 1994, when the tribunal would submit its annual report.

It seemed an impossible task. But the U.S. government, demonstrating Madeleine Albright's commitment to the new court, had come to the rescue. It had donated $2.3 million in computer equipment and seconded, or loaned, some twenty-two investigators, analysts, attorneys, and administrative experts from government jobs to the tribunal. By late summer a staff of about forty people had been assembled, albeit far too top-heavy with Americans for the Europeans' liking. The sleepy former insurance building that housed the tribunal in a leafy suburban neighborhood not far from the waterfront in The Hague sprang to life.

People bustled through the hallways. The lights burned late at night. There was much to do: because the tribunal was to be a mix of both common and civil law—and the two systems are quite different, so prosecutors, investigators, and other staff had to debate every detail. What, for example, should an indictment look like? In civil law, the level of proof is "serious and corroborated" evidence, while in common law it was a "prima facie" case. Which standard should be adopted? So untested was international humanitarian law that the tribunal's staff also had to struggle with defining particular crimes. Most legal systems, reflecting years of jurisprudence, have defined the elements that constitute a crime such as murder. But there were no standards for such crimes as genocide. "We were literally starting from scratch," recalled a prosecutor.

Some staff took to keeping sandwiches in their file drawers, as most worked into the late evening hours. They had a sense of zeal and historic mission, as well as an intimidating pile of data assembled by the UN Commission of Experts to sort through. Struck by the Commission's findings in and around Kozarac, Hamdija Kahrimanović's home town, prosecutors focused on who was responsible for the Omarska camp, where he had been incarcerated.

That September, when a team of Tribunal lawyers and investigators arrived in Bosnia to gather evidence, they anticipated the ongoing war would interfere with their work, if not endanger their lives. Even so, the realities of their mission were sobering. One prosecutor later recalled having to share a helicopter with the body of a dead Norwegian UN peacekeeper. And the team didn't expect that the UN and its associated agencies would do almost nothing to help their work in the field. They found themselves without cars, much less armored vehicles or satellite phones in a country where no conventional telephones functioned. Every request for supplies was immediately snarled with layers of red tape. Tribunal staff carried on, very much alone. "We were the red-headed stepchild of the UN," recalled one staffer. "We had to beg, borrow rides. And when we did get cars, they were shit cars." Ultimately, a $300,000 donation from philanthropist George Soros enabled the tribunal at least to buy radio receivers and transmitters and have them delivered in forty-eight hours.

So evident was the lack of support for the new court that some of the tribunal staff became disillusioned, if not downright suspicious. They wondered if the powerful UN member countries that had opposed the tribunal's creation now wanted it to fail. "There was such resentment and opposition to our creation. We weren't going to get support," remembered one prosecutor. "We were going to have to fight every inch of the way."

In November 1994, the president of the tribunal, judge Antonio Cassese, underscored his staff's misgivings in an address to the UN General Assembly. "How is it that twelve months after the establishment of this ground-breaking institution—the tribunal for the former Yugoslavia—no trials have yet been conducted at The Hague?" the Italian jurist asked. He went on to enumerate the tribunal's needs that had not been fulfilled, and called for additional funds. For example, there were only twenty investigators, the same number used in most countries to prosecute just two or three murder cases. (By contrast, the Nuremberg Tribunal had a staff of 996 in 1946.)

Despite this, the tribunal had been forging ahead. On November 1, Cassese said, the tribunal had issued its first indictment, against Dragan Nikolić, the head of the Sušica concentration camp in Vlasenica. (Goldstone later called this indictment a "political move" undertaken to appease the U.N.) And on November 8, the court had asked the German government to transfer a Bosnian Serb arrested in Munich—on charges of genocide, ethnic cleansing, and the torture, rape, and murder of civilians and prisoners of war—to the tribunal to stand trial.

The man in a Munich jail cell was no high-ranking Bosnian Serb nationalist leader like Radovan Karadžić. But he was certainly well known to at least one Bosnian: former school principal Hamdo Kahrimanović from Kozarac. The man whose case would become the tribunal's first trial was Duško "Dule" Tadić—the same young Tadić who had taught karate at Hamdo's school and had grown up just across the street from his home.

HAMDO AND FIRDESA were in Germany when they heard the news that Tadić was being sent to The Hague. Some 1.2 million Bosnians had fled abroad to avoid the war's ravages, and Germany, spurred by its World War II legacy, opened its arms and took in 400,000—the most of any country in Europe. From Munich to Berlin, Karlsruhe to Hamburg, Bosnians led lives of near invisibility, staying in refugee hostels or in the homes of relatives already employed as "guest workers" in German factories, supplementing state welfare benefits by picking up whatever jobs came their way. They learned just enough German to get by.

Firdesa felt fortunate that Hamdo had had the foresight to send her and their daughter to Austria, where the couple's son, Enes, had been working in a factory since just before the war began. For the first few months of the summer of 1992, the three had shared Enes's room at a worker's hostel. As the days went by with no word from Hamdo, Firdesa cried herself to sleep every night. She imagined him dead, by the side of the road in Kozarac, or held hostage in one of the concentration camps whose discovery dominated the news. Finally she decided to make her home with her brother, who lived in a small village near Karlsruhe in Germany. Firdesa wondered if she'd ever hear from Hamdo again.

But one day the phone did ring, and indeed it was Hamdo. He had gotten out of Bosnia on an aid convoy and was in Croatia. He made his way to Germany, and they rented a one-room apartment, eager to start a new life abroad. Firdesa, a trained nurse, became a cleaning lady in the offices of Siemens, the German electronics company. It wasn't the scrubbing and vacuuming she found humiliating. What was demoralizing was that she had lost her identity. In Germany, she had no name. She was no longer Firdesa Kahrimanović, wife of Hamdija, whose family had lived in Kozarac for as long as anyone could remember. She was simply a *Flüchtling*—a refugee. For the Siemens executives, dressed in their well-tailored dark suits and colorful ties, who bustled by her in the hallways wielding their briefcases, chatting about how German reunification was wrecking the economy, she might as well not exist. "Are you a Muslim?" the chef in the office canteen yelled at her, admonishing her for trying to take leftovers home. Firdesa desperately longed to move back home to Kozarac and to reclaim who she was.

But as long as there was war, that was not an option. Even those who had a hand in starting the war, like Duško Tadić, were leaving Bosnia. Tadić had moved to Munich to live with his brother Mladen; rumor had it he had quarreled with the Prijedor chief of police, Simo Drljača. News of his arrival whipped through the Bosnian refugee community and reached the German police as well. His arrest in February 1994 merited front-page headlines in Germany. By November he was en route to The Hague.

Firdesa felt happiness surge in her heart for the first time since Hamdo had returned home. After all they had suffered, justice was finally going to pay the Kahrimanović family a visit. Not only would Tadić be punished, she thought, but surely his arrest was a step toward stopping the war.

"NINETEEN NINETY-FIVE is the year when something *has* to happen," a well-informed British diplomat told a colleague of mine in Zagreb, "because 1994 was the year when nothing happened."

By the end of 1994, both the war and diplomatic efforts to end it were at a dead end. On the ground, fighting raged over incremental changes in front lines that had stayed essentially the same since the autumn of 1992. Every diplomatic effort was in stalemate, every threat of force seen as a bluff. In a humiliating visit to Sarajevo, Boutros Boutros-Ghali was booed by its residents and spurned by the rebel Serbs.

Over and over again, the rebel Bosnian Serbs had tested the West's commitment to its new safe-area policy—as well as the new combination of NATO air power along with UN troops—and found it wanting, as Europe and America could not decide what to do. By December, the UN–NATO partnership, which put the threat of air power behind UN troops, was on the verge of collapse. The sixteen-member NATO alliance was deeply fissured, with Europe and America at odds over the use of air power, a rift that developed in a showdown over a Serb attack on another "safe area," Bihać. And the United Nations was seriously talking about withdrawing its peacekeepers. All that had stilled the fighting was the heavy winter snow and a four-month cease-fire, the result of last-minute talks between former American president Jimmy Carter and Bosnian Serb leader Radovan Karadžić.

Events would occur in 1995 that would change the course of the war, as that British diplomat predicted. Many of them would unfold in the besieged UN safe area of Srebrenica, where Hasan Nuhanović and his family lived. To begin with, a fresh battalion took up command in the enclave, the 13th Battalion of the Dutch airmobile brigade—Dutchbat III. The Netherlands had been one of the very few countries to respond to the UN's call for more peacekeepers.

One of the translators for the UN military observers (UNMOS) accompanying Dutchbat III would be Hasan Nuhanović, by then a tall, skinny man whose tendency to knit his brows had etched long, vertical worry lines on his forehead. In the two years he had worked as a translator, Hasan had earned the respect of both the local Bosnian leaders and the surrounding Bosnian Serb commanders. The Bosnian Serb military—who used to hail the UNMOS over the radio using a prearranged numeric code—granted Hasan his own: "21" meant "send us Hasan Nuhanović."

The year began ominously, amid signs that the Bosnian Serbs, who had successfully attacked the several other "safe areas," would turn their attention to Srebrenica. Local Serb leaders stepped up rhetoric about wanting the Bosnian Muslims of Srebrenica to leave. The surrounding Bosnian Serb troops started halting aid convoys. Stockpiles dwindled, and warehouse shelves grew empty and dusty. Even supplies for the Dutch troops were stopped, and the men had to eat combat rations. Fuel was rationed, meaning the soldiers had to forgo the hot showers and movies their predecessors had enjoyed. They could patrol only on foot, not a particularly effective way of monitoring what went on in their territory, essentially an enclave that included the city and territory beyond. Their supplies of ammunition grew low, to only 16 percent of what they needed. After the Bosnian Serbs refused to allow the return to Srebrenica of Dutch soldiers who had gone on leave, their numbers dwindled to 450 men, only 150 of them combat-trained. The battalion's commander, Lieutenant Colonel Ton Karremans—a beanpole of a man with a scraggly mustache and an ineffective manner—complained repeatedly to his UN superiors, but his concerns were dismissed.

The Dutch soldiers in Srebrenica grumbled. They were peacekeepers in an unpleasant prison, and many of them had little sympathy for their fellow inmates, finding the Bosnian Muslims grasping, dirty, and smelly. They resented the sniveling kids who, spoiled by earlier UN troops, ran after them yelling, "Bon-bon! Bon-bon!" They resented the swagger of the local commander, Naser Orić, and his men, who had plenty of money while many in Srebrenica starved. And they were annoyed by the raids Orić and others still carried out on local Serb villages despite the fact that the safe area was supposed to be demilitarized.

That spring, as the snow began to melt in the jagged crags and gullies of the steep, dark mountains of Bosnia, hostilities, predictably, broke out anew. By now the Bosnian government's army was finally emerging as a real fighting force, reorganized with more intelligence and logistics. In April, the government's army succeeded in seizing back Mount Vlašić, a key telecommunications facility in central Bosnia. For the first time, it posed a threat to the rebel Bosnian Serb troops. The rebel Serbs decided they could no longer afford to keep their men pinned down around the so-called safe areas—islands of Bosnian Muslims in an otherwise Serbian sea.

What peace there had been disintegrated into war. Fighting also broke out in neighboring Croatia, when Croatian government forces conquered large parts of western Slavonia. Serbian leader Slobodan Milošević had begun to talk seriously to Western diplomats about peace measures in exchange for having the embargo against his country lifted. A rift between Milošević and Karadžić had grown and was widening. If the Bosnian Serbs wanted to join Serbia, it was now or never. It was time to do the job of ethnically cleansing the parts of Bosnia they needed.

In April the Bosnian Serbs bombarded Sarajevo. On just one day, 1,211 "firing incidents" were logged in the city—roughly 46 an hour. Once again the dead of Sarajevo stacked up, filling the city's morgues and cemeteries. The sense of protection offered by the label of "UN safe area" vanished, infuriating residents who felt cheated. "Politicians, UN diplomats," muttered Hedija Bosak, the matriarch of the family I had befriended in Sarajevo. "Nothing has changed."

Daily the rebel Bosnian Serbs humiliated the UN peacekeepers, constrained by their rules of engagement. Bosnian Serb soldiers stole light weapons and flak jackets from French UN troops, then brazenly showed up at a UN checkpoint to display them. They snuck into the UN weapons collection sites to steal arms and fire off their own guns. Across Bosnia, Bosnian Serb soldiers snarled UN convoys en route to deliver aid to the safe areas. Within the UN command, rifts appeared. The new head of UN forces in Bosnia, General Rupert Smith—a British general respected for his searing intelligence and his flexibility—pushed for a more robust response to Serb attacks on the safe areas than his superiors were willing to undertake. He believed force, not diplomacy, was the only way to get the rebel Bosnian Serbs to respect the UN and NATO's policies on the safe areas. But Smith would frequently find himself overruled by the commander of UN forces, Lieutenant General Commander Bernard Janvier of France, and the UN special envoy, Yasushi Akashi, when he called for air strikes.

Even so, by then the Bosnian Serbs knew all too well that the UN and NATO feared casualties in their ranks more than anything else. So when the UN did call in NATO air strikes on ammunition depots in Pale on May 25 and 26, 1995, as punishment for violations of the exclusion zone around Sarajevo, the Bosnian Serbs seized several hundred UN peacekeepers and unarmed observers, many of them French. The rebels even chained some hostages to bombing targets as human shields. NATO halted its raids. Ensuing negotiations between General Janvier and the rebel Serbs led to the hostages being released.

On May 29 an undoubtedly reluctant General Smith issued a new directive clarifying peacekeepers' responsibilities in safe areas. "Execution of the mandate [is] secondary to the security of UN personnel," it read, noting that force could be used only as a "last resort." It was rumored that Janvier had told Bosnian Serb General Mladić that NATO would no longer use air strikes if hostages were returned. (Janvier would later deny this.) But in a June 19, 1995, memo to the UN's Department of Peacekeeping, Akashi quoted Milošević as saying that he had been advised by French President Chirac of "President Clinton's agreement that air strikes should not occur if unacceptable to Chirac."

As the United Nations prepared to celebrate its fiftieth anniversary that summer, its peacekeeping mission in Bosnia was in shambles. The Bosnian Serbs denounced all UN Security Council resolutions and were again shelling Sarajevo. On May 30 an indignant UN Secretary-General demanded the Security Council withdraw UN troops or alter their mandate. Recent events, he argued, showed that coupling force, or NATO bombing, with peacekeeping did not work. If troops were to stay, he argued, they must act only as peacekeepers.

Just days before, Janvier had stated the same concerns when he spoke to UN diplomats. Janvier focused on the failure of the safe areas, such as Srebrenica and Sarajevo. The policy made no sense, he argued: Lightly equipped UN soldiers couldn't defend areas of key military significance from the heavily armed rebel Bosnian Serbs. He appeared to call for the UN to withdraw from safe areas. "In the absence of effective lightning rods, let us distance ourselves from the areas where lightning strikes," he said.

And lightning did strike—in Srebrenica, the very first of the UN's safe areas. It came in the form of a grueling Bosnian Serb artillery barrage that began on July 6.

THE BOSNIAN SERBS had just the man to lead that attack: General Radislav Krstić. Vain, ambitious, bitter, Krstić made no secret of his loathing for Bosnian Muslims. In late 1994, he had stepped on one of their land mines, crippling his right leg and forcing him to wear a prosthesis that earned him the nickname "Šepo," or cripple, behind his back.

Born in a small village near Nuhanović's hometown of Vlasenica, the forty-eight-year-old Krstić was a career army officer who rose through the ranks of the Yugoslav army and then became part of the Bosnian Serb Army in 1992. Tall and lean, he was an old-fashioned, strict soldier who enjoyed not only following orders but also dispensing them. He luxuriated in enforcing the army's petty rules, snapping at men who didn't stand at attention or comb their hair properly. His soldiers didn't like him, but his commanders did. By 1995 he had become the deputy commander and chief of staff of the Bosnian Serbs' Drina Corps. Eastern Bosnia, including Srebrenica, was his territory.

It was Bosnian Serb leader Radovan Karadžić who in March 1995 first ordered "combat operations" that would "create an unbearable situation of total insecurity with no hope of further survival or life" for Srebrenica. General Ratko Mladić relished the idea. The beefy, swaggering general had developed a particular loathing for Srebrenica, in part because of the raids its residents conducted on nearby villages. But it was Krstić who spent months planning Operatije Krivaja 95, assembling men and training them. That spring he replaced the elderly Serb farmers and shepherds guarding Srebrenica's perimeter with tougher fighting men. At a time when the NATO embargo made fuel difficult to find, Krstić gathered enough to power his tanks and scores of buses. He'd moved fifty men from one of his reconnaissance units, the Drina Wolves, to Srebrenica's south.

His artillery began pounding the south of the enclave before dawn on July 6. The sound of heavy guns rattled the night air, awakening the Nuhanović family. In the southeast, fighting erupted around the Dutch battalion's observation posts, as black-clad members of the Drina Wolves and camouflaged members of the 10th Expeditionary Unit fought their way forward, driving villagers out of their homes and setting haystacks alight to mark their advance.

At the Dutch battalion headquarters in an old battery factory in the village of Potočari to the north, Lieutenant Colonial Ton Karremans was worried. The Bosnian Serb tanks were firing directly at Dutch positions; shells had even hit as far north as his headquarters. Karremans didn't believe the Bosnian Serbs intended to seize the enclave, but their attack was clearly a violation of the UN safe-area policy. He called his superiors in Sarajevo, requesting that NATO planes deliver close air support and halt the attack. Under UN rules, NATO airplanes could bomb if UN soldiers had been directly targeted.

The chief of staff of the UN forces in Sarajevo, Brigadier General Cees Nicolai, was not sympathetic. He reminded Karremans that, according to the new orders, NATO force was to be used as a "last resort." It was better to watch and wait and see what the rebels were up to, he cautioned. Besides, air power could imperil talks a new European Union negotiator was holding with Milošević; some thought the discussions could lead to Bosnia's diplomatic recognition by Serbia and Montenegro and an end to the war.

And so neither the Dutch troops nor NATO airplanes responded to the attack. The Serbs pounded Srebrenica, shooting off tank rounds and artillery directly at the UN soldiers, narrowly missing their observation posts. It was the most resounding attack the Dutch troops had seen there. Yet that evening, when UN Secretariat officials met with European diplomats to discuss Bosnia, the attack on Srebrenica never arose.

Emboldened, the Bosnian Serbs kept attacking. By July 8 Karremans and his Dutch battalion had a full-scale crisis on their hands.

ADVANCING WITH TANKS, grenades, and small-arms fire, rebel Serb troops overran one Dutch observation post and took its soldiers hostage. Then they seized another and surrounded a third. A Dutch soldier was killed in what was mistakenly believed to be an attack by Bosnian Muslim fighters when his armored personnel carrier began to withdraw. Bosnian Serb troops advanced from the south of the city, driving hundreds of refugees northward. The Dutch commander asked his UN superiors in the cities of Tuzla and Sarajevo twice more for air power to halt the Serb attack; twice more he was refused.

Because of multiple misjudgments and errors, no one in the UN's higher echelons was informed about the continuing attack on Srebrenica. When Secretary General Boutros-Ghali convened UN officials in Geneva on July 8, there was no discussion of the enclave. Not until the next day, July 9, when news of the Srebrenica attack was finally relayed to Akashi, the UN special representative in Bosnia, and General Janvier, the head of UN forces, did Srebenica get their attention. Neither Akashi nor Janvier was an interventionist: Akashi was a weak-willed administrator who backed down in confrontations, and Janvier had made his doubts about the viability of UN safe areas very clear. Once informed of the attacks on Srebrenica, however, both men returned to their posts in UN headquarters in Zagreb, Croatia. Janvier, contacting the Bosnian Serb Army, threatened that NATO would bomb them in retaliation.

His threats—as was so often the case in Bosnia—were too little, too late. By the day's end, Krstić's Drina Corps had overrun five more UN observation posts. Thirty Dutch soldiers had been taken hostage, and nearly 3,000 refugees from the southern outskirts of the Srebrenica enclave were streaming into the city center. There was chaos, panic, and confusion.

And General Mladić, gauging the international community's tepid response to the attack, appeared to rethink his strategy: He decided it was time to seize the entire enclave and rid the Bosnian Serbs of the long-hated Bosnian Muslims once and for all.

THAT EVENING HASAN Nuhanović picked his way through the exploding shells and the whizzing gunfire back to his home on the city's outskirts. He was exhausted from reporting on the Bosnian Serb advance to the UNMOS, or UN Military Observers. But he had to tell his family what he knew: Bosnian Serb tanks were already on the nearest hills, and Srebrenica would soon fall into the hands of the rebel Serbs.

The Nuhanovićs had few doubts that the Bosnian Serb troops would be ruthless. After three years of the raids and counterraids on both sides, the enmity between local Bosnian Serbs and Bosnian Muslims ran as deep and dark as the waters of the nearby river Drina.

It was the safety of Hasan's younger brother, Muhamed, then eighteen, that worried the family the most. If the Bosnian Serbs did seize Srebrenica, Hasan would be protected by his UN ID card. Ibro and Nasiha thought they were old enough to be passed over. But Muhamed would be singled out and killed. Even though he had never hefted a gun, no one would believe a young man of his age wasn't a soldier.

"You have to make sure your brother is safe," said Ibro. The warning was unnecessary; Hasan had always looked out for Muhamed. It wasn't that long ago that he had beaten up men he believed had stolen his brother's shoes, a commodity as valuable as gold in snowbound Srebrenica. He decided to take him with him to the UN base north of Srebrenica. As long as he and Muhamed were near the UN, he figured, they'd be safe.

THE NEXT MORNING the Bosnian Serb army entered the southern edge of the city. The Drina Wolves' paramilitary chief, Milan "Legenda" Jovović, and his men swept from house to house, torching and looting and, reportedly, killing as they went. Families fled in terror, leaving clothes dangling on clotheslines, livestock in the fields. Smoke from burning homes hung in the air. Lugging suitcases and bags of food, refugees streamed toward the Dutch UN base in the heart of Srebrenica. Even though the lightly armed troops were few in number, people felt safer near them. Naser Orić, the local Bosnian Muslim commander, and his staff had left the enclave some weeks before and had not yet returned.

Early that morning Lieutenant Colonel Karremans dispatched fifty Dutch soldiers and six armored personnel carriers to take up positions on main streets leading into the city to block the rebel Bosnian Serb advance. Throughout the day the Serb attack intensified: Shells ripped through houses and bullets danced across the streets. But Akashi, who had flown from Zagreb to New York to brief the UN Security Council, painted a different picture. He said the Serb advance had stopped. And he repeated an inaccurate report made earlier in the day that stated that it was the Bosnian Muslims who had attacked a Dutch armored personnel carrier.

When asked by UN diplomats for a chronology of requests for NATO airpower, Akashi failed to mention that Karremans had already filed three requests and been refused. Amid the diplomats' confusion about what was happening in Srebrenica, the sense of urgency that had surrounded the crisis the day before waned.

Yet Srebrenica was teetering on the edge of collapse. By early evening Bosnian Serb infantry had appeared on the ridgeline overlooking the city from the south; the soldiers stood silhouetted against the sky, ghostly and threatening. Again Karremans requested NATO air strikes.

At the UN base at Potočari, Hasan watched curiously as several Dutch soldiers used wire cutters to cut a huge hole in the southern corner of the fence surrounding the camp. The base was a rickety affair: a series of rusty, metal-sided two-story buildings strung out in line, with several hangars for trucks. All that gave it the UN imprimatur was a large blue sign with white letters emblazoned DUTCHBAT atop one of the buildings.

Suddenly Hasan realized that the soldiers were opening a hole for the refugees to enter the base. He could see the future as clearly as if he held it in the palm of his hand: The Dutch, and their UN and NATO masters, were going to let the Serbs conquer Srebrenica.

What would the Bosnian Serbs do when they seized the enclave? Hasan asked himself. Had he been right to bring Muhamed, his brother, with him to the Potočari base? Just that morning he had dissuaded his brother from joining a large group of the enclave's military who planned to begin hiking out of Srebrenica. The men didn't believe the UN would protect them from the Serbs. But Hasan thought their plan foolhardy, given that they had to cross minefields and then rugged mountains before reaching safety. He stopped the boy from going along.

"Hasan!" yelled one of the Dutch liaison officers, interrupting his thoughts. "We have to go back to Srebrenica for a meeting and you need to translate." Hasan, exhausted, took off his glasses and rubbed his eyes. It was good news. If there was to be a meeting in Srebrenica, it meant the city hadn't fallen yet.

Toward midnight, Karremans strode into the Srebrenica post office with Hasan at his side. The Bosnian Army commanders and the city's civilian leaders awaited him. After four days of uncertainty and four days of nearly constant shelling, they were anxious for answers. Just what was the Dutch battalion—and the UN and NATO—going to do?

"Gentlemen, I have an important message," Karremans said. "The Serbs have received an ultimatum. They have to withdraw before 0600. Otherwise there will be bombing everywhere." Unrolling a map, he pointed out the potential targets. His audience was skeptical. Could Karremans guarantee that NATO actually would bomb the next morning? "Don't shoot the piano player," Karremans answered cryptically. Hasan looked at him blankly. What did he mean? Karremans repeated the phrase. Stumped by the colloquial expression, Hasan later recalled translating it as best he could. "Don't trouble the bringer of good tidings," Hasan said. He could feel himself relax, even as he said the words.

The UN and NATO were going to come to Srebrenica's rescue, after all.

WHAT WOULD UNFOLD over the next few days would prove a tragedy: a tragedy spawned by military incompetence, the UN's trepidation, and the international community's cowardice. In the dawn hours of July 11, all eyes were turned toward the sky, foggy as it was: the eyes of the Dutch officers, of thousands of Srebrenica's inhabitants, of Hasan Nuhanović. There was a glint of sun; then the fog slowly peeled back to expose a perfectly blue sky.

Perfect bombing weather. And so they waited for the buzz of the incoming NATO aircraft.

Somewhere, far above, NATO aircraft sent from Italy had been circling since 6:00 A.M., awaiting orders to unleash their bombs. But bureaucratic confusion had set in again. Lieutenant Colonel Karremans had assumed that NATO airplanes would bomb automatically. But his bosses were waiting for him to file yet another request saying NATO airpower was needed before giving the planes the go-ahead.

By 7:44 A.M., aware that something had gone awry, Karremans filed two successive requests for air strikes. But still nothing happened. The request took more than three hours to reach his superiors in Sarajevo, a delay later ascribed either to his failure to use the correct form or to a malfunctioning fax line. By then the NATO planes had been circling for nearly five hours and were short on fuel. They would have to fly back to Italy and refuel before returning.

No sooner had the NATO jets turned around—a move quickly spotted by Serbs following them on air defense radar—than the Bosnian Serb Army turned its guns on Srebrenica again.

"Howl like wolves!" shouted the blond, bearded "Legenda" to his men over a walkie-talkie as they prepared to enter Srebrenica itself. "NATO can do nothing to us!"

This time no one was going to wait in their basement for NATO to react. Hasan's parents hefted their small backpacks and joined the crowds streaming northward toward the last safe haven—the UN base in Potočari. The shells and bullets nipped at their heels, driving them northward like a sheepdog herding sheep.

By the time NATO planes returned to Srebrenica and dropped their bombs, it was 2:30 P.M. But it was too late. The pilots manning the

F-16 hit only a few targets—destroying one tank, disabling another—before the Bosnian Serb Army delivered an ultimatum to the UN: Stop the bombing, or we will kill the Dutch UN soldiers we have hostage, and we will shell the Dutch base at Potočari—killing all the UN soldiers and the refugees inside.

After frantic phone calls from the Dutch government, the UN called off the raids. By four that afternoon a Serb flag fluttered from the top of Srebrenica's post office, where two years earlier General Morillon had pledged to put the city under the UN's protection. The Serbs had met no resistance, and the UN safe area was no more.

A jubilant General Mladić, binoculars swinging from around his neck, strode through the streets. Behind him limped an equally buoyant General Radislav Krstić. "Take down that Muslim street sign," Mladić commanded a soldier. "Take it down. Climb up, man. Do I have to tell you ten times!" Up strolled "Legenda" and members of the Drina Wolves; Mladić embraced them, kissing them ritually on both cheeks three times. Next came the 10th Diversionary Unit; Mladić congratulated them all.

And then he turned to the camera carried by a Serb TV crew. "Here we are, on July 11, 1995, in Serbian Srebrenica just before a great Serb holiday." Mladić was exultant. "We give this town to the Serb nation reemerging from the uprising against the Turks. The time has come to take revenge on the Muslims."

He turned back to his men and impatiently directed them forward. "On to Potočari."

THOUSANDS OF PEOPLE swarmed toward the UN base. Elderly men, clad in the frayed suit jackets and berets they had worn for the last three years, hobbled on their canes. Mothers toiled under the burden of a backpack and a child pulling at each hand. Old women, colorful scarves swathing their hair, plodded forward, gnarled hands around battered suitcases. It was hot and chaotic. The dense air was full of the sounds of people wailing and crying. At the side of the road, abandoned luggage piled up as some travelers, too undernourished and exhausted to carry on, simply lay down by the side of the road.

Hasan, ordered to direct the refugees into the UN camp, waved people through the hole in the fence. Faces swirled by, some familiar, some not. Hasan's brows creased with worry. Where was . . . ? Could that be . . . ? Finally he spotted his parents in the crush. Thank God, they had made it.

Some 5,000 Srebrenica Muslims had entered the confines of the base when the UN soldiers, informed of the Serb ultimatum to bomb the compound, changed their minds. "Tell them no one else can come in except women with babies," a captain ordered Hasan. "Tell them they can stay in the surrounding buildings, just outside the camp." Hasan's mouth dropped open. He and a fellow translator, Emir, looked at each other, aghast. How could they tell the thousands of people jostling and pushing to get into the base to stay outside? As he shouted out the new orders through a megaphone, the crowd fell silent. The exhaustion on their faces gave way to disbelief, then horror. A few tried to shove their way past a line of UN soldiers, with no success. Not until shell fire rang out did the crowd panic, running, screaming, into abandoned factories nearby.

Inside the UN base, the air smelled of excrement, sweat, and fear. There was no water, food, or medical supplies. Outside, some 20,000 people cried and wailed. The hole in the fence had been welded shut just as General Mladić, General Krstić, and their soldiers arrived. All that stood between Muslim refugees and the Bosnian Serb fighters, flush with victory, was a line of blue-helmeted Dutch UN peacekeepers—some sporting their summer uniform of shorts—surrounding the UN base.

Years later Hasan would think that what happened up to this moment was the fault of the UN and NATO. Their reluctance to use airpower and their failure to grasp the seriousness of the attack had resulted in the enclave's capture. Only NATO bombs could have halted the rebel Serbs.

Yet what unfolded next, Hasan later came to believe, was the fault of the Dutch UN peacekeepers. The Dutch were under orders to protect the refugees. That evening, the UN in Zagreb issued strict guidelines to the peacekeepers: Negotiate for a cease-fire. Do not give up your weapons. Concentrate forces in the Potočari camp. Defend your forces with all possible means, including the use of close air support. Be prepared to receive and coordinate delivery of medical and other relief supplies. "Take all reasonable measures to protect refugees and civilians in your care," read the orders issued by the acting commander of the UN forces, Hervé Gobillard.

Twice that night the jubilant Mladić summoned Lieutenant Colonel Karremans to meetings at the Hotel Fontana in nearby Bratunac to discuss the fate of the refugees and the Dutch battalion. There, in the communist-era hotel ablaze with shades of purple—and cameramen filming with the earnestness of Leni Riefenstahl making a Nazi documentary—Mladić harangued the cowed Dutch commander. Offering Karremans a cigarette, he said with a sneer, "Don't worry, it won't be your last." Then the Bosnian Serb general drank a toast with the Dutch UN commander. "Ziveli! Cheers!" roared Mladić, as Serb cameras captured the moment.

In the two meetings—one conducted with a civilian representative of the refugees—Mladić pledged to evacuate the wounded according to the Geneva Conventions and to evacuate all the other Bosnian Muslims as soon as they surrendered their arms. He vowed to establish a cease-fire. Karremans, who had a reputation even within the Dutch military as being somewhat spineless, said little.

But Mladić's words proved a mockery. That night the group of Bosnian fighters, along with some women and children, began their long march out of Srebrenica through the woods toward Tuzla. Fewer than one-third of the men were armed, and their units were placed first, in case of attack. Progress had been slow as they snaked, single file, through the minefields. By dawn, they were heading toward Mount Kamenica. And then the first Bosnian Serb shells exploded in and around them. They were under attack. There was no cease-fire, after all.

ON JULY 12 Ibro Nuhanović, Hasan's father, found himself en route to the Hotel Fontana, one of the three people chosen to represent the refugees in what would be the third meeting with General Mladić.

"And the gentleman next to you?" General Mladić barked as the group began introducing themselves. General Krstić sat silently next to him.

"Nuhanović," Ibro replied. "I'm an economics graduate and a former businessman. Now I'm in the war. Now I'm here in Srebrenica. We're stuck here." Ibro, his white hair neatly combed, his short-sleeve blue shirt looking remarkably clean, was all business, as the Bosnian Serb propaganda cameras captured him on film.

"Will you speak a little louder, if you can?" Mladić demanded.

"Well, I'm saying we simply happened to arrive in Srebrenica during the war. Otherwise, I lived in Vlasenica."

"And where were you born?"

"I was born in the village of Stoboranj, Han Pijesak municipality." Ibro answered all of Mladić's questions calmly until the general was satisfied.

"I want to help you," Mladić said, his beefy face beaming, his camouflage uniform well pressed. "But I absolutely want cooperation from the civilian population. Your army has been defeated. Your people need not die. Not your husbands, or your brothers, or your neighbors. All you have to do is say what you want. And I told that to a gentleman last night. You can either survive, or vanish."

In a rush of unstoppable rhetoric, General Mladić repeated his demands of the night before. Everyone will be free to go, once the Bosnian Muslims disarm. But all able-bodied men between the ages of seventeen and sixty must be screened against a list of war criminals. Then the Dutch battalion and their employees will be evacuated separately. Mladić adjourned the meeting before anyone could disagree. Swiftly cabling his UN superiors with Mladić's demand, Karremans noted that the general threatened to shell the compound and its refugees if his orders were not followed. "I am not able: a) to defend these people; b) to defend my own battalion," wrote Karremans.

At the UN base, Ibro relayed Mladić's demand to the deputy commander of the Dutch battalion, Major Robert Franken. Franken, an ambitious commander, would virtually assume command over the next few days, as Karremans became ill. Franken—dubbed "Franco" behind his back for his dictatorial manner—was not well loved by the Dutch battalion. He was professional, but some thought him heartless. Still, Franken listened intently to Ibro's report. As Hasan translated his father's words, he became increasingly concerned.

Screen for war criminals? Hasan thought. There were some 25,000 people camped in and around Potočari, mostly young boys and old men. All of the enclave's fighters had already fled in the column headed through the woods; surely Mladić knew they wouldn't be stupid enough to stay. The general's suggestion sounded like a way to detain as many men and boys as possible. In fact, it sounded like a prelude to slaughter.

Ibro, along with the other representatives of refugees at the base, swiftly drew up a plan designed to foil the Bosnian Serbs' worst possible aims and gave it to the major. Already Karremans had told Mladić that Dutch soldiers would accompany the evacuation to ensure that it was carried out correctly. Their suggestions took his idea a step further. They recommended that the Dutch inform their UN superiors—and the media—of what was happening in Potočari. Make sure the world's eyes were on the evacuation, they wrote. Place Dutch soldiers on every bus. Mix the men and boys in among the women.

As Major Franken read their plan, Hasan heard the sputtering of one of those typical Yugoslav buses whose motors rasped and spat like a rusty saw. He rushed out to the gate of the compound. Dozens of buses lined the road, clearly assembled to evacuate the population. There was Sembirja Transport of Bijeljina, far to the north, and Drina Trans buses from Zvornik, and Auto Transport from Banja Luka.

How had so many been assembled in such a short time? Where had they gotten the fuel? Clearly, the meeting Ibro had attended had been a farce; there were to be no "plans" for an evacuation. This evacuation had been planned long ago.

Outside the UN compound, Mladić walked to the wire fence separating the refugees from the road. Like a political candidate courting votes, he patted a child's head here, handed out a candy bar there. In a calm, soothing voice, the general, who had vowed vengeance just the day before, explained how the evacuation would proceed. "Don't be afraid," said Mladić. "*Polako*, take it easy. Let women and children go first. . . . Don't be afraid. Nobody will harm you." Everyone would go to Kladanj; everyone would be safe. As the general strolled away, a UN military observer noticed Mladić's soldiers snatched the candy back. It was, the observer reasoned, all one big propaganda stunt.

Back inside the UN base, an argument had broken out. The Dutch decided they had no choice but to comply with Mladić's wishes. But Ibro and Hasan begged Major Franken to halt the evacuation. The Serbs will separate the men from the women and then murder them, they said. They have done it before.

"You're asking me to make the choice between thousands of women and children and the men?" Franken answered, incredulous. Ibro nodded in response; okay, the evacuation had to go ahead. Instead, the Dutch major suggested Ibro draw up a list with the names of all the men ages sixteen to sixty-five both inside and outside the base, to try to protect them by identifying them. Ibro had time to collect a list of only 251 names.

Outside the UN compound, Hasan's and Ibro's worst fears were being confirmed. As people lined up to board the buses, Bosnian Serb soldiers were pulling aside every man roughly over fifteen and under seventy. Even worse, Dutch UN peacekeepers were watching—even helping—as the Bosnian Serb soldiers separated the men from the women.

As the buses packed full of women drove off, the UN peacekeepers looked on as the rebel Serbs led the men to a white house not far from the UN gate. There the soldiers stripped the men of their belongings. The pile of the knapsacks, suitcases, and discarded IDs grew larger and larger. Some of the men, placed on a waiting truck, begged the UN soldiers for help.

"You know these people are going to kill us and you are not doing anything about it," they said, tears streaming down their cheeks. The Dutch UN peacekeepers stared at the ground.

Later, a Dutch UN officer would say the experience was like watching a cross between the movies *Sophie's Choice* and *Schindler's List*. A Dutch private, Paul Groenewegen, looked on, aghast, as Bosnian Serb soldiers led a man to a wall and shot him in the back of the head. One peacekeeper watched as two men were slain near the UN compound's exit; another saw five men being led away and then heard gunshots. A team of Dutch soldiers later stumbled across nine bodies by a stream, all killed with a shot to the heart.

As the sun sank behind the hills, the screams of those outside the UN base echoed off the surrounding hills. The Bosnian Serb soldiers swaggered into the nearby hangars and factories, still packed with refugees. Shining their flashlights, they chose the prettiest girls and raped them. Or they led young men outside and slit their throats.

Inside the base, the Dutch peacekeepers passed on reports to their commanding officers that they had seen Bosnian Muslim men separated from the women and that several had been executed. Major Franken, informed that men had been pulled aside, called ahead to Kladanj, where the first buses had arrived, to see if only women had arrived. To his dismay, he learned that the Dutch peacekeepers who were to escort the buses with refugees had been taken prisoner by the Bosnian Serbs, who had stolen their weapons and their cars. UN staff in Kladanj also told Franken that although no men had arrived on the buses, they weren't overly worried.

Franken, ever practical, concluded that the men had been killed. Yet apparently neither he—nor anyone else—passed such fears up the UN chain of command, despite the fact that the UN Security Council had assembled to discuss the crisis. News of the isolated executions didn't reach New York, either. That night, when the UN Security Council adopted a resolution calling on the Bosnian Serbs to withdraw from Srebrenica, there was consequently no outrage about the killings. The rebel Bosnian Serbs were not reminded that they were party to the Geneva Conventions or that the civilians who had surrendered were protected under international humanitarian law.

It is possible that the Dutch commanders in Srebrenica had dismissed what their soldiers had seen as just random revenge killings. But they weren't isolated executions; they were portents of what was to come.

HASAN'S ONLY THOUGHTS were of Muhamed. Rumors of executions had reached him, and all night long Hasan had begged one UN peacekeeper after another to help him save his younger brother. He was frantic. He knew that many of the thousands camped outside had been evacuated; soon it would be time for the those inside the UN base to go.

The buses arrived on schedule the next morning at 7:00. Groups of Bosnian Muslim refugees lined up, numb with worry. The Bosnian Serb soldiers, flashing their AK-47s, brusquely separated the men from the women. By noon the sun was hot and stifling and all those outside the base had left. To ensure that evacuees inside the base exited in an orderly fashion, Dutch peacekeepers had stretched two yellow plastic tapes from the door of the main UN building to the gate.

"What am I supposed to tell people?" Hasan asked.

"Everyone is to leave in groups of five," a Dutch soldier replied.

"And what about the men?"

"The men should come along with their families, but in groups of five," the soldier responded, then turned away.

Hasan walked back into the building. It was hot and crowded with refugees. Men and women plucked at his sleeve. Their fear hung in the air. "Hasan," they cried, "what is going to happen to us?" Hasan turned to them. At twenty-seven, he felt eighty-seven. He looked at their faces, carved by exhaustion, hunger, and fear.

"They will kill us all," he said. A moan arose from the crowd.

What could he do? What could he say? He wasn't even sure he could help his own brother, let alone thousands of others. He had asked the UN military observers to let Muhamed hide in their Jeep; they had refused, saying they had too much luggage. He had tried unsuccessfully to get a fake UN ID made. Finally, he had begged another UN military observer to add the boy's name to a list of UN employees to be evacuated with the Dutch troops.

Picking up the list of UN employees and scanning it, Hasan realized that even this last desperate attempt to save his brother had failed. Muhamed's name was not on the list.

Hasan ran in search of Major Franken, in charge of the evacuation. His office was empty. He sprinted up and down corridors, searching. He found Franken in a hallway, issuing orders. Hasan interrupted, demanding to know why his brother wasn't going to be evacuated.

"I did not want to jeopardize those who have ID cards by putting your brother's name next to theirs," Franken snapped, by way of explanation.

"Please, Major Franken," Hasan pleaded. "The military observers agreed they would tell everyone that my brother has been working for the UN as a cleaner. The Serbs won't know the difference."

Franken, as Hasan recalled it years later, was brusque. "I am busy now. I do not have time to talk to you. Leave me alone."

Hasan had failed.

Downcast, he walked slowly back to the office where his parents and brother were waiting. Hasan could not bear it; he had pledged to save his brother's life. But he could not think of how to do so. How could the UN soldiers and military observers who knew him—who knew his family—let this happen?

His brother was going to die. Grief choked him, as Hasan swayed down the hallway. Oh, this was betrayal far worse than that of the Serbs. This was betrayal by the Dutch peacekeepers in the employ of the United Nations, an organization which he had counted on to save his family. How could he have been so naive?

He pushed open the door to the office. Inside, Muhamed looked up. "What now?" he asked.

Hasan told him. "Fuck them all," spat Muhamed. "Do not beg them for me anymore. I will go with other boys. Whatever happens to them will happen to me too."

The Nuhanović family sat and waited for the word to join the evacuation. Outside, buses and military trucks stood in rows as the people of Srebrenica lined up. Off to one side, Bosnian Serb soldiers with German shepherds began sweeping the cornfields for escapees. They didn't want anyone left behind.

Finally the door opened. Three Dutch UN military observers—the men Hasan worked for—stood there, embarrassed. "Hasan," they said, "your family must leave now." Hasan broke down in tears. It was the most difficult moment of his life.

"Hasan," said one observer, more firmly. "There is no time for waiting."

Muhamed stood up.

"I am coming with you!" Hasan screamed. "I am not letting you go there alone!"

Ibro, ever the family patriarch, interrupted. "Hasan, let your brother come with us. The three of us will go as a family. Do not worry, he will be with his parents. Nothing will happen."

Hasan did all he could to ensure the Bosnian Serbs would not mistake Muhamed for a soldier. He yanked his expired UN card from his wallet and gave it to him. He insisted Muhamed take off the leather jacket he was wearing over his Dutch battalion UN T-shirt and swap it for Hasan's denim jacket; it made him look less tough.

Together, the Nuhanović family exited the main building. Ahead of them stretched the path—outlined with yellow tape—to the compound's main gates. Muhamed began to walk toward the gate.

Hasan yelled after him. "I am coming with you!"

Muhamed pivoted around. "You are not coming with me," he yelled back. "You can stay, so stay. You will not come with me."

Nasiha turned to Hasan and kissed him. Slowly she walked up to join his brother. Ibro paused to say farewell to his oldest son. The moment hung in the air, taut with unspoken regret and sorrow. And then a shout interrupted them.

Ibro and Hasan turned their heads: It was Major Franken. Hasan almost fainted with delirium. A thousand possibilities danced before his eyes. The Dutch had reconsidered! Muhamed could stay! Maybe the whole family could stay! Franken, as always, was direct. "Tell your father that he is one of the three representatives, and their names are on the list of those who can stay," he said. Hasan translated, his hopes sinking.

"What about my family?" Ibro implored.

"Tell your father that if he does not want to stay, he can leave with his family," Franken told Hasan. "It is his choice."

Ibro didn't hesitate. "I am going with my wife and son," he said. Stretching his hand out, Ibro shook Franken's hand and smiled, then shook Hasan's hand. "Kiss Braco for me," said Hasan, using his brother's nickname. Ibro strode off briskly, to catch up with Nasiha and Muhamed, who had already disappeared from sight.

It had taken General Krstić and his Drina Corps a mere six days to seize the enclave and expel its population. As UN leaders dithered, as the Dutch government hesitated, as Washington fretted, the Bosnian Serb forces had exposed the ineffectiveness of the safe areas the UN had created.

"The world is allowing us to do this," one Bosnian Serb soldier outside the UN compound said with a laugh.

A soft evening breeze rustled over the piles of knapsacks, bags of potatoes, half-empty suitcases, and identity cards stripped from the evacuees. That was all that was left of the men and women of the UN safe area of Srebrenica.

Standing out on the road, one of the UN military observers watched as three members of the Nuhanović family walked to the waiting bus. Then an armed Bosnian Serb soldier grabbed Muhamed and pushed him off to one side, separating him from his parents.

ON JULY 12 Akashi, the UN's special representative, noted in a fax that there is "reason for concern" that some 4,000 men from the Srebrenica enclave appeared not to have arrived in the nearby city of Bratunac for "screening" by the Bosnian Serb Army. But in his missive to Kofi Annan Akashi added confidently: "There continues to be no reports of the BSA [Bosnian Serb Army] mistreating any Bosnian civilians. Allegations that refugees were threatened at [the UN base] of Potočari," he wrote, were "quite false." The Bosnian Serb soldiers were found to be distributing "sweets and cigarettes, instead."

Mass executions of the men and boys from Srebrenica began on the next day. When they ended on July 19, more than 7,000 Bosnian Muslim men had vanished, presumed missing or dead. The Srebrenica massacres would prove to be the single largest massacre on European soil since the Holocaust.

There were dozens of warning signs as Srebrenica was captured. The Dutch battalion had filed many reports on what was happening in and around Potočari, reports that apparently never reached UN headquarters: the executions the Dutch soldiers witnessed at Potočari; the shocking sights that those who traveled with the female refugees being evacuated to Kladanj described to their superiors later. Corporal Hans Berkers saw nearly 1,000 men gathered in a field with hands on their heads, clearly prisoners, guarded by the armed Bosnian Serbs. "It's all over for those men," he thought; and indeed, the next day the field was empty. Private Ynse Schellens saw a truck stuffed with at least fifty bodies and observed dozens more corpses on the road. Others among the Dutch UN troops saw men in rubber gloves and trucks full of corpses—clean-up crews at work.

Even as of July 14, rumors of mass executions were beginning to surface. Bosnian Foreign Minister Mohamed Sacirbey relayed his fears about possible atrocities that day to Madeleine Albright, who alerted the National Security Council. The U.S. ambassador to Bosnia, John Menzies, passed on reports from Bosnian officials that thousands of men had been collected in a soccer stadium in Bratunac and that a call for bulldozers had been issued, indicating a need to dig mass graves. Bosnian officials brought word of killings to General Smith. The American ambassador to Croatia, Peter Galbraith, passed on his concerns to the State Department upon hearing reports that women had been separated from their husbands; he saw it as an ominous indication that the men would soon all be killed. There were times the Bosnian Muslim government had exaggerated their fear of massacres, but increasingly this did not seem to be one of them. "By the fifteenth or sixteenth [of July]," Galbraith recalled later, "it was clear to anyone who followed the Balkans what had happened."

From the start, world leaders had been divided as to the seriousness of the attack on Srebrenica and what could be done to halt it. And once the enclave was captured, there was no agreement as to whether the West should try to retake it. French President Jacques Chirac, upon hearing the news of Srebrenica's capture, exploded with anger and urged military action to get it back. In a phone call to President Clinton on July 13, Chirac warned that military-age men had been separated from the women and might be slaughtered. But Clinton told Chirac he wanted to focus on saving the other enclaves.

Then, amid the chaos and conflicting reports coming out of Srebrenica, world leaders and the United Nations were slow to focus on executions as a possibility for what was happening to the men separated from the women at Potočari. On July 16, UN staff in Tuzla were reporting that some 5,000 Bosnian men had been taken to Bratunac for questioning about war crimes and that the Bosnian Serbs were not allowing any aid group access to them. General Smith and other UN officials, meeting with General Mladić on July 17 and again on July 19, believed the men to still be held prisoner and lobbied for the International Red Cross (ICRC) to visit them.

Meanwhile, thousands of women and children were pouring into the Muslim-held city of Tuzla, camping out under the hot sun on the grass of the airfield. "I am asking the world to help the people who were arrested by the Chetniks," sobbed Šera Vesović as she held my hand, telling me how the men and women had been separated. Each story was more horrific than the last: rapes in the UN compound, poisonous gas used on the fleeing column, young boys whose throats had been slit, rebel Bosnian Serbs dressed in UN uniforms. While there were then no reports of executions, one thing was clear: there were hardly any men or boys to be seen. But as a few men, survivors of the column that had hiked out of Srebrenica, came stumbling into Tuzla, it became easier to hope that all the men had survived than to contemplate the prospect of their mass execution.

Then the Bosnian Serbs attacked another safe area, Žepa, and Srebrenica became yesterday's news. Boutros-Ghali, traveling in Africa, suggested the story had been overplayed. The media made the battle for Srebrenica, he told reporters, sound "like Stalingrad." The Dutch battalion, successfully evacuated from Srebrenica, reached Zagreb on July 21, where exuberant troops belted back beer and danced the can-can in celebration. Lieutenant Colonel Karremans described Mladić's capture of Srebrenica to reporters as a "well-prepared military operation." (Major Franken, before leaving Srebrenica, had signed a document pressed on him by the Bosnian Serbs saying the evacuations had been carried out "correctly.") Even when some Dutch officials suggested "genocide" might have been the motivation behind Srebrenica's capture, General Hans Couzy, the Dutch Army's chief of staff, dismissed the idea. "I can't comment on what happened to refugees when the Dutch left," he told reporters at a July 23 press conference in Zagreb.

But some of the Dutch UN troops knew better. A few let it slip to reporters that they'd told commanders they'd witnessed single executions. A journalist reporting from Serbia near the Bosnian border found local Serbs bearing stories of mass executions of the Srebenica men. Some had seen buses taking bodies to a field to be burned. Others talked of mass burials. On July 25, Ambassador Galbraith cabled Secretary of State Albright with the news that human-rights observers interviewing Srebrenica refugees had found a man, claiming to have survived a Bosnian Serb massacre, who said "many if not most" of the missing men had been executed. By July 27, John Shattuck, an assistant U.S. Secretary of State, was on the ground in Bosnia, interviewing a few massacre survivors.

And on August 10, Madeleine Albright stood before the UN Security Council with U.S. satellite imagery showing that an estimated 2,700 bodies had been dumped in a mass grave near Srebrenica. It was graphic proof of the UN's and NATO's failure to act.

By then, Hasan who, as a UN translator, had been evacuated to safety along with the Dutch UN troops, had begun frantically hunting for news of his mother, father, and brother. He buttonholed UN officials; he contacted friends and family. But no one knew what had happened to Nasiha, Ibro, and Muhamed. They had simply vanished.

To Hasan, "justice" had once seemed as simple as getting out of Srebrenica and reclaiming his prewar life. But no longer. Wracked with guilt and worry, justice for Hasan came to mean uncovering the role the United Nations had played in his family's disappearance. It meant making a commitment, as one of Srebrenica's few survivors, to ensure that the world did not forget what happened to the former UN "safe area."

And it meant dedicating his life to retracing his family's final steps. He was determined to know what had happened to Muhamed, Ibro, and Nasiha after they left the UN base and turned toward the waiting buses, only to disappear forever—like shadows—from Hasan's life.

Book Two

TRIALS AND TRIBUNALS

7

PEACE WITHOUT JUSTICE

While they look for me everywhere
I wait in the ambush of the dawn.

—Radovan Karadžić, "A Morning Hand Grenade"

The man sitting across from me and my translator in November 1996 was an indicted war criminal. A ten-page indictment issued by the Yugoslav Tribunal had accused him of grave breaches of the Geneva Conventions, violations of the laws and customs of war, and crimes against humanity. But the Bosnian Serb mayor of the town of Bosanski Šamac had been every inch the Balkan gallant when I showed up uninvited at his office: ushering me in, offering me a rickety chair, snapping his fingers for coffee—"for the ladies, please."

Sinking into his plush red-velvet chair, Blagoje Simić smoothed his dark blond curls back over his slightly balding pate, straightened his gray jacket, and graciously explained why he had not yet been arrested by the 60,000-member NATO-led force that was overseeing a newly struck peace deal in Bosnia. He hadn't even been questioned by the American troops whose base was just down the road. How had he avoided detection? Simić shrugged.

"I'm not uncatchable. I think someone important still hasn't ordered the arrests to be done." And who would that be? "President Clinton," Simić said, his round baby face beaming. "Absolutely."

The fall of the UN safe area of Srebrenica in 1995—and the ensuing massacres of thousands of men and boys—pushed Bosnia along the road toward peace. On the ground, battlefield lines had finally shifted. With the capture of Srebrenica and then of another UN safe area, Žepa, by the Bosnian Serbs, Bosnia became more easily divisible along ethnic and political lines. At the same time, Croatia seized that moment to grab back the Krajina region from Serb control, sending thousands of its Serbs fleeing—the same people whose revolts had touched off the first war between Croatia and Yugoslavia in 1991. This time Serbian leader Slobodan Milošević did not lift a finger to help them. It was a signal that he was tired of the economic sanctions that had driven his country into poverty and was ready for peace.

Peace looked possible, and Western leaders, stung by humiliation and guilt, finally decided to take firm action against the Bosnian Serbs. President Clinton's top policy advisors, especially the National Security advisor, Anthony Lake, and the UN ambassador, Madeleine Albright, pushed for a far more aggressive policy in Bosnia. Hesitancy in Bosnia had cost the president dearly, and he would be up for reelection in 1996. When a Bosnian Serb shell exploded in Sarajevo in August 1995, killing thirty-eight and injuring eighty-five, NATO finally, at American urging, delivered punishing air strikes against the Bosnian Serbs, their first major military action in nearly fifty years. And a shrewd, ambitious American diplomat, Richard Holbrooke—a good match for Milošević—entered the peace process and kick-started it down the road.

By the end of 1995, both Rwanda and Bosnia were poised at much the same point. Each was making the transition from war to peace, moving from counting their injustices to confronting them, recognizing wrongs needed to be righted, amends made, punishment delivered. The war crimes tribunals in both countries were called upon to begin delivering justice, replacing collective guilt with individual responsibility. "Those accused of war crimes, crimes against humanity and genocide must be brought to justice," said President Clinton in 1995. "There must be peace for justice to prevail, but there must be justice when peace prevails."

But it soon became clear that peace and justice do not always go hand in hand, at least not right away.

THE THREE MEN most blamed for Bosnia's carnage—the tens of thousands dead and missing and the more than 2 million driven from their homes—were once again under one roof on November 1, 1995: Serbian strongman Slobodan Milošević, Croatian president Franjo Tudjman, and Bosian Muslim leader Alija Izetbegović. War had joined them for more than three years, but now they were gathered to talk peace at the optimistically named Hope Hotel and Conference Center at Wright Patterson Air Force Base in Dayton, Ohio.

Milošević, with his jutting chin, looked like a bulldog. Tudjman, with his paunch, like a South American dictator. Izetbegović, downcast and disheveled, like an absentminded professor. Enclosed on the 8,000-acre base in America's heartland, they would be tasked for the next twenty days with resolving the differences that had divided them for so long. On the table were not only the grievances between the warring parties in Bosnia, but also those between Croatia and Serbia. Recognizing the importance of the talks, the Hope Hotel had gone so far as to waive its no-smoking ban, as no self-respecting Balkan does business without a cigarette and a cup of coffee or a glass of slivovitz, or plum brandy, in his hand.

Noticeably absent from the gathering, however, was Bosnian Serb leader Radovan Karadžić, indicted for genocide by the Yugoslav Tribunal in July 1995. UN Secretary-General Boutros Boutros-Ghali later told chief prosecutor Richard Goldstone that the indictment was inadvisable given the absence of peace. But in the hectic pace of the summer's news, the indictment had gone all but unnoticed, and it worked to the negotiators' advantage. An international arrest warrant had been issued for Karadžić, making it impossible for him to leave the region; if he had been able to come to Dayton, Izetbegović might not have attended the talks. In Karadžić's absence, Milošević, who, after all, had masterminded the war, was to negotiate for the Bosnian Serbs.

Karadžić, however, cast a large shadow. His absence highlighted that being indicted by the Yugoslav Tribunal did have some drawbacks. No longer could he enjoy the comforts of swank hotels in Geneva, London, or Paris, as he had during other peace conferences. That fact was not lost on other Balkan leaders, and certainly not on the one man every Western negotiator hoped would clinch a peace deal: Milošević—the same man former U.S. secretary of state Lawrence Eagleburger had labeled an alleged war criminal back in 1992.

No matter how you looked at it, Dayton meant doing a deal with the devil. Only Milošević, the man who had started the war, could end it, and at issue were just what terms he would exact in return. The West was desperate for peace; the Clinton administration, in particular, didn't want the specter of a war-torn Balkans clouding its 1996 reelection campaign. Milošević, his country impoverished by economic sanctions, was also anxious to bargain. Striking a deal meant that sanctions could be lifted and that Milošević, ever the political chameleon, could metamorphose from war criminal to peacemaker. If Milošević delivered the stubborn Bosnian Serbs, the West might think twice about putting him behind bars.

And that left the Yugoslav Tribunal worried about just what kind of horse-trading was going on behind Dayton's closed doors. Judge Gabrielle Kirk McDonald even wondered if the peace negotiators would simply announce there was no more need for the war-crimes court. By the fall of 1995, the Yugoslav Tribunal was finally up and running, with a staff of more than 200, a fully functioning courtroom, a jail, and nine indictments accusing 43 people of all ethnic stripes. It had one defendant behind bars, Duško "Dule" Tadić.

But it had become clear that the tribunal's mere existence did not deter atrocities, as many had hoped. The massacres at Srebrenica, orchestrated by Karadžić and General Mladić, occurred *after* the first war crimes indictments against the two had been announced. "I was hoping for deterrence," Judge Antonio Cassese, the tribunal's president, later recalled, "but after Srebrenica I realized they didn't care at all about the tribunal. The only impact we could have was to bring them to trial after the fact."

But bringing defendants before the court had proved no easy task. With no police force of its own, the tribunal had to rely on Serbia, Croatia, and the warring factions within Bosnia to surrender those charged with war crimes. Yet Milošević, Tudjman, and Karadžić had been unwilling to recognize the court as legitimate. Moreover, the Bosnian Serb government had refused to act on the first warrants the tribunal had issued for indicted war criminals in their territory.

Now Milošević and Tudjman were pivotal players in a peace process. Any number of things could happen. In their rush for a settlement, negotiators could offer amnesty from prosecution for war crimes, as had been done in Haiti just the month before. Or the final deal could fail to ensure that war criminals would be arrested and brought to The Hague. Either of these options would undermine the tribunal's already limited effectiveness. What its judges and prosecutors wanted was a guarantee that the court would have more defendants than Tadić—and high-ranking ones—to put on trial.

"The tribunal was pretty much ignored," Goldstone later recalled. Tribunal staff were not included in the Dayton talks and could only hope that the Clinton administration officials would make their case for them. So on the eve of the Dayton talks, Judge Cassese fired off a letter to Madeleine Albright, asking that the surrender of indicted suspects be a condition of any peace accord. Then, addressing the UN Security Council as the peace talks got under way in Dayton, Cassese made it clear that he believed the future of the tribunal was at stake. "At present there appears to be a real prospect for a lasting peace in the region. Should that day arrive, is the tribunal going to become useless?" Cassese thundered. "The answer must be a clear 'no'.... It is universally acknowledged that peace without justice is no peace at all."

Cassese had history to point to. His remarks came just days after the fiftieth anniversary of the first verdicts pronounced by the Nuremberg military tribunal against the Nazis.

THROUGHOUT THE DAYS and nights at Dayton, negotiators twisted arms, threatened, and cajoled. They waved the stick of economic sanctions, dangled the carrot of the region's ultimate integration with Europe. Balkan leaders shouted, cried, and tore up maps. Some nights there were dinners of lobster flown in from Maine, but much of the time the diplomats chewed on meals served at Packy's All-Sports Bar on the base. The mood veered daily, like a capricious ocean breeze, from optimistic to pessimistic, to clinching a peace deal to rejecting it outright. The only leader the American delegation developed a rapport with was, ironically, Milošević.

One of the first rumors to leak out of the closed-door sessions was the most ominous: The Bosnian Serb delegation had demanded immunity for Karadžić and Mladić in exchange for peace. Diplomats then—and now—deny that immunity was ever an option. But tribunal chief prosecutor Goldstone was taking no chances. Fearful that Western leaders might grant Karadžić and Mladić clemency, tribunal investigators and prosecutors had rushed to prepare a second indictment against Karadžić and Mladić for the Srebrenica massacres. On November 16, 1995, Goldstone announced the new indictments and told reporters he'd quit if immunity was put on the negotiating table. He then lobbied Clinton administration officials to include terms for the surrender of the two men in the Dayton peace deal. "I can see absolutely no contradiction between peace negotiations and justice," he explained, emerging from talks with key administration officials, including Central Intelligence Agency director John Deutsch and Defense Secretary William Perry.

Meanwhile, the Bosnian delegation in Dayton also tried to convince American and European negotiators that any peace deal must guarantee that indicted war criminals would be turned over to The Hague. The Bosnians had quarreled repeatedly among themselves about many issues, but on war crimes they were stubbornly united. Among other proposals Izetbegović and his aides put forward was one that economic sanctions against Serbia should not be lifted until indicted war criminals had surrendered.

Yet American negotiators feared that including terms for the surrender or arrest of war criminals would derail the peace talks. The Clinton administration's chief priority was for the Bosnian war to end. It rebuffed every suggestion to include the prosecution of war crimes in the peace agreement, recalled the Bosnian delegation's legal advisor, Paul Williams. As agreements were slowly struck—on eastern Slavonia, an important issue to Tudjman and Milošević; on the political partition of future Bosnia; on the unification of Sarajevo—diplomats in the talks' final days focused instead on the divisive issue of territory. Around the clock, the Balkan leaders argued over mountains and roads, cemeteries and cities, trading real estate like little boys with baseball cards. In the final twenty-four hours of the peace talks, a deal was struck, disintegrated, and put back together again. Finally, after working throughout the night, an agreement was reached on November 21.

The hero of the hour was, of course, Slobodan Milošević, who made the final concessions on behalf of the Bosnian Serbs. When he shook hands with members of the American delegation, he reportedly had tears in his eyes. The Bosnian Serbs, by contrast, boycotted the initialing ceremony.

The Dayton agreement, all sixty-three pages of it, promised peace: 60,000 NATO troops would take up position in Bosnia to separate and disarm the warring armies. Bosnia would nominally remain one country; it would be divided into two self-governing statelets, with 51 percent of the territory becoming a Muslim-Croat Federation and 49 percent a Serb republic. Sarajevo would remain with the Muslim-Croat Federation. The country would have an elected collective presidency, a two-house parliament, a constitutional court, a central bank, and eventually a single currency. The peace agreement also promised a new civil society. All sides agreed to hold democratic elections in 1996; a UN international police force would keep order; and a newly created Office of the High Representative would oversee, among other things, that the estimated 2 million refugees and displaced persons could return home or be compensated.

But the Balkan peace plan, unfortunately, was built on the gains of the war's chilling central practice—ethnic cleansing. The Dayton accord recognized Bosnia's external, internationally recognized borders, but it divided the country in half along the ethnic gains made by the rebel Bosnian Serbs. While the Bosnian Serbs were to return some of the territory they had seized, with the peace accord they had gained what they had always wanted: the Republika Srpska, a swathe of contiguous territory almost entirely populated by Serbs. In parts of northern Bosnia given to the Serbs, for example, the Muslim population had declined by 90 percent by 1995, according to statistics issued by the UN High Commission for Refugees.

Some experts feared the Clinton administration's drive to get a peace deal before the president's re-election campaign had sent the wrong message to Slobodan Milošević. "One consequence of this plan is that it will officially sanction large-scale ethnic cleansing," said Marshall Freeman Harris, who quit the State Department in protest when the first Bush administration failed to halt ethnic cleansing. "This is a wonderful signal to Milošević to step up the disenfranchisement of non-Serbs elsewhere."

Dayton, while consolidating the consequences of ethnic cleansing, also failed to guarantee punishment for those who had perpetrated it. The peace agreement did not promise that war criminals would be arrested or be forced to surrender. But it did state they would be barred from military and government office. Negotiators, dubious that they would have had a deal had they included the issue of arrest, were relieved that the accord mentioned the International Criminal Tribunal for the former Yugoslavia several times, and that all those signing the Dayton peace plan—Milošević, Tudjman, and Izetbegović—pledged to cooperate fully with the tribunal to bring the accused to justice.

No one had any illusions that Dayton was a perfect—or even a workable—peace agreement. Even Richard Holbrooke, the American negotiator most responsible for the deal, said: "On paper we have peace. To make it work is our next and greatest challenge."

Indeed, while negotiators and Balkan leaders were wrangling in Dayton, I had been in Bosnia, assessing the will for peace. Bosnia was then a ravaged country, its cities smashed by artillery, its villages desolate. War had turned the clock back. People still rode horses rather than drove cars—there was no fuel and no money to buy it; homes had no windows, only sheets of plastic that flapped when the wind blew. Checkpoints, once manned by surly nationalist thugs, had been dismantled, but driving was still hazardous, given the frequency of land mines.

The concerns I heard in Bosnia's battle-scarred cities and towns were best summarized by Bosnian Muslim leader Alija Izetbegović. He had arrived in Dayton calling for "peace with justice." But the day that Dayton was announced, Izetbegović sighed and said: "This may not be a just peace, but it is more than just a continuation of war." A just peace. Peace, in the minds of most Bosnians, whether they were Serb, Croat, or Muslim, was inextricably linked with the need for justice. On that level, the Dayton peace deal could only be a disappointment.

All sides had unfinished agendas. The rebel Bosnian Serbs, though they gained the Republika Srpska, had not realized their dream of a "Greater Serbia." The Muslim-led Bosnian government held on to Sarajevo but had not recaptured the territory they believed was theirs. Even more frustrating, peace was struck after Bosnian Army commanders had made their first battlefield gains. They still hungered to retake the city of Banja Luka from the Serbs. And the Croats continued to smart at being allied with the Muslims in a federation. "There is not even a stone in this country that is not sad," Janja Šunjić, a Bosnian Croat, told me. "All three nations here are bitter. The war here will go on for as long as the river keeps flowing."

Nor could the Dayton peace agreement deliver "justice" in the sense of restoring the country to its prewar state, as many wished. It promised that refugees could return to their original homes and guaranteed that all Bosnians would have freedom of movement across the former front lines. But multiethnic Bosnia was gone. By keeping Bosnia as one country divided into two ethnic halves, the Dayton peace deal had gerrymandered it along ethnic lines. As I walked the streets of Sarajevo, the perceived injustices of Dayton rankled. "I cannot live with a divided country," Sahza Muslić, a mother of two, told me. "Not after so many victims; not after so many deaths."

It remained unclear how there could be "peace with justice," when the Dayton peace agreement did so little to guarantee that indicted war criminals would see their day in court. Western leaders had no means to force Milošević to turn over indicted war criminals, save for the threat of renewed sanctions. "At Dayton," recalled a senior UN official, "you empowered the thugs."

It was a glaring omission, and U.S. negotiator Holbrooke, by his own account, knew it. He feared Karadžić and Mladić would stand in the way of the Clinton administration's strictly choreographed aims in Bosnia: Establish peace, yet take no casualties; hold elections by the fall of 1996; start the country down the road to democracy; and ensure that NATO troops could leave by year's end. Within hours of Dayton being signed, Holbrooke told President Clinton that if both men remained at large, they would imperil Bosnia's peace. Clinton concurred.

Arrests became a question of political will, a three-way tug of war among the Pentagon, the White House, and its European allies. As days, weeks, and then months passed without any indicted war criminals being arrested, the worst fears of chief prosecutor Richard Goldstone were realized. Dayton did give Bosnia peace, but at the price of justice. "The arrest of war criminals," he would say some years later, "was clearly bargained away at Dayton."

EVEN THE MOST cynical, war-weary Bosnian, knee-deep in December's heavy snow, could not help but be awed by the sight of thousands of NATO troops pouring into their land. The NATO soldiers' uniforms were as crisp as their salutes, their tanks as gleaming as their polished boots, their military might as formidable as anything Bosnia had ever seen.

Across the Sava River separating Croatia from Bosnia came the Americans, having thrown up a pontoon bridge that spanned the river's dark waters from icy bank to icy bank. Black Hawk helicopters whirred overhead. American M1-A1 tanks, Humvees, trucks, and Bradley Fighting Vehicles rumbled across the bridge to the applause of those standing on the bank. The tanks made an impressive display, towering far above the average person's head. The American soldiers, with their camouflage uniforms and weaponry and helmets and flak jackets, were especially imposing. Ordered to wear their full "battle rattle," the Yanks looked a little like the Michelin Man crossed with Darth Vader. The Bosnians watching them were overjoyed. If NATO troops were here, then surely all the other things that Europe and America stood for—democracy, justice—would not be far behind.

U.S. troops had been assigned to patrol Hasan's old territory, from Vlasenica to Srebrenica. British troops were on the ground in Hamdo's old stomping grounds of Prijedor and Kozarac. Russian troops were placed near Bijeljina in the north, where Petko and Gordana, who had fled Konjic for that Serb-held city, watched their arrival with relief. The NATO troops were called IFOR—the International Implementation Force. Their task was to swiftly disarm and separate the warring factions; to mark and enforce the zones between the Bosnian Serb Republic and the Muslim-Croat Federation; to clear minefields; and to ensure that all people, whatever their ethnic origin, could travel around freely and safely. Given the savagery Bosnia had seen, it was a tall order, even for 60,000 troops.

But Srebrenica survivor Hasan Nuhanović, impressed by the American show of force, was sure the troops were up to the job. He now lived in Tuzla, the city in Bosnia that was the country's main oasis of multiethnicity and home to most of Srebrenica's refugees. That was where the American troops were headquartered. One day he watched with awe as American soldiers unscrewed the blue-and-white UN sign at a military base outside the city and let it drop unceremoniously into the muddy snow. A massive green sign emblazoned EAGLE BASE was swiftly hammered up in its place.

The UN was gone; NATO was in charge. Hasan likened the moment to the Soviets planting their flag on the Reichstag in Berlin at the end of World War II. The good guys had arrived; soon all the bad guys would be behind bars or on trial. He was not alone in his expectation that Bosnia's indicted war criminals would soon be arrested. Most Bosnians hoped it would be just a matter of months before soldiers made their first armed snatch. How could they not arrest war criminals? There were so many NATO soldiers in comparison to the number of gangsters on the loose. Plus, these troops and their commanders were everything the

UN peacekeepers before them had not been: heavily armed, savvy, well briefed.

As NATO troops fanned across Bosnia, setting up camps in the snow and mud, Karadžić and Mladić, normally so conspicuous, kept a low profile. When news broke that a political rival of Milošević's—Vojislav Šešelj, the head of the Serbian Radical Party—had volunteered to testify to the tribunal about Milošević's involvement in the Bosnian war, some hoped that arrests might soon follow.

As the weeks ticked by, however, NATO troops didn't even try to arrest suspected war criminals. In theory, under the terms of Dayton, Milošević was to have turned Mladić and Karadžić over or, at least, to have forced them to step down. But the Serb leader, reveling in the fact that sanctions against his country had been lifted in November 1995, did no such thing.

The only Bosnian Serb leaders who fell into the tribunal's net were two senior officers who took a wrong turn outside of Sarajevo and were captured by the Bosnian Army, General Djordje Djukić and Colonel Aleksa Krsmanović. Chief prosecutor Goldstone—aware he had only one suspect in The Hague and hopeful that Djukić and Krsmanović could incriminate their higher-ups—pressed for the men to be handed over even though they were not indicted. General Ratko Mladić, himself indicated for genocide, promptly threatened to break off relations with NATO troops and the Bosnian government. Justice and peace battled, as the tribunal and Western military leaders quarreled over the two officers' fate. Both men were sent to The Hague, and Djukić was subsequently indicted. But he was released and charges dropped when it was found he had terminal cancer. (Krsmanović was released without being charged.)

The tribunal's overeager grab for a war crimes suspect aroused suspicions among Bosnia's Serbs that the tribunal offered only a "victor's justice." It also strained relations between the tribunal, NATO, and the UN officials on the ground in Bosnia. "It was a fuck-up," recalled one UN official, "they had nothing on him [Krsmanović], but they arrested him anyway." Eventually an agreement was reached that restricted all sides in Bosnia from capturing someone unless he had been already identified as a suspected war criminal.

By February 1996, Karadžić and Mladić, emboldened, emerged from hiding and strutted around freely. NATO troops did nothing to halt them. Karadžić, in his telltale Mercedes with its tinted windows, sailed past NATO troops en route to the city of Banja Luka to appear on a TV program entitled *Ask the President*. A few days later he campaigned on the city streets, waltzing past NATO soldiers, Western officials, and a group of Bosnian Muslim ministers. "Could you believe it? He feels safe!" Hasan Muratović, a Bosnian official, exclaimed. In the Bosnian Serb–held village of Pale, Italian troops turned around after running into Karadžić's armed guard, who cocked their guns at them.

Karadžić, seeking to undermine the aims of the Dayton accord, then tested NATO's commitment further. Preaching nationalist bile on radio and TV, he incited the 50,000 Bosnian Serbs in the half of Sarajevo he had occupied at the beginning of the war to leave before it returned to Muslim-Croat control as the Dayton peace deal decreed. This destroyed any hopes that the city would reintegrate. Abandoning their homes in panic, stripping them of everything from furniture to kitchen sinks, the Bosnian Serbs even dug up their dead and fled to Bosnian Serb territory. Those who chose to remain faced Karadžić's henchmen: Either they were beaten or their homes were looted, trashed, and set afire. As flames danced in the rubble, as those Bosnian Serbs who wished to stay called for help, NATO troops did nothing. They were not, they said, a police force.

A few weeks later, General Mladić, looking tanned and rested, was spotted skiing on the slopes of the Jahorina resort in Pale. He attended a funeral in Belgrade, passing through at least one NATO checkpoint en route. Indicted for genocide, the general regularly drove by NATO soldiers in his well-known armored green Jeep bearing a massive red, white, and blue Bosnian Serb flag. Dayton was looking less and less like a peace deal and more and more like a farce.

"WHY HAVEN'T THEY arrested Karadžić and Mladić?" asked my father, the ex-Marine, when I called him from Sarajevo one day. He believed the United States had fought World War II as much for ideals as for territory, and he was stunned at this morally shameful behavior. How could our soldiers—our boys—let two indicted war criminals walk free! This wasn't the same military he'd fought with back at Guadalcanal. "Why don't they just go get the bastards?" he muttered, insisting that soldiers weren't cut from the same cloth as they had been in his day.

I relayed his question to General William Nash, the blunt-talking, cigar-chomping head of U.S. forces in Bosnia. A veteran of West Point and Vietnam, Nash was no stranger to combat. But he was surprisingly terse on the subject of arrests. Why hadn't he tracked down and arrested any indicted war criminals, I asked.

"The simple answer is, I've been told not to," Nash replied. "Our rules are, if we come across them in a tactical situation, we will seize them."

Admiral Leighton Smith, the commander-in-chief of Allied Forces in southern Europe, explained the orders this way: "Our job is not to go hunt them." Soldiers could arrest indicted war criminals only if they came across them in the "normal course of duties," he further explained, adding that even then "security concerns would dictate how they would react."

What Smith meant by "security concerns" were, to a large extent, American casualties. Memories of Vietnam still haunted the American military, leaving them reluctant to become too involved in Bosnia. The Clinton administration, remembering how eighteen U.S. soldiers died in the 1993 attempt to arrest Somali warlord Mohammed Farrah Adid, decided its troops would not arrest Bosnian war criminals. "The decision was made at the highest levels," said one senior military official then on the ground in Bosnia. "We were given a special order not to pursue [war criminals]."

Pentagon officials, in fact, had warned President Clinton that NATO troops would carry out an arrest mission *only* if the president directly ordered it himself—an unlikely scenario, given that it was his reelection year. "Our definition of success was that we would take no casualties," a senior Pentagon official told me. "We were risk-avoidant. There were a lot of things we could have done, but we elected not to do them because we were simply not interested in justice."

Greece and Russia, two of Serbia's staunchest allies, were also opposed to NATO troops arresting indicted war criminals. Whenever the issue was raised before the North Atlantic Council, NATO's political decision-making body, Greece, a NATO member, vehemently objected. At the same time, the Clinton administration—anxious that Russia not block its plan to have former Eastern bloc countries join NATO—tried to accommodate Russian concerns, given that Russian troops were part of the NATO mission in Bosnia. "The Russians basically warned us off taking any vigorous action [on arrests in Bosnia] because they were there," later recalled one high-ranking State Department diplomat.

In The Hague, prosecutors and judges fumed. They were powerless. The tribunal could not proceed unless it had defendants to try. Judge Cassese blasted NATO for its lack of resolve. "Moral leadership is required," he charged in a withering speech to European and American leaders meeting in Florence, Italy, in June 1996. "It is imperative to take rapid measures, draconian enough to ensure that a genuine and definitive peace reigns once again in the former Yugoslavia." Prosecutor Goldstone delivered his own salvo after returning empty-handed from Washington, where he had begged Clinton administration officials to arrest Karadžić and Mladić. "I can't believe that 60,000 troops would have difficulty" arresting Karadžić, he told *The New York Times.* Such an arrest, he said, "seems to me not only in the interest of justice but in the interest of peace."

But there were no arrests. Karadžić and Mladić became more and more brazen, and NATO's efforts to avoid "encountering them in the normal course of their duties" all the more comical. Nearly every time I drove across former front lines to Pale, where Karadžić was still king, I ran into him. Karadžić's schedule was predictable. He swooped out of his whitewashed villa in his Mercedes, wending his way to the Bosnian Serb Parliament, or to his office in the Famos factory, or, on Sundays, to services at the local Orthodox church.

It was impossible to be a NATO patrol stationed in Pale, in fact, and not "encounter" Karadžić. One Western official finally explained how Italian soldiers based in the city would turn their backs when he drove by. "Almost on order, they executed a very crisp and military about-face and faced Sarajevo," recalled Bill Stuebner, then with the Organization for Security and Economic Cooperation in Europe (OSCE).

By May, pressure was mounting for something—anything—to be done about Karadžić. In the White House, it was becoming clear that the Bosnian Serb leader threatened to sink the administration's plans for Bosnia, which centered on having NATO troops march out on schedule after the country's first postwar elections at the end of the year. Elections could not be held unless Karadžić stepped down; the Dayton accord, among other things, barred indicted war criminals from holding public office. In Serb-held Bosnia, Karadžić mocked Western leaders' discomfiture with his continued power, holding public rallies at which supporters would don Karadžić masks or wave posters with his picture and the slogan: "Don't Arrest Him!"

The Clinton administration finally recalled Holbrooke—who had left the administration for Wall Street—and dispatched him to Belgrade to talk to Milošević. It would take him several trips, and the threat of renewed sanctions, before Karadžić was persuaded to relinquish power in July. He handed over his presidency to an equally vociferous nationalist, albeit a matronly one: Biljana Plavšić, a sixty-six-year-old American-educated former biology professor.

But no mention was made of Karadžić's arrest. Holbrooke had tried to get the Serbs to agree that Karadžić should leave Bosnia, possibly for Montenegro, but they refused. Karadžić continued to drive around Pale, still very much the symbolic leader of the Bosnian Serbs.

In Washington, Clinton administration officials took the attitude that "once Karadžić was out of power, they didn't care" about his arrest, recalled Ivo Daalder, then on the staff of the National Security Council. But by late summer and early fall, some administration officials as well as NATO leaders, military officers in particular, were wondering if Karadžić, in fact, should have been arrested.

They knew General Mladić was untouchable; the Bosnian Serbs loved him. He also had ensured that NATO's time in Bosnia was a casualty-free one. But Karadžić was falling out of favor. Mladić's deputy, General Zdravko Tolimir, once told NATO commanders that the army would not react with force should Karadžić be arrested. "We made a serious mistake in not distinguishing between Karadžić and Mladić," a senior NATO official in Bosnia later recalled. "We could have pursued a policy of divide and conquer."

Karadžić, in fact, was terrified of being apprehended—so much so that at several points in 1996 he had a senior member of his staff discuss his surrender with tribunal staff. Talks had reached the point where NATO commanders even had a plan for his surrender to take place that summer. "They had a military operation set up—where to meet him, who would meet him," recalled a former senior NATO official in Bosnia. "But every time he came close [to surrendering] he'd back off, convinced NATO wasn't going to arrest him," said one former tribunal staffer who knew of the negotiations.

That Karadžić, an architect of genocide, whizzed past NATO troops in his Mercedes while Duško Tadić, a freelance local thug, stood in a courtroom before the Yugoslav Tribunal's judges only underscored questions about just how effective the court could ever be. NATO's reluctance to arrest Karadžić undermined not only the alliance's reputation but also that of the war crimes court, both in Bosnia and abroad. "The war crimes tribunal is a farce," scoffed one Bosnian Serb soldier. "All they've done is go after the little guys."

INDEED, AS THE big guys strutted free in Bosnia, the little guy's trial had started, the first international war crimes trial since Nuremberg and Tokyo. The presiding judge in the case was Gabrielle Kirk McDonald.

In every case before her, Judge McDonald always tried to take the measure of her defendants—to scrutinize them, observe them, get to know them at a distance. Duško Tadić was no different. By the end of June 1996, she'd been sitting across a courtroom from him for more than a month, trying to understand how this short, darkly handsome man with a Kirk Douglas–style cleft in his chin could be charged with thirty-one counts of murder, sodomy, and torture at Omarska and other camps. The acts he was accused of constituted crimes against humanity (crimes committed as part of a widespread or systematic attack against civilians); violations of the laws and customs of war (violent crimes against civilians); and grave breaches of the Geneva Conventions of 1949 (depriving civilian prisoners of their rights, among many other crimes). One accusation against him was that he had forced a prisoner to bite another's testicles off. Tadić's was also to have been the first rape trial before a war crimes tribunal, but the charge was dropped when the sole witness was too frightened to testify.

How could anyone commit such cruelties, and why? McDonald wondered. From time to time, Tadić's dark eyes would lock with hers across the courtroom, a kind of nonverbal exchange of greetings. But in them she found no answer. She looked to her own experiences instead for insight. The month before, she had told Court TV, which was covering the trial, that she found striking parallels between Bosnia's ethnic divisions and America's struggle with racism. "What has happened in the former Yugoslavia of course is nothing that we would ever expect to occur in the U.S. but is an example of what can happen when you don't resolve your ethnic divisiveness," she had said.

On the trial's opening day, May 7, 1996, swarms of journalists from around the world descended on the tribunal. The first war crimes trial since Nuremberg was newsworthy. There were so many television cameras and radio microphones and reporters waving notebooks that the overflow had to be accommodated in two red tents on the lawns just outside the five-story tribunal building.

Inside, those lucky enough to gain admittance crammed into a public gallery separated by a wall of bulletproof glass from the newly constructed $900,000 courtroom, a wash of white punctuated by brown desks and the bright blue of the judges' chairs and the UN flag. Cameras mounted around the room captured every moment of the proceedings. Computer screens flickered in front of each attorney, enabling him or her to read simultaneous transcripts, focus in on an exhibit, or look at the televised proceedings.

Court TV, expecting legal pyrotechnics to match the courtroom's newfangled wizardry, had billed the proceeding as "the trial of the century." They planned to give it gavel-to-gavel coverage. But journalists soon realized it was unbelievably dull.

It was boring partly because listening to the trial being simultaneously translated was like watching a movie where the soundtrack is slightly off. Reporters could see witnesses, clearly moved, on the stand, but as the translators housed in glass booths interpreted the testimony, their voices droned through the audience's headphones, stripped of all emotion and with a brief delay. The result was a complete emotional disconnect.

The trial was also tedious because prosecutors, uncertain as to just what the judges would want, began by laying the grounds for Tadić's prosecution under the laws with which he was charged, rather than sketching a dramatic picture of the murders and beatings he had allegedly committed. For Tadić to be found guilty of grave breaches of the Geneva Conventions—considered one of the more heinous of war crimes—prosecutors had to prove that Bosnia's war was an international armed conflict in which Serbia had also played a direct role.

And so they began with expert witnesses. Historians and others called to the witness stand told of the region's past in incredible detail, sending the audience to sleep with the recitation of events that seemed far removed from Tadić's crimes. After the opening arguments, in fact, it would be nearly two weeks until Tadić's name was even mentioned again. Judge McDonald, frustrated, wondered quietly when the prosecution would get to the point.

Intent on proving their case to the judges, the tribunal's prosecutors failed to realize the significance of proving their case to the world. The Tadić case was being beamed by satellite to the Muslim-Croat portion of Bosnia and about 30 percent of the Serb half, thanks to an outside grant. But after a few days, people snapped off their television sets in exasperation. They couldn't understand what was happening in the courtroom. In The Hague, journalists stopped covering the trial. "This prosecution seems almost to be acting in disregard of its relationship to the cameras and the print media," observed a baffled Raymond Brown of Court TV. "Here's the one situation in which the world—especially victims and others to whom we hope this will have a deterrent value—need to know what is going on, and they [the prosecution] almost seem to be going in the opposite direction, and deliberately not doing this in a way that might dramatize... what can be a rather murky kind of proceeding."

In the end, however, what made the case so unsatisfying was that Tadić was a little fish in the scheme of Bosnia's horrors. He was no architect of mass murder, no evil genius who dreamed up ethnic cleansing. While his case was hyped as that of "the Butcher of Omarska," there were many others with more authority at the camp who were equally as cruel. It was clear that he was simply the only defendant the tribunal had to prosecute.

In fact, Tadić's defense lawyers argued his trial was not only a case of mistaken identity, but also the desperate act of a court anxious for a trial. Tadić, they said, was just a traffic cop, not a thug responsible for beatings at Omarska, a place he claimed never to have been. "The thirst for revenge must not be satisfied at the well of polluted justice," argued one of his attorneys, Michaïl Wladimiroff, an experienced and eloquent Dutch lawyer.

To rebut Tadić's defense attorney's argument that he had never been at Omarska, prosecutors needed people who could identify Tadić. They called some fifty-six eyewitnesses to place him at the scenes of beatings and murders.

And that is how Hamdo Kahrimanović came to be called to testify in front of the International War Crimes Tribunal for the former Yugoslavia.

Of all the testimony Judge McDonald would hear in the Tadić case, it would be Hamdo's that would haunt her the most.

IT WAS JUNE 25, 1996. Hamdo was seated at the witness stand in the courtroom at The Hague. His white hair was carefully combed, his face was plump; he'd regained the weight he'd lost in the Omarska camp. He had donned a beige jacket and slacks for the occasion, but no tie. He spoke with confidence—even with a dash of pomposity—leaning over the wooden desk toward the microphone. He, after all, had been the principal of Bosnia's largest elementary school, the Rade Kondić school of Kozarac.

He chose his words carefully, trying to answer the questions of Australian prosecutor Grant Niemann precisely.

Did he know Tadić? Yes, he knew Dule Tadić—they lived around the corner from each other most of their lives, and "therefore, I knew him a very, very long time," Hamdo added a little nervously.

He had been called to testify for this reason. He had not been beaten by Tadić at Omarska, nor had he witnessed any of the crimes Tadić was alleged to have committed. Plenty of gruesome reports had already been given on the stand, like that of Uzier Bešić, who described seeing Tadić jump up and down on prisoners stretched on the floor, injuring them to the point where one begged, "Please kill me." Sulejman Bešić, detailing the horrors at the Trnopolje camp where Tadić had also been spotted, made Judge McDonald recoil when he described a fellow inmate's wounds filled with maggots.

No, Hamdo had been called because he had known Dule all his life. He could identify the man beyond a shadow of a doubt.

Hamdo was not frightened to testify, but he also wasn't eager to do it. Some of the witnesses, as they left the stand, had told him they had found the experience cathartic. They felt years drop off their shoulders when they finally confronted Tadić in a courtroom and told of his crimes. Hamdo felt differently; he saw testifying as his duty. It wouldn't answer his needs for justice; only returning to Kozarac would. As he sat there, watching the judges in their black robes listening intently through their headsets, Hamdo was swept with a wave of nostalgia for Kozarac as it had been before the war. The cafés . . . the mountains . . . his family together . . . He longed to go home.

The prosecutor interrupted his reverie.

"Did you know his father?"

"I know him very well," answered Hamdo. "He was a man of prestige. He was the bearer of the 1941 Partisan badge. We are neighbors. We were very close. We must know each other. We had to see each other almost every day."

He went on, describing Tadić's growing involvement in politics, the outbreak of the war in Kozarac, and the Omarska camp. Had he seen Tadić at Omarska? Yes, Hamdo remembered, he'd seen Tadić swaggering around Omarska; he'd seen him there twice.

"Did you observe how he was dressed?" asked Prosecutor Niemann, who had once investigated Nazi war criminals.

"Camouflage, standard clothes," said Hamdo.

Although Hamdo provided few new revelations about Tadić, Judge McDonald was riveted by his testimony. The reason why she would never forget what he had to say, however, had nothing to do with Tadić at all. It was due to the fact that Hamdo had been the principal of Bosnia's largest elementary school—*its largest multiethnic school.* The school had been integrated. It had graduated class after class of students, who had added their sums, played catch, elbowed their way through the lunch line. Its teachers, like Hamdo, had preached the lesson of brotherhood and unity. And still ethnic strife had erupted in Kozarac?

What did this mean for the United States? McDonald wondered. What did it mean for the future of African Americans and white Americans and Chinese Americans and Latino Americans in the multiethnic United States? What did it mean about the success of the Civil Rights Act, or for the work she had done for the National Association for the Advancement of Colored People (NAACP), or for that time she had defeated the Ku Klux Klan? Did it mean Yugoslavia's ethnic strife and America's racial problems had even more in common than she had first thought?

Was harmonious multiethnicity impossible?

She wanted to ask Hamdo: Are you telling me that despite integration, people killed each other? She wanted to say: I'm black, and I'm a civil rights lawyer and I believe we can curb discrimination, that people can live together. Are you telling me we can't?

Why did this happen in Kozarac?

And so she asked him why.

"I gather that you have taught Muslims and Serbs in the school where you were a schoolteacher and then a principal. Is that correct?" asked McDonald, peering at Hamdo through her glasses.

"Absolutely." Hamdo explained at some length his climb up the educational career ladder in Kozarac.

"My question really related to your having taught Muslims and Serb children. I gather Serb children go to school with Muslim children?"

"Absolutely."

"You testified that you have persons of other religion in your family, that you lived in a neighborhood where there were Serbs. Is that correct? Is all of this correct?"

"My next-door neighbor was a Serb, a very good man."

"So I guess my question—"

Hamdo interrupted her. "He died in my wife's hands."

"—is perhaps not a fair question. I do not know that you could give a complete answer, but perhaps you can help me to understand since I am not from that area. How could you explain some of the atrocities that we have heard that have been committed. . . . Given your background, your experience, knowing that Serbs and Muslims lived together, went to school together, intermarried, how did that happen?"

Hamdo paused. "It is difficult to answer, this question," he replied. "I am also at a loss. I had the key to my next-door neighbor's [house] who was a Serb and he had my key. That is how we looked after each other. We visited each other for holidays. My best man at my wedding was a Serb. We were friends and he was the same one who threatened us. It is inexplicable what happened to those people. It was some kind of madness. I mean, one did not know whom to trust any more and I do not have a word of explanation for that."

"Thank you very much for coming," replied McDonald, and after checking with her fellow judges to see if there were additional questions, she dismissed Hamdo from the stand.

As he walked away from the courtroom, Hamdo wished he had talked about how the men responsible for that "madness"—such as Prijedor police chief Simo Drljača and the camp commander of Omarska, Željko Mejakić—were still in charge in Kozarac. Until they were arrested and behind bars, Hamdo doubted he could ever return home.

SOME MONTHS LATER, in the fall of 1996, I picked up the telephone and called the police station in the town of Omarska, in Bosnia's Serbian half.

"Željko?" said the receptionist. "He's not here at the moment, but he will definitely be here later."

I was looking for Željko Mejakić—indicted for crimes at the Omarska concentration camp but still working as the chief of police.

It wasn't just Karadžić and Mladić who roamed free across Bosnia in 1996. NATO's reluctance to let its troops arrest war criminals meant that dozens of those indicted by the tribunal remained at large and in positions of power, ruling their communities as firmly in peace as they did in war—and in utter violation of the Dayton peace accord.

In Omarska, a town so small that almost every house had some kind of view of the former concentration camp, residents denied that the notorious facility had ever existed. "I have no idea what you are talking about," snapped one housewife that autumn, as she hung her faded sheets on a laundry line that overlooked the camp. Mejakić clearly had Omarska under his thumb. And he was not the only one: Three others indicted for crimes at Omarska, I found out, were still police officers in the nearby city of Prijedor, also in violation of the Dayton peace accord.

As 1996 unfolded, NATO's hands-off policy toward war criminals was proving not only morally indefensible but also strategically shortsighted. Yes, the fighting had stopped and Bosnia's elections took place on schedule. Yes, there were no NATO combat-related deaths. But there was no *enduring* peace. As long as alleged war criminals continued to wield power—as hard-line mayors, police chiefs, security officers, and local political leaders—they undermined the very peace Dayton tried to establish and suppressed the truth about the worst war crimes Europe had witnessed in half a century.

In many communities, nationalists blew up homes that had been untouched throughout the war to prevent refugees from returning. They "ethnically cleansed" remaining Muslims, forcing them from their homes, confiscating their property, and then selling it for a high price on the black market. They threatened opposition politicians who preached unity or forgiveness. "The only thing that has changed since Dayton is that there is no shooting," one Muslim, living as a minority among Serbs in the city of Prijedor, told me. "We continue to live in fear."

Some indicted war criminals, including Karadžić, no longer focused on "ethnic cleansing" but trafficking in stolen cars, cigarettes, liquor, gas, diesel fuel, prostitution, drugs, and counterfeit money, just as they had during the war. Scratch the surface of a former war criminal and you'd find a successful racketeer. So brazen were they—and so successful at undermining efforts to root out corruption and restore Bosnia's economy—that both the Federal Bureau of Investigation and the Drug Enforcement Administration dispatched agents to Bosnia. "The old warlords have simply shifted their activities," said Colonel Pieter Lambrechste, of the European Union police, which aided Bosnian law enforcement, "and in this postwar period, crime is flourishing." Others indicted for war crimes, such as Omarska's Željko Mejakić, tightened their hold on their communities, intimidating political opponents, destroying evidence.

As did Simo Drljača. Technically, Drljača had not yet been indicted, although his name had surfaced so many times during the ongoing Tadić trial that it was hard to believe prosecutors weren't hard at work assembling charges against him. Drljača was typical of how those who thrived during the war were busy undermining the peace. Racketeering, extortion, blocking refugees from returning as Dayton required—Drljača flourished at them all. I could understand why people like Hamdo did not want to return home so long as he remained in power. "He is god around here," one Western official in Prijedor told me in the autumn of 1996.

Drljača was all the more flagrant in his abuse of power because he hadn't been indicted, and so he was an open book when it came to understanding how others, already indicted, operated. His center of operations was his restaurant in downtown Prijedor, the Aeroklub, where he spent his time, hatching his latest scheme like a spider waiting for a passing fly. So successful had he been at cleaning the city of Bosnian Muslims that Drljača had turned his attention to his fellow Bosnian Serbs. As police chief, he forced restaurants and businesses to pay him protection money, earning himself the moniker "Mr. Ten Percent." He demanded cash from fellow Serbs who didn't wholeheartedly embrace the nationalist line. For the right price, Drljača would give people new apartments: He controlled both the local Property Commission and the Commission on Displaced Persons and Refugees, which gave him a monopoly on the area's housing.

Skillful at extortion, Drljača also excelled at undermining Western plans to reform Bosnia. If businesses accepted foreign aid for reconstruction, he threatened to burn them down so that his company would receive the funding instead. He rounded up Bosnian Serbs foolish enough to talk to NATO peacekeepers and took them to the police station for more of his "informative talks." He drummed up mobs to threaten groups of Bosnian Muslims attempting to visit their homes. Everyone suspected that it was Drljača's doing in 1996 when ninety intact, unoccupied Bosnian Muslim homes were suddenly blown up.

Refusing to recognize the tribunal, Drljača went so far as to threaten witnesses who had been summoned to The Hague by Tadić's defense team to establish his alibi. Defense attorneys finally resorted to using a video link, so that witness testimony could be beamed in from Bosnia to the tribunal. "I don't respect that court," Drljača informed me, after I spotted him holding court with his cronies in the Aeroklub. "If any trial happens to me, it will happen here."

At first, British NATO troops stationed in the area accommodated Drljača, ensuring that one of his companies received a foreign contract at their behest just to guarantee good relations. But Drljača, the man who had terrorized Prijedor, Kozarac, and Omarska, repeatedly annoyed NATO officers and their troops. Finally, when soldiers stopped him in the summer of 1996 and tried to relieve him of his submachine gun, he fired it off, instead. NATO officials and Bosnia's civilian authorities called for his dismissal, but the Bosnian Serb government simply promoted him to the Ministry of the Interior instead.

And did he have greater respect for NATO troops, now that they'd called for his dismissal? I asked him.

"Oh, from now on, I am going to be a good boy," he told me sarcastically. "They are watching my every move."

When I questioned him about the prospect that he might be indicted and arrested for war crimes, Drljača turned belligerent. "These charges are unjustified," he shouted. "But it won't affect my personal life. I have protection. Any time of day or night, I am ready to resist."

Within a year his boastful words would prove more prophetic than either of us could have imagined.

8

SEARCHING FOR THE TRUTH

This: were we led all that way for Birth or Death?

—T. S. Eliot, "Journey of the Magi"

It was on a bitterly cold day in January of 1996—a day when the snow lay so white and thick across the mountains of eastern Bosnia that it erased all signs of war—that Hasan Nuhanović, survivor of Srebrenica, finally got the news he had longed to hear.

"I know what happened to your mother," the Bosnian Serb told him.

Hasan had been searching for Nasiha, Ibro, and Muhamed for five months—ever since Dutch UN soldiers had ordered them out of the compound in Potočari and into the arms of Bosnian Serb troops. In the days immediately following Srebrenica's capture, Hasan had commandeered the Dutch battalion's satellite telephone and frantically called around, hoping his family had made it to safety. Then, after arriving in Zagreb, Croatia's capital, with the evacuated Dutch battalion, Hasan had continued his search, buttonholing UN officials about the fate of the refugees. Finally he had moved to Tuzla, where most of the Srebrenica survivors sought refuge. Desperate with worry, burdened with grief, Hasan had spent day after wearying day talking to anyone who might have information. Were they dead? Alive? Captured? Killed?

But there was not a trace of Nasiha, Ibro, or Muhamed.

Hasan found he could not stop waking up in the middle of the night, wanting answers about the larger play of events as desperately as information about his missing family. Why had the UN and NATO let Srebrenica be captured? Why hadn't the Dutch battalion done more on behalf of the refugees? If massacres had taken place, which Bosnian Serb commander was responsible? If men and boys had been executed—Ibro and Muhamed—then where was Nasiha?

Hasan was not alone in being pursued by such thoughts. Some ghosts never let you go. In postwar Bosnia there were as many ghosts—of guilt, of betrayal, of wrongdoing—stirred by the war's end as people who had survived it. Many Bosnians set about putting those ghosts to rest by trying to find the truth: about where their loved one's body lay, about why their neighbors and best friends turned on them, about why they themselves had picked up a gun and killed.

Even I found myself obsessed with tracking down and confronting those responsible for the Srebrenica massacres. My own ghosts called out for reckoning. They had been stirred to wakefulness by Hasan's story, which he told me when we first met in the fall of 1995 in Tuzla. Hasan blamed himself for his family's disappearance, if not their deaths; he could not forgive himself for having believed the UN would protect Muhamed once he was on the Potočari base. I also blamed myself for a family member's death—that of my older brother, Dan. As Hasan and I sat in a drafty hotel restaurant in Tuzla, he talked about the weight of his guilt. I understood immediately.

I was not close to Dan. He was eight years older, emotionally difficult, and he had been absent from the family for much of my childhood. We became reacquainted when I was in college. One day, after he had badgered me repeatedly with urgent phone calls over nothing at all, I admonished him and then hung up the telephone. Tough love, I decided, was the best approach. A few days later he killed himself, throwing himself in front of a train as it passed through New Haven, Connecticut. I had been the last member of the family to talk to Dan, and mine was the only telephone number the police found on his body. They called me and I told my parents. Over the decades since, I had tried to decipher what role I'd played in his suicide, to understand what caused him to take his life, but a journey into a psyche, whether your own or someone's else's, is a baffling thing. My answers were incomplete.

In Bosnia, however, I could do for others what I had not been able to do for myself. I could find at least some of the answers for others. As a Western journalist, I had access to information about the Bosnian Serbs that no Bosnian, particularly no Bosnian Muslim like Hasan, could gain. And so, when my editor suggested I try to identify and track down those responsible for Srebrenica's massacres, it was an assignment I knew I had to take.

THE UN HAD taken Hasan's family away—or at least the bumbling decisions made by UN and NATO commanders had done so—but they had given him a job, and a means to find his family in return. His longtime girlfriend, Mirza, had joined him in Tuzla. There Hasan was an interpreter for the UN's International Police Task Force (IPTF), and the only interpreter willing to travel to the Serb-held side of Bosnia, just a half hour's drive away. Even though there was peace, most Bosnian Muslims were frightened to cross the former front lines. But Hasan happily volunteered for such trips. He hoped that by slipping the odd question about his family into conversations, he might learn something.

And that is how Hasan, a Bosnian Muslim, found himself in the hardline, Bosnian Serb–held city of Zvornik, just a little over a month after peace had been signed. Hasan may have been the first Muslim to return to the city since it was ethnically cleansed in 1992.

Zvornik was a logical place to start his search. The bustling city perched on the Drina River by the Serbian border had always been a major center for commerce, legal and illegal, in eastern Bosnia. Everything could be found in Zvornik for the right price. It had been Nasiha's hometown as well; her parents, Hasan's grandparents, had been ethnically cleansed from the city in 1992. The stark reminder that Muslims had once lived in the area was a handful of mosques, located just across the Drina River in neighboring Serbia.

By 1996 Zvornik was a city of shadows and darkness, of war profiteers and war criminals. It was the perfect beachhead for the UN police force's efforts in the area, so Hasan and his bosses were on a house-hunting mission on that January day when he stumbled across the first clue to his mother's fate.

Raw winds whipped off the gray-hued Drina River. The city lay buried in more than a foot of snow. Hasan suggested retreating to a restaurant to conduct their search. Indeed, no sooner had he and the IPTF officers sat down at a table than the red-faced, beefy owner came bustling over, anxious to make them welcome, eager to have them spend money. He could tell at a glance they weren't locals: They had to be Europeans—possibly Scandinavians—with their blond hair, jutting chins, and well-pressed uniforms. Where there were Westerners in postwar Bosnia, he knew, there would be dollars.

"Here's *rakija*—on the house, of course!" The restaurant owner beamed as he swooped down and offered them free glasses of the local brandy.

"Do you know of an empty house that these men could rent?" Hasan asked. "They are looking for an office. Something comfortable, but something reasonable."

The proprietor all but rubbed his hands with glee. He plunked himself down at the table. His restaurant was Zvornik's answer to Rick's Café in *Casablanca:* The powerful either supped here or were among those who kept him stocked with food and booze. He knew everyone in Zvornik, whether they were in Karadžić's hard-line Serb SDS party or in the local military command. Yes, he could help them.

"Another round of *rakija!*" he ordered his staff. The UN police officers smiled happily. In fact, the proprietor knew of just the right place: a house that had once belonged to a well-to-do Muslim heart surgeon. After several rounds of toasts, the UN police officers arranged to meet him there the next day.

Business done, Hasan slowly worked the conversation back around to Zvornik. Why, he had relatives from Zvornik. Maybe the proprietor had heard of them....

"Did you know Ibro Nuhanović? He was my father," Hasan said.

The restaurant owner's eyes widened. This young man was a Bosnian Muslim! He had suspected as much. But a member of the Nuhanović family! Of course he knew Ibro; everyone in eastern Bosnia knew him, given his job as the head of the region's biggest lumber concern. And he remembered Nasiha too, and her father, who had been one of the best-liked cobblers in the city. Hasan gave him a brief synopsis of his family's story.

"I am trying to find out what happened to them after Srebrenica."

The smile vanished from the restaurant owner's face. He looked down at the table. "I'll see you at the house tomorrow," he said, abruptly making his excuses and getting up from the table. Hasan, watching the man's hasty retreat, hoped he would actually show up.

The next day, the house proved just what Hasan's bosses wanted: a large multistory building, one of the biggest in Zvornik, with a wide front garden. As the UN police officers viewed its interior, the restaurant owner motioned Hasan outside, behind the house. They stood near each other, their boots sunk into the snowdrifts. The branches of a nearby tree groaned in the wind.

Hasan waited.

"I know what happened to your mother," the restaurant owner whispered, leaning close to Hasan, his breath forming a cloud in the freezing air with each word. "*Ona je umrla*. She has died."

A yell suddenly came from one of the IPTF officers, standing just outside the entrance. "Hasan!" he said. "What are you doing? Come over here, we need you." The conversation ended just seconds after it had begun.

Hasan wanted to grab the restaurant owner by his thick winter coat and shake the details of Nasiha's death out of him. But his bosses were in a hurry to retreat to the warm confines of Zvornik's best hotel, the Vidikovac, to clinch the deal. There, in the vast dining room overlooking the Drina River, Hasan remained outwardly composed while inwardly he was in turmoil. He smiled, he was gracious; he ably translated the niceties tossed back and forth between the IPTF officers and the local Serbs. One of them was a man he vaguely recognized, the head of the Zvornik police, Dragomir Vasić. Hasan had spotted his photograph on a calendar, snapped posing next to Zvornik's hometown hero, Milan "Legenda" Jović, the head of a Bosnian Serb army unit, the Drina Wolves.

Even as Hasan listened, he studied the Bosnian Serb men clustered around the dinner table. He watched them as they picked up their knives and forks, the simple act of deboning a fish taking on a sinister quality. *Did they murder my mother?* he wondered as he translated compliments about the wine. *Do they know who killed her?*

All the way back to Tuzla in the car, he was forced to keep up the same pretense. As he answered the IPTF officers' questions, a phrase kept swimming in Hasan's head: *ona je umrla*, she has died. It beat a rythym in his mind, as the car wheels thumped over the ruts in the road. The IPTF officers chatted about the beauty of a snowbound Bosnia; Hasan could think only of the skeletons the snow undoubtedly concealed.

Not until he reached his home in Tuzla could Hasan become the grief-stricken son. He stumbled into his apartment and into Mirza's arms. Only when he saw her—the last remnant of his past—could Hasan react as he had wanted to, when he had heard the words that had crystallized his mother's disappearance into her death. The perfectly dedicated translator broke down and cried.

OF COURSE, HASAN didn't know if the information was true. The news about Nasiha was tantalizingly oblique, and there had been no opportunity to ask questions. The restaurant owner had chosen his words in Bosnian carefully; the phrasing of his sentence made it clear that Nasiha either had been murdered or had killed herself. Hasan replayed the brief conversation in his head over and over again, puzzling over its meaning. He was like an archaeologist discovering only a few lines of his Rosetta Stone; he still lacked the key to unlock the past.

Hasan spent days wondering what to do next. A journey to find your family is also a journey into yourself, into the corridors of your memory and your emotions. Hasan traveled down them in his mind. Who else could give him information? Where should he go now? What if his UN police bosses didn't give him another chance to return to Zvornik and he could never talk to the restaurant owner again? It was impossible to call the man: Phone lines remained cut between the two ethnically divided halves of Bosnia, the Muslim-Croat Federation and the Republika Srpska. It was equally impossible to go on his own. Even if public transportation had been restored, or if he had a car, it just wasn't safe. At least if Hasan was accompanied by UN police officers, he had a better chance of not being killed.

Hasan took to pacing the corridors of the UN offices out by the Tuzla airfield late at night, trying to walk out his fears and worries. The UN staff came to learn his story, which particularly moved one civil affairs officer, an Israeli woman named Ilana Bet-El. She had grown up in the shadow of the Holocaust, surrounded by Jewish survivors still searching for the truth about their families, fifty years after the end of World War II. She understood the significance of what Hasan was trying to do. So when the opportunity came in April for her to travel to eastern Bosnia, she asked Hasan to accompany her as a translator.

She guessed, correctly, that a trip to Srebrenica and to Vlasenica, his hometown, would be helpful to him.

They set out on a beautiful day. The sky was full of fluffy white clouds and there were green buds on the trees. But as Bet-El sped eastward into Serb-held Bosnia in her regulation white Jeep with UN written on it in bold, black letters, she was nervous. Peace had held in Bosnia for nearly six months, but Europeans or Americans, much less UN staff, remained persona non grata in the Serb half of the country, viewed as accomplices in the worldwide plot against the Bosnian Serbs. That was the result of years of Karadžić's skillful propaganda.

Yet the day's meetings with various Bosnian Serb officials passed smoothly. Still, as their UN Jeep approached Srebrenica that afternoon, they fell silent. Srebrenica had been off limits since it had been captured by the Bosnian Serbs six months earlier. Returning, Hasan had the eerie sense he was watching his life as if it were a movie played in reverse. There was the Potočari base, still boasting its blue-and-white Dutchbat sign; then the yellow bridge at the entrance to Srebrenica; and finally the town itself. For a moment he could almost trick himself into thinking that time had wound itself backward too, that it was 1994, that Srebrenica was still a UN safe haven, and that around the corner would be Muhamed, walking down the street.

But in 1996 the Bosnian Serbs ran Srebrenica. The town's mosque, dynamited by entering troops, lay in heaps in the center of the main road. Piles of junk—books, furniture, crockery—were heaped in the streets, much of it heaved out of apartment windows by the rampaging Bosnian Serb army the summer before. Stray dogs wandered amid the decomposing piles of garbage.

A palapable sense of misery hung over the scene. Scores of Bosnian Serbs, convinced to flee Sarajevo by Karadžić, had been forced to take up residence in the filthy town, and it was almost as if they were being punished for the city's past sins. There was still no electricity or running water; no trees to chop down for fuel. The homes, where dozens of families had squeezed while Srebrenica was under siege, were full of fleas.

"We call it a cursed city, the town of spirits," one newly returned resident told me when I went to Srebrenica just a day or two before Hasan's own visit. "Nobody wanted to come back here." In a meeting, the local mayor rattled off a long list of complaints to Bet-El, and it was late in the day when he finished. There was just time to quickly visit the house where Hasan and his family had stayed. Hasan was hoping at least to retrieve some of the family photographs; he had only one or two snapshots of his brother and his parents to remember them by. As the UN Jeep pulled up to the house, however, he was taken aback to see three men lounging on the balcony.

For a moment, it was as if he were seeing his brother and father and himself sitting there, in their customary seats. Instead, it was three Bosnian Serbs, two in military uniform.

"Hey, do you have a cigarette?" asked one as Bet-El and Hasan walked up. Hasan shook his head; all he could think about was how cigarettes were as valuable as gold when he had lived here.

"Did the . . . former inhabitants of the house leave anything behind, like pictures?" Bet-El asked. Hasan translated.

"No, the place was completely ransacked," one of the soldiers replied. Hasan felt another small hope die inside him. He returned, disconsolate, to the Jeep.

Hasan was standing, his hand poised on the door handle, when the noise of a car chugging down the street caught his attention. He turned his head. It was a yellow BMW, and the man behind the wheel looked familiar. The car slowed. Hasan peered at it more closely. As the driver returned his gaze, there was a flash of recognition between the two men.

Hasan knew that face; it was Colonel Vukota Vuković, the head of the Bosnian Serb Skelani Brigade, whose forces had surrounded Srebrenica and whom Hasan had dubbed "the Fox." Hasan had frequently translated for him at meetings with the UN in Srebrenica. For a commander besieging Srebrenica, Vuković had always been pleasant enough.

Vuković jammed on the brakes. The two men stared at other for several seconds in utter astonishment, before Hasan walked over to Vuković's car and bent down to the open window. And then the composure he had maintained all afternoon evaporated.

"Colonel Vuković," he cried, pulling on the car door as if to open it. "Where is my family?"

Vuković shook his head. "I wasn't in Srebrenica when it fell," he said, locking the car door firmly. "I took care of myself."

"Can I have your phone number?" Hasan pressed.

"I have no phone number," Vuković replied. Pressing his foot down on the accelerator, he gunned the car, leaving only a swirl of dust and unanswered questions behind him.

IT WAS COLONEL Vuković's boss, the limping, bitter General Radislav Krstić, whom I was searching for even as Hasan made his trip to Srebrenica. My translator, Aleksandra Seratlić—Alex—and I had set out in early March to re-create the chain of command at Srebrenica and determine just who had ordered the execution.

At the time, I did not think it an unrealistic assignment. The war was over. More than half a year had passed since Srebrenica. Surely guilt would weigh heavily on some people's souls, making them anxious to talk. After all, three months earlier a member of a Srebrenica execution squad, Dražen Erdemović, had tried to turn himself in to a disinterested U.S. Embassy in Belgrade and then ended up confessing his crimes to the French newspaper *Le Figaro*. He had since been sent to The Hague. Others, I thought, would follow.

And Alex, a vivacious, dark-haired Montenegrin, was equipped not only with charm, good humor, and moral outrage but also with a long list of contacts she had acquired throughout the war. She also had a way of turning Serb men to putty. I felt confident that in a week or two we would have our story.

Instead, it took us nearly two months. We had underestimated the terror and repression in the Serb half of eastern Bosnia. Day after day we drove our rented white Opel up and down the route of the Srebrenica massacres, seeking information: in Vlasenica; in Srebrenica itself; in Bijeljina, the city in the north near the Serbian border where Petko lived. No one would talk—not the farmers, not the barkeepers, not the elderly; not the young. All shook their heads and denied any knowledge that anything had ever even happened in Srebrenica. Most days I never even opened my notebook.

Our experiences made for interesting talk around the dinner table, but not much else. We had, for example, found a new mass grave on Mount Kamenica and brought the tribunal's war crimes investigators there. We had spent the night on the mountain with an elderly Bosnian Serb shepherd and his wife—listening to the rats rustle in their kitchen—after I had driven the Opel into a ditch. (Thankfully, the *Boston Globe* accountants did not question the charge I put down for "oxen" on my expense account—the only available means of towing.) I had learned how to take notes under the table while drinking in bars with small-town Bosnian Serb thugs, all of whom boasted that they should really be in The Hague but refused to provide any specifics.

I had even acted as postwar mail carrier, bringing letters from Bosnian Muslims to their old friends—those they remembered as "good Serbs"—asking for their assistance. But it was to no avail. Upon receiving a letter from one of his best Muslim friends before the war, requesting his assistance, one Serb tore it into ever-smaller pieces that fluttered to the ground. "I cannot help you," he said.

Most interviews were like the one I had with a bus driver, Relja Ikonić. I knew that bus drivers from near Srebrenica had been forced to drive the refugees to their execution sites; some, in fact, had been made to take part in the executions. That civilians were intimidated into killing was typical of the Bosnian war. People often thought the war's atrocities reflected people's animosities. I found quite the opposite. Atrocities occurred because people had been close, and it was the only way to break those bonds forever. The first wave of heinous crimes was always committed by outsiders. Serbian paramilitary outsiders, with no ties to the community, would come in and kill. Yet as they did so, they implicated local Serbs or forced then to join in. And murder begat murder begat murder.

Ikonić, I suspected, had been forced, one way or another, to take part. He visibly paled when I showed up at his doorstep and uttered the word "Srebrenica." As the sweat poured down his face, he twisted his hands—his demeanor indicating he had a secret gnawing at his soul—and denied all.

"I didn't see anything," he said with a moan as his wife, standing next to him, threw her apron over her face, crying: "We are ruined! We are ruined!"

As long as Serb leader Radovan Karadžić and his top general, Ratko Mladić, remained in power, few dared step forward with the truth. They and their loyal henchmen ruled Bosnia's Serbs with a tight and terrifying hand. "Everyone is frightened," one Serb in the city of Bijeljina told me. "No one even knows if Karadžić and Mladić will ever be arrested." Added another Bosnian Serb: "I would tell you more, but even now, people disappear in the night."

We persisted; I was determined to write something. Eager to make use of every minute, we gave up lunch, often a time-consuming procedure in Bosnia. Instead, Alex and I zigzagged our way across the trail of death leading out of Srebrenica munching on cereal from small boxes given to us by American troops. We drove. We interviewed. We despaired, and then we vowed not to quit. By the time we finally stumbled onto the very few Bosnian Serbs willing to talk, we had eaten our way through the Wheaties, the Cheerios, the Sugar Smacks, and even the Froot Loops.

The Bosnian Serbs who finally answered our questions did so for the same reason the UN had created a war crimes tribunal: They wanted individual responsibility to replace collective guilt. They did not want every Serb to be blamed. "It is important for Serbs to know who is a war criminal and who is not," said one.

Still, the precautions we were forced to take bordered on the ridiculous. We had, for example, agreed to interview one source, a demobilized Bosnian Serb soldier, while he fed the pigs at a collective farm. As he tossed corn to squealing piglets, his discussion of the details of the attack on Srebrenica was interrupted by a nosy policeman making his rounds. To cover, we had to pretend we were reporters doing a story on the revival of Bosnian Serb agriculture. Returning late that night to finish the interview—this time, sitting in a field outside the barn—we were interrupted again by the farm's proprietor, who assumed our man was having an outing with two prostitutes. We played along.

Slowly we pieced together what had happened. The capture of Srebrenica had been assigned to Drina Corps' general Radislav Krstić. He apparently did a good job; a few days after the city was taken, General Mladić promoted Krstić to head of the Drina Corps. The Drina Corps, along with local police and the army's special forces, was part of the massacre plan. Indeed, all the massacre sites fell inside the Drina Corps' territory.

Some of the massacres had been committed by the Corps' diversionary units—comprised of men who had been trained to kill, a number of them recruited directly from prisons. There were ten such units, but two seemed the most involved. One, the Tenth, or Sabotage Unit, was headed by Milorad "Miša" Pelemiš; his unit had particular clout and reported directly to General Mladić. It was Pelemiš who was the boss of Dražen Erdemović, the Srebrenica execution-squad member who had confessed. As I would discover, he also was the boss of Marko Boškić, the alleged mass executioner I had tried to interview in the café in Bijeljina. The second unit was the Drina Wolves, and was headed by Milan Jovović, a man everyone called by his nom de guerre, "Legenda"—the Legend.

Krstić, however, had vanished. The last time anyone could remember seeing him was in late 1995, when he had met with General William Nash, the head of American forces. Oddly, it was Krstić who first brought up the topic of Srebrenica, lecturing Nash ad nauseam about the atrocities committed by the safe haven's Muslim inhabitants. "I couldn't believe he had the balls to raise the [Srebrenica] issue," Nash later told me. Despite his initial bravado, Krstić dispatched deputies to all meetings with the American troops thereafter. Krstić, we were told, had gone to Serbia for a "rest cure."

Discouraged by our inability to find out more, Alex and I had returned to our temporary abode, the Hotel Panorama in Vlasenica, to plan our next step. The Panorama was a threadbare establishment run by hard-line Bosnian Serbs, proprietors who were much better at spying on their guests than, say, providing seats for the toilets. Striding into the lobby that April 1996, I bumped into someone I never expected to see again, and certainly not in Serb-held Vlasenica: Hasan Nuhanović.

"Hasan!" I cried, so stunned to see him I yelled his distinctively Muslim name, which immediately singled him out to the men lounging around the hotel lobby. On cue, the hotel receptionist's head swiveled toward us, his eyes revealing concealed interest, like a lizard spotting an appetizing fly. Now, here was news: *a Bosnian Muslim.* There hadn't been any in Vlasenica since they were chased out of town at gunpoint in 1992.

After four years, Hasan Nuhanović had come home.

He had just arrived along with UN civil affairs officer Bet-El. His homecoming was proving bittersweet. On the drive from Srebrenica, Hasan had all but pressed his nose to the window, reveling in the familiar roll of the mountains, the way his hometown sat perched on the hill, catching the sun. He was elated yet terrified; overjoyed at seeing familiar landmarks, saddened that he was returning to Vlasenica with no family by his side. At each intersection, he scanned the faces of those trudging by, hoping to recognize someone. More than once he yelled, "Stop!" only to leap out of the car and greet amazed Bosnian Serb neighbors who had assumed he, like so many other Bosnian Muslims, was dead. Even before he had gotten to the Panorama Hotel, Hasan had quizzed the father of a math classmate and a goalie from the local soccer team for information about his family.

Now he was determined to make the rounds of the hotel, despite my imprudent gaffe that no doubt had the hotel receptionist on the telephone to the local police. I watched as he entered the dining room, packed with locals, touching those he recognized on the shoulder and offering to buy them a glass of cognac. Slowly, amazement would cross their faces: it was Hasan Nuhanović, Ibro's son! Alive, and in Serb territory! What are you doing here? You're working for the UN!

For nearly four hours Hasan cornered people he recognized, each time making his mission clear: to find out what had happened to Nasiha, Ibro, and Muhamed. He kept expecting the police to stride into the dining room and arrest him or for someone to whip out a gun and threaten him. As nothing of the sort happened, his confidence grew; he bullied, he threatened, he cajoled, hoping to coax even the slightest bit of information out of his former neighbors.

"You can count on me coming every week," he said. "I won't give up, I will dig as deep as necessary to find the truth about my family. If you want to kill me, kill me now; because I will never, never stop looking."

But the citizens of Vlasenica appeared to have collective amnesia. They knew nothing about Srebrenica. They hadn't been in Vlasenica at the time. They were at the beach in Montenegro. Or visiting an elderly aunt in Banja Luka. Or in Belgrade. And of those who had remained in Vlasenica, none had seen or heard a thing. Of course, they knew that the Drina Corps, headquartered here, had captured Srebrenica. But civilian massacres? Impossible. Ibro, Nasiha, and Muhamed killed? Unthinkable.

By the evening's end, whatever excitement Hasan had felt at returning dissolved into bitter frustration. It was bad enough to see his former neighbors; after all, in his mind, they'd betrayed him and his family, failing to warn them of the dangers of the Bosnian Serb takeover of Vlasenica back in 1992. Had the family known in time, they would have gone to Europe. Now he felt doubly betrayed. It was peacetime, and still nobody was willing to tell him anything.

But if former friends weren't willing to tell him the truth—if the bonds of affection could not prove stronger than those of fear and ethnic separation—how would he ever learn what had happened to his family?

It was a long, quiet journey for Hasan back to Tuzla that night.

PEOPLE OFTEN ASKED me what it was like being a female war correspondent in Bosnia. While it had many drawbacks, it had one advantage: Bosnian men loved women and adored being flattered by them. Many a time I had sailed through a checkpoint manned by armed Bosnian Serbs, thanks to a few choice compliments and a broad smile, while my male colleagues were left behind, answering a long string of questions.

What worked with ordinary soldiers would only work the better for war criminals, I reasoned. If evil, on one level, is viewed as ordinary men who do extraordinary things to gain power, then asking for an interview was a way of recognizing, even validating, that power. The men I wanted to interview had been nobodies before the war. Only the war had made them into somebody.

Vanity. The answer, I finally decided, to finding out more about who was responsible for the Srebrenica massacres lay in appealing to the vanity of those who had participated in the crime. I decided to interview those whom I knew to be directly involved in capturing Srebrenica. So Alex and I set about finding Marko Boškić, the alleged massacre squad member; his boss, Milorad "Miša" Pelemiš; and Milan "Legenda" Jović, head of the Drina Wolves. Wearing our tightest jeans and applying our lipstick heavily, as was the Bosnian Serb fashion, we sat in bars favored by these men's cohorts, putting out the word we wanted to interview them. I hoped they'd be lured—if not amused—to hear that an American journalist and her Montenegrin translator wanted to talk to them. The strategy worked.

"You want Legenda?" said the bartender at the most crowded, pulsing café in the Bosnian Serb city of Zvornik, a slice of bright neon on the otherwise gray St. Sava Street. "I'll get him for you."

And there was Legenda, in a booth in the back of the café he'd been given as a reward by the elders of Zvornik. He had named the café the Adonis. Alex and I grinned at each other. Yes, he was vain, all right. If the café's name wasn't a tip-off, then its interior was. Smoky and dark, it boasted little but purple neon, some battered white plastic tables and chairs, and dozens of posters of Legenda, his arms cradling an AK-47, his face blackened, his body clad in a camouflage uniform with its telltale Wolf patch. While we waited, we listened to the music of Serbia's well-loved pop star Čeča, the wife of "Arkan," another alleged war criminal who was responsible for having ethnically cleansed eastern Bosnia, including the city of Zvornik.

From Legenda's pictures, I had expected a grim, strutting, military type, but as he drew closer I saw he was handsome, blond, and gracious. Sinewy and tall, with a cleft in his chin and oddly catlike yellowish-gray eyes, he was less a Drina Wolf than a powerful, watchful lion. He had traded in his uniform for the postwar chic of tight-fitting jeans and a gray T-shirt that displayed his muscles. He extended his hand. His grip was strong.

"And so we will take my car," he commanded with a smile. The plan, we were told, was that we would go out for dinner. Politely opening the door of his red Jeep for us—the only one in Zvornik, he noted—he told us that he was taking us "to a very good restaurant—you know, Zvornik is renowned for its food." Alex, translating, rolled her eyes. This kind of boosterism often led to a lecture on the virtues of the Serbs and a harangue about their alleged defeat at Kosovo Polje by the Turks in 1389. But Legenda gave us no such speech, and the food at the Stadion restaurant, located next to the stadium where Karadžić and Mladić used to parade Bosnian Serb troops, was indeed good.

The aura was that of a Viennese café: white tablecloths, fawning waiters, an extensive menu and wine list. The proprietor came bustling up and we were ushered with great ceremony to our table. Across the room, people stood up at their tables and greeted Legenda as if he were royalty. He returned their greetings with a nod and then sat down. Only then did the other diners reclaim their seats.

Interviewing can be like seduction: You train the force of your personality on the person you are talking to, convincing him to trust you and confide in you. It is often a time-consuming process. I wanted to get Legenda drinking, hoping that while proclaiming his own virtues he would give us the information we were after and implicate someone else in the process. Within a few minutes, however, it was clear he was far, far smarter than we thought. When Alex and I ordered beer, Legenda ordered a Coke.

Our discussion became more like a game of tennis than a seduction, two opponents volleying back and forth, each seeking the other's weakness to score the match point. Legenda answered every question we asked but revealed little. Even his body language betrayed nothing: He readily met my gaze, not needing to drop his eyes. If anything, it was his gaze that was unnerving, mentally assessing me, undressing me, trying to outcalculate me.

I tried flattery. "Why are you called Legenda? Are you the stuff of legends?"

Legenda laughed. "I was in the special forces, and we address each other by nicknames; it was by accident, this nickname."

"And how did you end up running a café? You must be quite the businessman."

"It was a reward from the town," Legenda replied. He glanced down at the menu and changed the subject. "You must try the *karadjordjeva šnicla* [breaded pork stuffed with ham and cheese]," he urged. "It's wonderful here."

I tried the personal approach. "And what was your life like before the war?"

"I was a pentathlon competitor," said Legenda, noting that his wife was also an athlete. And he had been a movie buff; he loved James Dean and Cary Grant movies.

I tried a somewhat more direct approach. "I'm very ignorant of the Bosnian Serb military. Can you explain to me how your unit fit into the Drina Corps?"

Legenda happily obliged. The Drina Wolves, he said, were like the Green Berets—special forces—trained for difficult tasks. Sometimes the soldiers recruited were from less than savory backgrounds. It took a good commander, he said, to hold the men in line.

"And how did your men see you?"

"I'm respected as an honest and good commander."

Despairing that I would ever learn more, I began noting down what he looked like in my notebook. There was silence, while he ate his meal. Finally I asked him: "How old are you?"

"Why?" Legenda snapped, with a look at my notebook. "Does the tribunal need a portrait?"

"Do you have reason to worry about them?"

"No. I have never killed an enemy civilian or mistreated a prisoner.

Nor have my men. No matter how much they may hate them, they cannot do it. I would disobey an order if I was ordered to kill the weak, women and children, and the elderly." I noticed he did not mention men and boys in his list.

"You sound like you are frightened of the tribunal."

Legenda laughed. "Personally, I'm not afraid of The Hague. But I'm afraid of the setup. I'm afraid I'd be wrongly accused."

"So there were executions? And there are mass graves?"

"It is possible." Legenda was evasive. "But my soldiers did not commit executions and rapes—I would be responsible for them. I'm not in a position to say who did it, whose responsibility it was, and [if they had,] who should be sent to The Hague." He was on a roll now.

"I'll go to The Hague and deliver myself personally if they find out I shot at one civilian who was not carrying a gun," he exclaimed. "But the people who are responsible may want to deliver others in order to wash their hands of it."

He was impressive: noble, passionate. I could see why his men looked up to him. Listening to him talk about virtuous commanders and how they inspired their troops, I wanted badly to believe him. I wanted to believe he had not been involved. I could tell from Alex's expression that she did too.

Yet there was already information in my notebook that suggested otherwise. A Bosnian Muslim journalist who monitored military radio broadcasts during the fall of Srebrenica had a few weeks before read me a transcript of a July 14 conversation allegedly involving Legenda. It appeared to refer to an execution.

> 14:17 P.M. Anonymous soldier: "Legenda, I have thirty pieces."
> Legenda: "Finish with it. You know we are paid by the piece."
> 14:47 P.M. Anonymous soldier: "Boss, the job is done."

I *knew* he had to have taken part.

And soon he knew that we knew. Because a week or so later, when we next stopped by the Adonis café, we met a very different Legenda.

Gone was his casual air, his lectures about military honor, his flirtatious manner. This time he didn't bother to sit down with us at the table. He simply placed his hands on it and leaned over us, every inch a commander towering above subordinates.

"Think how unfortunate it would be if you were driving along the river one night and your car was to skid uncontrollably into it," he said pointedly. "Or you were to get a flat tire out on these lonely roads, and no one would come to your aid. What an easy way for you to disappear."

He was silent. Loud pop music pounded in the background. Slowly Legenda straightened up, his eyes not leaving ours. "You girls are asking some unpopular questions," he said. "Too much truth is a dangerous thing."

The next day, an old contact of Alex's, and a man well placed to know a great deal and eager to tell it, canceled a meeting with us. We were waiting for him at a hotel downtown, where he was holding a business meeting, and we watched him be summoned to the hotel's front desk for a telephone call. We saw him listen and then swiftly put down the phone. He returned to his meeting, dismissed it, walked his guests out into the parking lot—and never returned.

"The voice said: 'If my name appears in the newspaper—if you talk to those journalists—you and your family are dead,' " he told Alex a few days later. "If I stepped forward with names now, no one could guarantee my safety. I'm sorry."

SUCH THREATS—WHILE they convinced Alex and me to leave Zvornik right away—impeded but did not stop the truth from emerging. Investigators from the Yugoslav Tribunal continued to collect evidence on the ground about Srebrenica, the siege of Sarajevo, the abuses at the Čelebići camp. By July 1996 they were ready to reveal some of what they had gathered against Bosnian Serb leader Radovan Karadžić and General Ratko Mladić. Their forum was a "Rule 61" hearing—the very same hearing that Judge McDonald and Judge Cassese had battled over for so long. Rule 61 hearings are not trials in absentia, but they do allow prosecutors to present evidence against defendants—in this case, Karadžić and Mladić—so that the tribunal's judges can confirm international arrest warrants for them.

The hearing, which unfolded in the two weeks leading up to the first anniversary of the Srebrenica massacres, was a shrewd public-relations gesture. There was no ignoring that the hearing had no accused in the dock, no overlooking that world leaders were now refusing to arrest those the court had charged.

Prosecutors didn't hesitate to drive the irony home in the courtroom.

"Karadžić and Mladić's perfidious and cowardly deeds will long be remembered," prosecutor Mark Harmon told the three judges in attendance: Claude Jorda, Elizabeth Odio-Benito, and Fuad Abdel-Moneim Riad. "What should not be remembered is that the world had the ability to bring these two alleged architects of genocide to justice and did nothing. It will haunt the victims and shame us all."

The evidence was devastating. The stream of expert witnesses—UN personnel, tribunal investigators, historians, and Bosnian Muslim survivors—spelled out a tale of calculated killing. It began with the Bosnian Serb campaign to shell Sarajevo and its civilians into submission and ended with the premeditated butchery of Srebrenica. Karadžić and Mladić, charged Harmon, "instigated, planned and ordered the genocide and 'ethnic cleansing' of Bosnia . . . crimes which have shocked the conscience of the world." He added: "The fury and cruelty of . . . these attacks were limited only by the perpetrator's inability to imagine darker deeds."

Inevitably, not only Karadžić and Mladić were on trial, but also the UN and the Dutch battalion. As the hearing focused on Srebrenica, as members of the Dutch battalion were called to the stand—including their commander, Ton Karremans—the complete story of the safe area's last days emerged for the first time: the lack of support from UN headquarters; the air strikes that came too late; the chaos; Mladić's bullying orders for an evacuation; the Dutch troops' awareness that the male refugees were at risk; the fact that some peacekeepers had witnessed isolated executions.

Judge Riad, who would later describe Srebrenica as "evil written on the darkest pages of human history," went right to the question of the UN's, and the Dutch battalion's, mistakes of judgment. He bore in on Colonel Karremans. What had he done to stop executions once he was made aware of them?

"But did you include any mention, not to say protest, against the executions?" asked Riad.

Karremans floundered, unable to explain. He hadn't protested, he wasn't aware, there was no opportunity to evaluate. "To be frank," he concluded, "I had not thought about the idea of asking him [General Mladić] what happened with the refugees."

On July 11, 1996—on the eve of the anniversary of the massacres at Srebrenica—The Hague Tribunal issued international arrest warrants for Karadžić and Mladić. The warrants made them international fugitives from justice and, effectively, prisoners. Even if they couldn't be arrested in Serb-held Bosnia or Serbia, they could be picked up if they stepped foot outside of those areas. (While both men refused to recognize the tribunal, they dispatched lawyers to The Hague.)

The warrants gave fresh momentum to the call for Karadžić and Mladić to be put behind bars. Some nations, such as Germany, expressed frustration with the NATO's reluctance to arrest the two men. Inside the Clinton administration, fissures over the issue emerged: The Pentagon urged caution, while the new secretary of state, Madeleine Albright, pushed for arrests. Even public opinion in the United States shifted. In July, a poll released by the University of Maryland's Program on International Policy Attitudes revealed that nearly 70 percent of Americans favored having U.S. troops seize Mladić and Karadžić to deliver them to The Hague, even if casualties would result. But the Pentagon did not budge. There would be no NATO arrests of indicted war criminals in Bosnia in 1996.

BY THIS TIME Dušan Tadić was no longer the only defendant in The Hague. There were now seven. Austria and Germany had made some arrests; Croatia, under heavy pressure from the United States, had arranged one surrender and one arrest. And Bosnian Muslim authorities had complied with the call to arrest and turn over alleged war criminals. By late summer of 1996, the detention cells at The Hague had a distinctly multiethnic mix of Croats, Bosnian Serbs, Bosnian Croats, and Bosnian Muslims.

And among them were four men of great interest to Petko Grubač, the Serbian psychiatrist who had been held at the Čelebići camp: Zdravko Mucić, the camp's commander; Hazim Delić, the deputy commander; his sidekick, Esad Landžo; and Zejnil Delalić, the top Bosnian military officer in the Konjic area.

Since their escape from Konjic in 1992, Petko and Gordana Grubač had tried to put as much distance as they could between them and the

Čelebići prison camp. The camp was in the south; they had settled as far north as possible, in Bijeljina, a grim city by the Serbian border. But Petko and Gordana hadn't chosen Bijeljina because of its charm. They had picked it partly because Petko's sister lived there, but mostly because it felt safe. Once a mixed city, Bijeljina was now almost all Serb. As much as Petko and Gordana hated to admit it, they now felt safer surrounded by their own ethnic group.

Plus, the local hospital had need of psychiatrists. As Petko made his rounds along the hospital corridors, he would meet men traumatized by the evil they had either practiced or witnessed or, alternatively, had utterly denied. His psychiatric practice was full of lost souls, of men and women with flashbacks and nightmares and sweaty palms and anger and despair. These were people who lived in a twilight world in which the present is dominated by the past, reliving that moment they put a gun to a man's head, or burned a house down, or watched their best friend shot standing next to them.

Increasingly, they reminded Petko of Gordana and himself.

The couple could not stop talking and thinking about what had happened to them in Konjic and of Petko's time at the concentration camp. They could not stop asking the questions that seemed to be unanswerable: What had the war been for? How could it have happened? Why did Petko and Gordana—people who believed in multiethnic Bosnia—now find themselves more comfortable living among Serbs? Had the life they lived in Konjic, among that great circle of Muslim, Serb, and Croat friends, simply been an illusion? Had their friends always been their enemies?

And so when Petko and Gordana Grubač were asked to give evidence to the Yugoslav Tribunal about war crimes committed against Bosnian Serbs at Čelebići, the couple gave it serious thought, even though few Bosnian Serbs then respected the court. The request came to them in late 1995, at a time when both Bosnian Serb leader Radovan Karadžić and Serbian leader Slobodan Milošević openly opposed the tribunal. Even before his indictment for war crimes, Karadžić had argued that The Hague Tribunal was not a legitimate international court, given that it had been created by the UN Security Council and not by treaty.

Most of Gordana and Petko's friends and neighbors in Bijeljina agreed. Every newspaper, every television station, every radio station was full of condemnation of The Hague, a name that in the Serb-held half of Bosnia became synonymous with anti-Serb prejudice. Nearly every Bosnian Serb I interviewed at the time believed that, while justice was important, the Yugoslav Tribunal was not the right forum for it. The court, they said, was part of the vast European-American conspiracy against the Serbs. "To them, all Serb soldiers are war criminals," said Nedjo Krstović, a Sarajevan Serb. "The tribunal will never provide justice to a Serb."

Outside of Bosnia, in the Serb diaspora that stretched from Australia to Canada to the United States, other Serbs disagreed. They wanted Serb victims of the Bosnian war to have their day before the war crimes tribunal and show the world that not all of the war crimes had been committed by Serbs. It was these Serbs who ultimately reached out to the Grubač family. Their effort had begun when a member of the Serbian-American Women's Caucus, Mirjana Samardžija, attended a speech given in San Francisco by tribunal prosecutor Richard Goldstone in early 1995. She was struck by the fact that he mentioned investigations only into crimes committed against Bosnian Muslims and Croats.

"I asked him, 'Given your presentation, it doesn't sound like the tribunal is looking into crimes against Serbs. Is there a plan to do so?' " Samardžija recalled. "He couldn't answer my question. So after we left, I said to the others, 'Let's get to work. Let's prepare a report with documentation.' And we did."

Of course, Goldstone and his investigators weren't unaware of the issue. It was no secret that while Bosnian Serb leaders may have committed the bulk of the country's war crimes, they were hardly alone when it came to violating the Geneva Conventions. In 1992 a Helsinki Watch report concluded that "to varying degrees, all parties to the conflict in Bosnia-Hercegovina have violated humanitarian law, or the laws of war." Atrocities at the Čelebići camp were already known by 1992, when Acting Secretary of State Lawrence Eagleburger first pegged Karadžić—and Delić, the camp's deputy commander—as war criminals. Goldstone also knew that the Yugoslav Tribunal couldn't afford not to prosecute Bosnian Muslims and Croats for war crimes as well as Serbs. The court had to be seen as independent in order to have an impact.

Efforts to track down such crimes, however, had been halted at every turn by both Milošević and Karadžić. Belgrade had refused to issue visas to members of the Yugoslav Tribunal, making it impossible for investigators to set foot on Serb soil. Tribunal staff in Serb-held Bosnia found it difficult to convince local Serbs to meet with them. So the Serbian-American Women's Caucus, working with the Belgrade-based Association of Detainees, a victims' group, was able to do some of the tribunal's footwork, convincing war crimes survivors to come forward. Their hope was that the tribunal, confronted with evidence of war crimes committed against Bosnian Serbs, would be willing to prosecute a case accusing the Bosnian Muslims of genocide, too. The two organizations, after locating survivors living in the United States willing to testify, put together a team of ten scouts to comb Montenegro, the Republika Srpska, and Serbia for concentration camp victims, including those from Čelebići.

And that is how they found Petko and Gordana Grubač.

For days the couple debated what to do. They wanted the world to know the truth of what had happened in Čelebići, to understand that the camp was part of a larger Bosnian Muslim effort to round up and kill local Serbs, but what if they were found out? Would local authorities in Bijeljina, who, like Karadžić, opposed the tribunal, make life difficult for them if their cooperation became known? Would they lose their apartment, or would Petko lose his job?

Finally, they decided they had to testify no matter how risky it might prove. Petko and Gordana wanted to hear the truth as badly as they wanted to tell it. The Yugoslav Tribunal seemed their best—and perhaps their only—forum to do so.

So secretive were preparations for the trial that the first groups of survivors meeting with the tribunal investigators did so in Romania or Hungary. Gordana traveled to Timisoara, Romania, to meet with investigators. By the time it was Petko's turn, he had to go no farther than Belgrade. Milošević, after two years of barring tribunal investigators from his country, had finally allowed them to open an office in February of 1996.

Regardless, Petko traveled in secrecy, telling no one at the hospital why he had asked for a few days off, refusing to tell the friends he stayed with in Belgrade the real reason for his visit. As his bus crossed the border back into Bosnia, he was nervous about the consequences if someone found out.

Yet the only ones who learned about the Čelebići investigation were the men to be indicted. One day that March, the telephone rang in the Grubačs' two-bedroom apartment in Bijeljina, and Petko picked it up.

"Is that Petko Grubač?"

"Yes," he replied.

"Zdravko Mucić here."

Petko's mouth went dry. How had the head of the Čelebići concentration camp gotten his phone number?

"Have you heard this news—that I am about to be indicted?" Mucić demanded. "That I am going to be taken to The Hague?

"Can you believe it!" Mucić was off on a tirade, as indignant as if he had not spent the war as commander of an infamous concentration camp. He was outraged that people thought they could put him on trial; after all, he'd just been doing his duty. Then he hung up.

Petko wasn't sure if the call was a threat or a desperate effort to ensure that he would say kind things about Mucić if he testified. Some weeks later, on March 21, Mucić was indicted, along with Hazim Delić, the imperious camp thug, and his gratuitously cruel underling, Esad Landžo. And so was another man for whom Petko and Gordana had little sympathy: Zejnil Delalić, the Bosnian commander in charge of the region who had belatedly come to Petko's rescue, allowing him to leave the Čelebići camp.

News of the indictment spread quickly throughout Serb-held Bosnia. Even though prosecutor Goldstone had several times openly declared that his staff was working on such a case, few Bosnian Serbs had believed him. On the radio, on the TV, in public pronouncements, attention in Serb-held Bosnia focused on the case of *Prosecutor v. Delalić et al.*—otherwise known as the Čelebići case. The fourteen-page, forty-nine-count indictment listed atrocities that could have been plucked from a page of testimony at the Tadić case. Delić was indicted for four murders; Landžo, for five. Among the crimes with which the two men—both Bosnian Muslims—were charged was killing a man by beating him and nailing a Bosnian Muslim party badge to his forehead.

Bosnian Serb deputy leader Nikola Koljević—the Shakespearean scholar serving in the Karadžić government—hailed the indictment as "an obvious sign that the tribunal wants to present itself as being impartial, or at least less partial, and I would say just about time."

Throughout the summer and into the fall, the Yugoslav Tribunal's prosecutors assembled their evidence. They knew that just as the Tadić case had been scrutinized as the tribunal's first, the Čelebići case also would be carefully studied, if only by the Bosnian Serbs. It was the tribunal's first—and possibly only—chance to prove that the war crimes court did not take ethnic sides.

Prosecutors wanted the best possible line-up of witnesses to testify at the Čelebići trial, slated to start in The Hague in 1997. By the fall of 1996, they knew they wanted Petko and Gordana Grubać to be among them. Did the couple want to testify under pseudonyms? Did they want witness protection, to be relocated to another country?

No, Petko told the tribunal staff with whom he met in Belgrade. Gordana and I are going to testify, and when we do, we will use our names. We are not ashamed. We will live with the consequences. When it came to justice, it was truth, after all, that they were seeking.

9

BRING ME HIS BODY

just
to be able
to bury your body,
to have a place
where your mother
can go with
flowers

—Ariel Dorfman, from the poem
"Red Tape" in *Last Waltz in Santiago*

You could smell the grave long before you could see it.

Wafting through the dark pines, dancing down the rutted dirt track that ran by a stream, came a primeval scent, fetid and cloying. It hovered over the path. It massed like a cloud of flies around the American soldiers who sat in their Humvees trying to wave it away, distraction at least from the tedious job of watching a forensic team exhume a mass grave from a distance. "God, it stinks," said one soldier, tapping his fingers on the wheel, his M-16 propped nearby.

"Yeah, the investigators are up there digging," said the second, jerking his thumb up toward the path.

That was how one found the Cerska grave in the summer of 1996.

I still carry that stench in my memory. Photographs of mass graves can prepare you for what you might see—a jumble of skeletalized limbs, heads, bodies—but nothing prepares you for how it smells.

I had expected bones, which themselves present a kind of abstract, impersonal beauty, not a stinking stew of rotted clothes and outflung hands and hunks of flesh. Perhaps it was the shock of that sweet, cloying smell that made the morass of human remains in the Cerska grave seem so tangible, personal—intimate, even—that first time I gazed into it.

Or maybe it was the clothing strewn throughout the grave that made the decaying mess seem somehow so human. I could see a red high-top sneaker peeping out of the mud, the arm of a black leather jacket flung outward from a body, the tails of what appeared to have once been a man's white shirt. I was prepared to be horrified, but I was not prepared to be moved. At Cerska, there was no avoiding the fact that these were not just skeletons. These were the remains of human beings: someone's son, lover, brother, husband.

That was when I fully grasped that one of the most contentious issues for a society wishing to achieve justice in the wake of genocide would be how mass graves were exhumed. Bosnia would prove no exception.

Peace had only just arrived along with a host of Western agencies, but already groups were in conflict over the graves' exhumations. The Yugoslav Tribunal—charged with gathering proof that the thousands of men and boys executed after the fall of Srebrenica had been killed in cold blood, not in combat as the Bosnian Serbs had claimed—saw the mass graves in terms of evidence. Although they would exhume the bodies, they would seek to identify only some of them, just enough to prove their case. Already I could see Bill Haglund, the Yugoslav Tribunal's forensic expert, in the grave. He was directing the painstaking removal of each body, noting the bullet holes in the back of the head, how the wrists had been wired together.

But the hundreds of bereft women who had survived the fall of Srebrenica weren't seeking evidence but information. This grave was their best chance to discover what had happened to their brother, their husband, their son. It was their past and their future, their hope and their heartbreak. While they cared if those responsible for the massacres stood trial at The Hague, they cared even more about a proper burial, mourning, closure for their grief. "If the people who got killed in Srebrenica are not identified, not buried, in a human way," said Munera "Beba" Hadzić, who headed the Women of Srebrenica, an ad hoc support group, "then I deeply believe that there is no real justice, and that Srebrenica will, as a result, happen someplace else, some day."

Tribunal investigators and survivors, however, were not the only groups with a stake in the graves' exhumation. For political leaders among the Srebrenica refugee community, the mass graves were a powerful symbol of the world's injustice and the UN's treachery. Some were not sure they wanted the graves exhumed, believing their existence to be the most searing reminder of how the UN, the Western powers, and even the Muslim-led Bosnian government had let down the people of Srebrenica. Exhumation, they argued, would be the final "ethnic cleansing."

For the Bosnian Serbs, the graves were a liability, particularly for executioners whose fingers had been on the trigger. Bodies could link them to crimes and to prosecution by the Yugoslav Tribunal. Killing innocents was one thing; being found guilty of it, another. As soon as the first whispers of a peace blew across Bosnia in the autumn of 1995, some Bosnian Serbs began to take steps to ensure that the graves would never reveal their deadly secrets.

Local Bosnian government officials in the city of Tuzla, where the Srebrenica refugees had made their home, had their own reason to oppose the exhumations. They feared the digging would leave them with scores of bodies to bury. Privately they looked forward to the day when the Srebrenica refugees—and their associated corpses—would go home.

So it wasn't only the shifting weather, the slippery clay soil, the still-fragile peace that greeted Haglund when he arrived to exhume the Srebrenica graves in the spring of 1996. Like everything else in the Balkans, the graves had their politics, their conflicting agendas. In those deep trenches, after all, lay buried not only the bones of dead men and boys but also civilization's hope that evils such as genocide were a thing of the past.

EXHUMATIONS, TRADITIONALLY, ARE as much about survivors are they are about the dead. It was the women of Srebrenica who would care the most—and whose concerns would figure most prominently—when the Yugoslav Tribunal's plans to exhume the graves was first broached in early 1996. They were were the ones who had survived or at least had not been targeted for execution. Some had been raped, others had been beaten. A few came under gunfire as they fled with the column of men who left through the woods. Most were forced to watch as their menfolk were torn from them in Potočari by Bosnian Serb soldiers, who barked commands at their sons and husbands to march off in a different direction. And their men, more than 7,000 of them, were never seen again.

Evacuated by bus from Srebrenica to the safety of Tuzla—the nearest large Bosnian Muslim–held city—survivors lived a refugee's harsh life. They were jammed into temporary housing in schools and collective centers, eight or ten or sixteen squeezed into a room with makeshift bunk beds. Many came from the deep countryside, as evidenced by their traditional dress: gaily patterned headscarves and long baggy trousers, or *dimija*. These women were at a loss in the gritty, industrial city, a situation made worse without the support of their husbands and other male relatives. With no family to care for, no fields to tend, their days and nights were dedicated to one primary activity: grieving the loss of their loved ones. And with that grief came immeasurable guilt.

It was always difficult to interview the grieving in war-torn Bosnia; at some point the pain comes pouring out, far more pain than you can ever get into your reporter's notebook. But interviewing the Srebrenica women was all the more difficult because they expected reporters to have the answers about their missing men. As Western journalists, we could travel to Serb-held territory where their menfolk had disappeared, whereas they could not. Whenever I arrived to interview Srebrenica survivors, at least one woman always would pluck at my jacket to draw me aside. "My son, I heard he was last seen near Kosovo Polje," she might whisper. "Have you heard anything about survivors there?" I would shake my head in reply.

When Bosnian Serb soldiers brusquely separated these women from their husbands and sons at the Potočari base, there had been no chance to say good-bye, much less protest. They were determined to do so now.

By early 1996 survivors had banded together to form the Women of Srebrenica. They gathered in the Bosnian Family Aid Agency (BosFam) run by Beba Hadzić. Hadzić, a tall, dynamic woman with a head of black curls, was not a refugee herself; she had spent the war in Tuzla. But she came from Srebrenica, and her sister Džefa, who had spent the war there, had lost both her husband and her son. Quickly Beba's office became the center of operations, the family hearth, for the Women of Srebrenica.

Beba's first concern was helping the refugees find a way to support themselves, and the agency was transformed into a miniature emporium of handmade goods. Inside the glass storefront, women sat cross-legged on the concrete floor in front of looms weaving rugs or knitting multicolored sweaters out of whatever yarn had been donated to them. Voluminous piles of bright clothing and sweaters—orange and purple socks, iridescent green cardigans—were piled on the shelves, ready to be sold. But the agency also served another purpose: On any given day, a core group of the women would be jammed onto the battered couches in Beba's tiny back office, smoking, drinking coffee, and angrily discussing how the world had failed them.

More than six months after the fall of the UN safe area, their men were still not accounted for, and, they told me, no one was trying to find them. They were furious: In February 1996 they'd taken their anger to the streets, stopping cars in Tuzla and then setting upon the offices of the International Committee of the Red Cross, the humanitarian organization in charge of searching for the missing, smashing windows in protest. They accused Izetbegović of indifference. "They all promise help, but never deliver it," said Fatima Huseinović, the feisty former perfume-store manager who emerged as the group's primary spokesperson. (It was she who had organized the women to halt General Morillon's armored personnel carrier in Srebrenica back in 1993, a move that had led to the city being declared a UN safe area.) In the BosFam office, they wove their bitterness and their frustrated hopes into tapestries every bit as complex as those being created on the looms in the workroom outside.

Anecdotal evidence pointed to one conclusion: The missing men were dead. There were as many as twenty reported mass graves, several of which had been verified by NATO satellite imagery and survivors. Dražen Erdemović, the member of a Bosnian Serb army special forces unit who'd surrendered to the Yugoslav Tribunal in March, had admitted to having gunned down hundreds of unarmed Srebrenica men and boys at a collective farm in the town of Pilica. Among those identified as taking part in the execution was Marko Boškić.

But there had been a few survivors, enough to keep the women's hopes alive. Unbelievably, a group of eight men had stumbled out of the woods in November of 1995, having withstood the onset of winter by eating apples, nettles, and mushrooms. Some men came home in the first wave of prisoner exchanges after the 1995 signing of the Dayton peace plan. Each survivor, each fresh snippet of information came streaming into the BosFam office, into the hands of the Women of Srebrenica.

"As I was leaving the camp, the guard told me, 'More are coming,' " said Sakib Rizvić, newly released from the Batković camp in Serbia, to a crowd of women in Beba's office when I visited them one April day in 1996. Their eyes brightened hopefully.

"We are all aware that the mass graves are full of bodies," said Fatima, her eyes blinking with tears behind her glasses. "But we are still hoping to find those alive too."

The rumor most tightly embraced was that the men were being held in slave labor camps in Serbia and Serb-held Bosnia: a lead-zinc mine, a chicken farm, and a supermarket basement. "Take photographs of the men you see cutting brush along the roads in Srpska," Beba urged me one day. "These may be our men, forced to work, and we can identify them."

But even as they hoped and dreamed, the Women of Srebrenica had survived the war by being realists. So when they heard that the Yugoslav Tribunal's team was to begin exhuming the graves in early April, they dropped their weaving, huddled together in corners, and held hands. They stroked each other's cheeks. "Women have to know the truth," said Fatima, drawing herself erect and nodding her head sagely. "We know for The Hague it doesn't matter who was killed, but for the families, it is important to find out who was killed and where." Her husband had been separated from her outside the UN Dutch base at Potočari.

And identification would be easy, they thought. Most of the women knew exactly what the men were wearing when they had disappeared; after all, they'd mended those outfits again and again. And of course, they knew their son or husband's every scar, broken limb, and missing tooth as if it were their own.

"He was wearing a peculiar blue shirt and trousers, I'd made them," Sudeta Dizdarević told me, describing her son Selvedin. "He had a scar on his foot, and he had broken his left arm, near his elbow; he complained his arm hurt when the weather was changing. He was right-handed and had good teeth."

"You could easily recognize my husband by what he was wearing: a pink T-shirt, a reversible black jacket, green running shoes, Adidas," Mirsada Aljkanović said. "And a belt with a metal buckle. He was about

196 centimeters tall, right-handed, and the fifth tooth on the right side was broken. He had a deep scar that scratched the skull between the eyebrows."

"Just bring me his body," said a distraught Hatidža Hren, of her husband Rudolf. "I will recognize his bones."

With bones would come a burial; with a burial, a cemetery; with a cemetery, remembrance. For the first time in months, the Srebrenica survivors allowed themselves to fantasize about a positive step they could take in the future. Those who were religious dreamed about reclaiming their loved one's body, having it ceremonially washed, wrapped in a shroud, and buried in a cemetery, while they prayed in the traditional Muslim way. At least they would know his soul was at rest.

Those who weren't religious envisaged having a cemetery both to visit and to serve as a memorial to the dead. It would be like that cemetery in Washington—was it called Arlington?—women told me in those sessions in Beba's office. It would have rows and rows of white tombstones, a sparkling green lawn. It would be so vast that airplanes would be able to see it from the air.

"Oh, at least I would know where his bones are!" cried Mirsada, describing how she would faithfully visit the grave every day.

But exhuming all the bodies—and identifying them—was not what the Yugoslav Tribunal had in mind.

Its aims were limited and specific. Prosecutors were concerned with gathering forensic evidence that showed that executions had occurred at several key graves, in order to cement the case against Bosnian Serb leader Radovan Karadžić and his top general, Ratko Mladić, who had been indicted in 1995 for genocide in Srebrenica. Both men vehemently denied that atrocities had occurred: Karadžić claimed that those killed were soldiers fighting in battle. Mladić—who had, in those fateful days of July 1995, assured the Dutch UN commander and Hasan's father, Ibro, that the Srebrenica refugees would be escorted safely to Bosnian Muslim territory—suggested the Muslims had killed themselves.

WITH MORE THAN 7,000 people missing, skeletons were scattered for miles along the escape routes across the hills and valleys surrounding Srebrenica, some poking from mass graves, others glinting on the surface. White bones gleamed from the crevices of rocks. Skulls bared their teeth, sunk among the ferns in the woods. Broken tibias and femurs were sown across hillsides, looking from a distance like white flowers amid the green shoots. Driving up Mount Kamenica one day, where hundreds of Bosnian Muslim men and boys fleeing the Srebrenica enclave had been gunned down by the Bosnian Serbs, the wheels of my car rolled across what appeared to be a pelvis, smashing it with a resounding crunch.

There were nearly as many groups with conflicting agendas—and a stake in these skeletons' future—as there were sites in which to find them. In addition to the Srebrenica women and the Yugoslav Tribunal, the Bosnian government had its own forensic team. There were also Manfred Nowak, the UN's Special Rapporteur on Missing Persons, and Elizabeth Rehn, the UN's Special Rapporteur on Human Rights, who had a team of Finnish experts ready to collect bodies that lay on the hillsides.

The International Committee for the Red Cross, however, which has the international mandate to locate the missing, was opposed to the idea of opening the graves at all—unless the Yugoslav Tribunal had some idea of who was in them. "What are we to do? Line up hundreds of skeletons on the ground and ask the relatives to walk past?" said Jacques de Maio, a senior official with the ICRC, told *The Guardian* newspaper.

The Boston-based Physicians for Human Rights (PHR), which had been tasked with the job of coming up with an identification plan, was also uneasy about the fate of the bodies to be exhumed from the graves. With members who had exhumed bodies in Guatemala, El Salvador, and Kurdish-populated northern Iraq, PHR felt strongly that if bodies were going to be exhumed, they also had to be identified.

Yet the Srebrenica graves presented a challenge unlike any other. As the piles of discarded IDs that littered the roads testified, the Serb soldiers had removed the men's personal belongings. There were dozens of graves and thousands of bodies in them to identify.

The plan the PHR experts conceived was daring, never before attempted in the wake of a genocide. What they proposed was creating an ante-mortem database that would seek to match exhumed corpses to descriptions of the missing, compiled through interviews with relatives or witnesses to their disappearance. Dental records, distinctive injuries, and even DNA could then be used to make a firm identification. The database would require thousands of meticulous interviews and exacting forensic examinations. But if it worked, there was at least a chance that some of the Srebrenica dead could be returned to those who mourned them.

"Our chances of success are not good, but you have to do this for the living—not the dead," said PHR's lead pathologist, Dr. Robert Kirschner of the University of Chicago, as he explained the ante-mortem database to me in 1996.

It was an ambitious undertaking. But the sheer volume of the horror of Srebrenica's massacres—and the demands of families as well as the tribunal's prosecutorial needs—called for extraordinary efforts. With luck and hard work, those involved with exhumations thought, justice could be achieved: evidence gathered for the courtroom, answers given to grieving families.

But there was just one major problem, as the forensic experts would discover when they broke ground. These were no ordinary mass graves, and this would prove no ordinary exhumation.

THERE IS NO universally accepted definition of a mass grave. Some experts say a half-dozen bodies; some say a mass grave must have bodies in contact with one another. For the purposes of the two Yugoslav and Rwanda Tribunals, mass graves were sites where at least three victims of "extra-judicial, summary, or arbitrary" executions were buried. In other words, people had been executed and buried in an attempt to hide the evidence.

Exhumations to determine war crimes were not new. In the 1940s, Nazi exhumations in the Katyn Forest helped establish that Soviet troops had executed many of the more than 11,000 Polish officers and soldiers the graves contained. But it was not until the 1980s that full-scale exhumations to establish human rights violations became commonplace, ongoing in countries such as Argentina, Brazil, and Guatemala. In some Latin American countries, family members even stood by the grave, aiding the experts by recognizing the clothing on the corpses.

But the rules of the game changed in Bosnia and Rwanda. These were not shallow graves containing discrete numbers of known individuals. These were deep graves, often made by a backhoe, or bulldozer, filled with hundreds of bodies unknown to local survivors. As Haglund already knew from the exhumation he'd just completed in Kibuye, Rwanda, the sheer volume of modern, turn-of-the-millennium slaughter demanded a new approach. Until his exhumations in Rwanda, the single biggest mass grave to have been exhumed was the El Mozote massacre site in El Salvador, which contained 143 bodies, primarily children. In Kibuye, Haglund and his team exhumed 450 bodies.

Haglund cut a refreshing swath through the otherwise bureaucratic world of the tribunals as he shuttled between Rwanda and The Hague. His self-deprecating humor, his intense focus, and his occasionally eccentric manner quickly earned him his share of devoted allies and enemies alike. While other members of the exhumation team wore their regulation blue UN jumpsuits in the grave, Haglund always sported a shirt and tie and his trademark broad-brimmed brown felt hat.

Possessed of phenomenal drive and energy—some called him obsessive—he'd stay up all night to do his notes and then conduct a business meeting over breakfast, existing for days only on catnaps. His manner was that of an avuncular, somewhat distracted scientist, who lived and breathed his work and cared little if people thought him odd. "Snakes, insects, and death," he told me once brightly, "are so maligned." His comments veered from the endearing to the arcane, and he often referred to a corpse with a wave of the hand as "that gentleman."

His energy and quixotic style made him well suited to the challenges of the Rwanda exhumations. In one spot, well-meaning residents had picked up all the skeletons; he was greeted with separate mounds of femurs, skulls, and tibias. Then there was the fact that Rwanda's mass graves could be found in everything from dug-out latrines to deep crevices. To the surprise of his guides, Haglund insisted on being lowered into these sites to inspect them. "I found myself standing on a slick pyramid of human remains that sloped to the surrounding walls," he wrote in a September 1995 journal entry. "Backbones curved up the sides. Crania had rolled away from their skeletons, leaving mandibles abandoned. White teeth gleamed in the faint light from the opening. . . ."

Rwanda prepared him not just for the horror, but also for the quirks of the exhumations he would face in Bosnia. Haglund knew someone other than the exhumations team would have to be tasked with removing mines or unexploded ordnance as well as guarding the graves to make sure remains weren't tampered with. And he knew that modern methods of creating graves made his job more complicated. Graves were deeper and the bodies in them entangled, not laid out in neat rows. Haglund had consequently chosen to combat modern crimes with modern methods: He exhumed using a backhoe, directing the operator as he removed earth, inch by inch, until the first sign of a body appeared. Then he used trowels and shovels to remove dirt.

The Srebrenica graves, however, presented more obstacles. In Rwanda, Haglund had exhumed one large mass grave and several smaller graves and a latrine; in Bosnia he was expected to exhume six major mass graves or more. He also had a very short window of opportunity: In Bosnia, the summer is short and the digging season stretched only from April to October. And the Yugoslav Tribunal's prosecutors, eagerly mounting a case against Karadžić and Mladić, wanted evidence quickly.

Scribbling out schedules on the napkins he used as scratch paper, Haglund estimated that every second, every minute would have to count. He calculated and recalculated, drew up list after list of supplies. He had to get staff to Zagreb, then set up a morgue in Bosnia, and then there was the equipment needed, and a group of experts to assemble . . . the list was endless. Haglund thought he could do it, but to succeed the operation would have to function as efficiently as planes taking off from a major airport.

And so the clock was already ticking furiously when I caught up with him and his seven-member team on April 8, 1996. The group had done all it could to keep its movements a secret, but reporters had been trailing after them. We all wanted to be present for the first on-site, official confirmation of a mass grave.

Haglund was sniffling; he had a cold. He was standing near the entrance to a tunnel, bending over a group of whitened bones, sparking a frisson of anticipation in the crowd surrounding him. Slowly he craned farther toward the earth, haphazardly pushing his dun-colored tie inside his blue shirt.

Bones under soil, we thought, could only mean one thing.

Haglund murmured under his breath. We bent forward.

"An immature pig," he pronounced, amused, as his hands gently picked up the bones, turning them over with fingers gnarled from years of rough work. The crowd moaned with disappointment.

For days we'd patiently watched as Haglund and the others—armed with rubber gloves and spades, plastic bags and cameras, probes and trowels—undertook the painstaking job of determining if any of the suspected massacre sites were, indeed, mass graves. Each site had to be measured and photographed, each item carefully recorded and logged. Every detail lying on top of a suspected mass grave told a part of the story: the abandoned heaps of tattered shirts and scarves, jackets patched and mended at the elbow, an ambulance stretcher, a canteen, blankets, and a pile of well-worn ID cards. "How can General Mladić say mass graves hold the bodies of soldiers?" scoffed Jean-René Ruez, a former member of the French judicial police and the Yugoslav Tribunal's chief investigator on the Srebrenica case, as he surveyed a tangle of T-shirts and blue jeans.

Only after the surface of a grave had been carefully inspected did Haglund and his team test for bodies. Using a four-foot metal probe in the shape of a T, they gently speared the earth, gauged its resistance, trying to determine the mass grave's outline. And then the team's investigators—Haglund had been joined by crime-scene experts on loan from the FBI and U.S. Air Force—undertook a process eerily somewhat reminiscent of a French gourmand on a truffle hunt. Gently they pushed the probe into the earth. Respectfully they raised the tip of the probe to their noses. Then—*sniff*—a practiced nose could detect the telltale smell of decomposing bodies.

But there were no bodies; at least not as far as we knew, anyway. On April 10 the team set off for the village at Glogova, where reporters earlier in the year had spotted bones in a farmer's field outside the village about a little over twelve miles from Srebrenica and were sure it was a mass grave. Approaching the spot, one could well imagine the executioners choosing it. It was convenient: The field was off a dirt track, a few minutes' drive from the main road, making getaway easy. It was simple to dig: A former cornfield, the earth had been tilled repeatedly and tractor tracks would not raise too much undue suspicion. Best of all, the field was located just over a small rise, so it was not in full view as you drove up the dirt road. Here was a spot few would find, a grave that could easily hold its secrets.

But when the long convoy of fifteen vehicles snaked up to it early that morning—white UN Land Rovers bearing the tribunal team, NATO Humvees escorting them, NATO aircraft buzzing overhead, and a parade of journalists' cars—the field was not abandoned. Indeed, a small white

Renault with Belgrade tags was parked right on top of the suspected mass grave.

The tribunal team slammed on their brakes. Jeeps ground to a halt. The American soldiers manning the guns on the Humvees swiftly trained them on the car. Sabotage . . . an ambush . . . a battle? We all held our breath.

Nothing happened. The car was empty. Wait—no, it seemed to be possessed by spirits as it rocked up and down, up and down. As we stared with amazement, a man's head popped up in the windshield, like a Jack-in-the-box. Startled, he threw open the car door and looked at the cars, Jeeps, and soldiers with guns surrounding him. He was shirtless and his trousers were unzipped. "What's going on?" he yelled as a woman then sat up next to him, revealing her shoulders and naked breasts.

We had interrupted two lovebirds in a tryst atop a mass grave. The couple giggled with embarrassment as the team's translators explained their mission. The NATO soldiers, smiling, lowered their guns. Tribunal investigators guffawed. Still laughing, the two lovers threw on their clothes, gunned the car, drove off the field, and disappeared down the dirt track.

The mood of good humor quickly vanished, however, once the team began inspecting the field. The Renault was not the only vehicle to have visited the Glogova site. Tractor tracks, some months old, were still streaked across the field. Piles of dirt stood off to the side. One bank of earth appeared to have been churned repeatedly. A spot of white glimmered in it against the dark soil. Haglund picked up a small bone and muttered to himself under his breath, "Clavicle and rib, probably twenty-four- to twenty-six-year-old male."

But the rest of the body was nowhere to be seen.

As if there weren't enough evils to characterize the Srebrenica massacres, another had just been added to the list: Someone anxious to hide Glogova's nasty little secrets had robbed the grave.

Tribunal investigators weren't entirely surprised; they'd been warned about grave-robbing. As I learned talking to officials in Washington later that day, satellite imagery taken by U.S. spy planes had captured a series of disturbances at Glogova and Pilica, a mass grave farther to the north.

The graves had been disturbed in the fall of 1995, just as talk of peace was in the air; local Bosnian Serbs were clearly worried they might be sold out in any peace deal. So on September 27 of that year—as Bosnian Muslim, Croat, and Serb foreign ministers announced agreement on basic constitutional principles for a state, the first major step toward the Dayton peace deal—U.S. spy planes captured signs of digging at Pilica in the presence of a backhoe, front-loader tractor, flatbed trailer, and a deep trench. A snapshot taken on October 2 showed that the trench had since been filled in.

That same day, the exhumation team found a secondary grave, filled with body parts that had been moved, possibly from Glogova. That meant Bill Haglund would have to try to identify at least some of the bodies from the fragments that remained. Looking at the site, he knew his job had gotten much more difficult.

HAGLUND'S JOB WAS to provide forensic evidence to an international war crimes tribunal, something that had never been done before. Forensic evidence was not introduced at Nuremberg. In fact, forensic evidence as it related to human rights violations only made its debut in court in the 1980s, when it was used to help convict the deposed Argentine military junta.

Yet forensic evidence was key to the Yugoslav Tribunal's case against Karadžić and Mladić. If experience was any guide, the Bosnian Serbs had not left a paper trail that could be presented in court. Survivors could always be accused by defense counsel of exaggerating. But bones do not lie. A single gunshot wound to the head is hard to deny. So would be the evidence of blindfolds or hand restraints, hallmarks of an execution.

Yet as April turned into May and May into June, Haglund and his team were a long way from even beginning the exhumations. Haglund knew the Bosnia dig would be logistically complex, but his efforts to assemble what the team needed had been stymied. To begin with, Haglund wanted to use the same equipment he had used in Rwanda, but no plane large enough could be found swiftly in Rwanda to fly the equipment to Bosnia. That meant Haglund and his Rwanda team—Andrew Thomson, a New Zealand medical doctor; José Pablo Baryabar, a Peruvian anthropologist; Melissa Connor, an American archaeologist; Clea Koff, an American anthropologist; the two British logisticians, Geoff

Buchnell (known as "Mr. Fix-It"), and Carl Rhodes—ended up carrying what cameras, towels, and surveying equipment they could on their passenger flight from Rwanda. Then came the second obstacle: Haglund had assumed that supplies would be easy to get. Bosnia, after all, was in Europe. But it turned out that no money had been budgeted for the exhumation—the largest in modern history, aimed at providing evidence against two major indicted war criminals.

Thomson, in charge of logistics for the exhumations, howled when informed by the Yugoslav Tribunal that there were no funds available in the court's already meager budget, still being doled out on a quarterly, not annual basis. As UN budgets are drawn up months in advance—and consequently, before peace in Bosnia was assured—exhumations had not been included. Plus, UN spending cuts, provoked in part by the fact the United States was $1.2 billion in arrears in dues to the organization, so hobbled the court's work it could barely send investigators into the field to work on collecting evidence for the forty-three indictments.

The money for the exhumations would have to be raised from voluntary contributions elsewhere; the European Union had financed the Rwanda digs. "You gotta be joking—you want six graves dug and you are telling me there is no money?" Thomson shouted during a visit to the tribunal in The Hague. "Oh, shit," said Haglund, when told of the news. "It's going to be even harder than I thought."

So Haglund and his team turned from gravediggers into equipment scroungers: They begged and borrowed used equipment wherever they could find it. They needed everything: refrigerator trucks, backhoes, shovels, body bags, tables, X-ray equipment. They had to outfit not just the team at the dig but also a lab for pathologists to examine the bodies; no lab in postwar Bosnia was equipped to do so. Haglund and Thomson called every friend, every acquaintance, appealing for help. Finally, Physicians for Human Rights, to which Haglund belonged, dipped into its own pockets to float the team's early expenses. Ultimately the U.S. State Department pledged $1 million for the exhumations, although the funds would be months in arriving. The team finally got some leftover equipment from military bases shutting down in Germany and other supplies from old UN warehouses. But until the British government donated three Land Rovers in late May, the forensic experts had no cars.

NATO wasn't helping matters either. For months, the tribunal's chief prosecutor, Richard Goldstone, and Admiral Leighton Smith, commander-in-chief of Southern Allied Forces, had been battling over just how much support the heavily armed peacekeepers would give to the war crimes court. Goldstone, aware of how difficult the exhumations would be, had asked for wide-ranging assistance. He wanted NATO soldiers to de-mine the graves, guard them, and escort the investigators. The graves, after all, lay deep in Bosnian Serb–held territory where a well-placed shell lobbed by someone wishing to impede the tribunal's work could wipe out the whole team.

But Admiral Smith, along with the senior NATO commander, General George A. Joulwan, at NATO headquarters in Brussels, opposed any involvement. "Investigating mass graves is not part of my job," Smith told reporters. NATO feared the "mission creep" that had so compromised the Americans in Somalia. Since January Joulwan had ruled out even having NATO soldiers near the mass graves. "We will not be in a position of guarding sites," Joulwan had firmly declared.

Frustrated, Goldstone turned to the U.S. secretary of defense, William Perry, with whom he had also been butting heads over the Pentagon's reluctance to share intelligence with the tribunal. Perry was at least willing to guarantee that American troops, in whose area of responsibility the mass graves lay, would escort tribunal investigators to the graves and guard them as they worked. He also agreed to have mass graves sites put under twenty-four-hour aerial surveillance.

When grave tampering was discovered that spring, however, NATO commanders had to make some concessions. The head of American forces in Bosnia, General William Nash, pledged he would have daily drive-by patrols check on the mass graves. Yet that was as far as NATO was willing to go, and that left the tribunal team without a way to remove land mines from the sites.

Haglund and Thomson began the search for a de-mining team even as they struggled to nail down all the equipment for the upcoming exhumations. They were locked in a battle with Bosnian authorities over where the pathology lab could be located. Tuzla, the closest major Bosnian Muslim city, was the most logical place. But local officials, not entirely happy that Srebrenica refugees had overwhelmed their scant resources, did not want the corpses either. They were hoping all the refugees would go home.

So even as experts from Guatemala, the United States, Chile, Argentina, and fifteen other countries began arriving to take part in the summer's dig—some ninety people including pathologists, radiologists, archaeologists, and anthropologists—hundreds of details had yet to be resolved.

Things fell into place only at the last minute. Norwegian People's Aid, a refugee assistance organization, found a dog team to sniff the graves for mines. On the morning of July 6, as a NATO convoy escorted the exhumation team through Serb-held eastern Bosnia to their summer home at Camp Lisa, an American base, Tuzla authorities offered Haglund a site for the morgue in an old sewing factory in the town of Kalesija near Tuzla.

"The property didn't look like much," Haglund scribbled in his journal that evening. "Heaps of broken bricks, wood, metal siding, broken glass littered the ground, intermixed with garbage. The buildings were bereft of windows, electrical fixtures had been stripped from the walls.... Any room with plumbing had been gutted leaving only gaping holes. I'll take it, I said, and the deal was sealed... we raced back to the convoy. At least we had an exam area. We had two weeks to set it up. But there were so many details hanging in the air. I felt tense at the thought of one decision after another."

On July 7—more than a month behind schedule, and almost exactly a year after the executions had occurred—the exhumation team got to work. As Haglund recalculated the team's summer schedule for the umpteenth time, he hoped that the worst was behind them. In fact, the worst was yet to come.

HASAN NUHANOVIĆ MET Bill Haglund when he went to Tuzla to explain to survivors how the exhumations were progressing. Haglund told them that, in Latin America, families had been able to stand by the graves as they were opened, and he expressed his regret that the Bosnian Muslim women—who were terrified to travel to Serb-held Bosnia—could not do the same. He talked about how only some of the mass graves were going to be examined and noted that the chances of identifying more than a few bodies were unlikely, unless a lot more money was allocated to make DNA identification possible. Haglund would go away remembering Hasan, the tall, thin young man with the intense, beseeching hazel eyes.

Hasan only half listened to Haglund's talk. He wanted to believe that, somehow, his family was alive.

Just a few weeks before, a UN police officer Hasan worked for had handed him an outdated copy of a Serbian newspaper, *Revija '92.* "Hasan, have you seen this?" the Russian officer asked, pointing to an article entitled "Mladić's Truth Against Lies from The Hague." Hasan scanned it: There, in black and white, was *his father's name.* The author mistakenly identified Ibro Nuhanović as a Bosnian Muslim military commander but wrote at length that Nuhanović was one of "three eyewitnesses" at the Hotel Fontana meetings where General Mladić had guaranteed that the Srebrenica refugees would be safely evacuated.

Hope flickered in Hasan's heart once again. Perhaps his father had been kept alive so he could testify on Mladić's behalf before the tribunal. The article's timing underscored this theory: It was written just after the Yugoslav Tribunal had indicted Mladić and Karadžić for the Srebrenica massacres. Maybe through this article the Bosnian Serbs were trying to send out the word that they had witnesses who would testify that Mladić wasn't guilty at all.

The article's author, Hasan discovered, had gleaned most of its details from the former Bosnian Serb information minister, Milovan Milutinović. Formerly General Mladić's spokesman, Milutinović now lived in the Bosnian Serb city of Banja Luka, to the west of Tuzla. But Banja Luka might as well be in Australia. Phone lines were still not connected between the Serb and Muslim-Croat halves of Bosnia. And Hasan had no way to travel there. Finally he convinced a friend working for the UN in Banja Luka to act as a middleman, relaying his questions to Milutinović and then reporting back the answers.

It was good solution in theory, but maddening and time-consuming in practice. The responses that came back were vague and contradictory. Yes, Milutinović said there was information that Muhamed, Hasan's brother, was alive. No, he said, maybe there wasn't information about Muhamed but maybe about Ibro, Hasan's father. Yes, he was 60 percent sure they were alive. No, make that 40 percent. Hasan's thick brown hair began to fall out with frustration. He was short-tempered with his girlfriend, Mirza. He smoked incessantly, sometimes going through a pack of cigarettes in just one conversation. He knew the day would come when he would have to get to Banja Luka to confront Milutinović himself.

And that was when I ran into Hasan for the second time, in Banja Luka that summer of 1996. We bumped into each other one night in the parking lot of the UN building. Against the backdrop of the evening's darkness, his face had a whitish pallor, taut over his pronounced cheekbones. He had discovered it had all been a terrible mix-up. His friend had been asking questions throughout the summer of the wrong man—Milovan Martinović, not Milovan Milutinović. As soon as Hasan walked into the meeting the error became clear; Martinović had simply been trying to be helpful but knew little. Yet he did give Hasan the phone number for Milutinović. Retreating to the UN office, Hasan had picked up a telephone and called him.

"Hello, sir," as he recalled the conversation unfolding, "I am Hasan Nuhanović. I'm the son of Ibro, who attended the meeting at Hotel Fontana."

"Yes, I remember your father," Milutinović replied slowly. "Yes, I remember him; he was wearing a blue shirt. He was even demanding things at that meeting on behalf of the refugees."

"You were at the Fontana?" Hasan asked, surprised.

"Oh, I was at that meeting. The chief [Mladić] was there to give all the guarantees to your father. We filmed the meeting, and we have more than twenty hours of material about Mladić," Milutinović said. "Your father is on it. We are keeping this as an alibi for the chief if he needs it."

"And my father," pressed Hasan. "Do you know what happened to my father?"

Milutinović sighed. "I don't know. I don't know what happened to your father after the meeting."

Polite good-byes. The telephone clicked in the receiver. Hasan put his head down on the desk in despair. What was the point of all his research, of his constant phone calls, in trying to find out anything at all, when the truth seemed so elusive?

But discovery is as much accident as method, and Hasan's hard work would pay off. Some four months later, into his office in Tuzla walked a woman employed by the UN in Srebrenica. Hasan had once asked her as a favor to track down a close colleague of his father's there. "Just ask if my father is alive or dead," he had said.

She stood, holding out her hand. In it was a folded piece of paper. Hasan took it and opened it. On it was scrawled the following message: "Hasan, someone I know told me he saw your father alive—two weeks after the fall of Srebrenica, in the Zvornik police station."

Hasan clenched his hand around the piece of paper. The trail, it seemed, always led to Zvornik.

And now it seemed to point to the city's police chief, Dragomir Vasić, whom Hasan had met on his very first trip to Zvornik early in 1996—the city in and around which all the mass graves lay. Since then he had heard Vasić described as a dangerous, corrupt nationalist who hated Muslims. Everyone warned Hasan Vasić would kill him if Hasan approached him directly. Hasan decided he'd have to convince the tribunal—or someone else—to go after Vasić.

GIVEN THE POLICE chief's reputation, Ibro's trail might well have led directly from Zvornik to the Cerska grave, a little over twelve miles down the road. The exhumations were finally under way by then, and Haglund was standing at the site. It was a picturesque spot, alongside an embankment above a stream, which bubbled and ran noisily over the rocks. An abandoned mill stood by the flowing waters. The firs were thick and green, and the birds sang noisily. The killers, however, had chosen the site for its configuration, not its beauty. The embankment dropped off steeply from the dirt track, creating a natural hollow for a mass grave. Now, that hollow was filled in with dirt, and bullet casings were scattered on the top.

There were no known survivors of the Cerska massacres. Srebrenica refugees fleeing through the woods on that July day in 1995 had seen buses, filled with men, turn off the main road and down the dirt lane that led to the village. Following the bus was an armored vehicle and an excavator. *Pow. Pow. Pow.* They overheard execution-style shooting. When the buses returned down the road later, they were empty. Only one man, gasping, had somehow missed being buried. "His last words were, 'In this grave, there are 173 of us,' " said Lutvo Hodzahmetović, a resident of Cerska. "We carried him for 200 meters, and he died."

Even without a survivor, the bones of the Cerska grave would have a powerful story to tell.

Of all the graves I saw exhumed, it was Cerska that I would come to know the best. The Yugoslav Tribunal's forensics team looked impressive as it headed to the grave. So imposing was the caravan—the backhoe, the UN trucks, and the escorting Humvees, with soldiers manning their 50-caliber machine guns—farmers in the fields lay down their scythes to gape. A Bradley Fighting Vehicle—which looks like a small, squat tank—guarded the intersection of the main road and the dirt road that led to Cerska.

When I arrived, German shepherds were sniffing the dirt for mines. Members of the forensics team, using a plumb line and measuring tapes, were surveying areas the dogs had declared safe; someone wielding a metal detector was looking for bullet casings. Haglund, his hands on his hips, was looking down at the grave, possibly the first still moment in the frenzied pace he had maintained for days. He scanned the slope of the incline, the mounded earth on the top, his eyes darting over the grave the way a surgeon looks at X rays: calculating, measuring, assessing where best to open it and how.

There was a reason for this. A mass grave is a complex, reactive environment. The soil, the drainage, and the insects and plant life that exist in and around it play a role in how bodies decompose. So does the manner in which bodies fall into a grave: Were they twisted and compressed by a bulldozer? Or did they fall on top of each other? Or did they fall side by side?

Each grave is different; each grave is a new puzzle. For example, an arm might lie at the surface of the grave, but the torso and legs could be buried deep in it, underneath other bodies. You couldn't just pull at the arm to release the body; the bodies were so decomposed it would come apart in your hands. Haglund spent hours just gazing into the grave, puzzling out what limb connected to which body and at what angle and where next to dig.

I watched as he directed the backhoe up to the grave, at times to the horror of those archaeologists and anthropologists on the team who were used to working with trowels. The immense maw of the backhoe looked as if it would swallow the grave and the evidence within it, but Bucknall and Haglund wielded it as gently as a surgeon would a scalpel. Slowly Bucknall would raise the backhoe and scrape away the earth, an inch at a time, like a horse pawing with its hoof. Haglund, his eyes riveted on the ground, searched for something to emerge. At the slightest signal from Haglund, Bucknall would stop the hoe. Haglund wanted every corpse removed as intact as possible from the grave; the more complete a body, the more complete a story it would tell.

"Once you begin to uncover a body, it is important to delineate that body: to know where the individual's hands, arms, and legs are," Haglund explained to me. And linking hands to heads was going to be important in this dig: If these corpses had been executed, their hands would be bound. The bodies also might bear blindfolds and have execution-style bullet wounds in the back of the heads.

Every bone was carefully photographed as it was uncovered, so investigators would know just where it lay in the grave. Then, slowly, the anthropologists and archaeologists removed the dirt from around the bone with trowels, fine brushes, and bamboo sticks, making an effort to isolate it from others in the grave. The dirt was carefully sifted for any bone fragments. Each body, once exposed, was marked with a red identifying flag, measured, surveyed, and numbered as evidence. Finally it would be lifted from the grave, placed in a body bag, and put in a refrigerator truck to be sent to the morgue. It was a laborious process, but the tribunal's case would rest on the quality of the evidence.

About ten days later, when I next returned to Cerska, the bodies were exposed and were being removed. Haglund demonstrated how the executions had proceeded. A group of men had been lined up on at the top of the embankment, about a quarter of them with their hands wired behind their backs. They were then shot, sprayed by automatic weapons; the bodies, Haglund noted, were peppered with bullet wounds. One by one they fell on top of each other. The executioners used the natural incline of the hill to their benefit; they didn't have to dig the grave. They only used a digger to scoop out the gravel from a nearby trench and dump it over the bodies.

"See how the left wrist is crossed over the right?" said Haglund, directing my attention to a pair of wrists, just exposed in the grave. "And see there, there is the wire that bound them."

He was standing in the grave, motioning to me to walk down the slope that led into it and join him. I had asked him to let me do this, but suddenly I was reluctant to follow. In my naïveté, I'd envisioned an orderly grave: rows of skeletons with clothes on, not this stinking brew. I'd worn shorts and sneakers, dressed for standing around in the broiling sun, but Haglund had dressed for the grave: long pants, a long-sleeved shirt, and rubber boots.

Gingerly I tiptoed down into the grave, alternately feeling foolish and squeamish, past the investigators busily measuring and marking bodies with flags. Others peeled the corpses out of the earth—at times, throwing their arms around the remains in a physical embrace—the bodies making a sucking sound as the dirt released them.

"Here, you can see the head, the left shoulder, the left hand. The knees are up, and the skull is down; it's clear he fell backward," Haglund said, as he troweled around a body numbered 87. "And this body—you see it?—it is parallel to the ditch, with the feet heading downhill. Here's the right shoulder, and the left."

I wrote furiously in my notebook. I hoped jotting down every detail would distract me from the intimacy of the bones, the sorrow of the naked wrists bound with wire, the omnipresent smell. I felt sick. I wanted to leave, but I couldn't admit this to Haglund. He was having a great day. Moreover, he had just spotted a body on the slope in which he was particularly interested. He yelled over to those slowly excavating it.

"Can you give me a right elbow? Is it there? Or the hand? Or the wrist? Is there a left?" The team quickly worked to isolate body number 86. "Do you think this is faceup or facedown?" asked one, standing near the rib cage, covered in rotting clothes.

Body 113: a skull, a black jacket. Body 114: red sneakers. Body 119: a man in fetal position, his knees drawn up to his chest. His pants wrapped around his leg bones. His hands, I noted, are flung up the hill, as if in desperation.

To me, the grave appeared to be nothing more than a soup of skulls, bones, and shoes boiling under the hot July sun. I could just make out the outlines of bodies, which melted one into another. One, wearing a white shirt, its skull smashed, appeared to be curled in a fetal position. Another, lying on its back with its arms outstretched, had on black shoes. Many bodies were badly decomposed because they had been buried on an incline, under a loose layer of gravel; water had flowed through the grave, speeding their disintegration.

"Can I have a reading on the head?" yelled one of the investigators, standing next to a shattered mass that did not look like a head to me.

I couldn't imagine how Haglund and his team could spend twelve hours a day with all this. How can they face death every day? "One aim is to establish an irrefutable historic record," Haglund said, dodging the question of how he handled the job emotionally, "so we can convict the people responsible for these murders." Later he told me: "I feel undaunted by death. Your duties are your armor. It's the problems that I have to solve, the logistics, that get me down."

When I returned that evening to the apartment where I was staying in Tuzla, I showered once, twice, three times. Eventually I went on to other stories in Bosnia. But for weeks afterward, I had a recurring dream that revolved around a pair of high-top sneakers I had seen in the Cerska grave. In my dream they had feet in them with ankles that descended into the grave's morass. Yet no matter how hard I looked, no matter how hard I dug, I couldn't reach the rest of that one body, lost deep amid all the others in the grave.

IN REAL LIFE, however, the team at Cerska was finding plenty of bodies; in fact, far more than expected. The grave's exhumation was taking longer than planned, and Haglund stepped up the pace. The team had to stay on schedule.

The pool of corpses—over a hundred—had drawn the attention of the Bosnian Serb government, which so far had steered clear of the exhumations. One day the Bosnian Serb deputy justice minister, Goran Nešković, arrived and Haglund gave him a tour of the grave. As Haglund—politely, professionally—pointed out the men's bound wrists, their shattered skulls, their T-shirts and their trousers, Nešković's face appeared drawn, seemingly angered. But he spoke little. "He only said, 'There were a lot of massacres,' " Haglund told me with a shrug.

As the days passed and Cerska yielded more and more bodies, everyone worked double time. They all looked exhausted, but Haglund had a peculiarly exhausted yet frenetic energy. He was chain-smoking cigars, snapping at people, issuing orders imperiously. Some staffers thought he was glaring at them with displeasure, but the truth was he was glassy-eyed from lack of sleep. I found out why: He was sleeping at the gravesite. Security arrangements made with independent contractors to guard the graves had fallen through. Seizing on the fact that NATO troops were guarding the tribunal's exhumations team, Haglund and other members of team had been taking turns camping out at the grave. To protect the team members, the NATO troops had to stay at the site.

Haglund insisted he didn't mind, despite the deep circles under his eyes. He used the wheelbarrow as a lounge chair. He'd build a fire, crack open an emergency flare, and read a mystery novel. He kept beer and watermelons cool in the brook nearby. At first he and John Gerns, an American forensic expert who camped out with him, slept in the Land Rover, but then they got cots.

Sitting out at night, admiring the vast expanse of stars above and the rush of the river, Haglund thought about the men killed at Cerska: how it must have felt to have stood there, their arms tied behind their backs, listening to that stream and waiting for the bullet to hit.

"It's a beautiful spot, you know, with the water rushing in the brook, and the stars above at night," he later explained. "It is deeply philosophical, in a way. It is conducive to looking and thinking: Why were they killed here? Who are these souls lying in a grave?

"If you really believe in human rights, you have to believe in individuals. To die so ignobly, so clandestinely—it's important to give victims a voice. I liked to think that somebody would be able to tell how it happened, if it happened to me."

Naser Orić, the enclave's former military commander, had called for all the exhumed bodies to be identified. But Haglund was more realistic. "Identification is a matter of months, years, if ever," he said.

By the time the Cerska grave was completely exhumed on July 19, each and every fragment had been carefully lifted from the grave's embrace. Some were exposed bones; others still encased in flesh. Regardless, each rib, each femur, each tiny fingerbone had been mapped and measured and photographed and placed into a body bag. Some 150 bodies and various body parts were lying in the refrigerator truck, ready to head to the morgue in Kalesija. There a team of forensic pathologists, headed by Kirschner, PHR's lead pathologist, would document the injuries, the time and cause of death, and collect information that could lead to the body being identified. Kirschner, a dark-bearded, voluble, and hyperactive scientist, was one of the world's authorities on gunshot wounds.

In the morgue, each body would be fluoroscoped, a kind of X-ray process that shows the presence of bullets. X rays would also be taken to reveal fractures and the particular build of each body. Skulls would be cleaned, fitted together, and glued. Teeth would be examined. Bones would be scrutinized for details such as left- or right-handedness. The pattern of gunshot wounds would be studied. The information would go both to the tribunal and the PHR team, working on compiling the ante-mortem database.

But first the bodies had to get safely from Cerska to Kalesija. NATO was not going to escort the truck. As Andrew Thomson, the scientific coordinator, pondered this dilemma late one afternoon, up pulled the Bosnian Serb police in their cars, lights flashing. They were, they said, under order from Karadžić to provide a safe escort for the bodies to the Serb border; from there, the truck would be escorted by authorities of the Muslim-Croat Federation.

A police escort provided by the government that ordered the Srebrenica killings? Thomson was incredulous. But he had little choice. And so he reluctantly climbed into the truck with his translator, and they set off. At each bend of the road, each steep incline, he expected the police car to ram into the truck, sending it teetering over the road's edge, taking all the evidence with it. "I thought," he admitted later, "that was the end of it."

But Thomson and the bodies arrived safely. In the morgue in Kalesija—still missing most of its furniture and equipment—the team heaved a sigh of relief and congratulated one another that the work had gone smoothly, even though there were more bodies than expected. There had been no clashes with the Serbs. They were optimistic they could still finish in time. But after Cerska, the team's luck would begin to run out.

MIDWAY THROUGH THE next dig, at the mass grave by the Nova Kasaba soccer field, the Norwegian government dispatched the mine-sniffing dogs to a dig in Mozambique, and work was halted for three weeks. Without knowing if the graves were safe, Haglund was not going to let his team exhume them. Back at the Kalesija morgue there were still so many problems unresolved: not enough gloves, scalpels, doctors, whatever. The X-ray machine wasn't working. Not everyone liked working for Kirschner, who could be brusque and overcritical. Not everyone liked working for Haglund, who drove people as hard as he drove himself. "I need someone to be the social chairman on the *Love Boat*," he would complain when staff wanted to take time off. And there were so many delays. By the time exhumations began at the third grave, Lazete—more or less the unofficial halfway point—it was already late August. Haglund, desperate to make up for lost time, again put himself on double schedule.

Adding to his worries was the fact that he also was expected to oversee the exhumation at the grave at Ovčara in Croatia, which he had first visited back in 1993 when he was with the UN Commission of Experts. With no satellite phones and no two-way radio, Haglund regularly commuted the 155 miles between the two sites, a three- to five-hour drive, depending on traffic.

Then Kirschner had to return to the United States, and the morgue was left without a manager. Haglund assumed that job too. By late summer, his days had become a grueling routine of digging and driving between three different areas. He gave up his room and lived out of the back of his car, where his dirty clothes and mud-encrusted boots soon piled up. The car smelled of grave odor mixed with Scotch, from a bottle that had fallen off the seat and broken. To have more daylight hours to spend on the two simultaneous exhumations, Haglund commuted at night. He'd simply pull off the road for a nap. By 4:00 A.M. he'd be back on the road, following his circuit from Ovćara to the morgue at Kalesija to the latest Srebrenica exhumation site.

Haglund had instructed the teams at both sites to expose bodies but not to remove them until he arrived. As each corpse was put into a body bag, he would quickly dictate notes about the clothing into a handheld tape recorder. It was an approach that annoyed many of the anthropologists on the dig, used to developing their own relationship with a grave. After having spent hours delineating a body—wiping off the dirt and getting to know it intimately—they wanted the psychological resolution of removing it from the grave themselves. They resented Haglund's interference. Overtired and overworked, Haglund simply told them they'd do it his way. Increasingly he struck some of his colleagues not only as obsessive but also slightly megalomaniacal.

His avuncular manner faded, his humor vanished. Haglund pushed himself relentlessly to get the work done. As the exhumations proved more and more demanding, Haglund whittled a week's vacation with his wife, Claudia, down to three days. They hadn't seen each other since January, the longest stretch apart in twenty years of marriage. Perhaps by error or through annoyance, when Claudia arrived with the clean shirts Haglund so desperately needed, she brought the wrong size.

And then the autumn rains arrived, with a vengeance.

They came during the exhumations at Branjevo Farm at Pilica. The site, estimated to hold up to 1,000 bodies, was the most crucial for the Yugoslav Tribunal's prosecutors. By then, prosecutors had Dražen Erdemović, who had confessed to executing men there, in custody. They had satellite imagery that had captured the bodies strewn on the field, the grave being dug, and the ensuing grave tampering. And two men who had survived had agreed to testify at The Hague. ("I prayed for darkness," one told me that summer, describing how he fell to the ground during the execution and played dead, a bullet having passed through his jacket without hitting him. "All around me, there was a meadow of dead people. I had come to the field in the morning, and by the late afternoon they were still killing people."

Yet Pilica, the grave that was so important to the developing court case, was the hardest exhumation of all. Under the lashing rains, Branjevo Farm's fields oozed into mud, every surface becoming a slippery slope. The grave flooded, turning quickly from an exhumation site into a swimming pool. Every day the tribunal team had to pump out the grave before they could dig. It was a gruesome job: The water was mixed with mud and rotting flesh.

In the grave itself—33 yards long by 11 yards wide and 5½ yards deep—the mud had the consistency of quicksand, sucking at the investigators' boots and pulling them down with it. As they slipped and slopped around, they had no choice but to lean or step on corpses to brace themselves. The team's seven-ton backhoe was in constant danger of slipping into the grave. Under the barrage of water, an entire wall of the grave collapsed, nearly burying the team with it.

And then there were the bodies: gelatinous, oozing corpses, hardly skeletalized at all. Pilica's remains were just one pile of goo. The dead men had been bulldozed into the grave, and so the bodies were smashed and shoved together at one corner. For the team, standing out in the waterproof clothing, mud to their knees, it was difficult to discern where one body ended and another began.

Tempers were fraying among the team, which had been working without a break since July. Their entire life revolved around driving to a grave, digging in it, and then driving back to camp out with the American troops at Camp Lisa in Vlasenica. It was nearly a two-hour commute each way. At night the team showered, they ate, and they drank Scotch before collapsing into bed. Everyone was exhausted, and it showed.

"It is the grave from hell," Haglund said wearily when I saw him in Tuzla. He and his clothes stank. His beard was straggly; his eyes, bloodshot. People walking by clapped their hands over their noses, but Haglund didn't care. "I'm taking two, three showers a day," he said peevishly. Nonetheless, before our interview I ordered him into my shower. Then, partway through the interview, he fell asleep midsentence, sitting upright on the sofa. "It's Pilica, it's awful," he explained when he awoke.

Some of Haglund's team members accused him of being high-handed, complaining he hogged the media. (The tribunal had asked him to act as spokesman.) "Some people," one team member said later, "used this work as a means of self-promotion." Others found him too dictatorial for their tastes. Haglund—exhausted, worried, frantic, obsessed with getting things done—had lost the art of polite conversation. He'd cut people's sentences short, issued instructions that sounded like orders; he lost all tolerance for stupidity. Pulling up to Camp Lisa one day in his car—clothes scattered in the back, along with his shovels—Haglund drove away in a fury when a young soldier refused to let him in unless he unpacked every item. When he returned later, still in a huff, the soldier trained his gun on Haglund, convinced he was some kind of nut.

But it wasn't just the demanding hours, the monotonous and muscle-breaking work, the cramped quarters, and the smell of death that affected the team members who rotated in and out under Haglund's direction that summer. The bodies they were digging up weren't wearing garb from another century; they were dressed in Levi's and Nikes, reminding them of their own loved ones. It was impossible for team members to keep an emotional distance from the bodies. Yet they had little psychological support, cut off from their own families, their bosses in The Hague, even the families whose loved ones they were trying to uncover. And they were laboring to preserve evidence for a case that might never come to trial unless NATO troops began arresting war criminals.

"These people had never been involved with these things before, especially the archaeologists," Haglund told me. "They hadn't had to deal [in previous digs] with hands and feet, which are so empathetic, which prompt the thought, is this someone I know? They hadn't had to deal with contemporary clothing. So this thudded them across the noggin, with an extra zap of psychology. But I drove people hard," he added. "I drove myself hard."

"I never thought I would have to do more than one site at a time," he said some years later, reflecting on that summer of 1996. "I knew it would be horrible, and it was horrible. . . . That whole summer was beyond The Hague's vision. They didn't realize how much time it would take. There was no clear direction. And we didn't have a good sense of what we were getting into."

Even death-hardened Haglund all but broke into tears one day, exhuming a body so poignant it haunted him for weeks. It was a man with an artificial leg. Despite his handicap, his hands had been wired behind his back in preparation for his execution.

By October Haglund and his team had exhumed five of the graves the tribunal needed. Bosnia's graves had yielded 650 bodies; the Ovčara grave in Croatia, 200. Added to the two sites Haglund had exhumed in Rwanda that year, he had overseen the exhumation of approximately 1,200 bodies.

That summer's exhumations were one of the largest, most daring ever attempted. But they would come at a price Haglund never expected to pay.

ON ONE LEVEL, the Srebrenica case was proceeding well: Dražen Erdemović, the mass executioner at Pilica, had confessed to the Yugoslav Tribunal, providing valuable evidence of how he and other members of his execution squad, including Marko Boškić, had gunned down prisoners. Erdemović, a twenty-five-year-old Bosnian Croat with curly hair and an angelic face, had been a mercenary. He began the war in the Bosnian

Army but had drifted to the Serb side. When the war finished, he claimed, Serb members of his squad singled him out and harassed him because of his ethnicity.

He cried during some of his testimony. Because of his youth, his apparent remorse, his value to the Srebrenica investigation, and the fact that he committed the execution under duress, the young executioner received a ten-year sentence on November 29, 1996. In Bosnia, Srebrenica survivors including Hasan were outraged. Ten years for an estimated 1,200 lives? The news shook Hasan's confidence in the Yugoslav Tribunal. Even Judge McDonald was surprised. She thought the sentence should have been longer.

At the same time the United Nations was being accused of complicity in Srebrenica's capture and the ensuing massacres. The failure of the Dutch UN troops to protect Bosnian Muslim civilians in Srebrenica had become a major scandal in the Netherlands. A government inquiry was launched, but—much to Hasan's, and other survivors', distress—it absolved the UN peacekeepers, blaming UN commanders instead. Even in France, questions were being raised about UN general Bernard Janvier, who had refused three separate calls for air strikes before finally approving the bombing that had come too late to help.

On another level, the Srebrenica investigation had hit a major snag. After the exhumations ended, several members of the team complained to tribunal investigators that shortcuts had been taken that could compromise the evidence. Among the complaints, other than Haglund's management style, were that the graves had not been made secure. Animals had raided some of them, dragging off body parts. Other allegations centered on administrative sloppiness; some bodies and their parts had been wrongly labeled. Fearful that defense attorneys in the case might have been handed a powerful weapon, the tribunal and its lawyers launched an internal inquiry.

Haglund had no sooner returned to his home in Seattle for his first vacation in more than a year when he got the news he was suspended and his work was under review. He was furious, hurt, and outraged all at once. The tribunal had assembled a list of some twenty-seven complaints, from the picayune to the serious. But my God, he thought, the team had exhumed five mass graves in three months, as the Yugoslav Tribunal had asked him to do!

Haglund was not alone; serious complaints had also been raised about how Bob Kirschner, the PHR pathologist who oversaw the morgue, handled some of the pathology reports.

The tribunal inquiry lasted well over a year and deeply divided the exhumation team. Some saw the probe as a necessary precaution; critics saw it as a witch-hunt. Some thought Haglund was unfairly dragged through the whole mess; others believed sloppy mistakes had been made and that Haglund had no one but himself to blame. Predictably, Haglund loathed the whole process, which consisted of a review of the summer's work by the tribunal's registrar and then by an outside panel of forensics experts.

Yet when it was all done, Haglund would be fully cleared, and his suspension lifted in 1997; no action was taken against Kirschner. Even years afterward, tribunal staff disagree over whether the inquiry was necessary. Yugoslav Tribunal officials maintain that given the complaints that would undoubtedly be raised by defense attorneys at trial, they had no choice but to closely examine Haglund, Kirschner, and the summer's exhumation results. "We had to take a strict legal position," explained deputy prosecutor Graham Blewitt. "There were allegations that evidence was compromised, and we didn't know what the truth was."

Others, arguing that the Yugoslav Tribunal had something of a reputation for arrogance and high-mindedness, thought the court could have handled the complaints in a less inquisitorial manner. And had the tribunal not asked so much of Haglund and his exhumation team, there might not have been any complaints or possible shortcuts, they argue. "It was shameful," said one former Yugoslav Tribunal investigator.

In the end, it seemed that everyone was to blame: the tribunal, inexperienced in the demands of forensic work; PHR, which agreed to exhume the sites and pushed its team to finish; and Haglund and Kirschner, who took on more than they could handle. "Everybody got in over their heads," said Clyde Snow, the world-famous forensic anthropologist who also worked on the Ovčara exhumation while a consultant for PHR. "I don't think any one person can be blamed for this. They were trying to do too much, and they had to do it on a shoestring budget. If you took the medical examiners' offices in Chicago and Los Angeles and put them into one, it would equal what these guys were trying to do on an ad hoc basis."

Haglund would not return to work for the Yugoslav Tribunal, although he would go on to testify before both the Rwanda and Yugoslav tribunals. Even though the Srebrenica exhumations would continue, Haglund would not be part of them. But as he flew off to exhumations in Cyprus and elsewhere, his thoughts would turn to the bodies he had dug up so painstakingly in Bosnia during the summer of 1996. Under cover of darkness, they had all been carefully moved from the morgue at Kalesija into the city of Tuzla. There, shrouded in white body bags, they lay in an old tunnel that burrowed under a hillside. Haglund hoped against hope that those bodies would ensure another kind of justice for Bosnians: identification.

10

HAVING CLEAN HANDS

The word *performance* keeps rising. He sees he wrote down his nadir reached: Justice is a performance.

—Nadine Gordimer, *The House Gun*

"You should really go to Rwanda," Bill Haglund told me one day late in the summer of 1996. "Now, there's a story."

He was taking a short break from the graves, and my translator, Alex, and I had dragged him off for a beer. It was the sort of sultry afternoon that in Bosnia signifies the last gasp of summer; we'd ended up outside the city of Tuzla at a lake crammed with holidaygoers, picnicking and splashing in the water. There we sat at a table, watched the sunset, and tried to remember what our lives were like before Bosnia.

I asked Haglund how he came to be exhuming graves in Bosnia, and he began by telling me about his brief trip to Croatia with the UN Commission of Experts, which led to his later being dispatched to Rwanda. He described his Rwandan exhumations and how he and his team had preserved evidence of massacres for at least two upcoming trials. Yet the latest news out of Rwanda had shaken his hopes for several of the cases. Witnesses due to testify before the tribunal had been killed, he said.

"I know you are interested in postwar justice in Bosnia. But Rwanda," he said, standing up and wiping his hands on his less-than-clean corduroy jeans. "I mean, witnesses are getting killed off there. That's justice in the rough."

I tucked the idea away. Rwanda. Two parallel war crimes tribunals. Two countries racked with postwar hatred, which international leaders said must find a way to forget and forgive. I was intrigued by the idea, so I briefly mentioned a trip to Rwanda to my editor and then forgot about it. With the Dayton peace agreement barely limping along in Bosnia—most reporters were taking bets as to which side would restart the fighting first—traveling to Rwanda was unlikely.

But Rwanda came to me, or at least the request that I pack my bags and go there posthaste. It was early November 1996, and tens of thousands of Rwandan Hutu, camped out in refugee camps in Zaire since the end of the genocide in 1994, had come under attack from rebel Zairean Tutsi and were believed to have fled into the jungle. UN officials were warning of a "humanitarian crisis."

The crisis was actually as political as it was humanitarian, and it had been brewing for months, if not years. Zaire's corrupt dictator, Mobutu Sese Seko, had happily given shelter to some 700,000 Hutu, including many of the militia members who had taken part in Rwanda's genocide. Since 1994 the refugee camps had become a political embarrassment as well as a regional threat.

To begin with, the camps had, somewhat unfairly, become the focus of the West's humanitarian aid. As disease and hunger had swept through them, in 1994, killing tens of thousands, the United States and Europe had opened their purses. An estimated $2.5 billion in Western aid poured into refugee camps in Zaire, resulting in a shameful inversion of priorities: Those who perpetuated the genocide received more aid than those who survived it. Only $572 million went to Rwandans to rebuild their ravaged homeland.

Unwittingly, the West's largesse handed another weapon to the genocide's architects. Hutu extremists, ruling the camps like kings, seized the humanitarian aid and used it as a way to control the refugees in their power. Those who obeyed their extremist calls were rewarded; those who didn't were punished. The UN estimated that some 230 key leaders were in the camps, stockpiling food and medicine and selling them to buy guns in preparation for attack on Rwanda. Poised on Rwanda's border, the refugee camps allowed the killers they sheltered to conduct cross-border raids against Tutsi and continue the genocide.

As long as the camps remained, it was clear there could be no peace for Rwanda. But there appeared to be no peace for Zaire either. Discontented with Mobutu's corrupt rule, the Zairean Tutsi, or Banyamulenge, formed their own rebel army. Irate, the Zairean government had ordered the country's Tutsi—many of whom had lived there for generations—to leave. In turn, the rebels, led by fifty-one-year-old Laurent Kabila, a student of Che Guevara, struck back. With Rwandan military aid, they easily pushed Mobutu's forces out of eastern Zaire and by November occupied the city of Goma, right on the Rwandan border.

As Zaire and Rwanda headed toward war, the Tutsi rebels attacked the camps, hoping to send Rwanda's Hutu back to their own country. Their strategy misfired; many refugees in the chaos were believed to have fled to the west, deep into Zaire's jungle, instead of eastward to Rwanda. Aid officials were consigning many of the 700,000 Rwandan Hutu refugees on the run to illness or death.

Yes, Rwanda was back in the news again. "I think you should go," said my editor, and so I did. I arrived in Kigali late one evening, on a very dark, moonless night. I saw nothing of the city save the blur of streetlights on the ride from the airport. It was a symbolic beginning for me, underscoring what an American cliché I was; I was reporting from a continent that I knew only from reading Joseph Conrad's *Heart of Darkness*. And I was reporting from a country to which I had been dispatched only because genocide had torn it asunder and justice was to reconcile it. "The only cure for Rwanda is justice," Josue Kayijaho of Ibuka, a victim's association, told me. The question was what form the cure should take.

WHAT FIRST SURPRISED me was Rwanda's seeming normality. Unlike Bosnia, which in some ways resembled London after the Blitz, Rwanda was largely unscathed physically after the fighting of 1996. Only the bullet holes that pockmarked the side of the Parliament building in the capital, Kigali, bore witness to recent clashes. The rest of the city seemed peaceful: purple and pink bougainvillea along the roadside, gaily painted storefronts, villas with balconies perched on the hill, tall acacia and cypress trees.

And then there were all the people—crowds of people—streaming along the road with baskets of food perched on their heads, jamming the outdoor markets, strolling the streets. I had expected the streets to be desolate, the markets empty, because between 500,000 and 1 million people had perished and hundreds of thousands more had decamped to Zaire. I had thought I would have been able to see the legacy of the genocide in the absence of Rwandans themselves.

Yet Rwanda had been overpopulated to begin with, and after the RPF victory, some 750,000 Tutsi who had lived in Uganda or other African countries since 1959 had finally returned home with their families. They returned with a burning sense of justice, a desire to improve the land, but almost no knowledge of its customs, practices, or even its official language, French, much less its native language, Kinyarwandan. They spoke English, the language used in Uganda.

As a result of the influx, the country was oddly trifurcated. There were Tutsi survivors of the genocide, crippled, impoverished, and poor. There were returning Tutsi, more modern, more European, better off, who knew of genocide only from news accounts. And then there were the country's many Hutu—its majority—a mixture of those who had nothing to do with the genocide, those who were victimized by it, and those who took part in it.

At first, Rwanda's seeming normalcy made the pain and loss wrought by the genocide almost impossible to grasp. The restaurants were open, the banks in operation, and bustling markets offered everything from women's shoes to black-market foreign currency. It took me some weeks to realize that the legacy of Rwanda's genocide lived on in people's inner lives. Survivors, whether Tutsi or Hutu, went through the motions of everyday existence but not its emotions; they skated across their feelings, frightened of experiencing them too deeply. One of my translators, Françoise—whose family had been killed in the genocide—answered me this way, when I asked her how the slaughter had affected Rwandan society. "Look right in front of you," she replied. "We have all lost something. We even have an expression for it: *bapfuye buhagazi*. It means the walking dead. This is the land of the walking dead."

During the weeks and months I spent in Rwanda, I came to absorb what she meant. The people I befriended understood intellectually what had happened to them: they had lost their entire family or their homes, or they had been raped or had narrowly escaped death. But they were not yet reconciled with those losses. The speed with which the genocide took place—the killing lasted just 100 days—had deprived victims of the time to come to terms with it. So did the reality of living in Rwanda, as Tutsi and Hutu coexisted in an uneasy truce. Everyone I met had a family member who was either a victim of the genocide or accused of taking part in it. Rwandans, deeply private by nature, had become even more so; they didn't trust their neighbors, their friends, their family, or themselves. Conversations had the strained air of a Victorian-era tea party, at which emotions were never mentioned.

Who could live with such fear, suspicions, and anguish, day in and day out? No wonder people seemed to be sleepwalking through life. All that kept them together, other than deep ties to the land, was the promise of the future: the promise made by the RPF government that Rwanda would be for all Rwandans and would deliver an even-handed justice. Authorities vowed to follow the terms set down by the Arusha accords, which established power-sharing between the Hutu and Tutsi and different political parties. At first the Tutsi-led RPF tried to be all-inclusive: Of twenty-two government ministers, sixteen were Hutu and just five from the RPF. Symbolically, Rwanda's president was Hutu: Pasteur Bizumungu, one of the Hutu who had sided with the RPF before their invasion.

Yet the real power broker was the swashbuckling General Paul Kagame, the man behind the 1990 RPF invasion that preceeded the genocide. The government in reality was an uneasy alliance of conqueror and conquered that, by 1996, had all but fallen apart. Hutu officials, finding themselves disenfranchised by Kagame and his supporters, quit in disgust, claiming the RPF government was not one of national unity after all. First to go was the Hutu chief of staff, J. D. Ntakirutimana. He was followed by the Hutu prime minister, Faustin Twagiramungu. "Some of us believed the RPF victory would enable us to achieve real change," Twagiramungu said. "But the RPF has simply installed a new form of Tutsi power." Four others resigned and left the country shortly afterward, including Interior Minister Seth Sendashonga, a well-respected moderate, critical of what he believed to be reprisal killings of civilians by the RPF army.

While Hutu still dominated the Rwandan cabinet in 1996, their presence was more token than influential. The Tutsi, particularly those returning from Uganda, held the real power and dominated all other political, judicial, intellectual, and even economic institutions in the country. In every town I went to, the mayor, or burgomaster, was Tutsi, regardless of the area's ethnic mix. Consequently, the country's Hutu felt disenfranchised, particularly because Hutu were still being indiscriminately accused of war crimes, arrested and jailed. Reprisals for the genocide were common: The country's army, the RPA, once a highly disciplined force, had picked up new Tutsi recruits who reveled in violence and used their newfound power to harass and kill Hutu. Twagiramungu estimated that as many 310,000 Hutu had been killed.

By November 1996 Rwanda's strained peace faced a new challenge when events brewing across the border in Zaire finally bubbled over. The tens of thousands of Rwandan Hutu in the refugee camps were on the move. While many had fled westward—away from Rwanda—many more, coming under attack from Zairean Tutsi rebels, had turned to flee eastward, toward Rwanda. After two years, they were headed home.

THE FIRST TRICKLE of returning refugees—carrying battered leather suitcases and balancing dirty bedrolls on their heads—washed over the Rwandan border on November 11. As I stood by the metal gate manned on both sides by surly bureaucrats wielding rubber stamps with abandon, the refugees limped across, exhausted. The returning Rwandan Hutu told of hunger, of wandering for weeks in the jungle, of being attacked by Zairean Tutsi rebels. "I saw so many dead bodies I stopped counting," Devota Mukarusema, a mother of six, told me as she leaned on her wooden staff by the roadside, tears mingling with the sweat coursing down her face.

By November 15, however, that trickle had swollen to a flood, and standing at the border was like watching an angry river's swift, inexorable currents breach a breakwater. Tens of thousands of people were marching home. The undulating column of returning Hutu was nearly twenty-five miles long, moving and shimmering under the sun, and no matter how high a hill one climbed, it still stretched from one horizon to another. On and on and on they came, calabashes and plastic jugs of water on their heads, babies on their backs, bags of food in their arms, walking with bare feet or, in the case of one woman, in one golden slipper. So determined were the Hutu returnees that they crossed the border at the rate of nearly 200 people per minute. By midday a transit camp near the Rwandan border designed to hold 30,000 refugees was already full. All along the road from Zaire into Rwanda, the air smelled of pungent sweat and sweet eucalyptus. Families, tired after what had often proven to be a march of several weeks, camped out by the roadside and lighted brush fires.

And yet they continued, hips and heads and shoulders swaying, men and women and grandmothers and adolescents and children and crying babies. Some pregnant women, swept up in the return, gave birth on the road. "No, there is no name yet," said Elisabeth Nyiranfubakuze, holding up a corner of the *pagne* she had wrapped around herself, to show her newborn baby's wrinkled face. "I am just too tired."

To the surprise of Western aid officials, scurrying to set up makeshift camps and organize the distribution of humanitarian aid, many of the returning refugees looked the picture of health, carrying plenty of provisions with them for their march. Indeed, their return looked less like an urgent flight from armed rebels than a planned evacuation. "They're carrying firewood—how many people fleeing for their lives carry firewood?" wondered Russell Nielson of Save the Children Foundation, as he tried to wind his truck through the packed crowd at the Rwandan border.

That night I found myself struggling for ways to describe what I had witnessed, this mass movement of people. The flow had not abated by nightfall, and indeed it would take four days for all the refugees to cross. At a loss, I settled for the word "exodus" to describe the return of the Hutu in the story I wrote for the *Boston Globe*, even though the expression was a cliché. In retrospect, it was not such a bad choice, for it is in Exodus—the second book of the Old Testament—that questions of sin, justice, and forgiveness are first raised in the Bible. God is enraged when he discovers the people of Israel have made a golden calf to worship, despite his orders not to make any graven image. Moses pleads for forgiveness on their behalf. God, in turn, defines justice: "The Lord . . . forgiving iniquity and transgression and sin, but who will by no means clear the guilty. . . ."

Understanding evil, defining repentance, avoiding vengeance, delivering judgment, granting forgiveness: These were the issues three-quarters of a million returning Hutu now posed for Rwanda. Indeed, they were issues the country was already meeting head-on. That afternoon, President Bizimungu had climbed on top of a pile of potato sacks at the border and greeted the refugees through a bullhorn. "Your brothers are waiting for you in Rwanda," he bellowed. "Together we will build a new Rwanda where peace will prevail. Do not be afraid."

Unofficially, feelings were anything but hopeful. In tiny villages near the border, where Tutsi had been killed with a vengeance, small groups of survivors greeted the news of the Hutu return with as much enthusiasm as a death warrant. Nyundo, a small village that crept up a lush hillside some twenty miles from the border, was one such place. Its white cathedral, the largest building for miles, was where almost 500 Tutsi, including some 30 Catholic priests, were massacred in 1994. Outside the cathedral's wooden door a hand-painted sign read: "We must pray that those who committed genocide never return to their country. To kill is against God's words."

I found Suzanne Nyirantagorama sitting underneath that sign the day after the first Hutu returned. She had been crouched there for some hours, her thin arms encircling knees she had drawn up protectively to her chest. That morning she had seen the faces of two men she thought she would only see again in her nightmares: two members of the Hutu militia who had slaughtered her neighbors but somehow, in their frenzy, had missed Suzanne and her family. They had just returned to Nyundo. Had they come there for her, now one of only ten surviving Tutsi in the village? "I am frightened," she said, putting her head down on her knees, as if she could curl into a ball and simply disappear from sight. "I don't know if they came back with a good heart or if they will continue their killing."

Father Jean-Marie Vianney Nsengumurcmyi, Nyundo cathedral's priest and also a massacre survivor, strode out of the church, his green-and-white cape billowing. We stood on the cathedral steps and looked down on the road below, where the endless line of returning refugees marched past the smoke of roadside campfires. He shook his head. How easy it would be for Rwanda to erupt into violence again, for hatred to persist, for vengeance to take hold. "Justice must work here," he said firmly, as if to remind himself to add it to his prayers. "Without it, we can't advance."

Later that day I again returned to the border crossing just outside the graceful city of Gisenyi. As I scanned the crowd of returning Hutu, I wondered just who was whom and what role each had played in the genocide. What about that man in the pink shorts and red shirt, a yellow jerry can strapped to his hip, his well-muscled shoulders barely straining under the sack balanced on his head? Was he responsible for the killing at Nyundo? Or that teenager there, with the green windbreaker and the blue flip-flops, or even that woman, her purple-and-white *pagne* wrapped around her, a bedroll on her head. What had they done?

I was not alone in scrutinizing the tired, lined faces of the refugees marching home. Crowds of Tutsi and Hutu stood at the border, looking for enemies as well as friends and relatives. My translator, Françoise, broke into my thoughts as we stood there. All eight of her family had been slaughtered by Hutu militia in Gisenyi; she lived simply because she'd been at a neighbor's house when the killers arrived. Survivors' guilt was a burden she, a staunch Catholic who found solace in her faith, bore without complaint.

"See that one?" Françoise said, pointing to a small man shuffling along, bowed under the weight of his suitcase on his back. "I'm pretty sure he's the man who killed my neighbor up the street." She strained forward to look. "Yes, that's him." She nodded.

Françoise had told me earlier that she had a good idea of who had killed her family. So I asked, "What would you do if you saw those responsible for killing your family?"

"I've been looking at the crowd," she said, continuing to peer at the faces parading by. "So far I haven't seen anyone responsible for my family's death."

I persisted. "But what if you did?"

Françoise sighed. Conflicting emotions played across her broad face. She was quiet for a good five minutes, searching her soul, asking her God for guidance. "Vengeance," she said finally, "won't bring my family back. The answer lies in justice and in God."

WHO WAS TO deliver this justice? The International Criminal Tribunal for Rwanda was to prosecute the key leaders of the genocide, but most Rwandans had swiftly dismissed it as ineffective. For one thing, it promised an unequal justice. The Rwanda Tribunal intended to judge the genocide's most heinous criminals; yet the most severe penalty one could receive from the court was life imprisonment. That meant that the high-ranking architects of mass murder would receive a more lenient sentence than the smaller fry judged by Rwanda's own courts, which routinely handed down the death sentence. This seeming irrationality made little sense to anyone.

And the tribunal, Rwandans were swift to point out, still had yet to do anything. Twenty-one indictments had been issued and thirteen people were in custody. Yet nearly two years after the court's founding, trials had not yet begun. It was as if the United Nations and its member states had drawn no lessons from their peacekeeping mission in Rwanda, where underequipped and outnumbered soldiers watched helplessly as the genocide commenced, their cries for reinforcements ignored. The Rwanda Tribunal also had little funding. Like its sister tribunal in The Hague, it received money only on a stopgap basis, making it impossible to recruit staff. In January the UN Special Rapporteur on Rwanda had appealed to the UN to "increase the budget of the International Tribunal in order to provide it with the necessary human and material means to fulfil its mission as effectively as possible." Still, the Rwanda Tribunal received only $36 million in 1996, doled out in three-month increments, and the slow-moving UN bureaucracy was slow to respond to the court's needs.

The shortfall was obvious on the ground. Tribunal investigators arrived in Gisenyi, anxious to cross into Zaire and check the now-abandoned camps for incriminating evidence left behind by Hutu leaders. But no one had approved their travel orders and they couldn't enter Zaire without them. They were reduced to hanging around the hotel pool, pouncing on journalists who might have documents they could use. "You just back from Zaire? Did you make it to Mugunga [a refugee camp]? Did you find anything?" asked one tribunal investigator, as I arrived back late one evening clasping papers in my arms.

In the absence of an effective tribunal, Rwanda was left to itself to dispense justice. Justice was one of the RPF government's bywords and reforming the justice system one of their top priorities. But these goals would be difficult to achieve. Rwanda's justice system, which had suffered for decades from the whims of its various rulers, was partisan and corrupt. No independent association of defense attorneys had existed, just one appointed by the government, and its lawyers frequently lacked legal training. After the genocide, little remained of the country's judicial system. The majority of lawyers and staff had been killed. Out of 750 judges, only 244 had survived. Courtrooms and offices were smashed, furniture and equipment stolen or destroyed. The windows of the Ministry of Justice building in Kigali had been blown out and its case files set afire. Law books had vanished as had copies of the country's code of criminal procedure.

In the absence of a functioning police and judiciary, Rwanda's army was making sweeping arrests, in theory to ensure people did not take vengeance into their own hands. The country's prisons were filled to overflowing. But Rwandan justice, human rights groups warned, was far from even-handed. Some 80,000 Rwandans, nearly all Hutu, were behind bars. There were rarely case files explaining why someone had been arrested. Those being trained to fill the jobs of judges and prosecutors were almost all Tutsi, hardly a reflection of the country's ethnic mix. Now some 750,000 Hutu Rwandans—many implicated in the genocide—were on their way home. Who would judge them?

At the Ministry of Justice, Deputy Justice Minister Gerald Gahima had been assigned to bring the country's justice system up to speed. A tall man, thin as a drinking straw, Gahima was a Tutsi who had grown up in Uganda. An optimist about what Rwanda could accomplish, he noted with pride how far the country had progressed in a mere two years. With Western aid, the government had rebuilt courthouses, including the Supreme Court. It had installed a few telephones, collected law books, and begun training a handful of new judges and prosecutors. Some $44.6 million had been pledged to overhaul the justice system, although about $66 million was needed.

Still, Gahima admitted, because of the mass nature of the crimes, justice would mean distinguishing not only between good and bad but also between innumerable shades of gray. "The crimes committed here involve everyone," he told me. "If a million people died, then you have to figure at least 2 to 3 million are complicit in the crimes. But you can't prosecute them all. We must punish the leaders and find a way of dealing more leniently with the rest."

Agreeing how to do that was proving no easy task. Questions of justice divided the government. Its moderates, both Tutsi and Hutu, wanted only the most high-ranking, powerful participants in the genocide to be prosecuted, hoping to spur their country toward reconciliation. But RPF hard-liners wanted as many of the guilty people to be arrested and punished as possible.

It took months of heated debate before Rwanda's Parliament passed the country's genocide law in August 1996, a law that was actually more lenient than many desired. The law divided crimes into categories with different penalties, ranging from Category 1, the architects and planners of the genocide who would receive the death penalty, down to Category 4, or those involved with property crimes. Quite controversially, it allowed for defendants in Categories 3 and 4 to plea-bargain after a confession and an apology. The hope was that scores of the accused—dubbed *génocidaires*—would confess, emptying the prisons and clearing the docket so trials would move swiftly when they began in 1997.

Up in the hills, people were already publicizing the government's new law, hoping returnees would sign up to confess. I'd seen them there, using a megaphone to summon residents scattered in homes along the hillside, and then trying to explain the concept to them. I asked Gahima about those returning from Zaire. How did the government plan to ensure that suspected killers weren't the target of vengeance, rather than justice, when they moved back home? Gahima acknowledged the question with a nod. For now, the plan was to arrest only Category 1 offenders, the leaders, he explained. (Despite good intentions, however, an estimated 6,810 returnees were arrested by mid-January 1997.)

But what about those already in jail? I asked. How long would they have to wait for trials? What if innocent people had been put behind bars accidentally in the first wave of arrests? Both Rwandan and Western human rights groups were finding cases in which prisoners had been fingered by a neighbor jealous of his property or eager to settle scores. If the Rwandan government was trying to send a message that impunity was over and a new era of justice had begun, shouldn't the justice system have to meet the highest possible standards?

Silence. Then Gahima looked at me. "The problem isn't just one human being committing a crime against another," he replied. "But all human beings were doing things that no one could imagine a human could do. It was as if there was a kind of collective insanity. . . ." His voice trailed off.

"What you end up with in a post-genocide society is not justice," the deputy justice minister concluded. "Perhaps we should think of another word for it."

"**ANOTHER WORD FOR** it" certainly described Kigali Central Prison. A massive, red-brick Victorian edifice that stood on Avenue de la Justice, the prison was a forbidding place. When the black iron gates clanged behind me as I entered its first courtyard, I realized I had not only walked through a door, I had traded the world of light and space and movement for one of darkness, crowds, and fetid air. I could only just step inside; the prison was simply too packed with men, a mass of bodies, for me to walk any farther. In order for me to proceed through the prison yard, the warden forced the inmates to their feet; they had to hug each other as they crammed to one side to let me squeeze through.

"Out of the way, out of the way," a guard yelled. "Move, move, come on." The prisoners—8,764 of them, more than four times the prison's capacity—either stood, ramrod straight, jammed shoulder to shoulder, or sat, knees to their chest, tightly packed in with all the others, hour after hour. They had to negotiate with each other in order to move or stretch their limbs. Clad in pink shirts and shorts that made them look like beauticians rather than alleged mass murderers, the prisoners smelled of sweat, damp clothing, and unwashed feet. Fleas hopped up and down on their arms, their heads. Most lay in the rooms they were assigned to, some six or eight people to a rough-hewn wooden bunk. They stretched out in alternating reverse direction, feet to head to feet again, like sardines in a can. Above them, dozens of bright raffia or plastic bags holding their possessions dangled from the ceiling, like rows of cow udders.

As I talked with one prisoner who was lying at the outer edge of his bunk, I glanced down. Next to my foot I spotted a gleam of white in the darkness. It smiled at me. I recoiled; it was a man's head. So tightly packed was this room that men slept under the bunk beds, too. It was clear why there had been so many deaths from overcrowding or asphyxiation, tuberculosis, and dysentery. In one prison in the town of Gitarama, 884 prisoners died in just one seven-month period.

A voice piped up in English, asking a question that seemed surreal, given the context. "Where are you from? I went to the University of Chicago," it asked. The University of Chicago! That is how I met Leon Nsengimana, a doctor who had worked in the family planning section of the Ministry of Health in the former Hutu government.

Leon was not sure why he had been arrested, but he had been in Kigali Central Prison for two years. He and his wife, Marie Claire—both a mix of Tutsi and Hutu—had fled the capital during the genocide for the province of Kibuye. In the confusion and chaos that engulfed them, fifteen members of their immediate family were slain. When the RPF government seized control of Rwanda in 1994, it had called on former members of the government who had not taken part in the genocide to return. Leon and Marie Claire didn't hesitate. "I said to myself, 'Why not? I'm not a *génocidaire*,' " Leon said. They went back to Kigali and reclaimed their house. Leon was arrested twenty-eight days later.

Like 2,892 other prisoners in Kigali Central Prison, Leon had no case file. (In fact, the UN Special Rapporteur on Human Rights, René Degni-Ségui, concluded in a 1996 report that it was "rare for persons arrested and detained to have a case file.") That meant Leon had been arrested because someone had accused him of genocidal activities but no investigation into those charges had taken place yet. (In the Rwandan justice system, a relic of Rwanda's days as a Belgian colony, investigating police don't work for the prosecution but seek to establish the truth or falsehood of the accusation.) According to the gossip that had reached Leon's wife, a neighbor had accused him of killing the local handyman, a man who was somewhat mentally impaired, and of inciting others to kill.

Leon insisted he was innocent. His arrest, he said, was a setup: The neighbor who accused him had hungered for the new house he and Marie Claire had moved into just before the genocide. "This isn't justice, it's collective retaliation," Leon said as he plucked at the blanket on his bed. Despite the fact that the RPA had committed its share of civilian massacres, very few of its officers had been charged. Those charged had been low-ranking soldiers. The government talked about justice, Leon said, but it seemed somewhat one-sided.

I folded up my notebook to leave, but Leon waved at me to stay. He was eager to talk. Leon, incarcerated in his primitive cell, needed to connect with the civilized world. How was that Boston baseball team doing? And what about the jazz scene in Chicago? He was by nature upbeat. Even lying on his back, crammed into a fetid bunk, he was an entertaining host, cracking jokes, telling about how he had escaped death with patter almost reminiscent of Jay Leno.

Our talk turned back to justice. "We need trials," said Leon. "We desperately need them. Now each ethnicity thinks the other is guilty. People died by the thousands, and we want those who did it to be punished. We have to go through this process which will clear us, which will show that we have clean hands."

But how to ensure that justice didn't turn into the "collective retaliation" Leon feared? He wanted to believe that Rwandans themselves could sort out who was guilty and who was not. Leon hoped that reason would triumph over passion and for individual convictions, not attributions of collective guilt. But, he suggested, maybe there was something about killing—the very nature of a genocide—that made individual accountability irrelevant. "You live in Germany," he asked. "Do Germans and Jews still have that kind of hatred?"

When I told him that Jews were now one of the fastest-growing populations in Germany (admittedly, the result of anti-Semitism in the former Soviet Union), Leon was not reassured. "But that took fifty years," he said pointedly. As I closed my notebook, I told him I was sure he'd be on his way to trial in much less time.

Leon roared with laughter.

"You'll see me here in the next millennium," he said, winking. I laughed, thinking he was joking. But Leon was not. His prediction would be right on target.

MUCH OF THE weeks I had spent in Rwanda was in cities or big towns: Kigali, the bustling capital; Gisenyi, the tranquil city perched on Lake Kivu at the Zairean border. The time had come to climb the hills of Rwanda and visit its villages. After all, 95 percent of Rwandans are subsistence farmers living off the land in small hamlets. I wanted to know how the return of the refugees affected these tightly knit communities, particularly those that were the focus of investigations by the Rwanda Tribunal.

Among their many cases, tribunal investigators had been assembling evidence against Jean-Paul Akayesu, the mayor of Taba commune, a village about eleven miles west of Kigali nestled in rolling hills of coffee, banana, and eucalyptus. Taba was actually a collection of houses strung out haphazardly along the top of a high ridge. On a clear day, as you descended from the top of the ridge, the forests opened up to a sweeping vista: hill after hill after hill rippling toward the horizon like waves, with the tiny peak of one of Rwanda's volcanoes in the distance. To the extent that Taba had a hub, it was its outdoor market located near the charred remains of a burned-out bus, tipped to one side. The only other place people gathered was the Bureau Communale, something like the mayor's office. It was here that Jean-Paul Akayesu had stopped defending Tutsi villagers and encouraged the Interahamwe militia to kill, beat, and rape them instead.

My introduction to Taba came through its women and a remarkable social worker named Godelieve Mukasarasi. She was an uncommonly tall woman, well over six feet, with a burning energy that shone in her eyes and pulsed through her voice. Ever since the genocide ended, she had devoted all her energies to gathering Taba's women—mostly widows—together into an association. Once a week they would assemble, to cry and sing and dance and tell stories and learn new skills to help keep them and their children alive. Godelieve believed she owed it to these women to help them with their grief. She had been luckier than they.

"Long time ago, during the war, I prayed to God. I asked him for the safety of my children. I prayed a lot," Godelieve explained to me in heavily accented French. "I said to God, if they survive, I will do something important. As a miracle, all my children survived." She debated whether to open an orphanage but chose instead to help Taba's women, to show them "at least they are not alone," she explained.

I found them patient and hardworking, the women of Taba, women used to waiting: for the sun to rise and to set, for afternoon showers to pass, for the crops to ripen, for the next Sunday mass. Now they were also waiting for justice, in the form of a trial against Akayesu. They hoped it would bring them relief and consolation.

The genocide had been particularly cruel to Rwanda's Tutsi women, and Taba was no exception. As part of its campaign of genocide, the Interahamwe had beaten, violently raped, and even sexually mutilated thousands of women, whom their propaganda had portrayed as temptresses, spies, and whores. Rwanda's Ministry for the Family and the Promotion of Women had recorded 15,700 cases of rape, an estimate experts regarded as low.

Those women who survived found themselves doubly cursed. Rwanda was now a country of widows. Women, in addition to spending the day fetching fuel and water as well as preparing meals over a fire for their children, had to try to scratch out a living as subsistence farmers. Most failed, and they and their children were starving. Malnutrition was common, particularly among adolescent girls. Rwandan law also discriminated against women, ruling that only men could inherit or buy property. Women now farming the land had no more rights to it than squatters, and any surviving male in their family could turn them off it. Few women had savings, and they were always routinely denied credit.

The return of Hutu refugees threatened the already perilous life of Rwanda's Tutsi women. In Taba as in other villages, those whose homes had been destroyed during the genocide had moved into homes vacated by the fleeing Hutu. Now where would they live? Some of the women had stepped forward and given evidence to war crimes investigators—hardly discreet as they wheeled through the village in their large white Jeeps with UN painted on the side. Who would protect them? The tribunal had no witness protection program. "As you can imagine, they are having nightmares," Godelieve told me. "They keep thinking the men who raped them will come back. But let's go to the meeting at the marketplace. The women will tell you themselves."

Under the wooden eaves of the outdoor market, some forty women had gathered, immaculately dressed in their brightly patterned *pagnes*. Godelieve introduced me. The women applauded and immediately started talking. The tribunal investigators I had met in Rwanda had warned me that women would not discuss their rapes, but nearly every woman in Taba had a story to tell of the genocide, and her rape was usually at the heart of it. Like Xaviera: raped, then thrown into the river, then raped again, and again and again. She had told Rwandan police about her rape and also given details, she said, to investigators of the war crimes tribunal. "I'm angry nothing has happened yet," she said. "The tribunal has our dossier. I hope they will bring those responsible for my rape to justice, but I am not sure."

Or like Donathille: She was raped and then sexually mutilated. "He said, 'Do you know what a Tutsi looks like between her legs?' " she recounted. "Then he took a scissors from his pocket. He cut me between my legs. I bled so much. He said he wanted to take a piece and put it where everyone could see."

Or like Antoinette: raped by five men, one assault resulting in her son Emmanuel, age two, whom she gave me to hold. "Ah, you have no idea how much I want just to forget," she said. "Still, I want all of them to be brought to justice," she added, her fingers flying over knitting needles with which she was transforming a ball of pink wool into a sweater. "But I'm not so sure they will be."

Or like JJ, who was nearly poisoned by insecticide.

I did not know her by that name then. There was no ignoring her, tall and shy, with eyes that lit up when she smiled, as if someone had placed a bright candle inside a lantern. Something in her reticence was commanding, and she told me parts of her story, of how the Interahamwe threw her father in the latrine, of how she hid in the coffee fields, of how she gave her baby to a Hutu family who then killed him. I listened until Godelieve nudged me that it was time to go.

As I stood up, Godelieve gathered the women round. I shook hands and said good-bye, and got into the car. The women began swaying together and clapping their hands. Then they began singing: a chorus of soprano and alto, of hope and pain, of the future and of the past. I could not understand what they were saying. But as they stood there, transformed by the music, their blue and purple and yellow and red *pagnes* swaying from side to side, I thought it was one of the most hopeful things I had seen in Rwanda. The sound of their voices seemed to follow me, long after my car turned the corner and the women were out of sight.

A WEEK, A plane flight, and a bus ride later, I was in Arusha, Tanzania, standing in the dark concrete lobby of the Arusha Conference Center in the wing earmarked for the International Criminal Tribunal for Rwanda. It was my first visit. It was an instructive one.

"I have an appointment with your press spokeswoman, Beatrice LaCoste," I told the guard.

He scanned his sheet of telephone numbers. "We have no Beatrice LaCoste."

"I know you do," I persisted. "I spoke to her this morning. The main switchboard put me through to her. She told me to come and call up to her from the lobby."

He crossed his arms. His eyes flickered lazily down to the sheet of paper in front of him and back up to me again. "I am telling you there is no such person."

"Can't I go in and just try to find her?" I asked. "She said her office was up on the mezzanine."

He looked shocked. "This," he said drawing himself upright, "is an international tribunal!"

And so it went with the Rwanda Tribunal, an institution that in 1996 mixed the worst of African tribal politics with UN bureaucracy. Top officials, I would learn, were accused of mismanagement and some employees of corruption. It was an international tribunal, but one with no trials as yet ongoing; where prosecutors still lacked pens and paper, and security officers lacked guns; where reporters could not look at public indictments because someone had decided they should be classified. For a tribunal intended to set an example for Rwanda—where judicial corruption and impunity had long reigned—the court was off to a bad start.

"Theft, corruption, nepotism—that's the situation here," a high-ranking tribunal official in Arusha told me, deliriously relieved that complaints about the tribunal might finally make their way into print. "If this tribunal is going to consider the crimes it has, it must have clean hands," he said. "But what is our credibility now?"

The Rwanda Tribunal had always been the Yugoslav Tribunal's poor cousin, given less emphasis by top prosecutors in The Hague and fewer resources by the UN in New York. Just as the Rwandan genocide was so easily dismissed, so was the country's search for justice. Further complicating the mix was the physical division of the Rwanda Tribunal: The prosecutor's office was located in Rwanda, while the court, the judges, and the administrative staff sat in Arusha, Tanzania. Both offices were overseen by a chief prosecutor in The Hague.

Arusha, a sleepy town nestled between two tourist sites Mount Kilimanjaro and the Serengeti, was a poor choice for the court. The town had a commanding beauty: Nestled at the bottom of Mount Meru, its roads were lined with flame trees, jacaranda, and bougainvillea. Yet it was far better equipped to be a jumping-off point for camera-toting tourists on safari than for war crimes prosecutors in pursuit of bigger game. Judges arriving in January of 1996 found that the roof of the conference center leaked when it rained. The rooms they were assigned to came without a secretary or a telephone. Prosecutors finally made desks for themselves out of orange crates. Local markets might sell sunscreen but certainly not a legal pad, and prosecutors quarreled over the dwindling paper supply. The roads were rutted, the electricity intermittent, and the phone lines filled with static.

Kigali was even worse. What office equipment there had been was destroyed in 1994. Staff had nowhere to work. "They had no desks, no chairs, no computers and the employees were about to go on strike," recalled Timothy G. Connolly, the Principle Deputy Assistant Secretary of Defense for Special Operations. Upon hearing of the tribunal's plight, he located $3 million worth of surplus military equipment and flew it into Kigali in the spring of 1996 so investigators and prosecutors could have something resembling an office.

From the start, the Rwanda Tribunal was at a disadvantage, scorned as it was by the Rwandan government. In February 1996 RPA soldiers stopped a UN vehicle in downtown Kigali and beat up three tribunal investigators. In neighboring Kenya, where many of the high-ranking genocide leaders were sheltered, President Daniel arap Moi threatened to arrest tribunal staff if they came to that country in pursuit of them. In Zaire, Mobutu, harboring many of the genocide's henchmen, was not about to cooperate with a tribunal anxious to arrest them.

Yet this opposition could not account for everything that was wrong with the Rwanda Tribunal in 1996. It was an institution in disarray. The court was strangled by a huge bureaucracy—riven by political infighting, nepotism, incompetence, and vulnerable to petty fraud. Some staffers got their friends and relatives hired. Others rarely showed up for work. Simple requests, such as one for getting a car repaired, could disappear in the void of the tribunal's bureaucracy. The little legal work that the tribunal had accomplished by the fall of 1996 was jeopardized by its administrative failures; those good employees it had lured to its ranks were quitting. "The situation at the tribunal was so bad you couldn't imagine it was by accident, though it was," recalled Sara Dareshori, a former tribunal prosecutor now in private practice in New York.

Cries of outrage had reached the UN Inspector General, who conducted an inquiry. Investigators from the U.S. Agency for International Development and the State Department also began reviewing allegations against the tribunal. Other donor countries were threatening to follow suit.

The possible demise of the Rwanda Tribunal was the first challenge for its newly appointed chief prosecutor, Louise Arbour of Canada, who took over from Goldstone as chief prosecutor for the two war crimes tribunals in October 1996. Arbour, a law professor and jurist, like Goldstone had no prosecutorial experience. She had, however, been involved with human rights issues, both through her teaching and through having chaired a commission investigating conditions in women's prisons in Canada. Methodical and precise, Arbour had a direct, no-nonsense manner that some found harsh but others found refreshing. Flying into

Rwanda to listen to her staff's complaints, she handed over three hundred dollars of her own money so that office photocopiers could get fixed. She readily admitted the Rwanda Tribunal was in chaos. "Everything is not fine," she told me. "There is no point in trying to pretend otherwise." Still, she added, that the tribunal had accomplished what it had under the circumstances "was nothing short of a miracle."

The staff she met blamed the tribunal's deputy prosecutor, Honoré Rakotomana, based in Kigali, for some of the court's disorganization. Rakotomana, whose trial experience was limited, was said to have no sense of overall strategy. He was also a Francophone in an otherwise English-speaking world. Almost all his prosecutors spoke English exclusively, as did his bosses in The Hague. He needed an interpreter to communicate. Most of all, prosecutors complained Rakotomana did not always grasp the urgency of what they needed.

Every one of his prosecutors and investigators complained to me about how slowly Rakotomana was moving to put together a witness protection program. Without protection, witnesses had no incentive to testify, and those who did risked their lives. Bill Haglund had been right: Tribunal witnesses were getting killed. In 1996 alone 227 genocide survivors were murdered, several of them deliberately targeted as potential tribunal witnesses. Yet when I asked Rakotomana about this, the deputy prosecutor shrugged and said: "We will have to wait and see what happens."

"Rakotomana," recalled one former prosecutor, "was an empty suit."

The majority of the complaints about the tribunal's ineffectiveness were leveled at its registrar, Adronico Adede, based in Arusha. As in the Yugoslav Tribunal, the registrar, in addition to witness protection, which he had ignored, had control over all administrative issues: finances, staffing, and making some indictments and issuing arrest warrants. So desperate was one group of six investigators that they wrote to the chief prosecutor directly. "Our needs have been sadly neglected.... We feel that the United Nations has not lived up to its obligations or provided the necessary support for its staff." Administrative errors endangered what resources they did have: They desperately needed two cars that had sat in a garage for two months because the registrar's office had failed to pay $64 for repairs. Office phones once had been shut down for two weeks because of unpaid bills. Layers of bureaucracy hampered investigators' every move: They could not even send a fax without authorization.

The lack of administrative support also imperiled investigators, who found they could wait for weeks to get approval to get into the field and gather evidence to support prosecutors' indictments. Under the tribunal's laws, people could be arrested before being formally charged, but charges against them were to be filed swiftly, and a spate of arrests had brought thirteen people into custody.

At the same time, scores of jobs remained unfilled. The tribunal's finances were in chaos, simply because there wasn't enough staff to do the accounts. "The fact I am unable to provide the required level of service to the tribunal is directly linked to your constant reluctance to provide me with the staff I request," wrote former chief financial officer Peter Goddard in a letter to the then-chief of personnel, Abdoulaye Diallo.

Even the tribunal's first pending trial, against Jean-Paul Akayesu, the mayor of Taba, hung in the balance because his defense lawyer threatened to quit when the registrar failed to refund him his back expenses. The trial of Clement Kayishema, a high-ranking Rwandan official indicted for genocide, then had to be postponed because no protective measures had been put in place for witnesses so prosecutors could release their names to the defense. The trial was further compromised when copies of witness statements were mistakenly turned over to defense attorneys. Finally, someone in the registry nearly cost the tribunal an arrest, announcing news of the indictment of Elizaphan Ntakirutimana, a Seventh Day Adventist priest from Rwanda living in Texas, and his son Gérard before it had been unsealed. FBI agents barely made the arrest in time. "The Rwanda Tribunal is the most incompetent place I have seen in my life," one frustrated investigator said with a groan.

Part of the problem was Adede's management style, which his staff described as more tyrannical than judicial. He refused to delegate, insisting decisions could be made only with his permission, yet he was rarely in Arusha. Between December 1995 and October 1996 Adede spent more than five months traveling on tribunal business. "Nothing can get done," defense attorney Michael Karnavas complained. "You simply have to wait for Adede to return." Decisions lingered for months without being resolved. Cases of mismanagement and nepotism multiplied in his absence; one tribunal employee somehow collected $15,000 in salary advances while still receiving his salary.

Registrar Adede, for his part, defended himself on all counts. "My conscience is clear," he said.

So defeated and disillusioned were tribunal staffers that some believed that powerful countries within the United Nation that were implicated in the genocide—such as France and Belgium—were intent on ensuring that the court did not succeed. Others thought the United Nations itself, ashamed of its failure to halt Rwanda's slaughter, wanted to ensure investigators did not point the finger at it. Up and down the halls of the conference center in Arusha, paranoia reigned. "We could get the job done—if only they would let us," one investigator told me. A high-ranking tribunal official put it differently. "There is sabotage inside," he said, "and there is sabotage outside."

Despite the turmoil, the case against Jean-Paul Akayesu was finally slated to begin in January 1997, after months of delays. The tribunal's credibility would rest on just how well that trial proceeded. "Everything depends on the success of the Rwanda Tribunal," said Judge Yakov Ostrovsky, then the tribunal's vice-president.

A FEW WEEKS after I left Rwanda, Taba commune came under attack, on December 23, 1996. A gang of men, some wearing former Rwandan Army uniforms, attacked a shop, killing four people. The target appeared to be a man slated to give testimony to the Rwanda Tribunal in the case of Jean-Paul Akayesu. His name was Emanuel Rudasingwa, and UN investigators had visited him many times in their highly visible, marked cars. In Rwanda's small, clandestine society, a white person who drove up in a Jeep to a black family's doorstep was probably a UN tribunal investigator.

Rudasingwa was the husband of Godelieve Mukasarasi, the energetic social worker of Taba. She had not escaped the fate of the widows she worked with, after all. The assailants killed not only her husband but also her twelve-year-old daughter. On that December day, Godelieve joined the ranks of the grieving genocide survivors in Rwanda.

11

WHAT A TUTSI WOMAN TASTES LIKE

Rape was the rule and its absence the exception.

—UN Special Rapporteur René Degni-Segui

No one who heard the tall, shy Rwandan woman testify that day in 1997—the day when the past finally caught up with indicted war criminal Jean-Paul Akayesu—has ever quite forgotten it.

It was mesmerizing. The woman spoke as if in a trance, her large, luminous dark eyes focused somewhere in the distance, on a world only she could see. Words flowed from her in a steady, strong current that swept those sitting in the courtroom of the International Criminal Tribunal for Rwanda along with her as she spoke. She told of her rape by militiamen in the dirt of the sorghum field. Of her rape in the darkness of the forest. Then of her rape inside the grounds of the Bureau Communale of Taba, where Akayesu had been mayor. There were so many rapes over so many days by so many men she could no longer count them.

And then she spoke the words that helped seal Akayesu's fate. "He also told them, 'Never ask me again what a Tutsi woman tastes like,' " she said, recalling Akayesu's conversation with members of the Interahamwe after they had finished raping her and other women. "Tomorrow they will all be killed." Almost reflexively, everyone in the courtroom—even those in the spectators' gallery watching through a wall of bulletproof glass—turned to look at Akayesu, the haughty, handsome man in his beige jacket and tie, his face impassive as he studied the top of his desk. For a moment every gaze cast on the former burgomaster of Taba seemed full of horror and disbelief.

A year later, when the judges of the Rwanda Tribunal delivered their judgment, that unforgettable phrase—"Never ask me again what a Tutsi woman tastes like"—would help thrust Akayesu from the ranks of petty thugs into the ranks of notorious war criminals. Their 294-page judgment made Akayesu a famous man, doubly famous, in fact. He became the first man in history to be found guilty of genocide by an international tribunal. (The term "genocide" had not yet been coined when the Nazis were on trial at Nuremberg.) And his case became the first in which rape—one of the most ancient of war crimes—would be held by a court of law to be an act of genocide and a crime against humanity.

But that was still many months in the future. What was ironic about this powerful day of testimony was that Akayesu had not been originally charged with rape at all. Had it not been for another witness who linked Akayesu to the Taba rapes, the interest in the case shown by the court's one female judge, pressure from human rights and women's groups, and prosecutors skilled at winning over their witnesses, the former mayor might never have been tried for Taba's rape crimes. And he might never have been convicted for rape had it not been for the testimony of that tall, shy Rwandan—whom I discovered was one of the women I had met in Taba in 1996, a woman now known to the world as Witness JJ.

Some years later she would tell me how frightened she had been to board a plane and leave Rwanda and to confront Akayesu in court in Tanzania, where the tribunal was located. But her fear gave way to relief and a satisfaction that has stayed with her to this day. Now when she tells the story of her testimony, she begins with how her young daughter, flying with her, was convinced the airplane to Arusha flew right through the stars.

WAR AND RAPE often go hand in hand, and the wars in Rwanda and Bosnia were no exception. Over the centuries, the violent act of war and the violent act of rape have been linked together in a deadly dance. Open the dictionary: Rape is defined not only as "the crime of forcing a female to submit to sexual intercourse" but also "to plunder or pillage." Rape as a part of warfare is not just about having sex, it is also about having someone's else property. "Booty and beauty," historically, have simply been expected spoils of victory. As Thersites reminds Agamemnon during the battle for Troy in Homer's *Iliad*: ". . . what more do you want? Your tents are filled with bronze and with fair women, for whenever we take a town we give you the pick of them."

Even with the advent of chivalry in the Middle Ages, rape remained a socially acceptable by-product of war, whether waged in the name of politics or of religion. Commanders rewarded their poorly paid soldiers by allowing them to rape the women of a conquered village after looting it. Throughout the centuries of wars that followed, through World War I and World War II, sexual violence continued: the rape of Jewish women by Nazi soldiers in the ghettos and the death camps, the rape of German civilians by the conquering Red Army, the rape of Chinese women by the Japanese Army during the occupation of Nanking. It was just what boys did, after all, particularly if they weren't members of a well-trained army. "Can't he [Milovan Djilas, the Yugoslav commander who complained of the rape of Yugoslav women by Soviet forces] understand it," replied Joseph Stalin at the end of World War II, "if a soldier who has crossed thousands of kilometers through blood and fire and death has fun with a woman or takes a trifle?"

Which isn't to say that the law has ignored rape. During the Hundred Years' War, both Richard II and Henry V made rape during war punishable by death. But in practice the criminal statutes accounted for little. Henry V's law, for example, applied only to rape in cities not under siege. In 1474 Sir Peter von Hagenbach became the first man in history to be prosecuted by an international military tribunal for war crimes. Rape was among the charges, but only because his men had failed to inform the city in which they raped and plundered that it was officially occupied. In 1625, when Hugo Grotius, the father of international law, made the first thorough examination of conduct prohibited in war, he concluded that the "better conclusion" is that it is not permissible to rape women during war. He noted, however, that this "is the law not of all nations, but of the better ones . . . the more advanced peoples."

Not until the American Civil War, when the United States began to codify the customary laws of land warfare, did crimes against civilians, including the rape of women, become explicitly punishable. In 1863 the Lieber code, a military code used by the Union Army during the Civil War, made rape a capital offense. Despite the adoption of conventions prohibiting rape by various countries, the prosecution of wartime rape has remained the exception, not the rule. During the Nuremberg trials, for example, prosecutors barely discussed rape, although evidence was entered into the record of rape, sexual violence, forced prostitution, and mutilation committed by German troops against women in the Soviet Union and France as well as against Jewish women. When officials did mention rape, they were downright Victorian. "The Tribunal will forgive me if I avoid citing the atrocious details which follow," said the French prosecutor at Nuremberg, describing rapes in France.

The Tokyo Tribunal did prosecute and convict rape, but more as an afterthought than as a part of its judicial strategy. The ensuing Geneva Conventions made rape a war crime, but not very forcefully. Only two articles name rape specifically, and in the others it is only implicitly condemned, referred to vaguely as "inhuman treatment" or "outrages upon personal dignity." In international humanitarian law, the body of treaties and international agreements that govern countries during war, there is no specific name given to acts of systematic rape.

While wartime rape had been defined as a crime, it was never prosecuted. Women have generally been regarded as fair game no matter who they were, players in a game with rules no one ever followed. I had a taste of this myself one night in Bosnia in 1995, when I found myself stranded on Mount Igman, a mountain above Sarajevo, after my colleague's armored car jackknifed in a ditch. At that time in the war, the only way in and out of besieged Sarajevo was to drive along a mountain track the UN had thoughtfully enlarged just enough to accommodate a car. It was a night of heavy shelling: The Bosnian Army was making a concerted effort to push back the rebel Serbs, who were firing back with glee. So intense was the fighting that the Bosnian Muslims temporarily closed the Igman road to civilians so that ambulances could whisk the wounded down it. It was nearly midnight by the time we got under way, and we had no choice but to turn off our headlights, so as not to be spotted by Bosnian Serb gunners. Fireflies in the roadside brush helped light our way up the mountain, but darkness enveloped us once we crested the top. Blinded, we took a turn in the forest too swiftly; the rain-soaked earth gave way under the car's heavy weight, and we toppled upside-down into a ditch. Climbing out of the driver's door as if it were a submarine hatch, we dusted ourselves off and waited, hoping someone would come along and lend a hand.

Help did not arrive; a gang of drunken, boorish, and well-armed Bosnian Army soldiers did. One, his breath foul with drink, grabbed me roughly. "Sex . . . American sex," he murmured, locking his hands behind my neck and thrusting his groin into mine, his hips swaying. His intentions were perfectly clear. I was powerless, his hands swiftly traveling down my breasts. (Actually, to his surprise, his hands found only the plate inside my bulletproof vest.) It seemed like hours, but it was only minutes before my colleague, Rod Nordland of *Newsweek*, and I somehow convinced the soldier that the charms of the very expensive armored car in the ditch merited more attention than mine.

I was lucky; he abandoned me in exchange for "helping" us get the car out of the ditch while we swiftly searched for the nearest UN peacekeepers based on the mountain. No sooner had we found help than the car, resurrected, went sailing by us—the soldiers' booty. We were left to hitchhike off Mount Igman, as the shells rained down on Sarajevo below. We finally flagged down a ride with a French UN general whose code name over the UN radio was Napoleon—an ironic choice, given how much that French leader had done to codify war crimes law, albeit not on the issue of rape.

For a few minutes that night, I sensed all too well the powerlessness, terror, and shame that so many of the rape victims I had interviewed had known. I suddenly understood why sexual violence, in all its intimacy, is so different from other kinds of violence. Nothing had happened to me and yet I still felt degraded and ashamed.

Much later I pondered what recourse I would have had if the soldier had attacked me. One thing I did know: Had I been Bosnian or, for that matter, a Rwandan, at that time I probably would have been raped. During the war, rape became a weapon used to terrorize, punish, and degrade women of a specific ethnic group. As ethnicity in Bosnia is derived from one's father, some Bosnian Serb men deliberately set out to get Muslim women pregnant in an effort to "dilute" the ethnic group. "He took me to an office, when I asked why, he said, 'Because I want you to give birth to a little Serb,' " Tesma Elezović, a Bosnian Muslim, told me, recalling her rape at the Omarska prison camp in Serb-held Bosnia. The same was true in Rwanda. Rape, sexual mutilation, and sexual enslavement were the lot of Tutsi women during the genocide, often as a prelude to their murder.

When the Yugoslav war crimes tribunal was established in 1993, it was considered quite revolutionary that rape was included in its statute as a "crime against humanity." Chief prosecutor Richard Goldstone had made his commitment to prosecuting rape quite clear, appointing lawyer Patricia Viseur Sellers as his gender coordinator. During July 1996 hearings to establish genocide charges against Karadžić and Mladić, prosecutors pursued allegations that rape was a weapon of war, allowing tribunal investigators to testify that raping Bosnian Muslim women was part of the Bosnian Serb strategy of "ethnic cleansing." Goldstone created one team dedicated just to issues of sexual assault. Even if Goldstone hadn't been determined to prosecute rape, he could have hardly ignored the issue. So many letters and postcards supporting the position arrived at the tribunal that the mail was stuffed in canvas bags and carried into his office.

But it was one thing to *want* to prosecute rape. It was another actually to do so. The story of how Witness JJ got a chance to testify, I learned, made that perfectly clear.

BOTH THE YUGOSLAV and the Rwanda tribunals were born in part from the public outrage over the crimes of sexual violence in each conflict. The European Community, investigating rapes in Bosnia, touched off a firestorm in 1993 when it published a report stating that 20,000 Muslim women in Bosnia had been raped, a number that was later discredited. The UN Security Council then pronounced its first-ever resolution condemning wartime rape. News of the mass rapes, coming as human rights groups meeting at a 1993 conference in Vienna were lobbying for women's rights to be added to the UN's human rights agenda, swiftly angered and mobilized women around the issue. Investigations in the wake of the Rwanda genocide established that widespread, systematic rape had taken place across that country as well. As the UN Special Rapporteur on Rwanda, René Degni-Segui, put it: "Rape was the rule and its absence the exception." Calculating backward from the number of pregnancies caused by rape, Degni-Segui concluded that at least 250,000 women—and as many as 500,000—had been raped in Rwanda in 1994.

Rape during war, however, presented tricky questions of proof. Except in the case of sexual mutilation, it was unlikely that there was physical evidence to back up rape allegations in a trial. Many victims never saw a doctor until months after the attack occurred, if they were able to see one at all. Traumatized victims sometimes can and do exaggerate, particularly in a charged, political postwar atmosphere.

In making rape prosecutable under international humanitarian law, the Yugoslav Tribunal took a historic and controversial step, but not one without controversy. The only category under which rape was listed—"crimes against humanity"—was one of the most difficult for prosecutors to prove, due to the need to establish that the rapes were part of a "widespread" or "systematic" attack. Many human rights and women's groups, as well as legal experts, argued this was too limiting. They believed that rape also should be prosecuted under other articles within the tribunal's jurisdiction, such as genocide. Genocide is defined as certain acts committed with an intent to destroy, in whole or in part, ethnic, racial, national, and religious groups, and they pointed to the fact that much sexual violence is intended to terrorize or humiliate victims of a particular group. In both the Rwandan and the Yugoslav conflicts, advocates argued, sexual crimes were also aimed at interfering with a woman's reproductive capabilities, seeking either to mutilate their private parts—thereby preventing them from having more children—or to force them to have a child of mixed stock, thereby "destroying" their ethnic group.

Other human rights activists, however, disagreed. They argued that the 1948 Genocide Convention—governing the most heinous international crime, genocide—should be used sparingly, reserved for only the most horrendous acts of mass murder. By 1995, however, the U.S. Court of Appeals for the Second Circuit had established legal precedent on the issue. The judges, ruling on pretrial issues in a case brought by Bosnian refugees against Bosnian Serb leader Radovan Karadžić, found that rape could be an act of genocide.

It was against the backdrop of this highly charged debate that Jean-Paul Akayesu was arrested on October 10, 1995, in Zambia. Akayesu, like Duško Tadić in Bosnia, was a small functionary in the grand scheme of the genocide. His became the first case before the Rwanda Tribunal largely by an accident of timing. The tribunal's prosecutors and investigators had only just arrived in Rwanda. They didn't even have an office; they certainly didn't have an indictment. Akayesu was arrested because his name was on a list of criminals wanted by the Rwandan government, not the tribunal. "We didn't even know who he was," recalled former prosecutor Sara Dareshori. After he was arrested and held on suspicion of war crimes, prosecutors had ninety days under the tribunal's rules to decide whether to file charges. Chief prosecutor Goldstone, fearful that the Rwanda Tribunal would lack defendants just as the Yugoslav Tribunal had, pushed his staff to forge ahead.

From the start, the investigators approached the Akayesu case as if it were one of serial murder, seeking to link Akayesu to the more than 2,000 deaths in Taba. With little or no experience investigating sex crimes, they often didn't ask about rape or didn't consider it important enough to ask about. Nor did Rwandan women volunteer that they had been raped. Many found it offputting when investigators, mostly white males, roared into the villages in their white UN Jeeps and then treated survivors with condescension, as if they were stupid rather than traumatized. Taba women simply didn't want to open up to them. It wasn't surprising, then, that the first indictment lodged against Akayesu on February 16, 1996, made no mention of rape.

As new investigators, some of them women, joined the tribunal team, incidents involving sexual slavery, mutilation, and mass rape began to be reported. In the summer of 1996, Human Rights Watch published a 103-page document detailing sexual violence during the genocide, much of it gleaned from interviews with women in Taba. The report criticized the tribunal, noting that, despite the UN Special Rapporteur's conclusion that "rape was the rule," none of the twenty-one people indicted by the Rwanda Tribunal by the summer of 1996 had been charged with the crime.

"Unfortunately, the manner in which the International Criminal Tribunal for Rwanda has been conducting its investigations strongly suggests that unless it takes active steps, it may fail to mount even one rape prosecution," the report concluded. "If the Tribunal does not take immediate steps . . . by the time cases are brought before the Tribunal judges it will be too late to include rape charges."

Human rights groups, and particularly Human Rights Watch, fumed over the Rwanda Tribunal's failure to charge rape. They began lobbying for indictments to include acts of sexual violence. Yet in the Akayesu case, investigators kept coming up empty-handed, even after a sexual assault committee was formed. Prosecutors had enough evidence to prove a myriad of rapes in Taba, but not any with which Jean-Paul Akayesu had anything to do.

So when the first mention of rape surfaced at the trial—in January 1997, when *Prosecutor v. Jean-Paul Akayesu* had been under way just a few weeks—everyone was stunned.

WITNESS J—NOT JJ—was on the stand, describing Akayesu's role in various murders. As she told her story, she volunteered that her daughter—her six-year-old daughter—had been raped by three men. The three judges on the case—South African judge Navanethem Pillay, Senegalese judge and tribunal president Laity Kama, and Swedish judge Lennert Aspegren—immediately leapt in with questions. Who raped her daughter? The Hutu Interahamwe? Were they connected to Akayesu in any way? Judge Pillay, a respected women's advocate who had served on South Africa's Truth and Reconciliation Commission, was astonished by the revelation. Sitting on the judges' dais, watching the cross-examination, she was even more dismayed when Prosecutor Haile-Mariam failed to pursue the point. "I couldn't understand what the prosecutor was doing," she later recalled.

But the case tribunal prosecutors were building against Akayesu was one that centered around the betrayal of trust. In the scheme of the Rwandan genocide, he was not a machete-wielding killer, nor, for that matter, one of the genocide's top architects. He was a midlevel bureaucrat but one of extraordinary standing, a man who, because of Rwanda's rigidly hierarchical society, had absolute sway over Taba. As far as the village was concerned, Akayesu was like the local pope: the man who not only dictated the village's economic affairs but also its moral conscience. Tribunal prosecutors saw Akayesu as a man who had abused his authority, a man who set aside his duty to his people out of a lust for power.

Prosecutors intended to show that while Akayesu initially resisted the genocide, he joined the killing when he realized that his political future depended on it. It was not until Akayesu had attended a meeting in nearby Gitarama at which Rwandan leaders called on the differing Hutu political parties to unite and fight the Tutsi that he decided to become a killer. Akayesu, making a political calculation about his future, joined in the genocide with a vengeance.

Overnight Akayesu went from being Taba's protector to its predator. He donned military garb. He called on the populace to seek out Tutsi in hiding and kill them. He ordered the military to murder the community's intellectuals. He stood by while mud-brick homes of Tutsi villagers were destroyed and looted. And he refused to help the hundreds who fled to the Bureau Communale, the town hall, to seek refuge. Few had perished in Taba before Akayesu joined the genocide. But after he shifted sides, thousands died at the hands of neighbors, friends, and relatives, often at his urging. His case provided a window into the killing that had gripped the country, a frenzy partly rooted in the Rwandan belief in authority. If leaders said kill, it was easier for many people to follow suit than to question the order and face being killed themselves.

So the witnesses who came into the steamy courtroom of the International Criminal Tribunal for Rwanda were there to link Akayesu to specific killings. Their testimony was intended to show that after the fateful meeting of Hutu leaders, Akayesu had ordered and even participated in the genocide. As the weeks drifted by, the trial proved slow and difficult, for several reasons. Courtroom conditions were appalling. The electricity often failed. There was no air-conditioning in a courtroom that had only two narrow slits for windows. As prosecutors and judges fanned themselves, all they did was circulate the hot air. ("It was," recalled one participant, "like sitting in a sauna.")

Then, in the trial's second month, the UN Inspector General, reacting to reports of mismanagement and corruption within the tribunal, delivered a scathing report about the court's performance. The report, which investigated "serious operational deficiencies in the management of the Tribunal," was devastating. "Not a single administrative area functioned effectively," it concluded. Staff were "inexperienced and unqualified." The Office of the Prosecutor "had administrative, leadership and operational problems." Nothing short of an entire overhaul was needed before the tribunal would function effectively, the report by the Office of Internal Oversight Services concluded. "If the United Nations means to keep its promises to the Rwandan victims of genocide and other systematic violations of the law," it warned, "then the Secretariat must assist the Secretary-General in his task of ensuring that the body established to bring to justice the persons responsible for such grievous crimes becomes fully functional."

The registrar, the deputy prosecutor, and others resigned. As the office frantically reshuffled, the task of prosecuting Akayesu fell largely on Pierre Prosper, a former federal prosecutor with a smooth voice and a convincing manner. The thirty-four-year-old lawyer, a graduate of Pepperdine University's School of Law, was well prepared for the task, despite his youth. He had six years of trial experience under his belt, most of them spent prosecuting street gangs or drug cartels. (By contrast, many tribunal attorneys had no trial experience at all.) In addition, Prosper, the son of Haitian doctors who had settled in upstate New York, spoke fluent French.

Yet Akayesu proved a formidable adversary. As the weeks passed, Prosper would sweat out the trial, and not just because of the lack of air-conditioning. Akayesu, tall, elegant, and highly educated, was equally intelligent and charismatic. He was regal in his demeanor, with a long, narrow face accented by a small beard and mustache. He swept into the courtroom every day neatly dressed in a suit, tie, and well-polished wingtips. A gold watch flashed on his left wrist; gold wire-rimmed glasses perched on his nose.

Nothing escaped his scrutiny. He frequently interrupted the proceedings, like a quarrelsome professor, to object to how witness testimony was being translated from his native Kinyarwandan into French. He honed in on small, tiny discrepancies in testimony that served to buttress his version of events: that he had never wavered in his opposition to the genocide in Taba and was simply overwhelmed in his efforts to halt it. Each time he scored a victory against prosecutors, he smiled to himself, sure he would walk out of the courtroom a free man. As testimony unfolded, it was hard to reconcile the man in the courtroom with the person who had allegedly committed such unimaginable deeds. "He had two personalities, the stark, sinister, evil person and then the public persona, polite, respectful," Prosper recalled some years later. "He mentally separated himself from the man he was in 1994 to the guy today. He would refer to himself in the third person, saying: 'Akayesu did not do that.' My job was to bring the two personalities together."

And those two personalities collided one day in March 1997, when a woman named Witness H took the stand.

For three months the judges had listened to testimony concerning murder and torture and exquisite betrayal. Now before them came Witness H, who described yet another kind of horror: The Hutu military had raped women right on the grounds of Taba's Bureau Communale, she testified. There was no way Akayesu could have not known about the rapes.

As soon as she finished speaking, Judges Aspegren and Pillay pounced on the young witness. Each fired off nearly thirty questions, aimed at determining the burgomaster's responsibility for the rapes. But Witness H never wavered.

Judge Pillay went first. "Would you say that Akayesu was aware that these rapes were going on?"

"I don't know," said Witness H. "What I can tell you is that it happened at the Bureau Communale, and he knew that we were there."

Judge Aspegren followed. "In your opinion, if a burgomaster wanted to, could he stop what was happening?"

"Yes, he could stop what was happening."

"By what means?"

"I think that he could have stopped these events," said Witness H. "He didn't even try."

Judge Aspegren—openly critical of the tribunal and its disorganization—then asked Witness H if investigators had asked her for the names of the men who had raped the women at the Bureau Communale. Witness H said they had not. Aspegren was so incredulous at her answer, he repeated his question: "No one asked you for these names?"

The trial was scheduled to adjourn for several months that day to allow Akayesu's defense attorney time to research his case. Prosper was relieved. The prosecution clearly also had work to do. Witness H's entire testimony had been something of a gamble for Prosper. She had only mentioned the rapes at the Bureau Communale for the first time at pretrial preparation the day before; it wasn't included in the statement she had given investigators. Listening to Witness H, Prosper had suddenly realized that the refugees at the Bureau Communale were nearly all women, not both sexes, as he had first believed, and that they were there as part of a plan for their rape. For the first time, there was a connection between acts of sexual violence and Akayesu himself. Swiftly, Prosper had telephoned the court's gender coordinator in The Hague to see how best to proceed. They decided to let Witness H tell her story and, if the judges appeared interested in it, to proceed with a new indictment.

Now, the judges' response to Witness H augured well for adding rape charges to the indictment. Prosper, sitting in his cramped third-floor cubicle in Arusha, called The Hague again, this time to organize charges of sexual violence to Akayesu's indictment. Members of the newly formed sexual violence team were quickly summoned and put to work. They were to return to Taba and find women, if any were still alive, who had been raped at the Bureau Communale. They were to convince the women to testify. And they had just three months to do it.

NEWS OF WITNESS H's testimony rocketed through the international legal community. Those groups that had urged the tribunal to prosecute rape were outraged that tribunal investigators had failed to discover a direct link between Akayesu and rape. Now that the connection had been established in court, they were determined that prosecutors would follow up. That March, members of dozens of groups filed an amicus curiae, or "friend of the court," brief, outlining why crimes of sexual violence should be added to the case. The brief accused the prosecution of failing to include charges of rape "despite there being evidence of rape and criminal responsibility in relation to the accused," and warned of setting an "unwelcome precedent for prosecutions to come. . . ." If the tribunal didn't amend the Akayesu indictment, it was clear that forty-two women's and human rights organizations would have something to say about it.

Yet it was late spring before investigators could even get to Taba. Rwanda, in the first months of 1997, remained a dangerous place. Among the Hutu who returned the year before from neighboring Zaire were Interahamwe who still hoped to overthrow the government and continue the genocide. They and Interahamwe from surrounding countries staged deadly raids, swooping down on villages and killing off Tutsi survivors. As the Rwandan Patriotic Army retaliated, thousands of civilians were killed in the cross-fire. The fighting was at its worse in the northwest, where the Hutu were concentrated. In the first nine months of 1997, some 6,000 civilians were killed, albeit mostly by Rwandan government troops. Being a foreigner was no protection: In January insurgents had killed two Spanish aid workers; in February they killed two UN human rights observers and the Rwandans traveling with them. As a result, the tribunal staff was confined to Kigali.

By summer Rwanda was quieter. Tribunal investigators finally reached Taba, and luckily for them, Witness JJ did not prove difficult to find. Years later, she recalled having been interviewed by the tribunal in connection with the Akayesu case and said that no one had ever asked if she was raped. The only questions tribunal investigators put to her then were general ones, and she never heard from them again.

Now the tribunal had returned. They didn't want to talk about how most of her family had been murdered, nor about the destruction of the family's two homes, nor how the Hutu militia had tried to poison her with insecticide. No, they wanted her to talk about rape; and they wanted her to do it in front of a court. JJ was hesitant to relive the genocide all over again through her testimony.

To begin with, she was six months' pregnant, with a child conceived not out of rape but of love, sired by a man from Taba whose Hutu wife had fled during the genocide. Through prayer and hard work, JJ had started to piece together the semblance of a new life. Her body still hurt from the beatings and rapes; her heart often beat too quickly, she got debilitating headaches. Testifying, she was sure, would make her health worse. It would be dangerous; everyone was still talking about how Godelieve Mukasarasi's husband, who had been interviewed by the tribunal, had been killed by Interahamwe.

And they wanted her to talk about being raped? No, she wasn't sure she could bear testifying—the risk, the shame of it—at all. "Do I want to talk about those things?" she wondered. "Do I?"

Then in her mind she heard Akayesu's sneering voice that day at the Bureau Communale: "*Ntihzagire umbaza uko umututsikazi yari ameze, ngo kandi mumenye ko ejo ngo nibabica nta kintu muzambazo,*" he had said, "*Ngo ejo bazabica.*" Never ask me again what a Tutsi woman tastes like. Tomorrow they will be killed. Like she was a piece of melon, waiting to be carved, eaten, and thrown away. She had trusted him, and he had betrayed her, and his scorn weighed heavily on her. She could almost feel it, heavy on her heart. She wanted to be free of it: free of his hatred, free of the memories, free of the shame.

To be free of it. Yes, maybe she would testify, and tell of the bad things that had happened in Taba and across Rwanda to the women. If she told her story, maybe the world would listen.

Yes; she would testify, after all.

Several days later on June 17, 1997, Prosper returned to the courtroom in Arusha. He stood in front of Judges Aspegren, Kama, and Pillay. "Good morning, your honors, good morning, counsel," he said. "Firstly I would like to thank the Chamber for uniting us at such short notice. I realize that the Chamber at times would prefer to have written motions submitted, but because of the urgency that we feel in the matter and the time constraints, we asked for an oral hearing on issues of whether or not the Prosecutor would be allowed to amend the indictment against Mr. Jean-Paul Akayesu."

Prosper spoke for several minutes, outlining how Witness H had prompted a reinvestigation of the case. "The investigators went and did some investigations, took statements from witnesses which we received here in Arusha, late Friday evening last week. In reading these statements it is clear that the acts of sexual violence which occurred in Taba and specifically at the Bureau Communale, which my colleague will discuss, are horrific, they are shocking and they are acts that can be attributable to the accused."

Prosper moved to amend the indictment to include three additional charges of rape and sexual violence. The judges agreed. And the Akayesu trial continued once again.

IN TABA, JJ was counting not the days until her court appearance but the days until she was to give birth. As lawyers filed motions and heard witnesses and argued over fine points of the law in the courtroom in Arusha, she was getting closer and closer to her due date for her baby. In fact, by the time it came for her to testify, her baby boy would be ten days old.

Her infant provided her with the ruse for leaving town. The Rwanda Tribunal by then had only the most limited of witness protection programs, and much of that protection was provided in Arusha during trial. Prosecutors had assured JJ that she would stay in a "safe house" and that no one would find out her identity. But she had to account for leaving Taba. Everyone knew she was expecting, and it would seem odd if she just disappeared, especially since everyone knew she had nowhere else to go. The tribunal, wishing to keep her identity and her testimony a secret, dispatched an ambulance to fetch her at her home. Word went quickly round Taba that JJ and her newborn son were ill and in the hospital.

In reality, however, JJ was taking her first airplane trip on a UN ten-seater Beechcraft to Arusha, Tanzania. She had her infant and her young daughter with her when she climbed aboard the plane. She hated it immediately. She hated the roar the engines made prior to takeoff. As the plane rose, the change in elevation made her ears and head ache. But her daughter loved it. She kept her nose pressed to the glass, marveling at the sky. JJ was too sick, too worried, to pay much attention to the world outside the airplane window.

It was all so dizzying: a plane, and then landing, and then being whisked off to an unfamiliar place to stay. JJ felt so alone, so far away, even though there were other women who were also testifying about rapes in Taba. They were also terrified, but they all agreed it was worse for JJ. She was scheduled to go first. They could at least learn from her mistakes.

She had brought a favorite blouse—one of two she owned—and a patterned skirt to wear, hoping it would boost her spirits. But when she walked into the courtroom on October 23, 1997, JJ's heart sank. Who was she, a lowly peasant, in this world of lawyers and judges? The courtroom, with its white walls and sleek brown desks and raised dais and large blue UN flag, was antiseptic and imposing. There were all these bright lights and cameras and everyone seemed to know what to do. Why didn't she? There were so many people she didn't recognize: Who were all these young men and women, bustling around in black robes? Why was one of the judges a woman, and why did she knit her brows together so threateningly?

The tribunal president, Judge Laity Kama, immediately sensed JJ's fears. "She seems a bit frightened," he said to the interpreter, as he asked JJ to take the oath. "Does she wish to express herself in Kinyarwandan?" JJ, who did not speak French, most certainly did. She raised her right hand and took the oath. As soon as she was seated—and had spotted Prosper—she relaxed a little. She instinctively trusted the young prosecutor; he had a sympathetic manner and coaxing voice. He had listened to her carefully when they had gone over her testimony before the trial. Judge Kama, realizing that JJ was breast-feeding her newborn son, assured her she could leave to do so whenever she wished. "Just simply indicate this to the Court, and we will take a brief recess," Kama said. He then asked JJ to move closer to the microphone. She was still nervous. "Can we ask her to be more relaxed?" said Kama.

Gently, Prosper began leading her through the questions. What had happened on April 7, 1994, when President Habyiramana's plane had gone down? Could she identify Jean-Paul Akayesu? She looked at the tall, elegant man, flanked by two guards, wearing a light beige jacket. "There he is in the middle, and he is seated alone," she said, pointing.

It was confusing, answering the prosecutor's questions through an interpreter. She got rattled when Judge Aspegren told her to clarify her remarks. At one point she nearly interrupted him midsentence in her rush to clarify. "Just a moment, I haven't asked my question," the judge chided. "You wait for a question, and you will try to answer. I'll ask the question over again." Then, when Prosper handed her the laser pointer so she could show the judges where she and the other refugees sought shelter at the Bureau Communale, JJ couldn't get it to work. She tried twice before he came to her rescue. "I will go over the plan, and you can tell me when I get to the area," he said kindly.

JJ had just sighed in relief when Akayesu interrupted. "I think there is a nuance between saying he [i.e., Akayesu] was in the courtyard and he was in front," the former mayor said. "The translation was not authentic." JJ watched him. He still frightened her.

She continued with her story. She had first sought refuge in the forest, her baby on her back, along with her younger sister, wounded from the attack. Her sister had vanished. Then she had fled to a nearby village, where a Hutu peasant hid her in his field and gave her food. With her next few sentences, she demonstrated just why war crimes tribunals are so important to a society trying to recover from a genocide, as JJ established individual—not collective—guilt. "He was a Hutu, but one who cannot harm," JJ told the courtroom. "Not everyone killed."

Finally, she testified, the order had come from Akayesu for the Tutsi to give themselves up and go to the Bureau Communale. There she joined sixty other Tutsi, mostly women, hoping that the mayor would save them. So far, only Taba's intellectuals and men had been killed, and JJ hoped that the women might still be spared. But when Akayesu pulled up in a car with policemen, he ordered JJ and the other refugees to be beaten instead. He had changed his mind about the Tutsi, JJ said; they were "wicked people" who had no right to shelter. Aware that death was her fate, JJ had gone to Akayesu and begged to be shot instead of macheted to death.

"He told us there were no more bullets." Even if there had been bullets, JJ recalled, Akayesu said "he would not waste them on us." The judges, sitting and listening intently on their dias, rocked back a little farther in their chairs.

That morning JJ had two breaks to breast-feed her son and get some lunch. As the day wore on, the courtroom began to look a little less intimidating. She noticed there was a distinct back-and-forth to the questions and answers. If she got into the rhythm—as she often did, sowing seeds across one of her family's fields back in Taba—it seemed a little easier. It would be well after 3:00 P.M. by the time JJ would speak about her rape.

She began to correct herself in an effort to be more legally precise. "When we entered the house—here, I'll talk about what happened to me," said JJ, before either Akayesu or his lawyer or the judges had a chance to intervene.

"I apologize in advance about these questions, but I have to ask you in detail what happened to you," said Prosper. JJ, her confidence growing, began to tell her story. The Bureau Communale was a compound of three buildings, entered through a main gate on the dirt road. One day Akayesu was standing in front of the brick building inside the compound that housed his office, as a gang of militia dragged JJ and other women and girls into the building that was the town's cultural center. That's where the rapes took place. Some of the girls were as young as twelve years old.

She described how the men were drunk, high on victory and booze and marijuana, and of how the first man, a very young man carrying a knife, raped her twice. "To see a young child rape me, as you can understand . . . this is something very difficult," said JJ. "Then he said to me that on the day that they wanted, they would come and kill us." The second who raped her took off his trousers but kept his underwear on. She never had a chance to get off the floor. She was lying there, as if she were dead, when the third man came upon her. He entered her viciously, again and again. "It was very difficult for me . . . to put my two legs together, to put my thighs together," said JJ. "It was as if it was a duty . . . when they finished, they went away."

The courtroom was perfectly still.

JJ continued. She and the other women, barely able to walk, dragged themselves out of the cultural center. "I believed I was going to die," she said quietly. "I was wondering what type of death I was going to die." But there would be no death for her, just rape, over and over again.

It was on the second day of the rapes that Akayesu strode up outside the cultural center. JJ had been raped twice so far that day. He came in front of the center and spoke to the young militiamen, still pumped up, their adrenaline soaring from the sex they had had. "Never ask me ever again what a Tutsi woman tastes like," Akayesu told the young men, adding: "Tomorrow they will be killed." These men had heard enough propaganda on the radio to know what Akayesu meant. Now these Tutsi women, traitors to their country, would be killed. It was the natural order of things.

The next morning JJ left the grounds of the Bureau Communale to buy food for her baby, who was crying. After she did so, she ran into some youngsters. They grabbed her and told her that everyone at Bureau Communale had been taken away and killed. Panicked, she turned and fled with her baby, this time deep into another sorghum field.

JJ was on the run again. But she had survived it all—the rapes, the hunger, the near death by poison to tell her story, before a courtroom, before the world.

THAT WAS NOT the end, of course. Trials are not so well plotted as plays. Rarely does someone's most dramatic testimony signal an end to the trial, like a curtain ringing down on the end of a performance. Next it was Akayesu's lawyer's turn to cross-examine JJ, seeking to highlight contradictions and expose weaknesses in her tale. But now that she had told of her rape, she was no longer afraid of him, or of the courtroom, or even of Akayesu.

By the end of her testimony and cross-examination, when Judge Aspegren asked her why she had come to the Rwanda Tribunal, JJ raised her head and spoke loudly and confidently. "I was able to get close to him [Akayesu]. I talked to him directly, face to face," said JJ. "So I believe I am responsible, coming to give evidence of his evil deeds in the Taba commune.... When someone is leading killers, assassins, he is also a killer, also a murderer, also an assassin. We were exterminated in his presence."

Minutes later, after Judge Kama had thanked her for her testimony and dismissed the court, JJ looked around the courtroom one last time. The bright lights, the blue chairs, the furniture, the UN flag. She was leaving the courtroom a changed woman.

"Don't worry," she would later tell the other women waiting to testify, wringing their hands with fear. "You will feel a weight lifted from your heart."

And they did. Witness KK told of how a twelve-year-old girl was stripped naked in front of an exuberant Akayesu, who urged Hutu militiamen to have sex with her. Witness NN testified to being raped by six different men and then kept locked up by one of them as his sexual slave. Witness OO and Witness PP, and all the others, then testified as to how the Taba women were hunted down and raped and killed simply because they were Tutsi. Months later, when it was Akayesu's time to defend himself, he would deny knowing anything about sexual violence in Taba. By then no one believed him anymore.

THE AKAYESU TRIAL lasted for fifteen months. Nearly a year passed after JJ's testimony before the judges handed down their judgment on September 2, 1998, in the historic genocide trial. The spectators' gallery was packed in anticipation of the verdict. Akayesu, as neatly turned out as ever, had the cocky air of a prizefighter. Yet it was clear to anyone following the trial that the mayor of Taba had lost.

At the beginning of the trial, Akayesu and Prosper were like two heavyweights in a title fight, with Akayesu having the upper hand. But Prosper got the better of him in the last round, when Akayesu testified in his own defense. His account was so full of inconsistencies and contradictions that it undermined any credibility he might have had. At first, Akayesu tried taunting Prosper. "What's your question, Mr. Prosecutor?" he said.

Prosper refused to be intimidated. "Let's go back to the transcripts," he said. "Why don't you read that to us, Mr. Akayesu?" Soon the denials became more and more frantic: No, Akayesu never saw any bodies, in front of the town hall or elsewhere. Akayesu had heard of rapes, but not in Taba. "I was a puppet mayor," he whined. "But I got hold of information. I couldn't be everywhere at once. Perhaps I wasn't told. Nobody came to tell me that rape was committed here and there."

The coup de grâce came when Akayesu—who had denied attending the key meeting at which Hutu leaders urged that Tutsi be killed—admitted he had indeed been present. He then tried to parse the difference between attending a meeting and participating in it. The judges refused to buy his evasions. "So what do you mean by 'I did not participate in a meeting,'" asked Judge Kama. "Because people say that you changed after that meeting."

"Ah, Mr. President, I can't remember," replied Akayesu.

It took Judge Kama a full hour to read the tribunal's summary of the Akayesu decision. Was genocide committed in Taba? Yes. Was Akayesu part of it? Yes. And rape? Yes, rape had occurred, the judges ruled. In order to encompass the horrific violations that had been described to them—women penetrated by sticks and bottles as well as penises—they defined the crime broadly, as "a physical invasion of a sexual nature, committed on a person under circumstances which are coercive."

And did Akayesu know of the rapes? The judges decided that he had ordered, instigated, aided, and abetted acts of sexual violence. Because of his authority in Taba, his complicity sent the message that rape was officially tolerated, even encouraged.

And was rape an act of genocide? The judges ruled yes. "Sexual violence was a step in the process of destruction of the Tutsi group," the judges ruled, "destruction of the spirit, of the will to live, and of life itself... the rapes of the Tutsi women in Taba were accompanied with the intent to kill those women."

It was over for Jean-Paul Akayesu.

Back in Taba, Witness JJ heard Kama's lengthy recitation, as the judgment was broadcast on Radio Rwanda. She and others had the satisfaction of hearing "guilty" pronounced nine times, as Akayesu was found guilty of nine of fifteen charges. Like most of the Rwandan population, she didn't understand much of what was said in the judgment—but she understood when the judges spoke of Akayesu's role in the rapes. She smiled to herself with satisfaction.

Akayesu, for a change, wasn't smiling. As Judge Kama read out the verdict, his eyes darted around the courtroom. The only time he flinched was when he heard the word "rape."

When Judge Kama was finished, Akayesu stood up. He took off his gold-rimmed glasses and put them in his suit breast pocket. Then he picked up the papers on his desk.

Guilty of genocide; guilty of rape as a means of genocide and a crime against humanity. That is how history will remember Jean-Paul Akayesu.

He took a long last look around the courtroom, and then he walked out the door alone.

12

WHEN THE VICTIMS ARE THE SERBS

> However much a man loved the law he could not love so much of it as wound its sluggish way through the Palace of Justice at Nuremberg. For all who were there, without exception, this was a place of sacrifice, of boredom, of headache, of homesickness.
>
> —Rebecca West, *A Train of Powder*

Into the courtroom in The Hague swept the judges, resplendent in their long red-and-black robes adorned by sparkling white cravats. "All rise," intoned a young court clerk, in a voice infused with equal parts authority and boredom. It was March 10, 1997, shortly before 10:00 A.M. As the judges settled into their regulation blue UN chairs on the dais, defendants and their counsel, sitting below them, followed suit. Spectators, separated from the main body of the courtroom by a bulletproof glass wall, stirred expectantly.

"Case number IT-96-21-T," the clerk said. "The case of the Prosecutor against Zejnil Delalić, Zdravko Mucić, Hazim Delić and Esad Landžo."

"Are all the accused present?" asked Judge Adolphus Karibi-Whyte somberly. A continent away from the Akayesu trial, the Čelebići case—Petko and Gordana Grubač's chance for justice—had begun.

By 1997 the Yugoslav Tribunal, and to a lesser degree the Rwanda Tribunal, were established courts. The UN had exposed the scandals dogging the Rwanda Tribunal, and new administrators and prosecutors had been hired. In The Hague, testimony had finished in its first case, the trial of Duško Tadić, and the judges were expected to hand a judgment down soon. Judge McDonald and her colleagues on the bench would finish a four-year term that fall. Chief prosecutor Richard Goldstone, who had taken a two-year leave of absence from South Africa's

Constitutional Court, had already returned home. Louise Arbour of Canada had taken his place at the tribunal.

It was time for the two war crimes courts to start working on some high-profile, impressive cases.

Madeleine Albright, who had pushed for the courts' creation, had just become U.S. Secretary of State, which augured well for continued support to both tribunals. Not only had she visited the Yugoslav Tribunal, she also had repeatedly spoken about its importance and appointed an aide, David Scheffer, ambassador for war crimes issues and authorized a small staff. Both the Rwanda and Yugoslav tribunals had full dockets, with ninety-four indictments between them. Both had defendants to try: seven behind bars in The Hague, twelve behind bars in Arusha. And both had major trials in progress simultaneously in 1997, including the Čelebići case in The Hague and the case of Jean-Paul Akayesu, the mayor of Taba, which had begun in January in Arusha, Tanzania.

The Čelebići case was seen as significant for many legal reasons. It was the first multidefendant war crimes trial since Nuremberg and Tokyo. It was also the first prosecution using "command responsibility"—the principle that a commander is responsible for the acts of his soldiers—since the phrase was coined fifty years earlier. And hopefully it would be the first trial to end all comparisons between the Yugoslav Tribunal and the World War II–era tribunals and their victor's justice. In the Čelebići trial, the perpetrators were Bosnian Muslims and a Croat—and the victims were the Serbs.

Politically, the case was a chance to woo over the recalcitrant Bosnian Serbs, who accused the court of "anti-Serb bias." As if to prove them wrong, stretched across one side of the courtroom in The Hague was a multiethnic rogues' gallery with no Serb in it: Bosnian Croat Zdravko "Pavo" Mucić, the commander of the Čelebići camp, mustachioed and sporting dark glasses, who was accused of responsibility for the killings, acts of torture, plunder, and unlawful confinement of civilians; Esad Landžo, a baby-faced Bosnian Muslim with a shaven head, charged with murder, wilful killing, torture, and cruel punishment of the prisoners, including setting several on fire. Next to him sat Zejnil Delalić, also a Bosnian Muslim; haughty and proud, he was charged with command responsibility as the head of the Bosnian forces' First Tactical Group, which prosecutors alleged had authority over the Čelebići camp. Finally came the tall, bald, heavily muscled Hazim Delić, the camp's deputy commander, a glowering, gum-chomping Bosnian Muslim accused of acts of murder, torture, and rape as well as command responsibility for the offenses other than rape.

As the case limped along over the next nineteen months—through the testimony of 122 witnesses, the presentation of more than 1,500 exhibits, and enough talking by attorneys to fill 16,000 pages of transcript—it came to represent, however, a worst-case scenario of a war crimes trial. In fact, to observers and some of its witnesses, despite the best intentions of those involved, the Čelebići trial epitomized the limits of what war crimes tribunals could accomplish.

Years later Petko Grubač would diplomatically put it this way: "There is no justice that can please each and every one of us." And the first to be displeased with the Čelebići case were the Bosnian Serb witnesses whom it was meant to serve.

JUSTICE IS NEVER expected to be swift or easy before a war crimes tribunal. The Čelebići case, however, swiftly became mired in minutiae, running weeks behind schedule. The case was extremely complicated, full of motions and countermotions and arguments about the fine points of international humanitarian law or about which procedures to follow. By the sixth week of the trial—by the time the prosecution had originally calculated they would finish their case—only thirteen of seventy-five of their prospective witnesses had taken the stand.

As delays continued, bad luck certainly played a part: A judge fell ill with pneumonia. A key prosecution witness was hit by a car the day before he was to testify. The courtroom had to be shared with another equally difficult case, that of Croatian General Tihomir Blaškić, accused of war crimes in the Croat-Muslim war.

Yet incompetence and bureaucracy were also at fault. Video hook-ups became snarled. Defense attorneys couldn't get legal briefs translated for their clients. A Croatian newspaper published many of the names of the potential witnesses, including their promised pseudonyms, which halted the proceedings while an investigation into the leak was carried out. Defendants repeatedly dismissed their attorneys; one would have six before the trial ended in 1998.

Flamboyant defense attorneys harangued the witnesses; the judges often appeared either asleep or intent on belaboring procedural questions; defendants, obnoxious and disrespectful, glowered at witnesses and were rude to attorneys, sometimes causing the trial to be stopped; witnesses wanted to give speeches, and sympathetic and earnest prosecutors let them do so.

As these problems mounted, they raised larger questions about tribunal justice itself. Should the tribunal really be devoting time to prosecuting what were, ultimately, minor players in the war? Were trials before an international court the proper forum to address the needs of Čelebići camp survivors? Were qualified defense lawyers available to defendants?

Could a tribunal case ever be all things to all people? The clash of views over international justice itself snarled the trial. Victims had one view of proceedings and what they would accomplish, whereas prosecutors, defense attorneys, and judges had others.

Prosecutors, for example, did not want the Čelebići trial to be seen as the "Bosnian Serb" case. They did not mean for it to be about ethnic identity at all. Rather, they wanted to emphasize that individuals, not ethnic groups, were responsible for war crimes. "The religion or ethnicity of the perpetrators is of no consequence," Swedish prosecutor Eric Ostberg told the court in his opening arguments on March 10, 1997. "It is their serious violations of international humanitarian law we are going to try . . . not responsibility of a state or army or any such body—just their own individual responsibility."

Yet the Bosnian Serbs who came forward from Europe and the United States to testify—such as Petko and Gordana Grubač—had different hopes. They *wanted* this to be a case about the Serbs. Indeed, the Bosnian Serbs—many of whom saw themselves as victims of the CIA, President Clinton, NATO, and the Western press as well as the Bosnian Muslims and Croats—were where they thought they belonged: in the witness stand, describing the injustices, historic and otherwise, against them. Only then could the world see the Bosnian war as they saw it: a war in which the Bosnian Muslims and Croats were at least as guilty as the Serbs.

In fact, Bosnian Serb witnesses were outraged by the tribunal's failure to depict a larger picture of Bosnian Muslim treachery against them. Some, who had told investigators about abuses at several concentration camps, were annoyed that the indictment focused only on Čelebići. Others, who had pointed the finger at Bosnian Muslim president Alija Izetbegović—saying he'd visited the camp and knew of the conditions—were upset that the indictment reached no higher than Delalić, the tactical commander for the region. And everyone was outraged that the case did not charge the four men with genocide.

"Honorable Mrs. Arbour," wrote a disgruntled Gojko Kličković, the Bosnian Serb prime minister on March 6, 1996, to The Hague's chief prosecutor, "these late, disproportionately and unacceptably insufficient accusations . . . so far the only ones against the criminals responsible for the atrocities against the Serbs, make us completely unsatisfied. . . ."

Even Petko, never an ardent Serb nationalist, was disappointed that prosecutors had taken the Čelebići camp out of context. Surely if they were unbiased they would have concluded that there had been genocide against the Serbs in Konjic. What about Donje Selo? Bradina? The particularly brutal camp at Tarčin? Human rights investigators had reported on atrocities there. Wasn't justice about looking at all the evidence?

TRIBUNAL PROSECUTORS DID not see the Čelebići case as an opportunity to probe allegations of genocide in and around Konjic. They saw it as the tribunal's first chance to prosecute "superior responsibility" and an important test for future cases. Bosnian Serb leader Radovan Karadžić—if he were ever brought to trial—would be charged with superior responsibility for the crimes committed by his underlings. Superior responsibility is, however, difficult to prove. Prosecutors have to demonstrate that those charged have real power over those who commit atrocities and that they knew, or had reason to know, about war crimes being committed. It was all the more difficult in Bosnia's conflict, with its makeshift chains of command and its relative lack of a paper trail. Tribunal prosecutors, led by its purposeful American attorney, Teresa McHenry, would have to depend almost entirely on the Bosnian Serb camp survivors to prove the charges. Slowly, cautiously she mounted her case.

Indeed, those taking the witness stand did describe a life of unpredictable and inhumane cruelty at Čelebići committed either by or with the permission of the four defendants. They spoke of being imprisoned in underground tunnels, hangars, and even manholes without light, water, and food. Each day promised another round of indiscriminate terror—possibly torture with an electric shock, a beating with an iron bar, or being burned with hot implements.

"I was afraid of everyone," testified Witness F. "Whoever walked in, I was afraid of them, and prayed to God not to be taken out, because I was not sure that I would come back alive if I were taken out."

Witness Grozdana Čečez—the first woman to ever testify about rape before the Yugoslav Tribunal—summed up the camp's dreadful legacy. "I will never be able to be the woman that I was," she said. "They kill you psychologically."

Bosnian Serb witnesses, anxious to tell their stories, often resisted being reminded to keep them to the point. When one witness proved particularly long-winded, the frustrated defense attorney cross-examining him simply gave up and sat down while the man was still speaking. Rebuked by the judge, the attorney replied: "Your honor, if the witness wants to simply make speeches then I do not want to get in his way." The Čelebići witnesses, needing the therapeutic value of talking about what they had seen, had expected the tribunal's proceedings to be more like a truth commission than a trial. They were disappointed when prosecutors, defense attorneys, and judges tried to restrict their testimony. The hard-line nationalist Bosnian Serb press soon picked up their complaints. Soon the official Serbian news agency reflected witnesses' complaints that "the public was kept blind and uninformed about the shocking testimony of the Serbs."

Defense attorneys, of course, had other aims in the Čelebići case, including debunking the witnesses' testimony. They sought to prove that the witnesses were in fact armed rebels and not "protected" by the Geneva Conventions at all, and that they had lied about the beatings at the camp and falsely accused the defendants. If these witnesses wanted a sympathetic hearing—if they wanted a truth commission—this defense team was definitely not going to cooperate. The defense attorneys saw the trial as a legal and even political battleground.

Led by three American attorneys—who had earned their legal spurs in Texas and brought the freewheeling, combative style of the Lone Star State to the courtroom—the defense team was aggressive. They flooded the court with motions, challenged the prosecution at every opportunity, and submitted witnesses to grueling—and sometimes pointless—cross-examination in an effort to prove they were lying. "Texas litigation," said defense attorney Tom Moran, who typically appeared in court in black cowboy boots, "is a contact sport like football." Yugoslav lawyers, for their part, tried to replay the war in the courtroom. At times they delved unnecessarily into irrelevant questions of history, such as Bosnia's 1,000 years of statehood.

The judge presiding over the case was Adolphus Karibi-Whyte of Nigeria, who rarely stopped defense counsel or witnesses as they droned on. In fact, some observers suspected he slept through portions of the trial, given his propensity to sit with his eyes closed and breathe with a loud, snorelike rattle. When he did speak, his Nigerian accent was so difficult to understand that attorneys had to read the simultaneous text scrolling across their computer screens. Also sitting on the bench was Judge Saad Saood Jan of Pakistan, a well-liked and attentive judge with years of criminal experience, who attempted to keep the courtroom proceedings on schedule. But he received little assistance from Judge Elizabeth Odio Benito, a former human rights activist best remembered for barely speaking during the trial and for becoming vice-president of Costa Rica while in The Hague.

It was a combustible combination: traumatized witnesses who wanted to deliver speeches, earnest prosecutors, lax judges, combative defense attorneys. No wonder Mirko Klarin, an independent journalist who regularly attended the trial, would conclude that Čelebići had gained the reputation as "the trial where everything that could go wrong, did go wrong." And Klarin, from Belgrade, was typically a fierce advocate for the tribunal. It was he, writing in 1991, who had first called for a war crimes tribunal for the former Yugoslavia.

SOME OBSERVERS AND staffers in The Hague, watching the trial plod along, shook their heads knowingly. The Rwanda Tribunal had the high-profile problems: allegations of corruption, fraud, blatant mismanagement. The Yugoslav Tribunal's were more ordinary: poor management, bad planning, incompetence. Some of it was chalked up to the Goldstone years. Former chief prosecutor Richard Goldstone got high marks for having lobbied hard and wide for the court's survival, winning it allies around the world and raising its public profile. But the tribunal's more experienced lawyers felt his lack of prosecutorial experience had hurt some cases. His deputy, Graham Blewitt, while amiable, had a rather old-fashioned approach to war crimes, and tribunal investigators had consequently focused on building cases from the bottom up, which meant it could take years to mount the evidence against someone like Serb nationalist leader Slobodan Milošević.

Prosecutors hoped Arbour was different. A former professor of law who had served on the Ontario Supreme Court as well as its Court of Appeals, Arbour could focus on improving the quality of prosecutions now that Goldstone had assured the tribunal's reputation. Yet she was as media-shy as Goldstone was media-savvy, and her methodical nature could be maddeningly slow. She arrived, hoping to make arrests and stronger indictments a priority, but, like her predecessor before her, Arbour found herself battling the United Nations over money. In 1997 she asked for $63 million; she got $49.5 million instead. That meant funds for staff, investigations, translators, even defense counsel were limited. Top-notch American and European defense attorneys already shied away from the tribunal, finding its rates of $80 to $100 an hour too little to cover administrative costs, much less the loss of their regular salary.

Money wasn't the only problem. Complex UN hiring procedures meant that it could take up to a year to hire a prosecutor; as a result, many lawyers at the tribunal were on loan by their own governments. While some tribunal prosecutors and investigators were—or became—experts in the Balkans, others didn't. The result was a staff whose skills and dedication varied widely. One former analyst recalls being shocked when asked by an investigator, "Who is Franko Tudjman?" Franjo Tudjman was the president of Croatia.

Equally pressing was the tribunal's shortage of translators. One of the reasons trial days in the Čelebići case tended to be short—resulting in cases that moved slowly—was that there weren't enough translators. (In fact, the tribunal's first budget failed to allocate hardly any funds for any translation at all.) By the end of 1997, a General Accounting Office team investigating the tribunal found a backlog of 800,000 pages of documents, 9,000 photographs, and so much videotape that it would take one person two years to watch. The court's database was so poorly organized staff referred to it as "the black hole."

In the end, all it took was one look at Čelebići's defendants to make one wonder about the tribunal's overall strategy: Did the prosecution of these men satisfy the need to bring the region's most heinous war criminals to trial? Dušan "Dule" Tadić had been a small fish, but he had been the tribunal's first case. Čelebići was the tribunal's second case, and yet the defendants were still minor figures. Even assuming that the best way to get Bosnia's ringleaders was to prosecute those further down the chain of command, it was hard to see where Delić, Landžo, Mucić, and Delalić—who giggled, scowled, and slouched their way their way though trial like boys in junior high school detention hall—would lead anyone. During the trial Delić, the camp's deputy commander, threatened a defense attorney and made loud, disparaging remarks about witnesses while they testified. Landžo, the young guard, laughed and giggled in a high, whinnying voice. Mucić, the camp commander who always wore dark glasses to court, laughed inappropriately during witness testimony and passed notes to other defendants. In one memorable incident, he sarcastically blew kisses at one of the prosecutors—stalling the proceedings amid calls for an apology. Judge Karibi-Whyte, annoyed, referred to him as "a rascal."

Only Delalić stayed above the fray. But as the evidence was presented, it was hard to see how Delalić, a somewhat shady businessman–turned–tactical commander, had become a powerbroker. Was the tribunal, with its limited funds, doing the right thing by going after these defendants? "There is no strategic vision," said one tribunal staffer during the trial. "There is no idea of who we are picking off and why and where we are going."

Some of the tribunal's prosecutors had been lobbying to have the court focus on high-ranking defendants rather than lesser ones, if NATO could be persuaded to make arrests. By July their hopes would be realized—changing the course of the tribunal, at least in terms of the quality of its defendants, for the better.

AS THE ČELEBIĆI case got under way, the trial of Dušan Tadić had reached its conclusion. "Mr. Tadić," said Judge McDonald, about to deliver the court's judgment. "Will you please stand up?"

It was May 7, 1997, and she and the two other judges on the trial chamber had, after five months of deliberations, reached a decision. "For the foregoing reasons, having considered all the evidence and the arguments, the trial chamber find as follows . . . not guilty . . . guilty . . . not guilty . . . guilty . . . guilty . . ." On she read through the thirty-one counts.

Tadić, still standing, remained nearly motionless; it was exactly one year to the day after the trial started.

The judges delivered a mixed verdict: guilty on only eleven counts out of thirty-one. Dušan Tadić was found guilty of persecution and crimes against humanity, but not of murder. The case had been hurt, in part, by the discovery that a key witness had lied. On another eleven counts charging Tadić with violating the Geneva Conventions, two of the judges—with Judge McDonald dissenting—found the charges did not apply, as they decided that Bosnia's war was not an international armed conflict. (For the conventions to apply, a war must be an international conflict and the people affected must be "protected persons.") Incredibly, despite evidence that members of the Yugoslav National Army—which answered to Serbian leader Slobodan Milošević—had simply traded in their badges for those of the Bosnian Serb Army, two of the judges decided that Serbian troops were not involved.

The inch-thick judgment made clear, both in the details it revealed about Kozarac's takeover and the larger pattern of the war, that the Muslims had not begun the fighting or attacked themselves, as some Serbs claimed. Unfortunately, however, there were no Bosnians in the courtroom to hear the judgment summarized or to read it in depth. One difficulty with having a war crimes court located several countries away from the scene of the crime was that no one was on hand to watch the proceedings. Nor was it easy for detailed, unbiased coverage of proceedings to reach the Balkans. While the American and European press could afford to travel to The Hague to cover the Tadić trial, Bosnian reporters, particularly those from the country's fledging independent press, could not. The tribunal's press office was neither helpful nor forthcoming, frequently failing to return phone calls. And the region's nationalist press, part of the propaganda machine that had fed the conflict in the first place, simply skewed stories to fit their agenda without ever traveling to The Hague.

The nationalist Bosnian Serb news agency (SRNA), for example, incorrectly reported that "since Dušan Tadić was completely acquitted from accusations of murders and serious crimes, the sentence to be announced . . . would not be severe." The Belgrade newspaper *Politika*—at that time the chief tool of Milošević's propaganda—failed to report that Tadić had been found guilty. Its story hailed the judgment as a defeat for those in the international community who insisted that Milošević and his troops had taken part in the Bosnian war.

What received far more coverage was a lengthy interview by former Bosnian Serb leader Radovan Karadžić in the Belgrade daily *Novosti*. Coming amid a heightened NATO presence near Karadžić's home and a fresh rumors about his arrest, it stoked Bosnian Serb cynicism about the Yugoslav Tribunal. Karadžić, still so revered that many Bosnian Serbs had photographs of him on their walls or in their wallets, continued to shape public opinion. "If I could trust in that court, why not [go to The Hague]?" Karadžić lamented. "If that court would be impartial, if it wouldn't be a discriminating one, if it wasn't a political instrument... if, if, if. There are so many 'ifs.' "

Hamdo Kahrimanović, the former Omarska camp inmate, was in Bosnia when he learned of Tadić's conviction from friends who had heard it on the radio. That he was in his homeland when he heard the news was a victory; that he was not in Kozarac, a disappointment. So his reactions, a combination of joy and dismay, were as mixed as was the judges' verdict.

Not until the Yugoslav Tribunal chose to go after Simo Drljača and other leading nationalists in the region near Kozarac, thought Hamdo, would there be justice for him and his family. The couple, among the first Bosnians to volunteer to be repatriated from Germany, had arrived in their homeland only to discover that Simo Drljača still prevented them from returning home. Kozarac had fallen into the Serb-half of Bosnia under the Dayton peace plan, and Drljača, still the police chief in neighboring Prijedor, remained the local strongman.

Whenever Bosnian Muslims did try to return home—as was their right under the Dayton peace accord—Drljača did all he could to prevent them. He organized crowds of angry Bosnian Serbs, distributed weapons, and threatened each and every person as he or she arrived. It was too dangerous for Hamdo and Firdesa to move back to Kozarac. Instead, they settled in Sanski Most, the nearest city to it in Federation territory. Their home was only a half-hour drive away; but with Drljača in charge, it was as inaccessible as ever.

Unbeknownst to them, however, Simo Drljača was about to become the first indicted war criminal that NATO would try to arrest.

IT WAS A peaceful summer day in July 1997. Drljača was fishing with his son and brother-in-law at a reservoir near the former Omarska concentration camp he helped create. The sun beat down, making them drowsy, and dragonflies buzzed over the water. A boat rocked idly nearby. Not until a group of British SAS commandos appeared through the brush did Drljača have any idea that he was about to make legal history. Startled, he leapt to his feet, drew his gun, and ran toward the boat at the water's edge. A British soldier, hot in pursuit, tackled him; Drljača, turning, shot him in the leg. As he had bragged to me just the year before, in the event of a NATO arrest, "any time of day or night, I am ready to resist."

But four more shots rang out and Drljača was shot dead. It was not quite the result that the planners of "Operation Tango" had wished for, given that Milan Kovačević, Drljača's cohort in genocide, had been arrested quietly at the local hospital where he worked. Still, the arrest signaled a reversal in NATO's attitude. A year and a half after arriving in Bosnia, the sixteen-member alliance had finally consented to arrest indicted war criminals, as long as a special arrest squad did the work. In The Hague, the team of investigators and prosecutors assembling war crimes cases in the Prijedor region opened a bottle of red wine in celebration.

NATO's change of heart was spurred in part by changes in political leadership. With the re-election of President Clinton in 1996, Madeleine Albright, long an outspoken advocate of arresting war criminals, became U.S. secretary of state. Britain's elections in 1997 brought her an ally on the issue with the victory of Labour candidate Tony Blair. In Washington, while the Pentagon still opposed getting involved with arrest missions, there was increasingly a consensus among Clinton's foreign policy aides that something had to be done with Bosnia's war criminals. As long as indictees remained at large, they undermined Bosnia's peace, necessitating the need for NATO troops to stay longer. And the White House wanted its troops out of Bosnia, the sooner the better.

But NATO, under pressure from Greece and Russia, was too divided ever to sign off on arrests. The solution lay in a different strategy, hammered out in discussions between the Clinton administration and its European allies in late 1996 and early 1997. National troops, rather than NATO forces, would make the arrests to bypass the need for approval by the North Atlantic Council, NATO's political decision-making body. And they weren't just any troops, but specially trained troops, part of their own unit. Early in 1997, the United States and its European allies began training a group of 125 special forces soldiers—British, French, German, and Dutch—in Stuttgart, Germany. "They were brought in especially to nab war criminals," recalled a senior Clinton administration official. (It was British special forces troops, not members of Britain's NATO forces in Bosnia, that made up "Operation Tango," the mission to arrest Kovačević and Drljača.)

At the tribunal, chief prosecutor Louise Arbour decided that by indicting alleged war criminals secretly it would be easier for NATO to arrest them. Tribunal indictments had been made public because Balkan countries, under the terms of the Dayton peace accord, were to turn their war criminals over to The Hague. But neither the Bosnian Serbs nor the Serbs had complied, and the indictments only put war criminals on notice. With secret indictments in hand, NATO troops could more easily "encounter" an indicted war criminal—as their rules of engagement allowed—and no longer use the excuse that soldiers were not to hunt down indictees. In March, Arbour issued secret indictments for Kovačević and Drljača.

She had the luxury, however, of a trial run to convince NATO of the wisdom of the new approach. Arbour also had a sealed indictment for Slavko Dokmanović, a Serb who was the former mayor of Vukovar. It was his arrest on June 27—by unarmed tribunal investigators along with UN peacekeepers—that finally shamed NATO into action.

It helped that Jacques Klein, the brash American in charge of the UN Transitional Administration for eastern Slavonia—an area of Croatia occupied by the Serbs in 1992 and scheduled to be returned to the Croats—hungered to arrest Dokmanović, who had been charged with grave breaches of the Geneva Conventions, violations of the laws and customs of war, and crimes against humanity. (It was he who was held responsible for the execution of 260 patients from the Vukovar hospital whose bodies lay in the mass grave that Bill Haglund helped examine back in 1993.) Klein, anxious for the arrest to go smoothly, conducted trial runs and rehearsals until he was confident the mission would proceed flawlessly.

Dokmanović also made the arrest easy. It was he who had first contacted the tribunal, offering to testify against his rivals, the Croats. His complaints to tribunal investigators at the time—Dokmanović whined about not being able to get compensation for property lost during the war—gave them the pretext they needed to lure him to a spot where he could be easily arrested. They suggested he meet with Klein in Croatia, to discuss his difficulties, offering him UN protection from the Croats. A UN car met an unsuspecting Dokmanović at the border and whisked him to the nearest UN base. There, Dokmanović's "meeting" turned into his arrest by tribunal staff, instead.

His arrest, Prosecutor Arbour made clear, would not be the tribunal's last. "As long as there is no change to be seen in those who are supposed to carry out [arrests], we will use all legal means available to us to bring the indicted before the court," she warned. Meeting afterward with NATO commanders, Arbour put them on the spot. Said one UN source: "Louise told [NATO commander] General Crouch 'If the UN can arrest war criminals, then you can too.' " Within days NATO had a legal team en route to talk to Klein about the Dokmanović arrest.

That both Dokmanović's arrest—and that of Drljača and Kovačević—had gone off smoothly augered well for future arrest missions. That Drljača had died was a loss, but more important to NATO was that none of the soldiers had been killed in the raid. Nor, as American and European leaders had feared, was there any kind of armed backlash on the ground. (Western leaders, as they had during the war, persisted in believing that the rebel Bosnian Serbs were skilled, dangerous fighters.) Instead, the Bosnian Serbs—as they always did when confronted with force—retreated into gloom and self-pity. Rather than launching wide-ranging attacks on NATO peacekeepers, they held a massive state funeral for Drljača instead.

Two thousand mourners held candles while eleven Orthodox priests chanted prayers over his coffin, draped in a red, white, and blue Bosnian Serb flag. Bosnian Serb nationalists uttered a lot of menacing rhetoric; posters were plastered around Prijedor condemning Drljača's murder; and Momcilo Krajišnik, the Serb member of Bosnia's three-member collective presidency, sounded apocalyptic as he warned the Bosnian Serbs "not to take revenge" on NATO soldiers. Yet more than ever, the Bosnian Serbs defined themselves as victims rather than aggressors.

Soon, another decision from The Hague gave them all the more reason to do so. Five days after Drljača's arrest, Judge McDonald sentenced Duško Tadić—Kozarac's own war criminal—to twenty years in prison.

It was an emotional moment for McDonald. She had begun the trial believing in Tadić's innocence, and had presided over it for nearly a year while trying to keep an open mind in the face of horrifying evidence. But she believed the evidence pointed firmly to his guilt, and she wanted Tadić to acknowledge what he had done. She turned to Tadić and, looking him directly in the eye as she had done so many times during the trial, asked him why he had done what he did.

"You committed these offenses intentionally and with sadistic brutality, using knives, whips, iron bars, the butt of a pistol, sticks, kicking the victims and tightening a noose around the neck of one until he became unconscious," she said, her voice full of emotion. "Why?" She paused. Tadić said nothing.

It was a question that had haunted her throughout the trial. Why do people kill people of a different ethnicity, race, or religion? McDonald kept asking the question of each witness until one finally answered it. Because of prejudice, the witness had said; because we judge people by their differences. For months afterward, McDonald could still hear those words reverberating in her head. It confirmed her worst suspicions: that she, as an African American, had by her own experiences known the answer all along.

And so she decided to make clear—for history, for Bosnia and for Tadić himself—that what had happened in Kozarac was prejudice, racism at its most extreme. If people of different races were to coexist, they had to know that intolerance left unchecked could become genocide.

Still looking Tadić in the eye, McDonald spoke.

"The testimony of one witness explains your cruel and brutal conduct against your former friends and neighbors. The witness testified that you threatened the area 'would be a greater Serbia . . . and that [they], Muslims, will not be there, that there will be no place for them.' " She was overwhelmed with emotion as she pronounced Tadić's sentence.

"You—" her voice cracked—"must bear responsibility for your criminal conduct. To condone your actions even when committed in this context... is to give effect to a base view of morality and invite anarchy."

Both the prosecution and the defense moved to appeal.

AND THEN IT was Petko Grubač's turn to testify.

As a doctor at the concentration camp, he could speak with some authority about the injuries and deaths he had seen there, and which of the men—Delić, Delalić, Mucić, Landžo—were responsible for them. Because Gordana had managed to convince Delalić to release Petko, she could support her husband's testimony that as commander of the Bosnian First Tactical Group, Delalić was clearly in a position of command over the camp.

So Petko told the court of watching Delić beat prisoners senseless and of watching them die as he tried to staunch their wounds. He talked about treating prisoners who had been purposefully set aflame. He testified as to how Delalić had signed his discharge papers from Čelebići but made it clear that he did not consider Delalić a hero for doing so. Petko's release ultimately had only led to more captivity: house arrest in Konjic, and then incarceration in local jails for both Gordana and him.

When it came Gordana's turn to enter the courtroom—she was one of the very few women to appear before the Yugoslav Tribunal at that time—she described her visit to Čelebići. She told of finding Petko thin and white as sheet and one of her brothers, with his nose broken and his teeth knocked out. She spoke of how, in desperation, she turned to Delalić, the old family friend whom everyone said was in charge. Arriving at his house, she had begged for her husband's life.

"And then I started crying and asked him, 'Zejnil, why is my Petko in prison for two months?' I told him I had been to the prison that day and that I had seen him and that he was in a very bad condition and that he would die there." Delalić, she said, arranged for Petko to be released the very next evening.

Gordana was composed as she spoke. Like Petko, she was somewhat put off by the courtroom's proceedings and newfangled modernity: the television cameras, the computer screens, the headphones, and the legal mumbo-jumbo that ate up hours of time. Most of all, Gordana couldn't understand why no one seemed to be paying attention to her testimony. Her story seemed to be having no impact. Why did Judge Karibi-Whyte appear to be sleeping through her testimony? Why did some of the defense attorneys' questions seem so unrelated? What difference did it make if, as one defense attorney had just asked her, she had been a member of the communist party?

Finally, when one defense attorney asked her if the Serbs had lost important positions during the war, Gordana broke down. Lost? Lost? Didn't he know?

"The Serbs lost everything with this war, their land—" she said.

"Could you list a few of the most important people who lost their positions?" asked defense attorney Zejnil Olujić.

"It is not the positions that count, it is human lives." Gordana's eyes filled with tears. "They have lost their dearest ones, which is most important of all, and then after that they have lost everything, their identity—I am sorry, I am a bit upset. They have lost everything, everything. We are a people without a past."

SOME WEEKS LATER, a defense attorney asked another witness—Witness R, a schoolteacher from Bradina who had testified about some of the worst beatings at the Čelebići camp—if he had ever read Dante.

"Yes," the witness replied.

"Thank you, I have no further questions."

"You mean, 'you who enter leave all hope behind'?" the witness said, confused as to the question's relevance.

That remark could have summed up the Čelebići trial. As the months passed, as summer turned into fall and then into winter, as defendant after defendant took the stand, many involved in the case lost hope. From 1997 into 1998 so many pages of testimony and piles of exhibits collected that the case took on the trappings of the long-running proceedings in Charles Dickens's *Bleak House*. "Jarndyce and Jarndyce drones on," Dickens wrote. "This scarecrow of a suit has, in course of time, become so complicated, that no man alive knows what it means. . . ." Journalists, dubbing the Čelebići case the "forgotten trial," stopped paying attention. The tribunal judges' terms had to be extended so they could finish the trial. As proceedings dragged on, the trial did not enhance the tribunal's reputation among the Serbs: A group of leading Serbian intellectuals signed a declaration stating the tribunal was "exclusively an instrument for the persecution of Serbs."

The trial's glacial pace obscured other of the tribunal's real accomplishments. It had served a subpoena on the state of Croatia in the Blaskić case, opening a new chapter in the battle between the tribunal's universal jurisdiction and countries eager to hang on to their sovereignty. Investigators in a raid in 1997 swept through Banja Luka, Prijedor, and other cities, seizing documents that lay the foundation for new indictments. (There was indeed a Bosnian Serb document trail, it turned out, albeit not quite as complete as the one left by the Nazis.)

Yet there was still no sign of an indictment against Slobodan Milošević—the man responsible for the Bosian war in the first place. Rumors swirled: that the tribunal had been told not to indict him because of his cooperation at Dayton; that the tribunal had indicted him secretly. Tribunal prosecutors always insisted they were investigating the Serbian nationalist. But prosecutors did not seriously focus on him until the fall of 1998. Indeed, they then swiftly wrote the indictment in just fifty-two days.

Meanwhile, it wasn't until February 16, 1998—almost a year after the Čelebići trial had commenced—that the prosecution rested its case. Defense attorneys began their rebuttal, lining up a battery of 72 witnesses and 266 exhibits. Delalić's attorney hoped to prove that, while his client was commander of Tactical Group One, he had no authority over the Čelebići camp. The other attorneys set out to prove that Čelebići was not a concentration camp but a prison, whose inmates—allegedly Serbs who had rebelled against the Bosnian government—had been well treated.

It would take nine more months before a decision was handed down on November 17, 1998, the day the judges' extended terms were due to end. Their legal assistants had toiled to complete it. Even if the trial, at times, had seemed like a farce, it was clear that the judges intended the Čelebići decision to be taken seriously. The 483-page document had the air of an academic treatise, breaking new ground in international humanitarian law. For legal scholars, it was a goldmine.

The judges clarified what "torture" meant. For the first time, they ruled that "acts of rape may constitute torture under customary law."

They refined the definition of "superior responsibility," noting that it could apply not only to people whose *title* granted them authority over those who committed war crimes but also to those whose *power* granted them that authority. And, in a resounding repudiation of the defense attorneys' case, the judges ruled that the war in Bosnia was indeed an international armed conflict and that the Bosnian Serbs in the camp were therefore "protected persons." (The Čelebići case's findings on that issue now contradicted those in the Tadić case.)

Certainly justice—in terms of the application and development of international humanitarian law—had been delivered. What was less clear was whether justice—in the sense of telling the truth and delivering punishment—had also been handed down. As far as the trial's witnesses were concerned, the verdict was deeply mixed.

Only three of the four men accused of crimes at Čelebići were found guilty. Delalić, the businessman turned tactical group commander, was acquitted on all counts, much to the prosecutor's surprise and Petko and Gordana's horror. He returned to Bosnia to be greeted like a conquering hero by jubilant crowds.

Mucić, the camp commander, was found guilty, his conviction the first based on "superior responsibility" since the Tokyo and Nuremberg tribunals. But concluding that his actions were the result of "human frailty, rather than individual malice," the judges sentenced him to only seven years in prison. Petko and Gordana, along with other witnesses, were outraged. Only Delić, the camp deputy commander, and Landžo, his acolyte, received anything resembling what the Bosnian Serbs who had suffered at their hands thought of as justice. "We have been appalled by the details of your criminal actions," said Judge Karibi-Whyte, staring at Delić as he sentenced him to twenty years in jail for crimes including rape. "You've displayed a singular brutality in causing the deaths of two men. . . ." Landžo was sentenced to fifteen years. His crimes, Judge Karibi-Whyte said, were "suggestive of significant imagination and a perverse pleasure in the infliction of pain."

Delalić beamed. Delić chewed his gum. Mucić, behind his dark glasses, smirked. Landžo's jaw dropped. And both the prosecutors and defense attorneys—once they finished reeling from the verdict—moved immediately to appeal.

Some Bosnian Serb witnesses saw the verdict handed down by the tribunal as predictably anti-Serb. Others, like Witness R, thought the proceedings were ridiculous. "The trial," says he, "was a circus."

Petko and Gordana finally came to a different conclusion. The tribunal had done its best but had delivered only partial justice: selective, limited, less than they had hoped for.

Now, they asked themselves, was this *all* they could expect of justice?

Book Three

AFTER JUDGMENT

13

A TIME OF RECKONING

And what next?
Those who've wounded the night–had already murdered the day.
Will they at least know how to feign repentance?
What will happen when they come to, when they wake up
From this high-caliber dream?

—Rezak Hukanović, *The Tenth Circle of Hell*

Far from Judge McDonald's courtroom in The Hague, far from debates over international humanitarian law and the 302-page Tadić decision, stood the village of Kozarac—or what remained of it—at a lonely crossroads in northwest Bosnia.

Even by postwar standards, Kozarac in 1998 was remarkable for the sheer devastation it had suffered, haunting in its grimness. Mile after mile of charred, gutted houses lined its streets. Trees sprouted from what were once living rooms. Brush climbed up staircases that mounted to nowhere. The movie theater was burned to the ground. All that remained of the prewar town were artifacts that poked from the rubble: a charred sneaker, a melted pot, a stove tilted on its side.

The only people who moved through the town's ruins were the handful of Bosnian Serb families who remained after the Muslims had been forced out, inheriting the rewards of the battle for "greater Serbia." The only business still operating was the Tadić family's bar, Sensei, now run by Mladen Tadić, Dušan's older brother, who had returned from Germany.

It was a desolate place. But one day that spring, a parade of cars and buses pulled up to Kozarac, followed by a group of armed NATO soldiers. The buses opened their doors; car doors slammed. A small cluster of civilians stepped tentatively onto the road. They blinked with confusion, as if they had been in the dark and were unused to the sudden, bright light. Some covered their faces with their hands and sobbed. Others broke into the slightest of smiles.

Six years after they had been forced from their homes at gunpoint, the first of the surviving Bosnian Muslims of Kozarac had come home to visit. Hamdo Kahrimanović, once an Omarska camp inmate, was among them.

The spring wind ruffled his white hair. He looked around, not daring to move far from the bus. Was this his Kozarac? But as he ran his eyes over the scarred remains, he began to envision his former hometown. Like an architect, he sketched new buildings in his mind from the remaining skeletal foundations. Yes; that was the main street. And over there, that was the movie theater.

He smiled to himself. Justice was slow, but it was possible. The proof? He, a Bosnian Muslim refugee, was back in the town from which he had been chased by the rebel Bosnian Serbs. He was back in his beloved Kozarac, just as he had dreamed all those months and days that he had been in exile. Had Tadić not been convicted, had Drljača not been arrested (and killed), none of this would have been possible. Justice had been done. Or had it?

With a shiver, Hamdo realized he was still only a visitor in Kozarac; his bus stood waiting to whisk him away. Whether justice would pave the way for reconciliation—or for Hamdo to return home—was still unclear.

THE YEARS FOLLOWING the 1997 Tadić judgment were years of reckoning. Slowly the world became a smaller, more uncomfortable place for war criminals. Judges handed down punishments; NATO's more aggressive arrest policy inspired the first waves of surrenders. In Tanzania, the former Rwandan prime minister Jean Kambanda became the first high-ranking government official in history to plead guilty to genocide before an international tribunal.

Even as the war crimes tribunals on two continents wrestled with their shortcomings, human rights advocates moved to take their example a step further. Since Nuremberg, many had dreamed of a permanent international criminal court that would sit constantly rather than be called into being in the wake of atrocities. In July 1998 that vision finally became reality. Delegates from 120 countries gathered in Rome and approved a treaty creating a permanent International Criminal Court. In so doing, they rebuffed the Clinton administration's staunch opposition, which put the United States in the company of countries such as Iran, Iraq, China, Libya, Algeria, and the Sudan, which had also lobbied against the court. (The Pentagon, opposed to arresting war criminals in Bosnia, was also firmly against the creation of a permanent criminal court, fearful that American soldiers serving abroad did not have enough protection from politically inspired prosecutions.)

Tyrants, it seemed, might no longer sleep so easily in their beds. Creation of a permanent criminal court signaled an end to allowing former dictators to be sheltered by any country's laws. Indeed, in the fall of 1998, British police seized Chile's former dictator, General Augusto Pinochet, on an arrest warrant from Spain. That Spain—not Chile—wanted to try the dictator on charges of crimes against humanity for the deaths, torture, and disappearance of more than 3,000 people reflected the growing support for universal war crimes laws. Some crimes are so heinous, lawyers bringing the case argued, that it was appropriate for any country to bring charges, not just the one in which the crimes were committed. Britain's House of Lords, as if to signal the end to impunity for dictators, then rejected Pinochet's claim of immunity as a former head of state.

Nineteen ninety-eight and the years that followed were not, however, just a time of reckoning for war criminals. They also marked a period of self-criticism for the United States, European countries, the United Nations, and even the tribunals. Governmental hearings, commissions, and UN reports examined the West's failure to intervene in the Rwandan genocide or to halt the slaughter at Srebrenica. At the same time, doubts were raised whether the two tribunals were fulfilling their UN mandate. While no one in Bosnia and Rwanda questioned the symbolic value of the trials, increasingly some began to question their practical impact. The trials took years to complete; only a handful of targeted war criminals had been brought to justice; and verdicts, when they arrived, were often so misunderstood they further divided communities instead of reconciling them.

Increasingly, what Petko and Gordana, Hasan and Hamdo, Witness JJ and Anonciata wondered was just how relevant to their lives the tribunals' cases really were. According to their UN mandate, the courts were to play a role in the "restoration and maintenance of peace." Would this ever happen?

HASAN NUHANOVIĆ, IN the three years since the fall of the UN safe area of Srebrenica, had become a man obsessed with his cause: tracking down details about his family's disappearance and the West's failure to protect thousands of Bosnian Muslim men and boys from being executed. He repeatedly fired off faxes to UN officials demanding information. He penned letters to the UN's High Commission for Refugees, the Dutch government, and the International Commission on Missing Persons, formed by the Clinton administration in 1996. He never missed an opportunity to confront Western officials and ask them what they knew about Srebrenica. In the gritty city of Tuzla, the tiny one-bedroom apartment he shared with his girlfriend, Mirza, was stuffed with correspondence, UN documents, TV tapes, and books, anything that related to Srebrenica. With his sharp memory and eye for detail, Hasan had become a Srebrenica expert, sought after by journalists and activists alike. Even his dress was a sartorial commitment to his cause. Hasan deliberately favored T-shirts in various shades of green and army-style pants with pockets, his way of announcing that he was a soldier in search of the truth.

His path, and the paths of the investigators working on the Srebrenica case, frequently converged in Bosnia. Even as Hasan became disillusioned with other Western institutions in Bosnia—few ever answered his letters—he had continued to believe in the Yugoslav Tribunal. He had particular respect for the chief investigator on the Srebrenica case, Jean-René Ruez, with whom Hasan frequently swapped tips. Ruez, a French investigator, was dedicated and hardworking, nearly as obsessed with Srebrenica as Hasan.

But by 1998 Hasan was having his first doubts about the tribunal and its ability to provide justice for Srebrenica survivors. First, none of those indicted for the massacres had yet to be arrested. Second, he wanted the court to investigate the Dutch UN battalion's actions in the safe area and the failure of UN leaders to halt its capture.

But the tribunal was unlikely to do so, as Hasan realized during a 1997 trip to The Hague. Hasan had gone there to meet with the Dutch foreign minister, Joris Voorhoeve, whom he hoped would know something about his family. The meeting proved a disappointment: Voorhoeve, whose department had consistently defended the peacekeepers, was unwilling to answer any of Hasan's questions, particularly in front of the Dutch television crew that accompanied him.

But Hasan's second goal for that trip was to convince the tribunal to investigate those he blamed for the massacres, chief among them Zvornik police chief Dragomir Vasić. Hasan was increasingly certain that Vasić held the answers to the disappearance of his father, Ibro. Hasan knew Ibro had been seen in the Zvornik police station just days after leaving the UN base at Potočari. He knew that Vasić was present when General Mladić negotiated with the Dutch peacekeepers at the Hotel Fontana and that the vast majority of mass graves fell within the police chief's jurisdiction. On his first visit to Zvornik, Hasan had spotted photographs of Vasić, grinning as he stood next to General Mladić and Milan "Legenda" Jovović of the Drina Wolves—two men certainly implicated in the Srebrenica killings. If that wasn't evidence enough, Vasić had a track record of anti-Muslim violence: Not only had he played a key role in ethnically cleansing Zvornik in 1992, he and his police force dynamited homes refugees tried to return to in 1996.

Yet, as Hasan learned during his visit, the Yugoslav Tribunal was focusing on prosecuting more-prominent war criminals. At the beginning, with no guarantee that arrests would be forthcoming, chief prosecutor Goldstone had been forced to take a scatter-shot approach. With successful arrests now behind them, prosecutors who had been arguing for the tribunal to focus its scarce resources on high-ranking defendants finally won out. In 1998 Arbour dismissed eighteen indictments against lower-ranking indicted war criminals that the staff believed were unprovable. The move infuriated many Bosnian survivors, but it did also send a message: the tribunal wanted to see the chief architects, Radovan Karadžić and his general, Ratko Mladić, on trial. Presumably, the tribunal also wanted to try the general in charge of Srebrenica, Radislav Krstić, although he had not yet been publicly indicted.

Yet if the Yugoslav war crimes tribunal was not going to go after men like Dragomir Vasić, Hasan wondered, who would? The legal system in every part of the former Yugoslavia was in too much disarray to make war crimes trials fair. Some legal proceedings lacked any pretense of even-handedness; others, manipulated by the nationalists who remained in power, became political show trials. In Croatia, a former concentration camp guard was sentenced to twenty years in jail after a trial in which he was not allowed to call witnesses or conduct a defense. In Bosnia, the first war crimes trial held by Muslim-Croat military authorities ended in disgrace when the court condemned two Bosnian Serbs to death, only to have the men they had allegedly killed discovered to be alive and well and living in Sarajevo. A murder trial held by the Bosnian Serbs of the "Zvornik Seven"—a group of Srebrenica survivors who the Serbs claimed were war criminals—was condemned by international observers for relying solely on confessions that the UN said were extracted by torture. Three of the men were sentenced to twenty years in prison.

That the low-level henchmen who played a role in the Srebrenica massacres still swaggered around freely was not Hasan's only quarrel with the tribunal and the justice it sought to provide for Bosnia. He and the war crimes court also differed over the question of the Srebrenica dead. Investigators were focused on mass graves, but Hasan believed they should examine individual graves as well. And there was one grave he specifically wanted them to exhume: that of his mother, Nasiha.

Finally, Hasan had stumbled on the news of how and where his mother died. The information came from an unlikely source: Milan, an older friend of Hasan's brother Muhamed, who still lived in their hometown of Vlasenica. When they met in the summer of 1997, they talked for two hours nonstop, trading questions in rapid staccato. So hungry were the two friends for information they never bothered to sit down, firing questions back and forth while leaning against the wall of a hotel hallway.

Milan's candor was refreshing after the constant denials Hasan was used to hearing. Had Milan joined the Bosnian Serb Army? Sure, Milan replied. Had those in Vlasenica taken part in the Srebrenica attack? Yes; anyone who denied that or said they didn't know what was happening was lying, the man responded. Were there massacres afterward? Absolutely.

Hasan was sure Milan would know something about Muhamed; he had adored the younger boy. But when Hasan asked what Milan knew of Muhamed's fate, he only shook his head. Hasan was crestfallen.

"And my mother," Hasan said. "I hear rumors that she was in Vlasenica, at the Škorpion Café. What do you know?" He threw in the question almost offhandedly, for he despaired of discovering more clues about his mother's death. By then he had deciphered that Bosnian Serb soldiers, on that fateful day in July 1996, had separated his mother from his father and brother and put her on a bus with other women to be evacuated to Muslim territory. When the bus passed through Vlasenica, Nasiha had screamed and cried and begged to be let off so she could find her husband and son. The last anyone had heard of her was that she'd been spotted at the Škorpion Café, which had been used as police headquarters during the war.

Milan paused. Silence hung between them, taut as a wire. Minutes passed.

"I came just after she was killed," he finally said in a hushed voice. "It was terrible, I tell you. Her body was just terrible."

Hasan felt his heart pound. It was true then! Nasiha was dead. Suddenly he could visualize her body. Oddly, he felt no grief; instead, he felt an overwhelming sense of relief. Nasiha *was* dead. He felt that now for sure.

Hasan pushed for more details. How? Where? Why? Milan, puffing on his cigarette, just shook his head. "Hasan . . . it was terrible. That's it. It was terrible. Get on with your life." He motioned Hasan outside; it was time to leave.

Hasan walked his old friend out to his car in the hotel parking lot. He was hesitant to press Milan for more details, but he yearned for answers to the questions now buzzing in his head. Why? How? When?

"Tell me," Hasan implored. "How was she killed? Was it a bullet or a knife?"

"Hasan, leave this," Milan said curtly. "Have children. Move on. Don't search for any more information. It's hopeless." He refused to give any more details.

Hasan, however, did not give up so easily. In the months that followed, he persisted: asking here, asking there. By the time tribunal investigators next came knocking at his door, Hasan had received a tip as to where his mother's body was buried, in a small village outside Vlasenica. He begged them to help him locate and exhume her body. The investigators regretfully declined.

THE WORLD MAY not have focused on Srebrenica, but thanks to Hasan and others, it had not entirely forgotten it either. The shocking events surrounding the 1996 capture of the UN safe area had spawned a series of documentaries, books, newspaper articles, and human rights reports. Journalists from the Netherlands, France, and the United States, ferreting out new information, raised disturbing new questions about the West's failure to halt the slaughter. Why had the United States failed to raise the alarm about executions when American satellite imagery indicated that they had occurred? Had German intelligence, as some German newspapers reported, electronically eavesdropped on a conversation before the capture of Srebrenica that should have tipped off Western officials to what General Mladić was planning? If the Bosnian Army, hardly high tech, had managed to intercept conversations—including one in which Drina Corps commander General Radislav Krstić allegedly ordered, "You must kill everyone. We don't need anyone alive"—why hadn't UN and other better-equipped intelligence forces on the ground done the same?

Theories abounded. Bosnia's own government had wanted to be rid of Srebrenica. Europe and the United States, in their drive for peace, let the Bosnian Serbs capture Srebrenica because it finally made the country's ethnic division geographically more viable. General Janvier, the French head of UN forces for the former Yugoslavia, had deliberately failed to send NATO airplanes in time because he had made a deal with General Mladić during negotiations earlier in 1996 to get French UN hostages released. "I am convinced Janvier made a deal," insisted one senior State Department official five years afterward. "I believe he agreed there would be no further air strikes in order to free the French peacekeepers taken in 1995."

However it had happened, it was clear the world had failed Srebrenica. In 1998 Hasan said as much to the group of U.S. congressmen assembled for a hearing in Washington, D.C. The title of the hearing at which Hasan was to testify, called by Representative Chris Smith, Republican of New Jersey, echoed popular belief: "The Betrayal of Srebrenica: Why Did the Massacre Happen? Will It Happen Again?"

Hasan had pondered for days on his testimony while he had strolled the streets of Washington, the only place he could safely smoke. Visiting the U.S. for the first time, Hasan marveled at how much larger, grander, and more wasteful everything was. (He figured that his hotel room was double the size of his apartment back home in Tuzla.) Determined to spend his time working, Hasan allowed himself only one indulgence: a visit to the movie theater. He pondered his choices and then picked the new hit, *Titanic*, starring Kate Winslet and Leonardo DiCaprio, figuring he could identify with the movie's tale of how official hubris and miscalculation resulted in the loss of more than 1,500 lives.

And so, on March 31, Hasan strode into room 2172 of the Rayburn House Office Building, prepared to tell his story of official miscalculations in the UN safe area of Srebrenica to the House Subcommittee on International Operations and Human Rights. He was wearing his unofficial uniform of green T-shirt and army pants and carrying the scuffed black airplane bag in which he carried all his official documents. His fellow witnesses were all respected for their knowledge of Srebrenica's tragedies: Diane Paul, a consultant to Human Rights Watch; Eric Stover, director of the Human Rights Center at the University of California at Berkeley; John Heffernan, head of the Coalition for International Justice, a group supporting the two tribunals; and Bianca Jagger of Amnesty International.

Unfortunately, the witnesses outnumbered the congressional attendees at the hearing. Only three congressmen were present: Congressman Smith; Congressman Benjamin Gilman, a New York Republican, and Congressman Frank Wolf, Republican of Virginia. A handful of aides and a small audience also turned out to listen. Still, Hasan's testimony about the fall of Srebrenica and his family's disappearance made an impact. Those listening remember being impressed with his clarity, his sophisticated arguments, and his lack of bitterness for someone who had experienced so devastating a loss.

One of Hasan's conclusions, however, startled them. For many Bosnians like himself, Hasan argued, the justice being delivered by the Yugoslav Tribunal was not necessarily the "justice" they sought. "The families in Bosnia are told that the International Tribunal in The Hague is performing an investigation on war crimes in Srebrenica," he said. "War crimes and war criminals is a separate issue from missing persons. The families of missing persons like myself, we have no use of [Dražen]

Erdemović being in prison for five years. He is going to come out of prison in three years now. It is not going to change anything in my search for my family. . . . There must be some other body which will launch a thorough investigation, right now, not waiting for the politicians to decide when the political situation is suitable for such an investigation." There was the International Commission on Missing Persons in Bosnia, but it was charged with aiding all the families of Bosnia's missing—not just the Srebrenica survivors to whom, Hasan believed, Western leaders had a special obligation.

Representative Smith sought to reassure him. "Mr. Nuhanović, let me just say that I believe, and I believe every member of our panel and every Member of Congress believes, that you and people like you are entitled to answers, whether it be as a result of gross miscalculation, or cowardice, or complicity in these crimes of the United Nations, of which we are a part, even though the Dutch had the lead here. You are entitled, regardless of any political consideration, to know exactly what happened to your family. As you pointed out, you still harbor some hope that one or more may survive."

An aide dimmed the lights in the hearing room. Stover, the former executive director of Physicians for Human Rights, began showing slides of the bodies that Bill Haglund and his team had exhumed from mass graves in and around Srebrenica. The hearing room fell still as slide after slide flashed on the screen, each more graphic than the last. Congressman Wolf finally broke the silence.

"I guess I had two questions," he asked. "Where do you think most of the Serbs are who were involved in the killings? Where are they now?"

As Stover finished his answer, Hasan took the microphone and explained that "Serb authorities who were in charge of those towns (and were involved with the massacre) in 1995 when it happened, the mayors, the chief of police, the military commanders are all there talking to American soldiers every day, American officers, as if nothing happened, because these things are forgotten." "It is just simple" to find war criminals, he added. He was thinking of Dragomir Vasić.

"Just go there and talk to them," Hasan told the congressmen. "All Serbs involved in war crimes in Srebrenica are still sitting in the same positions as they were in 1995."

"Thank you," Congressman Wolf said into the stunned silence that followed.

Hasan kept on talking. He produced documents, answered more questions, and reiterated several points. Despite the fact that the Dutch UN soldiers had been charged with protecting the refugees at the Potočari UN base—their orders had read "Take all reasonable measures to protect refugees and civilians in your care"—the Dutch had not saved one person, he said. "All these facts show there was very little interest to save the lives of anybody," Hasan concluded. The hearing was gaveled to a close, with the recommendation that the U.S. Congress call for all relevant intelligence, as well as United Nations documents, to be declassified.

It was only 12:28 P.M., but Hasan was so exhausted from his testimony he felt as if he had lived every moment of his days in Srebrenica all over again. He wanted to believe that telling his story to a congressional panel would somehow make a difference: to Bosnia, to the tribunal, to his own search for justice. Yet he had his doubts. "Is it useful for a person looking for truth and justice to fly 3,000 miles?" he wondered. "Why doesn't justice come to us?"

BY THAT SUMMER, however, Hasan had his first taste of justice—or, at least, the sense that the years he had spent battling for the truth to emerge about Srebrenica had not been in vain. The Dutch UN battalion's failure to protect Srebrenica had become the Netherlands' longest-running public scandal. With the election of a new government in 1998, the actions of the Dutch UN troops again came under renewed public scrutiny. The mood, and the Dutch cabinet, had changed since 1997 when Hasan had had his unsuccessful meeting with Defense Minister Voorhoeve about his family.

Newly elected Defense Minister Frank de Greve, buffeted by continuing allegations in the media of wrongdoing by the UN peacekeepers and government efforts to hush them up, ordered a new independent inquiry. Topping the inquiry's list: whether the Dutch government had destroyed photographic evidence of massacres taken by a peacekeeper and ignored a senior military policeman's report calling for criminal investigations into the peacekeepers' actions.

Then, Captain Ron Rutten, the Dutch UN peacekeeper whose film had been destroyed, accused his own battalion in a television interview of "collaborating" with the Bosnian Serbs in ethnically cleansing Srebrenica. "I thought we were collaborating, I thought it then and I still think so today," said Rutten, explaining how he had watched some of his colleagues assist Bosnian Serb soldiers in separating men from women during Srebrenica's evacuation. He also accused top Dutch military officials of dismissing the concerns he and other officers raised that Bosnian Muslim civilians were being slain by Bosnian Serb soldiers.

The captain's remarks focused new attention on what had transpired during 1996, raising questions about the Dutch troop's moral, if not legal, liability for the more than 7,000 men and boys who died. It was clear that those who entrusted their lives to the UN peacekeepers—such as Hasan's father, Ibro, and his brother, Muhamed—had all been executed. By contrast, at least some of the men who had not sought shelter with the UN but had fled by hiking across the minefields and through the woods had survived.

By summer's end, three separate investigations were ongoing in the Netherlands: the new, independent inquiry; a probe by the Dutch public prosecutor into allegations that peacekeepers ran over and killed as many as thirty Srebrenica refugees with their armored personnel carrier as they retreated; and a study by the Dutch State Institute for the Documentation of War (RIOD), which had begun in 1996. (The independent inquiry later found administrative errors but no evidence of a government cover-up; the public prosecutor's case against the peacekeepers was dismissed for lack of evidence. The RIOD report has not yet been published.)

"The Dutch," Hasan mused when we met in Bosnia late that summer of 1998. "We never saw them as real people, as flesh and blood, we saw them as something special, the UN, an effort to bring peace and justice. We had this idea that they represented the international community, European standards, justice, not people who make mistakes. So we were polite to them, obeyed their orders, even as they kicked out our people.

"I should have done more," he said angrily. "I should have thrown my bloody ID card in their face."

He looked much older than when I last had seen him; perhaps it was the new, scruffy mustache and goatee he was sporting. He had also traded in his army green T-shirt for a new one: this one screamed "Liars!" on the front, with a quote from Oscar Wilde across the back: "If you want the truth, you have to invent it." Hasan said he wore it whenever he talked to Western officials.

Hasan was pleased by the pummeling the Dutch peacekeepers were taking. Yet he was more discouraged than ever about the Yugoslav Tribunal's Srebrenica case. Only some 1,500 bodies had been exhumed after nearly three summers of digging. Tribunal investigators, opening new graves to discover only partial remains, now believed that many more mass graves had been tampered with than they had first thought. NATO troops still had not moved to arrest those indicted for the massacres, Radovan Karadžić and Ratko Mladić. Local Bosnian Serbs showed no signs of ever accepting that the massacres had even occurred. Indeed, even though the Bosnian Muslims reclaimed the majority of seats in the Srebrenica city council in 1997's municipal elections—people could vote from their prewar address, even if they no longer lived there—the new city counselors had not been able to attend any meetings. Mobs hurling rocks prevented the Bosnian Muslims and their Western escorts from entering Srebrenica.

Most disappointing of all to Hasan was the news that the Zvornik police chief, Dragomir Vasić, had disappeared after being dismissed from his job, the result of a shake-up between moderates and hard-liners in the Bosnian Serb government. Although Vasić remained a member of the Zvornik municipal assembly, no one had seen much of him since. According to rumor, he had fled to Serbia.

Of course, Vasić wasn't the only bad guy to slip through the net. There was absolutely no indication that the two men most responsible for starting the region's wars—Serbian nationalist Slobodan Milošević and Croatian president Franjo Tudjman—would even be indicted by the Yugoslav Tribunal.

Hasan sighed, lit another cigarette, and promptly apologized. "I can never talk about Srebrenica unless I have a cigarette," he joked, "and a glass of brandy." Brandy proved appropriate, because Hasan had other news to announce: He was the father of an eight-month-old baby girl.

"What's her name?" I asked.

"Nasiha," Hasan said softly. After his mother. "But she looks a lot like my brother, Muhamed."

When he swept his baby into his arms, Hasan told me, he felt the surge of optimism a new generation brings to the world. But he also felt afraid for his daughter, afraid that if there was no justice for Bosnia, fighting would resume. Hasan vowed to redouble his efforts: to find out what happened to his family, to continue digging out new facts about Srebrenica, to make sure the Dutch and the UN were held responsible.

He had been thinking about a truth commission for Bosnia, an idea that had been well received by victims' organizations representing all three of the country's ethnic factions when it was first proposed in 1997. The idea gained the support of more than 100 nongovernmental organizations on all sides of Bosnia's ethnic divide and the backing of Richard Goldstone, former chief prosecutor of both the Yugoslav and Rwanda tribunals. Supporters in Washington and other capitals swiftly noted that the Dayton peace talks had originally included a proposal for a commission of inquiry into the war.

But hard-line Bosnian nationalists, who still held power, bridled at the idea or sought to manipulate it. At the same time, the Yugoslav Tribunal strongly opposed such a commission, fearful both that it might endanger its own investigations and that it would be manipulated by nationalists. Tribunal prosecutor Louise Arbour and Judge McDonald had been outspoken in their belief that Bosnia was not yet ready for a truth commission. Arbour, in fact, had actively lobbied against it in conversations with American diplomats, saying it would undermine the court by giving "those who had no intention of cooperating" a "plausible alternative for avoiding their obligations." By 1998 her opposition, combined with that from some Bosnian politicians, had all but dealt the idea a death blow.

"I don't want my baby to live in a world that allowed this to happen and not have justice satisfied," Hasan told me. He drew deeply on his cigarette, his brandy glass half raised. "Justice and truth are the most important things. Sometimes I think, why did God leave me alone? To try to find the truth. And that would be a kind of justice. . . . You need to know what happened to your relatives when he or she dies. You make a thousand scenarios. You have them in your dreams, in your head. To stop this, you need the truth.

"I had this dream I was flying over a graveyard," he added. "My mother came out and said, 'I hate you.' I decided it was because I didn't save my brother. I didn't do enough, and I will die knowing I could have done more. . . . But I cannot draw any conclusions. You know, it's more sure than in 1996 that they are all dead. But still, I don't want to bury people alive. . . ." His voice trailed off and his eyes stared into the distance. So intent was his gaze that for an instant I was convinced that, if I turned around, I would see Nasiha, Ibro, and Muhamed standing there.

JUSTICE HAD NOT arrived for Hasan. But by the end of the summer of 1998, justice appeared to be inching forward for Hamdo Kahrimanović, the school principal from Kozarac. In northwest Bosnia, regional Bosnian Serb officials dumbfounded Western aid personnel by granting them permission to begin rebuilding homes so local Bosnian Muslim inhabitants could return. Symbolically, the town the Bosnian Serbs suggested for reconstruction was among the first they had destroyed back in 1992: Kozarac.

Ironically, I heard the news from Mladen Tadić, the brother of Dušan Tadić, the war criminal whom Hamdo's testimony before the Yugoslav Tribunal had helped convict. Alex, my translator, and I found Mladen in the Tadić family's bar in Kozarac one August afternoon. There was no missing the Tadić family establishment—one of the few buildings with a roof on Kozarac's devastated main street—and no ignoring its incongruous décor, sort of Kung Fu–meets–communist bloc. Outside, an Asian-style wooden gate bore the café's name, Sensei; inside, the concrete walls were adorned with mottled photographs of the Tadić boys in their karate uniforms.

Mladen, a short, almost gnomelike man with large eyes, bald head, and a slightly crooked nose, was a hearty publican, always ready to chat. Unlike many other Bosnian Serbs, he did not deny that his fellow Bosnian Serbs committed their share of war crimes; in particular, he blamed Prijedor police chief Simo Drljača. "Drljača was the most responsible person here," said Mladen. "All of those who took part in the tortures and killings [here] should be punished." Yet he still didn't believe Dušan was among them. Mladen was certain someone else at the Omarska concentration camp had committed the crimes, a man who looked so much like his brother that "they were like two eggs," as he put it.

"How could The Hague have made such a mistake?" Mladen asked. "It's undeniable there were war crimes. But this court should be ashamed that these people who committed crimes are walking down the street. And those who did nothing are in prison. I don't think that can be called justice."

He sipped his coffee. The smoke from his cigarette drifted lazily in the air. We chatted: about war, about peace, about the six new roofs I had spotted that gleamed like spotlights in the otherwise devastated village. "Have you heard there are Muslims who are moving back to Kozarac?" Mladen asked, by way of explanation. "Hamdo has even been here a few times; he's fixing up his house."

I put my pen down, taken aback. I had never dreamed that Bosnian Muslims would return to Kozarac, much less those who had spent time in nearby concentration camps. It was as hard to comprehend as concentration camp survivors returning to Germany. And yet it was a sign of some changes inching across Bosnia, which held out the promise that the country's warlords might one day have their reckoning.

NATO—its forces newly under the command of U.S. Army General Wesley Clark—had kept on arresting war criminals, although not necessarily high-ranking ones, using secret indictments. By the fall of 1998, thirty-three of the eighty publicly indicted war criminals were in custody in The Hague, more than three times the number the year before. Some had surrendered rather than face arrest. Even the swaggering Bosnian nationalist Radovan Karadžić had gone underground amid continuing rumors of his apprehension.

In the village of Pale where he lived, the guard post at the entrance to his driveway was deserted. Western generals on the ground, fed up with Karadžić's continued meddling in nationalist politics, had at least tried to annoy him. NATO helicopters often buzzed over his various residences; troops had at times followed his wife as she drove through Pale. Either the harassment or the tempo of arrests had proved too much for the former Bosnian Serb leader. Some believed Karadžić had fled to Belarus and was poised to surrender, others that he had hired two American lawyers to represent him and was preparing his defense. "I suspect he [Karadžić] will be in The Hague quite soon," Elisabeth Rehn, the UN envoy in charge of the multinational police force in Bosnia, told reporters. Meanwhile, General Mladić, on whose good graces NATO operations in Bosnia depended, continued to strut around openly.

Yet divisions among the allies—and particularly between the French, on one hand, and the British and the Americans, on the other—stymied any arrest mission targeting the Bosnian Serb nationalist leader. The French had extensive ties, both diplomatic and commercial, to the Serbs. At the same time, more French UN peacekeepers had died during the Bosnian war than any other nationality. A mission to arrest Karadžić posed certain hazards, and within French government circles, in fact, there was wide division as to its value.

Then the already shaky cooperation between the French and its NATO allies was dealt a blow when the news broke that a French army officer had been recalled, suspected of having tipped off Karadžić to an arrest operation. Senior U.S. and Western officials, quoted in the U.S. press, alternatively confirmed and denied that the arrest operation, which had apparently been compromised, was aimed at Karadžić himself. Others who knew the French officer, who had been based in Bosnia since the beginning of the war, had other theories. The officer "was conducting meetings concerning Karadžić's surrender," a UN official told me. "He was exploring that option on behalf of the French."

Regardless, several months later *The New York Times* reported that a multimillion-dollar operation to arrest Karadžić, code-named "Operation Amber Star," had been dropped. Involving U.S. and NATO intelligence, FBI agents and U.S. Marshals, the mission was cancelled because the Allies couldn't agree on when and how to launch it. Senior State Department officials still aren't sure just why Karadžić had not been arrested. Neither is Louise Arbour. "I was told that efforts were being made [to arrest Karadžić] but it was difficult for me to verify the extent to which these efforts were genuine," said Arbour several years later. "There were a million theories advanced to explain the delays. I've yet to hear anything that has the ring of truth."

To be sure, Karadžić had more than NATO to worry about. Leaders within his own Bosnian Serb nationalist SDS party wanted to diminish his stranglehold on power and black market money. Even fellow nationalist Biljana Plavšić accused Karadžić of corruption and struggled for political control. Anxious to diminish Karadžić's power, in 1997 Western officials threw their support behind Plavšić, despite her nationalist leanings and the fact that she had served in Karadžić's wartime presidency. In 1998 Plavšić moved even more to the center, embracing moderate Milorad Dodik, a former businessman, after he won the prime ministership by a narrow margin. Among Dodik's unfulfilled pledges: to work for the return of some 70,000, mostly Muslim, refugees and to support the Yugoslav war crimes tribunal. Should Radovan Karadžić be arrested on charges of genocide? I asked Dodik in an interview. "I wouldn't protest," Dodik replied.

After Plavšić and Dodik appeared to begin implementing key provisions of the Dayton peace accords, Western aid, which had long been denied to the Bosnian Serbs because of their failure to comply with the peace deal, followed. An estimated $100 million from the World Bank, U.S. Agency for International Development, and other groups was targeted for areas controlled by the two officials. As a result, by 1998 Serb-held Bosnia was physically divided: The west, where Plavšić and Dodik had centered the Bosnian Serb seat of government in the city of Banja Luka, benefited from Western aid. Eastern Bosnia, still loyal to Karadžić, did not. (In Bosnia's second national election in the fall of 1998, Plavšić lost to a nationalist, but moderates gained more seats in the Parliament.)

Fortunately for Hamdo, Kozarac was also now governed by the moderates, who had come to power after the death of local strongman Simo Drljača in NATO's first arrest raid in 1997. In Prijedor—a city that had been brutally ethnically cleansed—Bosnian Muslims were allowed to take up city council seats. "Once Drljača was gone," said Chris Bennett, an official then with the International Crisis Group, which monitored the peace process in Bosnia, "that opened the gates." Economics also had a lot to do with the sudden change of heart by Bosnian Serb authorities: for every house that Western aid groups rebuilt in Kozarac (which would be Muslim dominated), they were to build one in Prijedor (which would be Serb dominated). "They smelled the money," noted one Western aid worker.

Indeed, rebuilding Kozarac would finally provide barkeeper Mladen Tadić with a clientele, which was one reason he insisted he was ready for the town's former Bosnian Muslim residents to return. "I grew up with Muslims," he told me. "People have agreed to the fact that others are coming back."

Yet there was one person whose arrival Mladen wasn't looking forward to: Hamdo Kahrimanović, whose home was just across the street from the Tadić bar. Mladen believed Hamdo had lied about seeing his brother at Omarska. "As a family, we will now be forced to talk to the people like him who directly accused my brother," he said. As Mladen mulled the prospect of again being neighbors with Hamdo, the late-afternoon light illumined his profile. It was a cameo of uncertainty.

"How can they move back?" he asked. "It's not clear to me."

IT WAS NOT entirely clear to Hamdo and Firdesa Kahrimanović either when they contemplated the reality of returning to Kozarac. The United Nations High Commission for Refugees had billed 1998 as "the year of return," hoping that 50,000 of 1.8 million people displaced by the war would return to their homes in areas controlled by another ethnic group. Yet only some 11,000 did; in Serb-held territory, only 859 Muslims and Croats went back. And the first five Bosnian Muslim families who had reclaimed their partially rebuilt houses in Kozarac were not greeted cordially. No sooner had they arrived than someone dynamited a newly restored home, a warning of what returnees could expect. To protect those repatriating, the local NATO patrol made regular rounds past their homes. Apache helicopters buzzed overhead, signaling to the local Bosnian Serbs that the West had its eyes on the village's new inhabitants.

To its recently returned Muslims, Kozarac didn't feel like a village, but more like a prison. The few families kept to their homes, too fearful to go outside unless NATO troops were nearby. Still, they refused to leave. "I decided I'm returning to my own place even if I end up killed," muttered Smail Jakupović, who had come back along with his wife, Isfeta. She sobbed as he spoke, certain they'd be killed in their beds one night.

Hearing of the terror felt by Muslims who had returned to Kozarac, Hamdo and Firdesa lived in an apartment abandoned by a Serb family in the nearby city of Sanski Most. They realized that moving back home did not mean turning the clock back. They could not simply pick up their lives in 1992 as if the war had not happened. Drljača's death did not change the fact that Kozarac now lay in Serb-held territory, Bosnia's Republika Srpska. They would be Bosnian Muslims moving back amid hostile Bosnian Serbs, not Hamdo and Firdesa being welcomed back by old friends.

Hamdo was undaunted, even though he realized things would not be the same. "I cannot be a friend to the Serbs the way I used to," he explained, professorially underlining each of his words with a jab of his tortoise-shell glasses. "It's true I have bad memories. Bad memories—some I am not going to be able to forget. But we can live next to each other." To do less, he argued, was morally wrong. "By not returning, we would do great injustice to the victims. We would legalize what happened. I would give away as a present what my father and grandfather achieved [the family property]. And that would be a great sin."

Firdesa, however, was frightened. She feared they would be killed in their sleep. "Of course I'm afraid to return right now," she said, casting a withering look at her husband. "Who wouldn't be afraid? But I have no option but to go with him."

Even the Tadić trial appeared to have done little to pave the way for Muslims to return to Kozarac. Tribunal prosecutors frequently talked about how trials would help with reconciliation, replacing collective guilt with individual responsibility and propaganda with historic fact. Judge McDonald had deliberately made a point of including a detailed section on the Omarska camp in the judgment, making its existence impossible to deny to Bosnian Serb revisionists. Yet no one in Kozarac had seen the trial—local television had not carried it—and none had read the hefty decision. With no summary, glossary, or index, the Tadić judgment would not be translated into Serbo-Croatian for two more years.

Thus there remained two versions of history in Kozarac, split along ethnic lines. Bosnian Serbs like Mladen clung to the views they had held throughout the war, believing that Kozarac had been attacked because the Muslims were preparing an armed rebellion, although he admitted that local Serbs profited from plundering the houses. "All we wanted was to stay in Yugoslavia," Mladen told me. "People didn't kill Muslims because they hated them, people killed them to get their money."

Likewise, the local Serbs denied that the Omarska concentration camp had existed. "I don't know anything of what happened there, and I just hear all kinds of lies," snapped one sixty-nine-year-old resident. Even Mladen—one of the few Serbs who admitted that camps had existed—refused to call them concentration camps. "I was in Trnopolje, and that cannot be called a concentration camp," he said in disgust. One of his Bosnian Serb patrons, sitting at the bar and overhearing our conversation, yelled: "Tell them about Jasenovac [the World War II concentration camp]!"

Other reporters found the same level of denial in Hamdo's hometown. Radio reporter Lauren Comiteau, also visiting Kozarac that fall, brought up the question of Serb denial in an interview with Judge McDonald. Why did so few Bosnian Serbs living in Kozarac and Omarska know about the Tadić verdict, much less believe that Omarska had been a concentration camp?

McDonald fumbled for an answer. "That's what people said in Nazi Germany, we didn't know, we didn't know what happened," she said in the interview, broadcast on the BBC. "After the Nuremberg judgment, they found out in fact that it did happen, but it also took an acknowledgment on the part of the leadership of Germany that it happened. So it's not just a judgment on its own that will convince people, it requires some movement on the part of the leadership."

Afterward, sitting in her office at the Yugoslav Tribunal, McDonald was reflective. She toyed with the rubber band she wore around her wrist to help her remember to stop smoking. She looked around her office—with its photographs of her children, the Texas flag in the corner, and a poster of the "most wanted" Bosnian war criminals on the door—and felt depressed. Nobody knew about the Tadić judgment?

She was not so naive to have expected a revolution in thought, but she had hoped that the Bosnian Serbs, when confronted with firm evidence about the camp, would begin to change their minds.

But the citizens of Kozarac had not seen the decision, and no one from the tribunal had come to explain it to them. Consequently, the question of Dušan Tadić's guilt stood between the Bosnian Serbs and Bosnian Muslims of Kozarac—and between Mladen and Hamdo—like a psychological Berlin Wall. What the tribunal had decided didn't matter.

Said Mladen of Hamdo: "If this man is not ashamed of lying [about Dule's innocence], all I can do is look at him as a person not good enough to be accepted by me." Noted Hamdo of Mladen: "There's that old saying: He who is bitten by a snake is afraid of a lizard. Whoever feels guilty or responsible will either not look at me, nor live with me. I cannot forgive people who did such deeds."

It was hard, hearing such outpouring of emotions, to feel hopeful about Hamdo's return home. "Come see us next summer in Kozarac," he had said, and I promised I would. Some weeks after I left Kozarac, however, another newly restored house was dynamited as a warning—the shards of its bright red roof flung skyward to rest on the dirty rubble from 1992 that still lined the streets.

14

JUSTICE MUST BE SEEN TO BE DONE

We are betrayed by what is false within.

—George Meredith

After the public executions in 1998, Anonciata Kavaruganda's visits to Rwanda never seemed quite the same.

The mother of five and widow of Supreme Court president Joseph Kavaruganda was living in Belgium with her children, having narrowly escaped Rwanda's genocide. Yet she returned to her homeland at least twice a year. Even though her home in Belgium overlooked a field of grazing cows—a scene reminiscent of her homeland—it seemed very different. She missed Rwanda's sunny skies and balmy weather and the fragrant smell of tropical flowers. She yearned for African bananas, sweeter and smaller than those that could be bought in Belgium, and the taste of the Rwandan white fish, tilapia. She missed her mother, still living in Kigali, and her late husband. Even though she still had no idea where his body lay, in Rwanda she felt closer to him in spirit.

Then the Rwandan government ordered the first executions of those found guilty of genocide by its courts. The country's Tutsi and Hutu population, already divided by the bitter legacy of the genocide, became even more polarized over questions of justice. With each visit, Anonciata, like many other Rwandans, found herself straddling an ever-growing ethnic divide.

It was April 24, 1998, when the executions took place, and the crowds, some 20,000 strong, were exultant. The condemned, in their pink prison uniforms and with black hoods slipped over their heads, were lashed to stakes in Kigali's sports stadium. Onlookers cheered wildly as policemen picked up their assault rifles and shot them to death. One woman held her baby aloft for a better look.

Human rights groups, the Clinton administration, and Pope John Paul II, concerned about the fairness of the trials and the divisive nature of the executions, had called for clemency for the twenty-two men and women slated to be killed. Yet the Rwandan government, under pressure to deliver justice and still bitter about the West's failure to halt the genocide, insisted executions were necessary. As Justice Minister Faustin Ntezliyayo explained to a CNN reporter, they would serve as a kind of catharsis. "Justice," he said, "must be seen to be done."

It was a time of reckoning for Rwanda, just as it was for Bosnia. Congressional hearings and parliamentary hearings probed leaders' responsibility for the slaughter. American and European leaders admitted their failure to halt Rwanda's bloodbath. President Clinton, who in 1998 became the first Western leader to visit Rwanda after the massacres, apologized during his visit for the international community's failure to intervene. "We did not act quickly enough after the killings began," he said. "We did not immediately call these crimes by their rightful name: genocide."

The Rwanda Tribunal, emerging from the chaos that enveloped it in 1996, was finally conducting several trials in courtrooms in Arusha, Tanzania. Before the end of the 1998, the court would deliver two precedent-setting verdicts, including a guilty plea by a former prime minister. In Rwanda, where just two years before courtrooms were in ruins, their legal personnel slain, trials were under way with newly recruited and trained lawyers and judges.

No one could say now that Rwanda lacked justice. Both the international community and the Rwandan government had followed through on their pledges to make justice a priority, to uphold the rule of law in the wake of slaughter. Yet the question troubling many Rwandans was this: What kind of justice and for whom?

The International Criminal Tribunal for Rwanda was delivering international justice. Yet Tutsi survivors tended to feel that justice came far too slowly and was too lenient; trials dragged on for months, if not years, and none of the twenty-five high-ranking architects of the genocide being tried before the tribunal faced the death penalty. "What is going on in Arusha today is a mockery of justice," said presidential advisor Seth Kamanzi in 1997. And many among Rwanda's Hutu, already questioning the validity of the Rwandan government, couldn't understand why the tribunal had not moved to indict leaders of the Tutsi-led Rwandan Patriotic Army for the thousands of civilians they had slain after the genocide.

Then there was Rwanda's own justice system. Tutsi survivors were annoyed the courts weren't wrestling with issues of compensation in a land where crops, homes, and land—as well as entire families—had been destroyed. Rwanda's Hutu, pointing to the arrests that sent the prison population soaring from 88,000 to 135,000, argued that justice increasingly resembled vengeance, even as Hutu serving in government posts suddenly found themselves branded as *génocidaires*. Despite an influx of new legal personnel, those arrested often didn't know the charges against them for months, if not years. Meanwhile, disease raced through the overcrowded jails, killing 3,300 in 1998 alone.

To be sure, Rwandan courts did have something of a Wild West quality to them. International observers monitoring trials manned by hurriedly trained lawyers and judges found that, more often than not, proceedings were flagrantly one-sided. Court investigators and judges tended to find most of the accused guilty: 220 of 332 prisoners were convicted in 1997. An extraordinary number of defendants—36 percent—were sentenced to death in 1997, even though one Rwandan prosecutor estimated that nearly 15 percent of all detainees were falsely accused. Witnesses caught lying in court were not punished.

At the same time, while the genocide was over in Rwanda, the killing continued. One reason the country remained deeply divided in 1998, despite the government's call for reconciliation, was because of fierce clashes between extremist Hutu, who had not forsaken their campaign of genocide, and the Rwandan Patriotic Army. Hutu militia, in violent cross-border raids from neighboring countries where they lived in exile, killed both Tutsi and moderate Hutu, released Hutu prisoners from jails, distributed hate literature, and repeatedly threatened to overthrow the Rwandan government. Government troops retaliated harshly, often with crushing security sweeps. Swept up in the crossfire were thousands of innocent Rwandan civilians, particularly those who lived in villages dotting the country's mountainous northwest, where most of the fighting took place. Thousands were rounded up, killed, or simply disappeared, often at the hands of the RPA. Noted the U.S. State Department: "The RPA committed hundreds of extrajudicial killings, including individuals and families, in the course of fighting the insurgency in the northwest."

By the fall of 1998, Rwanda was marching toward a larger war, one that threatened to divide central Africa. Its target was former Zairean rebel leader Laurent Kabila. Rwanda had supported him in 1996, helping him to overthrow corrupt Zairean dictator Mobutu Sese Seko, who had allowed Hutu extremists to regroup and rearm in his country. Mobutu, his palaces trashed, his power shattered, limped off with his cane and trademark leopard-skin hat to Morocco, where he died of cancer. Kabila took control of Zaire, which was renamed the Democratic Republic of Congo (DRC). But by 1998 Kabila had proven little better than the man he replaced. He blocked UN efforts to examine reports of massacres of Hutu in Congo and then failed to curb the raids launched by the Rwandan Hutu militias that remained in his country. As if to emphasize their impunity, the Hutu militia was allowed to swoop into Rwanda to kill civilians in 1998, even as President Clinton was due to arrive. Rwanda's troops attacked Kabila's and war ensued, pitting Rwanda, Uganda, and Burundi against Zaire, Angola, Zimbabwe, and Namibia, countries that continued to shelter Hutu extremists.

A growing climate of suspicion hung over Rwanda like one of its many mists. The Tutsi wondered which of the Hutu, who remained the country's majority, were linked to outside extremists. The Hutu began to feel targeted by the Tutsi-dominated Rwandan government and its security crackdowns. The country's justice system just gave them one more excuse to feel persecuted.

In fragile, postconflict societies, the perception of justice is often as important as its delivery. Justice must be done, but it must be seen to be done fairly. Neither the the Rwanda Tribunal's trials nor those held by the Rwandan government met that test in the eyes of many Rwandans. Increasingly, both Hutu and Tutsi saw themselves as victims of justice, not recipients of it. Collective blame, rather than individual responsibility, still reigned.

THE REASON WHY Rwanda's 1998 executions continued to haunt the country had nothing to do with people being put to death. Rwandans in general approved of the death penalty. What was troubling was that Rwandan lawyers and international observers had found the trials that resulted in the executions to be deeply flawed. As UN High Commissioner Mary Robinson noted, the trials did not follow international standards, "in which all guarantees of due process are strictly observed."

Even today the case of one of those executed in 1998 lingers on in popular memory, the yardstick by which lawyers and clients measure their results. Many Rwandans point to the trial of Silas Munyagishali as a sign that their country's justice system is not even-handed. "Now, when there is a hearing," one Rwandan lawyer told me, "people say, 'Try to be careful so the case won't end up like Silas's.' "

To some, Silas Munyagishali, Kigali's chief prosecutor from 1995 to 1997, was a dangerous figure. The short, balding man with a slight beard was accused of taking part in several killings in his neighborhood and failing to help people in danger, crimes that were classified by Rwandan law as genocide. He was also believed to have abused his prosecutorial powers, destroying files of key Hutu extremists so they could not be prosecuted. (Apparently he was not charged with this as a crime.) "He had destroyed more than 300 genocide files," alleged one high-ranking member of Rwanda's legal community.

To others, Munyagishali was an honest man whose arrest had more to do with politics than with genocide. He frequently accused the Rwandan government's "screening commissions"—which studied cases to find out who in jail was falsely accused—of political bias. The lawyer challenged the Rwandan military's widespread arrests. Sometimes he refused to imprison those for whom he believed there was insufficient evidence. In so doing, Munyagishali was following in the footsteps of François-Xavier Nsanzuwera, his predecessor as Kigali prosecutor. Nsanzuwera, who sparred with Rwanda's military over his efforts to limit detention to those with credible charges of guilt, fled to Belgium in 1995 after receiving death threats. "Silas was not an extremist," said Nsanzuwera. The execution, he said, "was a political decision . . . one to create fear, to intimidate those who were guilty, and also to intimidate the Hutu to do what the RPF said.

Whether Silas Munyagishali was a criminal or a crusader was impossible for me to determine; trial records of his case were not made available when I asked for them. Yet what people remember about the case were not the specific charges. They remember only that the trial was unfair.

To begin with, one of the lawyers slated to represent Munyagishali, Innocent Murengezi—one of Rwanda's very few defense lawyers—disappeared before the trial began. When witnesses, saying they'd been threatened, asked to give testimony in private, the court refused. When a key witness did give evidence, she was harassed so badly she was too frightened to return to complete her testimony. The judges then denied other terrified witnesses the chance to submit written testimony. "It was a complicated and atypical case," said one Belgian lawyer. "But I think he was innocent. I think they did not have the evidence."

Rwandan government officials argue it is unfair to judge the entire court system by one trial. "Suppose they can prove this one trial was unfair," said Attorney General Gerald Gahima, interviewed several years after the execution. "What does that prove? We should not try people for genocide?" Yet the Munyagishali trial and execution, along with the others, sent a clear message to those in Rwanda's jails awaiting trial: It was better to confess than to go to court. The number of confessions—which, like plea bargain in the American system, result in a lesser sentence—had soared to 8,615 by the end of 1998.

Another message, at least for many in the Hutu community, was not to trust Rwandan justice. Avocats sans Frontières, a Belgian legal aid group that arrived in Rwanda after the executions to provide defense attorneys for those facing trial, warned of the dangers of this attitude. (There were only forty members of the defense bar for the 135,000 accused in 1997.) "The legal system system is failing in its message if it is not perceived positively," argued the group. "Present and future coexistence depend on it."

IF RWANDAN JUSTICE was perceived as unfair, then the justice delivered by the International Criminal Tribunal for Rwanda in neighboring Tanzania was seen as slow. Anonciata Kavaruganda was still waiting for the trial of General Théoneste Bagasora, one of the highest-ranking military officers alleged to have helped mastermind the genocide. He had been in custody since 1996.

She hoped his trial might reveal something about how and where her husband, Joseph, had been killed. Anonciata, allied with neither side of her divided country, had found few answers on her trips home. To many Hutu in Rwanda, Anonciata was too pro-Tutsi, given Joseph's ties to the RPF. To those Tutsi, particularly those newly arriving from Uganda who didn't know her, she was automatically suspect by the mere fact of being Hutu.

With no one in Rwanda to assist her—in the strained climate she trusted none but her closest friends—Anonciata had prayed the United Nations, and its tribunal, might have answers. She and her children penned numerous letters to the United Nations, pleading for any available information about Joseph's fate after the UN guards assigned to protect him had handed him over to his killers. She felt it was the UN's duty, having pledged to safeguard her husband, to provide her with details of his death.

In three years, however, she had received no replies. Two meetings with tribunal investigators had revealed little. What remaining hopes she nurtured were pinned on testimony that might emerge in the trial of Théoneste Bagasora, the retired colonel and Hutu extremist who assembled the genocidal government. Bagasora, with links to known assassination squads, had openly opposed those Hutu, like Joseph, who had favored working with the Tutsi-led RPF to form a new Rwanda. When the Presidential Guard had arrived at the Kavaruganda home to arrest Joseph in April 1994, their captain said he had been sent by Bagasora.

Yet there was no indication that the Bagasora trial would come any time soon. The Rwanda Tribunal, with thirty-five defendants awaiting trial, was overwhelmed. By 1998, neighboring African states, after initially refusing to cooperate, had decided it was good politics to back the new government in Rwanda by turning over war crimes suspects. Raids in Kenya, once the most recalcitrant country, had netted about twenty additional alleged criminals. As a result, an array of high-ranking architects of the genocide, including the governors of Rwandan provinces, former military commanders, and government officials, were behind bars in the tribunal's jail in Arusha, with its state-of-the-art exercise room and wide-screen TV.

The sheer number of defendants was not the only reason the tribunal's court proceedings were glacially slow. Despite new management—in the form of a new deputy prosecutor, Bernard Muna, and a new registrar, Agwu Ukiwe Okali—bureaucracy, a lack of staff, and continuing incompetence had created a virtual logjam. The post of chief investigator languished unfilled for more than two years—the result of what Chief Prosecutor Arbour described as "UN bureaucracy... a system so inflexible as to border on nonsensical absurdity." According to a 1998 UN internal affairs report, the failure to hire lawyers and investigators in the prosecutor's office constituted "a critical gap given the number of major cases to be tried." The report also found continuing problems in "procurement, recruitment, personnel, witness protection and asset management."

Determined to pick up the court's pace, Arbour proposed a new, aggressive strategy: folding twenty-nine defendants into one case—a mega "national indictment" aimed at producing a Nuremberg-style trial, which would reveal how politicians, the military, and others all conspired to produce the genocide. The case, she argued, would "highlight the complete criminal landscape of the widespread and systematic massacres committed." But the plan was rebuffed by the tribunal's judges, which put the prosecution team even further behind schedule. In another blow to the tribunal's reputation, Judge Lennert Aspegren announced he was quitting early.

"Those who accept bribes and embezzled money are promoted," the sixty-seven-year-old judge told the Swedish daily *Svenska Dagbladet*. "Those who voice criticism are formally cautioned. That is why I am stepping down early." He added: "The UN has not understood what a court is. Of the some 500 employees, some 20 are lawyers, 10 to 15 involved in trials.... We don't have a reference library.... Nothing of our efforts is passed on to the people of Rwanda. They don't know we exist." His comments touched off a bitter retort from the tribunal's registrar, who accused Aspegren of taking weeks of vacation and having difficulty working in a "multicultural background." Once again the court was plunged into an atmosphere of infighting and intrigue.

Even when trials began at the Rwanda Tribunal, they often sputtered along. Motions could not be found or had not been translated. Witnesses, and sometimes defense attorneys, failed to appear. Prosecutors sometimes were noticeably unprepared. The more aggressive defense attorneys filed hundreds of time-consuming motions, aimed at delaying trials in the hope that witnesses would lose heart to testify. "Every time a schedule is produced," complained Judge Navanethem Pillay in 1998, "either the accused is ill, or the witnesses are unavailable, or the prosecutor or the defense asks for more time."

The ongoing trial of George Rutaganda, the vice-president of the feared Interahamwe militia, suffered from all these problems. Rutaganda was accused of genocide in two neighborhoods in Kigali as well as in his hometown. The case was interrupted so many times—due to the defendant's illness, court recesses, or technical foul-ups—that by May 1998, after thirteen months of trial, it had seen only thirty-nine days in court. UN forensic expert Bill Haglund was forced to halt his testimony that spring when Rutaganda claimed he had malaria and was too sick to continue.

"Even yesterday I said I was unwell," whined Rutaganda, sniffling. Haglund's testimony in the Rutaganda case was his second before the Rwanda Tribunal. In November 1997 he had presented the first forensic evidence ever to an international war crimes court in the case of Clément Kayishema, the prefect, or district official, of Rwanda's province of Kibuye, charged with genocide. Some of the worst of Rwanda's slaughters occurred there; a book of those slain in the province was 1,085 pages long and listed 59,000 names.

At just one grave, the Church of Home St. Jean and St. John, Haglund and his team exhumed 450 bodies, the largest exhumation in history. By the time they added the skeletons that littered the nearby hillside that sloped down toward the brilliant turquoise waters of Lake Kivu, the total hit 495. Some of the dead had had their Achilles' tendons cut, which made it impossible for them to run away.

Nearly 70 percent of the bodies recovered were women and children; 25 percent were children under the age of ten.

In the Rutaganda case, Haglund was testifying about a much smaller exhumation: One of the gravesites was a latrine. "I cleaned it out one day so I could begin on the bodies," he recalled years later, "only to return the next day and find that someone had shit in it." Twenty-seven bodies, eighteen of them complete skeletons, were exhumed from the sloping field behind Rutaganda's headquarters, the Amgar garage in Kigali.

On March 10, 1998, Bill Haglund's testimony began with the inevitable questions about the 1996 exhumations in Bosnia. Prosecutors felt obliged to raise the topic of the tribunal inquiry, if for no other reason than to make sure the defense attorneys didn't use the information to discredit him. "And did your work in the former Yugoslavia land you in some controversy, Dr. Haglund?" asked the prosecutor, James Stewart.

"That's correct."

"And what was the result of this inquiry?"

"The Internal Board of Inquiry found the allegations against me not supported," Haglund answered. (He told friends once he got over being annoyed, even humiliated by the investigation, he found watching people review his work "downright interesting.")

Stewart dimmed the lights so Haglund could show slides of the graves and the exhumed remains. Some of those killed were shot, Haglund explained, and others had been bludgeoned to death. One corpse, a woman's, appeared to have been burned. Haglund meticulously pointed out to the judges the wounds on the skeletons and demonstrated how the remains revealed each person's sex and age. "This is the youngest individual we did examine," he explained. "If we look at the hipbones here you will note that the hipbone is not one bone. The hipbone really as it develops from childhood is three separate bones: the ilium, the top part, and then the pubis and the ischium. This bone is now in two pieces and the ilium and the ischium have just joined. These are the kinds of age indicators that we look at. . . ." The bones revealed the child was between nine and thirteen years old.

In his testimony in this case—Haglund's last trial before he left the UN's employ that spring to continue doing exhumations around the world for Physicians for Human Rights—the forensic expert was finally able to do something he had yearned to do. After all those long, hard months of exhumation, he was finally able to put a name to two of the thousands of skeletons he had unearthed.

One of the bodies had an identity card. Haglund then located the man's brother. Saved only because of a bribe slipped to the killers, he had been forced by Rutaganda's henchmen to dig the grave instead. "They made me bury my big brother and other people," the survivor, Witness T, later testified, going on to tell of how he had recognized his brother's clothing and driver's license, which the team had painstakingly exhumed. DNA testing by a lab in the United States had confirmed the identification.

By the time of his court appearance, Haglund had spent nearly five years reflecting on the strange, cumbersome thing called "international justice" that he had watched take shape since the tribunal's founding in 1993. It was a beautiful ideal, despite all its flaws: a justice greater than national boundaries, a justice that sprang from a fundamental belief in human rights, a justice that attempted to replace collective guilt with individual accountability.

Increasingly, however, Haglund had begun to wonder if the justice that the Rwanda and Yugoslav tribunals delivered was what victims wanted, particularly when it came to bodies. While people cared about verdicts, Haglund had come to believe that they cared as much, if not more, about identifying the dead. While he agreed with the tribunal that mass graves should be exhumed to allow international war crimes tribunals to create a historic record of the massacres, he felt more effort should be made to identify the bodies, as difficult a task as it would be. If the tribunal wasn't going to do it, someone else should.

In the final moments of his testimony, the forensic expert drove that point home to the judges. "We hope to collect information to identify individuals so that these individuals can be returned to respective families to resolve the sort of limbo grief that family members find themselves in when people are taken away from them in a violent manner like this, and the other reason to do this, my personal reason, is that I believe that it's important to give voice to the victims, to give what their bones and their remains have to tell. Otherwise, they would have died in vain because the world could not see the conditions under which they died."

Justice: For Bill Haglund, it did not lie in the development of international law, or in the maturation of each tribunal, or even in the postwar politics of Bosnia and Rwanda. He cared about those things. But ultimately justice lay in identification of bodies and, through that, in diminishing people's pain. Only then could one ensure that husbands and wives, sisters and brothers, children and the elderly weren't haunted for a lifetime, wondering what had happened to the person whose head once lay on the pillow next to theirs—or whose chair at the dinner table was now empty.

UNFORTUNATELY, EVEN THE tribunal's biggest success—the guilty plea of Rwanda's former prime minister, Jean Kambanda, the first official to admit to genocide before an international tribunal in May 1998, was undermined by the year's end. Kambanda had admitted he had conspired with other government ministers to direct Tutsi massacres, armed Rwandans, and incited the population to kill—events that hardly sounded like the "civil war" revisionists often insisted had occurred in Rwanda in 1994. It was an extraordinary coup for tribunal prosecutors, particularly as Kambanda agreed to testify against his former colleagues. (In exchange for his cooperation, prosecutors promised UN protection for his family.) "I am pleased someone had the courage to admit there was a genocide in Rwanda," Deputy Prosecutor Bernard Muna told the BBC, after Kambanda's plea. Rwandan deputy justice minister Gerald Gahima grudgingly acknowledged to a *Washington Post* reporter that the tribunal should be "commended for this," but he added "they [the court] still have a long way to go."

Should future historians of Rwanda have any doubt about the destruction Kambanda had wrought, in the fall of 1998 the tribunal's judges sentenced him to life imprisonment. (His defense attorney argued he deserved two years in jail, as he had given hours of testimony incriminating other leaders of the genocide.) Judge Laity Kama, calling genocide "the crime of crimes," noted that Kambanda had yet to express remorse for crimes he could have halted. "The crimes are unacceptable because, as Prime Minister, Jean Kambanda had the duty and the authority to protect the population," said Judge Kama, delivering the sentence.

But Kambanda—dashing hopes that his would be the first case to be easily completed by the tribunal—appealed his guilty plea and his sentence and then dismissed his attorney, complaining he had not been given the lawyer of his choice and that he had not been represented fairly. In long letters to the tribunal, he spoke of being betrayed by the tribunal and its justice. "It's symbolic even if he doesn't succeed" with his appeal, noted Thierry Cruvellier, a reporter who had covered the tribunal for many years for the news service Ubutabera. "It lessens his confession."

DESPITE ANONCIATA'S HOPES, none of the testimony in the cases being tried by the International Criminal Tribunal for Rwanda had revealed anything about the fate of Joseph Kavaruganda at the end of 1998. Not even the testimony of Canadian general Romeo Dallaire, the former head of UN troops in Rwanda—subpoenaed to testify as a defense witness in the case of Jean-Paul Akayesu—touched on the issue. Restricted by the UN to discussing only his own experiences of the genocide, not UN matters, Dallaire openly wept on the stand as he spoke of not having enough troops to halt the killing. "I am adamant that entire regions of Rwanda could have been saved from the killings," the downcast general testified. "If we had had a force that could have convinced them it was riskier to go to the barricades than stay at home, we could have stopped it."

Yet news about Joseph *did* arrive. It was not the UN who called Anonciata, nor the Rwanda Tribunal. It was her friend Louise Mushikwabo, the sister of Landoal Ndasingwa, a member of the Rwandan transitional government who was assassinated on the same day as Joseph. Louise's news made Anonciata's blood run cold.

United Nations staff in Rwanda, Louise told her, had known more than *two months* before the genocide of plans to assassinate Joseph and Landoal. She had learned this from a former investigator for the International Criminal Tribunal, Michael Hourigan, whom she had met at a small discussion about the Rwandan genocide in Washington, D.C., where she lived. Hourigan, after hearing Louise's story, pulled her into the hallway, opened up his briefcase, and showed her a copy of a memo dated February 17, 1994, from a member of UN intelligence to the commander of UN forces in Rwanda.

"We have been informed that there's a serious threat against CHEZ LANDO Hotel. The 'Death Escadron' is planning to conduct sabotage in the building and murder against Mr. Lando and Mr. Joseph Kavaruganda, president of the constitutional court," the memo read.

Louise paused in her story. Anonciata was speechless.

She had always thought the UN peacekeepers' failure to protect her husband, herself, and her children was a despicable act of cowardice. The memo, however, transformed cowardice into culpability. To Anonciata it meant that the UN peacekeepers, aware that they had been assigned to guard her husband because he was in danger, had *knowingly* sent Joseph to his death when they laid down their weapons and allowed the Presidential Guard to march him off. In her mind, these acts made the United Nations, and its peacekeepers, complicit in Joseph Kavaruganda's death.

That was when Anonciata Kavaruganda suspected she knew why she had never gotten answers from anyone at the United Nations, and why it was unlikely any trial before the UN war crimes tribunal in Rwanda would examine the circumstances of Joseph's death. If Anonciata wanted justice, she was going to have to look elsewhere for it.

15

JUSTICE ON THE GROUND

Ima boga ma da je k'o mrav.
There is a God, even [if he is] the size of an ant.

—Bosnian Proverb

In July 1999, the arid, unrelenting heat of Bosnia's south enveloped the town of Čelebići. Each rise in degree was signaled by the growing buzz of the cicadas. The air was languid at this bend of the Neretva River, where young couples lay on a muddy beach tossed up by the swift-running river just outside the town. Bosnia's war seemed eons ago.

Mention the guilty verdicts in the Čelebići war crimes trial, however, and the town awoke angrily from its lethargy. "There were no killings in this area," snapped Ibro Makam, deputy head of the municipal office, holding court at the local bar. "Most of the people here have no idea about this supposed camp. . . . It's all lies. The Serbs are responsible for what happened." Makam rocked on his heels, a Bosnian version of a country sheriff with a cigarette dangling from the corner of his mouth. The Serbs' lies, he said, had cost the town humanitarian aid, jobs, and a promising future. "Now *that* is genocide," he added irately.

It had been just a year since I was last in Bosnia—and four since the fighting had ended—and yet some corners of the country looked as if war had never occurred. Along the main streets of many cities, such as Sarajevo, gleaming new gas stations and shiny office buildings rose up, as well as billboards advertising everything from Seimens electronics to Slovenian shampoo. Out in the countryside, new red roofs shone amid the cornfields.

But drive off the main routes and the rebuilding ceased. Despite the promise of just the year before, Bosnia proved something of a Potemkin village, a country where change remained superficial and where the transition toward peace, justice, and democracy looked better than it was. Rebuilding was massive but still largely cosmetic, and the same could be said for people's attitudes, despite efforts to do away with the ethnic propaganda that perpetuated them. NATO soldiers, for example, had seized radio and television transmitters held by hard-line nationalist Bosnian Serbs in 1998, opening the way to long-overdue media reform. No longer did official Bosnian Serb telecasts refer to events in the Muslim-Croat half of Bosnia as "foreign news," and even-handed broadcasts, not propaganda, had been appearing on the nightly programs.

Regardless, Bosnia had yet to break free of wartime hatreds, corruption, and infighting. Denial about war crimes, as reaction to the Čelebići case proved, was not unique to the Bosnian Serbs, targets of the most pernicious propaganda. The Bosnian Muslims and Croats were also still mired in their wartime enmities. Reconstruction—and the tribunal's justice—had done little to heal old wounds.

While Bosnians freely crossed former battlefield lines without fear, they continued to define each other as Serb, Muslim, or Croat and as enemies. Despite the election of a few moderates, the same nationalists who led the country into war still ruled it. In the country's parliament, ethnic leaders had traded in battlefield arms for the weapons of bureaucratic infighting. Had it not been for the international community's power to dictate solutions, few laws would have been passed. "Bosnia," reflected Jacques Klein, head of the United Nations mission in Sarajevo, "is a patient on life support."

Even in Konjic—which the UN had deemed an "open city," an area ethnically tolerant enough to receive extra funds—wartime animosities ran deep. Gordana Grubač discovered as much when she returned to the family's apartment that year. She knocked on the door, hoping to retrieve some of Petko's books. A UN police officer was there to protect her, but Gordana was optimistic that the passage of time—as well as the outcome of the Čelebići trial—meant she would be sympathetically greeted. She was wrong.

"You Chetnik," spat the occupant. "What are you doing here?"

Fear was one reason that the citizens of Čelebići and Konjic were determined to deny that the Čelebići camp had ever existed. The father of Hazim Delić, the brutal camp guard convicted in the Čelebići case, was the powerful head of the local Bosnian Muslim nationalist party, which still had a stranglehold over apartments and jobs. As a result, few dared applaud the convictions. "Don't use my name," said one young man, who knew Delić well. "He was a monster and deserved a longer sentence. These men—nobody is defending them. People don't think they are innocent. But they don't dare say so."

But ignorance was another reason for denial. Just as little was known about the Tadić verdict in Kozarac, so in Konjic and Čelebići few were aware of the complexities of the Čelebići verdict. The trial had not even been broadcast on television or the radio, and its decision, while translated, was not yet available in Bosnia. People knew that one defendant had been acquitted and three others found guilty. But they knew nothing of the powerful evidence at trial, which proved that some Bosnian Serbs had been victims of war crimes too. While Čelebići remained the exception and not the rule in the spectrum of Bosnia's wartime atrocities, the fact remained that civilians had been brutally tortured and died there. For Bosnia's Muslims, so clearly the war's victims, it was hard to accept that their own army had been engaged in war crimes. Indeed, it was a fact many of their nationalist leaders completely denied. Yet it was a truth that had to be confronted, if in the future Bosnia was to avoid having one ethnic group that defined itself just by its victimhood—as its Serbs had done so successfully in the past.

Gordana had been shocked at her reception; dismayed to discover how little people in Bosnia knew about the case. But a UN expert group assigned to study the Rwandan and Yugoslav tribunals would not have been surprised. "It is likely that, except for a very small proportion of the populations of the former Yugoslavia and elsewhere, there is large-scale, if not total, lacking of knowledge" regarding the war crimes tribunals, warned the November 1999 report.

And at least one other person at the Yugoslav Tribunal was already aware that questions of public outreach had to become paramount if the court was to be effective: Judge Gabrielle Kirk McDonald.

Back in the fall of 1998, when Judge McDonald had first found out that no one in Kozarac believed the Tadić verdict, she had despaired for the tribunal's future, even though by then it was a powerful, fully functioning institution. The tribunal had twenty-six defendants behind bars and charges pending against thirty more; there was actually more work than its investigators, judges, courtrooms, and administrative staff could handle. None of the ten ongoing investigations, with only fifty-two investigators between them, was fully staffed. McDonald often worked at her desk into the early-morning hours trying to catch up on the stack of appeals. While her staff was dismayed by some of her habits—McDonald had, for example, collected nearly every stuffed animal "Beanie Baby" there was—they marveled at her stamina and persistence. After much arm-twisting, the judge had just managed to convince the UN to supply three additional judges to the tribunal.

Yet what if the tribunal was having little impact in Bosnia?

As McDonald looked at her appointments that afternoon she felt even more downcast. One of her duties was to try to convince the Bosnian Serbs to cooperate with the Yugoslav Tribunal by turning over their indicted war criminals—something they and Serbia had staunchly refused to do. (Never before had McDonald worked at a court whose arrest warrants were routinely ignored.) With no police force of its own, all the tribunal could do was to report noncompliance to the United Nations Security Council, something it had done some half dozen times with no result.

That day McDonald was to meet with Branka Milošević—no relation to Slobodan—the Bosnian Serb liaison to The Hague. Normally McDonald was upbeat about the task of convincing the Bosnian Serbs to cooperate, but now she was as discouraged about the tribunal—and the role of international justice in rebuilding a society—as she had ever been. As the meeting got under way, McDonald, in her disarming, friendly manner, laid out her arguments why the Bosnian Serbs should cooperate: The tribunal was intended to bring justice to all the peoples of the former Yugoslavia, regardless of ethnicity; justice was important to ending cycles of revenge; the Dayton peace plan required . . .

And then, midsentence, McDonald—poised and seemingly self-confident—simply lost heart.

"You know, I am wondering if this is all worth it," she said suddenly. "I'm wondering if what we are doing at the tribunal is worthwhile."

It was one of those moments when common experience transcends differences, when two strangers communicate more powerfully than two old friends. Milošević, a former prosecutor herself, knew what it was like to battle on behalf of justice. As distress washed across McDonald's face, the Bosnian Serb lawyer empathized. Instead of disagreeing and arguing that the tribunal had been illegitimately created by the UN—a view held by many Serbs—Milošević told McDonald stories of how she had tried keep the rule of law alive even during Bosnia's bitter three-and-a-half-year war.

"Even in these difficult times," the short, stocky lawyer concluded, "I have never lost my commitment to justice."

McDonald was moved. If she and Milošević could reach out to each other—with little in common save their sex and their passion for the law—then perhaps there was a way for the tribunal to make a difference in the former Yugoslavia. It was a question of personal contact. The tribunal must develop a major outreach program, one that could educate Bosnians about the court, bring its cases and verdicts to them, and arrange for them to go to The Hague.

Typically that wasn't a court's job, but then the tribunal was no ordinary court. In most cultures, law develops by consensus, and a country's own courts deliver judgments. The tribunal, however, was imposing the law—international humanitarian law—on the Bosnians and doing so in a courtroom far removed from them. Somehow, the court had to become part of Bosnian society, McDonald believed. It needed to make Bosnians engage with justice, to make them feel the court was theirs.

And if news of the tribunal was not getting to Bosnia, then the tribunal was going to have to bring news of its judgments to the Bosnians themselves.

McDonald already knew that the tribunal needed better public outreach in the United States; whenever she flew home to her old stomping grounds in Texas, she got blank stares from friends when she mentioned the names of the cases she was working on. In the fall of 1998, she dispatched two staff members to Bosnia and Croatia to assess what people thought of the court. Their findings only confirmed her suspicions. Bosnians, whether they were Serb, Croat, or Muslim, had unrealistic expectations of what they thought a war crimes tribunal *should* do—and no understanding of what it *did* do. The tribunal risked transforming what little support it had in Bosnia into resentment, staffers warned in a memo, unless it moved to better educate Bosnians about the court.

McDonald resolved to make creating a public outreach program her first order of business. But before she could do so, questions about the tribunal's impact on Balkans would be raised by another set of events—as Slobodan Milošević began ruthlessly ousting tens of thousands of Kosovar Albanians from their homes in the Serbian province of Kosovo, the same spot from which he had launched his nationalist career a decade before.

NEVER HAD THE tribunal looked so impotent or its staff felt so helpless. For much of 1998 and into 1999, the Yugoslav Tribunal was forced to watch as war crime after war crime was committed in Kosovo, as television and newspapers reported that villages were burned and families chased from their homes at gunpoint. Ignored by Western diplomats, powerless to get its staff into Kosovo to investigate, the tribunal did nothing save protest the obvious expulsion of Kosovars from their province. "It was," recalled one former tribunal staffer, "the complete low point."

Not until European and American leaders decided to stop appeasing Milošević—and finally branded him a war criminal in the spring of 1999—would the Yugoslav Tribunal and its international rule of law be embraced as part of the solution for the troubled Serbian province. For the first time, the court and the Western allies had the same objective: to bring Milošević to heel. The tribunal's investigations and prosecution of Milošević, in fact, helped justify NATO's sixty-three-day bombing campaign in Serbia in 1999, at least in public opinion. (NATO had not sought prior permission of the UN Security Council, which technically made its military actions legally questionable.) The tribunal suddenly found itself in world headlines, as national governments pledged more cooperation than ever before.

Such cooperation had not always been the case. Since the 1995 Dayton peace plan, the Clinton administration and its European allies had seen Milošević as crucial to the peace in Bosnia. With NATO troops on the ground, Western leaders did not want to antagonize him, particularly in 1998 when he became the head for the former Yugoslavia (Serbia and Montenegro). Theirs was a policy of accommodation, so much so that Tribunal staffers, while never ordered not to work on indicting Milošević for war crimes in Bosnia, were well aware there was no political will for it. Judge McDonald couldn't even get the UN Security Council to take action against Serbia for its refusal to turn over indicted war criminals, which it was required to do. "There comes a time when such defiance cannot be ignored," she pleaded to the fifteen-member Security Council in a speech in 1998, when Serbia had once again taken no heed of arrest warrants.

But such defiance *was* ignored. The West's tolerance for Milošević, combined with its evident reluctance to arrest Karadžić and Mladić, had sent the message that some Balkan leaders could be above the law, even with a war crimes court in The Hague. General Mladić lived openly in Belgrade, frequently spotted at sporting events. Former Bosnian Serb leader Karadžić was less visible, leading a migratory life.

Not until late 1998 was there a growing realization that arrest efforts had to focus on Karadžić. Both Madeleine Albright and General Wesley Clark, then head of NATO forces in Brussels, agreed that there could be no real peace in Bosnia while Karadžić remained at large; he still controlled Serb nationalist politics. One downside of having focused on lesser indictees—the "low-hanging fruit," as one State Department official put it—was that their arrests appeared to make it all the more difficult to get to Karadžić. Alert to the prospect of arrest, the former Bosnian Serb leader was surrounded by an armed retinue and led a life on the run financed by the Bosnian Serb nationalist party. Senior NATO military officials in Bosnia claimed it was difficult to arrest Karadžić without fear that others would be killed or even that one of Karadžić's own bodyguards might shoot him in the process. (As was the case with the arrest of Drljača in 1997, NATO military officials wanted the arrests to be near perfect and problem-free, an operational standard that was hard to meet.) The United States, hoping greed would overcome nationalist loyalty, slapped a $5 million bounty on Karadžić's head in June of 1999.

As Milošević plotted his attack on Kosovo in 1998 and 1999, he almost certainly felt he had nothing to fear from the war crimes court. He was above the law, even international law. "If they had arrested Karadžić, then Milošević would have known what his future would be," Blerim Shala, the editor of the Kosovo weekly *Zeri*, told me. "He'd know the West wasn't just making a statement on paper, and Kosovo might not have happened."

But it did happen. Balkan experts had been predicting that Kosovo would erupt ever since the province was stripped of its autonomy in 1989. Yet Kosovo Albanians had heeded the call of their pacifist leader,

Ibrahim Rugova, and the province remained calm despite a brutal crackdown by Serb police. But in 1997 a militant group, the Kosovo Liberation Army (KLA)—financed by ethnic Albanians in Europe and America—emerged. Armed skirmishes between Serbian special police forces and the KLA resulted; in March 1998, a bloody Serbian police raid on a KLA leader's family compound left fifty-eight dead. Tensions mounted. Milošević swiftly began beating the drums of nationalism, rallied the Serbs around him, and over the next months began to launch another campaign of ethnic cleansing to rid Kosovo of the KLA and its Albanians. By August over 200,000 Kosovar Albanians had fled in advance of Serb troops, police, and paramilitary squads: their homes torched, their cattle killed, their families slain.

Once again the sixteen-member NATO Alliance was slow to react. Not until reports that fall of full-scale civilian massacres in several Kosovo villages did Western leaders threaten Milošević with NATO air strikes and dispatch former Balkan diplomat Richard Holbrooke to bring Milošević to heel. Reluctantly, the Yugoslav leader agreed to withdraw Serb troops from Kosovo and let civilian international monitors take their place. He vowed Serbia would try those responsible for atrocities in Kosovo. So glaring was his—and Holbrooke's—failure to mention the tribunal in their pronouncements that Western diplomats immediately speculated that Milošević had been granted immunity in exchange for peace. Judge McDonald shot off a letter in protest to the UN Security Council to remind them that the "obligation to cooperate and comply [with the tribunal] . . . is not subject to alteration, negotiation or abrogation."

But the shaky peace crumbled and further negotiations failed. In March of 1999, Milošević massed 40,000 army and special troops and 300 tanks around Kosovo and attacked. Hundreds of thousands of refugees fled across the border into Albania, Macedonia, and Montenegro, at times reaching the rate of 4,000 per hour. Serb forces shot, decapitated, stabbed, and executed scores of Kosovo Albanians in small villages, determined to stamp out KLA opposition. As spreading violence and hordes of refugees threatened to destabilize the region, the NATO Alliance reacted. After ruling out sending in ground troops, NATO bombed Belgrade on March 24.

Western leaders began changing their rhetoric toward Milošević. British prime minister Tony Blair was the first, warning the Serbian leader that he could face war crimes charges if further atrocities were committed in Kosovo. President Clinton then drew comparisons between Milošević's ethnic cleansing and the Holocaust. German foreign minister Joschka Fischer likened Milošević to Hitler and Stalin.

Suddenly the tribunal found Western allies, once loath to turn over intelligence, agreeing to help put a case together against Milošević. German defense minister Rudolf Sharping gave chief prosecutor Louise Arbour aerial reconnaissance photographs. British foreign secretary Robin Cook promised Arbour "one of the largest releases of intelligence material ever authorized by a British government." It was, as former chief prosecutor Richard Goldstone described that year with some envy, "a very big sea-change."

An indictment of Milošević had to follow. There was no longer any excuse. Legal experts and human rights groups had been calling for the tribunal to indict him since 1994. And Kosovo was the perfect opportunity. An indictment for war crimes in a province that was under Milošević's control in many ways would be easier to prove than one for atrocities in Bosnia, a country in which the Serb nationalist meddled but never actually ruled. (The tribunal's statute did not include the crime of "waging war," which could have been used to prosecute Milošević for starting the war in Bosnia.)

The indictment, however, was months in coming. The same cautious, legalistic streak that endeared Arbour to some prosecutors now infuriated those anxious for her to act in the face of war crimes in Kosovo. Human rights groups clamored for the tribunal to intervene swiftly and act as a deterrent. But Arbour, uncertain about the court's capacity to prevent bloodshed, wanted to assemble her facts carefully, particularly given how little was known about the KLA. She and her legal advisors debated for several months over whether the conflict qualified as an "international armed conflict" and the tribunal should investigate. (Expressing "a measure of prudence publicly," she later said, was also one strategy to ensure the tribunal got the information it then needed.)

Even once she decided the tribunal should investigate Kosovo's war crimes, Arbour moved cautiously. For example, while Serb authorities routinely denied visas to tribunal staff for the province, Arbour hesitated to make an issue of it. Those inside and outside the tribunal were deeply frustrated when Arbour—invited to Belgrade but refused a visa to Kosovo—cancelled the trip altogether. The consensus was she should have gone at least to the Serbian capital and made the public point that authorities were standing in the way of the tribunal's work. "She could have been a front page story," recalled one high-ranking tribunal official. Arbour was finally persuaded to make headlines several months later, after the massacre of forty-five ethnic Albanian men, women, and children in the village of Racak. Cameras then captured the diminutive fifty-two-year-old prosecutor, her passport in hand, as she was dwarfed by guards at the Macedonian-Kosovo border denying her entry.

But a certain measure of caution was needed given how difficult it was going to be to tie the Yugoslav leader directly to the commission of particular war crimes. Milošević rarely used the telephone and issued no written directives. Even in conversation, he preferred to drop hints, leaving it to his aides to draw their own conclusions. "He's covered his tracks," a senior Western defense official who frequently dealt with Milošević told me. "If ever the finger was pointed at him, Milošević would be able to say, I never told them to do this."

And tribunal prosecutors, as always was the case, were finding themselves begging for the intelligence they needed—satellite imagery, intercepts—to help them make a "command responsibility" case against Milošević, one in which he would be charged for crimes committed by those answering to him. Prosecutors would seek to prove that Milošević, as leader of the Federal Republic of Yugoslavia (Serbia and Montenegro), had legal (de jure) responsibility over Serbian troops and police in Kosovo as well as actual (de facto) authority. Command responsibility includes not only when a leader orders a subordinate to commit a war crime, but also that leader's failure to halt crimes committed by those in his power. To that effect, Arbour and McDonald repeatedly warned Milošević that war crimes were occurring in Kosovo on his watch.

In the winter of 1998, as Milošević carried on with his campaign of ethnic cleansing and no indictment was announced, even the court's staunchest advocates grumbled. Finally, on March 31, 1999, Arbour—trying to show that the tribunal could make some kind of legal response to ongoing war crimes—announced the indictment of Željko Ražnatović, or "Arkan," the notorious paramilitary leader who had carried out a campaign of violence in eastern Bosnia and was reported to be operating in Kosovo. His indictment remained sealed, but Judge McDonald used it as an opportunity to urge Milošević to "exercise his authority over his subordinates to prevent the commission of further crimes." Arkan, round-cheeked and baby faced, protested his innocence on CNN, the BBC, and *Good Morning America.*

But on May 27 history finally came full circle. Fearing that Milošević, by then in discussion with Western representatives, would be offered amnesty, the tribunal announced his indictment. Slobodan Milošević became the first incumbent head of state ever to be charged by an international war crimes tribunal. The man branded as a war criminal back in 1992 was accused of crimes against humanity and violations of the laws and customs of war, along with four of his top aides. The indictment linked the deaths of 340 Kosovar Albanians from sixteen villages all the way up the chain of command to Milošević himself. News of the charges against the Serb strongman was broadcast around the world, carried live on TV, radio, and the Internet. Arbour declared the indictment was a sign that impunity for war criminals, no matter how powerful, was no more.

"Now the world is a smaller place for them," she said.

Praise and criticism were heaped on the tribunal. The allies divided: President Clinton and Prime Minister Tony Blair applauded the indictment; French interior minister Jean-Pierre Chevenement called it a mistake. Some critics charged that the tribunal had abandoned its judicial independence, becoming a pawn in the NATO bombing campaign. (Arbour consulted with NATO leaders before issuing the indictment.) In Serbia, state-controlled media ignored news of the indictment, finally releasing a government statement that claimed "Louise Arbour is only a puppet in the hands of the warlords."

The indictment did not deter Milošević from finally pursuing peace. By June 10 NATO bombing was suspended; ten days later Serb forces withdrew from Kosovo. In a sign that the international community finally understood the tribunal's importance, when tens of thousands of international peacekeepers arrived in the Serbian province, war crimes investigators were by their side for the first time. In Bosnia, forensic teams had to wait more than six months to get access to Srebrenica's execution sites; in Kosovo, they were on the ground in a matter of weeks. More than 200 investigators, including detectives from the FBI, Scotland

Yard and forensic experts from around the world, identified at least sixty-nine mass grave sites. More than three thousand ethnic Albanians, many of them civilians, were estimated to have been slain during the ethnic cleansing campaign. NATO leaders also agreed to take a more vigorous approach to arresting war criminals than had been the case in Bosnia. But Milošević was off limits: "I do not believe that the NATO allies can invade Belgrade to try to deliver the indictment," said President Clinton.

It was a heady time for the Yugoslav Tribunal, rocketed into prominence with the announcement of Milošević's indictment carried live on CNN. Finally it seemed that NATO's political leaders had recognized the tribunal's importance and accepted that international justice was a partner in peace, not an obstacle to it.

Arbour, two weeks after announcing Milošević's indictment, stated she was leaving to join Canada's Supreme Court. Her successor, Carla Del Ponte, a Swiss prosecutor known for her tough prosecutions of the Russian Mafia, alienated Western allies by announcing that the tribunal was investigating allegations that NATO had committed war crimes during its bombing campaign. Whatever the reason, as Kosovo faded from the headlines, tribunal prosecutors found they were not receiving nearly the intelligence they had been promised. "NATO was trying to justify the war and used us as a pawn," said a senior prosecutor. "The reality was, we got intelligence from them, but not in the form or in the volume that the world has been told." Inside the halls of the office building in The Hague, the belief that world leaders had embraced their cause slowly faded.

And there still was no support in the UN Security Council for measures to ensure that war criminals were handed over to the tribunal. Judge McDonald, who had decided after six years to leave the tribunal, emphasized this point in a critical farewell address to the Council on November 8, 1999. As the *Washington Post* headline read the next day: "Judge Blasts UN War Crimes Effort."

"It is time, I submit, for this complacency to cease," McDonald told the Security Council. "Radovan Karadžić and Ratko Mladić were indicted in 1995 and Slobodan Milošević was indicted earlier this year. Yet these individuals remain at large. Their liberty makes a mockery of the pledge to would-be tyrants that they will be indicted, arrested and made to answer for their alleged criminal acts and violations of human rights. . . .

"Make no mistake about it: if the international community does not ensure that the orders of the court are enforced, it is bound to go the way of the League of Nations."

And with that, Judge McDonald left the tribunal, wiser than she had ever dreamed about the limits of international justice in a modern world. But the stories told by those who testified before her remain with her still.

IN BOSNIA, HOWEVER, for Hamdo Kahrimanović and his wife, Firdesa, there seemed no limit to what the Yugoslav Tribunal could do. In the summer of 1999—after another round of local warlords had been indicted and arrested—the couple decided it was safe to move back to their newly restored home in Kozarac. Indeed, upon arriving in the town, I stumbled on Hamdo at the last place I'd ever expected: standing outside the Tadić family café, the Sensei, chatting with Mladen Tadić, the brother of the man Hamdo's testimony helped convict.

The encounter was surreal, made all the more so because just a little over a year earlier Hamdo had needed a NATO escort just to set foot in Kozarac. Since then, however, nearly all those responsible for the Omarska camp—save for the former commander, Željko Mejakić—had been arrested or had died. Some 240 Bosnian Muslim families had returned to the town. For the first time in six years, Bosnian Muslims again outnumbered the Bosnian Serbs.

At first glance, Kozarac seemed on the verge of a renaissance. At the Kahrimanovićs' home, there were boxes of red geraniums in the windows, a garden full of ripening vegetables, and a doghouse. "That's Lassie," said Hamdo pointing to a lop-eared dog. "You know, instead of 'Lassie, go home' like it was in the TV show, this is 'Lassie, you've come home.' " He roared with laughter at his joke. Despite the family's fears about the local Bosnian Serbs, some had proved welcoming, arriving with gifts of food. Mladen had even helped Hamdo jerry-rig an illegal electricity supply. Local Bosnian Serb authorities were a little less helpful: There was still no running water, no hospital, no school, and no mosque. And there were the odd threats: One Serb recently walked up to Hamdo and said: "I'm sorry we didn't kill you back then."

"You know who's not thrilled about Muslims returning," explained Mladen, when I later told him this anecdote, "those who robbed their homes and made money during the war. But we all lost to those people. It's the same Mafia now that is trying to poison things."

As they tried to poison his brother Dušan's case. Mladen had long believed that local Serb nationalists like Prijedor police chief Simo Drljača had sabotaged his brother's trial. Now judges at the Yugoslav Tribunal were holding hearings into Tadić's claim that his lawyer, a Serb, had come under pressure from Drljača not to defend him adequately.

Mladen, by then a lot angrier at local Serbs than at the Bosnian Muslims, viewed the changes in Kozarac pragmatically. More people meant better business, and Mladen had his dreams, which included reviving the family name through civic-mindedness. "I'm planning to open a bakery, and I want to hire these Muslims who have no jobs," he told me.

Yet the longer I stayed in Kozarac, the more I realized that the seeming harmony between Mladen and Hamdo, between the town's Serbs and its Muslims, was as deceptive as it was inspirational. Like Bosnia itself, Kozarac had been repaired only on the surface; in the hearts and minds of its citizens, the scars of the war had not yet healed. All it took was sitting in someone's home and chatting over coffee to realize that while justice had been delivered in Kozarac, reconciliation had hardly begun. "People have realized the war is over, and they can return home and not get killed—but the real question is, do they really want to live with each other?" said Milburn Line of the Office of the High Representative, the agency in charge of Bosnia's civilian reconstruction, near Prijedor. "Are they sincere?"

Kozarac had yet not made up its mind. It remained two villages, still divided neatly by the Tadić trial and its verdict. The town's Serbs, as they had the year before, still believed the Bosnian Muslims were to blame for the war and that Tadić was innocent. The others maintained it was all the Bosnian Serbs' fault.

There was something comfortable about these dueling versions of history, which the people of Kozarac slipped into as easily as into an old, familiar bathrobe. The explanation for this came one day when my translator, Alex, and I started asking about a war monument just outside the town. The commemorative plaque noted that Partisans had been massacred on a nearby field, yet the names on the gravestones were all Bosnian Serb in origin. When I asked why Bosnian Muslims and Croats had not been killed at that site, Mladen and Hamdo each offered competing versions of what had happened fifty years before.

"Over 800 Serbs were slaughtered there back in 1941," explained Mladen. "I know because my father was a Partisan, a commissioner with the Kozara Battalion. Most of the Muslims, they fought with the Nazis, not the Partisans. But after the war, it was all hush-hush. No one was ever punished for those crimes. Those who killed, they just kept on living here."

"It's not true that Bosnian Muslims from Kozarac committed those crimes," Hamdo told me after I had recounted Mladen's version. "It was people from outside of Kozarac." He laughed bitterly. "And the Serbs thought they were getting the Muslims back in this war, but they were wrong."

Competing versions of war, massacres, mass graves, and concentration camps were Tito's legacy to Bosnia. The Yugoslav leaders' greatest miscalculation was assuming that by creating a sanitized history of World War II he could make Yugoslavia's ethnic groups put their grievances behind them. Atrocities cannot be so easily dismissed. Rather than putting to rest—or confronting—the horrors of the past, Yugoslavs had nurtured and mythologized them—so much so that when the deadly calls of nationalism were sounded in the early 1990s, people responded.

"Who bothered to destroy the health clinic, the school?" Hamdo asked sadly. "Most of this was done by my students, the students I was teaching about World War II, Tito's version of it. And that can mean only one thing: I was teaching all those generations about history the wrong way."

A better way was to confront the past rather than to rewrite it; to develop not different, ethnic-based versions of history but one common understanding of what had occurred. This was at the heart of the Yugoslav Tribunal's mandate, to render not only justice but also to contribute to the "maintenance of international peace and security" in Bosnia. The court had succeeded in delivering justice to Hamdo and Firdesa Kahrimanović, in that they had moved back home. But it had failed to push Kozarac down the road toward reconciliation. As Judge McDonald and her staff had realized, simply issuing a judgment did not mean that people—or their children—could accept it. That would require at least more education about the tribunal and the Tadić case, as a start.

The question was whether it was already too late. Before leaving Kozarac that summer of 1999, Alex and I drove up the mountain above the town to a different war memorial, this one a famous, 100-foot concrete tower inscribed with the names of more than 9,000 slain Partisans. It epitomized Tito's myth of brotherhood and unity.

Now it perpetuates a new myth, from this most recent war. Someone had made a rough-hewn wooden cross, inscribed it, and stuck it into the ground. The cross does not honor the Bosnian Muslims who died in Kozarac by the thousands. It memorializes only the far smaller number of Bosnian Serb dead.

JUSTICE: HASAN NUHANOVIĆ had accepted long ago that his was a lonely path, that he was a Generation-X Odysseus in aviator glasses and tennis shoes, hunting for his family rather than his home. The tribunal was not going to help him find Ibro, Muhamed, and Nasiha. Still, a major breakthrough had occurred in the Srebrenica case that gave Hasan cause for hope. On December 2, 1998, American troops in northeast Bosnia had swooped down and arrested the head of the Drina Corps, Lieutenant Colonel General Radislav Krstić, who had been secretly indicted in October with genocide, crimes against humanity, and violations of the laws and customs of war. Announcing the arrest, State Department spokesman James Rubin said: "All persons indicted for war crimes, including Radovan Karadžić and General Ratko Mladić, belong in The Hague." Five years after its creation, the Yugoslav Tribunal had finally netted a big fish.

Six months later, in July 1999, I found Hasan demonstrating in front of UN headquarters in Sarajevo to mark the fourth anniversary of the massacres at Srebrenica. About 300 people had gathered, waving signs reading "Remember Srebrenica!" or "No Cover-Up of Bosnia War Crimes!" Few in Sarajevo paid the demonstrators much attention. Still, Hasan—dressed in his trademark army green—was optimistic about his cause.

General Krstić's arrest meant he and others now had a trial to look forward to, one that would reveal the details of how the Bosnian Serbs carried out the massacres. After all, it was Bosnian Serb leader Radovan Karadžić who had promoted General Krstić afterward, telling the Belgrade-based daily newspaper *Telegraf*: "I was very satisfied with the speed at which he took Srebrenica."

But the general's arrest also had special meaning for Hasan. Krstić had been at the Hotel Fontana meeting between General Mladić and Ibro Nuhanović on July 12, 1995; Hasan hoped through him to find out more about his father. "He can't just say 'I know nothing,' " Hasan said sarcastically when we got together later to talk about Krstić's arrest.

Hasan hoped that Krstić could confirm the news he had heard about Ibro just a few months before: that his father had been killed in a mass execution.

Hasan's first reaction to the news was one of relief. After so many years, he finally had an answer—and one that made sense—even if there were no direct eyewitnesses to confirm it. Hasan lined up the facts: His father had last been seen in Zvornik. Pilica was due north of that city, just off the main road. His father had been among the last of the Bosnian Muslims ordered off the UN base at Potočari; Pilica was the last known execution to have occurred after Srebrenica was captured. Hence that was probably where Ibro was killed.

Pilica was also where Marko Boškić had allegedly gunned down thousands of men. "Hasan," I said, "I may have met the man who killed your father.

"How?" His hazel eyes flickered with surprise.

"Back in 1996 I tracked down and interviewed a member of a Srebrenica execution squad named Marko Boškić. He was one of the people identified by his fellow member of the execution squad, Dražen Erdemović—you remember, the guy who turned himself into The Hague and confessed."

"And?"

"He didn't admit to anything," I said. "But it's all there, in the tribunal transcripts. Boškić, along with Erdemović, was one of the squad at Pilica.

"And do you remember Bill Haglund? He exhumed Pilica. So maybe there is a chance of finding your father's body." Pilica was the grave so awash with rain in the autumn of 1996 that Haglund called it "the grave from hell."

A few days after this revelation, Hasan, along with hundreds of other survivors, returned to the UN base at Potočari for a commemorative service on July 13, 1999—four years to the day since the Nuhanović family disappeared.

En route the river Jadar, stirred up by recent rain, ran a deep red, but it was the only ominous note in a landscape otherwise replete with beauty. If you didn't know better, you'd find the scenery idyllic under the blue July sky. Rows of corn rippled across the fields. Purple thistles, blue cornflowers, and yellow dandelions lined the roadside. Amid haystacks, a man stood with a scythe thrown over his shoulder.

As the buses ground their gears and wheezed down the road from Kladanj toward Potočari, they went down a particularly agonizing memory lane, past landmarks whose names are now synonymous with death. You needed to be able to decode the scene to understand its sense of malice to the passengers. You needed to know the village names so well that you recognized which intersection was a mass grave, which a place of refuge. You needed to know that the graffiti on the houses were screaming the name Arkan—the indicted Bosnian Serb paramilitary leader whose men killed and looted as they drove Bosnian Muslims from their homes.

You needed to know that the poppies that sprouted from a particular spot by the side of the road were growing out of the earth piled on top of clothing stripped from the Srebrenica men. And you needed to know that the children along the road, seeing the kerchiefed women on the bus and guessing them to be Bosnian Muslim, were not waving but giving a defiant, three-fingered Serb salute.

By the time the buses reached Potočari, most of the women were weeping. All signs that it was once a UN compound were long gone; the blue-and-white "Dutchbat" signs had vanished; the sandbagged UN observation tower had been dismantled.

"It feels odd, peculiar," said Emir Suljagić, another former UN translator for the Dutch battalion. "It feels normal, like nothing ever happened here, and that is not normal."

Hasan disagreed. "My family is missing and most probably dead. Now, after four years, we bring people here and ensure that this is not forgotten. It took a long time, but something happened."

"I would like to be a Serb for a short while just to see how it feels," said Emir. "I would like to know how someone can live with this—how anyone can live with this."

"I say the Serbs like the fact that thousands of men and boys disappeared," Hasan shot back. "And if they could do it again, they would. I think they are happy. But that's nothing compared with what the UN did. The Serbs were just the sharks. The UN had a lifeboat, and they threw out all the passengers who didn't have tickets to the sharks swimming in the sea."

Suddenly the women wailed with grief. From bouquets provided for the ceremony, each picked a rose—white, yellow, red, or pink—and carried it into the heart of the former UN compound. Four years ago they, along with husbands, brothers, and fathers, came here expecting that the UN and its Dutch soldiers in Srebrenica would save them. Now they wailed and beat their chests with cries of pain at their betrayal by the Dutch, the Serbs, the Western world.

At the factory next door, a gang of local Serbs watching the mourners giggled. They pointed to the women and yelled at some of them. Denial still ran deep in this corner of Srpska. "Oh, those Muslims," said a youth lounging against a wall. "The whole thing is exaggerated. Maybe we killed some, but they mostly killed each other."

Hasan ignored them. He was concentrating on reliving the events of July 13. Like an old soldier giving a tour of a battlefield, he pointed out landmarks. "There, I was hiding my brother," he said. "See that bush? I was standing there. On July 12 I tried to get my brother on the bus—I hid him in the bush there—but it was impossible. . . ."

"And Mladić was standing over there." He waved in another direction. "See the fence? There wasn't any brush on it then. On the other side were the Serb soldiers with dogs. On that side were buses and trucks and Serb soldiers. We were surrounded from all sides.

"And here." He motioned with both hands, creating a pathway. "There were two tapes that led to the gate. People had to walk between them, these yellow tapes. Then they were separated at the gate. Five thousand people between noon and 6:00 P.M. on July 13."

Hasan paused and pointed to a place somewhere between the factory building and the parking lot. "That is where Franken stopped me and my father," he said. Behind Hasan stood a chain fence that bore a sign reading: ON JULY 13, UNPROFOR TROOPS HANDED OVER 3,000 MEN AND BOYS TO THE HANDS OF THE EXECUTIONERS.

Then the women left the interior of the compound and walked back to where we were standing, and I lost Hasan in the crush. I scanned the group, looked at one grieving face after another. When I finally spotted Hasan, he was standing off to one side, holding a red rose. He clasped it awkwardly, as if it were a lit candle, and it trembled in his hand. As the Muslim priest gathered the women together for a final round of prayers, Hasan walked off. He was retracing his family's final moments step by step.

He strode down the path he could see in his mind, the corridor delineated with yellow tape. As did his family four years before, he went slowly up to the stone post at the compound's exit. And then Hasan gently placed his rose on top of the gatepost.

It was where his father, mother, and younger brother, ordered off the UN base, walked into the hands of the waiting Bosnian Serbs. It was where his old life ended and another began. Hasan Nuhanović has finished this chapter of his search for justice: He knows that Ibro and Nasiha are dead.

But the men who killed them still roamed the land. The Dutch UN soldiers had not been punished. He will not believe Muhamed is dead until there is proof of it. It will take all of Hasan's life for justice to be complete—and maybe the span of his daughter's life too.

There was no time to waste. Hasan turned on his heel and walked on.

16

RWANDAN CRIMES, ARUSHA JUSTICE

I've been facing a slow death.
Let me tell the crude truth
Families with both parents are very
Few here in Rwanda.

—Anonymous

They have picked up the bones of the dead since I was last in Rwanda: the bones that littered the steep hills of Kibuye; the ribs, femurs, and skulls that dotted the fields above the École Technique Officiele outside Kigali; the gleaming white fragments of the some 20,000 slain in a church in Kibeho.

Skeletons that could be identified were buried in individual graves, marked with rough-hewn wooden crosses. Others were placed in large, consecrated mass graves that bear witness to the scale and anonymity of Rwanda's slaughter. But most of the bones left heaped in churches, hospitals, schools, or on hills across this country were so intermingled they could not be assembled into a body. These bones have been separated by their type—skulls, tibias, femurs—and laid out on tables for all to see at Rwanda's genocide memorial sites. Arranged in precise rows that speak to this country's love of order, these thousands of bones provide a compelling arithmetic of the dead.

Leg and arm bones, lined up in rows like matchsticks, are easily counted; skulls, placed in rows with their empty eye sockets carefully turned to the front, swiftly multiplied. Twenty-five skulls across by thirty-five deep on a table: 875 genocide victims. Mathematics lets you try to calculate an otherwise incomprehensible atrocity.

One place where the bones have not been collected, however, is the Ntarama church, a massacre site about an hour's drive from Kigali. Instead, there the skeletons lie where they fell, inside the ruins of the red-brick church shadowed by acacia trees. This genocide memorial makes no attempt to render order. Here, up and down the church's nave, there is chaos and the unheard screams of those who sought sanctuary only to be macheted to death.

At first, you cannot see the skeletons so much as their effects: clothes, rotted by nearly six years of mildew, drape the church pews, a bodiless congregation of skirts, shirts, and trousers. Belongings are strewn from the altar with its rough-hewn cross all the way to the broken stained-glass window at the rear. Things lie where they were dropped: a white shoe, a battered black suitcase with clothes tumbling out, an upside-down white enamel plate, overturned straw baskets, a child's tiny white knitted sock.

Once my eyes got used to the darkness of the church I could see the skeletons more visibly. A white jawbone with teeth lay next to my foot. In front of me a skull was tipped on its side, resting on an open school notebook displaying careful penmanship. Ribs poked through the weave of a rotting sweater. The bones of a hand lay near a straw bag. The only order in all this disorder was the natural process of decomposition, which had long ago stripped the flesh from these skeletons.

"Now you can see why it is difficult to bring justice to Rwanda," said Jean-Damascene, a Tutsi survivor, who accompanied me there in the spring of 2000. Had he not been visiting a friend in another town on that fateful April day in 1994, his bones would be lying in the church, along with those of his family. "It is very difficult," he added with a huge, painful shrug of his shoulders, like Atlas trying to rid himself of his burden.

He meant many things with that statement. One was that the sheer scale of Rwanda's atrocities confounded conventional efforts to bring justice. It was one thing to pick up the bones of the dead and arrange them in rows for viewers at genocide sites. It was another to bring all the killers to trial.

The arithmetic of justice was as discouraging as the arithmetic of the dead was overwhelming. Rwanda's courts had handed down 2,500 verdicts in three years and set some 3,500 prisoners free. Even so, 125,000 suspects—some 10 percent of the Hutu population—remained incarcerated, although some 15,000 have confessed. Nearly 40,000 of them still had no files containing the charges against them; the deadline to prepare them had once again been extended to 2001. Trials remained highly politicized. Moreover, while court proceedings had become more efficient, they weren't swift enough: Government officials estimated it would take 150 years at the courts' current pace to try all those in jail. One positive sign, however, was that no more executions had taken place.

Meanwhile, the Rwanda Tribunal—even with the addition of three more judges and the use of joint trials—had just seven verdicts to its name. With forty-four of the country's leading planners of the genocide behind bars in Arusha, Tanzania—thirty-five still awaiting trial—experts estimated the court needed at least ten more years to complete its work, far beyond its mandate. Even those cases in which verdicts have been delivered had proved a disappointment to many Rwandans. Despite regular broadcasts by Radio Rwanda, the trials seemed remote and incomprehensible. Rwandans craved a justice as intimate as the genocide, a chance to see its architects judged. The country's Tutsi survivors, struggling to scratch out a living, increasingly yearned for restitutive justice, or compensation, rather than retributive justice. Those Hutu whose family perished at the hands of the Rwandan Patriotic Army when it seized the country wanted to see the tribunal judge war crimes on all sides.

Justice—or at least conventional courtroom justice—increasingly did not answer the needs of many Rwandans. "For reconciliation, we need justice," said my guide, using the tip of his shoe to turn over the bones surrounding our feet in the Ntarama church. "But justice comes so slowly. What if it comes too late?"

THAT RECONCILIATION MUST be quick but justice was slow was only one of many contradictions to be found in Rwanda at the beginning of the new millennium. Rwanda was a country that claimed it was for all Rwandans, yet was still ruled by the Tutsi-led Rwandan Patriotic Front. The government had forced more and more Hutu leaders from its ranks, including its president, Pasteur Bizimungu, who resigned in March 2000. Its preoccupation with stamping out Hutu extremists had resulted in the deaths of tens of thousands of innocent civilians in government security crackdowns. It had dispatched a National Unity and Reconciliation Commission around the countryside to bring Hutu and Tutsi together, but still used arbitrary arrest and imprisonment as a means to control and intimidate the country's Hutu majority. Rwanda was a country committed to justice but whose government bristled when human rights groups suggested more army officials must stand trial for their share in the massacres, such as the killing of Hutu in the refugee camp in Kibeho.

Perhaps it was not surprising, then, that after three years of pursuing conventional courtroom justice—whether in the form of the Rwanda Tribunal's war crimes trials or the genocide trials held by the country's judiciary—many Rwandans wondered whether courts were indeed the right institutions to deliver "justice."

Discontent with "Arusha justice," as it was dubbed, reached the boiling point in November 1999, when the tribunal's appeals court judges ruled to dismiss charges against Jean-Bosco Barayagwiza, reportedly one of the highest-ranking architects of the genocide. The judges ruled that tribunal prosecutors had violated his rights, and ordered the case dismissed "with prejudice," meaning that the court could not try him again. Barayagwiza was ordered to be returned to Cameroon, where he had been arrested. Protestors immediately surrounded the tribunal offices in Kigali demanding that the decision be overturned.

Relations had always been strained between the Rwandan government and the tribunal, but this time the government went a step further. It severed relations with the war crimes court, denied its chief prosecutor a visa, and announced its refusal to cooperate with tribunal investigators. The tribunal's "incompetence should not come at the expense of the Rwandese," foreign ministry spokesman Seth Kamanzi told reporters. "As long as the decision on Jean-Bosco Barayagwiza is not reversed, we are not open for discussion . . . what is there to discuss?"

ISSUED ON NOVEMBER 3, 1999, *The Prosecutor v. Jean-Bosco Barayagwiza* was Judge McDonald's last decision before she left The Hague. She wrote it even as she packed up her belongings and while plans were being made for her farewell party. Inside the Yugoslav Tribunal, many viewed the sixty-seven-page decision by McDonald and four other judges of the Chamber of Appeals as a courageous decision. Despite political pressure not to do so, it upheld the rights of the accused—a notorious propagandist, responsible for much of the genocide's inflammatory rhetoric—while also delivering a slap on the wrist to the Rwanda Tribunal, still plagued with management problems. "Did you see what the appeals chamber *did*?" marveled one astonished Yugoslav Tribunal staff member.

As the judges themselves wrote in their decision: "As difficult as this conclusion may be for some to accept, it is the proper role of an independent judiciary to halt this prosecution, so that no further injustice results. Nothing less than the integrity of the tribunal is at stake here."

There seemed little question of Barayagwiza's guilt regarding the genocide. In a civil case brought against him in New York City, a U.S. District Court judge had awarded $105 million in damages, saying Barayagwiza engaged in conduct "so inhuman that it is difficult to conceive of any civil remedy which can begin to compensate the plaintiffs for their loss." At the same time, there seemed little doubt that the tribunal prosecutors had violated Barayagwiza's rights in a manner "tantamount to negligence," as the appeals court put it. His ability to receive a fair trial, the judges concluded, had been repeatedly compromised.

First, Barayagwiza had lingered for months in jail after his 1994 arrest in Cameroon before he was formally charged with genocide. By the time a judge at the Rwanda Tribunal confirmed the indictment against him, that document was months overdue. It then took Barayagwiza nearly a month to get a copy of the charges against him, and a further three months passed before he appeared in court. In the interim, the tribunal failed to schedule a hearing of Barayagwiza's habeas corpus motion challenging the legality of his arrest, even though he had spent eighteen months in jail. "We find this conduct to be egregious," the appeal court judges concluded.

The decision not only prompted irate protests, it further divided the Rwandans from the tribunal over what "justice" meant. To the judges, the decision exemplified the purest justice: a reminder that the war crimes court, in essence the highest court in the world, must hold itself to the most rigorous legal standards, which included protecting the rights of the accused. Yet to Rwandans, the decision was the highest injustice. They knew only that the international court created to prosecute the genocide's leaders had ordered one set free. To many it was tantamount to saying that Barayagwiza was innocent and that the genocide had never taken place.

"American people see justice in a different way than Rwandans," cried Rwandan justice minister Jean de Dieu Mucyo one day in exasperation. "In Western law, a man can be guilty but released because of some procedures. But in Rwanda, a man who is a criminal cannot be released without being punished. In Rwanda, the meaning is in the fact—not the form, not the procedures. Now can you understand why Rwandans don't have faith any more in this tribunal?" One of the few cabinet ministers who was a survivor himself, Mucyo fingered a framed photograph that stood on his desk of his children, nearly all who remained of a vast extended family. Hutu militiamen, he added, not content with simply killing one of his brothers, had tortured him by opening his abdomen and removing his liver while he was alive.

Extending his hands to either side like the scales of justice, Mucyo balanced Barayagwiza's role in the death of hundreds of thousands of Rwandans against the court's violation of his rights. His hands tipped one way, then the other, then back again, coming down against Barayagwiza. "Does the tribunal provide justice?" Mucyo asked.

MANY RWANDANS ASKED themselves the same question. Among them were a group of women survivors, gathered one afternoon in the cool shadows of the Presbyterian church in Rwanda's capital. As sunlight, streaming through the stained-glass windows above, cast pools of color on the scars some bore from the genocide—machete slashes on their cheeks, the stump of a severed arm—they spoke of Arusha justice.

They accepted that the tribunal, which prosecuted key leaders, would always provide a symbolic and not a particular justice for women like them, who had come face to face with the genocide's foot soldiers. Still, they had never expected justice to be so confusing, so abstract, and so remote. It wasn't just that they had lost faith in the tribunal; it was that, for them, the war crimes court had lost its relevance.

None had seen news accounts of the trials, in a land where only the rich have televisions or the electricity to run them. Only a few had read about the cases in the newspaper, given literacy rates of about 50 percent. Most tried to follow the tribunal and its case via the radio, which remained the main source of news for most Rwandans, just as it had been the main source of propaganda during the genocide. Yet radio is far better suited to the distribution of political slogans than to explaining the complexities of international law. Translated into Kinyarwandan, the tribunal's intricate proceedings often dissolved into meaningless words and phrases. All it took was a blip in the frequency or a squalling baby, and the whole gist of the transmission was lost. Only about a third of the women survivors said they had heard radio reports that former Rwandan prime minister Jean Kambanda had pleaded guilty to genocide.

Even those who knew about the confession were disappointed. It wasn't enough to hear a report that he had acknowledged his guilt, they explained; the real catharsis would have come if they could have *watched* him confess to the crimes. "We prefer to see and hear those who did those crimes," volunteered one survivor, Patricie, her voice quavering slightly.

A few women clapped their crutches together in a kind of applause, sending dust motes dancing in the sunlight. Patricie continued. Having trials outside of Rwanda, she said, deprived genocide survivors of something they need in order for reconciliation: the need to *confront* those whose orders left them mutilated or robbed them of their families. That confrontation could occur if survivors are sitting in a court's public gallery or even watching a film about the genocide. What would matter was that the accused was before them—and they could see his reaction to the charges.

"We have to *feel* that justice had been done in order to forget and move on," Patricie explained. "It's not the same if I am listening to it on the radio, as seeing it with my own eyes." In a culture where reconciliation begins with a formal admission of one's wrongs, these women wanted, at the very least, to see the expression on a defendant's face as the guilty verdict was delivered—if not hear him admit remorse—to validate their suffering.

"Why won't the UN let us have that justice here?" asked Patricie, her voice angry. In her mind, there was no difference between the UN that had failed to stop the genocide and the UN that administered the courts. "This is a court for Rwandans, isn't it?"

I wasn't sure what to say.

WOULD WITNESS JJ —and the other women of Taba who confronted Akayesu in the courtroom, as these survivors wished to do—say that she had found justice? It was harder than I had imagined to get an answer to that question. In a sign of how insecure Tutsi survivors still felt—despite a 1999 cease-fire with the neighboring Democratic Republic of Congo and the government's success in beating back Hutu extremists—JJ and the other witnesses from the Akayesu case were keeping a low profile.

"It is not like it was when you were last here," said Godelieve Mukasarasi, the Taba social worker whom I first met in 1996. She explained it might take several days to find them, if I could at all. "It is not safe for them any longer," she added, her dark eyes flashing. She then told me the story of her husband's death, killed by Hutu extremists just days before the beginning of the Akayesu trial, in which he had cooperated.

Even so, it was hard to understand her caution, given the obvious signs of renewal in Taba. Mud-brick homes sprouted from the foundations of those destroyed during the genocide. The streets brimmed with life: Rwanda's mix of Tutsi survivors, Tutsi who had returned from Uganda and other countries, and Hutu, both those who stayed in the village and those who fled after the genocide's end and then came back in 1996. Women swayed up the hill with clay pots filled with potatoes or cassava root balanced on their heads. Young boys, dressed in khaki school uniforms, pulled goats along on a string. Old men, their jackets patched at the elbows, wheeled their bicycles along.

The largest crowd of all, however, was gathered outside the local prison. Each day the families arrived bearing lunch for the some 1,100 alleged *génocidaires* jailed in two small buildings. The mass of visitors, several hundred in number, was a stark reminder that even though the Tutsi-led RPF ruled Rwanda, the Hutu remained the country's majority. Tutsi genocide survivors were a minority within a minority, which made them vulnerable to attack. And those survivors who had testified in front of the tribunal were the most vulnerable of all.

Despite court-ordered pseudonyms, their identity was generally known; as a result they were the target of harassment by Hutu extremists outside Taba as well as by Hutu from the town who had taken part in the genocide. Everyone viewed the women as informants and feared that they would now implicate them in future trials. "If the neighbors see them talking to someone who isn't from the village," Godelieve explained sadly, "they will think 'She is accusing us.'

"But you can come to the meeting of the widows' group and ask about justice and hear what the women of Taba have to say," she volunteered. "Maybe some of the witnesses will identify themselves to you afterward."

The widows called themselves *Urunana Rw'abashaka Amahoro Taba*—"the hugging of people in need of peace from Taba." That day thirty women had walked five miles down the rutted road from Taba to a church at a neighboring village for a lecture on how to mill and then sell a kind of high-nutrient gruel made out of sorghum. They sat on low wooden benches, their bare feet on the earthen floor. They were now the heads of the household in a rural country where 70 percent of the people lived below the poverty line. The women hung on to the lecturer's every word.

Survival was their priority. As they gathered to discuss the tribunal at the lecture's end—their voices often raised in anger—they defined justice in economic terms. Like the women survivors in Kigali, they were frustrated that Akayesu had not been tried in Rwanda so they could have confronted him themselves. But they were even angrier that they had not been compensated for their losses. In a country where family is one's riches, they had lost their husbands and sons, nearly everything; Akayesu, by contrast, comfortable in his UN-run prison, complete with a workout center, garden, television, and regular visits from his family, had lost nothing.

"There is no justice because Akayesu lives better than us," said one widow in a bright yellow blouse. "He doesn't have any problem: He eats, he has his family. But those of us who are survivors have no family and nothing to eat." Thinking of how the clothes these women were wearing had been donated by the Red Cross—and how they juggled farming for a living, preparing meals over an open fire, walking miles to fetch water, and looking after their children—I could well understand their fury. Akayesu and other prisoners once had the luxury of holding a hunger strike to protest the tribunal's assignment of defense counsel, while many of these women's children were malnourished.

As the meeting closed, the sun was sinking quickly. The mists rose from the fields with the chill of the oncoming night. As the widows of Taba stepped up to shake hands and say farewell, one sidled up to me, a wraith emerging from the shadows, barely visible in her old brown sweater and faded dark skirt. "Can you tell us more about the Akayesu trial?" she asked, dropping her voice to a whisper. "No one has come to tell us more."

She didn't need to say anything else. It was Witness JJ.

DARKNESS IS MORE menacing in places without electricity, and Taba was no exception that evening. Shadows loomed larger than people. The hours dragged. In Godelieve's house, where a light powered by solar energy dimly illuminated the living room, normal household noises seemed ominous: Godelieve's newborn granddaughter crying in the next room, the whish of a broom outside on the pavement, the wind rustling in the jagged leaves of the banana tree. Even the heavy ironwork door to the house rattled like the ghost of Marley dragging his chains, as Godelieve reached up and hung a large padlock on it, locking out the night.

She cast a glance at her husband's portrait, a black-and-white photograph hanging on the whitewashed wall, next to the pictures of Mary and Jesus. One husband lost, a daughter too, but Godelieve considered herself lucky. She lived in a home with some creature comforts: the solar light, a radio, a manual typewriter, a latrine attached to the house. She had children who were still alive and she had means to earn a living. The women she counseled were not so fortunate.

"How can a woman who has lost all her family reconcile with those in jail who still have someone to bring them food, to talk with?" she mused as we discussed Akayesu and the chances for reconciliation between Hutu and Tutsi in Taba. Part of the tribunal's mandate was to spur reconciliation here, but Godelieve was not convinced it was possible. She paused, mentally counting up the childless widows, considered blessed if they had any roof over their head at all. Reconciliation? She shook her head, her corn-rowed braids rustling.

"There are many women here who survived, but they act as if they are dead," Godelieve added. "They might as well be."

I stayed at Godelieve's house that night, and I found myself unable to sleep. For hours in my imagination, I relived the genocide in Taba. The *plings* and *plongs* of nuts dropping on the corrugated metal roof overhead were bullets. The rustling of the banana trees was the sound of a machete. The moans and sighs of Godelieve's family as they slept was the final cry of those dying.

And then my thoughts filled with images of the women of Taba who had survived the killings: the women without families, the women who are alive but "act as if they are dead." After a while I could not tell if I was still awake thinking about them, or if they were with me in my dreams.

WITNESS JJ—WHOSE testimony revolutionized international law in a case UN Secretary-General Kofi Annan called a "testament to our collective determination to confront the crime of genocide"—was one of those women: alone and struggling daily just to live. Even by Rwandan standards, her existence was one of abject poverty. Her three-room home of mud and straw bricks had a dirt floor and a corrugated tin roof. A single window let light into the main room. Her furniture consisted of a grubby foam mattress on the floor, a rush mat, a bench, two wooden stools, and a chair. In the corner of the room stood bags of rice—the family's food—in which rats busily rustled and squeaked.

Tall, thin as a reed, her face so deeply chiseled you could all but make out the contours of the skull under the skin, Witness JJ bore her trials with Christian faith. She thought about her five children who had survived, she said, not the son who died during the genocide. She focused on the fact she was living, not on how her health still suffered from the beatings and the rapes or how her last boyfriend had left her. She talked about how a group of women who heard her testify had been so moved by her story that they had raised $1,000 for her and the other witnesses from Taba, not the fact that her share of the money was long since gone.

"My faith in God helps to me to forget," JJ said, as she sat down in the rickety, hand-hewn chair to breast-feed her young son. "But in some situations the devil is brought in front of me, and I remember things I want to forget."

Joining her that day were two other of the Akayesu witnesses, Witness PP and Witness OO, both eager for news of tribunal. (The last time anyone from the court had visited Taba, they said, was in 1998, when prosecutor Pierre Prosper came to deliver a copy of the judgment to Taba's mayor.) Witness PP, a petite, vivacious woman whose energy exceeded her height, had been a key witness in the Akayesu case: She had told the court how she heard Akayesu order Tutsi to be killed, including any fetus found inside a pregnant woman's womb. Witness OO, a quiet, shy woman in her early twenties, had testified how she and other women had been raped when Akayesu told the militia, "Take them."

As the women sat down, ours was at first polite social chatter: of children and marriage, of the rigors of a woman's day in Rwanda versus one in the United States, of the virtues of wearing a traditional wrap-around *pagne* versus a skirt. But our talk turned to justice in general and the Akayesu case in particular, and how it had changed their lives. They hungered to talk about it. Witness JJ leaned forward.

Had testifying against Akayesu given them any sense of relief? I asked.

"When I saw Akayesu with my eyes in court, I was afraid," said JJ. "But at the same time, I had something heavy on my heart. After I testified, it went away."

Witness PP clapped her hands gleefully as she remembered testifying against Taba's mayor. "I chose to confront him," she said. "I felt better and I was happy to confront him, because I know what I saw was true in front of the eyes of God, and all people."

Testifying had been cathartic. The guilty verdict against Akayesu was confirmation of their suffering. It had uplifted their souls. The problem, the women agreed, was that it had done very little to improve their material and physical circumstances. If anything, testifying in some ways had made their lives worse, tarring them as pariahs, not heroines. Participating in international justice had left them isolated, alone and afraid. The local Hutu ostracized them: taxi drivers refused them rides, and some vendors wouldn't sell them food. Witness PP was once chased away from the local hospital when she arrived with a sick child. Both Witness JJ and Witness PP had received crude letters threatening their lives. Even Tutsi survivors in Taba shunned them, fearful that they also would be suspected of working with the Rwanda Tribunal and therefore threatened.

"Ever since we came back from Arusha," said Witness PP, carefully arranging the folds of her brightly patterned skirt, "we have had problems." "There are rumors about us," added JJ, softly. "I think the population here was waiting for survivors not to tell anything about the genocide. I think they figured if we don't talk, there will be peace. But we can't forget what we saw."

Not only can they not forget what they saw, they cannot forget that the men who raped them remain at large. Until they are arrested and convicted, Witness JJ and the others witnesses said, they cannot feel safe. And even then there is danger. As Witness PP said, "Some of those who raped are in prison, but who is to say after some years they will not be released? We are afraid for our life."

In theory, the women could have turned to the tribunal for witness protection; the court had relocated some twenty witnesses to other parts of Rwanda. Yet they were doubtful they could leave the only home they had ever known and unsure the tribunal would actually help them. One woman, Witness NN, had tried in vain to convince security guards at the gate of the tribunal offices in Kigali that she was a witness in need of protection, they said. Unable to get their attention and desperate to leave Taba, she moved in with relatives in another city. "Ooh, I am so afraid some days; I want to leave here," cried Witness PP. Witness OO heaved a scornful sigh. "Oh right," said OO. "Just where will you go, woman? And how will you get there?"

Witness PP looked down at her hands. All of these women had very few options; they were poor. Genocide is not just a crime, it is also a social condition in Rwanda. Their homes had been destroyed; their crops burned, and their land turned fallow; their husbands and sons and sisters and mothers and fathers all slain—all the measurements of wealth in Rwanda for them had disappeared.

While the Rwandan government had established a fund for survivors, little of it had reached Taba.

"Yes, I'm poor," JJ admitted, sweeping her eyes around the dirt floor, the rough-hewn bench, her own ragged white blouse. "In fact, I am much poorer than before the war. Yet if we talk about compensation, I don't count on it . . ." Her voice trailed off. "Nothing can replace the people I lost. . . . For me, the sentence against Akayesu will just have to be enough," she added.

And did she and the others know the Akayesu case had been appealed? I asked.

They had heard of "an appeal," they answered, although they were confused as to why it was taking so long. The judgment in the Akayesu case was handed down in September 1998, and why had the judges not yet ruled, a year and a half later? They feared Akayesu and his relatives would have the guilty verdict overturned. "Why did they let Akayesu appeal?" bemoaned Witness PP. "We are afraid that things could change during this appeal process," said Witness JJ.

"It's his right under the law," I answered. The women, knitting their brows, reflected on this.

"We will go to Arusha again if they need us," volunteered Witness JJ. "We want to be there, if it is necessary." The other two women looked at her proudly.

"If it is necessary to go back to Arusha and give our testimony all over again, we are ready," agreed Witness PP, emphatically. "*We want to follow this case to the end,*" she added, emphasizing every word.

The three women looked at each other and smiled. Justice delivered by an international war crimes court had made them no richer and no more secure. It was not the kind of justice they wanted, much less a justice they understood. Yet their participation in the Akayesu case had left them strong in the knowledge that, as victims, they had a court in which to tell their story. Gone was the look of helplessness that some years before had etched their faces. Replacing it was a look of steely determination.

WHETHER OTHER RWANDAN survivors would ever share in their resolve, however, still hung in the balance. In Arusha, Tanzania, the tribunal hastened to mend its relations with the Rwandan government in the wake of the Barayagwiza decision. The tribunal's chief prosecutor, Carla del Ponte—the hard-charging Swiss prosecutor who resigned her job battling the Russian Mafia to head the court in September 1999—decided to challenge the Barayagwiza decision. In late February, she appeared before the appeals judges in Arusha to make the case herself in court, the first chief prosecutor to do so. Thrusting out her jaw, peering over her black glasses, the fifty-two-year-old del Ponte called on the judges to consider new evidence and reverse their decision. "I am asking you, Mr. President, not to allow the accused, Barayagwiza, to decide on the fate of this tribunal," she thundered. The judges did indeed reverse the decision, and Barayagwiza was ordered to stand trial.

The decision to contest the Barayagwiza decision helped mend relations with the Rwandan government and allow the tribunal to carry on its work. But it had raised larger questions about the court, which weighed on the minds of its staff that winter. Did the errors made in the Barayagwiza case mean that the tribunal had not improved, three years after a UN report found it riddled with mismanagement? Was the tribunal providing a justice that had meaning for Rwandans? Could that justice—could any courtroom justice—help Rwanda heal?

Inside the cavernous conference center that housed the tribunal—where the court's ad hoc nature was emphasized by the giant stuffed zebra advertising a local taxidermist which stood by the elevators to the courtrooms—opinions were sharply divided. "Our mandate is to bring justice—we cannot say we have fulfilled this mandate," said Judge Yakov Ostrovsky, the seventy-three-year-old Russian judge and legal scholar. Ostrovsky was visibly impatient with administrative mishaps and legal delays that had left him without a trial to oversee since November of 1998. "We cannot say this tribunal is working." (He was not alone in his frustration: Tribunal president Navanethem Pillay and Judge Laity Kama had also not had trials before them since July 1999.)

"This is not the same tribunal you visited in 1996," insisted Kingsley Moghalu, legal advisor and spokesman for the tribunal's registrar, responsible for the court's administration. "We've gotten better. Remember, this was an institution that has charted uncharted waters. There was no roadmap."

But the Rwanda Tribunal, despite reforms, pronouncements, and new management, was still divided by infighting and plagued by administrative and legal errors. The most ordinary discussions gave way to bitter back-stabbing, where one department of the court readily blamed another and staff accused one another of everything from sloth to corruption. So plentiful were the complaints about the tribunal, particularly concerning the slow pace of its trials, that the UN had assigned a Commission of Experts to review its workings as well as those of its sister tribunal in The Hague. The commission's report, released in November 1999, commended the tribunal for its improvements and accomplishments but also highlighted many flaws. "In ICTR [the Rwanda Tribunal], the reasons for delays are multiple," its report concluded. It seems that for every step forward, mused one staffer, "it then takes two backward."

Some of the court's steps forward were obvious. Inside the courtrooms, for example, the air-conditioning worked. In the hallways, lethargic gloom had been replaced by a bustling, forced cheerfulness. Photographs commemorating key court appearances had been tacked up, including pictures of the seven men convicted of genocide and crimes against humanity. Three courtrooms had taken the place of one, and a staff of some 700 people from eighty-five countries jammed offices near to overflowing. The court's budget had more than doubled, from $29 million in 1996 to $75 million for 1999. February 1999 saw the first tribunal case concluded when appeals judges confirmed a fifteen-year prison sentence for Omar Serushago, a former militia leader who pleaded guilty to genocide.

Yet step into any court session, and the problems that still bedeviled the tribunal were evident. Glitches included a defense attorney who failed to appear; prosecutors confused about their cases; mistakes in indictments; constant adjournments; and a virtual tidal wave of unnecessary motions—more than 200 pretrial motions between 1997 and 1999. Compounding the problem were the prosecution's plans to group defendants for trial by theme—a military trial was planned—a strategy that often resulted in a flurry of delaying tactics by defense attorneys. "I can't think of a single hearing that has gone by without a hiccup," said one legal assistant. Said Judge Navanethem Pillay, the Rwanda Tribunal's president, with a sigh: "The problems are strategy, sloppiness, and incompetence."

More pressing than the continuing questions of the court's legal competence, however, was the problem of how removed the Rwanda Tribunal was from the country's realities. "The tribunal is staffed with qualified personnel lacking one essential thing," Rwanda's representative to the tribunal, Martin Ngoga, quipped wryly, "They have never been to Rwanda."

Chief prosecutor Louise Arbour had pushed to have the war crimes trials transferred to Rwanda before she left in mid 1999. Still, tribunal judges only made their first official visit to the country later that year. The tribunal had just begun to address issues of compensation; some $300,000 from the UN and other donors had finally been received to provide medical aid, counseling, and other assistance for its witnesses. "The witnesses come, tell us of the horrible things that happened to them, and then we ship them back to Rwanda and say 'You did a good job,' " said the tribunal's registrar, Agwu Ukiwe Okali, who had pleaded for the funds for several years. "You begin to realize there is another level of tragedy . . . they are no better from having participated in tribunal procedure."

Whether such measures would be enough to help Rwanda's genocide survivors understand that "Arusha justice" was indeed justice was unclear. Far larger measures would be needed to still the bubbling discontent among many of the country's moderate Hutu, who had quietly hailed the Barayagwiza decision as a sign that the court was willing to treat all Rwandans fairly. When the appeals court decision was overturned, they accused the court of pandering to the Rwandan government. Already the tribunal's failure to prosecute the Rwandan Patriotic Army for its war crimes had raised allegations that the court would provide only "victor's justice." (Off the record, several high-ranking tribunal officials confirmed that investigations were ongoing into RPA crimes.) "One grand objective of the tribunal was to help with reconciliation in Rwanda," said François Roux, a French attorney representing Ignace Bagilishema, a Rwandan mayor accused of genocide and crimes against humanity. "If people have the sentiment that the process is inequitable, they will be closed to it and it won't help with reconciliation."

At times, the tribunal's task seemed as challenging as trying to piece together a body from the bones at one of Rwanda's genocide sites. Complex judgments in a handful of symbolic cases—even at a level of efficiency the tribunal had yet to achieve—could offer Rwandans only so much.

Some who worked for the war crimes court despaired it could ever do more. "I think we should abandon the tribunal and all its resources to a new body in Rwanda to improve the justice system," one disillusioned legal assistant concluded. "All we've done is create an institution which has neither the resources nor the ability to deliver justice."

Yet, while "Arusha justice" was not enough for Witness JJ, it was better than no justice at all. We had met several more times in Taba, the last of which she had giggled over my efforts to wear a Rwandan *pagne*. "No, no, the folds are all wrong," she fussed, adjusting the skirt firmly around my waist. It defied her efforts to smooth it down and ripple as gracefully as hers to the floor.

"Maybe American women just can't wear these skirts," I said in despair.

"No, you have to accept it isn't perfect on you," JJ said.

"Sort of like your experience with the tribunal?" I joked.

"It was justice." JJ shrugged. "Now I wait for God to reveal if there will be more justice. Only God plans for me."

17

WHEN A TRIBUNAL IS NOT ENOUGH

Justice is not only in the end result. It is also in the process.

—South African Supreme Court Justice Albie Sachs

I had waited four years to see the tall, rumpled man standing before me. I had actually expected to wait for many more. But in the spring of 2000, Bosnian Serb general Radislav Krstić was in the dock, on trial for genocide at the International Criminal Tribunal for the former Yugoslavia in The Hague.

This gray-faced man in his oversized shiny gray suit was the man who helped mastermind the capture of the UN safe area of Srebrenica and the brutal killing of thousands of unarmed men and boys. It was his orders soldiers had followed when they picked up their guns and fired and fired and fired until their victims were mowed down as easily as sheaves of wheat. This was the man whose orders Marko Boškić—the alleged mass executioner I'd interviewed—had turned to for direction.

On the witness stand that April day was a man called Witness I, one of only two survivors of the execution at the killing field of Pilica where Boškić had reportedly done his work. Witness I was telling of how the bullets tore by him, grazing just his elbow. How he fell to the ground, pretended to be dead, and waited for his chance to escape. How he sprinted across a field of dead bodies into the brush. How, eventually so weary and so hungry and so outnumbered, he surrendered to the Bosnian Serb police and hoped for the best.

And he spoke of how the police had stopped at a café while he was in their custody. There, the waiter took pity on him, offering him and another Muslim prisoner their first sustenance in days.

"Have a cigarette," the Bosnian Serb waiter urged him, "have some juice."

"This was so good for us," Witness I recalled. "This saved us. I will never forget what this man did for us. He said, 'I treat everyone in the same way. I used to work in Germany. I like everyone. I respect everyone.' . . . I would really like to know his name. He was like a good friend of mine. He behaved like a man."

Throughout the testimony that day, Krstić had focused on the desk in front of him, never looking up at Witness I. From time to time he had absently rubbed his right hand against his left, the large gold ring on his hand glinting in the light. The only sign of emotion was the twinge of pain that crept across his face when he tried to move his injured leg.

At hearing this anecdote, however, he recoiled, shrinking into the folds of his suit like a punctured balloon. Shame washed across his face, and he bowed his head. How I wished that Anonciata, Witness JJ, Hamdo, Petko, and Hasan—indeed all of Bosnia and Rwanda—had been able to see the look on the general's face, as he heard the story of how one man's decency defied a campaign of evil.

Had it not been for the Yugoslav Tribunal, Witness I would have never told his story and General Krstić would not have been in the dock to hear it. Nor would another man have been on trial before the tribunal that day, Momcilo Krajišnik, the brooding, bushy-eyebrowed Bosnian Serb nationalist and former right-hand aide to Radovan Karadžić, recently arrested and charged with war crimes. In less than a year, these two high-ranking Bosnian Serbs would be joined at the court by a third accused of masterminding Bosnia's war, the grandmotherly Biljana Plavšić, the first woman charged by the tribunal of charges of genocide, crimes against humanity, and violations of customs of war. Then, Blagoje Simić—the mayor I found still in his job in 1996 despite his indictment for war crimes—surrendered to the war crimes court to stand trial. Even Slobodan Milošević was finally arrested and sent to The Hague to face war crime charges for killings and expulsions in the Serbian province of Kosovo.

All would have led lives of relative comfort, as immune from prosecution in their homeland as generations of war criminals before them, had the Yugoslav Tribunal not been created. Now, they are likely to serve time in jail. Their actions during Bosnia's war will not be enshrined in myth or propaganda but preserved in a detailed trial transcript and judgment. That record will one day make clear their individual guilt—or innocence—replacing the collective guilt ascribed to the Bosnian Serbs.

The Yugoslav Tribunal, and to a lesser degree its sister court in Rwanda, have accomplished much against difficult odds. Both courts, something of an experiment in international law, are now established institutions. Each has high-ranking suspects in Bosnia's war and Rwanda's genocide behind bars. Their judgments have made it possible for refugees like Hamdo Kahrimanović to return home. They have enabled victims to confront those responsible for their suffering, as Witness JJ did. They have pushed back the boundaries of international law, defining many war crimes for the first time. Their work has inspired the creation of a permanent international criminal court to judge the world's war criminals and prompted countries to prosecute those responsible for humanity's most heinous crimes, even if they are not their citizens.

Yet neither tribunal's justice is all it could be. While the UN's financial and moral commitment to the courts has grown, its understanding of what a tribunal needs to function effectively has yet to catch up. The international community still only grudgingly supports the tribunals when it suits their purpose. Many high-ranking war criminals are still not behind bars. Inside the courts, trials still move far too slowly, and in the Rwanda Tribunal, administrative mishaps repeatedly stall proceedings.

Most disappointing of all, the two tribunals do not reach the victims for whom they were intended. Theirs has become a justice aimed more at international lawyers than genocide survivors. As both Hamdo and Gordana discovered, too few people understand just what the tribunal is, much less what it does, much less know about the war crimes trial relevant to where they live.

That may change. Before leaving the tribunal in 1999, Judge McDonald convinced UN member states to donate nearly $1 million towards an outreach program. Since then, the court has become somewhat more accessible. A small staff based in the former Yugoslavia help educate Bosnia's lawyers and judges about the court. Many of the court's decisions have been translated, and trials can be followed live on the Internet, for those with access to computers. In both Bosnia and Rwanda, tribunal staff aid local journalists by supplying them with footage for radio and television broadcasts. The Rwanda Tribunal has opened an outreach office in Kigali and has plans to distribute a picture book to explain how the court works to those who cannot read. Some court decisions are now available in Kinyarwandan.

It is an important step at a time when independent media are beginning to replace propaganda. When a Western documentary about Srebrenica aired on an independent television station in Serbia, some Bosnians I know received tearful phone calls from friends in Belgrade, devastated by what they had learned. Their reaction demonstrates how powerful the kind of truth the tribunal brings to light can be.

But more commitment and money are needed if the courts' justice is to be brought home effectively. Outreach funds, for example, are not included in the UN's regular budget for the court and must be raised each year. The $1 million Judge McDonald collected is barely enough to do the job. Yet to be realized are satellite broadcasts of trial verdicts, documentaries of completed cases, and meetings organized in local communities to discuss verdicts and judgments that directly affect them. Coverage of the trial of General Krstić—pivotal to Bosnia's understanding of what happened at Srebrenica—could be seen on TV, but only at odd hours. "You can't see it anywhere in the news," complained Hasan Nuhanović. "People just don't know about it."

Equally unclear is whether the tribunal will hold trials in Bosnia and Rwanda. Judge Claude Jorda of France, who became tribunal president after McDonald left, has acknowledged that trials need to take place in the region. Prosecutor Carla del Ponte has held out the prospect of trials in Rwanda. Increasingly, advocates of international justice think future war crimes courts should be both local and international. There are plans, for example, to create a court to address war crimes in Sierra Leone in which the chief prosecutor would be an international lawyer answering to the UN and the deputy from the country's own judicial system. Trials, which would apply both domestic and international law to war crimes, would be held in Sierra Leone.

Tribunal judges have also recognized that victims deserve compensation, that they are entitled to restitutive as well as retributive justice. Still to be worked out by the UN is who will pay. And much more needs to be done to ensure that the tribunal's trials aid in reconciliation, as their mandate requires. Trials need to heal communities like Kozarac, rather than divide them; differing versions of the past must be confronted, not ignored. Even if the tribunal's verdicts cannot sway the opinions of those who lived through this war, they can influence their children, Bosnia's future generation. As Holocaust survivor Bruno Bettelheim once warned: "What cannot be talked about can also not be put to rest; and if it is not, the wounds continue to fester from generation to generation."

THE BODIES THAT Bill Haglund and his team exhumed now lie on wooden risers in a morgue in Tuzla. Against all odds—and in what seemed like a miracle to those grieving their missing—102 individuals have been identified using DNA samples from the bodies in the 4,400 bags containing the Srebrenica dead.

"I never believed an identification like that could happen," exclaimed Semir Bekrić, whose brother Suad was among the corpses identified in 1999. Tears glittered in his eyes as he sat in the crowded one-room apartment that he and his sixteen-year-old brother, Sedin—all that remain of a family of five—called home. "It is better to know which grave he was in, rather than looking for him in all the graves," he added.

His brother was identified with the help of the database compiled by Physicians for Human Rights, working on behalf of the International Commission for Missing Persons. Since 1996, staff had conducted interviews with more than 7,800 relatives of the missing, using a form with 200 questions. It wasn't enough to know if a jacket was patched; the interviewers needed to find out the color of the patch and the stitching that attached it. It wasn't enough to know if a jacket had buttons; they had to know if they were wooden, metal, plastic, colored, neutral, or engraved with a design. To ensure uniformity of description, PHR's staff used color wheels to make sure everyone agreed on a particular shade. Drawings of teeth helped people remember whether their son or husband had fillings, or extractions or even gum disease. Staff noted down any kind of identifying item a missing person had on him, from a cigarette lighter to a pendant.

Thousands of entries from the tribunal's pathology reports had been logged in. Identifications so far had been slow, but there was every hope that the computer database could make many more matches. "I had no idea it was going to be this laborious," said Dr. Laurie Vollen, heading up PHR's ante-mortem database effort in Tuzla, when I interviewed her in 1999 in the house that served as office and living quarters for the small staff. "But then, there has never been an effort to identify victims of a genocide on this scale." By contrast, the U.S. Department of Defense's Prisoner of War/Missing Personnel Office, which has fielded teams in Vietnam and North Korea to search for missing troops, has a $12 million annual budget.

In Suad Bekrić's case—body number 109 from the Lazete mass grave—identification began with his mother's identity card in his jacket pocket. Plugging her name into the database, PHR staff came up with a missing man with the same last name wearing clothing that matched that on the corpse. Semir had given them the information, and so PHR returned to him and took a blood sample. Shipped to analysts at the University of Washington, his blood and a bone sample from the corpse was examined for mitochondrial DNA, which demonstrates a link between mothers and their children, and is easier to analyze and more plentiful in the body. (Nuclear DNA, which can prove a link to either parent, is harder to analyze.) In May 1999 the results came back: a match.

Semir had been lucky. The database was still far from perfect, and identification was impeded by the same clash of aims that marked the graves' exhumations. Because tribunal investigators had been more interested in gathering evidence than making identifications, detailed records had not always been kept. Local Bosnian authorities in charge of the bodies after they were exhumed also accidentally destroyed key evidence. Confronted with a pile of body bags—and with no means in a postwar economy to ensure they were stored properly—Tuzla authorities simply piled them on top of each other in the man-made tunnels under the city's hills. Clothing that might have distinguished a few of the bodies rotted in the damp. Since then, a morgue has been built to properly store the bodies.

But the greatest obstacle to identification was the theft of bodies from the mass graves. Tribunal investigators discovered not only secondary graves—to which the bodies were first removed—but also tertiary and even quadrutiary graves. Thanks to those Bosnian Serbs who stole out under the cover of the dark, moonless Balkan nights to destroy evidence, the numbers of bodies exhumed may never equal all those killed at Srebrenica. The Serbs' logic must have been similar to that of the Nazis, who destroyed their records of concentration camps before the Allies arrived: that which cannot be proved beyond a shadow of a doubt can always be denied.

Identification has held out such promise, however, that the International Commission for Missing Persons took over the PHR identification project in late 1999. The commission, headed by former senator Robert Dole, had come to believe that identification of bodies was key to postwar Bosnia's peace. Its goal was to make the process more efficient and more accurate. Rather than trying to match the clothing or the physical characteristics of a corpse to a profile of a missing person in the database and then do DNA testing of relatives, the commission reversed the process. Acquiring nearly $7 million worth of equipment and opening up DNA laboratories in Bosnia, it then fanned its staff out across the country to take DNA samples from survivors. By putting that information into the database, the commission hopes to identify 80 percent of the Srebrenica bodies that have been recovered within three to five years.

Nearly 3,800 of the body bags hold intact or partial bodies, which are easier to identify; the remainder have intermingled body parts, which will be more difficult. With exhumations still continuing, the Commission also hopes to identify more of the Srebrenica dead.

"Getting my brother's body was a kind of justice," said Semir. "It is so much better to know, not to be wondering, any more." Bill Haglund agrees. For him, as he travels around the world, unearthing mass graves elsewhere, it is a comfort to know that some of the Srebrenica dead he exhumed now have names.

PETKO GRUBAČ DIDN'T need to identify the dead; he needed to confront the living to feel as if justice had been done. For months after the Čelebići verdict, unanswered questions nagged at him: Why had his friends betrayed him? Why had his neighbors chosen to see him as a Serb, not as an ally?

As a psychiatrist, he believed the best way for people to come to terms with trauma was by talking about it. Yet war crimes trials, as he knew from his own experience, presented no chance for dialogue and discussion. A truth commission for Bosnia, however, would.

"A truth commission would get people to talk, and that would make things clear," Petko told me when I visited him in Bijeljina in the summer of 2000. "If it's forbidden to discuss certain things, if it's a kind of taboo, then that creates fear and suspicions. And that is what happened after World War II—and look where that got us." The talkative Montenegrin waved his hands in the air, as if he were summoning into the room the spirits of the people from Konjic who had betrayed him. "I need to know why they did certain things. I need to know—did we pretend all this time, all of us, to be friends? Or were we really true friends? If we see what the consequences are now, it seems that everything was a lie, it was not real. But I cannot accept that it was that way. . . ."

Political feuding in Bosnia—and stiff opposition from the tribunal—had squashed the dream of a truth commission in 1998. But the idea was resurrected two years later when the new chief prosecutor in The Hague, Carla del Ponte, was persuaded to endorse it. In February 2000 more than a hundred activists of all ethnic backgrounds gathered in Sarajevo to discuss what form the truth commission should take. Of the approximately twenty truth commissions organized by countries wrestling with the legacy of their past, no two have been alike. In South Africa, amnesty was granted to perpetrators, and truth commission hearings were cathartic, emotionally charged sessions open to the public. By contrast in Chile, truth commission sessions were private, and names of the guilty were kept out of the final report.

What was envisioned for Bosnia was different still. The commission would not grant amnesty, but there would be public sessions and, it was hoped, a kind of catharsis. Members would travel around Bosnia, seeking to arrive at a common truth about the causes of the war by exploring the role of the church, the media, and other organizations. Unlike other commissions, Bosnia's also would highlight good deeds, acts of moral courage committed by individual citizens in the face of the campaign of ethnic cleansing.

Advocates pushed to move swiftly. "We are at a crossroads," said Jakob Finci, a leading Jewish civic leader in Sarajevo and supporter of a truth commission. "We either move forwards towards a lasting peace or we have a war or we divide into three parts. The only real alternative is reconciliation, and the precondition for that is the truth."

Indeed, Bosnia was at a political turning point. All of those who played a role into leading the country into war—Slobodan Milošević, Franjo Tudjman, and Alija Izetbegović—were finally out of power. Croatian nationalist leader Tudjman was the first to go, dying on December 10, 1999, at the age of seventy-seven, without ever having been indicted by the Yugoslav Tribunal. Croats elected a new, more democratic leader. Then, in the fall of 2000, Slobodan Milošević was handed his defeat at the polls when the Serbs elected Vojislav Kostunica, a fifty-six-year-old constitutional lawyer, to be Yugoslav's leader. Although Milošević initially refused to leave office, he was forced to relinquish power when thousands of protestors took to the streets. While Kostunica was an ardent nationalist—and no fan of the tribunal—he has called for the creation of a truth commission. "We cannot, and should not, avoid facing the consequences of war and responsibility for war crimes," said the new Yugoslav foreign minister Goran Svilanović. Serbs, he continued, should be told about "everything that was done either in the name of alleged Serb national interests or against the Serb people."

Indeed, by July of 2001 Milošević would be arrested and in the dock in The Hague. Within less than a year his political career had been transformed, from a man confident he would always lead Yugoslavia to a man who was to be the first former head of state to be tried for war crimes by the tribunal. Even Bosnian Muslim leader Alija Izetbegović had stepped down as member of the Bosnian presidency in 2000. While nationalist parties held on to power in Bosnia's elections in the fall of that year, for the first time since 1996 they garnered less than 50 percent of the vote in both the Muslim-Croat and Serb halves. It was a small sign that Bosnians were slowly realizing the deadly role nationalism had played in their country's war.

A CONTINENT AWAY in Rwanda, another alternative to courtroom justice was also being hotly debated in the year 2000: *gacaca*, or "justice in the grass." It had become clear that Rwanda's own courts, even working alongside the Rwanda Tribunal, would need generations to settle the cases of the 125,000 prisoners still in jail. In fact, returning to Kigali Central Prison I found that Leon Nsengimana, the Ministry of Health doctor I had met in 1996 was right: He was still in prison in 2000 with no trial in sight.

"Ma'am, maybe we will eat lobsters in the Sahara before I see a lawyer," said Leon, wryly. Government officials had yet again extended the deadline by which all investigations were to be completed and charges brought against prisoners, this time to 2001. Leon's wife, Marie Claire, was so despairing of his case ever coming to trial that she haunted the hallways of the prosecutor's office, begging that his case be moved to one of the new *gacaca* courts—once they were created.

Fiacre Bisara, the Rwanda government's point man on *gacaca*, agreed that traditional justice could no longer cope. "In normal justice, we begin with the people who died, and make a dossier—but that's one million murder cases," he said. "One million murders—who did these? It would take us one million years. Can we continue down this road? Logically, no."

Gacaca tribunals, working alongside regular courts, could clear the prisons in just three years. Bisara whipped out his calculator to show just how: *Clickety click*. The country's *gacaca* courts could try as many as two hundred cases per day, he estimated. "*Gacaca*," he exclaimed, "could try up to 75,000 people in one year!"

Under the proposed *gacaca* plan, Bisara explained, up to 10,000 tribunals would be established across the country at the Rwandan equivalent of town, county, state, and federal levels. In a tiny country like Rwanda—where there are few secrets and where even the genocide was carried out in broad daylight—local hearings might more easily shed light on the truth of what happened during the genocide. A *gacaca* tribunal would draw all the witnesses from one place together at the same time.

Elected judges (replacing the village elders of old) would assemble the community, hear testimony and investigate crimes. Drawing on the moral force of an assembled village, they also might be more successful than a panel of judges in getting the guilty to confess. There would be no prosecutors or defense attorneys to delay proceedings with legal wrangling, and sentences would reward confession and participation, offering a blend of jail time and community service. "In Western justice, only the accused, the judge, and the victims are involved—so you only get a small part of truth," Justice Minister Jean de Dieu Mucyo explained. "But if you involve many people in a trial together, you get the truth. Nothing stands between survivors and the implicated."

But *gacaca* justice, under discussion in Rwanda since 1998, has remained controversial. Many of Rwanda's Hutu have feared such tribunals will violate the rights of the accused, becoming Rwandan-style versions of the Salem witch trials. The trials have few legal safeguards—no defense attorneys—and *gacaca* judges would have limited training. So terrified were some Rwandans when the government approved *gacaca* trials that 5,000 people, mostly Hutu, fled the country to Tanzania. Human rights groups wonder if *gacaca* trials aren't just another form of state control. At the same time, genocide survivors argue that since a *gacaca* tribunal draws on the moral force of the village, it is more likely to represent the views of the Hutu majority than the Tutsi. Victims' groups worry judgments simply will grant blanket amnesty, denying justice to survivors.

Even Rwandan government officials admit that the *gacaca* tribunals will be an experiment, if not a risk. No one quite knows just how this kind of justice will turn out. "*Gacaca* will have problems—it would not be honest to say it will be perfect," said Gerald Gahima, who by 2000 had become Rwanda's attorney general. "You are requiring people to sit in judgment of their friends, their relatives. The conflict of interest is apparent." But with tens of thousands of cases still pending, he says, there's no other choice. "Ordinary courts can never deal with the backlog of all the cases. I think *gacaca* ought to be given a chance. If it doesn't work . . . then we will simply have to try something else."

SIX YEARS AFTER the disappearance of Joseph Kavaruganda, Anonciata had heard nothing from the United Nations—or anyone else—concerning her husband. The Rwanda Tribunal still had not scheduled the trial of General Théoneste Bagasora. While Belgium and France had held public inquiries, the United States gave no signs of examining its role in failing to halt the genocide. With no other avenue of recourse, Anonciata and her friend Louise Mushikiwabo—whose brother, Landoal Ndasingwa, had also been slain while under UN protection—decided to have lawyers make their case, in what promised to become the first-ever lawsuit against the United Nations.

They assembled a team of expert lawyers who puzzled over how to bring the precedent-setting—and possibly quixotic—lawsuit. To begin with, the United Nations was not so much an institution as a group of member states and, thus, an expression of collective will. How does one in essence sue the world?

Their prospective lawsuit gained momentum when Representative Cynthia McKinney, Democrat of Georgia, took up their cause. She persuaded an independent three-person commission, appointed by Secretary General Kofi Annan, to examine how the UN had erred during the genocide, to interview the two women. Finally, after so many years of waiting, Anonciata was able to tell her story to someone in a position to do something about it.

"I think the time has come for the UN to recognize what they did, and come to the rescue of helpless people that are left in Rwanda without any kind of help," Anonciata told the independent panel in December 1999. "Very importantly, Mr. President of the Commission, I would like to ask you to find out through the United Nations investigations what happened to my husband."

The commission's report, released on December 16, 1999, sharply criticized both the United Nations for its failure to heed calls for help from General Romeo Dallaire in Rwanda and the United States for blocking efforts to send a significant, follow-up peacekeeping force. More significant for Anonciata, however, was one of the report's conclusions: that the UN had been negligent on Joseph's behalf. "The President of The Constitutional Court, Mr. Joseph Kavaruganda, was taken away by armed elements of the Rwandese Army and was never seen again. In these cases, UNAMIR [UN mission in Rwanda] did not succeed in providing the protection [Joseph Kavaruganda and Landoal Ndasingwa] required," it concluded.

That the UN bore moral responsibility for failing to protect the two men seemed clear. Less certain was how to prove that the UN bore *legal* responsibility and that the women were entitled to financial compensation for their loved ones' deaths. The United Nations, under its founding charter, was granted immunity from many legal obligations, and the scope of that immunity had rarely been tested. (UN officials cannot be sued in national jurisdictions for their official acts.) There was very little legal precedent to support the two women's claims for reparations, other than the fact that the United Nations had made reparations in the 1960s, when Belgians in the Congo had been killed as a result of negligence by UN peacekeepers. The United Nations legal staff, in correspondence with the women's attorneys, has denied all liability, in part because the mandate given to the UN peacekeepers in Rwanda did not specifically include the protection of government officials. After nearly a year, Anonciata and Louise parted company with their legal team, but they have vowed they will not give up the case.

And Anonciata now knows a little bit more about where her husband may have died.

The answer came from General Romeo Dallaire. The former head of UN peacekeeping in Rwanda—a man whose experiences during the genocide have left him suffering from post-traumatic stress syndrome—was clearly pained when I raised the issue of Joseph's death. "My duty as force commander is finished only when the ICTR [Rwanda Tribunal] brings all those who perpetrated those killings to court," he said, sadly. "I consider myself accountable."

Joseph, he said, may have been killed at a military camp near the presidential residence where other officials from the transitional government were reportedly taken and slain—a series of executions that proved a turning point in the genocide Dallaire then tried so hard to stop.

"All I needed was three battalions . . ." said the general, his voice trailing off, his eyes looking into the past.

LET ME END as I began: in Bijeljina, at the Montenegro Café. In the summer of 2000 I returned to Marko Boškić's old haunt to find it completely changed. Gone were the surly soldiers in the camouflage uniforms; of Boškic there was not a trace. In fact, the café was shuttered, and cobwebs adorned its front door.

I had returned hoping to talk to Boškić again about Srebrenica. In particular, I wanted to talk to him about what the confessed executioner, Dražen Erdemović, had had to say while on the witness stand in the Krstić trial. Erdemović had revealed that he, Boškić, and several others in the squad—once they had finished the first round of killings—had refused to take part in a second execution when commanded to that same day. With that revelation, my understanding of Marko Boškić had suddenly grown far more complex.

Had Boškić been forced to take part in the first execution? Certainly, the tribunal's judges thought Erdemović had: they had cited duress as one reason for his participation when they granted him a lenient sentence. Or had Boškić, after killing one group of prisoners, simply had a crisis of conscience? What would be his version of events of what unfolded on that terrible day?

The answers, I now believe, are as complex as the human soul, one reason why there is no one explanation for evil and no one form of justice to combat it. Tribunals, truth commissions, local trials, government inquiries—are all part of the answer, and even then the answer will not be complete. Justice after such horrors is imperfect, slow, and frustrating. It never arrives all at once, but inches forward, in a slow, steady pace that spans more than a lifetime. There is no easy means to achieve it; just the human will to try.

It is that will—political as well as personal—that is so important. And so, as you end this book, remember the commitment we have not yet fulfilled: It is not only Marko Boškić but also many of the architects of the atrocities in Bosnia and Rwanda who still walk the streets of their homelands, free.

AFTERWORD

The world's most significant war crimes trial since Nuremberg and Tokyo began on February 12, 2002, not with a rhetorical flourish but with a quiet statement of fact.

"The Chamber will now begin the trial of this man for the wrongs he is said to have done—to the people of his own country and to his neighbors," Carla Del Ponte, the chief prosecutor of The Hague Tribunal, told the court's judges on the first day of the trial of former Balkan leader Slobodan Milošević. "How simple that statement is to make today; how easily those words pass into the record of these proceedings; and yet how remarkable it is that I am able to speak them here. Today, as never before, we see international justice in action."

It was, indeed, a day few in the former Yugoslavia had ever expected to see, the day when Milošević, the Serb leader whose bloodthirst and ambition led his own people into three consecutive wars, would stand trial for genocide and other war crimes. From Sarajevo to Belgrade to Zagreb, people snapped on their television sets and stared with amazement as the pugnacious strongman—looking more wan and less portly than in the past—stuck out his chin in defiance while court prosecutors detailed the crimes against him. His were crimes of a "medieval savagery" and "calculated cruelty." Motivated by his own obsession with his "maintenance of personal power," Milošević, prosecutors said, had operated a criminal enterprise with genocide as its aim, cleansing parts of the former Yugoslavia of ethnic Croats, Muslims, and Albanians with an aim to creating a "greater Serbia." The indictment against him spans his days in power, from 1991 to 1999, from his support for those fighting in Croatia and Bosnia to his actions in Kosovo, when his security forces brutally repressed ethnic Albanians.

Seated quietly in the courtroom, Milošević's only reaction that day was the briefest of smiles when prosecutors showed a film clip of him delivering his most famous speech, rallying the Serbs behind his dream of greater Serbia at Kosovo Polye in 1989.

But if few had predicted that Milošević would ever stand trial, then fewer still could have forecast what would happen next. Milošević, the man who had decried The Hague Tribunal since its inception—the man who had railed at its judges through months of hearings, declaring himself the victim of a kangaroo court—decided to defend himself. With that simple act, he ultimately acknowledged the legitimacy of the International Criminal Tribunal for the former Yugoslavia.

As this book went to press, Milošević had just been extradited to The Hague, becoming the first former sitting head of state to stand trial before the tribunal, a historic triumph by any measure. As I write this now, the frequently postponed trial of another alleged mastermind of crimes against humanity, Col. Théoneste Bagasora, is due to begin before the International Criminal Tribunal for Rwanda, yet another important milestone. (Newly declassified State Department documents have also come to light since this book went to press, showing that Americans were actually quite well informed about the savagery unfolding in Rwanda, with one official going so far as to call Bagasora in an effort to halt it.)

Two of the men most responsible for the most deadly violence perpetrated against civilians in recent memory will be in the dock. While Milošević will grandstand in the courtroom, seeking to go down in history as the man who defied the West, and while Bagasora will inevitably seek more trial delays, in the end the trials will do what the tribunals' founders hoped they would do. They will create a historical record of what had happened; replace collective guilt with individual responsibility; and, in their fairness of purpose and harshness of punishment, send a message to all the world's tyrants that they can never be above the law.

In the wake of the brutal terrorist attacks of September 11 on the World Trade Center and the Pentagon, the knowledge that these two ad hoc international war crimes tribunals can deliver justice to leaders who perpetrate heinous crimes is welcome news, indeed.

Yet even at this moment of triumph for the two tribunals, it is important to note their shortcomings. Both are ad hoc courts, with a temporary life; the Bush administration has suggested they will have their work done as early as 2008. And, as thrilling as the sight of Milošević in the dock for war crimes has been for thousands of Bosnians, for thousands more it still isn't adequate justice. Consider, for example, the reaction of Hasan Nuhanović to Milŏsević's trial.

"Sure, it's spectacular—the key player is in the jail," said Hasan, reached by telephone at his new job in Sarajevo with the UN's International Police Task Force. "But on the ground, the small fish still run free. On the ground here, this is what is going on."

What he meant was that The Hague Tribunal has dedicated itself to indicting and trying only those deemed most responsible for war crimes. (And, while Milošević was in prison, former Bosnian Serb General Ratko Mladić and former Bosnian leader Radovan Karadžić, both indicted for war crimes, remain at large.) Still, nearly every major center in Bosnia has its suspected henchmen and triggermen, the low-level perpetrators of war and genocide. Deemed too insignificant to be arrested by NATO troops and hauled before the tribunal, they live their lives without fear of prosecution.

Their constant presence haunts the hundreds of Bosnian Muslims who hoped to undo the war's curse—their country's division along ethnic lines—by returning home. For them, the trial of Milošević only underscored how much has not changed, how much further their country needs to travel before justice can be achieved.

"If I go to Vlasenica, I won't meet [Gen.] Mladić in the street," said Hasan. "But I may meet my mother's murderer—and who should I go to complain to?"

He added: "I'm afraid the world watching Bosnia will get the impression that its problems have been solved by indicting Milošević. But what about the rest of them? I'm more afraid now that when the Milošević trial ends, the world will have reason to close down The Hague. And so many of these guys will still be unindicted."

His concerns are ones that Pierre Prosper, the attorney who once prosecuted Jean-Paul Akayesu, understands. Now the U.S. Ambassador-at-Large for War Crimes Issues, Prosper is in a position to reflect on what has been learned from the two ad hoc tribunals. Among their lessons, he says: The courts were too removed from the people they were meant to serve, both geographically and emotionally. There was no sense of "ownership" of justice when it was delivered, he said, and too often the courts, which focused on those responsible for orchestrating war crimes, had to neglect the prosecution of those who actually performed them. As the two international war crimes tribunals finish their work, Prosper is working to ensure that countries themselves take on the responsibility for enduring that mid- to low-level perpetrators do not go free.

"The little fish," said Prosper, "do not get a free pass."

It remains to be seen just how the next chapter in the history of the two ad hoc war crimes tribunals will unfold. Their defeats and their triumphs will be lessons for us all. As we embark on our search for justice, hoping to put the memory of the September 11 attacks of the World Trade Center and Pentagon to rest, we are joined by many others traveling on similar paths around the world.

Like Hasan.

"I gotta go now," he said. "Good-bye."

EPILOGUE

BOSNIA AND THE FORMER YUGOSLAVIA

- Slobodan Milošević was arrested April 1, 2001, by Serbian police and charged with corruption and other crimes. He was transferred to The Hague on June 29, becoming the first former head of state to face a war crimes trial. Appearing in the courtroom on July 3, Milošević refused to enter a plea, saying he considered the court a "false tribunal" whose aim was to justify NATO's campaign in the former Yugoslavia. His trial for genocide and other crimes began on February 12th, 2002.

- Former Bosnian Serb leader Radovan Karadžić and General Ratko Mladić remain at large. Karadžić is said to be in the French-held sector of Bosnia; Mladić, in Serbia.

- Žjelko "Arkan" Ražnatović was assassinated in Belgrade on January 2, 2000. He never stood trial.

- General Radislav Krstić was found guilty of genocide by the Yugoslav Tribunal on August 2, 2001. "General Krstić, you agreed to evil," said Judge Almiro Rodrigues, imposing a forty-six-year sentence on the fifty-three-year-old Krstić, the harshest the court had ever delivered.

- Milan "Legenda" Jovović, the head of the Drina Wolves, is believed to be in hiding in Serbia. Tribunal investigators found evidence of a mass grave near his headquarters.

- Dragomir Vasić, whom Hasan Nuhanović believes was involved with his father's death, is a member of the Zvornik Municipal Assembly.

Hasan Nuhanović

- Hasan, Mirza, and Nasiha live in Sarajevo. There is still no news of Muhamed.
- Milorad Dodik apologized for the Srebrenica massacres while serving as Bosnian Serb prime minister in 2000.
- A memorial for the victims of Srebrenica will be built in Potočari.

Hamdo and Firdesa Kahrimanović

- Hamdo and Firdesa live in Kozarac. Some four thousand Bosnian Muslim families have also moved back to the town. The couple's dog, Lassie, was shot in what they believe was retaliation for their return.
- Mladen Tadić runs a bar and bakery in Kozarac and is touch with his brother, Dušan, serving out his prison sentence in Germany.

Petko and Gordana Grubač

- Petko and Gordana still live in Bijeljina. They plan never to return to Konjic.
- Advocates of a truth commission plan to introduce legislation for the commission's creation.

RWANDA

- Leon Nsengimana's case has been brought to the attention of the Rwanda government by Amnesty International. Authorities promised his file would soon be transmitted to the court.
- Preliminary *gacaca* sessions were held in May 2001 for those without case files or whose files are incomplete. In one session, four suspects held in prison for more than four years were released. Real *gacaca* trials have not yet started.
- A documentary about the Rwanda Tribunal, produced by U.S.-backed Internews and directed by filmmaker Mandy Jacobson, began airing

across Rwanda in 2001. In June, residents of Taba were stunned to see the film, which showed their former mayor Jean-Paul Akayesu on trial for genocide.

- Laurent Kabila, the head of the Democratic Republic of Congo, was assassinated in January 2001. His son, Joseph Kabila, assumed power and has had peace talks with neighboring countries, including Rwanda.

Witness JJ

- Witness JJ lives in Taba. On June 1, the tribunal's appeals court judges dismissed Jean-Paul Akayesu's appeals. He is now serving his sentence.

Anonciata Kavaruganda

- Anonciata lives outside of Brussels. She still hopes to pursue legal action against the United Nations.
- General Romeo Dallaire lives in Canada. He is writing a book about his experiences in Rwanda.
- The trial of Theoneste Bagasora began in April 2002, but was further delayed when Bagasora and his three codefendants refused to leave their cells, claiming they would not receive a fair trial.

THE TRIBUNALS

The Hague Tribunal

- As of June 1, 2001, thirty-eight defendants were behind bars in The Hague. Three more have been provisionally released, pending their trial date. Twenty-six alleged criminals have been indicted but remain at large; an additional twelve secret indictments have not yet been served. Four defendants are now serving jail time in prisons outside The Hague.

The Rwanda Tribunal

- As of June 1, 2001, forty-five defendants were behind bars. Of the eight convicted, six have finished their appeals and are now serving sentences. Eighteen indicted alleged criminals still remain at large.

Judge McDonald

- Judge Gabrielle Kirk McDonald presided over the trial of Japanese Military Sexual Slavery, or "comfort women" trial, in Japan in 2000. She is currently the special counsel on human rights to the chairman of Freeport-McMoRan Copper & Gold, a mining company.

Bill Haglund

- Bill Haglund lives in Seattle and works for Physicians for Human Rights, performing exhumations around the world.

New York City
June 1, 2001

ACKNOWLEDGMENTS

Every page of this book would not have been possible without the support and understanding offered by close friends, understanding colleagues, generous strangers. To you all, I owe a debt of thanks.

In particular, I would like to acknowledge the help given to me by four people whose dedication to their professions caused them to lose their lives in Bosnia and other far-flung lands: Fred Cuny, Leah Melnick, Kurt Schork, and Miguel Gil Moreno de Mora. They remain an inspiration.

Immense thanks must go also to those who allowed their lives to be profiled here: Hasan Nuhanović and his wife Mirza; Hamdo and Firdesa Kahrimanović; Petko and Gordana Grubac; Witness JJ and Anonciata Kavaruganda and her children. They tolerated my persistent questions, unfailingly offered me hospitality, and taught me a great deal about the resiliency of the human soul. This book was inspired by Hasan's life story, and to him I will always be grateful. Gabrielle Kirk McDonald and Bill Haglund also deserve my warmest thanks.

I would never have reported from Bosnia and Rwanda—much less written a book about these two countries—were it not for the *Boston Globe*. I will always be indebted to David Greenway for starting me on my career as a foreign correspondent by dispatching me to the Gulf War. Matt Storin, the *Globe*'s editor-in-chief, deserves my gratitude for assigning me to the *Globe*'s European bureau, where he encouraged me to report on the Balkans in depth and then proved his commitment to the story by visiting Bosnia. Greg Moore, Helen Donovan, and David Shribman were voices of encouragement along the way. John Yemma was a source of strength and guidance as my editor during the Bosnian war; Phil Bennett, a source of inspiration and energy as my editor after the war ended. He deserves my gratitude not only for his fine editing but also for suggesting that I track down war criminals in the first place.

To all those on the staff of the *Globe* library who have tirelessly tracked down facts for me, you most certainly know this book would not have been written without your help.

In Bosnia, I am grateful to Aleksandra Seratlić, for her courage and unflagging energy on so many reporting trips. In Sarajevo, Nela and Mirsad Hosic and Ivan and Hedija Bosak opened their doors to me many times. Amela Filipović and her father, Faruk always showed me good cheer. My reporting colleagues shared knowledge, armored cars, and good company: Christiane Amanpour, Martin Bell, Joel Brand, Ray Bonner, Dan DeLuce, Cathy Jenkins, Dean Murphy, Rod Nordland, John Pomfret, Samantha Power, Thom Shanker, Christine Spolar, Tony Smith, Stacy Sullivan, Neely Tucker, and Tracy Wilkinson. Carol Williams gets special thanks for her keen insights into the former Yugoslavia; Barbara Demick my gratitude for loaning me L. C. Green's *The Contemporary Law of Armed Conflict* and pointing out that war crimes tribunals had the makings of a good story.

In Rwanda, I am deeply indebted to Alison DesForges of Human Rights Watch, who generously gave of her time. Binaifir Nowrojee, also of HRW, paved the way for me to write about the Taba rapes. I am also thankful to Farah Stockman for her help and enthusiasm. Abdel, Agnes, and Ismael were friends as well as translators and drivers; Juvenal and Louise good company. Without the help of Godelieve Mukasarasi, I doubt genocide survivors would have so generously opened their hearts to me.

Special thanks must go to those reporters who cover the tribunals and generously shared their knowledge: Thierry Cruvellier of Ubutabera and Mirko Klarin of International War Report. At the Rwanda Tribunal, I am grateful to the judges, prosecutors, and investigators who explained the court's working to me and to Tom Kennedy, who tracked down testimony and stray details. At the Yugoslav Tribunal, I am similarly indebted to Jim Landale and Paul Risley as well as many prosecutors, investigators, and other staff who generously gave of their time.

I am particularly grateful to have had the good fortune to have had experts in the field—Kelly Dawn Askin, Sheila Berry, Mat Burrows, Alison DesForges, Robert Donia, Herb Okun, Kitty Ross and Bill Stuebner—who read the manuscript and saved me from fatal errors. Thanks also goes to Julia Steinmetz for her insightful comments and general support.

I owe a large debt to Les Gelb and the Council on Foreign Relations, who gave me a home for a year on East 68th Street where I began this book. Alicia Siebenaler provided invaluable research help while I was there; Leigh Gusts and her staff at the Council Library worked hard on my behalf.

Writing is also about retreating, and I am thankful to the Corporation of Yaddo for giving me a quiet, supportive place to work. The Rockefeller Foundation also generously recognized the importance of this project and gave me the honor of spending a month at their Bellagio Study Center writing it. The New York Public Library also made a home for me to do research. The Harvard Center for European Studies was generous in loaning me an office. And I am grateful to the Open Society Institute; this book was supported in part by a grant they gave me.

Many labored to make this book see the light of day. I will forever be in debt to Michael Carlisle, my friend and my agent, who believed in this book and made it a reality. At St. Martin's/Picador USA I was lucky to have an enthusiastic editor in Charles Spicer and a publisher committed to the cause in Frances Coady. Many thanks to Dorsey Mills, Amelie Littell, Bert Yaeger, and others at Picador USA who worked hard on this project.

My friends in New York, Boston, and far-flung parts have been steady and true; I thank you all. In particular, I am grateful to Diane Asadorian, for her loyalty and good humor; Gary Bass, for teaching me about the history of war crimes; Laura Jereski, for reading rough drafts and her keen insight that helped shape them. Tom Keenan deserves thanks for his friendship and creating JustWatch, the e-mail list about international justice where I found many articles. My warmest gratitude goes to Alison Smale, for sharing her knowledge of the Balkans over many dinners and for proofreading the entire first draft of this book. Her husband, Sergei, inspired me with his music and their daughter, Lucy, with her love.

But my greatest thanks of all goes to Peter Canellos, without whose support and love this book would never have been completed. He understood when I had to travel to parts remote and dangerous; he forgave me when I had to retreat and write without interruption. With good humor and keen insight he kept me going through difficult times and his fine editing burnishes many a page. This book is very much the product of his sacrifices. For that, I am forever grateful.

NOTES

PROLOGUE

Interviews
Marko Boškić, Gerald Gahima, Richard von Weizsächer.

Page

xii *Marko "Mačak" Boškić* Macak means tomcat.

xii *identify Boškić as part of the massacre squad* Testimony of Dražen Erdemović, July 5, 1996. International Criminal Tribunal for the Prosecution of Persons Responsible for Serious Violations of International Humanitarian Law Committed in the Territory of Former Yugoslavia,* Case No. IT-95-18-R61 and Case No. IT-95-5-R61. (*Henceforth referred to as ICTY in all the remaining endnotes.)

xiii *Boškić was actually a Bosnian Croat* Erdemović was also a Bosnian Croat.

xiv *as Archbishop Desmond Tutu once put* "Healing a Nation," an interview with James Brittain, ITN, May 1996. Reprinted in Index on Censorship, Vol. 25, No. 5 (September/October 1996), Issue 172.

xv *Where does the boundary fall* These themes are explored in Martha Minow's *Between Vengeance and Forgiveness: Facing History After Genocide and Mass Violence* (Boston: Beacon Press, 1998).

xvii *was later reversed* Michael Walzer, *Just and Unjust Wars* (New York: Basic Books, 1997), pp. 292–293.

xvii *"It is also in the process"* Speech, South African justice Albie Sachs.

CHAPTER 1: BLOOD TIES TO BLOOD FEUDS

Page

4 *"Don't leave a single one alive!"* *Tribunal Update:* No. 197, October 30–November 4, 2000, as posted at Institute for War and Peace Reporting, http://www.iwpr.net.

4 *"and remain passive"* *Ubutabera: International Criminal Tribunal for Rwanda.* No. 31, March 2, 1998, as posted on *Judicial Diplomacy* http://www.diplomaticjudiciaire.com. Also, Lara Santoro, "Rwanda Massacres Were Avoidable, General Says," *Christian Science Monitor*, February 27, 1998.

7 *in foreign debt* Jackson Diehl, "Economic Crises Test Yugoslavia's System," *Washington Post*, February 20, 1986.

8 *dollars and Deutschemarks* Duško Doder, *The Yugoslavs* (New York: Random House, 1987), pp. 79–89.

8 *percent in 1989* Roger Cohen, *Hearts Grown Brutal: Sagas of Sarajevo* (New York: Random House, 1998), p. 105.

10 *"be excluded yet"* Laura Silber and Alan Little, *The Death of Yugoslavia* (New York: Penguin Books, 1995), p. 77.

10 *ultimately into rivals* Cohen, *Hearts Grown Brutal*, p. 18.

11 *as the Bogomils* Robert J. Donia and John V. A. Fine, Jr., *Bosnia and Hercegovina: A Tradition Betrayed* (New York: Columbia University Press, 1994), p. 19.

11 *called themselves Bosnians* Ibid., p. 71.

11 *did not fight on ethnic grounds* Ibid., p. 27.

12 *at Kosovo Polje* Timothy Judah, *The Serbs: History, Myth and the Destruction of Yugoslavia* (New Haven: Yale University Press, 1997), pp. 29–30.

12 *Bosnia until 1463* Ibid., p. 31.

13 *contemporary French traveler* Noel Malcolm, *Bosnia: A Short History* (London: Macmillan, 1994), p. 192.

13 *boasted 170 mosques* *Baedeker's Yugoslavia*, p. 183.

13 *whole-hearted military support* Donia and Fine, *Bosnia and Hercegovina*, pp. 38, 209.

14 *its former glory* Donia and Fine, *Bosnia and Hercegovina*, p. 75.

14 *of the century* Vladimir Dedjier, *The Road to Sarajevo* (London: MacGibbon & Kee, 1967), p. 81.

15 *"in turn upon others"* *The Other Balkan Wars: A 1993 Carnegie Endowment Inquiry in Retrospect* (Washington, D.C.: Carnegie Endowment, 1993), p. 73.

15 *had invaded France* ICTY, Statement of Expert Witness Robert J. Donia Pursuant to Rule 94 bis (A).

15 *of those mobilized* Cohen, *Hearts Grown Brutal*, p. 130.

15 *"Muslim Croats" or "Muslim Serbs"* Malcolm, *Bosnia*, p. 165.

16 *"love their freedom"* *Kozara: Istorijske Fotografije* (Stampa: Beograde, 1989).

16 *settle the dispute* John B. Allcock, John J. Horton, Marko Milivojević, *Yugoslavia in Transition: Choices and Constraints: Essays in Honor of Frank Singleton.* (New York: St. Martin's Press, 1992), p. 51.

17 *including 4,000 children/war criminals of the 1990s* Misha Glenny, *The Fall of Yugoslavia.* (New York: Penguin Books, 1992), p. 81.

17 *killed or starved* Tonči Grbelja and Dušan Osasević, *Istorija za 2 razred srednjeg usmjerenog obrazovanja* (Belgrade: Zavoa za Zdravanje Udzenika, 1989).

17 *and the Partisans* Donia and Fine, *Bosnia and Hercegovina*, p. 142.

18 *and 614, 123 Croats* Ibid., p. 87.

19 *"felt a slippery wound"* Ivan Goran Kovačić, "The Pit" in *Trajno* (Beograde: Petar Kočić, 1976), Chapter VI, p. 24, verses 7–12.

19 *how it arrived* See Ružica Rosandić and Vesna Pejić, eds., *Warfare, Patriotism, Patriarchy: The Analysis of Elementary School Textbooks* (Belgrade: Center for Anti-War Action, 1994). In "History Textbooks Mirrors Their Time," author Dubravka Stojanović concludes: "The textbook for the eighth grade is . . . filled to the brim with massacred people, including even details such as the one about Serbs boiled alive at Jasenovac. These examples go beyond any historical analysis and fall rather under the category of socio-pathological research. And yet, the model of such atrocities, absorbed in early childhood, inevitably encourages aggressiveness and revanchism and can hardly constitute a basis for normal relations with other peoples" (99).

20 *and lumber industries* Historical background on Kozarac has been drawn from the following sources: *Stanovništvo Bosne i Hercegovine, Narodnosmi sastav po naseljima* (Zagreb: *Državni zvod za statistiku Republike Hravtske*, 1995); *Enciklopedija Jugoslavije, Separat o Bosni i Hercegovina* (Zagreb: Jazu, 1983); *Vojna enciklopedija* (Beograde: Vodno-izdavački zavod, 1969), Branislav Begovič, *Sumaska privreda Bosne i Hercegovina, 1918–1941.* (Sarajevo: Institut za istoriju, 1985); Iljas Hadžibegović, *Bosnakoherceogvacki gradovi na rezme /u 19 I 120 stoljeca.* (Sarajevo: Ostobodjerje Public, 1991); *Olsobedilački rat naroda Jugoslavije 1941–1945, knj. 112.* (Beograde: Vojno-istorijski institut, 1958); *Bosna i Hercegovina od najstarijih vremena do kraja drugog svjetskog rata (grupa autora).* (Sarajevo: Veselin Magle, 1994, 1997); *Kozara u narodnooslobodilačkoj borbi i socijalističkoj revoluciji 1941–1945* (Prijedor: Naucni skup, 1980).

21 *"Jew or a Serb"* Silber and Little, *The Death of Yugoslavia*, p. 92.

22 *"of reformist forces"* *Oslobodjenje*, July 30, 1990.

23 *"phase of agony"* Silber and Little, *The Death of Yugoslavia*, p. 139.

24 *was predominantly Serb* ICTY, Opinion and Judgment, Prosecutor v. Duško Tadić aka, "*Dule*" (Case No. IT-94-I-T, May 7, 1997), pp. 39–40.

25 *"Serb autonomous regions"* Ibid., p. 35.

26 *the rest Croat and Serb* In 1991, Konjic municipality was 54.3 percent Muslim, 26.2 percent Croat, 15 percent Serb, 3 percent Yugoslav, and 1.3 percent other. ICTY, Judgment, *Prosecutor v. Zejnil Delalić et al.* (Case No. IT-96-21-T, November 16, 1998), p. 49.

27 *17.4 percent Croat* Ibid., p. 42.

28 *"there is war"* Silber and Little, *The Death of Yugoslavia*, p. 237.

28 *of the Yugoslav Federation* Ibid., p. 241.

28 *answering to Belgrade* ICTY, Judgment, *Prosecutor v. Duško Tadić aka "Dule"* (May 7, 1997), p. 45.

29 *a greater Serbia* Silber and Little, *The Death of Yugoslavia*, p. 240; Tadić, p. 39.

29 *the Bosnian Serb Army* ICTY, McDonald Dissent, *Prosecutor v. Duško Tadić* (Case No.: IT-94-1-T, May 7, 1997), p. 7.

29 *several dozen dead* Silber and Little, *The Death of Yugoslavia*, p. 247.

30 *"there will be no war"* Quoted in Roger Cohen, "Conflict in the Balkans: The Overview," *New York Times*, November 1, 1995.

30 *by the United States* April 6 was the fifty-first anniversary of Belgrade's bombing by the Germans.

31 *had been "liberated"* Mark Thompson, *Forging War: The Media in Serbia, Croatia and Hercegovina* (Bedfordshire, England: University of Luton Press, 1999), p. 74.

CHAPTER 2: THE TRIUMPH OF THE UNDERWORLD

Interviews

Hamdo and Firdesa Kahrimanović; Omarska camp inmates including Smail Jakupović, Muharem Murselović, Jadranka Cigelj, Tesma Elezović, Nusreta Sivac; Hasan Nuhanović, and other Srebrenica survivors including Fatima Huseinović; Petko and Gordana Grubač, Witness R and other Čelebići survivors; Fred Eckhard, UN spokesman.

Page

34 *with non-Serbs* United Nations Security Council, Final Report of the United Nations Commission of Experts Established Pursuant to Security Council 780 (1992), Annex V, *The Prijedor Report*, S/1994/674/Add 2 (Vol. V. December 28, 1994), p. 19.

34 *campaign of "genocide"* Role of propaganda is discussed in the ICTY, Judgment *Prosecutor v. Duško Tadić* (Case No.: IT-94-1-T, May 7, 1997), pp. 30–35.

35 *bank and the radio station* Ibid., p. 51.

36 *Bosnian Serb Army instead* Ibid., p. 42. The judges note: "However, most if not all, of the commanding officers of the old JNA who found themselves stationed with their units in Bosnia and Herzegovina on 18 May 1992, nearly all Serbs, remained in command of those units throughout 1992 and 1993 and did not return to Serbia. This was so whether [they] were in fact in origin Bosnian Serbs." In the Čelebići case, judges also ruled that JNA troops simply reenlisted in the Bosnian Serb Army. See the ICTY, Judgment in *Prosecutor v. Zejnil Delalić et al.*, November 16, 1998, pp. 47–48.

37 *mainly Muslim SDA party* ICTY, Judgment, *Prosecutor v. Zejnil Delalić et al.*, Case No.: IT-96-21-T, November 16, 1998, pp. 50–54.

40 *on both ends* ICTY, *Prosecutor v. Duško Tadić*, May 7, 1997.

41 *"Not small at all"* Rezak Hukanović, *The Tenth Circle of Hell: A Memoir*

of Life in the Death Camps of Bosnia (New York: New Republic, 1993), p. 30.

42 *and kill them* Kovacević, Drljača, and Milomir Stakić were indicted for war crimes. See ICTY Case No. IT-97-24 (http://www.un.org/icty/index.htm).

42 *often singled out* Hukanović, *The Tenth Circle of Hell*, pp. 29, 88.

42 *commander Željko Mejakić* Željko Mejakić was indicted for war crimes at the Omarska Camp ICTY Case No. IT-95-4.

42 *"you beat me?"* Michael Scharf, *Balkan Justice: The Story Behind the First International War Crimes Since Nuremberg* (Durham, North Carolina: Carolina Academic Press, 1997), p. 160.

42 *his testicles off* ICTY, Judgment, *Prosecutor v. Duško Tadić*, May 7, 1997, p. 75.

43 *however, contrived to bully him* Kahrimanović believes he was released with several other men in July to impress Western aid groups who were suspicious of the camps. Other Kozarac residents, however, have suggested that Drljača ordered him released. The Tadić family suspects Kahrimanović lied about seeing Dule Tadić at Omarska as a way of protecting Drljača.

43 *later told me* Drljača, on at least one occasion, used his power to get a friend's relative released from Omarska. The Bosnian Serb who told me this story said Drljača did so less out of charity than as a demonstration of his power.

44 *were beaten frequently* For details of Čelibići camp. *See* ICTY, Testimony, Petko Grubač, Gordana Grubač *Prosecutor v. Zejnil Delalić et al.*, Case No. IT-96-21-T, August 12–13, 1997.

47 *Omarska camp appeared* Roy Gutman of *Newsday* won a Pulitzer Prize for his reporting about the camps.

47 *Omarska and Trnopolje camps* Ed Vulliamy of the *Guardian* and reporters with ITN News.

47 U.S. Senate Foreign Relations Committee Report, in possession of author.

47 *war crimes in Bosnia* Silber and Little, *The Death of Yugoslavia*, 285.

48 *"to be created"* Speech to the London Conference, found at www.un.org/icty/path.htm.

48 *"soon befall us"* Mirko Klarin "Nuremberg Now!" *Naša Borba*, May 16, 1991.

48 *keeping their promises* Cohen, *Hearts Grown Brutal*, p. 231.

48 *of humanitarian aid* Resolution 770, passed in August 1992, was adopted under Chapter VII of the UN Charter. It called upon states to take "nationally, or through regional agencies or arrangements all measures necessary" to deliver humanitarian aid in Bosnia. When NATO planners estimated that 100,000 troops would be needed to do so, UN member states had second thoughts. The Security Council then passed Resolution 776 in September 1992, which gave UNPRO-

FOR a mandate to protect humanitarian relief convoys in Bosnia. See William J. Durch and James A. Schear, "Faultlines: UN Operations in the Former Yugoslavia," *UN Peacekeeping: American Policy and the Uncivil Wars of the 1990s* (New York: St. Martin's Press, 1996), pp. 227–229.

48 *"no-fly" zone* UN Resolution 781, October 9, 1992.

49 *the most demanding* Ivo H. Daalder, "Knowing When to Say No: The Development of US Policy for Peacekeeping," *UN Peacekeeping*, p. 35.

49 *mission in Bosnia* On August 13, 1992, the UN Security Council passed Resolution 770, which provided for UN troops to be sent into Bosnia under Chapter VII of the UN's charter. On September 14, the Security Council passed Resolution 776, which gave the peacekeepers the mandate to protect humanitarian relief convoys. The resolutions were based on the premise that impartial intervention was nonintervention and should be seen as such by parties on the ground. Durch and Shear, "Faultlines," pp. 228–229.

51 *rich silver mines* Donia and Fine, p. 30.

51 *three times Turkish* Jiricek and Radonjic, "Istorija Srba," Vol. 2 (Beograde: 1912), pp. 324–325.

52 *practiced on them* UN Report of the Secretary-General Pursuant to General Assembly Resolution 53/35 (1998). *Srebrenica Report*, p. 14.

52 *"we have killed"* quoted in Chuck Sudetic, "After Eight Months, First Relief Reaches Bosnian Town," *New York Times*, November 29, 1992.

52 *city into submission* Chuck Sudetic, *Blood and Vengeance* (New York: W. W. Norton, 1998), p. 188.

53 *of Serb civilians* *Srebrenica Report*, p. 14.

55 *lice were rampant* UNHCR Report, February 1993, quoted in Jan Willem Honig and Norbert Both. *Srebrenica: Record of a War Crime* (Harmondsworth, England: Penguin Books, 1996), p. 82.

55 *children be evacuated* Honig and Both, *Srebrenica*, p. 84.

56 *evacuated to safety* *Srebrenica Report*, 15.

57 *prepared to surrender* Ibid., pp. 18–19.

57 *Iraq in 1991* The UN Security Council, acting under Chapter VII of its charter, passed Resolution 819 declaring Srebrenica to be a UN-protected "safe area" free "from armed attack or any other hostile act." In June 1991 the UN Security Council extended the mandate to include deterring attacks, promoting the withdrawal of all but government forces, monitoring cease-fires, occupying some key points on the ground, and acting in self-defense when necessary. It also allowed UN member states to "support UNPROFOR in the performance of its mandate." "In practice, these resolutions were interpreted to mean that UNPROFOR would take action if its forces in or near a safe area were subject to attack and could call for NATO air support in those circumstances. They were not interpreted by UNPROFOR's leadership or its major troop contributors to give the operation general responsibility for safe areas,

nor were they interpreted to give NATO carte blanche to do so," write Durch and Schear, "Faultlines," p. 230.

58 *Goražde and Sarajevo* UN Security Council, Resolution 824, May 6, 1993.

CHAPTER 3: SINCE UNHAPPILY WE CANNOT ALWAYS AVOID WARS

Interviews

Judge Gabrielle McDonald, Bill Haglund, Michael Scharf; Bosnians as quoted and others interviewed during my time in Bosnia from 1994 to 1998; Felice Gaer, Jacob Blaustein Center for Human Rights; Human Rights Watch staff; Minna Schrag, former tribunal prosecutor; Cherif Bassiouni, former head of the UN Commission of Experts; Ben Ferencz, former Nuremberg prosecutor; Judge Antonio Cassese, tribunal staff; Sylvie Junod of the International Committee for the Red Cross.

Page

61 *a "gross deception"* Letter obtained by author.

62 *an egg, $3* Barbara Demick, *Logavina Street: Life and Death in a Sarajevo Neighborhood* (Kansas City, Missouri: Andrews and McMeel, 1996), p. 50.

62 *crime to me* This bombing was never part of either indictment against Karadžić.

62 *a war crime* Some officials of the UN Protection Forces early in the war questioned whether Sarajevo was besieged, as humanitarian convoys were able to enter. But The Hague tribunal disagreed, going on to prosecute Karadžić and Mladić for besieging the city. For a longer discussion of Sarajevo and siege warfare, see Aryeh Neier's *War Crimes: Brutality, Genocide, Terror, and the Struggle for Justice* (New York: Random House, 1998), Chapter 10.

63 *attacks on civilians* The Yugoslav war crimes tribunal has charged Karadžić and Mladić with crimes relating to the shelling of Sarajevo.

63 *our collective memory* Julia Preston, "UN to Set Up Tribunal on Yugoslav War Crimes," *Washington Post*, February 23, 1993.

63 *the new court* UN Security Council Resolution 808. For more detailed discussion, see Michael Scharf, *Balkan Justice: The Story Behind the First International War Crimes Trial Since Nuremberg* (Durham, North Carolina: Carolina Academic Press, 1997), pp. 55–63.

63 *"of law, I hope"* Barry Schweid, "Serbs Must Answer for War Atrocities, Eagleburger Says," Associated Press, December 17, 1992.

64 *in the Balkans* "Foreign Policy, Stupid," Editorial, *Christian Science Monitor*, January 15, 1993.

65 *action was necessary* Report of the Secretary General Pursuant to Paragraph 2 of Security Resolution 808 (1993) S/25704, May 3, 1993. p. 4.

65 *Colin Powell* Colin Powell, *My American Journey* (New York: Random House, 1995), p. 576.

65 *to the UN* From author's notes of the speech, April 5, 1999.

65 *the former Yugoslavia* Report of the Secretary General Pursuant to Paragraph 2 of Security Council Resolution 808 (1993), S/25704, May 3, 1993, p. 7–8.

66 *those who surrender* Deuteronomy XX, 10–14.

66 *intent to destroy* Caroline Moorhead, *Dunant's Dream: War, Switzerland and the History of the Red Cross* (New York: Carroll & Graf, 1998), p. 23.

67 *"laws of arms" Henry V,* Act 4, Scene 7, lines 1–2.

67 *the Upper Rhine* George Schwarzenberger, *International Law as Applied by International Courts and Tribunals: The Law of Armed Conflicts* (London: Stevens & Sons, Ltd., 1968), pp. 462–466.

67 *"only by accident"* As quoted in Caroline Moorehead, *Dunant's Dream, p. 25.*

67 *as killed them* McBride, Sean. "The Legality of Weapons for Societal Destruction," *Studies and Essay in Honor of Jean Pictet,* ed. Christopher Swinarski (Geneva: Martinus Nijhoff Publishers, 1984), p. 401. Dumdum bullets were among the first bullets to be banned. See also Moorehead, *Dunant's Dream,* pp. 168–169.

68 *customs of war* Moorehead, *Dunant's Dream,* pp. 37–38.

68 *that surrounded Solferino* For more on Dunant and the battle, see Moorehead, *Dunant's Dream,* p. 27–29.

68 *"horrors of war?"* Henry Dunant, *A Memory of Solferino* (Geneva: International Committee of the Red Cross/American Red Cross, 1986), pp. 19, 41, 127.

69 *governing wartime behavior* The Red Cross carries on in this role today.

69 *and mutton-chop whiskers* "The portrait painted to celebrate the occasion, by Charles Edouard Armand-Dumaresque, shows a gathering of dark-suited men with beards, mutton-chop whiskers and lavish moustaches." Moorehead, *Dunant's Dream,* p. 44.

69 *know it today* The developing body of law did nothing to deter the outbreak of war by its example. In 1907 the Fourth Hague Convention codified the laws of war on land and established norms for wars between differing states, or international wars, but World War I broke out nonetheless. See Theodore Meron, *War Crimes Law Comes of Age: Essays* (Oxford: Clarendon Press, 1998), p. 191. The Geneva Conventions were revised in 1906, 1924, and 1949. Two additional protocols were added in 1977.

69 *"worthy of prosecution"* Aryeh Neier, *War Crimes: Brutality, Genocide, Terror and the Struggle for Justice* (New York: Random House, 1998), p. 19.

70 *top Nazi leaders* Gary Bass, *Stay the Hand of Vengeance: The Politics of War Crime Tribunals* (Princeton, New Jersey: Princeton University Press, 2000), p. 180.

70 *to extradite him* Ferencz, "From Nuremberg to Rome."

70 *ended in fiasco* Bass, *Stay the Hand of Vengeance.* See Chapters 3 and 4.

70 *a Nuremberg prosecutor* Telford Taylor, *The Anatomy of the Nuremberg Trials: A Personal Memoir* (New York: Alfred Knopf, 1992), p. 5.

70 *seventy-hour weeks* Joseph Persico, *Nuremberg: Infamy on Trial* (New York: Penguin Books, 1995), p. 111.

70 *evaluated as evidence* published in the pamphlet, "International Military Tribunal: The Nuremberg War Crimes Trials," (Oberlandesgericht Nürnberg, Further Strasse 110, 90429 Nürnberg.)

71 *eloquently put it* Bass, *Stay the Hand of Vengeance,* p. 203.

71 *seven prison terms* Text of Justice Jackson's Report to President Truman on the Nuremberg Trial, *New York Times,* October 16, 1946, p. 23.

71 *to President Truman* Ibid.

71 *the present day* Tina Rosenberg, "Tipping the Scales of Justice," *War Crimes: The Legacy of Nuremberg,* ed. Belinda Cooper (New York: TV Books, 1999), p. 276.

71 *"at the time"* Interview with author, 1998. See also Jörg Friedrich, "Nuremberg and the Germans," *War Crimes: The Legacy of Nuremberg,* ed. Belinda Cooper (New York: TV Books, 1999), pp. 87–117.

71 *never prosecuted before* Scharf, *Balkan Justice,* pp. 11–13.

72 *firebombing of Dresden* The Soviet Union insisted that the Germans be charged with the massacres at the Katyn Forest, according to Scharf, *Balkan Justice,* p. 12.

72 *"for its sins"* Rebecca West, "Greenhouse with Cyclamens II," *A Train of Powder* (New York: Viking Press, 1904), p. 3.

72 *"is the truth"* Scharf, *Balkan Justice,* p. 54.

72 *larger, planned attack* Ibid., p. 14.

72 *rape, torture, and imprisonment* Already defined as crimes against humanity were murder, extermination, enslavement, deportation, persecution on political racial and religious grounds, and other inhumane acts committed in either an international armed conflict (two warring states) or an internal armed conflict (a civil war). Ibid., pp. 57–63.

72 *an ethnic group* Diane F. Orentlicher, "Grave Breaches," *Crimes of War,* ed. Roy Gutman and David Rieff (New York: W. W. Norton, 1999), pp. 153–154.

73 *ten articles long* Jean Pictet, "The Formation of International Humanitarian Law" *International Review of the Red Cross,* Jan.–Feb. 1985. Annex 2, p. 12.

74 *to prosecute them* There is a duty to bring those who have committed grave breaches to trial. The Torture and Genocide Conventions impose a similar duty to bring offenders to trial.

74 *weren't quite sure* Geoffrey Best, *War and Law since 1945* (Oxford: Oxford University Press, 1994), p. 176.

74 *interpret the conventions* Jean S. Pictet, ed. *The Geneva Conventions of*

12 August 1949 Commentary: IV Geneva Convention Relative to the Protection of Civilian Persons in a Time of War (Geneva: International Committee of the Red Cross, 1958), p. 6.

75 *ongoing peace talks* The Commission, headed by Fritz Kalshoven, was given little money and staff. Kalshoven's successor, Cherif Bassiouni, frustrated with efforts to undermine the group, raised money himself—$1.4 million from private foundations—to document atrocities in Yugoslavia. He eventually created a detailed database with some 50,000 entries that served as the foundation for the Yugoslavia Tribunal's first indictments.

75 *help exhume it* For details of the exhumation, see Eric Stover and Gilles Peress, *The Graves: Srebrenica and Vukovar* (Zurich, Berlin, New York: Scalo, 1998).

76 *"they never forget"* Eric Stover, "The Grave at Vukovar," *Smithsonian Magazine*, March 1997.

77 *the Bosnian Croats* At the time there were actually six sides: Bosnian Muslim businessman Fikret Abdić launched his own breakaway state near Bihać, where his supporters would fight supporters of Izetbegović.

78 *on the bench* William Horne, "Judging Tadić: Former U.S. District Judge in Houston Answers State Department's Call," *American Lawyer*, September 1995, http://www.courttv.com/casefiles/warcrimes/reports/judge.html.

78 *"a Negress," he failed* Ibid.

80 *rules in all* Scharf, *Balkan Justice*, p. 67.

80 *"of political expediency"* "War Crimes Without Punishment," *New York Times*, February 8, 1994.

81 *end of 1993* William J. Durch and James A. Schear, "Faultlines: UN Operations in the Former Yugoslavia," *UN Peacekeeping: American Policy and the Uncivil Wars of the 1990s*, ed. William J. Durch (New York: St. Martin's Press/A Henry L. Stimpson Center Book, 1996), p. 235.

81 *"killing each other"* Roger Cohen, *Hearts Grown Brutal: Sagas of Sarajevo* (New York: Random House, 1998), p. 244.

82 *no-fly zone* American F-16s shot down four Serb jets after they bombed Novi Travnik.

CHAPTER 4: THE LAND OF 1,000 GRAVES

Interviews

Anonciata Kavaruganda, Guilliaume Kavaruganda, Julien Kavaruganda, Witness JJ. The following also helped paint a picture for me of the genocide: Josue Kayijaho, Ibuka; Charles Kagenza, survivor of Nyange massacre; the Reverend Ubald Rugirangoga of Kigali's College of St. Andre; the Reverend Octave Ugirashebuja; Boniface Sogokuru, survivor of Shyorongi massacre; Godelieve Mukasarasi of Taba; Innocent Niyonabura, of CLADHO, a human rights group; Jean-Paul Biramvu, Rwandan lawyer and human rights activist. Insight into the mind of the killers was gained from interviewing men who confessed to me: Emmanuel Habimana and Jean Hakizamungu, incarcerated in Kibungo Prison.

Page

84 *mile after Bangladesh* B. W. Ndiaye, "Question of the Violation of Human Rights and Fundamental Freedoms in Any Part of the World, with Particular Reference to Colonial and Other Dependent Countries and Territories. Extrajudicial, Summary or Arbitrary Executions," UN E/CN.4/1994/7 Add.1, p. 6.

84 *since the mid-1980s* Children and Women of Rwanda: A Situational Analysis of Social Sectors. UNICEF, 1997, p. 3.

86 *have mixed ancestry* David Newbury and Catherine Newbury, "An Inquiry into the Historical Preconditions of the Rwandan Genocide," as quoted in the Organization of African Unity's (OAU) report, *The International Panel of Eminent Personalities to Investigate the 1994 Genocide in Rwanda and the Surrounding Events*, July 7, 2000 at http://www.oau-oau.org/Document/ipep.

86 *Europeans in Africa* Today Hutu and Tutsi Rwandans have vastly differing perceptions of their history. I have drawn heavily on the accounts given by Alison DesForges, an American scholar and human rights activist with Human Rights Watch, in *Leave None to Tell the Story: Genocide in Rwanda* (New York: Human Rights Watch, 1999).

86 *Hutu, or followers* In this section I am indebted to Alison DesForges, *Leave None to Tell the Story: Genocide in Rwanda* (New York: Human Rights Watch, 1999), pp. 31–38.

87 *was among them* Gerard Prunier, *The Rwanda Crisis: History of a Genocide, 1959–1994* (London: Hurst and Company, 1995), p. 7.

87 *intelligence and ability* Philip Gourevitch, *We Wish to Inform You That Tomorrow We Will Be Killed with Our Families: Stories from Rwanda* (New York: Farrar, Straus & Giroux, 1998), pp. 50–52.

87 *Garden of Eden* Gerard Prunier, *The History of a Genocide: 1959–1994* (London: Hurst and Company, 1995), p. 8.

87 *in the northwest* Alison DesForges, interview. See also Gourevitch, *We Wish to Inform You That Tomorrow We Will Be Killed with Our Families*, pp. 48–55.

88 *the neighboring Congo* For a full discussion of this, see Adam Hochschild, *King Leopold's Ghost: A Story of Greed, Terror and Heroism in Colonial Africa* (New York: Houghton Mifflin, 1998).

88 *43.2 millimeters wide* Alan Zarembo, "Judgment Day," *Harper's*, April 1997.

88 *Tutsi, or Twa* Opinions differ as to whether Rwandans declared themselves along ethnic lines or were assigned to different groups, depending on the number of cows they owned. See OAU report, Chapter 2, p. 2.

88 *1 percent Twa* DesForges, *Leave None to Tell the Story*, p. 37.

88 *around on litters* Rosalind Halsey Carr, *Land of a Thousand Hills: My Life in Rwanda* (New York: Penguin Putnam, 2000), pp. 77–78.

88 *of Rwandan society* DesForges, *Leave None to Tell the Story*, p. 37.

89 *from the Hutu* International Panel of Eminent Personalities to Investigate the 1994 Genocide in Rwanda and the Surrounding Areas, July 7, 2000, OAU report, Chapter 2, p. 3.

89 *country's "suppressed masses"* Alain Destexhe, *Rwanda and Genocide*, p. 43.

90 *Hutu, looked on* Ibid.

90 *"inyenzi," or cockroaches* OAU report, Chapter 3, p. 2.

90 *to reclaim power* DesForges, *Leave None to Tell the Story*, p. 39.

90 *aided those outside* Ibid.

90 *"by another one"* Prunier, *History of Genocide*, p. 53.

91 *the civil service* Destexhe, *Rwanda and Genocide*, p. 44.

91 *left their country* Interview, Alison DesForges

92 *right to complain* UNICEF, "Children and Women of Rwanda: A Situational Analysis," 1997, pp. 102–106.

92 *"there is discord"* "Survey on Violence Against Women in Rwanda." Kigali, December 1999, p. 32.

93 *established in 1975* Mouvement Révolutionnaire National pour le Développement (MRND).

94 *became successful entrepreneurs* OAU Report, Chapter 4, pp. 2–3.

94 *exports, dropped sharply* Government earnings from coffee exports dropped from $144 million in 1985 to $30 million in 1993. OAU report, Chapter 5, p. 1.

95 *just four years* Mahmood Mamdani, *When Victims Become Killers: Colonialism, Nativism and the Genocide in Rwanda* (Princeton, New Jersey: Princeton University Press, 2001), p. 148.

95 *to feed themselves* Ibid., p. 2.

95 *"akazu," for advice* DesForges, *Leave None to Tell the Story*, p. 44.

95 *supporting the country* The OAU report criticizes foreign aid donors for failing to use their dollars correctly, concluding: "Few Rwandans felt the benefit of foreign assistance" (Chapter 5, p. 3). The authors also quote a study that concludes: "The priorities of aid in the early 1990s were largely unrelated to the challenges of increasing polarization, inequality, hatred, and violence Rwanda was facing at the time."

95 *border into Rwanda* DesForges, *Leave None to Tell the Story*, p. 44.

96 *the Rwandan Army* The French troops would remain for three years; Belgian troops for a month.

97 *new RPF incursion* As noted in OAU report, Chapter 6, p. 4, drawing on work done by Alison DesForges.

97 *of the Tutsi* Gourevitch, *We Wish to Inform You That Tomorrow We Will Be Killed with Our Families*, p. 93.

97 *well-orchestrated attacks* OAU report, Chapter 7, p. 3.

98 *to undermine them* Ibid.

98 *"a Tutsi woman"* "Shattered Lives: Sexual Violence During the Rwandan Genocide and Its Aftermath," Human Rights Watch/Africa, Human Rights Watch Women's Rights Project, Federation Internationale des Lignes des Droits de L'Homme (New York: Human Rights Watch, 1998), p. 17.

99 *to be dead* Copy of a letter given to the author.

99 *times in size* OAU report, Chapter 12, p. 4. "French troops assisted in the expansion of the Rwandan army from about 6,000 on the eve of the invasion to some 35,000 three years later."

99 *to Kalashnikov rifles* DesForges, *Leave None to Tell the Story*, p. 97.

100 *"of the Constitution? No."* Letter given to author.

100 *"of our country"* Quoted in DesForges, *Leave None to Tell the Story*, p. 73.

100 *off worrying cables* OAU report, Chapter 9, p. 4.

100 *"certain ethnic group"* Report by B. W. Ndiaye, Special Rapporteur, on his mission to Rwanda from April 8 to 17, 1993. "Question of the Violation of Human Rights and Fundamental Freedoms in Any Part of the World, with Particular Reference to Colonial and Other Dependent Countries and Territories," August 11, 1993, E/CN.4/1994/7/Add.1, p. 23.

101 *help implement them* The UN Security Council authorized UNAMIR on October 5, 1993. Its operation was dependent on the consent of the parties. Troops were to monitor the cease-fire; oversee a new integrated army; remove land mines; repatriate refugees; and help with humanitarian assistance. See Matthew J. Vaccaro, "The Politics of Genocide: Peacekeeping and Rwanda," *UN Peacekeeping, American Policy and Uncivil Wars of the 1990s*, ed. William J. Durch (New York: St. Martin's Press, 1996), p. 376.

101 *"what you deserve"* Xerox copy of Kangura cartoon (no date) in possession of author.

101 *of peacekeeping costs* Linda Melvern, *A People Betrayed: The Role of the West in Rwanda's Genocide* (London: Zed Books, Ltd., 2000), p. 77.

101 *waiting television crews* William J. Durch, "Introduction to Anarchy: Humanitarian Intervention and 'State-Building' in Somalia," *UN Peacekeeping, American Policy, and the Uncivil Wars of the 1990s*, ed. William J. Durch (New York: St. Martin's Press, 1996), p. 311.

102 *Bosnia as well* The Rwandan peacekeeping mission, created by UN Resolution 872, was a Chapter VI mission in which peacekeepers go in with the consent of the host party. The Bosnian mission was a Chapter VII mission, in which a peacekeeping mission can be imposed by the Security Council and has wider responsibilities.

102 *pushed for 500* William Shawcross, *Deliver Us From Evil: Warlords and Peacekeepers in a World of Endless Conflict* (London: Bloomsbury Publishing, Plc, 2000), p. 107.

102 *a small mission* UN Security Council Resolution 872.

102 *one from Ghana* Shawcross, *Deliver Us From Evil*, p. 108.

102 *peacekeepers in Bosnia* Melvern, *A People Betrayed*, p. 79.

102 *them Belgian soldiers* DesForges, *Leave None to Tell the Story*, p. 141.

103 *"such a predicament"* Romeo Dallaire, "The End of Innocence," *Hard Choices: Moral Dilemmas in Humanitarian Intervention*, ed. Jonathan Moore (Baltimore, Maryland: Rowman & Littlefield Publishers, Inc., 1998), pp. 73, 77.

103 *never formally responded* "Report of the Independent Inquiry into the Actions of the United Nations during the 1994 Genocide in Rwanda," December 15, 1999, p. 5. (http://www.un.org/News/ossg/rwanda_report.htm.) Dallaire sent a draft set of rules of engagement for his troops to the UN asking for the secretariat's approval.

103 *exchange for protection* -Copy in possession of author.

103 *seize the cache* January 11, 1994, Cable to Baril\DPKO\UNATIONS from Dallaire\UNAMIR\KIGALI. Copy in possession of author.

103 *with President Habyarimana* According to the OAU report, Dallaire tussled over the issue of weapons caches with Iqbal Riza, Assistant Secretary General in the UN Department of Peacekeeping Operations. Riza had written the response although it was signed by Annan, as was typical UN procedure. The OAU report would fault Riza for making the decision about the mandate, "apparently without consulting the Security Council." Chapter 13, p. 6. Also, January 12, 1994, cable to Booh-Booh from Romeo Dallaire, UNAMIR\KIGALI from Annan\UNATIONS, New York. Copy in possession of author.

103 *the Kigali stadium* DesForges, *Leave None to Tell the Story*, p. 155.

103 *of ethnic violence* February 2 cable from Roger Booh-Booh to Kofi Annan, cited in UN "Independent Inquiry," p. 11.

104 *arms and recruits* Interview with General Romeo Dallaire, March 2001, New York. Human Rights Watch published a report at the time showing Rwanda had entered into an arms deal with Egypt and South Africa.

104 *and Joseph Kavaruganda* February 17, 1994, UNAMIR Military Division Interoffice Memorandum. Copy in possession of author.

104 *remains unclear* Anonciata Kavaruganda says the UN never told her family of the Death Escadron plot. General Dallaire, however, believes Joseph was told he was targeted for assassination.

105 *"have catastrophic consequences"* "Independent Inquiry," p. 9.

105 *Hadn't they heard?* Controversy continues over who shot down the aircraft. It had been believed that the plane had been shot down by extremist Hutu who had turned against the president because he had agreed to share power with the RPF. But Michael Hourigan, a former UN investigator, has said his investigators had found three informants

who claimed to have been part of an elite strike team created by the RPF to shoot the plane down. They alleged that Paul Kagame, the former head of the RPA and now Rwanda's president, was the "operations commando" of the assassination. The Rwanda tribunal has ordered the memo containing these allegations to be submitted to the court but to be sealed. The tribunal has declined to investigate further, saying the plane crash was outside their mandate. See Steven Edwards, *Washington Post*, "Memo Contradicts UN Claims on Assassination Probe," March 31, 2000.

CHAPTER 5: OUR ENEMY IS ONE

Interviews

Anonciata Kavaruganda, Guilliaume Kavaruganda, Julien Kavaruganda, Witness JJ. The following, among many others, also helped paint a picture for me of the genocide: Josue Kayijaho, Charles Kagenza, survivor of Nyange massacre; the Reverend Ubald Rugirangoga of Kigali's College of St. Andre; the Reverend Octave Ugirashebuja, survivor of Centre Christus Massacre; Boniface Sogokuru, survivor of Shyorongi massacre; Godelieve Mukasarasi of Taba; Innocent Niyonabura, of CLADHO, a human rights group; Jean-Paul Biramvu, Rwandan lawyer and human rights activist. Insight into the mind of the killers was gained from interviewing men who have confessed to me to taking part: Emmanuel Habimana and Jean Hakizamungu, incarcerated in Kibungo Prison. Also helpful were Sheila Berry and Ambassador David Scheffer of the State Department's Office on War Crimes Issues during the Clinton Administration, former State Department assistant secretary John Shattuck, and former chief prosecutor Richard Goldstone. International Criminal Tribunal for Rwanda (ICTR) investigators gave me information confirming Captain Kabera's role; General Romeo Dallaire.

Page

110 *saw Joseph Kavaruganda* The Kavaruganda family was careful to write down what happened to them. This re-creation is based on the chronology they assembled, interviews with them and interviews with ICTR investigators.

110 *up her vagina* Alison DesForges, *Leave None to Tell the Story* (New York: Human Rights Watch, March 1999), p. 190.

114 *OPPOSITION HAS OCCURRED* Copy in possession of author. Cable is from Roger Booh-Booh, the special representative to the UN Secretary General in Rwanda.

114 *to exterminate them* Testimony of Jean Kambanda, International Criminal Tribunal for Rwanda (ICTR). Judgment, *Prosecutor v. Jean Kambanda* Case No.: ICTR-97-23.

115 *including seven priests* Interview with survivor Octave Ugirashebuja, *African Rights: Death, Despair and Defiance* (London: African Rights, 1995), pp. 863–865.

115 *and party militias* "The International Panel of Eminent Personalities to Investigate the 1994 Genocide in Rwanda and Surrounding Events," or OAU report, Chapter 14, p. 4.

116 *confiscating their weapons* International Criminal Tribunal for Rwanda (ICTR) Judgment, *Prosecutor v. Jean-Paul Akayesu*, Case No. ICTR-96-4-T, September 2, 1998, p. 91.

116 *mandate was granted* The Security Council, for whatever reasons, had "blurred, sanitized the summaries from Boutros-Ghali's staff depicting mutual and chaotic killing." Julia Preston, "Rwandans Confound UN Security Council: Humanitarian Impulse as Mission Impossible," *Washington Post*, May 8, 1994.

117 *and provide assistance* OAU report, Chapter 15, p. 1.

118 *escalated almost immediately* Holly Burckhalter, Physicians for Human Rights. Testimony to Congressional Subcommittee on Human Rights and International Operations, May 5, 1998.

118 *in a single afternoon* DesForges, *Leave None to Tell the Story*, pp. 617–618.

119 *"for Assistance/Protection"* Copy in possession of author.

119 *thought of reinforcements* Melvern, *A People Betrayed*, p. 139.

119 *and destroy them* DesForges, *Leave None to Tell the Story*, p. 201.

119 *"is the Tutsi"* Ibid., p. 203.

119 *"then break it"* As quoted in the documentary, "The UN and Rwanda: Abandoned to Genocide," produced by Bronwyn Adcock of the Australian Broadcasting Corporation.

120 *enemy, the Tutsi* DesForges, *Leave None to Tell the Story*, p. 273.

120 *of their treason* Ibid., p. 273.

120 *"judgment unto them"* ICTR, Judgment, *Prosecutor v. Jean-Paul Akayesu*, p. 119.

120 *was the enemy* Ibid., p. 139.

121 *"to stay here"* Author's interview with Witness JJ. See also ICTR, Testimony, Witness JJ, *Prosecutor v. Jean-Paul Akayesu*, October 23, 1997.

123 *"them on you"* Ibid.

123 *of the massacres* Melvern, *A People Betrayed*, p. 172; See also J. Matthew Vaccaro, "The Politics of Genocide: Peacekeeping and Rwanda," *UN Peacekeeping, American Politics and the Uncivil Wars of the 1990s*, ed. William J. Durch (New York: St. Martin's Press, 1996), p. 377.

124 *against the idea* DesForges, *Leave None to Tell the Story*, pp. 629–630. See also Melvern, *A People Betrayed*, p. 163.

124 *for "forceful action"* Paul Lewis, "U.N. Council Urged to Weigh Action on Saving Rwanda" *New York Times,* April 30, 1994.

124 *had already died* As quoted in Shawcross, *Deliver Us From Evil,* p. 118.

126 *later, if needed* UNAMIR II could consist of up to 5,500 troops. The peacekeeping force was not created under Chapter VII, but the Security Council did indicate troops could use lethal force to "prevent the obstruction of its task," according to Vaccaro, "The Politics of Genocide," p. 378.

126 *carnage and bloodlust* The International Committee for the Red Cross estimated between 200,000 and 400,000 Rwandans were dead, according to Taylor B. Seybolt in "Coordination in Rwanda: the Humanitarian Response to Genocide and Civil War," Conflict Management Group Working Paper (Cambridge: Conflict Management Group, January 1997) (http://www.jha.sps.cam.ac.uk/a/a027.htm.) Alain Destexhe puts the number as 1C0,00 by the end of April; 200,000 by the middle of May, and half a million by the end of May. Alain Destexhe, *Rwanda and Genocide,* p. 32.

126 *"scandal," he said* "World Has Failed on Rwanda," Reuters. See also James Bone, "UN Chief Hits Out at Response to Rwanda Plea," *Times* of London, May 26, 1994.

126 *for "humanitarian reasons"* Operation Turquoise lasted from June 22 until August 21, 1994. It had, at the most, 2,552 French troops and 508 soldiers from African countries.

127 *into neighboring Zaire* OAU report, Chapter 15, p. 12. The report notes that the French helped some escape by refueling their trucks and even driving them into Zaire. It also notes that ex-Rwanda Army (ex-FAR) continued to receive weapons while in the French zone and in Zaire. Some of those weapons came from France.

128 *in April 1995* DesForges, *Leave None to Tell the Story,* pp. 13–14.

128 *and ten priests* Ibid., p. 714. There is controversy over how many people were killed in Kibeho, with the Rwandan government insisting the number totaled as few as 300.

128 *suffered from it* Alain Destexhe, *Rwanda and Genocide,* pp. 58–59.

128 *sick and dying* Seyboldt, "Coordination in Rwanda," pp. 9–10.

128 *back were killed* Jane Perlez, "Rwanda Camps: Long-Term Refugees?" *New York Times,* August 6, 1994. See also Raymond Bonner, "Rwandans Say the Victors Kill Many Who Go Back," *New York Times,* August 5, 1994.

129 *"been set up?"* Nelson Graves, "Premier-Designate Compares Rwanda to Nazi Genocide," Reuters, May 26, 1994.

129 *country's Tutsi population* DesForges, *Leave None to Tell the Story,* p. 1.

129 *been a genocide* "Christopher Urges Trial Over Genocide in Rwanda," *Washington Post,* July 1, 1994.

130 *propping up Habyiramana* Raymond Bonner, "Top Rwandan Criticizes U.S. Envoy," *New York Times,* November 8, 1994.

131 *in the region* Violations of Additional Protocol II were included; Article Three of the 1949 Geneva Conventions was criminalized. Both tribunals were created under the UN's Chapter VII enforcement provisions. The ICTY, in the midst of an ongoing war, was aimed at addressing abuses spawned by an international armed conflict. It draws on a wide number of laws and is investigating war crimes from 1990 up to the present. The ICTR was formed after the genocide was finished. It is charged with investigating crimes committed in a discrete period of time and those that are of an internal armed conflict.

CHAPTER 6: NO SAFE HAVENS

Page

133 *Council members objected* Report of the Secretary-General Pursuant to General Assembly Resolution 53/35 (1998), *Srebrenica Report*, (www.un.org/News/ossg/srebrenica.htm), pp. 27–28.

133 *with inadequate equipment* Ibid., p. 34.

133 *guarding safe areas* Elizabeth Neuffer, "Bosnian Cease-Fire Hits Snag as Weapons Turnover Halts," *Boston Globe*, February 13, 1994.

133 *of humanitarian aid* The UN declared safe havens under Chapter VII of its charter, UN Resolution, 824, p. 138, passed on May 6, 1993, spelled out the peacekeepers' mandate. William J. Durch and James A. Shear, "Faultlines: UN Operations in the Former Yugoslavia," *UN Peacekeeping, American Politics, and the Uncivil Wars of the 1990s*, William J. Durch, ed. (New York: St. Martin's Press, 1996), p. 230.

134 *"very critical here"* Elizabeth Neuffer, " 'Ham Radios' for Besieged Bosnians, A Vital Lifeline; Families Gain a Source of News," *Boston Globe*, April 14, 1994.

134 *"war with Bosnia"* General Sir Michael Rose, *Fighting for Peace: Bosnia 1994* (London: The Harvill Press, 1998), p. 121. Rose argues that he was determined from the start to resist the Bosnian Muslim efforts to involve the UN as a combatant.

134 *the UN peacekeepers* On April 8, 1994, the UNPROFOR commander wrote to the Security Council that by choosing to guard the safe areas with lightly armed troops, it had decided that safe areas should be established by agreement, not force. It would later be concluded that the rebel Serbs used UN negotiations as a cover to pursue their attacks. *Srebrenica Report*, p. 35. See also Rose, *Fighting for Peace*, pp. 95–127.

134 ad hoc *basis* In 1993, the tribunal's budget was $276,000. In 1994 the UN General Assembly gave the court $5.6 million, but only for the first half of the year, making it impossible for the tribunal to sign any contracts, whether for rental equipment or employment longer than six

months. By the time another $5.4 million was allocated in April, the tribunal was six months behind in hiring. *The Annual Report of the International Tribunal for the Prosecutions of Persons Responsible for Serious Violations of the International Humanitarian Law Committed in the Territory of the Former Yugoslavia since 1991*, http://www.un.org/icty/rapportan/first-94.htm

135 *of* 60 Minutes Richard Goldstone, *For Humanity: Reflections of a War Crimes Investigator* (New Haven, Connecticut: Yale University Press, 2000), p. 81.

135 *its annual report* Ibid., p. 105.

136 *in forty-eight hours* Ibid., p. 84.

136 *for additional funds* Address of Antonio Cassese, President of the International Criminal Tribunal for the Former Yugoslavia, to the General Assembly and the Security Council, November 14, 1994.

137 *three murder cases* Ibid.

137 *996 in 1946* Telford Taylor, *Final Report to the Secretary of the Army on the Nuremberg War Crimes Trials Under Control Council Law No. 10* (Washington, D.C.: William S. Hein & Co., 1949), Appendix.

137 *camp in Vlasenica* "The Annual Report of the International Tribunal."

137 *to stand trial* Cassese, UN Address.

137 *country in Europe* Mary Williams Walsh, "Germany May Repatriate Bosnian Refugees," *Los Angeles Times*, December 23, 1995.

138 *"when nothing happened"* Conversation between British diplomat with Alison Smale, Vienna bureau chief for the Associated Press.

139 *what to do* In May 1994, Boutros-Ghali submitted a report to the UN Security Council concerning safe areas. He called on the Council to redefine the concept, making it clear that their intention was to protect people and not to defend territory, and that UN troops had limited resources to do so. The Council, divided, did not respond. The rebel Serbs would go on to test the West's willingness to defend and/or protect civilians in the safe areas by attacks on Sarajevo and Bihać. In December 1994, Boutros-Ghali submitted a second report. He concluded that a small number of UN peacekeepers, even backed up by air power, cannot effectively protect safe areas. *Srebrenica Report*, p. 48.

139 *for more peacekeepers* Jan Willem Honig and Norbert Both, *Srebrenica: Record of a War Crime* (New York: Penguin Books, 1997), p. 118.

140 *what they needed* ICTY Testimony, Major Robert Franken, *Prosecutor v. Radislav Krstic*, Case No.: IT-98-33, April 4, 2000.

140 *them combat trained* Ibid.

141 *Bosnia they needed* Also part of the Bosnian Serbs' calculations was the fact that Croatia reentered the war. The Croats seized western Slavonia, held by Serbia since 1991. There was a sense that the war was turning against Milošević.

141 *46 an hour* Elizabeth Neuffer, "War Ends One Dream of Sarajevo," *Boston Globe*, April 9, 1995.

141 *for air strikes* In March 1995, the Security Council restructured UNPROFOR. Missions in Croatia, Bosnia, and Macedonia were all placed under the command of the Special Representative of the UN Secretary, Yasushi Akashi. See *Srebrenica Report*, p. 48.

142 *a "last resort"* Ibid., p. 195.

142 *would later deny* *Srebrenica Report*, p. 195.

142 *"unacceptable to Chirac"* Text reprinted in: Dr. Smail Cekić, ed., *Srebrenica 1995: Dokmenti I svjedočenja I, knjiga 2* (Sarajevo, Institut za instraživanje zločina protiv čovječnosti I medunarodnog prava Sarajevo, 1999).

142 *"where lightning strikes"* Elizabeth Neuffer and Colum Lynch, "A UN Leader Had Learned of Disaster in 'Safe' Area," *Boston Globe*, October 31, 1995.

143 *"life" for Srebrenica* ICTY, Testimony, Richard J. Butler, *Prosecutor v. General Radislav Krstič*, Case No.: IT-98-33-T, June 28, 2000.

144 *a "last resort"* Honig and Both, *Srebrenica*, p. 8.

144 *Srebrenica never arose* *Srebrenica Report*, p. 58.

144 *discussion of the enclave.* Ibid., p. 61.

145 *and for all* ICTY, Testimony, Richard J. Butler, *Prosecutor v. General Radislav Krstić*, June 28, 2000. See also *Srebrenica Report*, p. 62.

146 *Dutch* *Srebrenica Report*, pp. 65–66.

148 *malfunctioning fax line* Ibid., p. 69.

148 *refuel before returning* For an excellent, detailed re-creation of these events, see Honig and Both, *Srebrenica*, pp. 18–26.

148 *air defense radars* Chuck Sudetic, *Blood and Vengeance: One Family's Story of War in Bosnia* (New York: W. W. Norton, 1998), p. 284.

149 *revenge on the Muslims* This scene is part of the PBS documentary *Cry From the Grave*, Corporation for Public Broadcasting, 2000.

150 *forces, Hervé Gobillard* In possession of author.

152 *"survive, or vanish"* *Cry From the Grave*, documentary.

152 *battalion," wrote Karremans* July 12, 1995, cable to Janvier, among others. Smail Cekić, ed. *Dokumenti I svjedočenia* I, p. 120.

154 *only 251 names* List in possession of author. In testimony in the Krstic trial, Franken says he faxed his list both to the Hague and UN Headquarters to ensure the men's safety. It was then some weeks however, before the fax was located, and only after human rights groups demanded it. See also Franken's Testimony, *Prosecutor v. Radislav Krstić*, Case No.: IT-98-33, April 4, 2000.

154 *from the women* ICTY, Testimony Captain Johannes Rutten, *Prosecutor v. Radislav Krstić*, April 5, 2000.

154 *to the heart* Elizabeth Neuffer, "The Witness to Atrocity: UN Troops Stood by Role in Bosnian Serb Killings Probed," *Boston Globe*, October 1, 1995. See also *Srebrenica Report*.

155 *had been killed* ICTY, Testimony, Major Robert Franken, *Prosecutor v. Radislav Krstić*, April 4, 2000.

158 *disappeared from sight* Hasan Nuhanovic had all three UNMOs sign documents stating that his family was ordered by Dutch officers to leave the UN compound on the evening of July 13, 1995. "They were last seen passing through the compound gate behind which the Serb soldiers were standing," it reads. Copy in possession of author.

158 *with a laugh* Nesib Mandžić, one of the other refugee representatives, heard Serb soldiers saying this and told it to the author in a September 1995 interview.

158 *military observers watched* Lieutenant Colonel Joseph Kingori told Hasan the news that evening. Interview with author.

159 *"and cigarettes, instead"* Outgoing code cable marked "most immediate," July 13, 1995. Copy in possession of author.

159 *the next day* There were two different sets of executions: those of the men that were captured or who surrendered from the column in the woods and those of the men who were taken away from Potočari. In the first massacre, on July 13, men from the column were executed in a warehouse in the village of Kravica. Executions followed at Nova Kasaba and other sites along the escape route taken by those who had fled Srebrenica. By July 15, executions were taking place north of Bratunac in Kozluk and Pilica. The victims were the men and boys ordered off the UN base at Potočari.

159 *crews at work* Neuffer, "The Witness to Atrocity: UN Troops Stood By; Role in Bosnian Serb Killing Probed," *Boston Globe*, October 1, 1995.

160 *to halt it* A UN rapid-reaction force had been deployed to Bosnia as of July 14, 1995. The day before, Jacques Chirac urged that the force be used to retake Srebrenica and protect the other enclaves. Chirac called the fall of Srebrenica "a major failure not only for the United Nations . . . and NATO but also for all democracies." See Christopher Burns, "France Appeals to 'All Great Democracies' to Help in Bosnia," Associated Press, July 14, 1995. Western leaders' attention was then distracted from Srebrenica to the attacks on the enclave of Žepa.

160 *the other enclaves* Testimony Jean-David Levitte. Assemblée Nationale, Commission des Affaires Étrangères, Commission de la Défense Nationale et des Forces Armées, Paris, *Mission Srebrenica*, January 30, 2001.

160 *sound "like Stalingrad"* Barbara Crossette, "UN Chief Focuses on Africa's Underdog Conflict," *New York Times*, July 23, 1995.

161 *conference in Zagreb* Author attended press conference.

161 *mass burials* Duško Doder, "Slaughter of Muslims Reported," *Boston Globe*, July 26, 1995.

CHAPTER 7: PEACE WITHOUT JUSTICE

Interviews

Paul Williams, Judge Antonio Cassese, Judge Richard Goldstone, Judge Gabrielle Kirk McDonald. At Dayton, among others, Paul Williams, Peter Galbraith, others in attendance at Dayton. In Bosnia, indicted war criminals Blagoje Simić, Simo Drljača, and Željko Mejakić; UN police force staff; and European Union monitors based in Prijedor; U.S. military, including General Bill Nash. Also, Ivo Daalder, formerly of the NSC; former ICTY chief prosecutor Richard Goldstone.

Page

165 *and political lines* Except for the Bosnian-Muslim city of Goražde, which remained virtually surrounded by Bosnian-Serb territory.

166 *to help them* Known as "Operation Storm," this military action—which would also leave hundreds of civilians dead—would later become the focus of a tribunal investigation.

166 *reelection in 1996* One key meeting on Bosnia between Lake, Christopher, Perry, Albright, Shalikashvili, and Berger took place on July 17, 1995, while executions were ongoing at Srebrenica. Accounts of the meeting do not mention a discussion of the missing men. See Ivo H. Daalder, *Getting to Dayton: The Making of America's Foreign Policy* (Washington, D.C.: Brookings Institute Press, 2000), p. 99.

166 *"when peace prevails"* Remarks made by President Clinton at the University of Connecticut, Storrs, October 15, 1995. White House press release in possession of author.

167 *in Dayton, Ohio* Description of Dayton based partly upon Richard Holbrooke, *To End a War* (New York: Random House, 1998).

167 *in July 1995* ICTY, Rule 61 Hearing, *Prosecutor v. Radovan Karadžić and Ratko Mladić*, Case No. IT-95-18-R61.

167 *absence of peace* Richard J. Goldstone, *For Humanity: Reflections of a War Crime's Investigator* (New Haven and London: Yale University Press, 2000), p. 103.

169 *Cassese thundered* Address of Antonio Cassese, president of the International Criminal Tribunal for the Former Yugoslavia, to the General Assembly for the United Nations, New York, November 7, 1995 (http://www.un.org/icty/rapportan/first-94.htm.)

169 *in from Maine* Chris Black, "A New Bosnia Airlift: A Lobster to Peace Talks," *Boston Globe*, November 19, 1995.

169 *was, ironically, Milošević* From an interview with participants, including then-ambassador to Croatia Peter Galbraith and aide to the Bosnian delegation Paul Williams. See also Holbrooke, *To End a War.*

170 *Secretary William Perry* Norman Kempster, "Prosecutor Bars Immunity for Serb Leaders," *Los Angeles Times*, November 17, 1995.

171 *of non-Serbs elsewhere* Elizabeth Neuffer, "A Bosnia Peace Built on Ethnic Cleansing," *Boston Globe*, September 17, 1995.

172 *"and greatest challenge"* Elizabeth Neuffer, "Far from the Congratulations, Rumblings Among Combatants," *Boston Globe*, November 22, 1995.

172 *"river keeps flowing"* Elizabeth Neuffer, "Vows of Revenge Veil Bosnia Peace Process; Factions Have Blood Debts to Settle," *Boston Globe*, November 12, 1995.

173 *day in court* *Dayton Peace Accords: General Framework Agreement for Peace in Bosnia and Herzegovina*, U.S. Department of State, December 14, 1995, Annex 1-A, Article IX, p. 9. Responsibility arresting war criminals lay with signatories.

173 *peace, Clinton concurred* Holbrooke, *To End A War*, p. 315.

175 *might soon follow* Dusan Stojanović, "Opposition Leader Offers to Testify Against Milosevic in Hague," Associated Press, January 23, 1996.

175 *and subsequently indicted* Holbrooke, *To End a War*, pp. 332–333.

176 *strutted around freely* Christine Spolar, "NATO Troops Spotted Karadzic this Week; Capture Too Risky, Spokesmen Say," *Washington Post*, February 28, 2000.

176 *Bosnian Muslim ministers* John Pomfret, "Bosnia's Serb Leaders Stages Show of Defiance," *Washington Post*, February 10, 1996.

176 *Bosnian official, exclaimed* Press TWRA. "Karadžić Walked by Prime Minister and Bildt," *Bosnet-digest* V5#83/Thursday, February 29, 1996, http://www.hri.org/news/agencies/bosnet/96-02-29-1.bos.html.

176 *guns at them* "Italian NATO Troops Nearly Miss Capturing Radovan Karadžić," Bosnet Digest V5 #76, February 23, 1996. http://www.hri.org/news/balkans/bosnet.

177 *"they would react"* Spolar, "NATO Troops Spotted Karadžić This Week."

178 *"the former Yugoslavia"* Alison Smale, "Tribunal President Demands Arrests of Bosnian Serb Leaders," *Associated Press*, June 14, 1996.

178 *"interest of peace"* "War Crimes Prosecutor Criticizes NATO," *New York Times*, May 22, 1996.

179 *power in July* Holbrooke, *To End a War*, pp. 339–344.

181 *"your ethnic divisiveness"* Interview on Court TV with Terry Moran, May 3, 1996.

182 *even mentioned again* "Five weeks of the trial had passed without a shred of testimony as to the alleged crimes of the defendant. Indeed, after opening arguments, his name had been uttered only a single time in the courtroom by a witness. When I interviewed Grant Niemann a few weeks later at The Hague, he explained why the policy-witness phase of the prosecution's case had become so drawn out: 'We had asked the judges to determine that the conflict was international and that the abuses were widespread and systematic as a matter of judicial notice on

the basis of the pre-trial submissions, and they said these were going to have to be proven in open court during the trial. As a consequence, we took a very cautious approach and elicited a lot of evidence in support of such a determination.' " Michael Scharf, *Balkan Justice: The Story Behind the First International War Crimes Trial Since Nuremberg* (Durham, North Carolina: Carolina Academic Press, 1997), p. 137.

182 *"kind of proceeding"* Transcript, Court TV, June 1996.

183 *a little nervously* ICTY, Testimony, Hamdija Karimanović, *Prosecutor v. Duško Tadić aka "Dule,"* June 25, 1996.

187 *"live in fear"* Elizabeth Neuffer, "Bosnia's War Criminals Enjoy Peacetime Power," *Boston Globe*, October 29, 1996.

188 *the area's housing* Human Rights Watch/Helsinki Report, *Bosnia and Hercegovina;* "The Unindicted: Reaping the Rewards of Ethnic Cleansing," Vol. 9, No. 1, January 1997, p. 22.

188 *establish his alibi* Scharf, *Balkan Justice*, p. 103.

188 *guarantee good relations* "The Unindicted: Reaping the Rewards of Ethnic Cleansing," Human Rights Watch, January 1997, p. 22.

CHAPTER 8: SEARCHING FOR THE TRUTH

Interviews

Ilana Bet-El, Hasan Nuhanović, Milan "Legenda" Jovović, Gordana and Petko Grubač, Miša Pelemiš, and many Bosnian Serbs who asked to stay anonymous; former ICTY chief prosecutor Richard Goldstone, Mirjana Samardžija, and tribunal staff.

Page

193 *the local brandy* Identity known to author; not revealed at Hasan Nuhanović's request.

199 *in the executions* ICTY, Testimony, Dražen Erdemović, in Rule 61 Hearing, *Prosecutor v. Radovan Karadžić and Ratko Mladić*, Case No.: IT-95-18-R61, July 5, 1996.

199 *"We are ruined!"* Elizabeth Neuffer, "Many Bosnians Are in a State of Denial," *Boston Globe*, May 20, 1996.

200 *the Drina Corps* Elizabeth Neuffer, "Ghosts of Srebrenica," *Boston Globe*, May 19, 1996.

201 *café in Bijeljina* ICTY, Opening Statement, Prosecutor Mark Harmon, *Prosecutor v. Radislav Krstić*. Case No.: IT-98-33, May 13, 2000.

206 *very different Legenda* Ibid.

208 *"shame us all"* ICTY, Prosecutor Mark Harmon, in Rule 61 Hearing, *Prosecutor v. Radovan Karadžić and Ratko Mladić*, June 27, 1996.

209 *"with the refugees"* ICTY, Testimony, Colonel Ton Karremans, Rule 61 Hearing, *Prosecutor v. Radovan Karadžić and Ratko Mladić*, Case No. IT-95-18-R61, July 4, 1996.

209 *casualties would result* John Omicinski, "Poll: Go Get Serb War Criminals—Even at Risk of American Lives," *Gannett News Service*, July 10, 1996. See also Jim Hooper, "Dayton's Mandate for Apprehending War Criminals," as posted on www.pbs.org/wgbh/pages/frontline/shows/karadzic/trial/hooper.html.

211 *"laws of war"* A Helsinki Watch Report, *War Crimes in Bosnia Hercegovina* (New York: Human Rights Watch, 1992), p. 10.

211 *as war criminals* Elaine Sciolino, "U.S. Names Figures to be Prosecuted Over War Crimes," *New York Times*, December 17, 1992.

213 *to his forehead* ICTY, Judgment, *Prosecutor v. Zejnil Delalić et al.*, November 16, 1998. Delalić was acquitted.

213 *"just about time"* "Tribunal Issues More War Crimes Indictments," Associated Press, March 23, 1996.

CHAPTER 9: BRING ME HIS BODY

Interviews

Bill Haglund, Andrew Thomson, Robert Kirschner, José Pablo Baryabar, Jake Sherman, and other members of the exhumation team; John Rene Ruez and Fred Buckley at the Tribunal; Hasan Nuhanović, Fatima Huseinović, Beba Hadzic, Dzefa Parić, Lutvo Hozahmetović, Reuf Mahmedović, Sakib Rizvic, Sudeta Dizdarević, Hatidža Hren, and others. At PHR, Suzanna Serkin and Laurie Vollen; Eric Stover.

Page

215 *could see it* Portions of this chapter previously appeared in Roy Gutman and David Rieff, eds. *Crimes of War: What the Public Should Know* (W. W. Norton: New York, 1999).

219 *Izetbegović of indifference* "Bosnia Women Ask to Seek Missing Men with UN Envoy," Andrew Hill, Reuters, February 3, 1996.

219 *town of Pilica* "Soldier Admits Srebrenica Massacre," as cited in *This Week in Bosnia Hercegovina*, March 13, 1996, http://world.std.com/~slm/twibo313.html.

219 *nettles, and mushrooms* "Bosnia-Hercegovina: To Bury My Brother's Bones," Amnesty International, EUR 63/35/96, July 1996, p. 9.

221 *"recognize his bones"* Elizabeth Neuffer, "For Women of Srebrenica Grave Sites Hold Few Answers," *Boston Globe*, July 30, 1996.

222 The Guardian *newspaper* Julian Borger, "Grisly Tussle for Bosnia's Dead;

Views Differ on the Plan to Dig Up Mass Graves," *Guardian*, April 6, 1996.

223 *executions were buried* William D. Haglund, Melissa Connor, Douglas D. Scott, "The Archeology of Mass Graves," *Historical Archaeology*, 2000, 35(1), pp. 57–69.

223 *on the corpses* Christopher Joyce and Eric Stover, *The Story Bones Tell: Witnesses From the Grave* (New York: Random House, 1991), pp. 233, 246.

224 *exhumed 450 bodies* The Rwanda Tribunal indicted eight people on charges of organizing the slaughter in Kibuye, where hundreds of survivors were killed at a local Catholic church and some 8,000 executed in the football stadium. Almost all of the Kibuye's Tutsi were killed.

226 *village at Glogova* This gravesite is also referred to as Tartar.

226 *a mass grave* John Pomfret, "Grim Evidence Points to Muslims' Graves," *Washington Post*, January 19, 1996.

228 *possibly from Glogova* Zeleni Jadar.

229 *the Rwanda digs* Joyce and Stover, *The Story Bones Tell*, p. 146.

229 *months in arriving* Ibid., p. 147.

230 *Smith told reporters* "Mass Execution Site Revealed," *This Week in Bosnia-Hercegovina*, January 16, 1996. (http://world.std.com/~5/m/twibo116.html.)

230 *had firmly declared* Jane Perlez, "NATO Backs Off Helping Bosnia War Crimes Panel," *New York Times*, January 20, 1996.

230 *twenty-four-hour aerial surveillance* John Pomfret, "NATO, Prosecutor Debate Bosnia Aims," *Washington Post*, January 22, 1996.

234 *go after Vasić* "War Criminals in Bosnia's Republika Srpska," International Crisis Group, Balkans Report, No. 103. (http://www.intl.-crisis-group.org.)

234 *missed being buried* Elizabeth Neuffer, "For Women of Srebrenica Grave Sites Hold Few Answers," *Boston Globe*, July 30. 1996.

238 *speeding their disintegration* William D. Haglund, "Recent Mass Graves: An Introduction," manuscript draft, p. 7.

240 *Muslim-Croat Federation* Some tribunal staff later surmised that Karadžić wanted to appear cooperative, as he tried to build an alibi that he hadn't known about the massacres.

242 *at The Hague* I interviewed one of the two survivors in 1996, on the condition I would not use his story or reveal his identity until the case had come to trial.

245 *November 26, 1996* Mirko Klarin and Vjera Bogati, "Last Week in The Hague" (November 25–29, 1996) Tribunal Update No. 5., as posted on http://iwpr.net.

245 *have been longer* Erdemović testified at the trial of Radislav Krstić in 2000. He finished his jail sentence and was released May 23, 2000.

245 *UN commanders instead* Elizabeth Neuffer, "Dutch Unit Defended on Death in Bosnia," *Boston Globe*, October 19, 1995.

CHAPTER 10: HAVING CLEAN HANDS

Interviews

Ray Wilkinson, spokesman for UNHCR; staff with the World Food Program and Doctors Without Borders; Mark Frohardt, with the UN Human Rights mission in Rwanda; Bernadette Kanzayire of Association des Voluntaires de Paix (AVP); Judith Kanakuzu of Duterimbere; Annonciata Nyiratamba of Avega; Josue Kayijaho of Ibuka. Also, Bill Haglund, Russell Nielson, Suzanne Nyirantagorama, Françoise, Gerald Gahima, ICTR investigators and prosecutors, Leon Nsegimana, Godelieve Mukasarasi, Donathille, Antoinette, JJ, Beatrice LaCoste, Tim Connolly, Honoré Rakotomana, Louise Arbour, Adronica Adede, Michael Karnavas, Yakov Ostrovsky.

Page

251 *with their families* "Report of the Secretary-General on Security in the Rwandese Refugee Camps," UNSCOR, November 18, 1994, Forty-Ninth Session, paras. 7–8. UN Doc S/1994/1308.

252 *from the RPF* Gérard Prunier, *The Rwanda Crisis: History of a Genocide* (New York: Columbia University Press, 1995), p. 329.

252 *of Tutsi power* Ibid., p. 367.

252 *the RPF army* Sendashonga joined the RPF in 1990. He fled to Kenya after quitting the Rwandan government. Forming an opposition group committed to political dialogue between all of Rwanda's ethnic groups, he reportedly was also compiling data of killings by the Rwandan military. He was assassinated in May 1998, a few weeks before he was to testify before the Rwanda Tribunal. Sendashonga was to address how the government had manipulated witnesses appearing before the court. Deborah Mendelsohn, "Analysis: The Trial of Sendashonga's Assassins—A Trial of Missing Links," *Internews*, December 19, 2000.

253 *had been killed* Report of UN Special Rapporteur, January 29, 1996.

257 *effectively as possible* As cited in the "United Nations Justice for Rwanda and Former Yugoslavia Undermined by Failure to Provide Adequate Support for Ad Hoc Tribunals," Amnesty International News Release, IOR 40/12/96, May 6, 1996. (http://www.amnesty.it/news/1996/I4001296.htm.)

257 *lacked legal training* The International Crisis Group, "Five Years After the Genocide in Rwanda: Justice in Question." April 7, 1999, http://www.intl-crisis-group.org/projects/cafrica/reports/rw01erepa.htm.

257 *244 had survived* Rwandan Ministry of Justice, *The Judicial System in Rwanda: A Report on Justice*, www.rwandemb.org/justice/justice.htm.

257 *files set afire* Lawyers' Committee for Human Rights, "Prosecuting

Genocide in Rwanda, A Lawyers' Committee Report on the ICTR and National Trials," July 1997, http://www.lchr.org/pubs/rwanda.htm.

258 *far from even-handed* Interview with Innocent Niyonabura of CLADHO, an umbrella organization of human-rights groups.

258 *were behind bars* U.S. Department of State, *Country Report on Human Rights Practices for 1996: Rwanda,* released by the Bureau of Democracy, Human Rights and Labor, January 1997.

258 *$66 million was needed* Krishna Kumar, *Rebuilding Postwar Rwanda: The Role of the International Community;* U.S. AID Evaluation Special Study No. 76, Center for Development, Information and Evaluation, U.S. Agency for International Development. David Tardif-Douglin, Development Alternatives, Inc., July 1996, DN-ABY-212, http://www.info.usaid.gov/pubs/usaid eval/ascii/pnaby212.txt.

258 *with property crimes* Lawyers' Committee for Human Rights, "Prosecuting Genocide in Rwanda."

259 *mid-January 1997* United Nations Human Rights Field Operations in Rwanda. Status Report as of January 1997, www.unhchr.ch/html/menu2/5/rwanda/rwa_str.htm.

260 *seven-month period* Lawyers' Committee for Human Rights, "Prosecuting Genocide in Rwanda."

261 "*a case file*" Report on Situation of Human Rights in Rwanda, January 29, 1996, p. 18.

263 *country of widows* "Children and Women of Rwanda: A Situational Analysis of Social Sectors," UNICEF, 1997.

263 *among adolescent girls* Ibid., p. 48.

264 "*am not sure*" Elizabeth Neuffer, "Women Wait to See If Their Attackers Will Face Charges," *Boston Globe,* December 14, 1996.

266 *a bad start* Elizabeth Neuffer, "Mismanagement and Red Tape Impede Tribunal," *Boston Globe,* December 11, 1996.

267 *the Rwandan government* Barbara Crossette, "Judge Urges World to Heed Rwanda Crisis," *New York Times,* December 31 1995.

267 *three tribunal investigators* Lawyers' Committee for Human Rights "Prosecuting Genocide in Rwanda."

268 *potential tribunal witnesses* United Nations High Commissioner for Human Rights, *Human Rights Incidents Involving Recent Returnees from Zaire and Tanzania,* Status Report as of January 27, 1997, http://www.unhcr.ch/html/menu2/5/rwanda_rwa_str.htm.

268 *based in Arusha* Neuffer, "Mismanagement and Red Tape."

268 "*for its staff*" From copy of letter given to the author.

269 *personnel, Abdoulaye Diallo* Copy in possession of author.

269 *had been unsealed* Both were charged with genocide, conspiracy to commit genocide, and crimes against humanity. See ICTR-96-10 and ICTR-96-17.

270 *receiving his salary* The employee, Saadou Moumouni, a former finance assistant, repaid the money, but he remained at the tribunal, despite a

recommendation from the UN Inspector General that he leave. See UN General Assembly, Fifty-First Session, Report of the Secretary-General on the Activities of the Office of Internal Oversight, "Financing of the International Criminal Tribunal for the Prosecution of Persons Responsible for the Genocide and Other Serious Violations of International Humanitarian Law Committed in the Territory of Rwanda and Rwandan Citizens Responsible for Genocide and Other Such Violations Committed in the Territory of Neighboring States Between 1 January and 31 December 1994." A/51/789, February 6, 1997. See also Report of Secretary-General on the Activities of the Office of Internal Oversight Services, A/53/428.

270 *visible, marked cars* Lawyers' Committee for Human Rights, "Prosecuting Genocide in Rwanda," p. 11.

CHAPTER 11: WHAT A TUTSI WOMAN TASTES LIKE

Interviews

Witness JJ, Witness PP, Witness OO, Witness NN, Witness KK. Judge Navanethem Pillay, Judge Lennart Aspegren, Sarah Dareshori, Pierre Prosper, Binaifir Bowrejee of Human Rights Watch, Eleanor Richter-Lyonette of the Coordination of Women's Advocacy, Kelly Dawn Askin, Felice Gaer, Jennifer Green, and James Stewart. I have relied heavily on the judgment in the Akayesu case and trial testimony (Prosecutor v. Jean-Paul Akayesu, Case No.: ICTR-96-4-T).

Page

271 *"all be killed" ICTR, Testimony, Witness JJ, Prosecutor v. Jean-Paul Akayesu,* October 23, 1997.

272 *crime against humanity* The trial chamber states that rape can constitute torture. The prosecution did not charge rape as an act of torture; it limited the acts of torture to beatings and interrogations. The first finding of guilt for rape as torture was in the Čelebići Judgment.

272 *plunder or pillage The American Heritage Dictionary of the English Language New College Edition* (Boston: Houghton Mifflin, 1976).

272 *spoils of victory* Simon Chesterman, "Never Again . . . and Again: Law, Order and Gender of War Crimes in Bosnia and Beyond," *Yale Journal of International Law,* Vol. 22, No. 2, Summer 1997, p. 299.

272 *"pick of them"* Homer, *The Iliad* (Roslyn, New York: Walter J. Black Inc., 1942), Book II, lines 225–229, p. 82.

273 *after looting it* Archer Jones, *The Art of War in the Western World* (Chicago: University of Illinois Press, 1987), pp. 216–219, describing the Thirty Years' War. During this war, Albert von Wallenstein, a military

contractor from Bohemia, implemented a system of creating a professional class of paid soldiers instead of allowing mercenaries free reign to pillage.

273 *"takes a trifle?"* Susan Brownmiller, *Against Our Will: Men, Women and Rape* (New York: Simon and Schuster, 1975), p. 71, citing Milovan Djilas, *Conversations with Stalin* (New York: Harcourt, Brace, 1962), pp. 89, 95. [Cornelius Ryan, *The Last Battle*; also in Kelly Dawn Askin, *War Crimes Against Women* (Martin Nihoff Publishers, Kluwer Law International, the Hague, 1997)]

273 *punishable by death* Ibid., p. 34.

273 *not under siege* Thom Shanker, "Sexual Violence," in *Crimes of War: What the Public Should Know*, Roy Gutman and David Rieff, eds. (New York: W. W. Norton, 1999), p. 323.

273 *was officially occupied* Shanker, "Sexual Violence," p. 323.

273 *"more advanced peoples"* Hugo Grotius, "The Law of War and Peace," (1625) reprinted in Leon Friedman, ed., *The Law of War* (New York: Random House, 1972), p. 158.

273 *a capital offense* The Lieber code was drafted by Francis Lieber in 1863 to serve as a military code for the Union Army during the Civil War. Article 37 states: "The United States acknowledge and protect, in hostile countries occupied by them, religion and morality; strictly private property; the persons of the inhabitants, *especially those of women*; and the sacredness of domestic relations. Offenses to the contrary shall be rigorously punished." *The Lieber Code: Instructions for the Government of Armies of the United States in the Field by Order of the Secretary of War* (General Orders No. 100) (1863), reprinted in Leon Friedman, ed., *The Law of War: A Documentary History* (New York: Random House, 1972). The Lieber Code served as a guide for other nations and the basis for the Hague Conventions of 1899 and 1907.

273 *not the rule* See Article 27 of the Fourth Geneva Convention and Protocols I and II.

274 *against Jewish women* U.S.S.R. Exhibit No. 51, read into evidence on February 14, 1946, *Trial of the Major War Criminals Before the International Military Tribunal Nuremberg, 14 November 1945–1 October, 1946* (Nuremberg: International Military Tribunal, 1947–1949) pp. 456–457. Despite this evidence, there was no charge of rape in the Indictment.

274 *rapes in France* Areyh Neier, *War Crimes: Brutality, Genocide, Terror and the Struggle for Justice* (New York: Random House, 1998), p. 181.

274 *its judicial strategy* General Iwane Matsui was charged as commander in charge of the "Rape of Nanking" invasion. *Record of Proceedings of the International Military Tribunal for the Far East: Court House of the Tribunal, War Ministry Building, Tokyo, Japan: The United States of America . . . [et al.] against Araki, Sadoa [et al.] accused.* (Tokyo: The Tribunal 1946–1948), Judgment of the International Military Tribunal

for the Far East 1012 (1948). The Tribunal found "approximately 20,000 cases of rape in Nanking." General Matsui was sentenced to death by hanging. The Tribunal concluded:

> Even girls of tender years and old women were raped in large numbers throughout the city, and many cases of abnormal or sadistic behavior in connection with the rapings occurred. Many women were killed after the act and their bodies mutilated.... the barbarous behavior of the Japanese army cannot be excused as the acts of a soldiery which has temporarily gotten out of hand when at last a stubbornly defended position had capitulated—rape, arson and murder continued to be committed on a large scale for at least six weeks after the city had been taken.

274 *"upon personal dignity"* Neier, *War Crimes*, pp. 179–180.

275 *Serb-held Bosnia* The International Criminal Tribunal for the Former Yugoslavia indicted numerous persons for the crimes committed in the Omarska camp, including crimes of sexual violence. See, for example, International Tribunal for the Prosecution of Persons Responsible for Serious Violations of the International Humanitarian Law Committed in the Territory of the Former Yugoslavia since 1991, *Prosecutor v. Željko Mejakić and Others*, Case No. IT-95-4, February 13, 1995. In this indictment, which included charges against nineteen persons, Mladen Radić was charged with numerous counts related to crimes of rape and sexual violence: grave breaches (great suffering for forcible sexual intercourse); violation of the laws and customs of war (cruel treatment); and crime against humanity (rape). Six persons were charged through command responsibility with rape and other crimes of sexual violence, as grave breaches, crime against humanity, and violations of the laws and customs of war. The case against four persons charged with committing crimes in Omarska, Keraterm, and Trnopolje camps, including Mlado Radić, opened in February 2000. ICTY, Second Amended Indictment, *Prosecutor v. Miroslav Kvocka, Milojica Kos, Mladen Radić, Zorah Zigić*, Case No.: IT-98-30-PT, May 31, 1999.

276 *of "ethnic cleansing"* Jennifer Scott, "Systematic Rapes," Reuters, July 13, 1996.

276 *was later discredited* The UN Commission of Experts estimated it had identified 800 victims, with 1,573 referred to by witnesses; other groups would have other estimates.

276 *Rwanda in 1994* United Nations, "Report on the Situation of Human Rights in Rwanda," submitted by René Degni-Segui, Special Rapporteur of the Commission of Human Rights, January 27, 1996.

277 *or "systematic" attack* Rape has subsequently been charged as a violation of the laws and customs of war (torture, cruel treatment, and out-

rages upon personal dignity), as well as grave breaches (torture), which brings with it universal jurisdiction.

277 *on the issue* Neier, *War Crimes*, pp. 177–178.

278 *women in Taba* Human Rights Watch/Africa, Human Rights Watch Women's Rights Project, Federation Internationale des Lignes des Droits de L'Homme, *Shattered Lives: Sexual Violence during the Rwandan Genocide and Its Aftermath* (New York: Human Rights Watch/Africa, et al., 1996).

280 *to seek refuge* ICTR, Judgment, *Prosecutor v. Jean-Paul Akayesu*, September 2, 1998, p. 39.

280 *"becomes fully functional"* Report of the Secretary General on the Activities of the Office of Internal Oversight Services, February 6, 1997, A/51/789.

282 *about the rapes* Testimony, Witness H, as quoted in ICTR Amicus Brief Respecting Amendment to the Indictment and Supplementation of Evidence to Ensure the Prosecution of Rape and Other Sexual Violence Within the Competence of the Tribunal, *Prosecutor v. Jean-Paul Akayesu*, March 6–7, 1997, http://www.ichrdd.ca/PublicationsE/amiceng.html.

282 *"didn't even try"* Ibid.

282 *"for these names?"* Ibid.

283 *"prosecutions to come"* Ibid.

283 *Rwandan government troops* Human Rights Watch World Report, "Rwanda: Human Rights Development, 1998," http://www.hrw.org/hrw/worldreport99/africa/index.htm.

283 *traveling with them* U.S. State Department, Bureau of Democracy, Human Rights and Labor, "U.S. Department Country Report of the Human Rights Practices for 1998: Rwanda," February 1999, http://www.state.gov/www/global/human_rights/hrp_reports_mainhp.html.

284 *from them again* Tribunal prosecutors remember this differently. They say they had never interviewed JJ before.

285 *and sexual violence* ICTR, *Prosecutor v. Jean-Paul Akayesu*, p. 28.

291 *"here and there"* Thierry Cruvellier, *Ubutabera: Independent Newsletter on the International Criminal Tribunal for Rwanda*, No. 32, March 16, 1998, as posted on the Judicial Diplomacy Web site, http://www.diplomaticjudicaire.com/uk/home.htm.

291 *"which are coercive"* ICTR Judgment, *Prosecutor v. Jean-Paul Akayesu*, p. 241.

291 *"kill those women"* Ibid., pp. 289–290.

291 *in the judgment* ICTR News, No. 5, November 1998.

CHAPTER 12: WHEN THE VICTIMS ARE THE SERBS

Interviews

Petko and Gordana Grubač; Teresa McHenry; Witness R; Simo Drljača; Mirko Klarin; Tom Moran; Judge Gabrielle Kirk McDonald; Jacques Klein; former chief prosecutor, Louise Arbour former ambassador for war crime issues David Scheffer; British officers in Prijedor who asked not to be identified; Hamdo Kahrimanović and Firdesa Kahrimanović; Teree Bowers; deputy prosecutor Graham Blewitt; ICTY staff who asked to remain anonymous; Lorna McDonald, Jon Cina, Katie Gallagher, John Ackerman; and members of the State Department and Clinton administration staffers who asked not to be identified. I have also reviewed select taped portions of the trial.

Page

294 *indictments between them* The ICTY had seventy-three indictments; the ICTR, twenty-one. Ewan Allison, "News from the International War Crimes Tribunals," http://www.wcl.american.educ/pub/humright/brief/v4i3/tribuna43.htm.

294 *bars in Arusha* George Rutaganda and Clement Kayishema. Also detained were Jean-Paul Akayesu; Joseph Kanyabashi, Eli Ndayambaje, Obed Ruzindana, Ferdinand Nahimana, Andre Ntagerura, Anatole Nsengiyumva, and Théoneste Bagosora.

294 *in Arusha, Tanzania* Also on trial was Croat general Tihomir Blaškić, charged with grave breaches of the Geneva Conventions, violations of the law and customs of war, and crimes against humanity in relation to events that occurred in Lasva Valley, Bosnia, in fighting between Bosnian Muslims and Bosnian Croats.

294 *of "anti-Serb bias"* Mirko Klarin and Vjera Bogati, *Tribunal Update*, No. 12, January 20–25, 1997, as posted at http://www.iwpr.net.

295 *pages of transcript* ICTY, Judgment, *Prosecutor v. Zejnil Delalić, Zdravko Mucić aka "Pavo," Hazim Delić, Esad Landžo aka "Zenga,"* Case No. IT-96-21-T, November 16, 1998, p. 13.

295 *taken the stand* unclear

295 *Croat-Muslim war* The Blaškić case would end up running even longer than the Čelebići case: 220 court days, with 158 witnesses.

295 *ended in 1998* In its judgment, the tribunal's judges noted: "the Defense for Zdravko Mucić in the course of these proceedings had adopted different positions in relation to the charges raised against him . . . which appear to be in part conflicting." ICTY, Judgment, *Prosecutor v. Zejnil Delalić et al.*, November 16, 1998, p. 265.

296 *"own individual responsibility"* ICTY, Opening Statement, Prosecutor Eric Ostberg, *Prosecutor v. Zejnil Delalić et al.*, March 10, 1997.

297 *"us completely unsatisfied"* Letter from the Cabinet of the Prime Minister, the Government of the Republic of Srpska, to Louise Arbour, No. 01-368-97, March 6, 1997, as reprinted by the Serbian Unity Congress at http://www.suc.org.

297 *on atrocities there* Helsinki Watch, *War Crimes in Bosnia-Hercegovina*, Vol. 2 (New York: Human Rights Watch), pp. 349–370.

298 *"were taken out"* ICTY, *Prosecutor v. Zejnil Delalić et al.*, November 16, 1997, p. 371.

298 *"kill you psychologically"* Ibid., p. 328.

298 *was still speaking* John Ackerman, quoted, was one of two lawyers representing Landžo; the other was Cynthia McMurrey.

298 *"in his way"* ICTY, Testimony, Witness R, *Prosecutor v. Zejnil Delalić et al.*, October 15, 1997.

298 *"of the Serbs"* From SRNA (Srpska Republika News Agency), September 28, 1997, as found at http://www.hri.org.

299 *"did go wrong"* Klarin was the former *Nasa Borba* reporter who first proposed a war crimes tribunal for the former Yugoslavia. His coverage, *Tribunal Update*, appears on the Institute for War and Peace Reporting Web site http://www.iwpr.com.

300 *their own governments* The United States was one of the tribunal's major donors. It had already contributed a $2.5 million computer system, a grant of $700,000 to go toward exhumations, and the services of sixteen lawyers. The UN had wanted it to pay an "administrative tax" on top of the lawyers' salaries. Of the three prosecutors on the Čelebići case, only one remained throughout the trial, chief prosecutor Teresa McHenry from the Department of Justice.

300 *years to watch* U.S. General Accounting Office, "Former Yugoslavia: War Crimes Tribunal's Workload Exceeds Capacity," Report to The Chairman, Committee on Foreign Relations, U.S. Senate. GAO/NS/AD-9-134, June 1998, p. 17.

302 *were not involved* Regarding grave breaches: In order for Article 2 to be applicable, the victims must be protected persons, and the conflict must be international in character. Two of the judges, taking a very literal definition of protected persons—"in the hands of a party to the conflict or occupying power of which they were not nationals"—ruled that those in Prijedor were not protected persons, and the conflict at that time was not of an international character. They argued that the Serbian Army would not only have had influence, but also effective control over the Bosnian Serbs, for the war to be international. In her dissent, however, Judge McDonald argued that the right test is "dependency and control," and "a showing of effective control is not required." She noted that the Bosnian Serb troops were really Serbian troops, with different badges. "The evidence proves that the creation of the VRS [Bosnian Serb Army] was a legal fiction. The only changes made after the May 15, 1992, Security Council resolution were the transfer of

troops, the establishment of a Main Staff of the VRS, and a change in the insignia. There remained the same weapons, the same equipment, the same officers, the same commanders, largely the same troops, the same logistic centres, the same infrastructure, the same source of payments, the same goals and mission, the same tactics, and the same operations. Importantly, the objectives remained the same: to create an ethnically pure Serb State by uniting Serbs in Bosnia and Herzegovina and extending that State from the FRY . . . to the Croatian Krajina along the important logistics and supply line that went through opstina Prijedor, thereby necessitating the expulsion of the non-Serb population of the opstina." Paragraph 7.

302 *"not be severe"* Srpska Republika News Agency (SRNA), May 7, 1997, www.hri.org/news/balkans/srna/97-05-07srna.html.

303 *"so many 'ifs'"* Dejan Lukic, "I Am Innocent," *Vecernje Novosti*, Belgrade, FR Yugoslavia, May 26–June 3, 1997.

304 *was shot dead* Re-created from interviews with British soldiers familiar with the arrest operation.

305 *mayor of Vukovar* Dokmanović was indicted on April 3, 1996, at the end of a Rule 61 hearing. His indictment was kept secret, while the indictment for three officers of the Yugoslav People's Army, or JNA, also accused of crimes was made public. The men have yet to be turned over to The Hague by Serbia. Dokmanović later committed suicide in his jail cell in The Hague. See Mirko Klarin and Vjera Bogati, "Last Week at The Hague," *Tribunal Update* Nos.: 34 (June 23–28, 1997), 35 (June 30–July 5, 1997), 43 (September 22–26, 1997), 50 (October 27–31, 1997).

306 *"court," she warned* Klarin and Bogati, "Last week at The Hague," *Tribunal Update* No. 35, June 30–July 5, 1997.

307 *rather than aggressors* There were several minor incidents. One American peacekeeper was injured in a bomb explosion; another peacekeeper was attacked by a man waving a sickle. Kovačević would later die of an aneurism while in tribunal custody. Many Bosnian Serbs accused the tribunal of "murder." Kovačević apparently requested a doctor several times before one arrived.

308 *"and invite anarchy"* ICTY, Transcript, *Prosecutor v. Duško Tadić aka "Dule,"* July 14, 1996.

309 *"without a past"* ICTY, Testimony, Gordana Grubač, *Prosecutor v. Zejnil Delalić et al.* August 12–13, 1997.

309 *the question's relevance* ICTY, Testimony, Witness R, *Prosecutor v. Zejnil Delalić et al.*, October 16, 1997.

309 *"what it means"* Charles Dickens, *Bleak House* (New York: Heritage Press, 1942), p. 18.

310 *"persecution of Serbs"* Mirko Klarin and Vjera Bogati, *Tribunal Update* No. 48, October 13–17, 1997, as posted at http://www.iwpr.net.

311 *"of the two men"* See ICTY Judgment, *Prosecutor v. Zejnil Delalić et al.*, November 16, 1998.

CHAPTER 13: A TIME OF RECKONING

Interviews

John Heffernan, Diane Paul, members of UNHCR staff, Hamdo and Firdesa Kahrimanović, Mladen Tadić, Judge Gabrielle Kirk McDonald, Hasan Nuhanović, Milburn Line.

Page

317 *slaughter at Srebrenica* The United Nations issued two sharply critical reports of its actions in Srebrenica and Rwanda. The *Srebrenica Report* was issued in 1998. The "Report of the Independent Inquiry into the Actions of the United Nations During the 1994 Genocide in Rwanda" was issued in December 1999.

319 *to in 1996* International Crisis Group Report on Sarajevo, "Minority Return or Mass Relocation?" May 14, 1998, pp. 19, 23.

320 *living in Sarajevo* Chris Hedges, "Jailed Serbs' 'Victims' Found Alive, Embarassing Bosnia," *New York Times*, March 1, 1997.

320 *extracted by torture* "Murder Confessions by Zvornik Seven Extracted by Torture Says UN," Reuters, May 21, 1997.

320 *hometown of Vlasenica* A pseudonym is used to guarantee this individual's safety.

322 *they had occurred* Charles Lane and Thom Shanker, "Bosnia: What the CIA Didn't Tell Us," *New York Review of Books*, May 9, 1996.

322 *"need anyone alive"* Roy Gutman, "The UN's Deadly Deal: How Troop-Hostage Talks Lead to Slaughter of Srebrenica," *Newsday*, May 29, 1996.

324 *"such an investigation"* Testimony, Hasan Nuhanović, House Subcommittee on International Operations and Human Rights, March 31, 1998.

326 *"today," said Rutten* "Former Blue Helmet Alleges 'Collaboration' in Srebrenica," Agence France-Presse, August 18, 1998.

330 *the year before* On March 31, 1998, the ambassador-at-large for war crimes issues, David Scheffer, noted that the number of indictees taken into custody in The Hague had more than tripled from eight to twenty-eight.

330 *than face arrest* Milan Simić and Miroslav Tadić of the Bosanski Šamac indictment surrendered in February. Dragoljub Kunarac, charged in the Foca indictment, surrendered in March 1998.

330 *Bosnia, told reporters* Guy Dinmore, "Time Running Out for Bosnian Serb War Crime Suspect," *Chicago Tribune*, April 10, 1998.

331 *at Karadžić himself* See R. Jeffrey Smith, "Secret Meeting Foiled Karadzic Capture Plan; US Says French Jeopardized Mission," *Washington Post*, April 23, 1998, and Steven Erlanger, "French Said to Hurt Plan to Capture Karadzic," *New York Times*, April 23, 1998.

331 *"Operation Amber Star"* Kevin Whitelaw, Richard J. Newman, and David E. Kaplan, "Time Is Running Out for Mr. Ethnic Cleansing," *U.S. News and World Report*, April 13, 1998.

331 *had been dropped* Tim Weiner, "U.S. Cancels Plans for Raid on Bosnia to Capture Two Serbs," *New York Times*, July 26, 1998.

332 *the prime minister* Elizabeth Neuffer, "Bosnian Serb Leader Turning Hate to Hopes," *Boston Globe*, March 29, 1998. Dodik became prime minister after Western officials dispatched a policeman to fetch a missing parliamentarian to give his party a one-vote majority. Hard-liners had left the parliament building confident of their victory. Dodik was one of the very few Bosnian Serb officials in power who had no record of hard-line nationalism or corruption during the war.

333 *some 11,000 did* U.S. Department of State, *Country Reports on Human Rights Practices for 1998: Bosnia and Herzegovina*, released by the Bureau of Democracy, Human Rights, and Labor, February 1999, http://www.state.gov/www/global/human_rights/hrp_reports_mainhp.html.

335 *it happened.* The interview was broadcast in October 1998.

CHAPTER 14: JUSTICE MUST BE SEEN TO BE DONE

Interviews

Aloys Habimana, Theobald Rwaka of LIPRODHOR; relatives and friends of Silas Munyagishala who asked not to be identified; members of the Rwandan legal community; Trish Huddleston, Human Rights Watch; lawyers at Avocats Sans Frontières; William Haglund, James Stewart, Judge Navanethem Pillay, Judge Gabrielle Kirk McDonald; others at the ICTY and ICTR; Françoise Xavier Nsanzuwera, Thierry Cruvellier; the staff of Ibuka.

Page

337 *Kigali's sports stadium* Victor Visathan, "Karamira, 21 Other Genociders Executed," *The New Times* (the Rwandan English-language daily) No. 34, April 27, 1998.

337 *a better look* James McKinley, "As Crowd Vents Their Rage, Rwanda Publicly Executes 22," *New York Times*, April 25, 1998.

338 *"to be done"* As quoted by CNN World News, "Rwanda to Carry Out First Executions for 1994 Genocide," April 22, 1998.

338 *for the slaughter* In 1997 the Belgium Senate launched an inquiry into the genocide. In 1998, members of the French National Assembly investigated France's role. In 1998, the Organization for African Unity launched its inquiry into the Rwandan genocide. In May of 1998, the

United States House of Representatives conducted a hearing, "Rwanda: Genocide and the Continuing Cycle of Violence," before the Subcommittee on International Operations and Human Rights of the Committee on International Relations. The United States has not yet conducted an investigation into its failure to respond to the genocide.

338 *"rightful name: genocide"* John F. Harris, "Clinton Cites 'Genocide' in Massacres," *Washington Post*, March 26, 1998.

338 *Kamanzi in 1997* As quoted in Jean-Baptiste Kayigamba and Charles Wachira, "Rwanda Doubts over Value of Genocide Tribunal," Inter-Press Service, January 12, 1997.

339 *own justice system* The Rwandan justice system is based on Belgium's, a combination of French civil law and Napoleonic codes. There are 145 local courts, then 12 courts of "first instance" and 4 appeals courts. In 1996, a new law created special chambers within the Courts of First Instance to try genocide cases. See "Prosecuting Genocide in Rwanda: A Lawyers Committee Report on the ICTR and National Trials," July 1997.

339 *branded as* génocidaires Report of the United Nations High Commissioner for Human Rights, "Question of the Violation of Human Rights and Fundamental Freedoms in Any Part of the World, with Particular Reference to Colonial and Other Dependent Countries and Territories," Human Rights Field Operation in Rwanda, February 14, 1998, E/CN.4/1998/61.

339 *in 1998 alone* U.S. Department of State, "Country Report on Human Rights Practices for 1998: Rwanda," released by the Bureau of Democracy, Human Rights and Labor, February 1999, http://www.state.gov/www/global/human_rights/hrp_reports_mainhp.html.

339 *flagrantly one-sided* Avocats Sans Frontières, "Justice for All in Rwanda," Annual Report, 1998, p. 6.

339 *convicted in 1997* Human Rights Watch, World Report 1999, "Rwanda: Justice and Responsibility, 2000," As posted at wysiwyg://9/http://www.hrw.org.reports/1999/rwanda.

339 *death in 1997* Avocats Sans Frontières, "Justice for All in Rwanda," p. 31.

339 *were falsely accused* The prosecutor of Ruhengeri. As noted in Human Rights Watch World Report, "Rwanda: Human Rights Developments, 2000," available on the Web at www.hrw.org.

340 *of the RPA* According to Amnesty International, 6,000 people, mostly unarmed civilians, are believed to have been killed by the RPA between January and August 1997. Two thousand were killed at the border between May and June, according to the U.S. Department of State.

340 *"insurgency in the northwest"* U.S. Department of State, "Country Report: Rwanda," February 1999.

340 *shelter Hutu extremists* Organization of African Unity, "The International Panel of Eminent Personalities to Investigate the 1994 Genocide

in Rwanda and the Surrounding Events," Chapter 20, http://www.oau-oau.org/document/ipep/ipep.htm.

340 *responsibility still reigned* Catharine Newbury, "Ethnicity and Politics of History in Rwanda," *Africa Today*, Vol. 45, No. 2 (1998), pp. 7–24.

341 *"are strictly observed"* "Rwanda Rejects Clemency Pleas and Begins Executions," reported on CNN, April 24, 1998.

341 *Rwanda's legal community* During a visit to Rwanda in February 2000, I asked to look at the records of the Munyagishali case and was refused. My account of his trial is based on interviews with those on both sides of the case, most of whom asked not to be identified because of lingering political sensitivities. It is also based on notes of trial proceedings kept by Aloys Habimana, who observed the trial as an independent human-rights observer with the group LIPROHDOR (the Rwandan League for the Promotion and Defense of Human Rights).

341 *than with genocide* Amnesty International, "Rwanda: Appeal Cases: No One Is Talking About It Anymore," AFRA 47/31/97, October 1997. Also various Amnesty International reports and press releases protesting the executions.

342 *trial was unfair* Alison DesForges, *Leave None to Tell the Story* p. 754. "In others, like that of Silas Muyagishali, there were apparently procedural errors as well as intimidation of defense witnesses," writes DesForges on p. 758. Also, p. 762: "Many observers, Rwandan and foreign, believe, for example, that the guilt of former prosecutor Silas Muyagishali was not proven in the trial, which resulted in his condemnation."

342 *the trial began* Amnesty International "Appeal Cases," October 1997.

342 *complete her testimony La Lettre du CLADHO* (A Rwandan Human Rights Group newsletter), No. 18, July/August 1997, p. 14.

342 *go to court* Ibid.

342 *end of 1998* DesForges, *Leave None to Tell the Story*, p. 762.

342 *accused in 1997* A bar association formed in 1950 never functioned. A new one started in 1997.

342 *"depend on it"* Avocats Sans Frontières, *Justice for All in Rwanda*, 1998.

343 *sent by Bagasora* Meeting between the survivors of the Rwandan Genocide and the Independent Inquiry into the United Nations' Role in the Rwandan Genocide, Washington D.C., December 8, 1999. Transcript in possession of the author.

343 *additional alleged criminals* The raids were known as "Operation NAKI."

344 *"on nonsensical absurdity"* Thierry Cruvellier, *Ubutabera:* International Criminal Tribunal for Rwanda, No. 38, June 8, 1998, as posted on the Judicial Diplomacy Web site at http://www.diplomatiejudiciaire.com/uk/home.htm.

344 *"and asset management"* UN General Assembly, Fifty-first Session, "Financing of the International Criminal Tribunal for the Prosecution of

the Persons Responsible for Genocide and Other Serious Violations of the International Humanitarian Law Committed in the Territory of Rwanda and Rwandan Citizens Responsible for Genocide and Other Such Violations Committed in the Territory of Neighbouring States between 1 January and 31 December 1994," Report of the Secretary-General on the Activities of the Office of Internal Oversight Services, A/53/428, February 1998, p. 22.

344 *"systematic massacres committed"* As quoted in Farah Stockman, "Anatomy of a Court: The International Criminal Tribunal for Rwanda," John Carey and R. John Pritchard, eds. *International Humanitarian Law: Origins, Challenges and Prospects* (The Edwin Mellen Press, Lewiston, Lampeter and Queenston, 1999).

344 *"know we exist"* "Critical Swedish Judge to Step Down From Rwanda Tribunal," Associated Press, July 18, 1998.

344 *a "multicultural background"* "Campaigning Judges," *Ubutabera*, as posted at http://www.diplomatiejudiciaire.com/uk/tpiruk/TPIRUK7.html.

345 *days in court* Cruvellier, *Ubutabera*, No. 35, Spring 1998.

345 *whined Rutagand, sniffling* As quoted in Cruvellier, *Ubutabera*, No. 33, March 30, 1998.

345 *age of ten* ICTR, Testimony, William Haglund, *Prosecutor v. George Anderson Nderubamwe Rutaganda*, Case No.: ICTR-96-3-T, March 10, 1998.

345 *exhumations in Bosnia* Ibid.

346 *Haglund answered.* ICTR, Testimony, William Haglund, *Prosecutor v. George Rutaganda*, March 10, 1998.

346 *the exhumed remains* Ibid.

346 *yearned to do* During the trial, a defense witness challenged Haglund's scientific method. In its decision, the ICTR ruled that the prosecutor failed to show a link between Haglund's findings and the indictment. The judges dismissed Haglund's findings. ICTR, Judgment, *Prosecutor v. George Anderson Nderubamwe Rutaganda*, December 6, 1999.

346 *confirmed the identification* ICTR, Testimony, Witness T, *Prosecutor v. George Rutaganda*, March 11, 1998.

347 *"which they died"* ICTR, Testimony, William Haglund, *Prosecutor v. George Rutaganda*, March 10, 1998.

348 *"way to go"* Stephen Buckley, "Ex-Leader in Rwanda Admits to Genocide; Hutu Premier Pleads Before U.N. Tribunal," *Washington Post*, May 2, 1998.

348 *delivering the sentence* James McKinley, "Ex-Rwandan Premier Gets Life in Prison on Charges of Genocide in '94 Massacres," *New York Times*, September 5, 1998.

349 *"have stopped it"* Cruvellier, *Ubutabera*, No. 31, March 22, 1998.

349 *court, it read* Copy in possession of author.

CHAPTER 15: JUSTICE ON THE GROUND

Interviews

Hasan Nuhanović, Hamdo and Firdesa Kahrimanović, Mladen Tadić, Petko and Gordana Grubač. At Physicians for Human Rights, Bill Haglund, Dr. Laurie Vollen, and Susanna Sirkin; also staff at the Podrinje Project. At the Yugoslav Tribunal, Deputy Prosecutor Graham Blewitt, Judge Gabrielle Kirk McDonald, José Pablo Barybar, Jon Cina, Jim Landale, Paul Risley, and others current and former who wish not to be identified; former chief prosecutor Louise Arbour, Ibro Makam, and others in Čelebići.

Page

353 *November 1999 report* UN General Assembly, Fifty-fourth session, "Report of the Expert Group to Conduct a Review of the Effective Operation and Functioning of the International Tribunal for the Former Yugoslavia and the International Criminal Tribunal for Rwanda," A/54/634, November 22, 1999, p. 42.

354 *staff could handle* U.S. General Accounting Office, Report to the Chairman, Committee on Foreign Relations, U.S. Senate. "Former Yugoslavia: War Crimes Tribunal's Workload Exceeds Capacity," GAO/NSIAD-98-134, June 1998, p. 24.

354 *was fully staffed* Ibid., p. 12.

354 *with no result* From October 1995 until March 16, 1999, the tribunal reported the noncompliance of the Federal Republic of Yugoslavia on eight different occasions.

355 *about the court* Among other findings, the staffers discovered that Bosnian Muslims were angry that high-ranking war criminals hadn't been indicted. Bosnian Serbs were outraged by the use of sealed indictments.

356 *actions legally questionable* See Steven Erlanger, "Rights Group Says NATO Bombing in Yugoslavia Violated Law," *New York Times*, June 8, 2000. Both Amnesty International and Human Rights Watch concluded the NATO bombing attack violated international laws aimed at protecting civilians.

358 *left fifty-eight dead* Independent International Commission on Kosovo, *Kosovo Report: Conflict, International Response, Lessons Learned* (New York: Oxford University Press, 2000), p. 68.

358 *their families slain* Ibid., p. 74.

358 *Milošević to heel* Human Rights Watch, "A Week of Terror in Drenica: Humanitarian Law Violations in Kosovo, 1999," http://www.hrw.org/hrw/reports/1999/Kosovo.

358 *exchange for peace* *Times* of London, October 13, 1998.

358 *"negotiation or abrogation"* October 22, 1998, letter, copy in possession of author.

358 *further negotiations failed* Unsuccessful peace talks were held between the Serbs, the KLA, and American, and European officials in Rambouillet, France, in February 1999.

358 *on March 24* NATO did not seek the authority of the UN Security Council. Hence the Independent International Commission in Kosovo concluded NATO's military intervention was "illegal but legitimate."

359 *committed in Kosovo* Transcript of speech given by British prime minister Tony Blair at NATO Conference, March 8, 1999. Posted on Justwatch-l@listserve.acsu.buffalo.edu.

359 *"a British government"* Transcript of press conference given by the foreign secretary, Robin Cook, London, April 20, 1990, posted on justwatch-l@listserve.acsu.buffalo.edu.

359 *war in Bosnia* Paul Williams and Norman Cigar, fellows at the Washington-based Balkan Institute in 1996, had assembled a prima facie case against Milošević for war crimes in Bosnia, which the tribunal did not use. The tribunal had been working more closely with governments to receive intelligence since it implemented its policy of sealed indictments. Part of the problem previously had been that few on the staff were trained in intelligence-gathering techniques, and they often failed to ask the correct questions of intelligence agencies. (Intelligence agencies are reactive, not proactive.)

361 *operating in Kosovo* The tribunal unveiled Arkan's arrest warrant; his indictment, and the specifics of the crimes therein, remain sealed.

361 *Good Morning America* His indictment was unsealed in 2001. Arkan was indicted for crimes against humanity, grave breaches of the Geneva Convention, and violations of the laws and customs of war. He was accused of command responsibility for crimes committed by his soldiers in Sanski Most in 1992. His soldiers allegedly beat, raped, imprisoned, and executed "non-Serbs," according to the indictment. The indictment mentions that Arkan and his Tigers were active in Zvornik and Bijeljina as well, but does not accuse him of crimes there.

361 *his top aides* Milan Milutinović, the president of Serbia, Dragoljub Ojdanić, chief of staff of the Yugoslav Army, Nikola Sainović, deputy prime minster, and Vlajko Stojiljković, the minister of internal affairs.

361 *to Milošević himself* Milošević, as civilian commander of the Yugoslav military and police forces, was charged with command responsibility for the crimes and with personal responsibility for them. In the Čelebići case, the judges ruled that command responsibility applies only to individuals in the direct chain of command who have power to issue binding orders and to punish those who violate such orders. The test is whether a superior has "effective control over the perpetrator." This ruling is likely to influence the Milošević case, when it comes to trial.

362 *mass grave sites* Kurt Schork, "Justice for the Balkans? War Crimes Tribunal Gains Momentum From Kosovo," Reuters, June 21, 1999.

362 "*War Crimes Effort*" Colum Lynch, "Judge Blasts UN's War Crimes Effort," *Washington Post*, November 10, 1999.

366 "*he took Srebrenica*" Hans de Vrelj, "NATO Arrests 'Butcher of Srebrenica,' " Radio Netherlands, December 2, 1998.

367 *to confirm it* There are at least two survivors of Pilica; I interviewed one in 1996, under the condition I would not reveal his full name. A second lives in hiding in Switzerland.

CHAPTER 16: RWANDAN CRIMES, ARUSHA JUSTICE

Interviews

In Taba: Witness JJ, Witness PP, Witness OO, Witness NN, Witness PP, Godelieve Mukasarasi, members of the widows group of Taba, Mayor Ephram Karangwa. In Kigali: At Ibuka, F. Regis Rukundakuvuga. At Avega, the Association of Widows of the Genocide, Geraldine Umugwaneza and Hilarie Mukamazimpaka; at the Rwandan Women Community Development Network, Mary Balikungeri; tribunal deputy prosecutor Bernard Muna and others of his staff who consented to be interviewed on the condition their opinions remain anonymous; Fiacre Birasa, Department of Justice, Kigali. In Arusha: Thierry Cruvellier of the newsletter Ubutabera; Martin Charles Ngogo, the Rwanda official in charge of relations with the tribunal; Judges Navanethem Pillay and Yakov Ostrovsky; Registrar Agwu Ukiwe Okali; Roland Amoussouga, chief of the tribunal's witness and support section; spokesman Tom Kennedy; prosecutor Holo Makwaia; and other tribunal staff who spoke on condition of anonymity.

Page

372 *15,000 have confessed* U.S. Department of State, "Country Reports on Human Rights Practices for 1999: Rwanda," released by the Bureau of Democracy, Human Rights, and Labor, February 2000, http://www.state.gov/www/global/human_rights_reports_mainhp.html.

373 *extended to 2001* Ibid.

373 *remained highly politicized* Human Rights Watch, "Rwanda: Human Rights Developments, World Report 2000," http://www.hrw.org/wr2k/Africa-08.htm.

373 *beyond its mandate* UN General Assembly, Fifty-fourth session, "Report of the Expert Group to Conduct a Review of the Effective Operation and Functioning of the International Tribunal for the Former Yugoslavia

and the International Criminal Tribunal for Rwanda," A/54/634, November 22, 1999, p. 95. In November 1999, the UN Experts Group estimated eight additional years. That number was revised upward with new arrests; some tribunal staff estimated as long as twenty more years.

373 *in March 2000* In 1999 the government announced it would not step down at the end of its five-year mandate as decreed by the Arusha accords. A series of government and parliamentary leaders then left or were forced from their posts. The country's parliament became heavily skewed toward the government. The entire Supreme Court was replaced.

374 *camp in Kibeho* U.S. Department of State, "Country Reports for Human Rights Practices for 1999: Rwanda," February 2000.

374 *Kamanzi told reporters* J. Coll Metcalf, "Barayagwiza's Ordered Release; Why It Happened, and What It Means," The Internews Network, November 24, 1999.

374 *November 3, 1999* ICTR, *The Prosecutor v. Jean-Bosco Barayagwiza*, November 1999, p. 28.

374 *Chamber of Appeals* Judges Mohamed Shahabuddeen, Lal Chand Vohrah, Wang Tieya, Rafael Nieto-Navia. Judge Shahabuddeen filed a thirty-one-page dissent.

375 *"at stake here"* ICTR, *Jean-Bosco Barayagwiza v. The Prosecutor*, November 1999, p. 28.

375 *"for their loss" Louise Mushikiwabo et al. v. Jean-Bosco Barayagwiza*, U.S. District Court, Southern District of New York, 94-CIV.3627 (JSM).

375 *court judges concluded* ICTR, *The Prosecutor v. Jean-Bosco Barayagwiza*, November 1999, p. 28.

376 *to run them* The Rwanda Tribunal began an outreach program in 1998. Among other measures, the court provided office space and logistical support for Radio Rwanda broadcasts of trials and judgments in Kinyarwanda, French, and English.

376 *to the crimes* Rwandan courts reflected this need. Those who confessed to crimes often also publicly apologized to their victims.

377 *validate their suffering* Human Rights Watch, "Rwanda: Human Rights Developments, World Report 2000," http://www.hrw.org/wr2k/Africa-08.htm.

378 *by Hutu extremists* Godelieve says her husband was slated to testify. Tribunal prosecutors disagree.

379 *children were malnourished.* Akayesu and other defendants called a hunger strike in October 1998 when the tribunal rejected his choice of lawyer, John Philpot, arguing there were too many Canadians acting as defense attorneys. Twenty-five detainees joined to protest the decision banning French and Canadian attorneys. The decision was reversed. See also The World Bank. *Rebuilding an Equitable Society: Poverty and Poverty Reduction After the Genocide*, World Bank Report No. 17792-RW, 1998, p. 6. Children in female-headed households also have a higher probability of malnutrition.

381 *"crime of genocide"* Comments made September 2, 1998. Quoted in ICTR News, No. 5, November 1998.

381 *to Taba's mayor* Tribunal witness-protection staff dispute this, saying they have visited Taba several times since the judgment was handed down.

381 *pregnant woman's womb* ICTR, Transcript, *Prosecutor v. Jean-Paul Akayesu*, November 4, 1997, p. 30.

382 *militia, "Take them"* Ibid., pp. 171–180.

384 *to stand trial* Barayagwiza's trial began in October 2000. He is part of the "media trial," in which three journalists are accused of conspiracy, incitement to commit genocide, and crimes against humanity.

385 *November of 1998* The trials ended in November 1998; the judgment was handed down in May 1999. Ostrovsky was not assigned another trial until October 2000.

385 *"was no roadmap"* The registrar, Agwu Okali, was replaced by a new registrar, Adama Dieng, in March 2001.

385 *and legal errors* "Infighting Cripples Rwandan Tribunal," Associated Press, August 16, 1999. The article describes infighting among the registrar, the judges, and prosecutors.

385 *its report concluded* United Nations, Forty-fourth session, "Report of the Expert Group to Conduct a Review of the Effective Operation and Functioning of an International Tribunal for the Former Yugoslavia and the International Criminal Tribunal for Rwanda," November 22, 1999, p. 20, UN document A/54/634.

386 *1997 and 1999* Ibid., p. 32.

CHAPTER 17: WHEN A TRIBUNAL IS NOT ENOUGH

Interviews

Anonciata Kavaruganda, Michael Hourigan, Geoffrey Robertson, Louise Mushikwabo; at UN legal affairs, Ralph Zacklin; at the tribunal, Judge Gabrielle Kirk McDonald, John Cina, Liam McDowall, Jim Landale, Bill Haglund, Laurie Vollen, Semir Bekrić; Ed Huffine of ICMP; Petko Grubač, Jakob Finci, Bill Stuebner; Fiacre Bisara, Gerald Gahima, and Yael Danieli.

Page

390 *to stand trial* Simić had fled to Serbia. His surrender came a week before Serbia was slated to meet a deadline mandated by the U.S. Congress to cooperate with the tribunal or risk losing thousands in U.S. aid.

390 *to The Hague* Milošević was arrested as the U.S. government was due to certify that Serbia had cooperated with the tribunal—a move that

would lead to millions in aid being released. After Milošević's arrest, the Bush administration agreed to release the money to Serbia, but emphasized it wanted to see him stand trial in The Hague.

391 *an outreach program* Money was raised from the Dutch, Finnish, and U.S. governments and the U.S.-based McArthur Foundation. Trilingual Internet broadcasting of tribunal proceedings is available at http://www.domavina.×s4all.nl. Few victims or victims' groups, however, have access to the Internet. Radio Liberty also broadcasts *Hague Chronicle*, a thirty-minute Serb-Croat summary of tribunal trials. South East News Service Europe also broadcasts regularly about what occurs in The Hague, but many Bosnians complain local networks continue to shift the time it is shown, making it hard to find.

392 *at odd hours* Portions of the trial were broadcast by SENSE, an independent TV service run by Mirko Klarin, who has plans to make a documentary about the trial for Bosnians.

392 *in the region* See letter dated May 17, 2000, from the ICTY president, Claude Jorda, to President Stipe Mesić, Republic of Croatia, JL/P.I.S./501-e, http://www.un.org/icty/pressreal/p501-e.htm.

392 *who will pay* ICTY Press Release, September 14, 2000, "The Tribunal's President, H. E. Judge Claude Jorda, will recommend to the Security Council and to the Secretary-General 'that methods of compensating victims of crimes in the former Yugoslavia be seriously considered by the appropriate organs of the United Nations.' "

393 *"generation to generation"* As quoted in C. Vegh, R. Swartz, trans., *I Didn't Say Goodbye* (New York: E. P. Dutton, 1984), p. 166.

393 *to a pendant* "Bosnian Projects: Antemortem Database Project," at http://www.phrusa.org.bonsia/an_intro.html.

399 *country to Tanzania* "Rwanda: Thousands of Refugees Flew to Tanzania," Integrade Regional Information Networks (IRIN), July 6, 2000.

399 *possibly quixotic—lawsuit* The lawyers included Geoffrey Robertson, the British barrister who represented Amnesty International in the 1998 case against former Chilean dictator Augusto Pinochet; Michael Hourigan, the former Rwanda Tribunal investigator; and Richard Middleton, president of the American Trial Lawyers' Association.

400 *up their cause* Michael Hourigan, who agreed to represent the two women early on, arranged this meeting.

400 *"to my husband"* Meeting between the Survivors of the Rwandan Genocide and the Independent Inquiry into the United Nations Role in the Rwandan Genocide. Representative Cynthia McKinney, U.S. House of Representatives, presiding, Washington, D.C., December 8, 1999. Transcript in author's possession. The women met with Ingivar Carlsson, Han Sung-Joo, and Major General Rufus M. Kupolati.

400 *"required," it concluded* "Report of the Independent Inquiry into the Actions of the United Nations During the 1994 Genocide in Rwanda," submitted to the Secretary-General by Ingivar Carlsson, Han Sung-Joo,

Major General Rufus M. Kupolati on December 14, 1999, available at http://www.un.org/News/ossg/rwanda_report.htm.

400 *by UN peacekeepers* UN legal staff argue the case is quite different. The UN mission in the Congo was an enforcement mission with a different mandate; the UN mission in Rwanda, a peacekeeping mission.

400 *up the case* Their attorneys were poised to file a lawsuit in New York against the UN in September 2000. News then broke out that Hourigan, while at the tribunal, had evidence that the Tutsi-led RPF shot down Habyarimana's plane, the act believed to have touched off the genocide. Louise Mushikwabo and Hourigan quarreled over the issue, and she subsequently instructed him not to proceed with the case. She is currently searching for new attorneys.

401 *that same day* This was revealed in both Dražen Erdemović's testimony during the Rule 61 Hearing and his testimony in the Krstić trial. See ICTR, Testimony, *Prosecutor v. General Radislav Krstić*, May 22, 2000, and July 5, 1996 for the Rule 61 Hearing, Case Nos.: IT-95-18-R61 and IT-95-5-R61.

BIBLIOGRAPHY

BOOKS

Allcock, John B., John J. Horton, Marko Milivojević. *Yugoslavia in Transition: Choices and Constraints: Essays in Honour of Fred Singleton.* New York: St. Martin's Press, 1992.

The American Heritage Dictionary of the English Language, New College Edition. Boston: Houghton Mifflin, 1976.

Andrić, Ivo. *Bosnian Chronicle.* Translated by Joseph Hitrec. New York: Alfred A. Knopf, Inc., 1963. First paperback edition 1993.

Andrić, Ivo. *The Bridge on the Drina.* Translated by Lovett F. Edwards. Chicago: The University of Chicago Press, 1977.

Askin, Kelly Dawn. *War Crimes Against Women.* Martin Nihoff Publishers, Kluwer Law International, The Hague, 1997.

Baedeker's Yugoslavia. New York: Prentice Hall.

Bass, Gary Jonathan. *Stay the Hand of Vengeance: The Politics of War Crimes Tribunals.* Princeton: Princeton University Press, 2000.

Bassiouni, M. Cherif. *The Law of the International Criminal Tribunal for the Former Yugoslavia.* Irvington-on-Hudson, NY: Transnational Publisher, Inc., 1996.

Begović, Branslav. *Sumsak privreda Bosne i Hercegovine, 1918–1914.* Sarajevo: Institut za istoriju, 1985.

Best, Geoffrey. *War and Law since 1945.* London: Oxford University Press, 1994.

Boissier, Pierre. *From Solferino to Tsushima: History of the International Committee on the Red Cross.* Geneva: Henry Dunant Institute/IRCR, 1985.

Bosna i Hercegovina od najstarijih vremena do kraja drugog svjetskog rata (grupa autora). Sarajevo: Veselin Masles, 1994, 1997.

Brownmiller, Susan. *Against Our Will: Men, Women and Rape.* New York: Simon and Schuster, 1975.

Buergenthal, Thomas. *International Human Rights in a Nutshell.* St. Paul, MN: West Publishing Co., 1995.

Buruma, Ian. *The Wages of Guilt: Memories of War in Germany and Japan.* London: Penguin Books, 1995.

Carr, Rosamond Halsey, with Ann Howard Halsey. *Land of a Thousand Hills: My Life in Rwanda.* New York: Penguin Books, 2000.

Cekić, Smail, ed. *Srebrenica 1995: Dokumenti I svjedočenja I, Knjiga 2.* Sarajevo: Institut za istrazivanje zlocina protiv covjecnosti I medunarodnog prava Sarajevo, 1999.

Cohen, Roger. *Hearts Grown Brutal: Sagas of Sarajevo.* New York: Random House, 1998.

Cooper, Belinda, ed. *War Crimes: The Legacy of Nuremberg.* New York: TV Books, LLC, 1999.

Daalder, Ivo. H. *Getting to Dayton: The Making of America's Bosnia Policy*. Washington, D.C.: Brookings Institute Press, 2000.

Dedjier, Vladimir. *The Road to Sarajevo*. London: MacGibbon & Kee, Ltd., 1967.

Demick, Barbara. *Logavina Street: Life and Death in a Sarajevo Neighborhood*. Kansas City, Missouri: Andrews and McMeel, 1996.

Des Forges, Alison. *Leave None to Tell the Story: Genocide in Rwanda*. New York: Human Rights Watch, March 1999.

Destexhe, Alain. *Rwanda and Genocide in the Twentieth Century*. New York: New York University Press, 1995.

Dickens, Charles. *Bleak House*. New York: The Heritage Press, 1942.

Disdarević, Zlatko. *Sarajevo: A War Journal*. Translated by Anselm Hollo. New York: Henry Holt and Company, 1993.

Djilas, Milovan. *Conversations with Stalin*. New York: Harcourt Brace, 1962.

Doder, Dusko. *The Yugoslavs*. New York: Random House, 1978.

Donia, Robert J. and John V. A. Fine, Jr. *Bosnia and Hercegovina: A Tradition Betrayed*. New York: Columbia University Press, 1994.

Drakulič, Slavenka. *The Balkan Express: Fragments From the Other Side of War*. New York: W. W. Norton & Company, 1993.

Dunant, Henry J. *A Memory of Solferino*. American Red Cross/International Committee of the Red Cross, 1986.

Durch, William J., ed. *UN Peacekeeping, American Politics, and the Uncivil Wars of the 1990s*. New York: St. Martin's Press/A Henry L. Stimson Center Book, 1996.

Enciklopedija Jugoslavije, Separat o Bosni i Hercegovini. Zagreb: JAZU, 1983.

Fromkin, David. *Kosovo Crossing: American Ideals Meet Reality on the Balkan Battlefields*. New York: Free Press, 1999.

Frye, Alton, Project Director. *Toward an International Criminal Court? Three Opinions Presented as Presidential Speeches*. New York, Council on Foreign Relations Inc.

Glenny, Misha. *The Fall of Yugoslavia: The Third Balkan War*. London: Penguin Books, 1992.

Glenny, Misha. *The Balkans: Nationalism, War and the Great Powers, 1804–1999*. New York: Penguin, 2000.

Goldstone, Richard. *For Humanity: Reflections of a War Crimes' Investigator*. New Haven: Yale University Press, 2000.

Gourevitch, Philip. *We Wish to Inform You That Tomorrow We Will Be Killed with Our Families: Stories from Rwanda*. New York: Farrar, Straus & Giroux, 1998.

Grebelja, Tonči and Duscan Otasevič. *Istorija za 2 razred srendnjeg usmjerenog obrazovanja*. Beograde: Zavod za zdravanje udzenika, 1989.

Green, Leslie C. *The Contemporary Law of Armed Conflict*. New York: Manchester University Press, 1993.

Gutman, Roy and David Rieff, eds. *Crimes of War: What the Public Should Know*. New York: W. W. Norton & Company, 1999.

Hadzibegović, Iljas. *Bosnakoherceogvacki gradovi na rezmedu 19. i 20. Stoljeca*. Sarajevo: Oslobodjenje Public, 1991.

Helsinki Watch. *War Crimes in Bosnia-Hercegovina.* New York: Human Rights Watch, August 1992.

Helsinki Watch. *War Crimes in Bosnia-Hercegovina,* Vol II. New York: Human Rights Watch, April 1993.

Henken, Alice H., ed. *Honoring Human Rights From Peace to Justice: Recommendations to the International Community.* Washington, D.C.: The Aspen Institute, 1998.

Hochschild, Adam. *King Leopold's Ghost: A Story of Greed, Terror, and Heroism in Colonial Africa.* New York: Houghton Mifflin Co., 1998.

Holbrooke, Richard. *To End a War.* New York: Random House, 1998.

The Holy Bible, Revised Standard Version. Cleveland: The World Publishing Company, 1962.

Homer. *The Iliad,* Book II. New York: Walter J. Black Inc., 1942.

Honig, Jan Willem and Norbert Both. *Srebrenica: Record of a War Crime.* London: Penguin Books, 1996.

Hukanović, Rezak. Translated by Colleen London and Midhat Ridjanovic. *The Tenth Circle of Hell: A Memoir of Life in the Death Camps of Bosnia.* New York: A New Republic Book/Basic Books, 1993.

Human Rights Watch/Africa, Human Rights Watch Women's Rights Project, Federation Internationale des Ligues des Droits de L'Homme. *Shattered Lives: Sexual Violence During the Rwandan Genocide and Its Aftermath.* New York: Human Rights Watch, 1996.

Ignatieff, Michael. *The Warrior's Honor: Ethnic War and The Modern Conscience.* London: Chatto & Windus, 1998.

Independent International Commission on Kosovo. *Kosovo Report: Conflict, International Response, Lessons Learned.* New York: Oxford University Press, 2000.

International Committee of the Red Cross. *Basic Rules of the Geneva Conventions and Their Additional Protocols.* Geneva: ICRC Publications, September 1983.

Jiricek and Radonjić. *Istorija Srba, Vol. 2.* Beograd, 1912.

Jones, Archer. *The Art of War in the Western World 216–19.* Chicago: University of Illinois Press, 1987.

Joyce, Christopher and Eric Stover. *The Stories Bones Tell: Witnesses From the Grave.* New York: Random House, Inc., 1991.

Judah, Tim. *The Serbs: History, Myth, and the Destruction of Yugoslavia.* New Haven: Yale University Press, 1997.

Junod, Marcel. *Warrior Without Weapons.* Translated by Edward Fitzgerald. Geneva: The International Committee of the Red Cross, 1982.

Kaplan, Robert D. *Balkan Ghosts: A Journey Through History.* New York: St. Martin's Press, 1993.

Karahasan, Dvevad. *Sarajevo, Exodus of a City.* Translated by Slobodon Drakulić. New York: Kodansha American Inc., 1994.

Keane, Fergal. *Season of Blood: A Rwandan Journey.* London: Penguin Books, 1996.

Kennan, George F. *The Other Balkan Wars: A 1913 Carnegie Endowment Inquiry in Retrospect with a New Introduction and Reflections on the Present Conflict.* Washington, D.C.: The Carnegie Endowment for International Peace, 1913/1993.

Kovačić, Ivan Goran. "The Pit" in *Trajno.* Beograde: Petar Kocic, 1976.

Kozı. [illegible] *narodnooslobodilackoj borbi i socijalistickoj reluciji 1941–1945.* Prejidor: Naunni skup, 1980.

Kressel, Neil J. *In Mass Hate: The Global Rise of Genocide and Terror.* New York: Plenum Press, 1996.

Levi, Primo. *Survival in Auschwitz: The Nazi Assault on Humanity.* Translated by Stuart Woolf. New York: Macmillan, 1993.

Making Justice Work: The Report of the Century Foundation/Twentieth Century Fund Task Force on Apprehending Indicted War Criminals. New York: The Century Foundation Press, 1998.

Malcolm, Noel. *Bosnia: A Short History.* London: Macmillan, 1994.

Mamdani, Mahmood. *When Victims Become Killers: Colonialism, Nativism and the Genocide in Rwanda.* Princeton: Princeton University, 2001.

Mazower, Mark. *The Balkans: A Short History.* New York: The Modern Library/ Random House, Inc., 2000.

Melvern, Linda. *A People Betrayed. The Role of the West in Rwanda's Genocide.* London: Zed Books, Ltd., 2000.

Meron, Theodore. *War Crimes Law Comes of Age: Essays.* Oxford: Clarendon Press, 1998.

Minow, Martha. *Between Vengeance and Forgiveness: Facing History After Genocide and Mass Violence.* Boston: Beacon Press, 1998.

Moore, Jonathan, ed. *Hard Choices: Moral Dilemmas in Humanitarian Intervention.* Landham: Rowman & Littlefield Publishers, Inc., 1998.

Moorehead, Caroline. *Dunant's Dream: War, Switzerland, and the History of the Red Cross.* New York: Carroll & Graf Publishers, Inc., 1998.

Mousavizadeh, Nader (ed). *The Black Book of Bosnia: The Consequences of Appeasement.* New York: New Republic Books, 1996.

Neier, Aryeh. *War Crimes: Brutality, Genocide, Terror, and the Struggle for Justice.* New York: Times Books/Random House, 1998.

Omar, Rakiya. *Rwanda: Death, Despair and Defiance* (Revised Edition). London: African Rights, 1995.

Oslobodilacki rat naroda Jugoslavije 1941–1945, knj. 1 i 2. Beograde, 1958.

Persico, Joseph E. *Nuremberg: Infamy on Trial.* London: Penguin Books, 1994.

Pictet, Jean. "International Humanitarian Law: Definition," *International Dimensions of Humanitarian Law.* Henry Dunant Institute/UNESCO, 1998.

Pictet, Jean S. (ed). *The Geneva Conventions of 12 August 1949 Commentary: IV Geneva Convention Relative to the Protection of Civilian Persons in Time of War.* Geneva: The International Committee of the Red Cross, 1958.

Prunier, Gerard. *The Rwandan Crisis: History of a Genocide, 1959–1994.* London: Hurst and Company, 1995/1997.

Rhodes, Richard. *Why They Kill: The Discoveries of a Maverick Criminologist.* New York: Alfred A. Knopf, 1999.

Robertson, Geoffrey. *Crimes Against Humanity: The Struggle for Global Justice.* New York: The New Press, 1999/2000.

Rosandic, Dr. Ruzica and Dr. Vesna Pejić (eds). *Warfare, Patriotism, Patriarchy: The*

Analysis of Elementary School Textbooks. Belgrade: Center for Anti-War Action, 1994.

Rose, General Sir Michael. *Fighting for Peace: Bosnia 1994*. London: Harvill Press, 1998.

Rosenberg, Tina. *The Haunted Land: Facing Europe's Ghosts After Communism*. New York: Vintage Books, 1995.

Ryan, Cornelius. *The Last Battle*. New York: Simon and Schuster, 1966.

Sarinic, Hrvoje. *Svi Moj Tajni Pregovori Sa Slobodanom Milosevicem 1993–95 (98)*. Zagreb: Globus International, 1999.

Scharf, Michael P. *Balkan. Justice: The Story Behind the First International War Crimes Trial Since Nuremberg*. Durham, North Carolina: Carolina Academic Press, 1997.

Scharf, Michael P. and Virginia Morris. *The International Criminal Tribunal for Rwanda, Vol I*. Irvington-on-Hudson, NY: Translational Publishers, Inc., 1998.

Schwarzenberger, George. *International Law as Applied by International Courts and Tribunals: The Law of Armed Conflicts*. London: Stevens & Sons Ltd., 1968.

Selimović, Mesa. *The Fortress*. Translated by E. D. Goy & Jasna Levinger. Illinois: Northwestern University Press, 1999.

Shakespeare, William. *The Riverside Shakespeare*. Boston: Houghton Mifflin Company, 1974.

Shawcross, William. *Deliver Us From Evil: Warlords and Peacekeepers in a World of Endless Conflict*. London: Bloomsbury Publishing Plc., 2000.

Silber, Laura and Allan Little. *The Death of Yugoslavia*. London: Penguin Books, 1995.

Stanovnistvo Bosne i Hercegovine, Narodnosni sastav po naseljima. Zagreb: Drzavni zvod za statistiku Republike Hrvatske, 1995.

Stover, Eric with photos by Gilles Peress. *The Graves: Srebrenica and Vukovar*. Berlin: Scalo, 1998.

Sudetic, Chuck. *Blood and Vengeance: One Family's Story of the War in Bosnia*. New York: W. W. Norton & Company, 1998.

Taylor, Telford. *The Anatomy of the Nuremberg Trials: A Personal Memoir*. New York: Alfred A. Knopf, 1992.

Thompson, Mark. *A Paper House: The Ending of Yugoslavia*. New York: Pantheon Books, 1992.

Thompson, Mark. *Forging War: The Media in Serbia, Croatia, and Bosnia and Hercegovina*. Bedfordshire, UK: University of Luton Press, 1999.

Vegh, C. *I Didn't Say Goodbye*. Translated by R. Swartz. New York: E. P. Dutton, 1984.

Vojna enciklopedija. Beograd: Vojno-izdavacki zavod, 1969.

Vulliamy, Ed. *Seasons in Hell: Understanding Bosnia's War*. New York: St. Martin's Press, 1994.

Wakin, Malham M., ed. *War, Morality, and the Military Profession*. Boulder, Colorado: Westview Press, 1979.

Walzer, Michael. *Just and Unjust Wars*. New York: Basic Books, 1977.

West, Rebecca. *Black Lamb and Grey Falcon: A Journey Through Yugoslavia*. London: Penguin Books, 1994.

West, Rebecca. *A Train of Powder*, New York: The Viking Press, 1955.

West, Richard. *Tito and the Rise and Fall of Yugoslavia*. New York: Carroll & Graf Publishers, Inc., 1996.

Zimmerman, Warren. *Origins of a Catastrophe: Yugoslavia and Its Destroyers*. New York: Times Books, 1996.

ARTICLES

Agence France-Presse (AFP). "International Tribunal Jails Two Bosnian Moslems for War Crimes," November 16, 1998.

Agence France-Presse (AFP). "Former Blue Helmet Alleges Dutch 'Collaboration' in Srebrenica," August 18, 1998.

Akhavan, Payam. "The International Criminal Tribunal for Rwanda: The Politics and Pragmatics of Punishment," *90 American Journal of International Law*, No. 3, July, 1996.

Akhavan, Payam. "The Yugoslav Tribunal at a Crossroads: The Dayton Peace Agreement and Beyond," *Human Rights Quarterly*, Vol. 18, No. 2, 1996.

Akhavan, Payam. "Justice and Reconciliation in the Great Lakes Region of Africa: The Contribution of the International Criminal Tribunal for Rwanda," *Duke Journal of Comparative and International Law*, Vol. 325, 1997.

Allison, Ewen. "News from the International War Crimes Tribunals. The Human Rights Brief," *The Human Rights Brief*, The Center for Human Rights and Humanitarian Law at Washington College of Law, American University, 1999.

Alvarez, Jose E. "Crimes of States/Crimes of Hate: Lessons from Rwanda." *Yale Journal of International Law.*

Alvarez, Jose E. "Rush to Closure: Lessons of the Tadic Judgement," 96 *Michigan Law Review*, No. 7, June 1998.

Amnesty International News Release, "Amnesty International Condemns Unfair Trial of "Zvornik Seven," EUR 63/07/97, April 24, 1997.

Askin, Kelly Dawn. "The International Criminal Tribunal for Rwanda and Its Treatment of Crimes Against Women,"*International Humanitarian Law: Origins, Challenges & Prospects*, ed. John Carey and R. John Prichard.

Associated Press. "Tribunal Issues More War Crimes Indictments," March 23, 1996.

Associated Press. "Infighting Cripples Rwandan Tribunal: In Five Years the Court Has Spent $209m and Dealt with Five Cases," August 16, 1999.

Association of Rwandan Genocide Widows (AVEGA). "Survey on Violence Against Women in Rwanda," Kigali, Rwanda, December, 1999.

Bassiouni, M. Cherif. "Former Yugoslavia: Investigating Violations of International Humanitarian Law and Establishing an International Criminal Tribunal," *18 Fordham International Law Journal*, No. 4, April, 1995.

Bennett, Christopher. "The Propaganda Battle Stretches Well into the Past. Official Serbia Boasts of Its Defiant and Heroic History. The Only Problem Is the Facts," *IWPR's Balkan Crisis Report 22.*

Biserko, Sonja. "Reporting from the Writing Fields, or 'How to Prepare Genocide in Five Years,' " *Helsinki Committee for Human Rights in Serbia,* 1997.

Black, Chris. "A New Bosnia Airlift: A Lobster to Peace Talks," *Boston Globe,* November 19, 1995.

Bone, James. "U.N. Chief Hits Out at Response to Rwanda Plea," *The Times* (of London) May 26, 1994.

Bonner, Raymond. "Rwandan Says the Victors Kill Many Who Go Back," *New York Times,* August 5, 1994.

Bonner, Raymond. "Top Rwandan Criticizes U.S. Envoy," *New York Times,* November 8, 1994.

Borger, Julian. "Grisly Tussle for Bosnia's Dead. Views Differ on the Plan to Dig Up Mass Graves." *The Guardian,* April 6, 1996.

Bosnet Digest. "Italian NATO Troops Nearly Miss Capturing Radovan Karadzic," February 23, 1996.

Buckley, Stephen. "Ex-Leader in Rwanda Admits to Genocide; Hutu Premier Pleads Before U.N. Tribunal," *The Washington Post,* May 2, 1998.

Chaney, Kevin R. "Pitfalls and Imperatives: Applying the Lessons of Nuremberg to the Yugoslav War Crimes Trials," *14 Dickinson Journal of International Law,* No. 1, Fall 1995.

Chesterman, Simon. "Never Again . . . and Again: Law, Order and Gender of War Crimes in Bosnia and Beyond," *22 Yale Journal of International Law* 299, 325.

Cibelli, Kristin and Guberek, Tamy. *Justice Unknown, Justice Unsatisfied: Bosnian NGOs Speak About the International Criminal Tribunal for the Former Yugoslavia.* A Project of Education and Public Inquiry and International Citizenship at Tufts University, 1999.

Cohen, Roger. "Conflict in the Balkans: The Overview," *New York Times,* November 1, 1995.

Corder, Mike. "Tribunal Adds a Courtroom to Speed Trials: Hague Court Faces Backlog," Associated Press, 1998.

Corder, Mike. "Bosnia Serb War Criminal Given 20-year Prison Term at Sentencing Today," Associated Press, July 14, 1997.

CNN World News Online. "Rwanda to Carry Out First Executions for 1994 Genocide," April 22, 1998. As posted at www.cnn.com.

CNN World News Online. "Rwanda Rejects Clemency Pleas and Begins Executions," April 24, 1998. As posted at www.cnn.com.

Crane-Engel, Melinda. "Germany vs. Genocide," *New York Times,* October 30, 1994.

Creta, Vincent M. "The Search for Justice in the Former Yugoslavia and Beyond: Analyzing the Rights of the Accused Under the Rules of Evidence and Procedure of the International Criminal Tribunal for the Former Yugoslavia," *Houston Journal of International Law,* Winter 1998.

Crossette, Barbara. "Judge Urges World to Heed Rwanda Crisis," *The New York Times*, December 31, 1995.

Cruvellier, Thierry, Ubutabera. Independent Newsletter on the International Criminal Tribunal for Rwanda. As posted on the Judicial Diplomacy Web site www.diplomatiejudiciaire.com/UK/Home.htm. No. 32, March 16, 1998; No. 33, March 30, 1998; No. 35, Spring 1998; No. 38, June 8, 1998.

D'Amato, Anthony. "Peace vs. Accountability in Bosnia," *88 American Journal of International Law*, No. 3, July, 1994.

Daalder, Ivo H. "Knowing When to Say No: The Development of US Policy for Peacekeeping," in *UN Peacekeeping: American Policy and the Uncivil Wars of the 1990's*, ed. William J. Durch. New York: St. Martin's Press (A Henry Stimson Center Book), 1996.

Dallaire, Romeo. "End of Innocence, Rwanda 1994," in *Hard Choices: Moral Dilemmas in Humanitarian Intervention*, ed. Jonathan Moore. Maryland: Rowman & Littlefield Publishers, Inc., 1998.

Diehl, Jackson. "Economic Crises Test Yugoslavia's System," *The Washington Post*, February 20, 1986.

Diljas, Alesksa. "A Profile of Slobodan Milošević," *Foreign Affairs*, Vol. 27 No. 3, Summer 1993.

Dinmore, Guy. "Time Running Out for Bosnian Serb War Crime Suspect," *The Chicago Tribune*, April 10, 1998.

Doder, Duško. "The Slaughter of Muslims Reported," *The Boston Globe*, July 26, 1995.

Driessen, Christoph. "UN War Crimes Tribunal Finds It Hard to Convict the Real Culprits," *Deutsche Presse-Agentur*, 1998. Web site. Accessed 5/13/1999.

Drozdiak, William, "Dutch Troops Absolve UN Troops in Fall of Srebrenica to Serbs," *The Washington Post*, October 31, 1995.

Durch, William J. and James A. Schear. "Faultlines: UN Operations in the Former Yugoslavia," *UN Peacekeeping: American Policy and the Uncivil Wars of the 1990's*, ed. William J. Durch. New York: St. Martin's Press (A Henry L. Stimpson Center Book), 1996.

Edwards, Steven. "Memo Contradicts UN Claims on Assassination Probe," *The National Post*, March 31, 2000.

Evenson, Brad. "Broken Dallaire, Haunted by Rwanda, Lies Drunk in Park," *The National Post*, June 29, 2000.

Erlanger, Steven. "French Said to Hurt Plan to Capture Karadzic," *New York Times*, April 23, 1998.

Fenrick, W. J. "Some International Law Problems Related to Prosecutions Before the International Tribunal for the Former Yugoslavia," *6 Duke Journal of International Law*, No. 1, Fall 1995.

Ferencz, Benjamin. "From Nuremburg to Rome: Towards an International Criminal Court." Policy Paper No. 8. As posted on Web site http://www.bicc.de/sef/publications/pol-pap/no8/text.html.

Finnegan, William. "The Next War: As Milosevic Empire Shrinks, New Resentments Inflame Outer Serbia," *The New Yorker*, September 20, 1999.

Forsythe, David P. "Politics and the International Tribunal for the former Yugoslavia," *Criminal Law Forum*, Vol. 5, Nos. 2–3, 1995.

Friedman, James. "Arendt in Jerusalem, Jackson at Nuremberg: Presuppositions of the Nazi War Crimes Trials," *Israel Law Review*, No. 4, Autumn 1994.

Friedrich, Jörg. "Nuremberg and the Germans," in *War Crimes: The Legacy of Nuremberg*, ed. Belinda Cooper. New York: TV Books, L.L.C., 1999.

Gec, Jovana. "Serbs Describe Rape, Torture by Croats, Muslims," *Associated Press*, April 27, 1996.

Goldman, T. R. "Recent Hague Rulings Could Complicate Pursuit of Milosevic," *Legal Times*, April 5, 1999.

Goldstone, Richard. "Justice as a Tool for Peace-Making: Truth Commissions and International Criminal Tribunal," *International Law and Politics*, No. 485, 1996.

Goldstone, Richard. "Assessing the Work of the United Nations War Crimes Tribunal," *Stanford Journal of International Law*, No. 1, Winter 1997.

Goldstone, Richard. "War Crimes: A Question of Will," *53 The World Today*, No. 4, April 1997.

Goodwin, Jan. "Rwanda, Justice Denied," *On the Issues: The Progressive Women's Quarterly*, Fall 1997.

Gordon, Melissa A. "Justice on Trial: The Efficacy of the International Criminal Tribunal for Rwanda." *ILSA Journal of International Law*, No. 1, Spring 1995.

Graves, Nelson. "Premier-Designate Compares Rwanda to Nazi Genocide," Reuters, May 26, 1994.

Green, Leslie C. "War Crimes, Crimes Against Humanity, and Command Responsibility," *NWC Review*, Spring 1997.

Green, Leslie C. and Michael N. Schmitt. "Levie on the Law of War." *International Law Studies*, Newport, Rhode Island: Naval War College, 1998.

Grotius, Hugo. "The Law of War and Peace (1625)," reprinted in *The Law of War: A Documentary History, Vol. I*, ed. Leon Friedman, New York: Random House, 1972.

Gutman, Roy. "Death Camp Horrors: Survivors Detail Serbian Atrocities." *Newsday*, October 18, 1992.

Gutman, Roy. "Death Camp Lists: In Town After Town, Bosnia Elite 'Disappeared,' " *Newsday*, November 8, 1992.

Gutman, Roy. "Prisoners of Serbia's War: Tales of Hunger, Torture at Camp in North Bosnia," *Newsday*, July 19, 1992.

Gutman, Roy. "War Crime Unit Hasn't a Clue: UN Setup Seems Designed to Fail," *Newsday*, March 4, 1993.

Gutman, Roy, "The U.N.'s Deadly Deal: How Troop-Hostage Talks Led to Slaughter of Srebrenica," *Newsday*, May 29, 1996.

Haglund, William D., Connor, Melissa, and Scott, Douglas D. "The Archeology of Mass Graves," *Historical Archaeology*, Vol. 35, No. 1, 2001.

Harris, John F. "Clinton Cites 'Genocide' in Massacres," *The Washington Post*, March 26, 1998.

Hedges, Chris. "Jailed Serbs' 'Victims' Found Alive, Embarrassing Bosnia," *New York Times*, March 1, 1997.

Hill, Andrew. "Bosnia Women Ask to Seek Missing Men with UN Envoy," *Reuters*, February 3, 1996.

Horne, William. "Judging Tadic: Former US District Judge in Houston Answers State Department's Call," *The American Lawyer*, 1995. As found at Court TV Web site www.courttv.com.

Horne, William. "The Real Trial of the Century," *The American Lawyer*, September 1995. As found on Court TV Web site www.courttv.com.

Hooper, Jim. "Dayton's Mandate for Apprehending War Criminals." Frontline, online. www.pbs.org/wgbh/pages/frontline/shows/karadzic/trial/hooper.html.

ICTR News, No. 5, November 1998.

ICTY. Press Release. "The Judges of the ICTY Acknowledge the Right of Victims of Crimes Committed in the Former Yugoslavia to Seek Compensation," September 14, 2000. The Hague, September 14, 2000. JL/P.I.S./528-e.

Integrade Regional Information Networks (IRIN). "Rwanda: Thousands of Refugees Flee to Tanzania," July 6, 2000. http://www.reliefweb.int/IRIN/cea/countrystories/rwanda/20000706.phtml.

International Committee of the Red Cross. "What Are the Essential Rules of International Humanitarian Laws? International Humanitarian Law: Answers to Your Question," December 1, 1999.

"International Military Tribunal: The Nuremberg War Crimes Trials" (pamphlet), Oberlandesgericht Nürnberg, Further Strasse 110, 90429 Nürnberg.

Judicial Diplomacy, "Campaigning Judges," as posted at http://www.diplomatiejudiciaire.com/UK/Tpiruk/TPIRUK7.htm.

Junger, Sebastian. "The Forensics of War," *Vanity Fair*, October 1999.

Kayigamba, Jean-Baptiste and Charles Wachira. "Rwanda: Doubts Over Value of Genocide Tribunal," Inter-Press Service, January 12, 1997.

Kempster, Norman. "Prosecutor Bars Immunity for Serb Leaders," *Los Angeles Times*, November 17, 1995.

Klarin, Mirko and Vjera Bogati. As posted on the Institute of War and Peace Reporting Tribunal Update No. 5: Last Week in The Hague (November 25–29, 1996); No. 12: Last Week in The Hague (January 20–25, 1997); No. 35: Last Week in The Hague (June 30–July 5, 1997); No. 34: Last Week in The Hague (June 23–28, 1997); No. 43: Last Week in The Hague (September 22–26, 1997); No. 48: Last Week in The Hague (October 13–17, 1997); No. 50: Last Week in The Hague (October 27–31, 1997); No. 197: Last Week in The Hague (October 30–November 4, 2000).

Klarin, Mirko. "Nuremberg Now!" *Nasa Borba*, May 16, 1991.

Koenig, Dorean M. and Kelly Dawn Askin. "International Criminal Law and The International Criminal Court Statute: Crimes Against Women," in *Women and International Human Rights Law*, eds. Askin and Koenig. Vol. 2. Ardsley, New York.

La Lettre du CLADHO, No. 18, July/August 1997.

Lane, Charles and Thom Shanker. "Bosnia: What the CIA Didn't Tell Us," *The New York Review of Books*, May 9, 1996.

Lieber, Francis. "The Lieber Code: Instructions for the Government of Armies of the United States in the Field by Order of the Secretary of War" (General Orders

No. 100) (1863), reprinted in *The Law of War: A Documentary History Vol. I*, ed. Leon Friedman, New York: Random House, 1972.

Lewis, Paul. "U.N. Council Urged to Weigh Action on Saving Rwanda," *New York Times*, April 30, 1994.

Lynch, Colum. "Judge Blasts UN's War Crimes Effort," *Washington Post*, November 10, 1999.

McBride, Sean. "The Legality of Weapons for Societal Destruction," in *Studies and Essay in Honor of Jean Pictet*, ed. Christopher Swinarski. Geneva: Martinus Nijhoff Publishers, 1984.

McDonald, Avril. "Sex Crimes at the Ad Hoc Tribunals," *Nemesis*, 1993.

McKinley, James. "As Crowds Vent Their Rage, Rwanda Publicly Executes 22," *New York Times*. April 25, 1998.

McKinley, James. "Ex-Rwandan Premier Gets Life in Prison on Charges of Genocide in '94 Massacres," *New York Times*, September 5, 1998.

Meltzer, Bernard D. " 'War Crimes': The Nuremberg Trial and the Tribunal for the Former Yugoslavia," The Seegers Lecture, *Valparaiso University Law Review*, Vol. 30, 1996.

Mendelsohn, Deborah. "Analysis: The Trial of Sendashonga's Assassins—A Trail of Missing Links," *Internews*, December 19, 2000.

Meron, Theodore. "Rape as a Crime Under International Humanitarian Law," *American Journal of International Law*, No. 3, July 1993.

Meron, Theodore. "War Crimes in Yugoslavia and the Development of International Law," *American Journal of International Law*, No. 1, January 1994.

Meron, Theodore. "International Criminalization of Internal Atrocities," *American Journal of International Law*, July 1995.

Meron, Theodore. "Answering for War Crimes: Lessons From the Balkans," *Foreign Affairs*, Vol. 76, January/February 1997.

Metcalf, J. Coll. "Barayagwiza's Ordered Release; Why It Happened, and What It Means," *The Internews Network*, November 24, 1999.

Milinković, Branislav. "The Hague Tribunal's Practice So Far," *47 Review of International Affairs*, September 1996.

Moore, Patrick. "Serbian Soldiers Confirm Massacre, Then Disappear," *Omri Daily Digest*, No. 50, March 11, 1996. BosNet NEWS.

Neier, Aryeh. "Watching Rights: Media Propaganda in Serbia," *The Nation*, 1994. Accessed database.

Neuffer, Elizabeth. "Serb Turns Himself in on War Crimes Charges," *Boston Globe*, March 13, 2001.

Neuffer, Elizabeth. "Mass Graves," in *Crimes of War: What the Public Should Know*, eds. Roy Gutman and David Reiff. New York: W. W. Norton, 1999.

Neuffer, Elizabeth. "Bosnian Serb Leader Turning Hate to Hopes," *Boston Globe*, March 29, 1998.

Neuffer, Elizabeth, "Women Wait to See If Their Attackers Will Face Charges," *Boston Globe*, December 14, 1996.

Neuffer, Elizabeth. "Mismanagement and Red Tape Impede Tribunal," *Boston Globe*, December 11, 1996.

Neuffer, Elizabeth. "Bosnia's War Criminals Enjoy Peacetime Power," *Boston Globe*, October 29, 1996.

Neuffer, Elizabeth. "For Women of Srebrenica Grave Sites Hold Few Answers," *Boston Globe*, July 30, 1996.

Neuffer, Elizabeth. "Many Bosnians Are in State of Denial," *Boston Globe*, May 20, 1996.

Neuffer, Elizabeth. "Ghosts of Srebrenica," May 19, 1996.

Neuffer, Elizabeth. "Far From the Congratulations, Rumblings Among Combatants," *Boston Globe*, November 22, 1995.

Neuffer, Elizabeth. "Vows of Revenge Veil Bosnia Peace Process; Factions Have Blood Debts to Settle," *Boston Globe*, November 12, 1995.

Neuffer, Elizabeth. "Dutch Unit Defended on Deaths in Bosnia," *Boston Globe*, October 19, 1995.

Neuffer, Elizabeth. "Witness to atrocity: UN Troops Stood By. Role in Bosnian Serb Killings Probed," *Boston Globe* October 1, 1995.

Neuffer, Elizabeth. "A Bosnia Peace Built on Ethnic Cleansing," *Boston Globe*, September 17, 1995.

Neuffer, Elizabeth. "War Ends One Dream of Sarajevo," *Boston Globe*, April 9, 1995.

Neuffer, Elizabeth. "Bosnian Cease-Fire Hits Snag as Weapons Turnover Halts," *Boston Globe*, February 13, 1994.

Neuffer, Elizabeth. "British Plane Assisting UN Is Shot Down Over Gorazde: World Body Asks Review of Role in Bosnia," *Boston Globe*, April 17, 1994.

Neuffer, Elizabeth and Column Lynch. "A UN Leader Had Learned of Disaster in 'Safe' Area," *Boston Globe*, October 31, 1995.

Newbury, Catherine. "Ethnicity and the Politics of History in Rwanda," *Africa Today*, Vol. 45, No. 2, 1998.

Newbury, Catherine. "Ethnicity and the Politics of History in Rwanda," *Africa Today*, Vol. 45, No. 1, 1998.

Newbury, David and Catherine Newbury. "An Inquiry into the Historical Preconditions of the Rwandan Genocide," *The International Panel of Eminent Personalities to Investigate the 1994 Genocide in Rwanda and the Surrounding Events*. Organization of African's Unity. http://www.oau-oua.org/Document/ipep/report/rwanda-e/EN-02-CH.htm.

New York Times, Op-Ed. "War Crimes Without Punishment," February 8, 1994.

Niarchos, Catherine N. "Women, War and Rape: Challenges Facing the International Tribunal for the Former Yugoslavia," *Human Rights Quarterly*, 17:4, November 1995.

Lukić, Dejan. "I Am Innocent." *Vecernje Novosti*, Belgrade, May 26–June 3 1997, http://www.cdsp.neu.edu/info/students/marko/evnovosti/evnovosti7.html.

Omicinski, John. "Poll: Go Get Serb War Criminals—Eve at Risk of American Lives." Gannett News Service, July 10, 1996.

Omri Daily Digest, No. 65, Part II, 1 A.

Paul, Diane. "Aiding and Abetting: Reconstruction Projects Are Seen as a Sort of Insurance Policy," *Balkan War Report*, May 1997.

Perlez, Jane. "War Crimes Prosecutor Criticizes NATO," *New York Times*, May 22, 1996.

Perlez, Jane. "NATO Backs Off Helping Bosnia War Crimes Panel," *New York Times*, January 20, 1996.

Perlez, Jane. "Rwanda Camps: Long Term Refugees?" *New York Times*, August 6, 1994.

Pictet, Jean. "The Formation of International Humanitarian Law," *International Review of Red Cross*. January–February 1995. Annex 2.

Pomfret, John. "Weapons, Cash and Chaos Lend Clout to Srebrenica's Tough Guy," *Washington Post*, February 16, 1994.

Pomfret, John. "Grim Evidence Points to Muslims' Graves," *Washington Post*, January 19, 1996.

Pomfret, John. "NATO, Prosecutor Debate Bosnia Aims," *Washington Post*, January 22, 1996.

Pomfret, John. "Bosnia's Serb Leaders Stages Show of Defiance," *Washington Post*, February 10, 1996.

Press TWRA. "Karadžić Walked by Prime Minister and Bildt," Bosnet-Digest V5#83, February 29, 1996. http://www.hri.org/news/agencies/bosnet/96-02-29_1.bos.html.

Preston, Julia. "U.N. to Set Up Tribunal on Yugoslav War Crimes," *Washington Post*, February 23, 1993.

Preston, Julia. "Rwandans Confound UN Security Council: Humanitarian Impulse as Mission Impossible," *Washington Post*, May 8, 1994.

Radin, Max. "Justice at Nuremberg," *Foreign Affairs*, Vol. 24, No. 3, April 1946.

Reuters. "NATO's Smith Says Unearthing Bosnia War Graves Not Troops' Job," January 14, 1996.

Reuters. "Bosnian Serb Police Reservists Found Guilty of War Crimes by UN Tribunal," 1997.

Reuters. "Christopher Urges Trial Over Genocide in Rwanda." July 1, 1994.

Rosenberg, Tina. "Tipping the Scales of Justice," in *War Crimes, The Legacy of Nuremberg*, ed. Belinda Cooper. New York: TV Books, L.L.C., 1999.

Rubin, Alred P. "Dayton, Bosnia and the Limits of Law," *The National Interest*, Winter 1996/1997.

Santoro, Lara. "Rwanda Massacres Were Avoidable, General Says," *Christian Science Monitor*, February 27, 1998.

Scharf, Michael P. "A Critique of the Yugoslavia War Crimes Tribunal," *Denver Journal of International Law & Policy*, No. 2, 1997.

Schork, Kurt. "Holbrooke Agrees New 'Rules of the Road' for Bosnia," Reuters, February 12, 1996.

Schork, Kurt. "Justice for the Balkans? War Crimes Tribunal Gains Momentum From Kosovo," Reuters, June 21, 1999.

Schrag, Minna. "The Yugoslav Crimes Tribunal: A Prosecutor's Views." *Duke Journal of International Law*, Vol. 6, No. 1, Fall 1995.

Schrag, Minna. "The Yugoslav War Crimes Tribunal: An Interim Assessment," *Transnational Law & Contemporary Problems*, Vol. 7, No. 15, Spring 1997.

Schweid, Barry. "Serbs Must Answer for War Atrocities, Eagleburger Says," Associated Press, December 17, 1992.

Sciolino, Elaine. "U.S. Names Figures to Be Prosecuted Over War Crimes," *New York Times*, December 17, 1992.

Sciolino, Elaine, Roger Cohen, and Stephen Engleberg. "Tense Start, Tough Talk and Sleepless Final," *New York Times*, November, 24, 1995.

Scott, Jennifer. "Systematic Rapes," Reuters, July 3, 1996.

Seybolt, Taylor B. "Coordination in Rwanda: The Humanitarian Response to Genocide and Civil War," Conflict Management Group Working Paper, Cambridge: Conflict Management Group, January 1997. www-jha.sps.cam.ac.uk/a/a027.htm posted on July 5, 1997.

Shanker, Thom. "*Sexual Violence*," in *Crimes of War: What the Public Should Know*, ed. Roy Gutman and David Rieff. New York: W. W. Norton and Company, 1999.

Smale, Alison. "Tribunal President Demands Arrests of Bosnian Serb Leaders," Associated Press, June 14, 1996.

Smith, R. Jeffrey. "Secret Meetings Foiled Karadzic Capture Plan; US Says French Jeopardized Mission," *Washington Post*, April 23, 1998.

Spolar, Christine. "NATO Troops Spotted Karadzic This Week; Capture Too Risky, Spokesmen Say," *Washington Post*, February 28, 2000.

SRNA (Srspska Republika News Agency) "News Review," March 21, 1997, as found at www.hri.org/news/balkans/srna/97-03-21.srna.html.

SRNA (Srpska Republika News Agency), May 7, 1997. 97-05-07 http://www.hri.org/news/balkans/srna/97-05-07.srna.html.

SRNA (Srpska Republika News Agency) "News Reviews" September 28, 1997, as found at [TK]

Steinmetz, Greg. "Her Way: A Daughter-in-Law of 'Old Blue Eyes' Takes a Tough Case," *Wall Street Journal*, 1999.

Stockman, Farah. "The Anatomy of a Court: The International Criminal Tribunal for Rwanda," *International Humanitarian Law: Origins, Challenges and Prospects*, eds. John Carey and R. John Pritchard. Robert M. W. Kempner Collegium/The Edwin Mellen Press, Lewiston, Lampeter and Queenston, 1999.

Stojanović, Dusan. "Opposition Leader Offers to Testify Against Milosevic in Hague," *Associated Press*, January 23, 1996.

Stover, Eric. "The Grave at Vukovar," *Smithsonian Magazine*, Vol. 27, March 1997.

Sudetic, Chuck. "After Eights Months, First Relief Reaches One Bosnian Town," *New York Times*, November 29, 1992.

Text of Justice Jackson's Report to President Truman on the Nuremberg Trial, as reprinted in *New York Times*, October 16, 1946.

Tutu, Desmond. "Healing a Nation," an interview with James Brittain, ITN, May 1996. Reprinted in *Index on Censorship*, Vol. 25, No. 5 (September/October 1996), Issue 172.

Vaccaro, J. Matthew. "The Politics of Genocide: Peacekeeping and Disaster Relief in Rwanda," *UN Peacekeeping, American Policy and the Uncivil Wars of the 1990's*, ed. William J. Durch. New York: St Martin's Press (A Henry L. Stimson Center Book), 1996.

Visathan, Victor, "Karamira, 21 Other Genocides Executed," *New York Times*, April 27, 1998.

Walsh, Mary Williams. "A Tribunal in a Time of Atrocities," *Los Angeles Times*, December 23, 1995.

Walsh, James. "Was It a Real 'War'?" *Time* Magazine, May 19, 1997.

Watson, Geoffrey R. 1996. "The Humanitarian Law of Yugoslavia War Crimes Tribunal: Jurisdiction in Prosecutor v. Tadic," *Virginia Journal of International Law*, No. 3, Spring 1996.

Weiner, Tim. "U.S. Cancels Plans for Raid on Bosnia to Capture Two Serbs," *New York Times*, July 26, 1998.

Whitelaw, Kevin, Richard Newman, and David E. Kaplan. "Time Is Running Out for Mr. Ethnic Cleansing: But the Case Against Karadzic May Be Weak," *U.S. News & World Report*, 1224: 14, April 13, 1998.

Williams, Carol. J. "The Last Days of Yugoslavia," *Los Angeles Times, Sunday Magazine*, November 24, 1991.

Wilmer, Franke. "Identity, Culture and Historicity: The Social Construction of Ethnicity in the Balkans," *World Affairs*, 1997. Accessed 9/27/1999. Electric Library.

Zarembo, Alan. "Judgment Day: in Rwanda, 92,392 Genocide Suspects Await Trial," *Harper's*, April 1997, 68–80.

BROADCASTS

Adcock, Bronwyn. "The UN and Rwanda: Abandoned to Genocide." *Australian Broadcasting Corporation*. www.abc.net.au/rn/talks/bbing/stories/s19237.htm.

BBC Broadcast. Lauren Comiteau interviews Judge Gabrielle Kirk McDonald. October 1998.

PBS/Corporation for Public Broadcasting, "Cry From the Grave," January 2000.

Court TV, "Bosnian War Crimes Tribunal," July 8, 1996.

Court TV, "Interview with Terry Moran," May 3, 1996.

Danner, Mark. "The Horrors of a Camp Called Omarska and the Serb Strategy," *Frontline* (PBS).

De Vrelj, Hans. "NATO Arrests 'Butcher of Srebrenica,'" Radio Netherlands, December 2, 1998.

Scott, Pippa and Kevin Sim. "The World's Most Wanted Man," *Frontline* (PBS), May 26, 1998.

COURT DOCUMENTS

Cases

INTERNATIONAL TRIBUNAL FOR THE PROSECUTION OF PERSONS RESPONSIBLE FOR SERIOUS VIOLATIONS OF INTERNATIONAL HUMANITARIAN LAW COMMITTED IN THE TERRITORY OF FORMER YUGOSLAVIA SINCE 1991 (ICTY)

Prosecutor v. Duško Tadić, aka "Dule." Case No. IT-94-1.

Prosecutor v. Željko Mejakić, Dragoljub Prcac, Momcilo Gruban, Dusan Knezević, Case No. IT-95-4.

Prosecutor v. Radovan Karadžić, Ratko Mladić. Case. No. IT-95-5.

Prosecutor v. Dario Kordić and Mario Cerkez, IT-95-14/2.

Prosecutor v. Zejnil Delalić, Zdravko Mucić aka "Pavo," Hazim Delić, Esad Landžo aka "Zenga," Case No. IT-96-21.

Prosecutor v. Drazen Erdemović, Case No. IT-96-22.

Prosecutor v. Miroslav Kvocka, Milojlca Kos, Mladen Radić, Zoran Žigić, Case No. IT-98-30.

Prosecutor v. General Radislav Krstić, Case No. IT-98-33.

Prosecutor v. Slobodan Milošević, Milan Milutinović, Nikola Sainović, Dragoljub Ojdanić, Vlajko Stojiljković, Case No. IT-99-37.

International Criminal Tribunal for Rwanda (ICTR)

Prosecutor v. Clemente Kayishma and Obed Ruzindana, Case No. ICTR-95-1.

Prosecutor v. Jean-Paul Akayesu, ICTR-96-4.

Prosecutor v. George Anderson Nderubamwe Rutaganda, Case No. ICTR-96-3.

Prosecutor v. Gerard and Elizaphan Ntakirutim, Case No. ICTR 96-10 and ICTR 96-17.

Prosecutor v. Jean-Bosco Barayagwiza, Case No. ICTR-97-19.

Prosecutor v. Jean Kambanda, Case No. ICTR-97-23.

Testimony

ITCY, TESTIMONY IN *PROSECUTOR V. DUSKO TADIC,* CASE NO. IT-94-1-T

Hamdija Kahrimanović, June 25, 1996.

ICTY, TESTIMONY IN *PROSECUTOR V. RADOVAN KARADŽIĆ, RATKO MLADIĆ* CASE NO. IT 95-18-R61 AND IT-95-5-R61

Jean-René Ruez, July 3, 1996.

Prosecutor Mark Harmon, June 27, 1996.

Dražen Erdemović, July 5, 1996.

Col. Ton Karremans, July 4, 1996.

ICTY, TESTIMONY IN *PROSECUTOR V. DARIO KORDIĆ AND MARIO ČERKEZ* IT-95-14/2

Expert Witness, Robert J. Donia, July 19, 1999.

ICTY, TESTIMONY IN *PROSECUTOR V. ZEJNIL DELALIĆ, ZDRAVKO MUCIĆ, HAZIM DELIĆ, ESAD LANDŽO,* CASE NO. IT-96-21-T

Opening Statement, Prosecutor Eric Ostberg, March 10, 1997
Petko Grubač, August 12–13, 1997.
Gordana Grubač, August 12–13, 1997.
Zejnil Olujic, August 12–13, 1997.
Witness R, October 16, 1997.
Esad Landžo, July 27, 28, 29, 1998,

ICTY, TESTIMONY IN PROSECUTOR V. GENERAL RADISLAV KRSTIĆ, CASE NO. IT-98-33

Opening Statement, Prosecutor Mark Harmon, May 13, 2000.
Johannes Rutten, April 5, 2000.
Major Robert Franken, April 4, 2000.
Dražen Erdemović, May 22, 2000.
Richard J. Butler, June 28, 2000.

ICTR, TESTIMONY IN *PROSECUTOR V. GEORGE ANDERSON NDERUBAMWE RUTAGANDA* CASE NO. ICTY-96-3-T

William Haglund, March 10, 1998.
Witness T, March 11, 1998.

ICTR, TESTIMONY IN *PROSECUTOR V. JEAN-PAUL AKAYESU,* ICTR-96-4-T

Witness JJ, October 23 & 24, 1997
Testimony of General Romeo A. Dallaire, February 25, 1998.
Testimony, Witness H, March 6–7, 1997
Testimony, Witness J, January 27, 1997

JUDGMENTS & OPINIONS

International Criminal Tribunal for the Former Yugoslavia (ICTY)

Judgment. "Prosecutor v. Zejnil Delalić, Zadravko Mucić aka "Pavo," Esad Landžo aka "Zenga." Case No. IT-96-21-T, November 16, 1998.

Opinion & Judgment. Prosecutor v. Duško Tadić aka "Dule," Case IT-94-1-T, May 7, 1997.

Sentencing Judgment of Duško Tadić; and Separate Opinion of Judge McDonald. The Hague: 1999.

Judgment, *Prosecutor v. Mejakić and Others,* IT-95-4-I, February 13, 1995.

International Criminal Tribunal for Rwanda

Judgment, Prosecutor v. Clemente Kayishema and Obed Ruzindana, Case No. ICTR-95-1-T, May 21, 1999.

Judgment and Sentence, *Prosecutor v. Jean Kambanda,* Case No. ICTR 97-23-S, September 4, 1998.

Judgment, *The Prosecutor v. Jean-Paul Akayesu,* Case No. ICTR-96-4-T, September 2, 1998.

Judgment, *Prosecutor v. George Anderson Nderubamwe Rutaganda,* Case No. ICTR-96-3-T, December 6, 1999.

Louise Mushikiwabo et al. v. Jean-Bosco Barayagwiza. U.S. District Court, Southern District of New York, 94-CIV.3627 (JSM).

Associated Legal Proceedings

Amicus Brief Respecting Amendment of the Indictment and Supplementation of the Evidence to Ensure the Prosecution of Rape and Other Sexual Violence Within the Competence of the Tribunal Re: *The Prosecutor of the Tribunal against Jean-Paul Akayesu,* Case No. ICTR-96-4-T.

International Court of Justice, Advisory Opinion on the Immunity of the Special Rapporteur, paragraph 66. http://www.icj-cij.org/icjwww/idecisions/isummaries/inumasummary19990429.htm.

FORMER TRIBUNALS

Record of Proceedings of the International Military Tribunal for the Far East: Court House of the Tribunal, War Ministry Building, Tokyo, Japan: The United States of America . . . [et al.] against Araki, Sadao . . . [et al.], accused. Tokyo: The Tribunal, 1946–1948.

Trial of the Major War Criminals Before the International Military Tribunal, Nuremberg, 14 November 1945–1 October 1946. Nuremberg: International Military Tribunal, 1947–1949.

GOVERNMENT TESTIMONY

Testimony, Hasan Nuhanović, House Subcommittee on International Operations and Human Rights, Washington D.C., March 31, 1998.

"Rwanda: Genocide and the Continuing Cycle of Violence," Hearing Before the House Subcommittee on International Operations and Human Rights of the Committee on International Relations, May 1998.

Meeting Between the Survivors of the Rwandan Genocide and the Independent Inquiry into the United Nations Role in the Rwandan Genocide. Representative Cynthia McKinney presiding, U.S. House of Representatives, Washington, D.C., December 8, 1999.

Transcript of Jean-David Levitte's Address to the French National Assembly, *Mission Srebrenica*, Paris, February 15, 2001.

Reports

Amnesty International. "Bosnia-Herzegovina: To Bury My Brother's Bones," EUR 63/15/96, July 1996. http://www.web.amnesty.org/ai.nsf/index/EUR630151996.

Amnesty International. "Rwanda: Appeal Cases: No One Is Talking About It Anymore," AFR 47/31/97, October, 1997. http://www.amnesty.it/ailib/aipub/1997/AFR/14031 97.htm.

Amnesty International. "Rwanda and Burundi, The Return Home: Rumours and Realities." February 20, 1996.

Avocats San Frontières. "Justice for All in Rwanda." *Annual Report*, 1998.

British Home Office's Immigration and Nationality Directorate Country Information and Policy Unit. *RWANDA. Asylum in the UK. Rwanda Assessment*, April 2000.

Human Rights Watch. *World Report 1999. Rwanda: Justice and Responsibility*, 2000.

Human Rights Watch. *World Report 1999. Rwanda: Human Rights Developments*, 2000.

Human Rights Watch. *Federal Republic of Yugoslavia: A Week of Terror in Drenica. Humanitarian Law Violations in Kosovo*, 1999.

Human Rights Watch. *World Report, 1998. Rwanda: Human Rights Developments*, 1999.

Human Rights Watch/Helsinki Report. *Helsinki Watch on Prijedor's War Criminals*, 1997. www.hrw.org.

Human Rights Watch/Helsinki Report. *Bosnia-Hercegovina: The Unindicted: Reaping the Rewards of "Ethnic Cleansing,"* Vol. 9, No. 1 (D), January 1997.

Human Rights Watch/Helsinki Report. *Bosnia-Hercegovina: Politics of Revenge; The Misuse of Authority in Bihać, Cazin, and Velika Kladusa*, Vol. 9, No. 9 (D), August 1997.

Human Rights Watch/Helsinki Report. *Bosnia-Hercegovina: The Continuing Influence of Bosnia's Warlords*, Vol. 8, No 17 (D), December 1996.

International Crisis Group Report. *Five Years After the Genocide in Rwanda: Justice in Question, Part I*, April 7, 1999.

International Crisis Group Report. *Minority Return or Mass Relocation*," Sarajevo, May 14, 1998.

Kavaruganda Family. *Pourquoi a-t-il été assassiné? Le President de la Cour de Cassation et de la Cour Constitutionnelle, Mr Joseph Kavaruganda.*

Lawyers' Committee for Human Rights. *Prosecuting Genocide in Rwanda, A Lawyers Committee Report on the ICTR and National Trials*, July 1997. www.lchr.org/pubs/rawanda.htm

Organization of African Unity (OAU), *The International Panel of Eminent Personalities to Investigate the 1994 Genocide in Rwanda and the Surrounding Events*, July 7, 2000.

The Rwandan Ministry of Justice. *The Judicial System in Rwanda: A Report on Justice.*

Taylor, Telford. *Final Report to the Secretary of the Army on the Nuremberg War Crimes Trials Under Control Council Law No. 10.* Washington, D.C.: William S. Hein & Co., Inc. August 15, 1949.

UNITED NATIONS

Report of the Independent Inquiry into the Actions of the United Nations During the 1994 Genocide in Rwanda, submitted to Secretary-General by Ingvar Carlsson, Han Sung-Joo, and Major General Rufus M. Kupolati on December 15, 1999.

UN General Assembly, Fifty-fourth Session, *Report of the Expert Group to Conduct a Review of the Effective Operation and Functioning of the International Tribunal for the Former Yugoslavia and the International Criminal Tribunal for Rwanda*, prepared by Jerome Ackerman in pursuance to General Assembly resolutions 53/212 and 53/213 of 18 December 1998, A/54/634. November 22, 1999.

Question of the Violation of Human Rights and Fundamental Freedoms in Any Part of the World, with Particular Reference to Colonial and Other Dependent Countries and Territories. Extrajudicial, Summary on Arbitrary Executions. Special Report on his mission to Rwanda from 8–17 April. Submitted by B. W. Ndiaye, to the Secretary General E/CN.4/1994/7 Addl.

UN General Assembly, Report of the Secretary-General on the Activities of the Office of Internal Oversight. *Financing of the International Criminal Tribunal for the Prosecution of Persons Responsible for Genocide and Other Serious Violations of International Humanitarian Law Committed in the Territory of Rwanda and Rwandan Citizens Responsible for Genocide and Other Such Violations Committed in the Territory of Neighbouring States Between 1 January and 31 December 1994.* A/53/428, February, 1998.

UN General Assembly, Report on the Situation of Human Rights in Rwanda submitted by Rene Degni-Ségui, Special Rapporteur of the Commission on Human Rights, under paragraph 20 of resolution S-3/1 of 25 May 1994. *Question of the Violation of Human Rights and Fundamental Freedoms in Any Part of the World, with Particular Reference to Colonial and Other Dependent Countries and Territories,* E/CN.4/1997/61, January 20, 1997.

UN General Assembly, Fifty-second session, Report of the United Nations High Commissioner for Human Rights on the Human Rights Field Operation in Rwanda. In accordance with General Assembly resolution 51/114 of 12 December 1996. *Human Rights Questions: Human Rights Situations and Reports of Special Rapporteurs and Representatives.* A/52/486, October 16, 1997.

UN Commission on Human Rights, Fifty-third session, Report of the High Commissioner for Human Rights on the activities of the Human Rights Field Operations in Rwanda. *Question of the Violation of Human Rights and Fundamental Freedoms in Any Part of the World, with Particular Reference to Colonial and Other Dependent Countries and Territories.* E/CN.4/1997/52, March 17, 1997.

UN Commission on Human Rights, Fifty-second session. Final Periodic Report on the Situation of Human Rights in the Territory of the Former Yugoslavia submitted by Mr. Tadeusz Mazowiecki, Special Rapporteur of the Commission on Human Rights, pursuant to paragraph 42 of Commission resolution 1995/89, *Question of the Violation of Human Rights and Fundamental Freedoms in any Part of the World, with Particular Reference to Colonial and Other Dependent Countries and Territories. Situation of Human Rights in the territory of the Former Yugoslavia.* E/CN.4/1996/9, August 22, 1995.

Report on the Situation of Human Rights in Rwanda submitted by René Degni-Ségui, Special Rapporteur of the Commission of Human Rights. January 27, 1996.

Report of UN Special Rapporteur, January 29, 1996.

UN Security Council, Forty-ninth Session, *Report of the Secretary-General on Security in the Rwandese Refugee Camps*, S/1994/1308.

UN General Assembly, Fifty-second Session. *Human Rights Questions: Human Rights Situations and Reports of Special Rapporteurs and Representatives.* A/52/486 October 16, 1997.

UN High Commissioner for Human Rights, United Nations Human Rights Field Operation in Rwanda. *Human Rights Incidents Involving Recent Returnees From Zaire and Tanzania. Status Report as of January, 27 1997.*

UNHCR Report on Situation of Human Rights in Rwanda, January 29 1996.

UN High Commissioner For Human Rights. Human Rights Field Operation in Rwanda. *Report Of the United Nations High Commissioner for Human Rights*, February 14, 1998. E/CN.4/1998/61

UN Security Council/IFOR.3122nd Meeting. Resolution: S/RES/781. October 9, 1992. http://www.nato.int/ifor/un/u921009a.htm

UN General Assembly, Fifty-first Session, Report of the Secretary-General on the Activities of the Office of Internal Oversight. *Financing of the International Criminal Tribunal for the Prosecution of Persons Responsible for Genocide and Other Serious Violations of International Humanitarian Law Committed in the Territory of Rwanda and Rwandan Citizens Responsible for Genocide and Other Such Violations Committed in the Territory of Neighbouring States Between 1 January and 31 December 1994.* A/51/789, February 1997.

UN Security Council, Report of the Secretary-General, Annex: Statue of the International Tribunal. *The Establishment of the International Tribunal to Prosecute Persons Responsible for Serious Violations of International Humanitarian Law Committed in the Territory of the Former Yugoslavia Since 1991*: Res 808, Res. 827.

United Nations, Report of the Secretary-General Pursuant to General Assembly Resolution 53/35 (1998) *SREBRENICA REPORT*, http://www.haverford.edu/relg/sells/reports/UNsrebrenicareport.htm.

UN Security Council, *Final Report of the United Nations Commission of Experts Established Pursuant to Security Council Resolution 780 (1992) Annex V: The Prijedor Report.* Prepared by Hanne Sophie Greve. S/1994/674/Add.2 (Vol. V), December 28, 1994.

Report to the General Assembly and the Security Council, *The Annual Report of the International Tribunal for the Prosecution of Persons Responsible for Serious Viola-*

tions of International Humanitarian Law Committed in the Territory of the Former Yugoslavia Since 1991, 1994.

UN General Assembly, Fifty-second session, UN Security Council, Fifty-second year. *Report of the International Tribunal for the Prosecution of Persons Responsible for Serious Violations of International Humanitarian Law Committed in the Territory of the Former Yugoslavia Since 1991*. A/52/375;S/1997/729, September 18, 1997.

United Nations. Report of the Secretary General Pursuant to Paragraph 2 of Security Council Resolution 808 (1993). S/25704, May 3, 1993.

United Nations Children's Fund (UNICEF), *Children and Women of Rwanda: A Situation Analysis of Social Sectors*, 1997.

United States AID Evaluation Special Study No. 76, *Rebuilding Postwar Rwanda the Role of the International Community by Krishna Kumar, team leader Center for Development Information and Evaluation U.S. Agency for International Development*. David Tardif Douglin Development Alternatives, Inc. with Carolyn Knapp, Kim Maynard, Peter Manikas, and Annette Sheckler Center for Development Information and Evaluation, U.S. Agency for International Development, PN-ABY-212, July 1996.

U.S. Department of State. *The Dayton Peace Accords: General Framework Agreement for Peace in Bosnia and Herzegovina*, December 14, 1995.

U.S. Department of State. *Country Report on Human Rights Practices for 2000: Rwanda*. Released by the Bureau of Democracy, Human Rights, and Labor, February 2001.

U.S. Department of State. *Country Reports on Human Rights Practices for 1999: Bosnia and Herzegovina*. Released by the Bureau of Democracy, Human Rights, and Labor, February 2000.

U.S. Department of State. *Country Reports on Human Rights Practices for 1998: Bosnia and Herzegovina*. Released by the Bureau of Democracy, Human Rights, and Labor, February 1999.

U.S. Department of State. *Country Report on Human Rights Practices for 1998: Rwanda*. Released by the Bureau of Democracy, Human Rights, and Labor, February 1999.

U.S. Department of State. *Country Report on Human Rights Practices for 1996: Rwanda*. Released by the Bureau of Democracy, Human Rights, and Labor, January 1997.

U.S. General Accounting Office. Report to the Chairman, Committee on Foreign Relations, U.S. Senate. *Former Yugoslavia: War Crimes Tribunal's Workload Exceeds Capacity* (Letter Report, 06/02/98, GAO/NSIAD-98-134). http://www.fas.org/man/gao/nsiad-98-134.htm.

The World Bank. *Rwanda Poverty Note: Rebuilding an Equitable Society: Poverty and Poverty Reduction After the Genocide*. (World Bank Report No. 17792-RW), 1998.

Cable

UNAMIR to UN Headquarters in New York, in possession of author.

Speeches

Address of Antonio Cassese, President of the International Criminal Tribunal for the Former Yugoslavia to the General Assembly of the United Nations, November 7, 1995.

Address of Antonio Cassese, President of the International Criminal Tribunal for the Former Yugoslavia to the General Assembly of the United Nations, November 14, 1994.

Address of Judge Gabrielle Kirk McDonald to the United Nations General Assembly, November 19, 1998, and November 8, 1999.

Address of Judge Gabrielle Kirk McDonald to the United Nations Security Council, November 19, 1998.

INDEX